T0164569

STILL ON THE ROAD

Also by Clinton Heylin:

So Long As Men Can Breathe: The Untold Story of Shakespeare's Sonnets

Revolution in the Air: The Songs of Bob Dylan Vol. 1 (1957–73)

The Act You've Known for All These Years: A Year in the Life of Sgt. Pepper & Friends

Babylon's Burning: From Punk to Grunge

From the Velvets to the Voidoids: The Birth of American Punk

All Yesterdays' Parties: The Velvet Underground in Print 1966–71 [editor]

Despite the System: Orson Welles Versus the Hollywood Studios

Bootleg—The Rise & Fall of the Secret Recording Industry

Can You Feel The Silence?—Van Morrison: A New Biography

No More Sad Refrains: The Life & Times of Sandy Denny

Bob Dylan Behind The Shades—Take Two

Dylan's Daemon Lover: The Story of a 450-Year-Old Pop Ballad

Dylan Day by Day: A Life in Stolen Moments

Never Mind the Bollocks, Here's the Sex Pistols

Bob Dylan: The Recording Sessions 1960–94

The Great White Wonders: A History of Rock Bootlegs

The Penguin Book of Rock & Roll Writing [editor]

Gypsy Love Songs & Sad Refrains: The Recordings of Sandy Denny & Richard Thompson

Rise/Fall: The Story of Public Image Limited

Joy Division: Form & Substance [with Craig Wood]

STILL ON THE ROAD

THE SONGS OF BOB DYLAN, 1974–2006

Clinton Heylin

CHICAGO
REVIEW
PRESS

An A Cappella Book

To Tony Lacey, for twenty years of friendship and faith.

Interior design: Sarah Olson

© 2010 by Clinton Heylin
First edition
Published by Chicago Review Press, Incorporated
814 North Franklin Street
Chicago, IL 60610
ISBN 978-1-55652-844-6
Printed in the United States of America
5 4 3 2 1

{ Contents }

||||| 1974 |||||

||||| 1975–6 |||||

||||| 1977–8 |||||

▌▌▌▌ 1979–80 ▌▌▌▌▌

||||| 1980–1 |||||

▖▌▌█ 1982–3 █▌▌▖

▌▌▌ 1984–6 ▐▐▐

▏▎▍▌ 1987–9 ▌▍▎▏

▌▌▌▌ 1990–5 ▌▌▌▌

||||| 1996–9 |||||

||||| 2000–1 |||||

▌▌▌▌▌ 2002–6 ▌▌▌▌▌

{ Just Like Another Intro }

I never opened up my own thinking. My stuff was never about me, per se, so everybody who . . . thought it was about me . . . they took the wrong road. —Dylan, 2007

I'm not a playwright. The people in my songs are all me. —Dylan, 2009

||||▮▮▮▮▮|||

Still on the Road, the sequel to my previous volume on Dylan's songs, *Revolution in the Air,* tells quite a different tale. Like that volume, its nature is dictated by the material it addresses, as it tells the stories of the next three hundred songs. But whereas the first three hundred songs were essentially written in a thirteen-year period, it took the man some thirty-three years to complete this second series. As a result, the songs herein are intersected by several periods of creative abeyance which last anywhere between six months (the first halves of 1975 and 1977, the second half of 1981) and six years (1991–6).

Nonetheless, both books share the key structural aspect—each is divided into two blocks of creative time: the first, when songwriting generally came easily and plentifully; the second, when the pipes got rusty, and supply became intermittent at best. In that first volume, the period 1961–7 saw Dylan write 236 songs in the white heat of inspiration, and a mere 52 songs in the years from 1968 to 1973—the so-called amnesia (see my discussion in *Behind the Shades,* pages 294–96). The differential is not quite so acute in this second volume, but the book still

1

ends up being divided between the 163 songs he wrote (or cowrote) in the years 1974–83, and the remaining 137 songs, which occupy the years from 1984 to 2006.

I would personally argue that the years 1974 to 1983 saw Dylan write as many great songs as he managed in those wild mercury years. After reestablishing his genius credentials with the devastating *Blood on the Tracks*, he reinforced them with *Desire* and completed the cycle with perhaps his most lyrically ambitious work to date, *Street-Legal*, before surrendering himself to God. A trilogy of testaments to his newfound faith followed (*Slow Train Coming, Saved,* and *Shot of Love*), before he signed off on those halcyon days with the 1983 "comeback" album, *Infidels*, which for all its (largely self-inflicted) flaws, again proved that no one wrote Dylan quite like Dylan.

But what truly marks out these years for Dylan the singer-songwriter was how, on every occasion he entered the studio to record an album, he always had the *material* to make a classic—just like the early-to-mid-sixties. The fact that he only managed to transfer such potentially first-class material onto tape in fits and starts, limiting himself to just two truly classic albums in this ten-year period, *Blood on the Tracks* and *Slow Train Coming*—and a couple of close calls, in *Street-Legal* and *Infidels*—does not devalue his output as a *songwriter* one jot. I would go as far as to argue that if Dylan emerged fully formed in 1974, with no track record to date, his body of work in just those ten years would still make him the most important songwriter of his generation.

Thankfully, because of the likes of the *Blood on the Tracks* notebook; the recollections of his collaborator on *Desire*, Jacques Levy; a December 1977 piano run-through of the *Street-Legal* material; and Dylan's determination to debut material in rehearsal at Rundown through 1981, ordering the songs by composition remains a viable methodology all the way up to *Shot of Love*. After that, *Infidels* may be a crapshoot, but from 1984 to 1990 we return again to surer footing, thanks in part to Dylan resuming recording his songs in a series of sessions, rather than in a single block. The exception—*Oh Mercy*—is also the one instance where Dylan's own *Chronicles* comes to our aid.

After 1983, though, the process itself starts to distend. Rather than the one writer's block of the late sixties and early seventies, Dylan became more and more inclined to bouts of creative forgetfulness. But, for all that, he had by no means written his last great song. Even during the remainder of that erratic decade, he still found the wherewithal to compose the likes of "New Danville Girl," "When the Night Comes Falling From The Sky," "Tweeter and the Monkey Man," "Most of the Time," "Shooting Star," "Dignity," and "Series of Dreams," all songs which no other songwriter could have conjured.

But as he told one familiar interviewer in 1991, as the most severe of his writer's blocks set in, "There was a time when the songs would come three or four at the same time, but those days are long gone." After a lull that lasted the first half of the nineties, he finally returned in 1997 with *Time Out of Mind*, the first in another trilogy of critically acclaimed albums dealing with mortality and fear, further advanced via *"Love and Theft"* (2001) and concluding in 2006 with *Modern Times*.

The difference now was that—even with longer and longer gaps between albums—he almost never came to the studio with enough of the kind of songs required for a classic collection. And, in fact, both times in the past two decades when he did manage such a coup—*Oh Mercy* and *Time Out of Mind*—he was so overwhelmed by producer Daniel Lanois's intrusive role in the process that he allowed the opportunity to slip from his grasp.

Lanois is not the only one who has failed to understand the artist's instinctual approach in a studio situation and/or has sought to impose an unsuitable sound on this last bastion of "live in studio" recording. When Dylan told assembled journalists at a 2001 press conference, "I have often been let down. All those people who thought they knew how to record me hadn't the slightest idea about what needed to be done,' I imagine Arthur Baker and Mark Knopfler loomed as large in his mind as Mr. Ambient.

For the past three albums, Dylan has in fact produced himself. It had taken him a long time to arrive at this juncture, secure in the faith it would sound all right. Without any kind of sounding board, it really has been a case of "trust yourself." By the time he decided he could do without a producer—with *"Love and Theft"*—it had been seventeen years since he had even test-run any of his material in front of an audience before pressing record. The resultant decision, to just get the songs down and move on, was one even Dylan was prepared to admit had its upside and its downside:

> Songs need a structure, stratagems, codes and stability. And then you hang lyrics on them. I'm speaking here as someone who sings a song that he's written. When we transfer all that to the stage, that's where all those elements come into play. They don't come into play on a record, 'cause my cohorts at the time never really develop any of that stuff, and I can't do it at the time of recording 'cause the song at the time is new to me. (2001)

Of course, he was keen to give the impression that this aspect was somehow beyond his control. Not so, Roberto. It was his call. The expressed rationale underlying his decision—a fear of bootlegging—I find frankly pathetic (and demonstrably untrue—when Dylan toured for six months in 1979–80 playing an entire set of new songs, not a single bootleg album ended up competing with the official releases).

And so, from the summer of 1984, when Dylan started the *Empire Burlesque* project, fans have had to learn to expect albums in which the songs have not always been developed fully, or been worth developing. Sometimes the results soar high. They also sink low. But not one of the seven albums of originals released in those twenty-three years—the same number he managed between 1974 and 1983—could be considered clunker-free by even the most blinkered fan.

But then, he long ago stopped considering the recorded version the be-all and end-all of the process. Rather, as he put it back in 1978, "Songs aren't any good really unless they can be sung on stage." After a decade of the Never Ending Tour, he remained convinced that such an endless slog of one-night stands would serendipitously provide the songs' right setting. As he repeatedly told any journalist who came his way, post-1987, he was a performer first and a songwriter second. And the accumulation of songs was no longer deemed a necessary by-product of any reinvention of self; rather, he now considered his own songs just a part of the musical patchwork that made up the endlessly unraveling "on the road" odyssey he began in June 1988 (which trundleth on still).

Dramatic rearrangements of a song's sensibility—a feature of all the tours from 1974 through 1984—became an ever rarer phenomenon, while there has been a dispiriting lack of lyrical reinvention in the hundreds of live performances post-1987. Even when there has been a new lyrical twist—say, on "Down Along the Cove" or "Workingman's Blues #2"—one has been left wondering as to the point of the exercise: novelty for novelty's sake?

Yet there was a time, and for a decade or so, when the reinvention of lyrics in performance had been a substantive part of his songwriting craft, as he allowed a song's lyrical template to be ever-open to reinterpretation. In the years 1975–84, a number of songs were given significant new sets of lyrics in performance—including two of the three perennial selections from *Blood on the Tracks*, "Simple Twist of Fate" and "Tangled Up in Blue." Other seventies compositions, like "Knockin' on Heaven's Door" and "Going Going Gone" regularly underwent the same transformative process.

Since 1984, such reinterpretative possibilities have been left for the studio, where he has certainly not abandoned his lyrical sculpting and resculpting. If anything, he has become more and more prone to use magnetic tape to tweak a song's words, rarely entering a studio with a defined set of words. And thanks to both the unofficial and the official *Bootleg Series*, it has been possible to document this process with reasonable thoroughness. However, for all his talk of "structure, stratagems, codes," once the recorded lyric is the released lyric, it is destined to become the live lyric too, whether verbatim or mumbled.

As such, 1984 proved a turning point when it came to the way Dylan recorded *and* performed those songs he planned to release. After his third summer tour of the arenas and stadia of Europe in six years, he stopped springing unreleased Dylan originals on unsuspecting fans. At the time few would have predicted such a sea change. Dylan had spent much of the 1979–80 shows performing his *next* set of recordings, while in 1981 he previewed the bulk of *Shot of Love* in performance prior to its August release.

Five years of intermittent chaos and confusion followed that 1984 tour, before Dylan reclaimed his position at the head of the welcome table for the Songwriters Convention, with *Oh Mercy*. He also now felt comfortable enough with his new house band, fronted by the ever-intuitive G. E. Smith, to again deliver shows which maintained a degree of intensity throughout. The shows from summer 1989 through spring

1990 were often as good as anything he had delivered in the previous two decades; but *under the red sky* and a second Traveling Wilburys collection spent the last round in his current locker, while G. E. Smith's departure at the end of October marked a key change in Dylan the performing artist.

His decision to mix it up in concert coincided with the onset of his most sustained "amnesia" as a songwriter. With the departure of bandleader G. E. Smith, he also abandoned the practice of breaking in new standing bands every two/three years, instead instituting piecemeal changes that made for a uniformity of sound and purpose that marked the end of the "genuine" Never Ending Tour (just as he suggests in the *World Gone Wrong* sleeve notes).

With a vast repertoire of originals (now totalling over 500 songs) and a seemingly inexhaustible supply of covers across every genre of popular song he could bend to his will, this ongoing tour was no longer a diversion from the album/tour treadmill, but a lifestyle choice. As a result, even when the songs dried up (and they did—very quickly), the tours kept rolling along. Between October 1990 and May 1997, Dylan not only instigated a series of distinct phases for his ever-rolling revue (something he also sent up in his *World Gone Wrong* notes), he found a way to pour himself entirely into performance, finding precious little time for other distractions. His focus, at times, was something to behold. But by 1996 the whole ethic had become tired, as had the arrangements and the band.

Only with the recording and release of *Time Out of Mind* did the identity of the Never Ending Tour change again. At last, he had a set of new songs he wanted to play; and it was here that he really began to explore the stratagems of those works he felt had barely transcended their demo status when placed in the hands of Lanois. If radical rearrangements of former songs became rarer still, and even those precious few were often ill-conceived (say, the various attempts to do "All Along the Watchtower" any which way but the one that worked originally), a whole new slew of spiritual covers helped sustain the shows into the twenty-first century. Gradually these, too, gave way to the post-*TOOM* songs he had begun penning, which by 2002 almost invariably received an identikit bludgeoning by a disappointingly derivative backing band.

At the same time, the endless parade of influences—soon to be displayed in his newfound vocation as a radio DJ—seems to have had a deleterious effect on his own creativity. He had claimed in one interview that he had recorded the two acoustic albums of covers in 1992 and 1993 "so I could personally get back to the music that's true to me." Well, whatever the intent, he had begun to lose a sense of where influence ended and plagiarism began.

Any analysis of the trilogy of albums released between 1997 and 2006 needs to address the way a mature Dylan has again chosen to foreground the kind of influences which used to rattle every line in the formative years (1961–3). This has proven a highly controversial methodology, with evidence of the scale of debt continuing to be uncovered thanks to the ever-expanding web-based forums on the man and his art (only very recently, an interesting thread on the Expecting Rain website concerned itself with Dylan's wholesale use of generally out-of-copyright literary sources to provide his 2004 memoir, *Chronicles*, with thoughts he could call his own, but weren't—a criticism previously leveled at *"Love and Theft"*).

The self-proclaimed "thief of thoughts" must sometimes wonder what all the fuss is about. It is forty-six years since he addressed the issue head-on in his eighth outlined epitaph. It is also the third time that he has succumbed to a form of wholesale lyrical appropriation in his post-conversion career. Nor has it been the most controversial. When it comes to controversy, Dylan's decision to base his entire oeuvre in the period 1979–80 on the Good Book directly challenged the cozy liberal consensus to which his songs had served as a soundtrack for so long and asked important questions of his own audience.

The scale of that debt is dealt with at length in this book, because it charts his progress from interpreter to zealot back to artist. The way that he began writing songs sparked by a particular Bible passage (e.g., "Do Right to Me Baby"), only to then revert to writing lyrical commentaries on sections of the scriptures in song (e.g., "In the Garden"), before finally, and with renewed artistry, sifting the message through his own unique vision again (e.g., "Caribbean Wind"), is one of the more revealing processes documented herein.

The process whereby he began to insert sections of dialogue from films and TV shows into the songs he was writing in the mid-eighties (1984–6) proved an infinitely more depressing spectacle. This form of appropriation went from deft to heavy-handed in the twinkling of an eye. He began by using it sparingly and judiciously, to dazzling effect, in the magnificent "New Danville Girl" (aka "Brownsville Girl"), but by the time he came to *Knocked Out Loaded*, he was all but content to set sub-Hollywood dialogue to old rockabilly tunes and call the results his own. This worrying direction led straight down to creative dearth.

Thankfully, with 1989's *Oh Mercy* Dylan abandoned this dubious experiment in favor of a fusion of styles that was once again all his own. But he soon exhausted that particular vein of inspiration (1988–90); and when he started writing complete songs again, six years hence, fragments of interpolated text were back in favor. With *Time Out of Mind*, he again slipped into the habit of using lines and ideas from the traditional lexicon and/or literature; at first sparingly and judiciously, and then, post-*TOOM*, with nary a care for whether it worked or it didn't.

The results have not been unremittingly awful—unlike, perhaps, those of the mid-eighties—but the resultant songs, spanning the last three albums, suggest Dylan himself is no longer in control of the process, or crafting his material with due diligence. Rather, he is letting the words fall as they may, trusting to instincts that once were consummate, but are fitful at best in these end days.

But he has not only survived, he has endured. The release of a new album in April 2009 shows that the man ain't done yet, even if the stylistic shifts over the past four albums have become nigh on imperceptible. They have certainly all been cut from the same cloth, perhaps because Dylan has decided to agree with a younger self who in conversation with Sam Shepard claimed, "I've always been real content with the old forms. I know my place." If so, songs like "Huck's Tune," "Nettie Moore," "Ain't Talkin'," and "Forgetful Heart" suggest he hasn't quite drained the well and that he is not quite ready to pen his last restless farewell . . .

—Clinton Heylin, June 2009

{ Some Further Notes on Method }

Criteria for Inclusion—If Volume One contained its fair share of songs covered in the dust of rumor, just about every song in this volume can be said with a degree of certainty to still exist, on tape or on paper. The central problem is not so much one of preservation, but of authorship. This is less of an issue with copyrighted songs since they *assert* his authorship (though, even here, a coauthor credit can be problematic, q.v. #537, "Heartland"). But when—as in 1978—Dylan spent many a soundcheck working on new songs, some of which sounded like him, some of which more resembled Shel Silverstein, the question of attribution becomes fraught, especially as he abandoned each and every one when he responded to a call from Calvary.

And because for most of the post-Rundown period we are reliant on studio logs more than actual tapes to discern what Dylan laid down, the songs which he recorded but never copyrighted cannot always either be dismissed as covers, or fully embraced as lost originals (especially given a recent penchant for using titles of well-known songs for new originals). At such times, I have had to make a personal judgment call—fully aware that I may yet be shown to be fallible when the latest tape drops through the ether and/or onto the web.

At least one song I was convinced would turn out to be a Dylan original—the 1981 outtake "I Wish It Would Rain"—I have been assured is nothing of the sort. It really is his version of the Marvin Gaye classic. The *Shot of Love* sessions are particularly problematic, simply because

9

the documentation itself is a mess, and Dylan was having a great deal of fun coming up with silly song titles ("Walking On Eggs," anyone?). One song specifically listed as an original—"She's Not for You"—is nothing of the sort (it is the Willie Nelson standard). Other songs we have in recorded form—"Yes Sir, No Sir," "Almost Persuaded"—bear no real relation to their titles, which coincide with those of familiar songs from well-known contemporary artists.

To add a soupçon of chaos to the confusion, Dylan in the mid-eighties began to "revise" rockabilly standards to his own, not-so-exacting template. As such, throughout the tours with the Heartbreakers and even at the *Knocked Out Loaded* smorgasbord-sessions, Dylan would often spring songs on the band that even they didn't know; which, as keyboardist Benmont Tench put it, would often "sound like they may be delta blues songs. [But] sometimes I'm not sure if they're . . . a new arrangement of 'It's Alright Ma.'"

Again, I have had to make a judgment call as to how much of himself Dylan need introduce for a song to become—at least partly—his and not merely a newly arranged cover. Half a dozen "hybrid" songs from the mid-eighties are a necessary part of the story and not just because of any nominal merit they may contain. In fact, he has resumed this practice, just with a great deal more guile, on his twenty-first-century collections. For instance, the credits to "Sugar Baby" should not read "Words and music by Bob Dylan," but rather, "Music: Gene Austin and Nat Shilkret; Lyrics: Nat Shilkret; Additional lyrics: Bob Dylan."

Manuscripts and Typescripts—Unfortunately, the paper trail dries up early in this second period. There are, however, three distinct and relevant resources that have become available to me, the first of which is by far the most important written resource currently unpublished. They are as follows:

1. ***Blood on the Tracks* notebook:** The crown jewel of Dylan manuscripts, the little red notebook into which Dylan entered handwritten drafts of eight of the album songs, and seven other titles, now resides at the Morgan Library. Its contents are discussed fully in the relevant section, but suffice to say such a full

depiction of the most important collection of twentieth-century lyrical love songs has only been possible because of access to said document.

2. *Shot of Love* **typescripts:** Because of the unique setup at Rundown Studios in Santa Monica, and Dylan's working methods in the period 1980–1, a lot of material was recorded in rehearsal and then forwarded for copyright purposes to New York. Usually, it would appear, both a tape and a transcript were forthcoming, though not all of the transcripts tally with the recordings. Copies of a number of these transcripts were kindly provided by the estimable Arthur Rosato, while others turned up accompanying a set of 1980–1 publishing demos circulated to potential beneficiaries. Hopefully such resources may yet form the basis for "correct" sets of lyrics to some of the songs which appear in *Lyrics* in denuded form. Also apparently coming from this period is a single handwritten song lyric that went entirely unrecorded (as far as we know), "Let Me Begin to Love." It turned up at a memorabilia auction in the late eighties.

3. The 2004 *Lyrics***:** Though the decision to reproduce a page of lyrics in draft form at the head of every section in the 2004 *Lyrics* sounds mouthwatering, the reality is less innervating. The core manuscript material, most of it acquired from collector George Hechter, is reused whenever the scattershot trawl has yielded a chronological blank, which is how we end up with *Blood on the Tracks* drafts in sections for *Pat Garrett, Down in the Groove*, and *Oh Mercy!*

Nonetheless, there are a handful of surprises here—a fragment of a draft typescript to "Changing of the Guards"; a typescript for "Handy Dandy" that is Typo City and radically different from its recorded self; and, finally, a handwritten draft of "Bye and Bye" on hotel notepaper. The reverse imaging makes it hard work deciphering Dylan's scrawl, but these three items doubtless represent the tip of a veritable iceberg of drafts to Dylan's modern lyrics.

Studio Logs—Starting in 1971, Dylan has been less inclined to use CBS Studios as the default locale of his album sessions (though he still recorded *Blood on the Tracks, Desire,* and *Modern Times* at current or former New York locales of CBS/Sony). He also as of 1974 started to allow his vocals to be overdubbed on occasions, making his previous "live and only live" method of recording not such a hard-and-fast rule. In fact, from 1983 on he has rarely released a track in its unalloyed live-in-studio state. In the late eighties, he also started running a live two-track DAT at (some) sessions, meaning that there is a whole raft of recordings that remain unlogged on the various multitracks. For all of these reasons, the cataloging of his studio recordings herein—and especially the assigning of a specific take to an album track—requires qualification.

The Michael Krogsgaard sessionography, issued in instalments in *The Telegraph* and *The Bridge* fanzines, becomes less and less reliable as the years roll by, until it finally stutters to a stop in 1990 (and as a guide to the *under the red sky* sessions, it verges on the useless). Even with the *Blood on the Tracks* and *Desire* sessions, where Dylan almost invariably stuck to the "live in studio" method, our discographer omits or misreads information (no details are given for an August 1, 1975, session; while he seems hopelessly confused as to the corelationship of "Call Letter Blues" and "Meet Me in the Morning"). No great crime there. But the problem is that he never explicates the basis for his information and rarely reproduces the track sheets to which he has had recourse. It is as if he *wants* to cover his tracks.

Despite such concerns, whenever Dylan sticks to recording live in a recognized studio on the East Coast or down south, said sessionography remains a useful and generally reliable guide. Thus, *Blood on the Tracks, Desire, Slow Train Coming, Saved,* and *Infidels* are all reasonably well-documented (save at the overdub stage). Where Dylan decides to record something out West, well away from Sony HQ, at his own whim in his chosen setting—i.e., *Street-Legal, Shot of Love,* the LA-based *Empire Burlesque* sessions—the Dane's sessionography is little more than a starting point for a credible chronology. And by *Oh Mercy,* Krogsgaard seems ready to throw in the towel, providing contradictory take information and omitting documented takes and overdubs, while ignoring take information already published (and substantiated) in my own *Recording Sessions 1960–1994.*

Since our fellow archivist gave up on his self-appointed task, Dylan has recorded some four albums of original material. However, of these, only *Time Out of Mind* appears to have generated any substantial body of outtake material—covered with unexpected breadth on the eighth official Bootleg Series, *Tell Tale Signs* (2008). The various versions of the 2008 set also included reproductions of tantalizingly trimmed track sheets and studio logs hinting at yet more mouthwatering content (and even other, unused outtakes—q.v. #562, "All I Ever Loved Is You").

Thankfully, the combination of these reproduced sheets and the recollections of musicians and engineers, some given to fanzines at the time, others in a recent bumper issue of *Uncut*, have enabled a reasonably accurate picture of these sessions to emerge, even if it has been painted with broad brushstrokes. I have also been permitted to hear a few of the outtakes that almost made the 2008 set, which also helped me fill in the dots. But full track details for these important sessions have still to be collated and compiled—hence, the lack of specificity in track information given here and on *Tell Tale Signs* for the *Time Out of Mind* material.

The session information for *"Love and Theft"* is somewhat more straightforward, largely because Dylan reverted to recording the old way—live to analog tape—and only recorded songs he wanted to use. The tape logs have also proven accessible (and informative). The *Modern Times* sessions followed along similar lines—as the two track sheets reproduced for *Tell Tale Signs* confirm—but tape logs have sadly not been available, so guesswork is again king.

However, the fulsome *Uncut* interview with engineer Chris Shaw (published online in its entirety) has proven invaluable in piecing together some kinda history of these sessions. So although we are still some way off a definitive documentation of Dylan's studio sessions—something akin to Ernst Jorgensen's Elvis Presley sessionography—I shall still claim that the session information herein is the most accurate of any would-be researcher and that any departure from or substantive addition to information found in the Krogsgaard sessionography has come about because of my own work on the sessions at Sony or through recourse to other reliable sources. I found common sense helped, too.

{ Still on the Road }

***Lyrics* & Other Lyrics**—As with *Revolution in the Air*, I again recommend that the reader does not rely solely on the official *Lyrics* but, where possible, checks out other versions of lyrics, as published *and* as recorded. Because the two editions of *Lyrics* published officially in this period—1985 and 2004—seem on occasions to delight in their own perversity, I suggest any reader also check out the Words Fill My Head section of Olof Björner's unofficial About Bob website, where many of the missing lyrics can be found. Thankfully, the radically different versions of the songs included on the 2008 volume of the (ongoing) Bootleg Series, *Tell Tale Signs*, have been assigned their own section.

As to when we can expect a more complete, nay annotated, version of *Lyrics*, your guess is as good as mine. But a good start could be made by simply reorganizing the existing edition so that it adhered to the modus operandi of *Writings and Drawings*, organizing songs in a way that doesn't insult readers' intelligence (*The Basement Tapes* coming between "George Jackson" and *Pat Garrett* is unforgivable, as is the assigning of songs written in 1961–2 with the first album, when almost everything dates from the *Freewheelin'* period) and maybe even getting some important songs retranscribed by someone who knows his (or her) Dylan. Guess what—the line forms here.

{Song Information}

Published Lyrics—References the two latter-day editions of Dylan's *Lyrics*, published in 1985 and 2004 respectively. Where relevant, *The Songs of Bob Dylan 1966–1975* (1976) has also been cited. Those instances in which the Dylan fanzine *The Telegraph* published a lyric first have also been referenced. For any other lyrical variants, the *Words Fill My Head* website is generally the best starting point.

Known Studio Recording—Information is derived from my own *Recording Sessions 1960–1994*, the Michael Krogsgaard sessionography (up to 1990), an up-to-date printout of the Sony database, tape logs for the *Time Out of Mind* and *Modern Times* sessions reproduced in the *Tell Tale Signs* booklet/s, and the tape logs for the *"Love and Theft"* sessions obtained independently. The code for the albums, singles, and CDs on which studio recordings have been officially released is as follows:

45	45 rpm single
ATB	*Across the Borderline* (1993)
BoB2	*Best of Bob Dylan Vol. 2* (2000)
BIO	*Biograph* (1985)
BoTT	*Blood on the Tracks* (1975)
CHR	*Chronicles* promo CD (2004)
DES	*Desire* (1976)
DSYS	*Divine Secrets of the Ya-Ya Sisterhood* soundtrack (2002)

{ Still on the Road }

DIG	*Down in the Groove* (1988)
EB	*Empire Burlesque* (1985)
G&G	*Gods and Generals* soundtrack (2003)
GSoBD	*Gotta Serve Somebody—The Gospel Songs of Bob Dylan* (2003)
GH3	*Greatest Hits Vol. 3* (1994)
HoF	*Hearts of Fire* soundtrack (1987)
INF	*Infidels* (1983)
JM	*Jerry Maguire* soundtrack (1996)
KOL	*Knocked Out Loaded* (1986)
L+T	*"Love And Theft"* (2001)
LYS	*Lucky You* soundtrack (2007)
MoTT	"Most of the Time" CD EP (1990)
MT	*Modern Times* (2006)
NRTC	*No Reason to Cry* (1976)
NCS	*North Country* soundtrack (2006)
OM	*Oh Mercy* (1989)
R+C	*Renaldo & Clara* [movie] (1978)
R&H	*Rattle and Hum* (1988)
SAV	*Saved* (1980)
SoL	*Shot of Love* (1981)
STC	*Slow Train Coming* (1979)
SftND	*Songs for the New Depression* (1976)
S-L	*Street-Legal* (1978)
TTS	*Tell Tale Signs: The Bootleg Series Vol. 8* (2008)
TBS	*The Bootleg Series Vols. 1–3* (1991)
TOOM	*Time Out of Mind* (1997)
TW1	*Traveling Wilburys Volume One* (1988)
TW3	*Traveling Wilburys Volume Three* (1990)
TWC	*The Traveling Wilburys Collection* (2007)
UN	*Unplugged* (1995)
utrs	*under the red sky* (1990)
WB	*Wonder Boys* soundtrack (2000)

1974

{ Blood on the Tracks }

*On January 3, 1974, Dylan returned to the road (save for 1982–5, for good).
On December 30, 1974, having returned "home" to Minnesota for Christmas,
he completed the album he had spent most of the year working on, recording,
thinking about, and rerecording.* Blood on the Tracks *was the result of a year
of letting his soul bleed into the songs again. And of putting his marriage vows
on hold. The process, though, of getting an album out of the fifteen songs he
scribbled into his notebook that summer—and two that he didn't—had proven
the most tortuous since* Blonde on Blonde. *Probably because he knew how good
they were, he was determined not to let this opportunity go to waste . . .*

{301} **LILY, ROSEMARY, AND THE JACK OF HEARTS**
Published lyric/s: Lyrics 85; Lyrics 04.
*Known studio recordings: A&R Studios, NYC, September 16, 1974—1 take;
Sound 80, Minneapolis, MN, December 30, 1974 [BoTT].*
First known performance: Salt Lake City, UT, May 25, 1976.

> The uses of a ballad have changed to such a degree. When they were singing
> years ago, it would be as entertainment . . . A fellow could sit down and
> sing a song for a half hour, and everybody could listen, and you could form
> opinions. You'd be waiting to see how it ended, what happened to this person
> or that person. It would be like going to a movie . . . Now we have movies,
> so why does someone want to sit around for a half hour listening to a ballad?
> Unless the story was of such a nature that you couldn't find it in a movie.
>
> —Dylan, to John Cohen, June 1968

17

Just six months after *John Wesley Harding*—"the amnesia" having barely set in—Dylan was trying to figure out how to reconfigure the most ancient form of popular song for an audience brought up on "going to a movie." Six years later, he pulled it off. "Lily, Rosemary, and the Jack of Hearts" sets out to tell, and succeeds in telling, a story "of such a nature that you couldn't find it in a movie" (though Jonathan Taplin at one point thought it could make the transition to celluloid). A ménage à quatre involving the three title characters and Big Jim, the tangled tale ends with only the fair Lily and the Jack of Hearts escaping with their lives.

This epic ballad appears to have been wholly inspired by Dylan's experience of making the movie *Pat Garrett and Billy the Kid* in a genre which suited both ballad and b movies: the Western. "Lily, Rosemary, and the Jack of Hearts" even acts like a shooting script at times. When Big Jim pulls a gun on the Jack of Hearts, only to find that "the cold revolver clicked," one's mind's eye immediately sees the empty gun in close-up, then the expression of Big Jim ("ya couldn't say surprised"), before focusing on Rosemary ("steady in her eyes") behind him. Only in the next-but-one verse do we find out that she (or Lily) has not only emptied his gun but has stabbed him with a penknife, a beautiful touch—the penknife being the favored instrument of murderers in every traditional ballad from "Love Henry" to "The Cruel Mother."

How long the idea gestated after those days in Durango we can only guess. But it should come as no great surprise that he wrote such a song separate from—and antecedent to—the pouring forth that makes up the rest of his 1974 album. It may have been something he had already started to sketch out on the road. (In his on-tour diary, he broods about the fact that Billy the Kid died when he was only twenty-one.) Certainly, the impetus here is quite different to the other nine cuts. In this song, he idealizes an outlaw who is part Billy the Kid, part Robin Hood, but mostly that archetypal "stranger" who arrives in town, turns everything on its head, and rides out.

Not that his model for this character comes from any movie. Rather, it can be found in a pack of cards, itself a running motif throughout the song (and, indeed, album). The Jack of Hearts is the Magus, the Magician of the Tarot, a juggler, "the mountebank who surprises yokels by his sleight-of-hand, the trickster in the commercial world, the subtle deceiver" (*Oracle of the Tarot*). Nor is it a coincidence that at the feet of the Magus, in the classic Rider-Waite tarot deck, are two flowers—the lily and the rose. Both appear, in appropriately Madonna-esque guises, in the ballad: each in thrall to the master magician. One is even prepared to spill blood to preserve his freedom of movement.

The sophistication of this narrative, both in its symbolism and as a carefully woven tapestry, is really quite remarkable, even for a man brought up on the "big ballads." That copy of Child's *English and Scottish Popular Ballads* which Allen Ginsberg remembered sitting on Dylan's shelf in MacDougal Street had been well thumbed. This was not a song Dylan ran off in an afternoon.

He presumably worked on "Lily, Rosemary, and the Jack of Hearts" in the immediate aftermath of a six-week tour. Certainly, by the time he was ready to crack open a new notebook and transfer the scraps of song he'd been working on, "Lily, Rosemary, and the Jack of Hearts"— his most ambitious lyric in almost a decade—was already a realized piece of work in need of very little tweaking.

Its position at the start of the *Blood on the Tracks* notebook—that fifty-cent purchase whose contents are now priceless—suggests not only that it was already to hand, but also that it was not a song he worked on much down on his Minnesotan farm, where most of the album was penned. Of the sixteen verses, just two are given a light makeover in the notebook—the twelfth ("Lily's arms were locked around . . .") and the fifteenth ("The next day was hangin' day . . .").

Dylan, it seems, was never entirely satisfied with the former scene, in which Lily entwines herself about the Jack of Hearts, and tried a number of ways to make the dialogue work. When he rerecorded the song in Minneapolis in December—for what became the album take— he omitted this verse altogether, even though its final line sums up the song's theme better than any other: "Just another night in the life of the Jack of Hearts." As it happens, he forgot to amend the songbook, so the verse has always appeared in the printed lyric:

Lily's arms were locked around the man she dearly loved to touch,
She forgot all about the man she couldn't stand, who hounded her so much,
"I've missed you so," she said to him, and he felt she was sincere,
But just beyond the door he felt jealousy and fear.
Just another night . . .

The "hanging" verse troubled Dylan, too, as he sought to make Rosemary's acceptance of her fate appear suitably stoic. In the process, he transforms the perfectly acceptable "And in the final moments, it was said she gave a wink / Toward the purple hills, or maybe to the Jack of Hearts" into something less satisfactory: "Nobody knew in those final moments what she did think." As a result, he forces the narrator to awkwardly introduce himself: "But I'm sure it had something to do with the Jack of Hearts." He also required the poet within to focus on the sober hanging judge, introducing the tautological "hadn't had a drink" to rhyme with "blink," so that he could introduce the memorable get-out clause, "The only person on the scene missin' was the Jack of Hearts." The whole song had been "just another night in the life. . . ."

The one challenge left now was to see if he could record this epic fifteen-verse narrative with a similar minimum of fuss. Which it appears he did. And again it came first. On day one of the sessions at the old Studio A in New York (now known as A&R Studios)—before the band called up to lend a hand had even arrived—Dylan had cut the song in a single take, making it the first song to be assigned to the album. Nor did he feel throughout the New York sessions the slightest need to return to the song.

Only at a second set of sessions in late December, set up in the frozen Midwest by his brother David, did he make it one of five songs "reworked" with a less minimalist touch. Before the tape rolled, the younger Zimmerman instructed the local Minneapolis musicians, "This is a long song; just keep playing. When you think it ends, it doesn't, so just keep on playing." It was a smart call. Unerringly, Dylan did it again: cutting the song in a single take after only a partial run-through (such was his haste that he was stuck playing harmonica in the wrong key—A, not D—throughout).

Dylan was less tempted to try his luck live. This compelling, convoluted narrative has been attempted just once in performance, as a duet with Joan Baez—who cut the song herself for her own live album, *From Every Stage*—at the final Rolling Thunder Revue show in Salt Lake City. He didn't think he could remember all the words and ended up writing a series of cue phrases on the sleeve of his shirt. He apparently still managed to pull it off (just as he had memorized Guthrie's equally epic "Tom Joad" fifteen years earlier). Unfortunately, Mormons don't appear to own tape recorders. The concert was not recorded, leaving this particular gathering of the Jack of Hearts and friends just a memory for the fortunate few.

{302} TANGLED UP IN BLUE

Published lyric/s: Lyrics 85; Lyrics 04. *[Variants 74–8: I Can Change I Swear; 1984 lyric: Words Fill My Head/In His Own Words 2.]*
Known studio recordings: A&R Studios, NYC, September 16, 1974—1 take; September 17, 1974—2 takes [TBS]; September 19, 1974—6 takes; Sound 80, Minneapolis, MN, December 30, 1974 [BoTT].
First known performance: New Haven, CT, November 13, 1975 [early show].

It's like this painter who lives around here . . . He might take a barn from twenty miles away, and hook it up with a brook right next door, then with a car ten miles away, and with the sky on some certain day, and the light on the trees from another certain day. A person passing by will be painted alongside someone [who's] ten miles away . . . That's more or less what I do.—Dylan, to John Cohen, June 1968

This description of "what I do" given to John Cohen can hardly be said to apply to those songs Dylan wrote in 1968—all three of them. It was another technique he was saving for a rainy day. Indeed, he only confirmed he had been working on the "real" follow-up to *John Wesley Harding* throughout the "lost" years when he began introducing "Tangled Up in Blue" at a number of American 1978 shows as "a song it took me ten years to live and two years to write."

During the spring of 1974 he finally began painting the words to this particular story, in which the past, present, and future intersect on the same tangled plain. As with previous momentous breakthroughs—like "Mr. Tambourine Man" and "Like a Rolling Stone"—"Tangled Up in Blue" became one of those songs Dylan seemed quite happy to talk about, welcoming the opportunity to explicate upon a breakthrough no less profound or enduring.

Invariably on such occasions, the two themes he sought to address were the way the narrative played with time and how it was essentially an aural version of a painting in his head; as "Lily, Rosemary, and the

21

Jack of Hearts" had been the aural equivalent of a motion picture. As late as 1991, he still talked about "Tangled Up in Blue," and the album it spawned, as products of "my painting period . . . learning how to paint on canvas. . . . It's like they are paintings, those songs, or they appeared to be. . . . They're more like a painter would paint a song as [opposed] to compose it."

This "painting period" came about because of time spent that spring in the company of an elderly teacher called Norman Raeben, in New York, while deciding what to do about his failing marriage. At the time, Dylan avoided discussing the connection with Raeben, but after spending a year and a half of his life applying the same methodology to a four-hour movie, *Renaldo and Clara* (1977), he opened up about their common inspiration.

Raeben was clearly a remarkable man, who pushed Dylan to unify the visions that had always come his way. As the songwriter informed poet-friend Ginsberg, "I had a teacher that was a conscious artist and he drilled it into me to be a conscious artist. So I became a conscious artist." There was very little practical about what Raeben taught his pupil/s. To him, it was all about vision, not technique—something Dylan wisely expounded over a number of interviews in 1977–8:

> He didn't teach you how to paint so much. He didn't teach you how to draw. He didn't teach you any of these things. He taught you [about] putting your head and your mind and your eye together. . . . He looked into you and told you what you were. . . . If you were interested in coming out of that, you could stay there and force yourself to come out of it. You, yourself, did all the work. . . . My mind and my hand and my eye were not connected up. I had a lot of fantasy dreams. . . . It wasn't art or painting. It was a course in something else. . . . After that I wrote *Blood on the Tracks* . . . Everybody agrees that that was pretty different. . . . There's a code in the lyrics. . . . You've got yesterday, today and tomorrow all in the same room.

Having been reintroduced to his "true self," it took Dylan a while to recognize a number of these former selves. If he felt like he had become an entirely different person, he was not alone: "I went home after that and my wife never did understand me ever since that day. . . . She never knew what I was talking about, what I was thinking about, and I couldn't possibly explain it." Having married a mathematician, she'd woken up with a poet.

He later informed Ron Rosenbaum, "I haven't come to the place that Rimbaud came to when he decided to stop writing and run guns in Africa." Which is not what he says in "Tangled Up in Blue"—and I'd rather trust the tale than the artist. The couplet "Then he started into dealing with slaves / And something inside of him died" explicitly equates Dylan's Woodstock period with Rimbaud gun-running in Abyssinia. With "Tangled Up in Blue," he threw off the shackles and was astounded to discover that his memory again served him well. By his own admission, having previously "tried to force-learn it . . . [but] I couldn't learn what I had been able to do naturally on *Highway 61 Revisited* . . . I learned in '75 [sic] that I have to do it . . . consciously; and those are the kind of songs I [now] wanted to write. The ones that do have the break up of time, where there is no time, [while] trying to make the focus as strong as a magnifying glass under the sun."

In order to lock in such intensity, Dylan was obliged to insert himself into his own story—as an omnipresent narrator looking at all these past selves. The ménage à trois element thus introduced ("I lived with them. . .") reflected a Gemini at war with himself. Even if he liked to introduce the song in concert as something he "wrote . . . about three people in love with each other all at the same time," it was his twin, "that enemy within," who was his opponent—as he almost admitted to Australian journalist Craig McGregor, describing "Tangled" as "the first [song] I ever wrote that I felt free enough to change all the . . . he and the she and the I and the you, and the we and the us. I figured it was all the same anyway."

A decade after he had flicked the switch and found his muse again, he went further, telling *Musician's* Bill Flanagan, "I was trying to do something that I didn't think had ever been done before. In terms of trying to tell a story and be a present character in it without it being some kind of fake, sappy attempted tearjerker. I was trying to be somebody in the present time while conjuring up a lot of past images."

The efficacy of the technique allowed autobiography to entwine around the very roots from which his art sprang, while putting some distance between real life and Art. When discussing this song with Matt Damsker in 1978, he felt able to claim, "There might be some little part of me which is confessing something I've experienced and I know, but it is *definitely* not the total me confessing anything."

The lines that ring truest are the opening and closing couplets: where he is lying in bed, remembering the past; and at the crossroads, looking to the future. When he sings, "Me, I'm still on the road, heading for another joint," he is contrasting his peripatetic life with the one his wife wanted for them. It proved to be an urge he never entirely killed off. Even in May 1971, at the height of his domestic hiatus, he told one biographer, "The important thing is to keep moving . . . Or else to stop by the side of the road every once in a while and build a house." He had done both and knew which worked for him. If past and present selves are reconciled at song's end, the lovers are not.

As part of the process, this conscious artist had become a rather self-conscious lyricist. If Dylan's references to Rimbaud and Hesse are oblique, for the first time in a lyric he was owning up to reading some real poetry. Thus, the mysterious girl from the topless bar (Hermine again— see "Went to See the Gypsy" in the previous volume) hands him a book of sonnets in which every word "rang true and glowed like burning coal." He even kept up the gag by informing McGregor "that [the] poet from the 13th century" was Plutarch, knowing full well it was Petrarch, the founding father of the love-sonnet—who was actually from the 14th century, but who's counting. (My prime candidate for the specific sonnet from Petrarch's *Canzoniere* Dylan is recalling would be #107: "I see no way now I can free myself / those lovely eyes have warred with me so long / that, alas, I fear this burden of care / will destroy my heart that knows no truce. / I want to flee: but those loving beams . . . are in my mind day and night.")

Like "Lily, Rosemary, and the Jack of Hearts," "Tangled Up in Blue" underwent surprisingly little reconstructive surgery after it was added to the notebook, suggesting it also was largely realized by the time it entered there. But her words to him, as they "split up on a sad dark night," originally tied him closer to the wheel of Fate on which they were bound; "Hell, this ain't no end / We've been through too much together / And we're bound to meet again . . ."

Once he started singing these words, he doubtless found such a word-rich construct left him tongue-tied. Likewise, "I muttered somethin' underneath my breath" is a lot more visual than "I made a joke, she didn't laugh." Otherwise, the words he set about recording at the end of the first *Blood on the Tracks* session (September 16) were the same ones he entered in the notebook back in spring.

Its recorded self, though, did not come at all easy. Having already recorded eight of the ten songs he intended for the album in his first, six-hour session—at least four of them with some permutation of Deliverance—it seems Dylan deliberately held off cutting "Tangled Up in Blue" until the very end of the night. This version—supposedly issued in 1991 on *The Bootleg Series Vols 1–3*[1]—suggests he quickly abandoned any idea of putting a band behind the song/s. A second guitar (Weissberg's?) picks out the parts of the melody Dylan's scratchy rhythm has left unsaid, while Tony Brown's bass underpins the clack-clack of the singer's jacket-buttons. But something ain't right. Weissberg recalled how "Bob . . . seemed a bit ill at ease in the studio, as though he wanted to get it over with." Having hurried through the song, he knew he'd have to return to it.

By the time work resumed the following evening, Dylan had dispensed with all the ancillary musicians. His only musical prop would be Tony Brown's bass notes. Yet three more takes failed to do the song justice, and rather than keep plugging away, he held back, knowing its time would come—a technique which would prove a feature of the New York sessions. As drummer Richard Crooks discovered on day one, "He'll do one take of one song, then just move on to another song, and maybe an hour or two later he'll come back and do that first song again, just so you don't lock on it too much."

In the case of "Tangled," Dylan only came back to it on the final session, the 19th. Again, he tried it a couple of times and then turned to other songs before returning to it at the end of the night, capturing it a couple more times. In fact, he had already caught it earlier that evening—as he discovered when reviewing the tapes, sequencing the album on or around September 25. This time the vocal had that edge of desperation the song required—even if his jacket was still providing percussion.

Yet enough doubt remained for him to try running it down again in Minneapolis at a second late December session. Having intended to rework just a couple of the songs cut in New York, he slowly became convinced that half the album could benefit from the kind of full-on accompaniment he had previously disdained. It was with "Tangled Up in Blue"—which had now acquired an intro awfully similar to Jefferson Airplane's "Volunteers"—that he elected to start work on December 30.

According to guitarist Kevin Odegard, he still "produced a small red notebook in which were scribbled the verses to [this] first song he wanted to record that night." Which begs the question: did he come up with the new sixth verse—wholly absent from said notebook—on the spot? One thing is sure: he is no longer "too busy, or too stoned." Rather, he is living "with them on Montague Street," consciously evoking a time when "there was music in the cafes at night / And revolution in the air." It was a sentiment to which he would adhere through every rewrite to come—and there have been a fair few.

Once he began to see this twisting tale as an ongoing narrative of his life to date, there was very little stopping him. Between 1975 and 1984 the song underwent a number of dramatic reworkings, of which the versions performed in 1978 and 1984 proved especially powerful. In 1975 the job that had drifted down from L.A. to New Orleans in its passage from A&R to Sound 80 was transplanted to Santa Fe. In 1976 it was a gear-crunching heavy-metal arrangement that signalled a change in direction, not any change of words. While in 1978, he decided he had another tale to tell, which is presumably why he told Matt Damsker he'd never been happy with the original recording/s: "I didn't perform it well. I didn't have the power to perform it well, but I did write the [*Blood on the Tracks*] songs. They can be changed [now], but the idea was right."

The vocal he applied to the song during the fall 1978 shows was not only "fighting sentimentality," as he once claimed, it was also battling against any vestiges of the gorgeous melody to which he had been singing the song earlier the same year as part of a guitar–saxophone tour de force. Meanwhile, two lyrical elements now entered the song: one there originally, but toned down in the recording process; the other entirely new. An overriding sense of destiny, first emphasized by the modified line "We're bound to meet again on the avenue," is reinforced when the dancer informs him, "It ain't no accident that you came."

The new element reflected a reconstructed worldview which concerned itself more with the poetry of the King James Bible than some medieval sonneteer. From mid-November 1978, the topless lady "opened up the Bible, and started quoting it to me . . . Jeremiah Chapters One to Thirty Three." Jeremiah 31:31, concerned with a new covenant between Jehovah and his chosen people, would later be quoted on the inner-sleeve of *Saved*. The change presaged by these lines led Dylan to abandon "Tangled" at the turn of the year, along with a whole slew of mid-seventies masterpieces.

It took until 1984 before he felt any need to revisit this song, and even then he still felt obliged to rework it. Whereas "Simple Twist of Fate" was given a banana-republic makeover, "Tangled Up in Blue" acquired an anti-romantic slant. A new ending suggested not only that the trail was now cold, but also that his pursuit of True Love had been a mistake all along. Coming from a man who in the interim had prayed to the Lord to take away "this trouble in mind," one line in particular—the penultimate one below—seemed like a statement of intent:

> So now I'm going on back again, to that forbidden zone,
> I got to find someone among the women and men whose destiny is unknown.
> Some are masters of illusion, some are ministers of the trade,
> All of them strong [on] delusion, all of their beds unmade,
> Me, I'm still walking towards the sun/Son,
> Trying to stay out of the joints . . . [Brussels, June 7]

This version, rivetingly debuted at a show in Rotterdam in early June, was released in a disappointingly emaciated form on *Real Live*, from a tired Wembley show a month later. Yet the new lyric seemed to please the man himself. He revealed the thinking behind the rewrite the following year, "The old ones [*sic*] were never quite filled in. I rewrote it in a hotel room somewhere. I think it was Amsterdam. I wanted to sing that song so I looked at it again, and I changed it. When I sang it the next night I knew it was right."

Yet the original lyrical construct—one of his most poetic—continued to bother the man even after the song reverted to its 1974 guise in performance, as it did from 1987 onward. In 1991, he would tell Robert Hilburn, "I always thought ['Tangled Up in Blue'] was written too fast, too rushed . . . just too many lines, as if I were racing to get from here to there." Actually, the only thing rushed about the song was the Never Ending Tour electric arrangement, which seemed in a particular hurry to complete the story (in marked contrast to the performance in Dortmund, Germany, in September 1987—probably the last live rendition to *really* do it justice). As one of the frustratingly few songs from the mid-seventies he has allowed to hang around, we should perhaps be grateful for the small mercy of its continued presence, pale shadow or not. Meanwhile, back in 1974, "Tangled Up in Blue" spawned song after song bound to the same wheel of fate, in a summer bonanza of inspiration.

{303} YOU'RE A BIG GIRL NOW

Published lyric/s: Lyrics 85; Lyrics 04.
Known studio recordings: A&R Studios, NYC, September 16, 1974—1 take; September 17, 1974—2 takes [BIO—tk. 2]; September 19, 1974—1 take; Sound 80, Minneapolis, MN, December 30, 1974 [BoTT].
First known performance: Hattiesburg, MS, May 1, 1976.

> I had a couple of years there where I went out to be by myself quite a bit of the time, and that's where I experienced those kinds of songs on *Blood on the Tracks* . . . I'll do anything to write a song . . . [Well,] I used to anyway. —Dylan, to Lynne Allen, December 1978

If the New York recording of "Tangled Up in Blue" ultimately failed to satisfy its author, the version of "You're a Big Girl Now" recorded the same week seems to have made him plain uncomfortable. The first of a punnet of ultrapersonal songs (#s 303–10) now entered in the notebook, it would be one of only three which would make the album. "You're a Big Girl Now" was pain personified, that pain remaining red raw when he cut the exquisite New York version originally intended for the album (only released ten years later, on *Biograph*). It is to just such a recording that *Blood on the Tracks* engineer Phil Ramone is surely alluding when he suggests, "Emotionally he was in a state of revealing his life, and most writers don't want to tell you they're writing their autobiography, but it's there in the atmosphere, as you hear the songs unfolding."

In "You're a Big Girl Now," Dylan is writing from the vantage point of someone who, having reached the top, discovers he is really "on the bottom." Without any secrets to conceal, he discovers a brutal honesty in the pain of loneliness ("I'm going out of my mind / With a pain that stops and starts"). He also finds an inner strength. As he told the sympathetic Julia Orange, in 1978, "There's strength in that loneliness. You must have that kind of strength coming from an unbearable place to remain focused . . . Everything else must go. If there's anything in the way, it will interfere."

Here, nothing is allowed to interfere. Even on its entry into the notebook, barely a word is out of place. But time not only heals, it sometimes deceives. And when Dylan's brother convinced him that the album was a little too pared down (to the bone) it was this song, along with "Idiot Wind," that he decided to rerecord, i.e., the two most naked, searing expressions of hurt on the whole album. On a radio show, shortly after the album's release, Dylan expressed mystification that, "People tell me they enjoy [*Blood on the Tracks*]. It's hard for me to relate to that. I mean, people enjoying that type of pain." The strength that had led him to write and record this song had drained away by the time he entered Sound 80 Studios on December 27, to be replaced by a ghostly memory of its all-consuming hurt.

Not surprisingly, the song went unattempted live after he and Sara became ostensibly reconciled. Only on the second leg of the Rolling Thunder Revue, in the spring of 1976, did he remember why he wrote it, playing it long and hard enough to warrant inclusion on the *Hard Rain* album. Though there have been subsequent restorations, he has not returned to said "unbearable place" since (save perhaps for the Rundown rehearsal version from February 1, 1978). Throughout 1978 and the G. E. Smith era of the Never Ending Tour (1988–90), as Dylan waved a fond farewell to Love Minus Zero, it acquired a nonchalance not altogether befitting such a baring of the soul.

{304} SHELTER FROM THE STORM

Published lyric/s: Lyrics 85; Lyrics 04.
Known studio recordings: A&R Studios, NYC, September 17, 1974—5 takes.
[BoTT—tk. 5] [JM—tk. 1].
First known performance: Clearwater, FL, April 17, 1976.

Though "There Ain't Gonna Be Any Next Time" [#308] actually appears next in the notebook, that song belongs with two other songs of a similar hue, which also failed to make the grade—as a mere footnote to the ongoing outpourings of guilt. It was immediately followed by a lyric worthy of any poet laureate, racked with the same grief as his "big girl" song and suffused with remorse. "Shelter from the Storm," though, was not as fully honed when transferred to the page. Perhaps it was the first song entered into the notebook in the *immediate* aftermath of its composition (assuming, as I do, that he'd been carrying the previous songs around with him).

Another long song, the "Shelter" narrative descends from some mythopoeic realm, its mournful message operating almost as "Wedding Song Part 2." This time he does not explicitly state that "she" saved his life, rather describing how he was "burned out from exhaustion, buried in the hail." Or, as he originally wrote it, "Bushwhacked on the prairie, rolled on New Year's Eve / Poisoned in the orchard, buried in the leaves." In its original guise, "Shelter from the Storm" also contained an extra verse, at the midpoint of its eleven verses:

Now the bonds are broken but they can be retied,
By one more journey to the woods, and the holes where spirits hide.
It's a never-ending battle for a peace that's always torn,
Come in, she said . . .

That first line represents the only moment in the song where he explicitly expresses the hope that she may once again provide shelter. This could be why it stayed a part of the song long enough to be recorded,as fans discovered when an alternate take was used for the soundtrack to Cameron Crowe's *Jerry Maguire* movie. This first run-through on the seventeenth has no bass accompaniment, possibly because he was showing Brown the song. Taking a pause to work on other songs, he only returned to "Shelter" later the same evening, wisely deciding the sixth verse added very little to the song. Trimming it to ten, he found a way "to cross the line."

That word-perfect fifth take survived all the reconfigurations the album underwent, emerging as one of its real highlights. And though Dylan went on to perform it a number of different ways—almost always effectively—the nature of the song remained fixed. Whether singing it loud and clear to its subject at Fort Collins in 1976, introducing a full-blooded arrangement as "the story of my life" in 1978, noodling back to a mellower self in 1987, or getting back to the country at the Warfield in 1992, the song has endured as long as that yearning for "a place where it's always safe and warm."

305} BELL TOWER BLUES

Published lyric/s: Lyrics 04 *[1 verse in ms.]*
Lyric included in Blood on the Tracks *notebook, c. summer 1974.*
Known studio recordings: ?A&R Studios, NYC, September 17, 1974.

It is perhaps a tad surprising that *Blood on the Tracks* draws so little on the blues, a form which Dylan had fully mastered and lent itself to all that he was feeling. Yet there is no such shortage of blues songs among those he was sketching out in his notebook that summer. Almost every song he removed from the process prior to recording falls into this category. In the end, he allowed them just a single slot, so every blues song which knocked upon his door had to jockey for that one position. ("Buckets of Rain," the second blues song on the album, was an afterthought.)

The couple of blues songs he did get as far as recording in New York were also set to the exact same twelve-bar arrangement. Aside from "Meet Me in the Morning" and "Call Letter Blues"—both ultimately released— there is a third, unknown blues track attempted at the second September session, listed simply as "Blues." This could be one of those two titles, but it would be odd for the engineer to list either so vaguely, given that they are both correctly identified elsewhere on the track sheets. It is tempting to believe that Dylan toyed with the idea of running down a "third" lyric, still set to the self-same template, to see if it suited this suite of songs better.

If so, the song "Bell Tower Blues" is the most likely candidate. It actually came first, clearly providing the model for "Call Letter Blues," and, to a lesser extent, "Meet Me in the Morning." The first verse, reproduced from the notebook on page 310 of the 2004 *Lyrics* (to "illustrate," er, *Pat Garrett and Billy the Kid*), sets the tone: "Climbed upon the bell tower, to gaze around at the terrain / I couldn't find you anywhere, you were gone like a northern train." He proceeds to wait for her at the schoolyard, where she is supposed to be (!), only to envisage her then running toward a windmill. Finally giving up the chase, he instructs himself, "Gotta learn to keep my distance." The best line in the song has no obvious bearing on his quest: "Fishing in the river, using my radio for bait." Underneath that apple-sucking tree, I presume.

{306} IF YOU SEE HER, SAY HELLO

Published lyric/s: Lyrics 85; Lyrics 04 *[new lyric]. [Variants 74–78:* I Can Change I Swear.*]*

Known studio recordings: A&R Studios, NYC, September 16, 1974—2 takes [TBS]; September 19, 1974—1 take; Sound 80, Minneapolis, MN, December 30, 1974 [BoTT]. First known performance: Lakeland, FL, April 18, 1976.

> A lot of myself crosses over into my songs. I'll write something and say to myself, I can change this. I can make this not so personal. And at other times I'll say, I think I'll leave this on a personal level, and if somebody wants to . . . make up their own minds about what kind of character I am, that's up to them. Other times I might say, "Well, it's too personal, I think I'll turn the corner on it." —Dylan, to Scott Cohen, 1985

By the time Dylan wrote "If You See Her, Say Hello," he had certainly reached that point in the writing process where the songs in the notebook were being entered as they were being written. Previously the lyrics were already sculpted, even those he was inclined to refine, but "If You See Her, Say Hello" has been written down with the ink still wet from last night's tears. Verses snake up and down the page, and when Dylan reaches the end, he starts rewriting two (of originally six) verses. The original fourth verse he scrapped entirely:

> Didn't mean to fail her, I guess I should have known,
> That another person's happiness can never be your own,
> And though you can't mistake the emptiness, the bitterness is gone,
> The pleasures of those days with her still linger on and on.

A little too close to the bone. Even an attempted rewrite of that second couplet—"If I seem preoccupied, there's nothing much to tell / It is the pleasures of those days with her that keeps me in a spell"—fails to turn the requisite corner. A further change, to the third person, making it so that "the pleasure of those days with her still bothers *him* at night," fails to mask the still visible scars. Eventually he decides the verse has to go.

The third-person narrator sticks around for a while, though. He even acquires a nickname—"the kid." It is "the kid" who directs the third verse not to her, but to the man who is making love to her; and who, unable to fully "express his love," "respects her for what she done, it lifted up the veil / . . . that covered up his eyes and kept his mind in jail."

This is one seriously mixed-up kid, sure of only one thing—he wants her back. That feeling only grew stronger; which is perhaps why, when he got to New York, Dylan couldn't wait to get this one down. One of those songs he recorded solo on day one while waiting for Weissberg and his band to appear, it was the first song he rolled tape on. That initial version would later appear on *The Bootleg Series Vols 1–3*, in all its tentativeness, but it was not the one he was looking for, and he recut it in a single take, three nights later, with Tony Brown's burbling bass beautifully complementing the man's sly rearrangement of that old favorite, "Scarborough Fair." It is no coincidence that he has set the song to the same melodic paradigm as "Girl of the North Country," another lyric addressed to a third party, asking him to send his best to a gal who left him behind.

But still he wondered whether the end result was "too personal, too probing," and it duly became another song he elected to put through the Minneapolis mangler. By the time he rerecorded the song at Sound 80, "I" has replaced another, and he is no longer the cuckold. "If you get close to her, kiss her once for me" is an antiseptic replacement for the displaced intimacy of "If you're making love to her, kiss her for the kid"—and one instantly revealed on the album's release, accompanied as the first pressing was by Pete Hammill's sleeve notes, which quoted the line as he recorded it in New York. Though the song came out the other side still shimmering, only the merest hint of the hurt which had spilled across those manila pages remained.

However, the bitterness which "disappeared with the love that he kept hid" returned with a vengeance when he decided to rewrite the song in a more vituperative vein in the weeks preceding the start of the fall 1975

Rolling Thunder Revue. Inspired by what he had done with "Simple Twist of Fate," Dylan turned to this sister song during tour rehearsals, as witnessed by reporter Larry Sloman, who notes how Dylan had turned "the mournful lost-love ballad into a revenge song." The reporter even quotes a couple of lines: "If she passes through this way, most likely I'll be gone / But if I'm not don't tell her so, just let her pass on." (Though Dylan semi-slurs much of the 1975 rehearsal version used in *Renaldo and Clara*, the last two lines are clear enough, "If she's passin'" back this way most likely I'll be gone / But if I'm not just let her know it's best she stays gone"—so this may very well be the version Sloman witnessed.)

It would be April 1976 before he unveiled the whole of the new lyric, which he did as an acoustic opener on the first night of the Gulf Coast Revue tour. When he did, the shock to the system was palpable. This was no passive cuckold. Revenge sat in his soul, as he fired off lines like:

> If you see her say hello, she might be in San Juan,
> She left here in a hurry, I don't know what she was on . . .

> If you make love to her, watch it from the rear,
> You'll never know when I'll be back, or liable to appear.
> Oh, it's [as] natural to dream of things, as it is for rules to break,
> But right now I ain't got much to lose, so you better stay awake.

Her possible return, rather than something devoutly to be wished, has become a cause for concern. On the final line of the breathless Lakeland performance, he expresses this concern in one of his great love–hate couplets: "I know that she'll be back some day, of that there is no doubt / But when that moment comes, Lord, give me the strength to keep her out." Though he performed the song just once more during that fiery tour, in Tallahassee, he went on to explore similar emotions on the 1976 versions of "Idiot Wind" and "Tangled Up in Blue," the blood on these tracks threatening to be *hers*.

Having passed through the fire, the song returned in 1978 with an altogether more resigned rearrangement, also destined to last less than a week. Aping the seesaw of emotions in the lyric with an old-fashioned waltz, Dylan beautifully sums up the impasse these two star-crossed lovers have reached: "'Though our situation, oh, it hurt me to the bone / She's better off with someone else and I'm better off alone.'" By 1994, when the song began its never-ending journey, he was back with the red notebook, singing those original lyrics (save for a last line in which he sings "If I'm still on her mind"). Initially he tried a little tenderness. Post-1995 versions—and it was still being performed in 2008—have rarely pulled off the same tightrope trick.

{307} CALL LETTER BLUES

Published lyric/s: Lyrics 04 *[complete version:* Words Fill My Head*].*
Known studio recordings: A&R Studios, NYC, September 16—3 takes [TBS—tk. 3].

Another no-punches-pulled exploration of the emotions of loss, "Call Letter Blues" betrays a blatant debt to its predecessor, "Bell Tower Blues"—as explicated by its original title, "Church Bell Blues." It also appears to have utilized a couple of lines left over from "If You See Her Say Hello" (and one from "Hollis Brown"):

> Way out in the distance,
> I know you're with some other man,
> I try to keep an open mind and understand.

Such self-consciously autobiographical imagery probably told for it in the end. I just can't imagine Dylan releasing the line "Children ask for mother, I tell 'em mother took a trip" into the world back in 1974. But at least he got as far recording this one with Weissberg's band on that first night, cutting it in three takes, before deciding that he would rather replace it with an entirely fanciful morning blues, aka "Meet Me in the Morning." The tune, he kept. Literally. As the 1991 release of "Call Letter Blues" fully revealed. (See #319 for further discussion.)

Note: The published lyric contains only the first four verses, though the full seven verses feature on the 1991 release. Presumably this is an oversight, as it was certainly copyrighted in its entirety.

308} THERE AIN'T GONNA BE A NEXT TIME

309} WHERE DO YOU TURN (TURNING POINT)?

{310} IT'S BREAKIN' ME UP

#308–10 lyrics included in Blood on the Tracks *notebook, c. summer 1974.*
#308 First verse + chorus in Lyrics (2004) *[p. 524].*

At this point in the proceedings, high summer, the line between therapy and threnody is becoming more than a little blurred. After "Call Letter Blues," Dylan adds two more blues lyrics to the notebook, making it five out of the first ten songs when we include "Bell Tower Blues" and "There Ain't Gonna Be a Next Time" (entered either side of "Shelter from the Storm"). At this juncture, he seems to have been planning to make another *Bob Dylan's Blues*. If so, the scheme was scuppered by further breakthroughs in rock lyricism.

In the case of "There Ain't Gonna Be a Next Time," once again the first verse and chorus of this "lost" *Blood on the Tracks* song has been inserted out of context in the back pages of the 2004 *Lyrics*. In this snippet, we find Dylan admonishing himself in the second person for having lost her scent ("You were always thinking about her / But you slipped away and lost her trail"). Once again "the kid" recognized (too late) that she "always understood" his tune "better'n you do." Castigating himself for treating her like a possession, while keeping "the world on a string," the whole tenor of this potentially promising song can be summed up thus: mend your ways, boy.

And the next two blasts of the blues—"Where Do You Turn?" and "It's Breakin' Me Up"—continue the self-flagellation. "Where Do You Turn" does so by asking where one turns when the lights burn out, when fate leads you astray, when your dreams fall down, when doubt replaces belief, and so on. Setting himself on the road to the 1976 "If You See Her, Say Hello," he finally asks the Lord for the strength to resist.

The other diversionary song penned before again picking up her trail is equally direct. "It's Breakin' Me Up," a simple blues, harps on three lines at a time about how "it's breakin' [him] up." He longs for the days when whipping out a guitar was all it took to win her back. But he knows it is time to put such twelve-bar therapy on the backburner and rediscover the "kind of strength [that's] coming from an unbearable place."

{311} SIMPLE TWIST OF FATE

Published lyric/s: Lyrics 85; Lyrics 04. *[Variants: I Can Change I Swear; Words Fill My Head.]*

*Known studio recordings: A&R Studios, NYC, September 16, 1974—5 takes;
September 19, 1974—3 takes [BoTT—tk. 3].*
*First known performance: "The World of John Hammond," Chicago, IL,
September 10, 1975.*

Though it would appear "Simple Twist of Fate" was another lyric
formulated on the farm, the impetus for such a nostalgic song was much
older. As "Girl from the North Country" had been triggered by the break-
up with Suze Rotolo, casting him back to an older affair, so "Simple Twist
of Fate" set him reflecting not on Sara, but on Suze—hence the song's
subtitle in the notebook, "4th Street Affair." That his former true love had
been on his mind is evidenced by a phone call he had made on arriving in
New York that spring. As Rotolo told *Rock Wives* author Victoria Balfour,
"Out of the blue he called. He was with Lillian and Mel Bailey, old friends
of both Bob and me. As I remember it, Mel was annoyed with Bob for
calling me up again, 'Leave her alone, she's married.' I felt nervous."

For all its references, implied or explicit, to the time Rotolo sailed
away to Italy, one rewrite he performed at a show in London on June
30, 1981, really gave the game away: "I remember Suze and the way that
she talked." "Simple Twist of Fate" is another song where Dylan felt
"free enough to change all the . . . he and the she and the I and the you,
and the we and the us." And even in the song "his" Suze remains out of
reach, because he is actually recalling how he sought solace in another
lady's arms when Suze was in Italy during that painful summer of 1962.

By jumbling up the narrative, Dylan ensures that the listener never
knows whether he is suggesting Suze was his lost twin, or the one-night
stand he is now recalling in such delicious detail. (He still hadn't made up
his mind by the time of *Chronicles*, wondering aloud if "maybe we [Suze
and I] were spiritual soul-mates.") The juxtaposition of an overwhelming
sense of loss with a slightly sordid liaison is masterful, enhanced by
Dylan's decision to rewrite the one verse that explicated the occasion as
a liaison with a prostitute:

A flute upon the corner played, morning taps like a promenade,
As the light busts through a cut-up shade, and sprayed upon the bed.
She raised her weary head. And couldn't help but hate
Cashing in on a simple twist of fate.

On one level, the whole song is about the tricks memory plays. Ten years later, Dylan will reuse the idea on the even more impressive "New Danville Girl." As he once said, "Certain things I can remember very clearly. Others are a kinda blur, but where I was and what was happening I can focus in on if I'm forced to." Forcing himself to "focus in" for this song, his mind wanders into the same memoryscape already mined on "Tangled Up in Blue": another love just out of reach. Like those star-crossed lovers, he knows that "chance is the fool's name for fate."[2] Indeed, the final verse of "Simple Twist of Fate," in draft form, almost replicates the former's finale. He has once again "picked up her trail / She's either there or back in jail." This time, though, he succumbs to the vagaries of fate with a metaphorical shrug of the shoulders; "She was born in spring, I was born too late."

Refusing resolution to such a moving narrative is one of the song's greatest strengths. It also permitted Dylan to toy with the narrative for another decade, beginning in September 1975, when he took some of the lessons he had acquired from *Desire* colyricist Jacques Levy and applied them to the previous album. On the final verse of the version he debuted on a TV tribute to John Hammond, he is again stuck at the docks, but this time he feels "She should have caught me in my prime / She would have stayed with me / 'Stead of going back off to sea / And leaving me to meditate."

Interestingly enough, he suggested at one point that the song "was recorded, I think, two times—and one time it had one set of lyrics and another [time] it had another set of lyrics. But the difference in lyrics wasn't that detrimental to the meaning of the song." The Hammond version had evidently become, in his mind, another *recording*. In reality, he stuck doggedly to the notebook lyrics at the *Blood on the Tracks* sessions, though he began his ongoing experiments with the arrangement. On the first night, it was the one song he attempted both solo acoustic and "with band" (as clearly indicated on the tape log). Three days later he reverted to a stripped bare, bass/guitar arrangement, putting it on the record immediately after that other song where memory and fate played games, "Tangled Up in Blue." Which is where it stayed through all the second guesses.

In concert, too, "Tangled" and "Simple Twist" seemed to enjoy an almost symbiotic relationship. Through 1984, both continued to benefit from significant revamps at every pitstop, with "Simple Twist of Fate" in particular seeming to bring out the best in Dylan the revisionist lyricist, year in, year out. In 1980–1, he even made the lady of the night a close cousin of those other "witchy women," Angelina and Claudette, as the pair "stepped into a waterfront hotel, with the neon burning dim / He looked at her and she looked at him / With that look that can manipulate." And still he continued to tap into the experience like it was yesterday.

By 1984 precious few vestiges of the original "4th Street Affair" remained. Instead, the duo had seemingly stepped out of a Malcolm Lowry novel to find themselves at the Grand Hotel "where the desk clerks dress in white / With a face as black as night." This time, the narrator ends up throwing the woman out, accompanied by a characteristic verbal volley, "I taught you all you know. Now don't bother me no more." Evidently, he was no longer prepared to let "witchy women" ru[i]n his life.

1987 marked another sea change. The song reverted to its original lyrical template—as did all the *Blood on the Tracks* songs he now performed. And still, vestiges of the song's beating heart remained well into the Never Ending Tour, Dylan rarely failing to invest this, one of his most personal songs, with power and passion. Perhaps the version that reignited the song came early in the 1987 Temples in Flames tour, when he was again finding it hard to stop his libido a-wanderin'." At a show in Helsinki (September 23), he seemed to remember everything about the song that mattered, in that moment demonstrating the full restoration of his performing powers.

312} **IDIOT WIND**

Published lyric/s: Performing Literature *[original New York version]*; Lyrics *85*; Lyrics *04*.

Known studio recordings: A&R Studios, NYC, September 16, 1974—5 takes [TBS—tk. 5]; A&R Studios, September 19, 1974—3 takes; Sound 80, Minneapolis, MN, December 27, 1974 [BoTT].

First known performance: Bellevue Biltmore Hotel, Clearwater, FL, April 17, 1976.

If you've heard both versions [of "Idiot Wind"], you realize, of course, that there could be a myriad of verses for the thing. It doesn't *stop* . . . Where do you end? . . . It's something that could be a work continually in progress. —Dylan, to Paul Zollo, 1991

{ Still on the Road }

From those summer days on the farm to the first Minneapolis session in December 1974, "Idiot Wind" quite literally remained "a work continually in progress." The red notebook vividly bears out girlfriend Ellen Bernstein's recollection that this song "was one in particular that I remember changing a lot. Whole verses would come and go." Though he got the whole song first time, a full four-verse version coming immediately after "Simple Twist of Fate," nine of the remaining twenty-three pages are devoted to the greatest love–hate song of the twentieth century.

But even before he moves on to another song he has begun reworking the final verse, rebuilding the stanza from line one, across two pages, until it has been dramatically realigned to (one imagines) ongoing events: "I hadn't called you Friday, it must have been because you were hard to reach . . . [or] I hadn't received my (goodbye) part of the speech."

He was a long way from finished. After penning "Don't Want No Married Woman" and "You're Gonna Make Me Lonesome When You Go," he decides to throw out verses three and four and start again. Again the changes spill across the pages of the notebook, occupying three sheets, the third of which starts with a line that shows in what direction the song is now going: "Politicians hold me up, while imitators steal me blind."

And even after he had latched onto a potential album closer, in "Up to Me"—which was itself reworked in the notebook—he wasn't quite done with "Idiot Wind." On the last coupla back pages, he starts again, not from verse one, which stays "same as before," but verses two through four. From page 33 to page 55, then, he allowed this catharsis to unwind as follows:

- p. 33–5 The full four-verse version of the song in its initial draft form, directly after "Simple Twist of Fate."
- p. 35–6 After drawing a line under the song, Dylan spends a page and a half rewriting—multiple times—the last verse of the song. Page 36 is reproduced on page 518 of the 2004 *Lyrics*, i.e., in the *Down in the Groove* section, but is almost impossible to read because of the blurry reverse image.

p. 40–1 Having written "Don't Want No Married Woman" and "You're Gonna Make Me Lonesome," Dylan returns to "Idiot Wind," spending a further two pages on the last two verses, with the last verse again preoccupying him greatly.

p. 53–5 The last entry in the notebook finds Dylan working on verses two to four of the song. Finally, he begins to sketch out new couplets and verses, some of which connect to "Idiot Wind," some of which do not.

In the rewriting process, a song that started life as a bittersweet song of regret ends up being "all about my steady hatred directed at some point that was honest"—which was the way Dylan described the original ten-page version of "Like a Rolling Stone." The initial draft of "Idiot Wind" probably bore a strong resemblance to the "vomit" draft of "Like a Rolling Stone." The one aspect of the 1974 song that didn't change was the first verse, which memorably begins in draft one, "Someone's got it in for me / They're planting stories in the press . . ." Already, Dylan has no doubt as to the source of the "Idiot Wind." As he once opined, apropos of criticism of a later offering, "If [critics] are off to say something, they're gonna say something and there's very little you can say against it, unless you defend yourself against *the wind*" (my italics).

For the narrator of "Idiot Wind," gossip has a power all its own ("Gossip is a weapon traveling through the air. It whispers. But it does have a tremendous influence. It's one of the driving forces"—Dylan, November 1977). Taking a leaf from Hank Williams—whose "Be Careful Of The Stones That You Throw" he had covered back in 1967, but whose "Mind Your Own Business" offers the closer template—this sixties survivor has the gossipmongers in his sights. Taking another leaf, this time from the F. Scott Fitzgerald tree, he makes the narrator a Gatsby-like figure, who it is said "shot a man named Gray, and took his wife to Italy." Upon her (unexplained) death, he inherits a million dollars (originally three million).

Only at the end of this magnetic verse does he reveal the real source of his enmity, the "sweet lady" who is a part of the blizzard of lies that is covering the entire land post-Watergate. Though the lines change, her complicity does not. "Idiot wind, blowing thru the circles round your eyes / Blowing thru the hot and dusty skies"—which is the way those lines appear in the first draft acquire an epic sweep when conjoined with "from the Grand Coulee Dam to the Mardi Gras," widening further "to the Capi-*tull.*"

The narrator's attempt to retain his sanity in a world full of lies is his primary concern at the start of the second verse. Looking for direction, he throws the I-Ching, a book he sang the praises of as far back as 1965 ("It's the only thing that is amazingly true, period . . . It's a whole system of finding out things . . . [and] besides being a great book to believe in, it's also very fantastic poetry"). He throws hexagram #51, which deals with The Arousing Thunder, while "waiting for the weather to change." But it doesn't provide the answer he's looking for. Nor does the Christ-like "lone soldier on the hill," who "won the war / After losing every battle." He thinks back to another, unnamed prophet who "told me once that too much pride is a disease / [And] always stand back a step from someone who's too eager to please."

However, he can't get "her" off his mind, nor forgive her for hurting the ones he loved best. No longer in "Rolling Stone" mode, imagining his victim as "swimming in lava . . . in the pain [she was] bound to meet up with," he finds an equally morbid image, her lying in a ditch (or, with greater finality, "grave" in the 1976 version). At the end of the first half of the song, he envisions laying flowers on her tomb, for the idiot wind has done her in.

Close to the point of no return, Dylan pulls back from the brink. As with "She's Your Lover Now," he has spent his fury by the end of verse two, allowing himself to reflect on his own failings. He is no longer sure what it is that he wants to say, or how he wants the whole affair to end. Having castigated those who profit from gossip, he finds himself indulging in the most intense examination of his own conduct in-song, and does not like what he finds.

He has a choice to make—stand naked before unknowing eyes again, or clothe the song in more mythopoeic attire. Sensing that he may be laying just a little too much of himself on the line, he instigates a series of second-guesses intended to make the initial, naked portrayal *seemingly* personal. He admitted such concerns were ever-present when discussing this song's composition a decade later with Bill Flanagan:

> I thought I might have gone a little bit too far with "Idiot Wind." I might have changed some of it. I didn't really think I was giving away

too much. I thought that it seemed so personal that people would think it was about so-and-so who was close to me. It wasn't. But you can put all these words together and that's where it falls. You can't help where it falls. I didn't feel that one was too personal, but I felt it seemed too personal. Which might be the same thing . . . Usually with those kinds of things, if you think you're too close to something . . . your feelings are going to change a month later, and you're going to look back and say, "What did I do that for?"

At this formative stage, he was still blaming *her* for six years of writer's block: "I tamed the fury in your soul / And you put out the fire in my heart." Which is an extraordinary claim, as even he quickly realized. Almost immediately, he began to reconsider. And so, after conjuring up that exquisite image, "I tamed the lion in your cage," he inverts the image so that she now tames *him*, while questioning his performance as a lover: "After I waited forever for you, you said that I came too fast." It's a line he was wise to forsake, even if it suggests he had been reading some Jacobethan sonnets.

The "original" fourth verse comes dangerously close to a 1974 "Ballad in Plain D." Thankfully, he allowed himself the time and opportunity to turn it into something else. Despite which, the song's focus is clear. The man can claim he set out to write something that "seemed so personal that people would think it was about so-and-so" till he is blue in the face. "Idiot Wind" began life as a letter to a Sara:

> I haven't called you for days and days,
> And it hurts me more than it bothers you,
> It wasn't that I didn't care,
> It was just something that I must've been going through.
> I figured I'd lost you anyway,
> What's the point of past desire?
> There would be your voice and mine,
> Trying to talk through wire.
> Finally got my eyesight back,
> And saw you for what you are,
> No reason to get all messed up,
> I think I'll watch you from afar.

The barest hint of reconciliation, introduced at the end of this verse, is begrudging at best: "It would be nice to work it out, but we would have to do it for love / Let's not do it for the money." This surprisingly honest sentiment would stay intact all the way to New York's A&R Studios, though the way he puts it in the studio is a tad more poetic: "You can have the best there is, but it's gonna cost you all your love / You won't get it for money." (To hear the way he alights on that final word, like a bird on the wire, on the oft-bootlegged test-pressing take is to *know* that the song remains tethered to his heartstrings.)

When he returns to the final verse—just before writing two songs for current paramour Ellen Bernstein—he has stopped merely targeting a former love. Everyone who has fucked with him through a turbulent decade is in his sights: "I've had so much stolen from me, some times I think I must be blind / With [so many] copycats and imitators, I guess the real thing is hard to find." Not that the "sweet lady" herself is entirely off the hook. She is accused of deceit, typecast as one of those "sweethearts [who] load dice on me." "I thought you were someone else / It must have been the mask you wore" is one such couplet he might easily have transferred to "Up to Me"; as is "I knew what we were going to say, but I hadn't received my part of the speech."

Reconciliation at this stage seems a long way off. The process of obfuscation for public consumption, though, continued apace. Having begun by revealing too much, he was intent on making the lyric increasingly cryptic. In the grip of the "Up to Me" mindset, he suggests, "I saw your brother later on, he gave your shoes to me and then he wept." But he soon kills the brother off, preferring to trade insults with that unfeeling heartbreaker at the center of this raging storm: "After you stepped over my head, you said you never wanted to see my face no more."

Despite everything, he continues searching for her "in the jail" and "in the sad cafes" of earlier songs. Soon, however, it is time to take a break from all the recriminations. By the time he returned to the song for the fourth time, he already had an album's worth of songs that reclaimed every inch of the territory lost in the forgotten years. But he still feared a return to those times, as he made clear with the new opening to verse three:

In a backroom full of refugees, blue strangers tell me where I've been,
But I don't remember anything; to me it's like amnesia has set in.
Now everything's a little upside down . . .

Meanwhile, he allows the fourth verse to go off on an astrological tangent—"The connection finally broke, and one day I felt the power of the storm / A hound dog bayed behind your trees, silhouetted by a moon in Capricorn." But even after writing out this "final" draft, he can't help rewriting one last couplet, which for now read, "I woke up on the roadside and was daydreaming about the way things used to be / Until a vision of your yellow horse trampled me straight back into reality."

By now, Dylan had started playing the new songs to friends, a practice that had once been the norm. But even way back when, never had he done such market research as he did now. Among the lucky recipients given their own private demonstration of genius rekindled were guitarist Michael Bloomfield, songwriter Shel Silverstein, country musician Pete Rowan, Dylan's cousin and assorted Hassidic friends, and, perhaps first of all, Stephen Stills and Tim Drummond, who were playing a concert in nearby St. Paul (with Crosby and Nash) when he and Ellen traveled up from the farm in early August. Drummond told Ben Fong-Torres the following day, "It's completely different from *Planet Waves*. It's gutsy, bluesy, so authentic."

"Idiot Wind" was surely shaped by this process, as Dylan faced up to the very public scrutiny such a song was bound to engender. By the time he arrived at A&R Studios on September 16, the sweetheart who loaded dice on him had become "ladykillers," the brother was now her "driver" (who "came in after you left, gave [all your bags] to me, and then he resigned"), and the "lovesick prophet" was no more. The femme fatale, though, continued to use her feminine wiles: "You close your eyes and part your lips and slip your fingers from your glove."

Initially, Dylan set the song to a simple bass accompaniment. However, though he twice pulled off complete takes on that first evening, he felt he had failed to "make the focus as strong as a magnifying glass under the sun." When he returned to the song three nights later, he persevered with a simple guitar/bass arrangement, only overdubbing some atmospheric organ—courtesy of Paul Griffin—after the fact. That version from the nineteenth was assigned to the original test pressing of the album, with said organ overdub and even a four-line vocal "punch in" (thus refuting engineer Ramone's claim that "we only punched in things like a bass part or an organ note that went sour. Not on him. Definitely not on him!").

Another previously rejected version, though, was selected for the 1991 *Bootleg Series* set. Though credited to the nineteenth, a close comparison with versions of "Tangled Up in Blue" and "If You See Her, Say Hello" attributed to the sixteenth, also included on the set, make it probable that this cut is from the same first session. It shares the same slightly mannered tone and a hesitancy in the delivery, which is slightly surprising given the number of times he had previewed the material.

On the other hand, the one earmarked for the "New York" version of the album is one of the most chastening, bittersweet vocals the man ever committed to tape. By this juncture Tony Brown is no longer burbling away in the background—he is *leaning* into every line. Brown himself remains in no doubt about the merits of the test-pressing take: "I really thought that what Paul Griffin and I did was far superior to what was used on the final version of the album. Nothing can touch our version of 'Idiot Wind.'" Even as he sinks into silence, the singer finds a certain sweet release, surrendering the song to one of his most plaintive harmonica codas. A full-on tour de bloody force is what it is.

And yet it seems Dylan couldn't wait to redo "Idiot Wind" when he reworked some of the songs—i.e., half the album—in Minneapolis, in late December. Once again, he found his emotions had taken a tectonic shift. He'd been applying the red marker-pen to those last two verses in the interim, honing his invective, and winding himself up for a grand finale which suggested recrimination may well best be served cold:

I been double-crossed now for the very last time and now I'm finally free,
I kissed goodbye the howling beast on the borderline which separated
   you from me,
You'll never know the hurt I suffered nor the pain I rise above
And I'll never know the same about you, your holiness or your kind of love.

Indignation has now replaced introspection. The tone of that final verse is almost sneering, making the change of heart that comes in the chorus with "*We're* idiots, babe" wholly unexpected, and not altogether convincing. Nor do the Minnesotan musicians add a great deal to the song, playing with a singular lack of flair, as if wary of challenging Dylan musically. The new version may have come quick—apparently four takes—but the song was now caught between two conflicting stools. It was still a mightily important song and garnered more than its share of praise when the album appeared the following February ("My favorite is 'Idiot Wind' . . . its intensity scares me."—Stephen Holden, *Rolling Stone*).

Even so, it was destined to remain "a work continually in progress" as long as the narrative still mirrored the narrator's life. All it took, really, for the next stage of its evolution was for Dylan to find himself back in the rain. By the spring of 1976, the recriminator had gagged and bound his more timid twin. Having broken into the song at a birthday jam session for Eric Clapton at Shangri-La Studios in March, wiling away the wee hours in those arid confines rather than going home to the wife, he recast it the following month as the centerpiece of the 1976 Revue, ready to twist the blade on his "sweet lady."

The work-in-progress had resumed its travels. If "Isis" and "Sara" had been the lyrical lynchpins of the fall 1975 shows, "Idiot Wind" now superseded them. At Fort Collins, the penultimate show of the Rolling Thunder Revue, the mobile truck was out back recording a live album, the cameras were on him, and his wife was in the pit, as sound and fury melded in the maelstrom. The performance that afternoon, in miserable weather, reflected three days of pent-up frustrations holed up in a hotel in the mountains with the rain falling harder and harder, and three years spent trying to mend a marriage inexorably falling to pieces.

He even threw in a couple of rewrites that seemed to be aimed directly at the orchestra pit. No longer haunted by visions of her chestnut mare, it is her "smoking tongue" which he can't stand. And just to prove this *was* personal, it was no longer her books he can't bear to read. Rather, he spits out the lines, "I can't even touch the clothes you wear / Every time I come in your room / You leave me standing in the middle of the air." Ouch. This man was airing dirty laundry to several million unknowin" eyes. And when the performance was made the finale of his *Hard Rain* TV film, the camera work, courtesy of Howard Alk, was as in your face as the delivery. At least it now seemed to be out of his system.

Like most other songs from that furnace of desire, Dylan left this "Idiot Wind" to blow away with the *decree nisi*. On the brink of resuming touring as a way of life in the fall of 1985, he even observed, "The stuff before '78, those people have kinda disappeared . . . If you see me live, you won't hear me sing too many of those songs."

So imagine the collective shock when word spread beyond the Antipodeans that Dylan had started performing the song again, night after night, at a solid set of Australian shows in the winter of 1992. Nor did Dylan disappoint. The rage had gone, but what had replaced it was the kind of fatalism that infused the best of his post-conversion work. He had returned to the heart of the song as it was when he got to New York. (He even kept tripping himself up at the start of the second verse, singing of "a lone soldier on the hill . . . You'd never know it to look at him, but in the final shot . . .," two vestiges of the original recording.)

Those last two verses had continued to concern him and were now truncated into a single verse, combining elements of both but leaving most of the real invective back in Colorado. And still those 1992 performances just got better and better from the NET debut in Melbourne on April 2 through one night in San Francisco (May 5), when Jerry Garcia put down his ham sandwich long enough to play on—and inspire the author of—this epic song about a marriage not so much on the mend as around the bend. Dylan even restored the harmonica coda, playing it with all the insouciance of a fifty-year-old man who had survived every storm life had thrown at him with his ineffable gift for performing intact. (A well-shot audience video of this performance is worth checking out just to see Dylan's expression at the end, knowing he has just delivered the goods.)

{313} DON'T WANT NO MARRIED WOMAN

Lyric included in Blood on the Tracks *notebook, c. summer 1974.*

{314} YOU'RE GONNA MAKE ME LONESOME WHEN YOU GO

Published lyric/s: Lyrics 85; Lyrics 04.

Known studio recordings: A&R Studios, NYC, September 16, 1974—8 takes; A&R Studios, September 17, 1974—3 takes [BoTT—tk. 3].
First known performance: Bellevue Biltmore Hotel, Clearwater, FL, April 22, 1976.

"I didn't want to get married, and I wasn't being asked to leave."
—Ellen Bernstein, to the author

Having bared his soul to the crosswind, Dylan chose to write two songs of light relief, both designed to appeal to his companion at the time, the young Columbia A&R lady Ellen Bernstein. The first of these, another twelve-bar blues, seems to be him having a little fun, portraying married women as being "too much aggravation," forever digging through his pockets and looking through his clothes. He lists all the various things he'd rather do, which include enlisting in the army, drinking muddy water, and looking into the devil's eye.

By the sixth and final verse, he appears to be targeting a particular married woman again, someone whom he's been trying to avoid because of her capacity for making his heart sink "like a ship . . . when you kissed my lips." Though the song made it no further, that final verse would reappear verbatim at the end of the last song written for the album, "Meet Me in the Morning," proving that all these *Bloody* blues were a mongrel breed.

If he was looking to amuse his one-woman audience, he was making a more serious point with the next devilish ditty, originally called "You're Gonna Make Me Miss You When You Go." Written with Ellen very much in mind, the song came pure and easy, with little changed from notebook to studio save for two lines in verse five, "Up till now the road's been steep / I been killing time, fighting sleep," which are then replaced by the lovely "compare / affair" couplet. Also, in the final verse, a very personal vision of heaven replaces the patently inferior "But I'm gonna have to change my gears / Or else you're gonna have to get back here."

The version recorded in New York—which suggests he'll see her "in the sky above"—comes across as a coded way of saying "so long, good luck, and good-bye." He tried it both fast and slow, preferring the former for the album (the latter was shortlisted for *The Bootleg Series 1–3*, but was cut when it was reduced to three disks). And Dylan retained a certain affection for the song even after he resumed his relationship with the married woman who made his heart sink like a ship (though he avoided rekindling any relationship that resembled "Verlaine's and Rimbeau"). It was no great surprise when he gave the song a gorgeous country-rock reinvention on the second Revue tour. With an even stronger melody, it cut quite a contrast to the other, angst-ridden arrangements given the 1974 songs in 1976. Rehearsed early on for the 1978 world tour and at least once during the G.E. era, it has nonetheless become the forgotten song from perhaps his finest album side.

{315} UP TO ME

Published lyric/s: Lyrics 85; Lyrics 04.
Known studio recordings: A&R Studios, NYC, September 16, 1974—1 take; A&R Studios, September 19, 1974—7 takes [BIO—tk. 7].

> It's a fine line between where I am and where I'm projecting [or] what I know about; what I'm familiar with; what I know to be the truth . . . it's a *very fine line* on what I tend to make personal of other people's situation.
> —Dylan, to Lynne Allen, December 1978

In its own way, "Up to Me" is as masterful an achievement as "Tangled Up in Blue," using much the same technique to create a well-crafted juxtaposition of "what I know to be the truth" and what "I'm projecting." As a rule of thumb, the sentiments expressed herein are real enough, but set within scenarios almost entirely derived from the worlds of fiction and film. In verse ten, he even taunts his second-person audience with the dangers of believing gossip, safeguarding against another blast of the idiot wind: "There's a note left in the bottle, you can give it to Estelle / She's the one you been wond'rin' 'bout, but there's really nothin' much to tell."

He is having such fun that he can even afford to discard some one-liners that a lesser poet might have saved, say for "Black Diamond Bay." Before he refused to "be governed by enforced insanity," he had "made the trade with an ounce of jade and gave up my vanity." The whole song could almost be the life story of "a man named Gray," such are the surreal things that seem to happen to the song's main character as he embarks on the eternal quest. Just like "Tangled Up in Blue" and "Simple Twist of Fate" and "Shelter from the Storm," "she" remains ever elusive. But unlike those earlier songs, he does not allow himself to be distracted from the search:

> Oh, the Union Central is pullin' out, it's smoking up my room,
> It's been floating in my memory ever since I left the womb,
> And the loan sharks up on St. Peter's Square questioned my morality,
> Somebody's got to find your trail, I guess it must be Up to Me.

Betwixt the carnival of coincidence that gives the song its loose narrative, he allows himself to express the pain he is still feeling, "Well, I just can't rest without you, love, I need your company," when not talking about the barriers he must constantly hide behind, "She's everything I need and love but *I'd never tell her that*" (later changed to "I can't be swayed by that"). Even in Dylan's canon, few lines are as poignant as the opening line to the final verse of "Up to Me": "And if we never meet again, baby, remember me . . ."

He is setting us up for an unhappy ending. Which may well be the rub, for "Up to Me" was surely written as the album closer. Save for a couple of throwaway ideas, it is the last song in the notebook (where it is written out twice). It almost segues from "Shelter from the Storm" melodically, completing a circle of sorts with the two opening songs of the album. When exactly Dylan gave up on making this song the album closer is less clear—presumably some time after he recorded "Buckets of Rain," the song which replaced it. Yet he spent much of the final session in New York working on "Up to Me." Even when he finally got a take he liked, he kept going. Two takes of the song were under consideration for the album right up to the final sequencing, six days later.

In the end, a desire for a more redemptive conclusion—and/or the dawning realization that he was making an *awfully* long album—did for it. (The released album is already over 52 minutes long. With "Up to Me" replacing "Buckets of Rain," it would have been over 55 minutes, an unheard-of length for a "rock" album in the vinyl era, until *Desire*.) As a result, for a decade or so fans had to make do with Roger McGuinn's respectable "Rolling Thunder" arrangement on his second solo album, *Cardiff Rose* (1976), before *Biograph* (1985) finally delivered the real deal.

{316} AIN'T IT FUNNY
{317} LITTLE BIT OF RAIN

Both lyrics included in Blood on the Tracks *notebook, c. summer 1974.*

> I wrote all the songs for *Blood on the Tracks* in about a month, and then I recorded them, and stepped back out of that place where I was when I wrote them and went back to whatever I was doing before. Sometimes you'll get what you can out of these things, but you can't stay there.
> —Dylan, to Bill Flanagan, 1985

Before Dylan "stepped back out of that place" where this extraordinary body of songs came from, he made two last attempts to write something short and bittersweet. Neither amounted to much, perhaps indicating that the well was already almost dry. "Ain't It Funny" amounts to four verses of familiar phrases about the inevitable falling out, though the suggestion that someone has drained "the fountain of our youth" and is now trying to bottle it is a corker.

"Little Bit of Rain" also seems to be trampling over familiar territory. Taking its title from a well-known Fred Neil song Dylan would have heard in the cafes when "revolution was in the air," the song again uses the standard repeated blues couplet to suggest that, come rain or shine, "there's sorrow in my heart." Though the song never made it from page to tape, the rain stuck around long enough to fill buckets . . .

{318} BUCKETS OF RAIN

Published lyric/s: Lyrics 85; Lyrics 04. *[Bette Midler version:* I Can Change I Swear*]*
Known studio recordings: A&R Studios, NYC, September 17, 1974—2 takes; A&R Studios, September 19—5 takes. [BoTT—tk. 4]; Bette Midler Session, NYC, October 1975 [SftND].
First known performance: Detroit, MI, November 18, 1990.

It would appear that Dylan had been playing some of his favorite contemporaries, looking for inspiration. Hence "Little Bit of Rain." Also probably on the Minnesotan turntable had been Tom Paxton's "Bottle of Wine"—a song Dylan's old friend had been performing for the past ten years, "as kind of a walking-on-home kind of thing, and usually the audience jumps right in." Dylan jumped right in and copped the melody for "Buckets of Rain," "Bottle of wine, dew on the vine" here becoming "Buckets of Rain, buckets of tears," as Dylan takes a jaunty celebration of the juice of the forbidden fruit and turns it into a modern "Que sera, que sera."

Like the other song completed after leaving the farm—and the notebook—behind, "Buckets of Rain" began life as a stray couplet intended for another destination. As Dylan puts the finishing touches to "Idiot Wind," he is still scribbling stray couplets and comes up with "Little red wagon, little red bike / I ain't no monkey but I know what I like." The thought is not expanded on, Dylan preferring to wrestle with visions of her. But by the time of the second New York session, he had written an alternative album closer, one that may not have them dancing in the streets at album's end, but might at least allow listeners to leave the razor blades in the bathroom cabinet. This fact alone ensured it kept its place from the day in late September when he arrived at a "provisional" album sequence to its eventual post-Minneapolis configuration.

But barely a year passed before he was disowning even these inoffensive sentiments. At the same time as he was rewriting "Simple Twist of Fate" and "If You See Her, Say Hello," he took up an invite to a session with Village diva Bette Midler to record a duet for her next album, *Songs for the New Depression*. Presented with a set of the original lyrics, he immediately set about rewriting them, suggesting changing "misery" to "ecstasy" (as in, "Everything about you is bringing me . . ."), and informing those assembled that he "must have written" the line "I like the way you love me strong and slow" when he "was ten years old."

Even the title of the song is changed to "Nuggets of Rain," though only after Midler suggested singing "rockets, fuck-its, or nuggets." By his own (later) admission, Dylan "was just sloppy drunk and I guess somebody led me there by the nose . . . I was lucky to get out of there." Yet once they start playing around with the song, he sounds like he's having a lot of fun, and when Midler asks him, "Are you a one-take guy?" he salaciously replies, "No, I can last all night." In fact, just when Midler seems happy with the song, and asks, "Are we gonna keep that take?" Dylan tells her, "No, we're gonna erase it to fuck with your head."

The session shall indeed continue a while longer, as he turns the song into a seduction: "I like the heavenly way you look at me / Everything about you is bringing me ecstasy," before trumping that sentiment with, "I like the way you monkey around / Stick with me baby, and we'll never be found." Even the moral of the song gets a shot in the arm: "Life is happy, life is sad / Life is a bust, when you think you've been had." Surprisingly, he willingly allows the results to appear on Midler's album, leaving it at that. Fifteen years later, for no obvious reason, he opens the final show of 1990 in Detroit with another "sloppy drunk" version, just not one shot through with the same joie de vivre.

{319} MEET ME IN THE MORNING

Published lyric/s: Lyrics 85; Lyrics 04.

Known studio recordings: A&R Studios, NYC, September 18, 1974; September 19, 1974—7 takes [BoTT ?tk. 2—backing track rec. September 16]; ?Sound 80, Minneapolis, MN, December 27, 1974.

In keeping with established practise, Dylan hadn't quite finished writing songs for his new album when he entered Studio A on September 16, 1974. The second of two songs recorded for *Blood on the Tracks* but absent from the notebook, "Meet Me in the Morning" was seemingly triggered by a dissatisfaction with the various blues he had penned to date, starting where a couplet from "Don't Want No Married Woman" left off. If the song was written to self-consciously fill the slot earmarked for "Call Letter Blues," it soon stepped into that song's shoes, Dylan taking the backing track of the earlier song, recorded with Deliverance, and overdubbing an entirely new vocal, before letting Buddy Cage add some steely riffs of his own.

If Dylan had never been exactly trepidatious about reusing a melody he'd already made his own, the hijacking of an entire backing track was unheard of, for him, especially as it required him to overdub a vocal using headphones, a process he had rigorously resisted for the past thirteen years. But a close examination of the tape log for the sixteenth, in tandem with the most cursory listen to the released "Call Letter Blues," shows that both backing tracks come from one and the same session. The tape log clearly lists three takes of "Call Letter Blues." Then, written in *after* the fact, next to take two, is the legend, "Meet Me in the Morning." (There is also an almost exact correspondence in timing between the two songs as released, "Call Letter Blues" clocking in at 4:28, "Meet Me in the Morning" at 4:26.)

The latter song does not appear (again) until two nights later (unless the unknown blues on the seventeenth is an early attempt at the song), "Meet Me in the Morning" presumably being written in the interim. According to the studio log, there were a further seven attempts on the nineteenth, though it is not clear whether these were an attempt to cut the song in the same acoustic guise as the remainder of the New York album or whether they were Dylan applying a new vocal to the "Call Letter Blues" backing track. (I suspect the latter). Either way, what was recorded on tape was evidently pruned to the length of "Call Letter Blues," even though the published lyrics, then and now, have a fourth verse absent from the album: "The birds are flying low, babe / Honey, I feel so exposed (x2) / Well, now, I ain't got any matches / And the station doors are closed."

According to a contemporary report in *Rolling Stone*, the song was then cut again in Minneapolis in December, though no such version has ever appeared, and one musician present at those sessions is adamant it was *not* recorded at Sound 80. (It is certainly not listed on the two-inch Sound 80 master tapes which reside at Sony.) Whatever the case, by the end of 1974 Dylan had decided to leave the song at 56th and Wabasha, making it the one *Blood* track destined never to appear in concert. He also apparently left behind the Martin guitar he'd been seen brandishing at the "Friends of Chile" concert in May and the September A&R sessions. As he subsequently told a U.S. journalist, he did so because after using it to write and record all the songs for this album, he just felt he "had squeezed it dry."

1975–6

{ Desire }

It seems unlikely that Dylan planned to record another album seven months after finishing Blood on the Tracks. *That is, until he ran into lyricist Jacques Levy on or around July 5, 1975. At the time he had written barely a handful of new songs, and even those were causing him trouble. He certainly had nowhere near enough for an album of his own songs. But once Levy was on board, taking soundings, the songs flowed easily; and a remarkably fruitful collaboration produced enough songs in just three weeks for a double album (the released single album is only five minutes shorter than the Stones' legendary double platter* Exile on Main Street*). This collaboration also led directly to a new tour, bound around an idea for a film that was part-documentary, part-performance, and part-fantasy.*

But then Dylan took his eyes off the lyrical prize again, writing almost nothing through the whole Rolling Thunder period, his creativity being directed elsewhere. Any personal trauma he directed outward on stage, not inward in song. From July 1975 to the end of 1976, we have evidence of just one completed song coming from the man's pen, and that one he gave to Ronnie Wood. Strange days, indeed.

{320} MONEY BLUES

Published lyric/s: Lyrics 85; Lyrics 04.
Known studio recordings: Rehearsal session, Minneapolis MN, Winter 1975; Columbia Studios, NYC, July 28, 1975—1 take; July 29—1 take.

I don't plan albums. All that pressure's off. I don't have to go in and make an
album every six months . . . I just continue to play my guitar and if there's
a song in my heart to do, I'll do [it]. —Dylan, to Mary Travers, April 1975

The past eighteen months had been pleasingly productive, yet Dylan
did not bathe long in the afterglow of a critical return to form before
wondering, What next. A still rocky reconciliation with Sara left him disin-
clined to continue in the same vein as his second chart-topping album
in a single year. And so at some point that winter he co-opted a local
Minneapolis band, Willie Murphy and the Bees, to jam on some new material, and though the results were hardly the equal of the songs cut at Sound
80 the previous December, he seemed happy to be making music again.

The "Money Blues" he recorded with Murphy and his fellow
Minnesotans bears almost no resemblance to the song he would end up
recording under that title in July, save for one key aspect, a "big band"
sound. Almost a jump-blues, the song has the full complement of brass
instruments on hand to help him stretch the thing out to six minutes, forty
seconds on the thinnest of lyrical threads: "Money, whole lotta money / So
I can get you a wedding ring / So I can get you everything / I need money."

He had little more he wanted to say when he got around to
mentioning the song idea to Jacques Levy, probably after they escaped
to the Hamptons to finish writing *Desire*. With someone to bounce ideas
off, Dylan managed to rustle up a couple of better lines, including, "Well,
the man came and took my Chevy back / I'm glad I hid my old guitar."
Used as a single-take warm-up to both "big band" album sessions at the
end of July, it was never a serious contender for official status, though it
soon ended up in folio form, in *The Songs of Bob Dylan 1966–75*.

Note: In Glen Dundas's *Tangled Up in Tapes*, the session with Murphy's
band is dated August 1975, but this version of "Money Blues" clearly
precedes the *Desire* version. A winter 1975 date is altogether more likely,
probably January or February. He had returned west by March.

{321} FOOTPRINTS IN THE SAND

Known studio recordings: Rehearsal session, Minneapolis, MN, Winter 1975.

This song idea—also recorded with Willie Murphy and the Bees—
has even less legs than "Money Blues," though a snatch of lyrics

distinguishes it from the two instrumental jams also recorded on the day. The only line he repeats was presumably intended to serve as the song's burden: "Till I saw these footprints in the sand." The melody also suggests a half-remembered idea for a song along the lines of the Shangri-Las' "Remember Walking in the Sand," lost when the following day's tide washed it away.

{322} ONE MORE CUP OF COFFEE (VALLEY BELOW)

Published lyric/s: Lyrics 85; Lyrics 04.
Known studio recordings: Columbia Studios, NYC, July 28, 1975; July 30, 1975—3 takes [DES].
First known performance: Plymouth, MA, October 30, 1975.

> Of all the aches of the elderly, the loss of power is the most terrible to bear. The strong old man, the leader of the tribe . . . demands love as a tyrant demands tribute; and, bereft of power, he must, like Lear, plead for it like a beggar. —Orson Welles, proposal for a film of *King Lear*, March 1985

There is something rather symbolic about Dylan beginning work on a successor to his first seminal album of the seventies on his thirty-fourth birthday, May 24, 1975. And something quite surreal about him starting to compose it while living in the south of France. It had been some eleven years since he had last written a song in Europe and, as he told biographer Robert Shelton on his next visit to said continent, "Creatively, I couldn't live anywhere but America, because I understand the tone behind the language. I'd love to live somewhere else, but only for a while."

Well, he had been living "somewhere else" for the past six weeks or so when his host, American painter David Oppenheim, suggested they pay a visit to a local gypsy festival. As Dylan later revealed to *Songtalk*'s Paul Zollo, "['One More Cup of Coffee'] is a gypsy song. That song was written during a gypsy festival in the south of France one summer. Somebody took me there to the gypsy high holy days which coincide with my own particular birthday . . . But the 'valley below' probably came from someplace else." That "someplace else" is the disconcertingly classical concept of the afterlife, Hades. The man whose point of view Dylan is adopting in song was a real person, as he informed Australian journalist Karen Hughes:

> [The gypsy king] was an old man at this time and the person that I went to see him with knew him . . . ten years earlier, when he was still vital and active. And at that time he had maybe sixteen to twenty wives and over a hundred children . . . He'd had a heart attack so the smell of death was all around and most of his family had abandoned him. Fifteen or sixteen of his wives had left him and gone, and he only had two or three children there, so he was pretty much alone.

He was intrigued to meet such a man, someone from another world entirely. He had found over the years "a lot of times [when] people open Up to Me . . . I can tell it's jaded . . . [they've] some ulterior motive . . . So where I get my source of material is the characters in my life who are there, and just the back routes that I'm on . . . Most of the people I talk to in different . . . areas of life don't really know who Bob Dylan is. So I seek those places out. I'm more comfortable with a person who doesn't know who I was [sic]." At this time, he was feeling particularly anxious to escape his usual social circles. On his return from France, he told incarcerated boxer Rubin Carter that he had "just had to get away. . . . People just suck my soul, just suck me dry."

Needless to say, Dylan was fascinated by the kind of figure who once exercised such power over his people (and had not the slightest idea who this wiry American with the piercing blue eyes was). Here was somebody who had genuinely lived outside of society. But rather than just tell the old man's story, Dylan adopts the viewpoint of a man who is lying with a young gypsy consort, by implication the gypsy king's daughter, but is only going through the motions, every thought being occupied with "the valley below."

The experience seems to have inspired Dylan to wrap this lyric—and most of the songs that follow in the next two months—in a "gypsy" sound. And some time in June 1975 he found a young woman with a gypsy air and a violin, wandering the streets of the Village. He took the lady, who went by the enticing name of Scarlet Rivera, to a local studio and there they jammed on "One More Cup of Coffee." Though no tape of that jam exists, they evidently didn't forget the experience because, during a break from filming the aborted Clearwater TV special in April 1976, they struck up something similar, turning the song (back) into an elongated, flamenco-inflected wail of regret.

In the studio, the song was given two quite different treatments. One has to wonder how it was ever even considered for a "big band" arrangement. But it was—a version being attempted at the July 28 session. Two days later, its truncated intro was now dominated by Stoner's descending bassline, and each chorus was sung as a duet with country singer Emmylou Harris, who found the experience more than a little daunting ("I'd never heard the songs before, and we did most of them in one or two takes . . . live"). The result was a standout album track, but one ripe for reinvention live.

In performance on the 1975 Rolling Thunder Revue, all the best parts of the two previous arrangements now came together as a contiguous whole, supporting a truly haunting lead vocal. And Dylan continued working at the song through all the rehearsals and the first week of shows in mid-April 1976, but by tour's end it had made way for the return of *Blonde on Blonde* and *Blood on the Tracks*, as songs of *Desire* faded from the frame.

Thankfully, this sultry song returned to the set at the sixth Japanese show in February 1978, by which time it had undergone another refit. Congas and a wailing sax had replaced the guitar / violin mix. If he left the new lyric he'd been toying with in rehearsals ("Your sister raised a fortune / She was born to read my mind . . .") at Rundown, the song itself was played for musical kicks. It remained one of just two staples from *Desire*—along with "Oh Sister"—performed at these shows, acquiring its own pre-song rap at the fall U.S. shows, which seemed to suggest it was about, er, coffee:

Well, about four years ago, on the day I was born, it happened to be a high holy gypsy holiday. So I went over to check it out. The gypsies have a party for a week, in the south of France. Well, I went because I had nothing else to do, and I partied for a week. So I met the king of the gypsies there . . . So after this week of partying with the gypsies, it was time to go our separate ways. And . . . I'll never forget this one man played Russian roulette with five bullets in the chamber! Yes, he did. And someone else was playing guitar right next to him. Anyway, things went on and it was time for me to go. So I, they said, "What you want Bob, as you're leaving us?" Seeing that I'd been there for at least a week and done everything at least twice. I just asked for a cup of coffee. Just One More Cup of Coffee for the road. They put it in a bag and they gave it to me. And I was standing there looking out at the ocean, and it was like [I was] looking at it in the valley below where I was standing.

After December 16, 1978, though, the song suffered the same fate as most other songs from his most successful album. The post-conversion Dylan decided "the songs on the *Desire* album, [they're] kind of a fog to me." It would be 1987 before a single *Desire* song was restored to the set; and June 15, 1988, before "One More Cup of Coffee" was resurrected (a recently emerged soundboard of that Denver performance shows the song to have lost none of its power in the interim). It remained a rare beast indeed, enjoying just eight outings in the first six years of the Never Ending Tour.

{323} GOLDEN LOOM

Published lyric/s: Lyrics 85; Lyrics 04.
Known studio recordings: Columbia Studios, NYC, July 30, 1975—4 takes; July 31—1 take [TBS].

> I wrote [most of *Desire*] with somebody else, but I always kept it on the track of where I thought it should be going. . . . When that particular album was happening, I didn't know what was happening at the time . . . I wanted to do more harmonica and violin together but we never got a chance to do that. —Dylan, to Lynne Allen, 1978

"Golden Loom"—along with its sister song, "Abandoned Love"—is one of the "forgotten" self-composed songs which got lost in the shuffle when Dylan decided to go with an album of cowritten narratives and not a collection of songs based on a particular principle he had expressed in a contemporary conversation with Allen Ginsberg: "The more pleasure I got, subtly there was as much pain. And I began to notice a correspondence . . . and saw it was a balance."

Like "One More Cup of Coffee," "Golden Loom" was clearly conceived as a harmonica/violin piece. Recorded for *Desire* on July 31 at a session largely reserved for those songs he wrote alone (and with his wife largely in mind), the song had lost its spark somewhere down the line. And though Rivera gamely tried to rekindle whatever spirit it had when she first heard it, presumably at that jam session in the Village, Dylan had already made up his mind in which direction *Desire* would go. And it meant omitting several songs of desire.

{324} OH SISTER

Published lyric/s: Lyrics 85; Lyrics 04.
Known studio recordings: Columbia Studios, NYC, July 28, 1975—1 take; July 29—8 takes; July 30—5 takes [DES—tk. 5]
First known performance: "World of John Hammond," Chicago, IL, September 10, 1975.

"Oh Sister" at one time was another remnant from that lost, pre-Levy successor to *Blood on the Tracks*. Probably written in those early days in the Village in June, it was apparently one of the songs rehearsed with Rivera alone. Set around a harmonica figure counterpointed by that omnipresent, slightly off-key violin, it had much the same gypsy feel as the one song he had written in France; and like "One More Cup of Coffee," it was a survivor.

Even when he struggled to extract its essence as madness reigned at the "big band" sessions in late July, he persevered. And indeed, when Stoner advocated a more naked sound, it was this song that they tried first—a last throw of the dice on the night of the twenty-ninth. The next night they followed the same template for the entire session, with dramatic results. Yet the song had more still to say. Indeed, the very best live version may well be the first—in a TV studio in Chicago in September 1975, when Dylan was paying tribute to his first producer, John Hammond, by singing it to a select audience of invitees. Here, he managed to inject a real yearning into his vocal, all the while swooping around Rivera's violin with a series of frantic harmonica bursts.

Intriguingly, it was introduced that evening in slightly ominous fashion, with a dedication to "someone watching tonight—she knows who she is!" The suspicion has long been voiced that the "someone watching tonight" was none other than Joan Baez. Indeed, the timeline of the song's composition suggests it was probably Dylan's idea of an answer-song to the title track of Baez's latest LP, issued in early May 1975, *Diamonds & Rust.*

It seems likely that he first heard her song, which was obviously about Dylan, on his return from France towards the end of May. This would tie in with him writing a "reply" song in June, before meeting Levy, who ultimately brought his own input to bear. Baez, it seems, could not resist continuing this peculiar dialogue-in-song on her next album, *Gulf Winds*, issued in November 1976, which would include the pointed "Oh Brother":

> I've known you for a good little while,
> And would you kindly tell me, mister,
> How, in the name of the Father and the Son,
> Did I come to be your sister?

Dylan himself never settled on the right setting for this modest prayer to some unspecified sister, trying it every which way at both the *Desire* sessions and in subsequent live performances. A song which relied heavily on Emmylou Harris's harmony vocals on the album, it was the one song performed as part of the closing set at the 1975 Revue shows which really showed off the harmonica/violin sound he had originally been looking for.

By 1976, the song no longer sat so comfortably in a set that now included "Idiot Wind," "You're a Big Girl Now," and "I Threw It All Away," but was nonetheless preserved on the live album of the tour, *Hard Rain*. And when Dylan came up with an even less worthy arrangement on the Far East leg of the 1978 world tour, that broody travesty was also given official status, on *At Budokan*. As one of the few songs from this period that has a strong religious dimension—being a precursor to the rapturous "Covenant Woman"—it is slightly surprising that it was cast aside in the wake of his conversion. Maybe he felt the sentiments no longer held good.

{325} ABANDONED LOVE

Published lyric/s: Lyrics 85; Lyrics 04. [*Live lyric:* I Can Change I Swear]
First known performance: Other End Club, NYC, July 3, 1975.
Known studio recordings: Columbia Studios, NYC, July 31, 1975—2 takes [BIO—tk. 1].

A rather fitting name for a song which was recorded under the title "Love Copy," and bootlegged under the title "St. John the Evangelist,"

"Abandoned Love" marks the very point at which Dylan decided to (temporarily) abandon love, and particularly forsaken love, as the prime subject matter for his songs. Written in that exciting period when he was cruising the streets of the West Village and popping up in the clubs that had once fueled the folk revival, "Abandoned Love" is the one original we have in its pre-*Desire* guise, recorded from the cheap seats during an impromptu "guest" appearance at a Ramblin' Jack Elliott gig in early July.

That performance is one of the finest documented stolen moments Dylan ever spent on a stage. Thankfully, all that time spent taping Bruce Springsteen shows stood the taper in good stead. His recording provides a rivetingly atmospheric, intimate insight into what those nights must have been like. Having warmed up with a little dose of Lead Belly, the conscious artist decided on the spur of the moment to see how this sophisticated Village audience liked his new stuff. After a few gentle strums he launched straight into a narrative no less haunting or lovelorn than the songs on his most recent album: "I can hear the turning of the key / I've been deceived by the clown inside of me . . ." And for eight magnetic verses he never lets up, not revealing the thrust of the song until those last two verses, when the correspondence between pain and pleasure is searingly magnified by these closing couplets:

> So send out for St. John the Evangelist,
> All my friends are drunk, they can be dismissed
> My head says that it's time to make a change,
> But my heart is telling me, I love you but you're strange.
> So step lightly, darling, near the wall,
> Put on your heavy make-up, wear your shawl,
> Won't you descend from the throne, from where you sit
> Let me feel your love one more time before I abandon it.

The punchline to this compelling narrative induces whoops from an audience who have for the past four minutes been collectively holding their breath. It's a winner, and Dylan knows it. But only a couple of days later he runs into Jacques Levy, and the album he has been working on for the past six weeks skids off its preordained path. And though he does not quite abandon the song, saving it for that final *Desire* session,[3] on this evidence his later claim that he "always kept [the album] on the track of where I thought it should be going" does not stand up to scrutiny.

In the studio, this heartwrenching song is given a jaunty, clippety-clop arrangement, a strangely disembodied vocal and a handful of lyrical changes that, while technically impressive, lighten the load. Lines like, "I've given up the game, I've got to leave / The pot of gold is only make believe / The treasure can't be found by men who search . . ." read effectively enough. Yet they do not betray the heavy heart of a lovesick ex-Lothario anything like as well as the original: "I can't play the game no more, I can't abide / By their stupid rules which get me sick inside / They've been made by men who've given up the search . . ."

Yet even so emaciated, the song begged to be included on the album. But it did not even make the short list. It would be ten years before *Biograph* gave us the song in its studio guise, from which the Everly Brothers subsequently took their own diversionary take. Ex–Green on Red guitarist Chuck Prophet, on the other hand, took the Other End performance as his template, and his high-flown version (on the 1995 tribute CD, *Outlaw Blues Vol. 2*) is all the better for it. Dylan himself was about to have another bout of selective amnesia when it came to abandoned love songs.

{326} ISIS

Published lyric/s: Lyrics 85; Lyrics 04.

Known studio recordings: Columbia Studios, NYC, July 30, 1975—2 takes; July 31, 1975—2 takes [DES—tk. 2].

First known performance: [Other End Club, NYC mid-July 1975] Plymouth, MA, October 30, 1975.

> [It] was almost a funeral dirge when we first worked on it. It was so slow and rather stately and sad . . . [and it] was slightly different at that time—we had a chorus at the end that was different from the final version.
> —Jacques Levy, *Isis* #90

Magnificent as the final song is, what one wouldn't give to have heard this "original," pre-Levy "Isis"! It evidently partially survived their initial collaboration, as on its live debut, less than a week after his other Other

End set, a *Rolling Stone* reporter described it as "an extraordinary, folky love song with a refrain that changed one word each verse, very much in the style of 'Visions of Johanna.'" Which is sure not how it sounds on record.

As to how Dylan ended up working with Levy the lyricist, he gave his account to Sloman at the time: "We ran into each other and we had seen each other off and on throughout the years, so we wound up . . . at his place sitting around and I had a few songs. I certainly wasn't thinking of making a record album, but I had bits and pieces of some songs I was working on and I played them for him on the piano and asked him if they meant anything to him. And [so] he took it someplace else, and then I took it someplace else, then he went further, then I went further, and it wound up that we had this song ['Isis'], which was out there."

One suspects that "this song which was out there," with a "chorus," was not as reconciliatory as the one he later recorded. Dylan even felt inclined to mess around with those closing lines in subsequent editions of *Lyrics*, replacing the triumphant, "She said, 'Ya gonna stay?' I said, 'If you want me to, yes'" with a slice of B movie dialogue: "I said, 'Yeah, I jes' might'" (which now rhymes with "not quite," as opposed to, "Well, I guess").

In conversation with *Isis* editor Derek Barker, Levy later elucidated why the pair worked on that particular song that first night: "The only reason that 'Isis' was chosen as the song to work together on was that we were at my loft apartment and Bob didn't have a guitar with him . . . but I had a piano, and 'Isis' was the one song that he had started to write on the piano. . . . We are sitting at a piano together and we are writing these verses in an old Western ballad kinda style. Y'know, the kind of thing that he spent a couple of years doing with The Band in the [Big Pink] basement."

According to another interview Dylan's colyricist gave *Melody Maker* at the time, once he started working on the song with Dylan, it came quickly: "He had the general feeling of the song when he came around [to my place] but he hadn't got further. We started to work on it at night and by the following morning it was finished. We did it together, going back and forth and trying things out on each other to see what would work and what wouldn't."

Dylan seems to have been relieved to find a sympathetic spirit who could provide some old-school craftsmanship, easing him back into the lyric-writing process. As he said in the early nineties of that night, "['Isis'] was a story that meant something to Jacques. It just seemed to take on a life of its own."

Levy, more theater-man than musician, was already known to Dylan through his earlier collaborations with Roger McGuinn, most memorably "Chestnut Mare," a song alluded to on the released "Idiot Wind." But Dylan wasn't entirely up-front with Levy, who continued to believe that the only thing "Isis" "has to do with the Egyptian goddess is that we threw in the pyramids, which were a substitute for the hills of Wyoming." In fact, the song was a thinly veiled rewrite of the oldest story of them all—the quest of the hero to prove himself worthy of the woman he worships—a tale found in all the mythologies of the classical world, Egypt included (in all likelihood, Dylan took such a conceit directly from Joseph Campbell's *The Hero of a Thousand Faces*, as has been suggested elsewhere).[4] As for the grave-robbing element ("I broke into the tomb, but the casket was empty"), I doubt there had ever been much of a call for said activity in "the hills of Wyoming."

Curiously, this was the only song on *Desire*—that last-minute inclusion, "Sara," excepted—which Dylan made no attempt to record at "big band" sessions on July 14, 28, and 29. He seemingly had in mind a stripped-down sound from the outset, one dominated by the instrument he originally composed it on—the piano. Bassist Rob Stoner—who had witnessed, and probably played on, the song's live debut at the Other End—seemed to know what Dylan needed, convincing him to record it with just his bass, Scarlet's violin, and the drummer from Stoner's own band, Howie Wyeth.

Stoner's ballsy self-confidence saved the song, and the album which was going nowhere fast. He even got to provide backing vocals on the released take, which comes from the session on the thirty-first (the version recorded with Emmylou Harris the previous night was rejected, for reasons unknown). They did two takes on the thirtieth, both complete, after which Dylan complimented Stoner on his choice of drummer, forming an instant musical bond with one of the great Dylan rhythm sections. Just about every completed track on the thirtieth made the album (or, in the case of "Rita May," single). So one wonders what made Dylan recut "Isis" the following night. Perhaps it was simply the presence of his wife at the session which made him revisit this song "about marriage."

"Isis" in turn became the centerpiece of the first set at every fall show, highlighting this ballad in its most dramatic guise. With no piano to chain him down, Dylan becomes the circus master, stalking the stage, harmonica in hand, letting the momentum of the narrative build and build, until that single, explosive expletive, "Yeah!!" triggers one last mad musical dash to the finishing line. (No one witnessing the footage from Montreal used in *Renaldo and Clara*—and as a bonus DVD to *Live 1975 [Bootleg Series Vol. 5]*—can avoid being blown away by the theatricality of the performance, which culminates in Dylan spitting out his harmonica and catching it in a single movement, as he heads stage right at song's end). But, like "One More Cup of Coffee," "Isis" was edged out of the set in 1976, and since then it has been enveloped by the fog that has clouded Dylan's memory of when the song of the sirens rang in his head.

{327} JOEY

Published lyric/s: Lyrics 85; Lyrics 04.
Known studio recordings: Columbia Studios, NYC, July 14, 1975—7 takes; July 30, 1975—1 take [DES—tk. 1].
First known performance: [Other End Club, NYC, mid-July 1975] Foxborough, MA, July 4, 1987.

> If you wanna write what you call topical songs [now], [it's] hard to find the frontier. —Dylan, to Mary Travers, April 1975

> One of the most mindlessly amoral pieces of repellently romanticist bullshit ever recorded. —Lester Bangs, *Creem*, April 1976

"The Ballad Of Joey Gallo"—or "Joey" as it became known—proved to be the most controversial inclusion on *Desire* in January 1976. Though its grasp of the facts of gangster-renegade Joey Gallo's life was at least as sound as Rubin Carter's in the album's other long ballad, "Hurricane," and Dylan's recorded performance was exemplary, Gallo was a violent white man. Whereas Donald White, George Jackson and Rubin Carter could always blame the color of their skin—and did—Gallo was just plain nuts. Hence his moniker, "Crazy Joe." Dylan probably saw some of the flak coming. He certainly was keen to defend his choice of subject when discussing the song with Larry Sloman, a full three months before its release:

> You want to know how the song "Joey" came about? . . . I was with Jacques. I was leaving town and Jacques says he was going up to some place to have supper and I was invited to come if I felt like it and I was hungry so I went with him and it was up to Marty and Jerry Orbach's place and as soon as I walked in the door, Marty was talking about Joey. She was a good friend of Joey's. They were real tight. I just listened for a few hours, they were talking about this guy, and I remember Joey. At that time, I wasn't involved in anything that he was involved in, but he left a certain impression on me. I never considered him a gangster, I always thought of him as some kind of a hero in some kind of a way. An underdog fighting against the elements. He retained a certain amount of his freedom and he went out the way he had to. But she laid all these facts out and it was like listening to a story about Billy the Kid, so we went ahead and wrote that up in one night. I was living around Little Italy so I was always walking around there.

At the time, Levy confirmed that the impetus for the song was as much Dylan's as his (a statement we can probably trust a tad more than Dylan's recent assertion that "Jacques Levy wrote the words. Jacques had a theatrical mind and he wrote a lot of plays. So the song might have been theater of the mind. I just sang it"). Levy, by his own admission, had "spent a lot of time with Joey in that last year he was alive . . . [but] Bob became very interested in it all." And Dylan was rather proud of what they produced. Having written the song one night, he was at The Other End the following night, playing it to the late-night crowd. It was also the first song he set out to record for the album, at a hastily assembled session set up barely a week after he wrote it, something he'd not done since "George Jackson." Already he was convinced he had an outlaw ballad as epic as the medieval Robin Hood ballads. ("To me ['Joey'] is like a Homer ballad . . . [It] has a Homeric quality to it that you don't hear every day." —Dylan, 1991.)

The version he cut on July 14 was his most grandiose recording to date—and a full-on preview of his next album, *Street-Legal*. At the session were ten musicians and three backing singers. And initially he seemed satisfied with the outcome, because when work resumed on the album two weeks later, after a sojourn in the Hamptons, he made no attempt to rerecord this song at either of the "big band" sessions. Only when, at Rob Stoner's suggestion, he stripped the whole sound down did "Joey" get an exhumation. Amazingly, the quartet cut this eleven-minute epic in a single take, Dylan delivering one of the best vocals of the session, dramatizing the life of a modern-day outlaw, while repeatedly letting the chorus ask the one question the song fails to answer: "What made them want to come and blow you away?"

And when it came time to sequence the album, Dylan was determined to include "Joey" as opening cut on side two, a mirror reflection of the album's opener, "Hurricane"—even though it meant an unheard-of twenty-eight-minute side. But the reviews of the album, which were almost universally laudatory, still tended to single out "Joey" for their opprobrium (Dave Marsh described "Joey," in his March 11 *Rolling Stone* review, as "a hymn to Joey Gallo, the self-educated Mafioso who . . . precipitated, with his brothers, the most vicious modern mob war. . . . Gallo was an outlaw, in fact, only in the sense that he refused to live by the rules of the mob").

And when that spring Lester Bangs wrote his famous *Creem* piece, "Bob Dylan's Dalliance with Mafia Chic," the case for the prosecution began to paint a compelling portrait of just how unpleasant Gallo could be. Aside from his extracurricular reading of philosophy in jail, he also took "part in a homosexual gang rape about which he bragged at a cocktail party after his release." And in having Joe Colombo "taken out," Gallo lived up to his nickname, effectively signing his own death warrant.

But Dylan continued to defend his right to write about a wrong 'un like Gallo. Matt Damsker heard a familiar mantra in 1978: "Even the old ballad singers . . . used to lay it out . . . in the same way. The singer . . . could decide for you, the listener, which side was right and which side was wrong." What's good is bad, then. At times it seemed as if, whenever the subject of outlaws arose in an interview, it was to this song that Dylan would turn the conversation. His longest and most lucid defence of the song—or at least the vantage point adopted therein—came in an interview designed to promote *Shot of Love* [!], with Dave Herman:

> I grew up admiring those type of heroes, Robin Hood, Jesse James . . .
> the person who always kicked against the oppression and had high moral
> standards. I don't know if these people I write about have high moral

standards, I don't know if Robin Hood did, but you always assumed they did. . . . There is some type of standard I have for whoever I'm writing about. I mean, it amazes me that I would write a song about Joey Gallo . . . but that's an old tradition. I think I picked that up in the folk tradition. There are many songs, a lot of Irish ballads [celebrating outlaws], Roddy McCorley . . . Jesse James, Cole Younger . . . Billy the Kid. . . . The English ballads had them and the Scottish ballads had them and that just carried over with me into whatever this special brand of music that I play now is.

In the light of such a comment, it should have come as no surprise when he reintroduced the song at a mercifully short set of shows with the Grateful Dead in the summer of 1987. But any surprise turned to stupefaction when Dylan began singing the song at an open-air Independence Day gig having only the vaguest idea of how the twelve long verses went. Inflicting this massacre-disaster blues on the folk of Foxborough, Massachusetts, was bad enough, but he made it ten times worse by playing the song at all first four stadium shows with the Dead, only to then put the first and worst version on the official album of the tour.

Restored to favor, the song has sporadically reared its head throughout the Never Ending Tour, with generally mixed results. Always committed vocally, he has been less committed to learning this tendentious version of events, stumbling over the lyrics just about every time. But he has continued to implicitly glorify Joey's kind, performing the song with especial gusto at a show in Brixton in late March 1995, the night after they buried East End hoodlum Ronnie Kray. So much for having "some type of standard . . . for whoever I'm writing about."

{328} RITA MAY

Published lyric/s: Lyrics 85; Lyrics 04.

Known studio recordings: Columbia Studios, NYC, July 14, 1975—7 takes; July 30, 1975—4 takes [45].

First known performance: New Orleans LA, May 3, 1976 (late show).

The other song which Dylan and Levy wrote that second week in July—also about a real person—contained a lot more levity than the saga of the Gallo clan. "Rita May" was a humorous send-up of the views of well-known lesbian novelist and activist Rita Mae Brown, whose first novel, *Rubyfruit Jungle* (1973), had caused quite a stir on publication because of its explicit portrayal of lesbian sexuality.

However, what really seems to have prompted this pair of male songwriters to challenge the lady's worldview was her role in founding a lesbian feminist newspaper collective, the Furies Collective, that held heterosexuality to be the root of all oppression. The song's narrator is understandably worried that, if he hangs around with her, he'll go blind (from self-abuse, presumably). Consumed by feelings of unworthiness, the narrator decides he's "gonna have to go to college / 'Cause you are the book of knowledge, Rita May." But the real burning issue he needs to know is again framed as a question, "How'd you ever get that way?"

Not exactly a major work, then. And yet "Rita May" was one of two songs Dylan was determined to record at the July 14 session—expending seven takes' worth of creative energy on it. On this original recording, the girl singers he co-opted as a chorus sing about how they "like the boys with the dreamy eyes . . . Don't think twice, it's so nice" on the fade, as if taunting the lady with what she might be missing. These gals had evidently not been culled from the Furies Collective.

In the end, Dylan decided that this version was a little too stodgy for a song that would not have been out of place on his other 1975 album (*The Basement Tapes*), giving it the same treatment as "Joey," stripping it down to fit the Scarlet–Stoner–Wyeth sound. For a while, it was even given a slot on *Desire*, as the side-one closer, before the exigencies of a sixty-minute album did for it. But the joke refused to pall, and Dylan worked up a live arrangement in time for the 1976 tour, where he gave it a couple of outings, before issuing the July 30, 1975, version as a stand-alone single, ostensibly to help promote the *Hard Rain* LP. But for all his huffin' and a-puffin'," it failed to tickle the general public's funny bone—perhaps because precious few knew of, or cared about, the lady and/or her views.

There is nonetheless an interesting corollary to this song's history. Bassist Rob Stoner likes to tell of when he walked the streets of Chicago with Dylan, the night of the John Hammond tribute, discussing old rockabilly singles (a shared interest). Finally, Stoner asks Dylan if he knows the relatively obscure Johnny Burnette Trio cut "Bertha Lou," from 1957. Dylan says, "Sure," only for Stoner to point out its similarity to one of the songs they just recorded (meaning "Rita May"). Dylan cuts the conversation short.

{329} HURRICANE

Published lyric/s: Lyrics 85; Lyrics 04.
Known studio recordings: Columbia Studios, NYC, July 28, 1975—3 takes; July 30—1 take; October 24—10 takes [DES—tk. 2+6]
First known performance: "World of John Hammond," Chicago, IL, September 10, 1975.

> The next song we did was "Hurricane" . . . but I said that I didn't want to write a song like "George Jackson" . . . I wanted to try to take the part of an attorney almost, and tell the story to the jury. —Jacques Levy, *Isis* #90

Though Dylan and Levy started on "the story of the Hurricane" in the immediate aftermath of writing "Isis," they abandoned it almost as soon as they began. As Levy would later say, "We had to do some research, so we could finish that song; and we went on to another one." Up to now, Dylan's idea of research had been the same as with "George Jackson," i.e., reading the self-serving account of an incarcerated "murderer" and believing this extremely violent young man had been railroaded. This time the book in question was *The Sixteenth Round*, Carter's own account of his "spiritual journey," published in spring 1974, as momentum for a retrial continued to build.

Carter—and his fellow accused, John Artis—had been in jail for more than eight years, serving three life sentences for the murders of bar owner James Oliver, customer Fred Nauyoaks, and waitress Hazel Tanis in what was presumed to be "retaliation" for the murder of black bar-owner Roy Holloway by white business rival Frank Conforti earlier the same evening (in what turned out to have been a straightforward dispute over money). (The three victims had no association with Conforti, but no other explanation for these apparently motiveless murders has ever been offered.) The two black men who entered the Lafayette Bar & Grill at two-thirty in the morning of June 17, 1966, carrying a shotgun and a handgun, were not holding up the bar. They set out with the clear intent of killing everyone who was there—including the one drinker who survived the bloody massacre, William Marins, who was shot in the head, losing an eye; he later proved unable to identify the killers through his "one dying [*sic*] eye."

The one reliable witness to the shooting—Marins himself remembering almost nothing—was Patricia Valentine, who lived above the bar and, awoken by the gunshots, got up just in time to see two black men jump into a white car with out-of-state plates and "butterfly" taillights. At 2:34 A.M., an all-points-bulletin went out for such a car. Just six minutes later, Sgt. Theodore Capter pulled over a car matching that exact description. Inside the car were Carter, Artis, and a third man. Because Capter knew Carter, who was by then an extremely well-known boxer, he let them go, which rather contradicts the version of events in Dylan's song:

> When a cop pulled him over to the side of the road
> Just like the time before and the time before that.
> In Paterson that's just the way things go.
> If you're black you might as well not show up on the street,
> 'Less you wanna draw the heat.

It turned out there was another witness—Alfred Bello. On lookout duty while his partner-in-crime Arthur Dexter Bradley broke into the warehouse of a local sheet-metal company, he also heard the shots and apparently phoned the cops independently, describing the identical car and two black assailants. Once he gave his testimony to the cops, they decided both accounts indicated Carter's white car, stopped earlier, and the word was put out to apprehend Carter and Artis.

They were soon pulled over again, and were requested to drive to the Lafayette Bar, where both Valentine and Bello confirmed that the white Dodge Polara was similar to the car they saw leaving the bar. When it came to the trial, much would be made of Carter's choice of car that night. He owned a black Eldorado convertible with his name stencilled in silver on the side, and yet he had chosen to drive this less conspicuous vehicle which was leased to his company as a business-tax concession. Carter later claimed the Polara was blocking the Eldorado in his drive, which was why he took the Polara.

By June 1966, Carter was a well-known figure in Paterson, having been one of America's better middleweights for the past five years. Indeed, Dylan is quite right to sing, "One time he could have been the champion of the world"—Carter had lost on points to then-champion Joey Giardello in a December 1964 bout. But he is quite wrong to claim that Carter was "the number one contender for the middleweight crown" at the time of the crime. When the shooting occurred, he was nothing of the sort. Since that defeat in 1964, his career had nose-dived, thanks to six defeats and a draw in thirteen interim bouts. And as his career began to crash, he began to revert to old ways, knocking out a man in a nightclub just for sitting at his favorite table and getting into numerous barroom brawls. (He already had "form," having spent time in two separate reform schools and spells in Rahway and Trenton state prisons for previous violent assaults.)

Initially, though, the police were not convinced of Carter's guilt, releasing him and Artis after they both passed lie-detector tests, even allowing Carter to fly to Argentina the following August, where he lost the final fight of his career to Juan "Rocky" Rivero. But on October 14, 1966, Carter and Artis were finally arrested and charged with the murders. In the song, Dylan (and Levy) imply that the cops were simply "lookin' for someone to blame," having always wanted to "put his ass in stir" for being an uppity n-word. And they had a point. Carter had a chip the size of a turnpike tollbooth on his muscle-bound shoulder and knew how to make enemies.

But the evidence was also hard to refute—at least it was as long as Bello stuck to his story (he changed his testimony at least twice over the years): two witnesses, one highly distinctive car, two shells found in Carter's car of the same calibre as the bullets used in the shooting (though *not* an exact fit), and no credible explanation for their where-abouts. Damning him further, at his (first) retrial in 1976, the one witness who Carter claimed would corroborate his whereabouts at the time of the shooting testified instead that the boxer had asked him to corrobo-rate a false alibi, and that he had *not* been drinking with him at the Nite Spot at the time, as Carter repeatedly claimed in his book. Carter was given two consecutive life sentences and one concurrent, while Artis received three concurrent terms.

Dylan, who had been contacted by Richard Solomon of the Hurricane Carter Defense Fund shortly before traveling to France in late April

1975, returned in mid-June to find a copy of Carter's book awaiting him. Having sat down and read the thing, he once again allowed himself to see the world in black and white. Almost immediately, he trekked out to Trenton to see the man in prison and felt a genuine rapport:

> The first time I saw [Carter], I left knowing one thing. That this man's philosophy and my philosophy were running on the same road, and you don't meet too many people like that . . . [and] I took notes because I wasn't aware of all the facts and I thought that maybe sometime I could condense it down and put it into a song. . . . Was I doing my bit for Rubin? I wrote that song because it was tops in my mind, it had priority in my mind at the time to get that song done.

Like "Isis," there was a quite different working version of "Hurricane" which Levy initially got to hear—by implication, this was a lot "like 'George Jackson.'" The more fastidious Levy thought they should first check their facts. He also thought the song should be like a mini-movie, the first verse acting like the opening credits: "The beginning of the song is like stage directions, like what you would read in a script . . . Bob loves movies, and he can write these movies that take place in eight-to-ten minutes." The author of "Lily, Rosemary, and the Jack of Hearts" was bound to respond to such an idea.

The two partners-in-rhyme finished up the song in the Hamptons, where they retired for ten days around July 15, hoping to complete an album's worth of Dylan/Levy songs. Already the song was intended to be a centerpiece of said album. Dylan the protest singer had been itching to find a suitable cause. As he had told Ben Fong-Torres one afternoon in January 1974, "Protest is an old thing. Sometimes protest is deeper or different—the Haymarket Square [riots] or the Russian Revolution . . . [But] there's always a need for protest songs. You just gotta tap it."

Having hooked up with Jacques, it seemed like all he wanted to do was protest. With a big-band "Joey" already in the can, Dylan used the first of four consecutive all-night sessions on July 28 to cut three complete takes of his new protest ballad, but some sixteen musicians were cluttering up the narrative. Two nights later he was down to just three, and a nervous harmony vocalist, cutting it in a single take. That version provided the requisite springboard for an album of protest narratives and tall tales. "Hurricane" fit both briefs.

Unfortunately, even after Levy cross-checked many of the details, they had gotten certain salient facts wrong. In particular, they were hopelessly confused about the roles of Bello and his partner-in-crime, Bradley. Bradley was accused in the song of "robbing the bodies," of cutting a deal with the cops, and having "baldly lied" on the stand. In fact, Bradley had been nowhere near the bar. It was Bello who robbed the register (not the bodies). Aside from confirming Bello's description of the car, Bradley contributed nothing significant to the police case.

The song also implied that Valentine had been the barman's lover, not simply the waitress's friend; and that she had corroborated Bello's description of the car, as opposed to providing a similar description to the police in her first, frenzied phone call, before she had even encountered Bello. It was "Talkin' John Birch" all over again; and when Dylan sang these potentially libelous lyrics on a prerecorded TV special for John Hammond Sr. in September, the CBS lawyers called him in, and told him he'd have to re-record the song and/or change the lyric.

For a man who liked talking about *truth*, Dylan remained blithely disinterested in the facts of the case, and although he agreed to change the line about "robbing the bodies," and to remember that the name of the guy on the scene was Bello, not Bradley, he continued to imply that Bradley cut a deal and "baldly lied" while accusing Valentine and Bello of concocting a consistent version of events "for the cops." Not surprisingly, he ended up being sued—by Valentine, who claimed invasion of privacy. (She finally had her case dismissed in 1983, on the grounds that for the purposes of the crime in question she was a public figure, though only after Dylan had been obliged to give a sworn deposition justifying his version of events.)

Only after his meeting with the label did Dylan have to face up to the fact that he could not simply "punch in" the new lyric, something he had finally learned to do on *Blood on the Tracks*. Having allowed producer Don Devito to record much of the album live with a minimum amount of sound baffling, even sharing a mike with backing singer Emmylou Harris (who was no longer available to redo her vocal anyway), he realized the song would have to be cut all over again. And so, in the middle of tour rehearsals at SIR Midtown, Dylan took his trusted trio, augmented by actress-singer Ronee Blakley and Leon Luther on congas, back into Studio E to do it all over again.

The night of this second "Hurricane" proved to be quite a frustrating session, none of the ten takes having the same kind of feel as the one-take wonder from July 30. In the end, Dylan left it to Devito to splice together two separate takes (two and six), rush-releasing the results as his new single. As with "George Jackson," he refused to give radio stations an alternative, putting an edit of the song (minus the n-word) on the A-side, and the full song on the B-side.

At the same time, he began performing the song in the second half of every show on the fall tour, set up partially to spread the word about this "injustice" (Dylan later commented, "Somebody getting beat up, or going to jail for a crime they didn't commit, that's injustice . . . not politics"). He duly admitted that the case had provided a large part of the motivation for touring—"I wanted to spread the message." And yet, as Dylan fully recognized, a real protest song always has a wider theme, like the next song the pair would write ("Black Diamond Bay"): "It really doesn't come out [being] about Hurricane. Really, the essence of it is never what it's about. It's really about you. Unless you're standing in somebody else's shoes you just don't know what it feels like."

No sooner was Carter finally granted a new trial, and released on bail on March 17, 1976, than the song was dropped from the set, never to reappear. But the real-life saga had not yet run its course. Carter's retrial began in November, but on December 22, both men were again found guilty on all charges. Meanwhile, allegations that six weeks after his release Carter had punched and kicked a bail bondswoman until she lost consciousness, after she had been working for his release for over a year, refused to go away. It would be another nine years before Carter was finally granted his freedom—on a technicality, or two. Federal Judge H. Lee Sarokin ruled that the state had "violated the constitutional rights of Carter and Artis on two separate grounds" by failing to disclose the results of the lie detector test given by Alfred Bello and by claiming that the killings were prompted by a desire for racial revenge. Sarokin ruled that such an argument "should never be permitted to sway a jury or provide the basis of a conviction," and without such an assertion the prosecution lacked any motive for the crime.

Despite such a verdict, Dylan still believed in Carter's innocence, putting a long sequence about Carter into his 1977 movie, *Renaldo and Clara* (in which he again used parts of the potentially libelous July recording)—only to later imply it was a hollow gesture. When he talked to Allen Ginsberg on the film's release, he seemed to suggest he had failed in his duty. "It comes back to the idea of getting out of prison. Clara will do what Renaldo will only dream about—get a man out of jail. Renaldo may be thinking about it, singing about it, but Clara does it, directly, in present time."

Shortly after Carter's eventual release Dylan invited him to a July 1986 show in New York, at which he said "hello to my friend," and after which they apparently embraced and talked animatedly for a full half-hour. A few days later, at a show in New Jersey, when someone in the crowd shouted for the song Dylan snorted, "Do you know what this state *did* to that man?" Others who were along for the ride in 1975 had never been so convinced. That shrinking violet Joni Mitchell told tour-chronicler Larry Sloman, "I talked to Hurricane on the phone several times and I was [seemingly] alone in perceiving that he was a violent person and an opportunist. I thought . . . 'This is a bad person. He's fakin' it.'" All in all, a rather fitting subject for the last protest song from the pen of the man previously responsible for "Ballad of Donald White," "The Lonesome Death of Hattie Carroll," and "George Jackson."

330} BLACK DIAMOND BAY

Published lyric/s: Lyrics 85; Lyrics 04.

Known studio recordings: Columbia Studios, NYC, July 29, 1975—12 takes; July 30—5 takes [DES].

I don't feel that to live in this country you have to watch the TV news. You learn from talking to other people. You have to know how people feel, and you don't get that from television news. —Dylan, to Neil Hickey, 1976

"Black Diamond Bay" is something of a lost gem. The one song from *Desire* Dylan has never played in concert, it leads directly on to the likes of "Changing of the Guards" and "No Time to Think" on *Street-Legal*. Lyrically the most ambitious of all the *Desire* songs, it was inspired by that storyteller par excellence Joseph Conrad. Determined to write narrative songs, and demonstrably ill-equipped to document real life, Dylan and his colyricist Levy began talking about their mutual love for Conrad's exotic tales (of which the novella *Heart of Darkness* remains the best known).

Conrad's inspiration would remain a general one. As Levy confirmed to *Isis*, "The narrative in the song is strictly original fiction, based on nothing else." A fantastic story, fully worthy of Joseph, it is set in a hotel on a tropical island when a volcano erupts (a single phrase, "from the mountain high above," apparently triggering the song). Hardly your Hollywood ending then, even if all the characters are straight out of a forties Warners' picture, and the coconspirators' intention all along was to write a screenplay-in-song, as Levy readily recalled:

> When we started to write the song there was this image of a mysterious woman on a veranda somewhere, with a Panama hat and a passport. Then there was that kind of slightly seedy hotel with a gambling room. . . . After that, the thing began to open itself up to us. . . . The sense that I was feeling was like in the movies, where they have all those jungle birds screeching loudly and you just know that there is some imminent danger. . . . The desk clerk, well, he's straight out of a Sidney Greenstreet movie. . . . That is what I was trying to achieve. The hotel is probably run by Humphrey Bogart; it is that kind of exotic setting.

Not content with telling such a texturally layered narrative, Dylan decided to set the lyrics to a 6/8 rhythm that would have represented enough of a challenge without introducing a series of internal rhymes he sure didn't find in no rhyming dictionary ("veranda"/ "necktie and a"; "open"/ "rope and"; "second floor"/ "Ambassador" ; "vous plaît"/ "fly away"; oh, and my personal favorite, "the basement blew"/ "je vous aime beaucoup"). Such outlandish rhyme schemes only affirm the whole song's rich exoticism.

Perhaps Dylan felt that the released version of "Lily, Rosemary, and the Jack of Hearts" had simply not been musically interesting enough to sustain an equally intricate story. After all, as Levy was learning fast, "One of the things about Bob's songs is that they don't take on the traditional pop song with two verses and then a bridge and then a verse. . . . They are more based on the idea of an old ballad where the verse keeps repeating in the same form over and over for as many verses as you need it to go." And Dylan knew that the old story-song genre represented a challenge to his audience's attention span. The two lyricists addressed it by constructing a fast-moving story line—which they then send up with a final verse that shows us that the whole story had been the backdrop to an item on the seven o'clock news.

This coda, actually the starting point for the song, stemmed from an offhand comment by Levy: "We were talking about the state of music at the time . . . [and] I made some kinda joke that instead of sympathy for the Devil, people had apathy for the Devil . . . All this [stuff] was happening around them and they paid almost no attention to it. . . . That final verse was intended right from the beginning. . . . Now I must confess that I didn't know exactly how to get there from the beginning but I had to get that apathy. . . . To make the song work you have got to turn the corner and get into another place, and look at it from another view altogether."

Like "Hurricane," the pair had begun writing this song in New York, finishing it off in the Hamptons, Levy specifically recalling that they "wrote two of the verses in New York and the rest of it out there in the Hamptons. . . . The style wasn't any different out there; we just kept on writing, but it was more relaxed and more conducive to work." Dylan delighted in the easy camaraderie and loose working regime. As he later informed Paul Zollo, "Writing with Jacques wasn't difficult. It was trying to just get it down."

One suspects they challenged each other to fill in ever more details, to color in the lives of these doomed souls. And some of the touches achieve a rare pathos, whether it is the Greek who is trying to hang himself when the lights go out and, rather than complete his suicidal act, "appears on the second floor / In his bare feet with a rope around his neck"; the dealer who tells the gambler, "You can take your money / But I don't know how you'll spend it in the tomb"; or the mysterious female who, at song's end, "sheds a tear and then begins to pray / As the fire burns on and the smoke drifts away."

Only after six sixteen-line verses does the camera-in-song pull back to reveal someone "sittin' home alone one night / In L.A. watchin' old Cronkite / On the seven o'clock news," thus reiterating Dylan's assertion that, "Unless you're standing in somebody else's shoes you just don't know what it feels like." The moral of this story is not the expected one—nor is it directed at the ill-fated characters from Black Diamond Bay, but at us.

Not surprisingly, the song proved one of the more difficult to record right, Dylan spending much of the July 29 session slugging it out with mandolin, trumpet, violin, harmonica, slide guitar, and backing vocals, trying to tease the story out. Even the stripped-down band that stepped in the following night found the song a challenge, but in the end—and with a little help from a crossfade intro—listeners got to find out about those lives consumed by an event that "left nothin' but a Panama hat / And a pair of old Greek shoes."

{331} CATFISH

Published lyric/s: Lyrics 85; Lyrics 04.
Known studio recordings: Columbia Studios, NYC, July 28, 1975—3 takes; July 29—2 takes [TBS].

Jacques Levy told Larry Sloman that he and Dylan wrote, or finished, some fourteen songs in East Hampton. Yet we can account for barely half a dozen songs. All of the major songs on the album were already conceptualized by the time they headed there. Even after the two songwriters continued toying with the longer narratives, any time not spent drinking in the local bars was expended writing "filler" songs like "Money Blues," "Mozambique," and "Catfish."

"Catfish," a sincere attempt to celebrate one of baseball's Hall of Famers—"Catfish" Hunter, pitcher for the Oakland Athletics when they achieved three World Series wins in the seventies, before defecting to the Yankees for a million dollars a year—had "outtake" written all over it. And yet it acquired official status as part of the scattershot 1991 set *The Bootleg Series 1–3*. By then Dylan was already rewriting history, claiming that *Desire* was "an album where I didn't have anything and I wasn't even thinking of making a record. I ran into Jacques downtown and we went off and just wrote some songs . . . [and] an album came out of it."

{332} MOZAMBIQUE

Published lyric/s: Lyrics 85; Lyrics 04.

Known studio recordings: Columbia Studios, NYC, July 29, 1975—7 takes; July 30—4 takes [DES].

First known performance: Clearwater, FL, April 17, 1976.

Another ditty dredged up from the bottom of the barrel, "Mozambique" came in for some residual stick when it was slotted onto the A-side of *Desire*, a comfy cushion propped between the rock that is "Isis" and the hard place called "One More Cup of Coffee." At a time when the sunny beaches were not the focus of the world media's attention—because of the bloody civil war then ensuing—the decision to depict the place as if it were a life-size replica of the movie set for *Flying Down to Rio* upset a small but noisy constituency among his critical fan base.

Such ire seems to have had the opposite effect to any intended. Dylan promptly, and perhaps predictably, issued the weakest song on *Desire* as the album's second single (when everyone was demanding he make it "Sara") and then introduced it into the 1976 live set, just as most other songs he had played hard and fast in the fall were falling by the Floridian wayside. One suspects that however much time he planned "to spend . . . in Mozambique," it would be in weeks what this song took him and Jacques to write in hours.

{333} ROMANCE IN DURANGO

Published lyric/s: Lyrics 85; Lyrics 04.

Known studio recordings: Columbia Studios, NYC, July 28, 1975—6 takes [DES].

First known performance: Plymouth, MA, October 30, 1975.

According to Levy, the bulk of the "Romance in Durango" lyric is his. Having jointly "established the beginning of the song," he "stayed up almost all night and . . . wrote the rest of the verses." When he presented the finished lyric to Dylan in the morning, it prompted a semiserious retort from the main man: "I can't leave you for a minute." If he was annoyed, he didn't let it affect his appreciation of the results. In fact, the song became one of the pivotal points on the fall tour, Dylan dramatically segueing from this "hills of Mexico" cowboy story to those mythical hills of Wyoming for the archetypal "Isis."

Again, conversation sparked a song idea. Dylan's time in Durango, November 1972 through January 1973, had filled the man with cinematic visions of a Mexico he had never quite transferred to song. When Levy coaxed him in this direction, it became more *Butch Cassidy and the Sundance Kid* than *Pat Garrett and Billy the Kid*—save that this time the Madonna figure, Magdalena, is there at the hero's side when he exclaims, "Oh, can it be that I am slain?"

But in one crucial sense the song *directly* addresses the movie he helped to make back in Durango, and which the studio took away from the director. "Romance in Durango" is about a man who is haunted by his own murder of a close friend ("Was it me that shot him down in the cantina? / Was it my hand that held the gun?"). At the point of his own death he recalls, in detail, the earlier slaying—the very technique Peckinpah intended to utilize in his 1973 film. The whole of *Pat Garrett and Billy the Kid* was intended to be a flashback from the vantage point of Pat Garrett, as he himself is gunned down by Poe—only for the producer Gordon Carroll to recut it at the studio's behest without this pertinent preface. Was Dylan making a subtle joke about the Movie That Never Was? (The film was later restored to reflect Peckinpah's original intent. Indeed, the 1973 version is now almost impossible to find.)

"Romance in Durango" was probably the last song the pair wrote for the album. It may even have convinced Dylan that his writing association with Levy had run its course, the song, for all its clever narrative touches, being another weirdly exotic script in the vein of "Isis" and "Black Diamond Bay." They had written a handful of modern protest songs and reinvented the popular ballad—but it was probably time to move on (or back), as soon as they captured everything on tape. According to Levy, "At some point out in East Hampton [after] we had about eight or ten songs finished, Bob got on the phone and called CBS and said, 'I'm in town, we've got enough songs for an album, let's schedule a date' . . . [but] when Bob went into the recording studio to make that record he was not all that familiar with some of those songs. This was a new experience for Bob; he was actually using lyric sheets to sing the songs."

"Romance in Durango" was one such song. The lyric wasn't at all straightforward, with phrases like "the serpent eyes of obsidian" (surely a

Levy touch) and "When they rode with Villa into Torreon," plus a chorus that was part Spanish, and elements of the song had never been seared into Dylan's subconscious by the act of composition. Not surprisingly, the vocal he gave it on the first night of sessions, July 28, is a tad half-hearted. He is concentrating on the words, not in the usual, intuitive way, but rather like someone trying real hard to recall how the whole thing turns out.

This, combined with the fact that he was using a band who were uncertain of both the material and the man's working methods—for this is the session at which Eric Clapton, backing singer Yvonne Elliman, English pub-rockers Kokomo, and every Village muso Dylan invited to the session attempted to gatecrash every song—means the results weren't so much counterintuitive as counterproductive. Eric Clapton summarized the problem to *Rolling Stone*: "He was trying to find a situation where he could make music with new people. He was just driving around, picking musicians up and bringing them back to the sessions. It ended up with something like twenty-four musicians in the studio, all playing these incredibly incongruous instruments."

Not surprisingly, almost everything recorded those first two nights was scrapped. The single exception was "Romance in Durango," which Dylan did not even attempt to second-guess. There was supposedly a discussion at the August 1 "mixdown" session as to whether they should try this song slimmed down, but everyone agreed it was fine as it was. It wasn't—as subsequent live performances amply demonstrated. In November and December 1975, "Durango" exploded with passion and attack, a blistering beacon irradiating all around it. All the nuances submerged beneath the black muddy mix at Studio E bubble up to the surface—flamenco guitars, Howie Wyeth's snappiest snare sound, and a chemically enhanced vocal beamed in from the planes of Intuition. The ending has also been fatalistically clarified. As *Telegraph* editor John Bauldie wrote in his *Desire* monograph, "On the record, the hopeful chorus is allowed to conclude the song; in later concert performances such hope is abandoned."

All of this was captured on film at a show in Montreal. That December 4 live performance, included in *Renaldo and Clara* (and on *Biograph*), is everything the sedate studio original is not, a master class in how the man

can reinvent nightly. But once the song was deemed surplus to requirements, reflecting neither the insanity of the 1976 tour nor the overblown
big-band sound of 1978 (though it *was* rehearsed at Rundown), it got lost
in the fog that enveloped this material post-conversion.

That is, until November 24, 2003, when "Romance in Durango"
became one of those remarkable one-off performances that the Never
Ending Tour used to be all about. Playing Hammersmith Odeon (sorry,
Labatts Apollo) for the first time in a decade, Dylan rekindled the spirit of
his 1990 residency and gave a high-voltage charge to the whole evening
when he began a slow, mournful arrangement of "Durango" that was
word-perfect and entirely heartfelt (a coda that repeated the opening
couplet even making the flashback technique explicit). Immediately,
Dylan realized it was far too good for these shows and dropped it like a
hot potato. But at least it made it through the night.

{334} SARA

Published lyric/s: Lyrics 85; Lyrics 04. [*Live lyric:* Words Fill My Head.]
*Known studio recordings: Columbia Studios, NYC, July 31, 1975—5 takes
[DES—tk. 5].*
First known performance: Plymouth, MA, October 30, 1975.

> Well, some songs you figure you're better off not to have written. There's
> a few of them layin' around. —Dylan, to Craig McGregor, March 1978

Such was Dylan's response to a question about "Sara" by the one
Australian journalist who interviewed him in both 1966 and 1978. By
then, the song was well and truly back in its locker, having been last
performed at the second "Night of the Hurricane" in Houston in January
1976. Like a number of songs (and one unreliable memoir) which appear
to be honest expressions but really play hard and fast with the facts,
"Sara" was Dylan's way of creating a certain distance from reality for the
sake of himself, first, and his audience, second. He almost admitted as
much to *Rolling Stone*'s Jonathan Cott, when the song again came up for
discussion on that exhausting world tour, in the contentious context of
truthfulness and art:

I've heard it said that Dylan was never as truthful as when he wrote *Blood on the Tracks*, but that wasn't necessarily true . . . "When people say 'Sara' was written for 'his wife Sara,' it doesn't necessarily have to be about her, just because my wife's name happened to be Sara. [pause] Anyway, was it the real Sara or the Sara in the dream? I still don't know."

Once again, he chose to write a song to appease his soul mate, not to satisfy his muse; and like the earlier "Wedding Song," it was written as an album closer. According to Levy, "Bob had been fooling with 'Sara' for a long time. He'd got the choruses down, but the verses were actually written out at this place on Long Island where we stayed. Out there are all the dunes and beach and all that stuff mentioned in the song. He would try things out on me, but it was a very personal song for him to write." Nearing the end of the process, and writing in self-imposed isolation, Dylan had returned to writing about himself, but in a way that suggested he was still shying away from reality.

In his famous article on "Joey," Lester Bangs bluntly asked perhaps the most pressing question the *Desire* songs raise: "Why, in 1975, should Dylan return to what . . . passes for activism? Because he's having trouble coming up with meaningful subject matter closer to home, that's why; either that or whatever is going on in his personal life is so painful and fucked up he is afraid or unwilling to confront it in his art." In the winter of 1976, when banging out such Bangsian bile, there was no evidence to support this interpretation of Dylan's affairs. He was relying solely on his critical instincts. In the ensuing months this supposition acquired biographical weight, as Dylan's marriage again entered free fall, at the same time as he summarily replaced "Sara" in the live set with "Idiot Wind."

On "Sara," her husband is surrendering to sentimentality all the way down the line. Even the line about "staying up for days in the Chelsea Hotel / Writing 'Sad-Eyed Lady of the Lowlands' for you" smacks of snake oil. Coming from the pen of a man whose "personal life is so painful and fucked up he is afraid or unwilling to confront it in his art," it makes an awful kind of sense that Dylan was trying to retie the bond in song. Unfortunately for his personal well-being, that "enemy within" was just as anxious to unlace the selfsame straps. Are we expected to believe it mere coincidence that he chose to sandwich the five takes of

"Sara" he recorded on the thirty-first between "Abandoned Love" and "Isis"? Or did his other self know that, for all such protestations, he would not hold on to her very long?

{335} SIGN LANGUAGE

Published lyric/s: Lyrics 85; Lyrics 04.
Known studio recordings: Shangri La Studios, Malibu, CA, March 1976 [NRTC].

After penning "Sara" in the Hamptons, Dylan returned to New York to find that at least one song about a fucked-up personal life was still swimming around in his subconscious. When he hooked up with his old friend, Eric Clapton, he played him said song, which he told the guitarist was called "Sign Language" and that "he'd woken up that day and just written down the whole thing. And he didn't understand why or what it meant. And as I listened to it, I realized it didn't have any kind of story line to it, it was just a series of images and powerful vocals put together. It was very stirring."

This was how Clapton described the song to a *Rolling Stone* reporter some five months before he set about recording the song himself. Perhaps a song like this, which hadn't "any kind of story line to it [but] was just a series of images," was Dylan's subconscious telling him what an opportunity he had scorned when he turned to writing travelogues. And yet, just like "I Don't Want to Do It"—a song he previously donated to Clapton's close friend George Harrison—Dylan had no intention of responding to this song's calling.

"Sign Language" did not feature at any of the *Desire* sessions, even though it was presumably during the first session—or a day or two before—that Dylan played the song to Clapton (who had been in town since at least the twenty-second, when he guested at a Rolling Stones concert). One suspects that would have been that, if it had been down to Dylan. But the song had been played to a fellow musician, who recognized its worth. And its potential. Three months later, conversing with *Rolling Stone*, it was still on Clapton's mind; and a further five months down the road, he was looking to rework "Sign Language" himself.

Fortunately for Clapton, the sessions for his new album, booked through March 1976 at the Band's Shangri-La Studio in Malibu, contained more than enough elements to entice Dylan into joining in. Having already recorded "One of Us Must Know," Clapton cajoled Dylan into sharing the microphone with him on another song where its author was "surrounded by fakery," targeting a capricious woman who has been "taking advantage / and bringing me down." In a couple of shakes the English guitarist had rescued a remnant from that lost continuum to *Desire*'s bloody predecessor.

336} WIRETAPPIN'

Known studio recordings: Columbia Studios, NYC, July 28, 1975.

We are reliant on Larry Sloman's *On the Road With Bob Dylan* for any record that such a song was performed, and presumably recorded, at the first of the *Desire* "big band" sessions. According to Sloman, a song of this name, with the burden "Wire tapping / It can happen," was one of "seven tunes" they ran through that night (the studio log lists only six). No such song has been located on the multitrack reels, and the possibility remains that it was a song Dylan ran down, perhaps at the piano, but never recorded; just as he ran down a number of songs as a warm-up at the October "Hurricane" session without Devito ever pressing record.

Note: Another possibility is that this is the mysterious "Devito's Song," attributed to the August 1, 1975, "playback" session—that is, if said song is anything more than some impromptu jam.

337} PATTY'S GONE TO LAREDO
338} WHAT WILL YOU DO WHEN JESUS COMES?

Known studio recordings: SIR Rehearsals, NYC, October 1975 [R+C].

Between the end of July 1975 and April 1978, when Dylan finally got around to recording *Desire*'s successor—a gap almost as great as the more famous one between *New Morning* and *Planet Waves*—there is very little evidence he was bothering to write song ideas down, at least not until the summer of 1977, when he began working on the first batch of *Street-Legal* songs. Like the equally undocumented period which separated *Blonde on Blonde* from the back wheel of his bike, the handful of extant songs from the eight months during which Dylan grappled with his Rolling Thunder Revue exist only because he was captured in rehearsal, in impromptu mode, by the film crew and/or some strategically placed tape recorder.

Perhaps that "Riding Down the Highway" he broke into at an April '76 Clearwater rehearsal was the start of a new song and not some Delta blues lodged in his id. Likewise, who knows what treasures may lie among the "three hundred songs [he played] one after the other"—according to Mick Ronson—at the October 1975 SIR rehearsals, while "there were tape machines [rolling] and everything [was] getting set up."

Just two new songs from those rehearsals later popped up, both on the soundtrack to the *Renaldo and Clara* film, and neither in a state which made it entirely clear what Dylan was singing or where said take may be going. "Patty's Gone to Laredo" could be the song Dylan was rumored to have written about Patty Hearst around this time, though most of its words are drowned out by the dialogue that Dylan (and coproducer Alk) have superimposed over a two-minute excerpt of a full-band performance, leaving us with just the hint that "she'll be back soon" and the statement that "the door is locked."

"What Will You Do When Jesus Comes?" is another full-band performance, complete with backing vocals and fully intelligible lyrics—which does rather presuppose it was not entirely worked up from scratch. A cross between "I'd Hate to Be You on That Dreadful Day" and "When You Gonna Wake Up," it lasts barely a minute before an exponent of the shopping-list school of poetry intrudes. Lines like "What will you say, when Jesus comes? / Will you kick him out in the street, will you drive him into the heat?" naturally assume a certain prophetic importance in the light of his subsequent conversion. For now he had only questions, like the ones he presented to Ron Rosenbaum in conversation at the time of the film's release: "What is it that attracts people to Christ? The fact that it was such a tragedy, is what. Who does Christ become when he lives inside a certain person? Many people say that Christ lives inside them: Well, what does that mean?" The answer, my friend . . .

{339} SEVEN DAYS

Published lyric/s: The Telegraph #13; Lyrics 85; Lyrics 04.
First known performance: Bellevue Biltmore Hotel, Clearwater, FL, April 17, 1976.

As the only completed original definitely written in the twelve months after *Desire*'s release, "Seven Days" takes on an importance its slight nature barely warrants. Again, there is precious little to suggest someone addressing his pain head-on. We are back in *Nashville Skyline* territory—simple rhymes going with straightforward yearnings—though thankfully sung with a great deal more urgency than that earlier material. In fact, it is sung with the same urgency—and libidinous promise—as the raunchy rearrangements of "Lay Lady Lay" and "Tonight I'll Be Staying Here With You" he was performing live at this time. He certainly makes no secret of the lustful impetus underlying this yearning—"I been good while I been waitin'," maybe guilty of hesitatin' / I just been holdin' on."

If there is a secondhand lyrical influence at work it is not so much Chuck Berry's "Thirty Days"—as Paul Williams suggests—but rather John Sebastian's "Darling Be Home Soon." Dylan puts his own spin on Sebastian's choral plea: "It's not just these few hours, I've been waiting since I toddled," which in "Seven Days" becomes "She been gone / Ever since I been a child." Any tenderness, though, is stripped bare, much like the new version of "Lay Lady Lay." Dylan even admits as much during the song's final couplet: "Trying to be tender, with somebody I remember / In a night that's always sadder than the day." Maybe he was addressing his pain, after all.

This is how Dylan sings it on the song's final tour performance in Orlando, as well as two nights earlier in Tampa (the version included on *The Bootleg Series 1–3*). However, the song was not copyrighted from one of these performances, but rather from a "dress rehearsal" run-through at the Biltmore Hotel in Clearwater on April 17, when Dylan was still singing "Seven more days that are connected, just like I expected"—as opposed to the contradictory "Seven days she'll be going, I can hear that whistle blowing." The former was evidently the version given to Ron Wood, who would record the song this way—and issue it as a rather feisty single—after receiving it in March, while both friends lent a hand on Eric Clapton's new album. With no plans to record it himself, Dylan happily gave his buddy the song, dropping it from the set within five days of the start of the spring tour, having perhaps realized he had really not 'been good while I been waitin.'"

1977–8

{ Street-Legal }

Though just a single nine-track album resulted from this intense two-year period, Dylan indulged in four distinct periods of songwriting, only the second of which was represented on LP: songs directly inspired by the break-up of his marriage, about which we have almost no information (or proof that they have survived in any form); songs written in the summer of 1977 on his Minnesotan farm, which constitute almost all of Street-Legal; a group of songs he wrote with backing singer Helena Springs in the spring and summer of 1978; and, finally, those songs he began working on at soundchecks during the U.S. fall tour for the planned natural successor to Street-Legal, which never came.

Instead, Dylan found Christ, and a new kind of inspiration, reflected in the last two songs he wrote while on tour. Both of these—"Slow Train" and "Do Right to Me Baby"—would be salvaged by the "holy slow train," which had now acquired a new passenger. As a result, a great deal of material covering more familiar terrain went unused, nine months of solid songwriting being discarded as an unworthy accompaniment to the revealed word of God . . .

{340} I'M COLD

Written circa winter 1977. No recording known.

This single song title, remembered by Rolling Thunder Revue musician Stephen Soles, is the only solid information we have regarding the material Dylan wrote during the winter of 1977, when he was preoccupied by a divorce and custody battle with his wife of eleven years. That there were a number of songs written at this time Dylan himself confirmed in conversation with the *L.A. Times*" Robert Hilburn the following May: "I cut that whole experience right off. I had some songs last year which I didn't record. They dealt with that period as I was going through it. For relief, I wrote the tunes . . . Some people around town heard them. I played them for some friends. But I had no interest in recording them. I wanted to start off new on the album."

None of these songs survived to *Street-Legal*, if we are to believe a comment Dylan made after being asked directly, by Australian Craig McGregor in March 1978, whether his new songs addressed the end of his marriage. "We were breaking up for a long time. So [the next album] doesn't reflect too much of that." The one *Street-Legal* song that sounds like it perhaps came out of these earlier efforts is "We Better Talk This Over." But most of the lyrics on his new album were so rich in archaic symbolism that it would be hard to prove their relationship to his personal predicament one way or the other—which was doubtless Dylan's intention. Any songs he wrote "for relief" were probably closer in vein to those he would write in the months after recording *Street-Legal*. Indeed, when it comes to titles like "You Don't Love Me No More" and "(Daddy's Gonna Take) One More Ride," it is tempting to speculate whether they may be one and the same.

341} CHANGING OF THE GUARDS

Published lyric/s: Lyrics 85; Lyrics 04.

Known studio recordings: Rundown Studio, Santa Monica, CA, April 25+27, 1978 [S-L].

First known performance: Paris, July 5, 1978.

I have new songs now that are unlike anything I've ever written . . . I mean, unlike *anything* I've ever done. You couldn't even say *Blood on the Tracks* or *Desire* have led up to this stuff . . . it's that far gone, it's that far out there. —Dylan, to Ron Rosenbaum, November 1977

There is a goodly amount of circumstantial evidence that "Changing of the Guards" was the first song written for Dylan's seventeenth studio album. It was certainly the first song recorded for, and opening song on, the resultant album. As often happened when he became enthused by a new way of writing, the template established with this powerful song generated an album of similar-minded brethren. However, the starting place for this song and the resultant album was not as far removed from its predecessor as he suggested to Rosenbaum. It fully reflected the same fascination with rhyme and structure shared with Jacques Levy for those three weeks in July 1975, when they talked at length about the technical side of lyric writing. As Levy later recalled:

> One of the very nice things about working with Bob is that he loves rhyme, he loves to play with it and he loves the complications of it . . . When you have a certain kind of rhyme scheme in [a song], it becomes interesting to solve that puzzle. That's rather fascinating to me, and I think that Bob found it fascinating too; that you could do that and still connect to the content of the song.

The verse structure on "Changing of the Guards" in a sense takes up where the likes of "Black Diamond Bay" left off, though this time he made assonance more of a stakeholder. For once, he was determined to spend time working on his craft, just like the other poets do. Only years later, in conversation with Leonard Cohen, did he discover that his fellow poet-lyricist had taken two years to finish "Hallelujah." One doubts somehow that "Don't Go Home With Your Hard-On," the song Dylan helped Cohen record that winter, took quite so long. However, they may well have discussed the (conscious) art of songwriting during the laborious *Ladies' Man* sessions. *Something* dramatically changed Dylan's approach to his craft; because "Changing of the Guards," and the half a dozen other songs written contemporaneously, crawled their way to completion.

The idea for the *Street-Legal* opener seems to have sprung from a Tom Paxton song that had been playing on his mind. "Peace Will Come," the title track from Paxton's 1972 album, was a message-song directed at oneself: "Peace will come / And let it begin with me . . . Oh, my own life is all I can hope to control / Oh, let my life be lived for the good, good of my soul." Given the turmoil surrounding Dylan's life in the months after the dissipation of the Rolling Thunder Revue, it was a message which was bound to strike a chord. Paxton's song is specifically mentioned in a most intriguing document, published some time in the summer of 1976, a long poem with the title "An Observation Revisited" which appeared under the name "R. Zimmerman" in (of all places) the first issue of a magazine called *Photography*. Ostensibly about a photographic exhibition, the poem suggests an ongoing search for the next sound and vision:

> Below is West Broadway
> a parking lot across the street
> people strolling.
> Am I a part of them?
> Or am I a part of what's going on
> in these photographs?
> Where's my music? . . .
> I'm making scribblings
> I'm always making scribblings
> A minstrel collecting words
> For an eventual song
> In my mind I keep humming Tom Paxton's
> "Peace Will Come"
> And all sorts of images
> Are flashing across the sky at once.

This long poem—it runs to 179 lines—hardly replicates the style of Dylan's previous poetry, but its discursive style does to some extent resemble the tour diary he kept in 1974, from which the *Planet Waves* sleeve notes came. And it would be quite a coincidence if said poem was written by some *other* R. Zimmerman, especially given that its author is described by said periodical as "a one-time kid from the mid-west. A poet and sometime musician who has taken a sabbatical from his instruments and is writing in the seclusion of the woods." Dylan's use of the exact same expression on the very last verse of "Changing of the Guards"— "Peace will come / With tranquility and splendor on the wheels of fire"—surely seals the case for his authorship of said poem.

{ **Still on the Road** }

Such a quasi-anonymous publication, appearing the summer before
he even began work on *Street-Legal*, suggests he was unsure as to any
future direction. It took a long time for those "scribblings" (prompted
by Paxton's song) to take any real shape, and for his muse/ic to return.
"Changing of the Guards" was surely one of those songs he started
writing in the summer of 1977, probably at the same farm where he
wrote most of *Blood on the Tracks*, but with a different woman at his side,
though given its role as the "Tangled Up in Blue" for another album of
farm songs, it could have been conceptualized, if not partly written, by
the time he arrived there with the kids' ex-teacher, Faridi McFree.

It is therefore slightly surprising that when Dylan "previewed" two-
thirds of the album at an impromptu post-rehearsal piano workout in
late December 1977, "Changing of the Guards" was not among the
songs performed, even though it preceded the "seven or eight" songs he
says he "wrote . . . in the fall . . . before this tour," to Craig McGregor the
following March. Asked for some song titles he came up with two: one
he never recorded (or at least not under the title given to McGregor); the
other was "Changing of the Guards."

The lady he took to the farm this time around was almost certainly
the first recipient to hear these magical words. As McFree told me some
years later, "He would show me some of the songs that he was writing.
[It was] practically the entire album . . . It started when we were on the
farm . . . He was very down. He was suffering when I met him. He was
in a bad way." One can well imagine him praying for peace to come.
But at this point the song was probably very different. The one verse
published in draft form—the penultimate verse, which gives the song
its title—reproduced in the 2004 *Lyrics,* bears only a resemblance to the
finished lyric:

> Baby be still she said, can y spare me a moment's passion
> Can I shine yr shoes, print yr money or mark yr cards
> What frozen truths can yr brave souls imagine
> Does yr hearts have the courage for the Changing of the Guards.

Dylan himself implied that the song changed almost out of recognition, telling *Songtalk*, "A song like ['Changing of the Guards'], there's

no way of knowing, after the fact, what the motivation was behind it, unless somebody's there to take it down in chronological order." (No one was.) He evidently felt at the time that its original, jumbled guise had come to him on a wave of familiar inspiration, informing Jonathan Cott, "'Changing of the Guards' might be a song that might have been there for thousands of years, sailing around in the mist, and one day I just tuned into it."

"Tuned into" is bang on. This really was a song from another lifetime. It surely was just what he had in mind when describing his new songs to Karen Hughes a matter of weeks before he recorded it: "I don't know where these songs come from. Sometimes I'm thinking in some other age that I lived through. I must have had the experience of all these songs because sometimes I don't know what I'm writing about until years later it becomes clearer to me."

"Changing of the Guards" may have been one that became *less* clear during the rewriting process. The introduction of a messianic figure in that penultimate verse ("Gentlemen, he said / I don't need your organization, I've shined your shoes / I've moved your mountains and marked your cards . . .") gives it an unexpectedly apocalyptic dimension, but I'm not sure this transition, marked by a change from first to third person (the reverse of "Tangled Up in Blue"), is entirely convincing. What had begun as a conversation between two lovers the morning after their tryst at the dawn of battle has changed into a prophetic pronouncement of the End Times.

It is a lyrical lurch that the music does its best to presage, but it still jars slightly. And yet the song manages to retain its magical hold. We really are transported back in time to some Babylonian narrative of lust and betrayal, to a period of mortal combat ("sixteen banners," "the captain waits," "a messenger arrived," "dog soldiers"). The fortunes of this war are told in the cards, divined by the fortune-teller of his soul, who may be "torn between Jupiter and Apollo" but knows that her fate—and his— will be ultimately decided by the King and the Queen of Swords.

The narrative is so compelling, and the structure so interwoven, that the listener barely notices a surprising absence of rhyme. There are just two consistent rhymes in each five-line verse—lines three and five. And even then he cheats on verse two, where the first rhyme comes mid-line.

It is "Merchants and thieves hungry for power . . ." which rhymes with "On midsummer's eve, near the tower" rather than ". . . my last deal gone down"—hardly the last image on *Street-Legal* he copped from Robert Johnson. Likewise, in verse eight, he rhymes another word in the "wrong" place—"organization" with "elimination."

In fact, one suspects the Johnson song title is something Dylan has jammed onto the end of the line, probably as a last minute interjection. It is missing from the "final" typed version, which was displayed seven years after the fact at an ASCAP exhibition—where an un-Dylanesque hand has added the line at a later date. Further evidence that Dylan is having to stretch and tighten lines in situ comes as one realizes there is meant to be a rhyme between lines two and four ("shadows" and "meadows"), but these lines have been thrown off kilter. Verse two should in fact read:

> Fortune calls
> I stepped forth from the shadows
> To the market place,
> Merchants and thieves hungry for power
> My last deal gone down,
> She's smelling sweet like the meadows,
> Where she was born,
> On midsummer's eve, near the tower.

Dylan the oral-poet knows he need not be hidebound to the page, and sure enough, when he sings the song, this is exactly how he sings it. This leaves the first and last verses with just a single rhyme holding them in place, perhaps indicating he mislaid some lyrical threads in the rewriting process. He was nonetheless rather pleased to find such a musical way of resolving this intricate narrative—hence his enthusiasm to Rosenbaum in November 1977, when he was still focusing on the writing process and not the recording process (which would again let him down).

Problems only arose when he returned to Santa Monica in April, ready to record the results at his own rehearsal studio, Rundown. "Changing of the Guards" was the song with which he started what proved to be another challenging series of sessions. The entire first day of sessions was spent working on what was surely already penciled in as the album opener. But Dylan was not satisfied, and after two further days of work had produced working versions for most other cuts, he returned to "Changing of the Guards," apparently cutting it again in twenty minutes of studio time.

Having greatly restricted his options for overdubbing by the method of recording—live vocals, without any baffling—there was very little postproduction possible on a song which announced one of Dylan's more challenging albums with an entirely unexpected fade-in and an equally abrupt fade-out (corrected on the remixed version of the CD, issued in 1999, which adds a full half a minute to said "fade-out"). What we hear on the album captures a moment, as Dylan intended.

Although "Changing of the Guards' got a great deal more attention than most of its compadres, it suffered from a mix that was almost all vocal, burying one of Dylan's most sophisticated set of studio musicians in one muddy mass (a problem only partially solved by the digital remix that producer Devito did for the 1999 CD reissue). This was presumably what he was referring to when he told Robert Hilburn, immediately after *Street-Legal*'s completion, "On this album I took a few steps backward, but I also took a bunch of steps forward because I had a lot of time to concentrate on it."

In concert, the song fared better, though Dylan took his own sweet time adding it to the set. He was two-thirds of the way through the European leg of the world tour before he soundchecked the song—and debuted it—at the third of five Paris arena shows, the first week in July. Clearly delighted to have released the song from its Rundown bonds, Dylan sashays through the verses like a man who has found the dancing child within. Once he made the song a set-closer and a showstopper, he stuck with it to the bitter end. By the time he was ripping through the song on December 2, 1978, at a show in Nashville, for the benefit of Italian TV cameras,[5] he felt he had discovered what he had been "writing about" all along.

It turns out he had been addressing the End Times before he really knew what they were. This song was truly a prelude for the peace to come. But for all its prescience, the song departed at tour's end, Dylan suffering the amnesia of a new convert. The fact that he later insisted, in a 1985 interview, "I never went to the holy mountain to find the lost soul that is supposed to be a part of me," suggests this vital song became one of those permanently lost to him when changing his point of view.

Note: The published lyric has always printed line four of the penultimate verse as "But Eden is burning, either *brace yourself* for elimination," though Dylan sings "get ready for elimination," both on the album and in performance.

{342} IS YOUR LOVE IN VAIN?

Published lyric/s: Lyrics 85; Lyrics 04.
First known performance: Tokyo, February 28, 1978.
Known studio recordings: Rundown Studio, Santa Monica, CA, December 26, 1977; April 26+28, 1978 [S-L].

> You gravitate toward people who've got somethin' to give you, and maybe you've got somethin' that they need. —Dylan, to Sam Shepard, 1986

"Is Your Love in Vain?" (or, as it was originally copyrighted, "Is *Her* Love in Vain?") was the one *Street-Legal* song Dylan debuted in performance prior to the album sessions. In fact, it was recorded for a Japanese live album on its February 28 debut, though the version selected for *At Budokan* actually comes from the following night. One of a number of perverse decisions made on that album's behalf, this meant that the one time Dylan used a harmonica intro to the song was not the one Sony released.

Quite what prompted Dylan to spring this song on the band in the middle of the Japanese leg is not clear. It was not a song they had rehearsed at Rundown. In fact, Dylan can be heard specifically complaining that he "can't spring anything new on this band" immediately after he has run this song down for Rob Stoner, Stephen Soles, and Joel Bernstein at an after-rehearsal piano preview on December 26, 1977. It took a while for him to take them into his trust. As Helena Springs recalls, "Sometimes he'd write a song, and we'd just get the

song in soundcheck. Like 'Can you cook and sew, make flowers grow . . .'
. . . we got that just like that." They were already in Japan when he
sprang it on them.

Even at Budokan, it received one of the more attractive melodies
from a period when Dylan had rekindled his interest in tunes. It was
perhaps this that prompted its inclusion as a "taster" in Japan, where it
survived just four shows. Its reappearance as opener to side two of *Street-Legal* prompted some criticism, as if Dylan's (and indeed, rock singers")
inherent chauvinism had been revealed for the very first time by lines
like, "Can you cook and sew, make flowers grow? / Do you understand
my pain?"

In truth, "Is Your Love in Vain?" adopted the exact same confessional
mode as songs like "Abandoned Love," or "You're a Big Girl Now." It
was a mode he adopted in conversation if the woman-interviewer was
pretty enough, and knew how to hold her tongue, as he demonstrated
on a couple of occasions in the months preceding the recording of
the song. The *Chicago Daily News'* Barbara Kerr got to interview Dylan
three or four times over a three-week period leading up to the world
tour, and on one occasion the voice of "Is Your Love in Vain?" rang
loud and clear:

> At one time I did have the idea that I'd find the "right girl," though I
> never expected to find the "one woman." But I got off the idea, became
> disillusioned about finding the "right girl"—or the right anything, for that
> matter. Women are sentimental . . . They get into that romantic thing
> more easily. But I see that as a prelude. Women use romance and passion
> to sweeten you up. A man is no more than a victim of that passion. You
> give me a woman who can cook and sew and I'll take that over passion
> any day.

The vulnerable figure who in 1974 lay naked before unknowing eyes
has begun to grow bitter. The opening couplet of the final verse says it
all: "All right, I will take a chance, I will fall in love with you / If I'm a fool,
you can have the night, you can have the morning, too." We know he
has no such intention; he has made this mistake before. He had already
given up looking for a partnership of equals. In Karen Hughes's company
in April he felt a similar need to confess. After Hughes remarked about

how "the other night, you were saying how difficult you found it to have girlfriends because they always had to fit into your life," and wondered aloud whether he had any reason to continue clinging to his expressed "belief in equality," Dylan admitted, "Anyone who is in my life at all respects [the fact] that I don't come home every night."

Such honesty, largely absent on the songs of *Desire*, had come at quite a price. He was duly rewarded with a series of right-on critics reading their own lives into his entirely unique predicament. Dylan, who was particularly aggrieved by Greil Marcus's condescending review in *Rolling Stone*, revealed exactly what he thought of Marcus and his creed in an interview he did for the same paper two months later: "When a man's looking for a woman, he ain't looking for a woman who's an airplane pilot. He's looking for a woman to help him out and support him, to hold up one end while he holds up another." Or as he told another North American journalist around that time, rather than continuing to "believe we can find that [one] person if we know ourselves real well, . . . I'd settle for someone who could just sew my pants right now."

"Is Your Love in Vain?" marked a refreshing change from the search for his twin which had occupied an unhealthy chunk of his creative output—and psychic energy—since *Planet Waves*. He was content to reiterate the message in concert, playing the song far more times on the American fall tour than the other two legs of the 1978 world tour combined. I wonder if he was making a point. Prior to the fall 1980 shows, with witchy women back on the agenda, it was again rehearsed, but this time in vain.

{343} SEÑOR (TALES OF YANKEE POWER)

Published lyric/s: Lyrics 85; Lyrics 04.

Known studio recordings: Rundown Studio, Santa Monica, CA, December 26, 1977; April 26+28, 1978 [S-L].

First known performance: Universal Theatre, L.A., June 1, 1978.

Since December 1978, "Señor" has become the sole survivor from the wreckage of Dylan's *Street-Legal* persona. The one song from this period he continues to relate to, it was played at the Boxing Day '77 Rundown piano preview. Indeed, Stoner specifically requested the song, which he called "Armageddon" (at this stage, the narrator is heading for either "Portobello Road or Armageddon"). Dylan proceeds to sing a couple of verses, but refrains from teaching it to the band until the April '78 album sessions are upon them. And despite the song's relatively ornate arrangement, "Señor" was captured successfully in that rehearsal space, garnering much praise on its release.

In concert, the song was invariably introduced by its subtitle, making "Señor" merely a convenient shorthand for its underlying content. In a sense, the song has the two titles because it is two separate songs. One is a conversation with a mysterious, all-seeing figure who allows the singer to expend himself asking questions, without answering a single one. An increasingly frustrated singer goes from the muted query, "Can you tell me where we're headin'?" to an almost histrionic, "Can you tell me what we're waiting for, Señor?"

The other narrative, contained within the two bridges, is more Dylanesque. On the boulevard of broken American dreams, he stands at a personal crossroads while another seer—"a gypsy with a broken flag and a flashing ring"—states, matter-of-factly, "Son, this ain't a dream no more, it's the real thing." Though there is no obvious religious import to the song—save for a single image in the last verse, "let's . . . overturn these tables"—the fact that the song presaged him finding some answers, and became the one *Street-Legal* song retained after said personal revelation, has encouraged commentators to read much into the song's "message."

Dylan himself obviously rated the song, it being one of just two (the other being the "hit" single) he introduced in concert immediately upon—actually, slightly ahead of—the album's release. And though he felt little need to expound on the song in interviews, by the tail-end of the world tour he was introducing it with a long, weird rap about an old, strange man, which he began doing less than a week after someone threw a silver cross on stage in San Diego (November 17), and a night or two after he had sensed the presence of Christ in his hotel room. Read into this what you will, but in Houston, on November 26, 1978, he began expounding on how he instinctively felt this señor had something to tell him:

I was riding on a train one time, from Mexico to San Diego. I fell asleep one whole day and then I woke up. And I was dreaming the train was at Monterey. This family was getting off the train with about fifteen children and all. I was looking through the glass and it was like a mirror, you know. And I saw this old man get on the train. He sat down next to me on the other side of the aisle—wearing a blanket. Anyway I took a glance at him. I could see both his eyes, they were burning like they were on fire and there was smoke coming out of his nostrils. I [thought], This is the man I want to talk to. Anyway I looked at him again, trying to find something to say.

As Dylan grew ever more gregarious between songs, the "Señor" rap continued developing through December 1978, with the train imagery becoming ever stronger after Nashville (December 2), the night he sound-checked a new song, "Slow Train." By the time he reached Savannah on the eighth, he was passing from the "trainload of fools bogged down in a magnetic field" to the holy slow train smoking down the tracks:

I was riding on a train one time from Mexico, from Monterey to San Diego. Anyway, I'd fallen asleep and when I woke up this train was in (the yard). A family was getting off the train, an old man stepped up on the train. I was still in a daze, so I was looking, I was watching it all through the window which was looking like a big mirror. And I watched all the time through this mirror. This old man stepped up on the train and walked down the aisle, took a seat by me across the aisle. Wearing nothing but a blanket. He must have been about 150 years old. Anyway, I kept looking at him in the mirror. I felt this strange vibration so I turned to look at him. When I turned and looked at him both his eyes were burning. There was smoke coming out of his nostrils. I immediately turned away, but I kept thinking that this was a man that I wanted to talk to. So I waited a little while longer and the train pulled out of the station. Then [when] I turned to talk to him, he'd disappeared. I searched for him at the next town, but he was gone.

It would take another twenty-three months before Dylan tracked "Señor" down again, but when he did, the beautiful piano-based arrangement was even more powerful, and the message more potent—especially when David Grisman blessed it with some florid mandolin work at a show in Portland (December 3, 1980), after Dylan dedicated the song to a woman he had met in Durango in 1972. The song had undergone only a couple of minor lyric changes—"broken hand" had replaced "broken flag," while "Seen the stripes of the dragon / Ain't slept in three days, may be more" constitutes a partial rewrite of verse three. But the key change comes from being sung by an older, less worldly-wise narrator, who no longer expects the answers to his questions. Spared a makeover by the Dead in 1987—though they did rehearse it—a live "Señor" by the G. E. Smith–era remained a rare sighting indeed. Only after a seemingly impromptu revival at a show in Indianapolis, in November 1991, was it restored to favor, even if its singer did not always have smoke in his nostrils or fire in his belly.

{344} NO TIME TO THINK

Published lyric/s: Lyrics 85; Lyrics 04.
Known studio recordings: Rundown Studio, Santa Monica, CA, December 26, 1977; April 27, 1978 [S-L].
First known performance: Gothenberg soundcheck, July 12, 1978.

"No Time to Think" was a hugely ambitious undertaking, and Dylan knew it. The most contentious song on his 1978 collection, not as regards the views expressed but the success of the treatment, this eighteen-verse opus gives "Changing of the Guards" more than a run for its money for scale of ambition and complexity of structure but falls well short of its more successful sibling. Its closest kin in the canon is not a song, but a film, *Renaldo and Clara*, the completion of which occupied the same period in which this no less extravagant gesture was conceived.

Dylan's one on-the-record comment about the song, to Cott, makes the connection explicit: "We're all dreaming, and . . . songs [like 'No Time to Think'] come close to getting inside that dream." One suspects this was meant to be another of Renaldo's dreams (just like the film, so Dylan tells us). Here, though, he really has ventured into a mythical place, perhaps one he thought might suit another movie he had in his head. He had already informed Ginsberg that the next movie "will be different. It will be about Corruption, about Pride, about Vanity and about Obsession," the very themes which pervade "No Time to Think."

{ Still on the Road }

If the crushing reception for his first movie killed any possibility of a second cinematic venture (for another quarter of a century, anyway), he was still allowed to record songs about "Loneliness, tenderness . . . Memory, ecstasy . . . Mortality, reality . . . Nobility, humility." All he needed to do was condense a four-hour narrative into a seven-minute song.

When he came to sing the song at the rented space in Santa Monica on December 26, 1977, he still wasn't sure how to make this jumble of phrases, many poetically potent, others pretentiously portentous, into a narrative. The tune—quite different from its eventual self—he was equally unsure about. But most of all he needed to figure out how to pull together a set of verses, some running to four lines, some to five, and jam-full with some of the most impertinent rhymes ever attempted in popular song, so that they constituted a cohesive whole.

Using "black letter" internal rhymes at every turn, he once again decided line-breaks were for squares ("You're a soldier of mercy / You're cold and you curse, He / . . ."; "I've seen all these decoys / Through a set of deep turquoise / Eyes. . ."). Whether rhyming "mirr'r" with "clear," or "one real" with "Camille," he is King Rhymester again, minus the reason. Unlike the profound part of his canon, "No Time to Think" claimed to address deep, dark issues, but really just served as a way of demonstrating that his best lines are not always found in his best songs. 'Cause there is no shortage of great lines herein—"The magician is quicker and his game is much thicker / Than blood and blacker than ink" is fully matched by "Stripped of all virtue, as you crawl through the dirt, You / can give but you cannot receive." But for once, such lines fail to take the listener anywhere new.

And though Dylan doubtless thought the experiment "far gone" at the point of inception, when he took the time to think, he realized he could leave such impulses alone. As he told Julia Orange, a few months after he wrote the song, "I used to write about rejection, obsession, compulsion, but . . . I'm [now] at this kind of crossroads where I can let it be." Hence why, save for a single run-through at a July 1978 Gothenberg soundcheck, he never took the song on the road after recording it at the third *Street-Legal* session.

{345} TRUE LOVE TENDS TO FORGET
{346} WE BETTER TALK THIS OVER

Published lyric/s: Lyrics 85; Lyrics 04.
*Known studio recordings: Rundown Studio, Santa Monica, CA, December 26,
1977; April 26–27, 1978 [S-L].*
First known performance [#343]: Dortmund, June 27, 1978.
First known performance [#344]: Paris, July 4, 1978.

> "True Love Tends to Forget" isn't like a possession trip, when you've been
> wronged—that type of thing—I was [just] trying to get the most out of
> that [idea]. —Dylan, to Lynne Allen, December 1978

I imagine Dylan had a certain amount of fun working on "True Love"
and its twin song, "We Better Talk This Over," songs that were partnered
on *Street-Legal*, and were, for a while, interchangeable in performance
(being debuted a week apart). Dylan even played them one after the
other at the December 1977 Rundown run-through, toying with both
songs, teasing the half-formed lines out. On the former, he comes up
with the kinda series of rhymes that tells us he is still some way off a
finished lyric, not having yet defined good and bad. "I left my pride on
the doorstep where we met" is good enough to belong on a lost *Blood
on the Tracks* song; "I'll be on top of a world that's upset" is not. He is
still gerrymandering reason and rhyme into one rickety construct, at one
point even delivering an ultimatum it is hard to take seriously: "I hope
you finally decide to accept / The love I can provide, or shall I ride into
the sunset?"

The bridge also requires work. He has the basic idea, "I was lying
down in the river when you dreamt of me / Letting the water come
by me," but then he is stumped and has to revert to humming the next
couplet. What he does come up with, in the end, works beautifully, fully
suggesting a love that crosses time and space: "I was lyin' down in the
reeds without any oxygen / I saw you in the wilderness among the men/
Saw you drift into infinity and come back again . . ." Great stuff.

At last, he is back addressing the great theme, "true love," not from
some mythical plane but in the here and now of recrimination and

regrets. He still hadn't made up his mind whether such an ideal really existed ("The soul mate would be the physical mate of the soul. But that would mean we're supposed to be with just one other person. Is a soul mate a romantic notion, or is there real truth in that, señor?"—Dylan, 1978). "True Love" plays around with such a "romantic notion." Should he stay or should he go? It never resolves itself—how could it? And by the time we move on to the next *Street-Legal* song, any romantic notion has been thoroughly disclaimed: "Don't think of me and fantasize on what we never had . . ."

The counterpoint song "We Better Talk This Over" also remained a work-in-progress when Dylan tested out the black keys on the Rundown piano the day after Christmas '77, though most of what he has got at this point—four months before he returns to Rundown, recording truck in tow—he will ultimately retain:

> I think we better talk this over
> Maybe by next October
> You'll unnerstan' I'm only a man
> Doin' the best that I can.

He stumbles through one more verse ("This situation's only gonna get rougher . . .") and a bridge ("You don't have to be afraid . . ."), but the song stutters out, just as it does on the sheet of memo paper on which he wrote—actually, typed—an early draft of the lyric. Unlike at Rundown, where Dylan simply moves on to another song he's planning to record, he perseveres on paper, beginning again after drawing a line under those original verses. And this time he lets some feelings about the (ex-)missus, her lawyer Marvin Mitchelson, and general money worries spill out:

> We don't need any back seat drivers
> Hypocrites, meddlers or cheap connivers
> Both of us are survivors.
> Don't be confused,
> You'll only be used
> We can work this out,
> There is no doubt,

Without having to shout.
Notify yr new advisor
That yr not greedy & I'm not a misor.

Fortunately, a new bridge breaks into this disturbing line of thought. "You don't have to yearn for love, you don't have to be alone," offers Mr. Magnanimous. The typed lyric—unless it carries over the page—peters out with one last piece of impertinent advice: "Opportunity's knockin' / get out of here / Go disappear."

But old working methods die hard, and he is soon back with pen in hand, scribbling up, down and around these typed lines, searching for thoughts that take the song *somewhere*. A line like "My feelings will be kept confidential" reads more like a legal epistle than a love letter. Still, he can't resist dishing out advice, some of it as mixed up as his metaphors. "Keep your head in the clouds but don't be [fooled?] by the devil" heads the list, if I'm reading that spidery scrawl right. He also finds a rhyme for "Opportunity's knockin'" with the singular warning, "The door to your future is locking," which he then rejects. However, the line "Before we decay," added after "go our own separate way," he retains. (This surely deliberate allusion to Elvis's own "divorce" song, "Separate Ways," makes it to the album.) Rapidly running out of space, he scribbles one last line that defines the song's theme for good: "I don't think we oughta go any further."

And he doesn't. At least, not for now. However, he is back working on the whole song—lyric, arrangement, and tune—at a session designed to break in the new bassist Jerry Scheff, just days before his standing combo begins recording *Street-Legal*. At this April 10 session, "We Better Talk This Over" is more concerned with what went wrong than what the future holds. Setting the song to the kind of big-band arrangement more suited to one of the Louis, he has another bridge he'd like to try out:

Every time we'd be alone, nothing is ever right,
Even when we're making love, it winds up in a fight.

Two weeks later, he comes up with something a little more poetic and a lot less personal: "Why should we go on watching each other through a telescope / Eventually we'll hang ourselves on all that tangled rope." By then, the confessional element to the song has been pretty much removed, along with any suggestion (he hoped) that this might be thought of as a "divorce song." Just one couplet from that more personal self proved too good to discard—"The vows that we kept are now broken and swept / 'neath the bed where we slept."

Another *Street-Legal* track Dylan introduced at the Paris residency in July, "We Better Talk This Over" slotted easily into a set which on a good day could include both its twin song and 1978 rewrites of "The Man in Me" and "Going Going Gone." All were part of the wholesale cull at tour's end, as *Street-Legal* was excised from the post-conversion canon (somewhat contradicting Dylan's claim in a 1985 interview, "I liked *Street-Legal* a lot").

The inclusion, then, of "We Better Talk This Over" at an intimate warm-up show in Anaheim in March 2000, ahead of another year of sustained touring, looms large in the pantheon of Never Ending Tour surprises. Did the version performed that night suggest he had been listening to the remixed version of the album, issued a few months earlier, or that he was just looking to shake things up? Either way, such an invigorating rendition argued for retention in the set. In his finite wisdom, though, Dylan decided it really was something he had "gone beyond."

{347} WHERE ARE YOU TONIGHT? (JOURNEY THROUGH DARK HEAT)

Published lyric/s: Lyrics 85; Lyrics 04.

Known studio recordings: Rundown Studio, Santa Monica, CA, December 26, 1977; April 26–27, 1978 [S-L].

First known performance: Blackbushe Festival, Surrey, England, July 15, 1978.

"Where Are You Tonight?" stands alongside the best album closers Dylan has written to order throughout his long career. Though not the last song written for *Street-Legal*—he still had a couple of filler songs to pen—it nonetheless marked the end of a process which resulted in another album radically different from any predecessor. Addressing recent traumas in the same convoluted code as "Changing of the Guards" and "No Time to Think," it shares their metaphorical approach.

Another song he almost certainly conceived at the farm, before atypically spending six months fine-tuning it, "Where Are You Tonight?" was the last song he previewed at Rundown in the season of good cheer. Not that there is anything cheerful about his performance that Yuletide afternoon. Sung slow, Dylan is again only prepared to go as far as the first chorus. But the second and third verses sung that day suggest he had yet to settle on the right tone:

> There's a neon light ablaze in this green smokey haze
> Where the cows used to graze overnight
> And a lonesome bell tone in that valley of stone
> Where she bathed in a stream of pure light.
>
> Her father was a prince and he had me convinced
> To go onward and follow my heart.
> In the ashes and dust, he predicted too much
> What would happen [???] fall apart.

By the time he had finished the song, that second verse had been transplanted to the West Village, and the father was predicting "the time and the place that *we'd part*" (which seems to have been a last-minute change. The published lyric has "the time and the place *the trouble would start*," rather than what he *sings*). The structure changed not a jot, though—three four-line verses,[6] each with internal rhymes on lines one and three, followed by a five-line bridge-chorus, rhyming AAABB. Again, though, he keeps his audience guessing at song's end, slipping in an extra verse before that redemptive final chorus, "I can't believe it, I can't believe I'm alive / But without you it just doesn't seem right."

And so he ends another album with the narrator figure "still on the road / heading for another joint," chasing that chimerical (and disavowed) "romantic notion." Evidence of the existence of another path is hinted at earlier in the song, when he "left town at dawn, with Marcel and St. John / Strong men belittled by doubt." Being Dylan, he doesn't make these figures" identity any clearer than the earlier St. Augustine. St. John is surely "the Divine." Not that the author of the Book of Revelation demonstrated any such doubts about the world to come. If the other figure is also a man of faith, it is not Proust—the obvious recipient—but could be Gabriel Marcel, a twentieth-century Christian existentialist (huh!), whose belief that we are living in a "broken world" was one Dylan could fully take on board. Dylan knew full well that such name-checks would breed rampant speculation—especially as they are the only two proper names used on the entire album, the generic Camille excepted. One suspects he is being playful.

But then, "Where Are You Tonight?" is not actually about his traveling companions. It is only about one strong man "belittled by doubt," and this man is at war with that most deadly enemy—the one within. Dylan's struggle with his Gemini nature lies at the heart of both the song and the album. This is why he quoted the proverb "No man can fight another like the man who fights himself" twice in contemporary conversations. To Barbara Kerr, he proceeds to ask, "Who could be a stronger enemy? Who can do you more harm than yourself? It is true that a man is his own worst enemy, just as he is his own best friend. You can either do yourself in, or do yourself a favor." He repeats the same mantra to his old friend Robert Shelton, in London that June, and this time explicitly tells us where to look for further explication: "If you deal with the enemy within, then no enemy without can stand a chance . . . It's all in those two verses of that last song [on the album]."

The evocative couplet which opens that penultimate verse, "I bit into the root of forbidden fruit / With the juice running down my leg," certainly takes the song to a different place. Both lines are about temptation, f'sure. But this imagery comes from that "weird ol' America," not from any well-thumbed book. Dylan has cleverly combined two images from the lexicon—"The juice of the forbidden fruit" being the title of a well-known traditional anti-drinking song recorded by Alan Lomax on one of his southern travels in the 1950s, and was undoubtedly known to Dylan. The other phrase comes from Robert Johnson, a man who gave in to temptation and paid the ultimate price (poisoned by a woman, or some jealous man). On Johnson's compelling recording of "Traveling Riverside Blues," he leaves no doubt as to his meaning when he sings, "You can squeeze my lemon 'til the juice run down my leg," adding as a spoken aside, "You know what I'm talking about." (Such juxtapositioning shall become a mainstay of Dylan's lyrical art come 2001, but with diminished artistry.)

These lines address Dylan's own struggle with temptation. It is a recognition that "you can't hide on a dark street from the demon within"—which was exactly how he described (to Ron Rosenbaum) the struggle Renaldo faced, in the film he was piecing together when he penned this other "Journey through Dark Heat." Those last four verses could almost be a belated coda to "Idiot Wind." And like that song, one suspects he worked on them right up to the last minute. When three takes on April 28 failed to suffice, work resumed the following day, and this time he nailed it. His struggles with "the demon within" were also ongoing enough for him to make the song a centerpiece of the second set at U.S. shows in the fall, as he continued to be "belittled by doubt." When certainty dawned, this song went the way of all flesh.

{348} FIRST TO SAY GOODBYE

Known studio recordings: Rundown Studio, Santa Monica, CA, December 26, 1977.

"First to Say Goodbye" is mentioned in a *Melody Maker* report by Harvey Kubernik concerning the Santa Monica rehearsals for the world tour, but does not appear on any of the circulating tapes from those sessions (though we are probably a good sixty hours shy of hearing what was actually recorded). However, the one unknown tune Dylan previewed on December 26, 1977, could well be the song in question. The opening line he sang reads as follows: "Just be kind to me and say goodbye / There's somebody waiting 'neath the window / And I cannot tell you why / [???] reflection in your golden eye." At this point, Stoner begins to play along, suggesting that he knows this one. But when it comes time to record these songs legitimately, Dylan has another bassist, Jerry Scheff, who has been less fully briefed, and no one saw fit to remind him about this one when the Wally Heider mobile truck was parked out back.

{349} HER VERSION OF JEALOUSY

Mentioned in conversation, March 12, 1978.

"Her Version of Jealousy" is one of two song titles Dylan gave to Craig McGregor in March 1978 as examples of the kind of thing he was currently working on. Since the other song was "Changing of the

Guards," we can probably assume it was a genuine title, and an intriguing one at that, but it seems to be one he gave up on when he began another bout of coauthoring, this time with backing singer Helena Springs.

{350} **IF I DON'T BE THERE BY MORNING**

{351} **WALK OUT IN THE RAIN**

Published lyric/s: Lyrics 85.

Known studio recording [#350]: Rundown Studio, Santa Monica, CA, May 2, 1978.

Known studio recording [#351]: Rundown Studio, Santa Monica, CA, May 1, 1978.

> We were together in Brisbane one evening [March 12–15], and he was playing on the guitar and we were just goofing around, laughing, and I said I can't really write [songs] . . . He said, "Well, come on, I'll write something with you. We'll write something together." And I said, OK. He said, "You start singing some stuff and I'll start playing." So he started strumming his guitar and I started to sing, just making up lyrics. And he'd make up stuff and that was when we got "If I Don't Be There By Morning" and "Walk Out in the Rain." —Helena Springs, to Chris Cooper, *Endless Road* #7

Having recently cowritten an album's worth of songs in a matter of weeks, Dylan knew that collaborating on songs could be fun. Throw in a good-looking young backing singer, fresh out of high school and eager to learn, and it is not too surprising he threw himself into joint composing sessions with alacrity. These sessions with the feisty gal also helped alleviate the boredom that came with the endless road. The fact that he and Springs wrote two songs that first night in Australia—replicating his experience with Levy three years earlier—boded well for the association, even if neither song suggested they'd tapped a similar lightning rod of inspiration.

"Walk Out in the Rain," the better song, carries on where "We Better Talk This Over" left off, with lines like "If you've said all that you've got to say / Please don't feel the need to linger." The tone is strictly *Street-Legal*—an intoxicating blend of mock-nobility and resigned acceptance. "If you don't want my love, it's a pity / I guess I can't see you no more." It also has an attractive, bluesy quality, at least as recorded by Eric Clapton on *Backless*.

"If I Don't Be There By Morning" is more forced and, whether Springs realized it or not, Dylan was probably drawing on "Friend of the Devil," the 1970 Garcia-Hunter song he later made his own in concert. Rather than a sheriff on his trail, he has a "private eye on my trail" and rather than a woman in Chino and Cherokee, he has "a woman living in L.A. / I got a woman waiting for my pay." This time it is this woman—rather than the devil—who takes his last twenty dollars. The song proves one thing at least: it really is possible for Dylan to write a worse imitation of the Dead than they could manage themselves.

All of which prompts the question, why did Clapton decide to cut these particular songs for *Backless*? According to Springs herself, "We had [decided] to put them down [on tape] for other people to hear . . . Those [particular songs] were given to Eric while we were on tour in Europe . . . We played them to him on guitar, in Holland [*sic*]. Then when we got back to do Blackbushe, he had them demoed and he'd done a really great job on them." According to Clapton, those weren't no demos; they were the finished tracks, even if Dylan didn't seem to realize this:

> He just laid this cassette on me with [those two songs]. He was hooked up with this girl called Helena Springs. They were co-writing, and I think he was very proud of it and laid it on me when we were in Nuremberg [July 1]. I've still got that cassette of them two . . . When I get down sometimes, I listen to them and it will bring me right out, because I know that no one else has got it. This was a gift to me . . . At Blackbushe I sat in a coach and played him [my versions]—I'd gone into the studio by then and done the two numbers—and I played them back and he said, "Well, when are they going to be finished?"

According to the studio logs, Dylan "put down" his own version of "Walk Out in the Rain" at the "last" *Street-Legal* session on May 1, along with another Dylan–Springs composition, "Coming from the Heart." However, there is no record of a Rundown version of "If I Don't Be There By Morning." Nonetheless, a four-track demo was circulated at one point, with these three songs—plus "Stop Now"—so evidently some kind of rough demo *was* recorded prior to the European tour. Clapton seems to imply that he was only given these two songs—and then only after the pair "had played them to him on guitar." One can't help thinking that if Clapton had been given a choice of all four, he would have gone with the third song the pair wrote, which hits the mark in a way these do not . . .

{352} COMING FROM THE HEART (THE ROAD IS LONG)

Published lyric/s: The Telegraph #3; Lyrics 85.
Known studio recordings: Rundown Studio, Santa Monica, April 10, 1978; May 1, 1978.
First known performance: St Paul, MN, October 31, 1978.

Helena Springs says "Coming from the Heart" was the third song she wrote with her bandleader, a few days after their initial writing session in Brisbane, with the end of the six-week Far East tour at last in sight. Hence, presumably, the song's subtitle and chorus: "The road is long, it's a long hard climb / I been on that road for too long at a time." This time the feelings expressed seem real, the longing in the lyric acute.

On the evidence of the so-called Scheff audition-tape recorded on their return to L.A. in early April, Dylan may have been considering cutting the song for *Street-Legal*, where it could well have become as big a radio hit as "Baby Stop Crying." Otherwise, why attempt a full-band arrangement a mere fortnight before they began recording said album? Springs insists she had no such expectation: "Bob doesn't use collaboration songs on his albums, per se. It's just a rule he has . . . [So] I never expected any of the songs to go on [the album]." (Er, what about *Desire*, Helena?)

Any such possibility had indeed abated by the time the album sessions came around, probably because Dylan managed to write a solo variant of this shoulder-to-cry-on seduction song in the interim, exchanging what Springs and Dylan had written—"Another man has hurt you honey / Why must I pay for the part? / Your love can't be bought with money, / 'Cause it's coming from the heart"—with a singer who is pleading for his baby to stop crying: "You been hurt so many times / I know what you're thinking of."

Nonetheless, after recording the whole of *Street-Legal*, Dylan did record "Coming from the Heart" (and two other tunes the pair had written in the past month), using the mobile truck he'd hired to record the album. The impromptu nature of the single take, though, makes it clear that this was for demo purposes only, as the backing singers seek to remove any adjective from their trade description, obliging Dylan to compete with them, not complement them. The band join in only after they see who's winning.

Dylan hadn't entirely given up on using the song himself. Sure enough, six months later at a Halloween show in St. Paul, Minnesota, he decided to give his home-state fans a special treat, closing the first set with this song, which received one of the most impassioned vocals on the whole 115-date world tour. Dylan is tonally breathing every doggone word. What a shame that he forgets—or at least omits—the best verse ("Make me up a bed of roses / Hanging down on the vine / Of all my loves you are the closest / That's ever been on my mind"). It still suggests a perverse spirit was abroad for this to become the only time he prepped the song to paying punters. And by the end of the year, he had another kind of song he wanted to record, so this mighty fine song was demoted to demo-tape status, from where it was temporarily rescued by the Searchers, making their first album in many a moon. Their (rather rare) eponymous 1979 LP features the entire song given the full pop-harmony monty it assuredly deserved.

Note: All four of the Dylan–Springs compositions included in the 1985 edition of *Lyrics* have been removed from the latest edition, one imagines for reasons of space, further negating the point of the exercise.

{353} NEW PONY

Published lyric/s: Lyrics 85; Lyrics 04.

Known studio recordings: Rundown Studio, Santa Monica, CA, April 26+28, May 1, 1978 [S-L].

First known performance: Paris Pavilion soundcheck, July [4], 1978.

I resist getting fully into the blues; that would be limiting. I just do it for my own self. I found out that the [Robert] Johnson songs aren't played the way I always thought they were; I hung out with [Robert] Lockwood

[Junior] and learned a lot. Those tunes are a real revelation for me. There have been times when I have been on the edge of becoming Lead Belly, but I did resist it. —Dylan, to John Mankiewicz, November 1978

Here is another of those genuinely revealing comments on his art, from a time when he proved surprisingly willing to discuss his inspirational approach. Given that he had been prefacing every single show that year with a stomping blues cover, be it Billy Lee Riley's "Repossession Blues," Buddy Wilson's "Lonesome Bedroom Blues," Tampa Red's "Love Her With a Feeling" and "Love Crazy," or, on one magical occasion, Robert Johnson's "Steady Rollin' Man," one might have expected Dylan to deliver the blues album he had been promising to record since his third Columbia session back in April 1962.

But he shrewdly recognized that, however much "real revelation" he personally found in the blues, musically it was highly restrictive in the emotional range and sentiments it could accommodate. Nonetheless, he was determined to slot at least one semi-original blues onto *Street-Legal* while he had that big band sound to hand—"New Pony." This simple four-chord blues initially failed to reflect the right spirit in this Rundown environment, and Dylan was obliged to return to the song twice before he was happy with the results. The song itself seems to have been a spur of the moment thing, Dylan even sending up the exercise by calling it "New Pony," lest it was burdened down by the many "Pony Blues" that came before.

We need not wonder whether Dylan was personally conversant with the recordings of Charlie Patton, Big Joe Williams, Son House, Big Bill Broonzy, and the like, all of whom had at least one pony, usually of a darker hue, whom they felt a need to rhapsodize about (or rebuke). He was up to his ears in the shared imagery of such folk, Son House's take probably providing "Well, the horse that I'm ridin'," he can foxtrot / He can lope and pace, lope and pace," perhaps witnessed in person during the 1964 Newport Folk Festival at which they both appeared.

However, for the true spirit of the "New Pony," we should turn to one of the founding fathers of rock and roll, Arthur "Big Boy" Crudup, who recorded his own take on House's "Black Pony Blues" with a simple guitar-drum accompaniment in 1941. And his version doesn't just roll, it *rocks*. Dylan tries to transmute that feeling, with a little help from his newfound friends. He may also be alluding to Crudup's "Mr. So-and-So," recorded for the same label as "Black Pony Blues," when he christens his own pony "Miss X" (she reappears in "Trouble in Mind" as "Miss So-and-So").

On the one hand, "New Pony" demonstrates a breadth of styles on Dylan's part—"Hey, I could do this kinda thing all night long, if I wanted to. . . ." On the other, it is a way to put his band (and backing singers) through their paces. He even attempts to embellish that legendary final verse in Robert Johnson's "Me and the Devil Blues" ("Early this mornin', when you knocked upon my door / And I said, Hello, Satan, I believe it's time to go"), imagining his reaction should Lucifer ever really come a-knockin'":

> It was early in the mornin'; I seen your shadow in the door, [x2]
> Now I don't have to ask nobody, I know what you came here for.

This verse, though, got edited from the version on the album, presumably because of time restrictions. That it was an integral part of the song—and should surely have been restored when the album was remixed for CD in 1999—Dylan demonstrated by including it in the album lyric sheet and singing it during the one "live" version known to have been attempted, unfortunately to an empty arena, during a Parisian soundcheck in July. But it never made it into the same set as his nightly dose of Tampa Red. I guess he thought it sounded too much like Lead Belly.

{354} BABY STOP CRYING

Published lyric/s: Lyrics 85; Lyrics 04.
Known studio recordings: Rundown Studio, Santa Monica, CA, April 28, 1978 [S-L].
First known performance: Universal Theatre, LA, June 1, 1978.

> The man in ["Baby Stop Crying"] has his hand out and is not afraid of getting it bit. —Dylan, to Jonathan Cott, September 1978

Dylan provides a fairly obvious clue in the chorus to this mawkish torch ballad that he has been immersing himself in the blues again. When he sings "Baby please stop crying, stop crying / It's tearing up my mind," he is yearning to rework Robert Johnson's "Stop Breaking Down" ("Baby, please stop breaking down . . . you're gonna make me lose my mind"). Unfortunately, the end result hardly qualifies for the same first-class berth as Johnson's coruscating plea, well known to all seventies rock fans from the Stones' sinuous cover on *Exile on Main Street*.

Written as a companion piece to the mostly lightweight songs of supposed heartbreak he had begun writing with his nubile backing singer, "Baby Stop Crying" was classic album filler. In fairness, it had an attractive melody and showed off his new band to great effect, so its immediate inclusion in the live set, straight after he promised to "Love Her With a Feeling," betrayed a certain kind of logic. But when it was then promptly released as a single and rode the high tide of Dylanmania in Europe to the Top Five, it had perhaps overextended itself. In America, the sentiments, and the song, were treated as badly as the woman, and Dylan promptly removed the song from the live set on his return stateside. To add insult to injury, when his label decided to issue a *Greatest Hits Vol. 3* worldwide, in 1994, they had the unmitigated gall to omit this, his last big hit, making a mockery of the concept; continuing to pretend that one of Dylan's best-known songs did not exist simply because *Billboard* spurned it.

{355} STOP NOW

Known studio recordings: Rundown Studio, Santa Monica, CA, May 2, 1978 and June 8, 1978.[7]

"Stop Now" was another song seemingly written to highlight the backing singers and to provide potential future revenue for the classy Ms. Springs. But there is more to it than that: it appears to have been under serious consideration for *Street-Legal*, hence its inclusion on a compilation tape by producer Don Devito. An alternative to "New Pony," this is a raspin'," stonkin' blast of blues-driven libido as Dylan discovers the delights of big, black, and beautiful (in both known versions Dylan delights in describing her "big arms, big hips, big belly, big lips," before pleading with her to "Stop now, before it's too late").

If there are two versions of "Stop Now" now in circulation, both recorded in L.A. in the hiatus between Far East and European legs of the 1978 world tour, confusion reigns as to which is which, thanks to the bootlegger responsible for their emergence (on Vols 1+2 of *The Genuine Bootleg Series*) failing to credit them correctly. On Devito's compilation cassette they are clearly dated; surprisingly, it turns out that the May version is the proper studio recording, whereas the June version is a rehearsal demo. The "Stop Now" recorded on May 2 is in full stereo, with separation on both guitar and sax parts and has a full band arrangement that allows Dylan to insist he has loved her with a feeling, but now it is time for her to go because his true love (or at least, another "fine woman") is due home any time now.

The May 2 take appears to have been cut the same day that Dylan began adding overdubs to the last song he wrote for *Street-Legal*. So it could have been another of his last-minute try-it-and-see songs. ("If I Don't Be There By Morning" may also have been recorded the same day.) Either way, the full capabilities of the Wally Heider truck, parked out back to capture a full sixteen-track sound, were brought to bear on "Stop Now." Indeed, it is slightly surprising it did not become the set opener, at the expense of blues covers of a similar hue. The so-called June 8 version, on the other hand, sounds like a demo. It starts with piano, the lyrics are somewhat garbled, and the song is taken at no great pace.

Another possible version of the song is attributed to the May 1 session in Krogsgaard's sessionography, where it was supposedly cut after the "Coming from the Heart" demo. Conceivably, the June 8 version could actually date from May 1—being mistakenly attributed to June 8 because this was when it was placed on a demo reel (all four Dylan-Springs songs being copyrighted on June 22). Or he could have taken the band back to the rehearsal room, the day after a week-long residency at the Universal Amphitheater, for one last run-through of a potential addition to the set prior to his first London shows in twelve years.

{356} **AFTERNOON**

{357} **ROMANCE BLUES**

{358} **SATISFY ME**

Published lyric/s: #362: Words Fill My Head.

All songs written by Bob Dylan and Helena Springs, circa 1978, copyrighted 1979–80.

At least ten of the songs Dylan cowrote with Helena Springs during the 1978 world tour were not copyrighted until 1979–80; with a further four being copyrighted in the late nineties (#356–8 and 368). The bulk of the songs (the six asterisked, plus "More than Flesh and Blood") were copyrighted in October 1979, in what was presumably a clearing-up exercise; probably from demo versions recorded by Springs for this very purpose. "Responsibility," "Tell Me the Truth One Time," and "The Wandering Kind"—which was then covered by Paul Butterfield—all circulate as solo piano demos sung by Springs. The other asterisked songs probably exist in a similar form.

These three demos have very little to recommend them, either lyrically or melodically. Hence, presumably, why almost no one took up the opportunity to record an album's worth of unreleased Dylan semi-originals. Also, none of the above songs seem to have been rehearsed at Rundown or tried out at any U.S. 1978 soundcheck. The best of them is probably "Responsibility," which has some decent couplets, at least one of which could be a comment on her coauthor's situation: "Well I walk into your life, and I take a vacant seat / Just to watch you scandalize every one you meet."

According to Springs, during a 1985 interview with Dylan researcher Chris Cooper, one of the more memorable songs they wrote was called

"Pain and Love," but in all likelihood this is one of the songs later copy-righted under another title, just as the song she calls "Red Haired Girl" is doubtless the same one copyrighted in 1980 as "Brown Skin Girl." There may well be yet more Dylan-Springs songs. As Springs says, "It just kinda kept flowing, and we never stopped writing. We got a lot of . . . stuff." On the evidence of what has been heard, though, it seems unlikely there are any more pearls to be plucked from the files of Dylan's publishing company.

{369} MORE THAN FLESH AND BLOOD

First known performance: New Haven, CT, soundcheck, September 17, 1978.
Known studio recordings: Rundown Studios, Santa Monica, CA, September 1978.

> I can't stand to run with women anymore. I just can't. It bothers me. I'd rather stand in front of a rolling train. —Dylan, to Matt Damsker, September 1978

Interviewed by Damsker on the afternoon of the opening gig to a daunting sixty-five-date North American tour, Dylan could well have been talking about "More than Flesh and Blood." It was one of two new songs he intended to debut at the upcoming shows, both of which displayed a misaligned misogyny borne of the misery suffered at the hands of previous madonnas (the other song is "Stepchild").

Although cowritten with Springs, "More than Flesh and Blood" is shot through with Dylan's own antiromantic worldview and maybe even a dawning awareness of the need for a higher calling (at one point, s/he seems to be singing, "I'm going down to find a [church] that I can understand"). This could have been Springs's contribution. She had been brought up a good Catholic girl (Dylan questioned her about her faith as he started to question his own). There is even a point at which the singer threatens to call out the evil spirit's five-letter name:

> I see you at a party, trying to converse,
> The room is going round and round, and now it's in reverse,
> Don't give in to the spirit, 'cause the spirit is adverse . . .

{ Still on the Road }

Originally listed as part of the repertoire for these shows—an alternate first-set closer to "Going Going Gone"—the song failed to appear. And yet, Dylan was not only working on the song at a sound-check to the New Haven show, two days into the schedule, but had not forgotten it by November 4, when he again soundchecked the song in Omaha, Nebraska. Even when the song went the way of all those post–*Street-Legal*, pre-conversion songs—and there were quite a few—Dylan and/or Springs decided it was far too good a song to discard, cutting a version for a Helena Springs single, backed by the tour band, produced by Knack drummer Bruce Gary. The formation of a label of Dylan's own, Accomplice Records, in late January 1979, was probably intended to create an outlet for such a release. Unfortunately, that project fell by the wayside when Dylan realized that Satan was indeed alive and well.

{370} I MUST LOVE YOU TOO MUCH

Published lyric/s: The Telegraph #17; Lyrics 85; [Lyrics 04.]
Known studio recordings: ?Rundown Studios, Santa Monica, CA, September 1978.
First known performance: Binghamton, NY, September 24, 1978.

> You like someone and then you don't want to like them any more because you're afraid to admit to yourself that you like them so much. —Dylan, to Jonathan Cott, September 1978

"I Must Love You Too Much" appears to have been one of the last songs Dylan wrote with Springs (assuming, as I do, that #356–68 date primarily—or wholly—from the spring and summer months). Like "More than Flesh and Blood," he envisaged making it part of the live set. In fact, he did fleetingly introduce it at shows in Binghamton and New York City at the end of September, before it faded away. Even then, the song kept cropping up at soundchecks, sometimes sung by the girl singers, sometimes by Dylan (it appears on all three recorded by tapers in late October/early November: Carbondale—October 28, St. Louis—October 29, and Omaha—November 4).

While it is not clear what the original lyrics are, at least as Dylan sang them at the September shows—the two audience tapes concerned lack a certain clarity—he certainly sings about how this affair has already cost him his car and his wife and is now threatening his life, all because he loves her too much. Evidently, he was still obsessing over witchy women ("I'm crazy 'bout you, lover, and I carry a torch / You can take me without any force"). On the evidence of the version finally copyrighted in early January 1979—which appears to be the one given to *The Telegraph* in 1984—Dylan kept tinkering with the verses even after he dropped the song from the set, as he continued to be concerned with that familiar theme of disaffected love: "One minute you love and the other you don't / You want me to leave but I won't / I love you too much."

One wonders what this copyrighted version was taken from—a rehearsal, a soundcheck, a lyric sheet? Whatever the case, it certainly bears more resemblance to the song he reworked in rehearsals and soundchecks than the un-Dylanesque drivel published in the 1985 edition of *Lyrics*, now credited to Dylan, Springs, and ex-ELP bassist Greg Lake. Lake, who wanted to put his stamp on the song before releasing it, decided he could "improve" on the original. His version, the basis for this reconfigured lyric, suggested any brain surgery hadn't worked.

{371} STEPCHILD

Published lyric/s: The Telegraph #7. *[Alternate versions: Words Fill My Head]*
First known performance: Augusta, ME, September 15, 1978.
Known studio recordings: Rundown Studios, Santa Monica, CA, September 1978.

In an interview given backstage in Nashville on December 2, 1978, Dylan discussed the one new original he was playing consistently at these shows—which he called "Baby, Am I Your Stepchild?"—telling said interviewer, "It's a more simplified version of just a man talking to a woman, who is just not treating him properly." Five days later, he claimed it was written some six months earlier, after "a horrible love affair." Already he was thinking of phasing out the song, stating, "I don't know if I'll record it." He never did, though he played it at all sixty-five North American shows. (It was copyrighted initially from a board tape of the first live performance, in Augusta, Maine, on September 15, subsequently replaced by another live version from Oakland in November).

{ Still on the Road }

The first song written in a while without Helena's helping hand, "Stepchild" is a close cousin of the two coauthored compositions he had been laying on his new band. Once again, some mean woman is messing with his mind, even after he has expressed his devotion with extraordinary deeds:

> I crawl across the desert for you, girl,
> And you say, "So what!"
> I bring you all the diamonds from the mine,
> And I find your door is shut.

On other occasions, he claims to have pulled her "out of dope scenes, orgies and jam sessions, too." But if he really was still being mistreated so, he hadn't been telling the truth when he informed *Playboy*, "I don't single out women as anything to get hung up about . . . [But] in the past I was guilty of that shameless crime." The distasteful portrait of the "stepchild"—the narrator in the song equating himself with the dirt beneath her feet—seems an odd one coming from a man who had legally adopted Sara's daughter Maria. Perhaps there was hope, though. As he told Matt Damsker the night he debuted the song: "Even in my sinful ways, I see some morality coming out of the ashes." It would take a strong, monotheistic, patriarchal code to truly convince him to let such women be.

{372} YOU DON'T LOVE ME NO MORE

{373} THIS A-WAY, THAT A-WAY

{374} TAKE IT OR LEAVE IT

{375} (DADDY'S GONNA TAKE) ONE MORE RIDE

First known performance: #372–4: New Haven, CT, soundcheck, September 17, 1978; #375: Carbondale, IL, soundcheck, October 28, 1978.

> I've been doing a lot of writing, got a bunch of new songs. We're gonna record them next year sometime . . . I've got a lot that no one has heard yet. —Dylan, to John Mankiewicz, November 1978.

Throughout the American leg of the 1978 world tour, Dylan regularly took the opportunity to work on new songs at the sometimes lengthy soundchecks the kind of aircraft hanger he was now playing demanded. No longer of the opinion that he couldn't spring anything on his tour band, he knew there was little need to work on songs from the set list, all of which were now firmly bedded in. Instead, he found another way to put the musicians through their paces, setting the unfamiliar to this now familiar framework. Nor was Mankiewicz the only journalist to be informed that the songs he was working on would form his next album. He confided in Cott, "I'm writing songs on the run again—they're dear to me, the songs I'm doing now . . . So if I can block time out, here and there, I can work on an album the way the Eagles do." We should all be grateful that such a disturbing aspiration was short-circuited.

Some of the songs, though, sound like a loss—even if the lack of even a halfway decent tape of any soundcheck from those three inspired months on the road makes assessing their merits problematic. A number of tunes he attempted at the half a dozen soundchecks taped by members of the audience on crude cassette recorders have no words, or only the barest of lyrics. These may well have been worked on further. Or not. Of the songs that seem to qualify for realized status, three songs [#373–5] were attempted at least twice on the circulating soundcheck tapes, all of which are a hard listen.

"You Don't Love Me No More," the first of five new songs he works on at a long soundcheck in New Haven—which included the two Dylan-Springs songs he was minded to introduce into the set—he only does on this occasion, but it is clearly more than just an idea, having presumably been worked on at Rundown. It already has its own full-stop ending, and instrumental breaks in all the right places, while the lyric reproaches some unspecified woman who won't explain why she doesn't love him no more. He wonders aloud, "Did I say something wrong?" All in all, pretty enjoyable.

The other two songs rehearsed in New Haven have more than their fair share of dummy lyrics, but "This A-way, That A-way" has a gorgeous tune and Dylan isn't about to give up on it (or her), still playing with the song at the very soundcheck where he first performs his next album's title track, at Nashville in early December. "Take It or Leave It," on the other hand, sounds more like some country cover— and given the number of Shel Silverstein songs he performed at these soundchecks, could well be some lost cowboy tune—but the lyric appears to be his, with its stock-in-trade line about getting ready to leave another gal behind (this time in the form of an ultimatum, "take it or leave it, one more time").

Again, the song lingers, cropping up more than a month later at a soundcheck in Carbondale, when he introduces a song, "(Daddy's Gonna Take) One More Ride," that is in a similarly mawkish vein, mirroring (but not emulating) a song soundchecked the following day, Silverstein's own "Daddy's Little Girl." The most formulaic of the songs he was using to while away these stateside soundchecks, "One More Ride," reappears in an empty Omaha arena a week later, but this proves to be its last go-round. He would soon be "low-down and disgusted" with himself.

{376} LEGIONNAIRE'S DISEASE

Published lyric/s: Lyrics 85; Lyrics 04.

First known performance: [Olympia Stadium, Detroit, MI, soundcheck, October 13, 1978.]

"Legionnaire's Disease" was among the songs Dylan was working on at soundchecks up and down the land. Performed at a Detroit soundcheck, it was promptly sidelined, though not before guitarist Billy Cross had got the song in his head. And so, when he got his hands on a tape of the soundcheck, he decided to record his own version, which he duly released on the Delta Cross Band's 1981 LP, *Up Front*. Cross either took some liberties with the lyric or—more likely—the published lyric made a bad job of transcribing whatever source was to hand. In the second verse of Cross's version, he sings:

> Now I wish I had a dollar for everyone that died within that year,
> It grabbed them by the collar, and many a maiden shed a tear.

The published lyric suggests the disease "got 'em hot by the collar, plenty an old maid shed a tear," which manages to be ghastly *and* nonsensical. Likewise, whereas Cross sang, "it him 'em like a tree," the published lyric suggested "it came out of the trees"—as opposed to the air-conditioning, from where this disease would be somewhat more likely to come. Bizarrely, this is the one wholly unrepresentative song from this fertile little period to survive to the 2004 *Lyrics*. So much for producing a definitive edition of the man's work as a lyricist.

{377} SLOW TRAIN

Published lyric/s: Lyrics 85; Lyrics 04.
First known performance: Nashville, TN, soundcheck, December 2, 1978.
Known studio recordings: ?Rundown demo, April 1979; Muscle Shoals, Sheffield, AL, May 3, 1979 [STC].

> the songs on this specific record are . . . exercises in tonal breath control . . . the subject matter—though meaningless as it is—has something to do with . . . the holy slow train. —*Highway 61 Revisited* sleeve notes, 1965

It had been thirteen years since Dylan last wrote about "the holy slow train" when he began soundchecking the song that became "Slow Train" the first week of December 1978. The tune he sang at the December 2 Nashville soundcheck has already acquired at least two verses—frustratingly, all but inaudible—as well as a recognizable chorus, "There's a slow train coming up around the bend."

The only other couplet that *is* audible ("She said get out of town / before the sun goes down") confirms this is not quite the song it would become. One suspects that it began life addressing his personal journey on the "holy slow train"—the very train he is alluding to in the pre-song rap to "Señor" at these shows—not the judgments of a modern Jeremiah which it became. If so, just one verse ("I had a woman down in Alabama . . ."), and a single couplet in the final verse of the released version reflect such a starting point:

> Well, my baby went to Illinois,
> With some bad-talkin' boy she could destroy,
> A real suicide case, but there was nothing I could do to stop it.

In the released song, this verse and stray couplet are little more than incongruous asides to the state of the world he is going to such pains to address as part of a general forewarning to repent. In the five months separating the soundcheck from the famous Alabama studio, he arrived at a view he shared some years later with Denise Worrell: "All the comforts are real deceiving as to what life's all about. All the crutches. Society, you know. Western civilization." Yet, even in its realized state, "Slow Train" contains no specific allusions to the Bible, and only a single reference to the source of all the world's misery ("Fools glorifying themselves, trying to manipulate Satan"). It is an Old Testament rant, but very much in the modern-day protest singer's vernacular. One must, as such, presume it was finished before he underwent the next stage in his doctrinal education, the Bible School in Reseda. The fact that he had demoed the song even before the album sessions suggests he recognized the song as kicking off a new phase. (Such a demo, apparently instrumental, is logged in the Sony system.)

The soundcheck tryout confirms that it was the slow train itself which set Dylan off, an archetype that had cast a spell on him ever since he was a child ("in my youngest days I used t kneel / by my aunt's house on a railroad field . . . as I waited till I heard the sound / a the iron ore cars rollin' down." —*Joan Baez in Concert/2* sleeve notes, 1963). Indeed, he took to prefacing the song at fall 1980 shows with a rap about those times: "When I was a young kid growing up I used to sit around all the time, the trains used to roll through town three or four times a day. And I used to watch them trains just wondering where they were going. And one day I knew I was gonna go where those trains were going."

And the redemption train had stayed ever on his mind. One of his earliest songs, "This Train Ain't Bound for Glory," adopts a similar litany of condemnation to "Slow Train," as does 1962's "Train A-Travelin'." "People Get Ready," Curtis Mayfield's gospel plea to join the glory train, with its evocative opening, "People get ready, there's a train a-coming . . . All you need is faith to feel those wheels a-hummin'" was a song Dylan recorded at least three times—in 1967, 1975, and 1989—each time with the passion of a true believer, even if those first two times he remained belittled by doubt.

By 1979, the holy slow train carried far more apocalyptic contraband, Dylan invariably prefacing performances with a rap suggesting that "this world is going to be destroyed, we know that. Christ will set up his kingdom in Jerusalem for a thousand years where the lion will lie down with the lamb. Have you heard that before? . . . This is called 'Slow Train Coming.' It's been coming a long time and it's picking up speed."

In fact, there is little in the sentiments of "Slow Train" that would have required Dylan to embrace the Pilgrim Fathers' faith. Even his castigating of "nonbelievers . . . talkin' in the name of religion" attacked their falsehood, not their faith. Only in the context of an album so explicit in its profession of Christianity did the song take on evangelical connotations distasteful to the left-leaning liberalists that had for so long accepted the man as a prophet (and whom he sent up in concert by stating, "I told you the answer was blowing in the wind, and it was. I told you the times they were a-changing, and they were. And I'm telling you Christ is coming back—and He is!").

In such a context, "Slow Train" was bound to get beaten with a critical stick. The line that seemed to upset critics most was not even one of those which damned them personally—it was his attack upon "Sheiks walkin' around like kings / Wearing fancy jewels and nose rings / Deciding America's future . . ." Chris Bohn, in *Melody Maker*, found his view on such "worldly topics" to be "frighteningly inflammatory and positively dangerous," and called "Slow Train" "possibly the most irresponsible song Dylan has ever written." *NME*'s Charles Shaar Murray was worried by a Dylan who "has divided the world into Good and Evil according to the precepts of a narrow and fundamentalist creed. . . . What Dylan is preaching talks not of liberation but of punishment, and in sour and elitist terms." *Rolling Stone* editor Jann Wenner, on the other hand, decided that "Slow Train" was "unequivocally in the tradition of the 'state of the union' songs that Dylan has put on every record he's ever done [!]. . . [and] is nothing less than Dylan's most mature and profound song about America." We just disagree.

Dylan would hardly have considered his attack on the Arabs to be a "worldly topic." He was responding to the chapter in Hal Lindsey's inflammatory *The Late Great Planet Earth* (1970) in which Lindsey suggested that (many) Arabs were intent on wiping Israel from the face of the earth. The relevant chapter, "Sheik to Sheik," suggested "this kind of . . . smouldering hatred against Israel will keep the Middle East a dangerous trouble spot," a view fully vindicated in the forty years since he wrote it—*unlike* his belief that an attack in the near future on Israel by Arab leaders would spark the final battle between good and evil, Armageddon. Dylan's own views continued to be colored by Lindsey's apocalyptic scenario as late as 1983's equally provocative "Neighborhood Bully," while "Slow Train," for all its flaws, would remain in the live set every night through 1981. But save for an occasional outing in 1987, when the song was taken at almost the same clip as those glory-bound carriages (having lost its anti-Arab verse), this "holy slow train" has subsequently been shunted off into a siding.

{378} DO RIGHT TO ME BABY (DO UNTO OTHERS)

Published lyric/s: Lyrics 85; Lyrics 04.

First known performance: Miami, FL, December 16, 1978.

Known studio recordings: Muscle Shoals, Sheffield, AL, May 4, 1979—4 takes [STC].

On December 16, 1978, in Miami, Dylan completed a 115-date world tour that had started with such promise but which by halfway through the American leg had become another rerun of the 1974 tour, about which he later said, "There was nothing other than just force behind that [tour]. I've fallen into that trap." The one thing that seems to have sustained him in those last few weeks was his newfound faith, the first public intimation of which came on the last night of the tour, when he debuted the first song he had ever written around a Biblical proverb.

The song in question, "Do Right to Me Baby," took as its philosophical fulcrum a chapter from the gospel according to Matthew, which he had recently begun quoting chapter and verse in "Tangled Up in Blue." Written to demonstrate that Christ fulfilled all the Old Testament prophecies of the Messiah, Matthew's gospel has its fair share of sayings that have been wilfully misread, one of the most misinterpreted being, "Therefore all things whatsoever ye would [wish] that men should do to you, do ye even so to them: for this is the law and the prophets" (7:12).

Dylan himself is one of those guilty of misreading said dictum. As Paul Williams has pointed out, "'*If* you do right, then I will' is not the

Golden Rule at all, but a perversion of it." Christ, in the Sermon on the Mount, requests not an exchange of goodwill, but a commitment to doing good. Dylan also (mis)appropriates another verse from the same sermon for the song's opening line, transforming "Judge not, that ye be not judged" (7:1) into, "Don't wanna judge nobody, don't wanna be judged."

There is where the biblical lesson ended—for now. The rest of the song is mostly a list of things he no longer believes in, but once did. "Don't wanna marry nobody if they're already married" and "Don't wanna touch nobody, don't wanna be touched" are the expressions of a man who, above all else, is looking to abandon the pursuit of a romantic ideal he now knows he will never find. For now he has but one concern—cleverly hidden away in verse three: "Don't wanna be burned." For the first time, he is talking about the eternal flames of damnation, not some fair deal gone bad.

The version Dylan sang to a mystified Miami audience comes at an appropriate point in the set—after "It's Alright Ma (I'm Only Bleeding)," before "Forever Young"—and features just three verses, the first and third verse as released, plus a second verse where he yearns to not be deceived or lied to anymore. The song in its studio form continues the catechism of things he'd rather like not to do, or have done to him, but is essentially the same song he sang in Miami, minus the guitar and organ fills left over from the previous song (at one point he apparently recorded it with just acoustic guitar and piano, à la "Dirge"). The simplicity and sincerity of the message was lost amid the howls of displeasure that greeted the album as a whole, but Dylan continued to imbue the song with a certain grace throughout 1979–80, even if it retained worrying vestiges of time spent listening to Eagles albums.

1979–80

{ Slow Train Coming; Saved }

The two songs Dylan began writing in the last two weeks of the fall 1978 U.S. tour would prove to be but the first flutterings from a reborn songwriter. By December 1979 he was telling one radio interviewer, "I don't sing any song which hasn't been given to me by the Lord to sing," as the songs of disaffection which had occupied his waking hours on the road were all replaced by bulletins from the road to Calvary. Initially, these heartfelt testimonies directly addressed a Christ who had rescued him from "the death he's bound to die." But after attending a two-month course in "Discipleship" at a makeshift school in Reseda, California, the songs became not only inspired by the spirit of the scriptures, but also infused by the very phraseology of the King James Bible.

This transition was charted through the writing of Slow Train Coming *(from December 1978 to April 1979). By the end the songs were little more than versified expositions of the Scriptures. Thankfully, even these dogmatic ditties were saved by the sheer intensity with which Dylan imbued them in live performance, those fall 1979 shows including a further nine songs penned after completing such a strident statement of Faith. Any movement back to a more Dylanesque turn of phrase on hold. Instead, he recorded a second collection that was concerned largely with salvation (and less with damnation).*

Saved was recorded in February 1980, but it would be summer before it appeared, as his record label wondered what to do with another gospel record. Dylan almost immediately began penning songs with a more personal approach to the Christian message. In April, he debuted three of these—"Ain't Gonna Go to Hell," "Cover Down (Pray Through)," and "I Will Love Him"—at the same time expounding at length on the underlying message in a series of pre-song raps. By the end of May 1980, he had decided to suspend "preaching the gospel from place to place," retiring to the Midwest, where he continued to mine new songs from this rich new vein of religiously inspired lyric-writing . . .

{379} GOTTA SERVE SOMEBODY

Published lyric/s: Lyrics 85; Lyrics 04.
Known studio recordings: Muscle Shoals, Sheffield, AL, May 4, 1979—4 takes [STC].
First known performance: Saturday Night Live, NYC, October 20, 1979.

> And if it seem evil unto you to serve the Lord, choose you this day whom ye will serve. —Joshua 24:15

"Gotta Serve Somebody" seems to be another song which sprang from Dylan's close reading of the Gospel according to Matthew in the immediate aftermath of his own Pauline moment, on the road to Miami. Like "Do Right to Me Baby," it was a list-song inspired by another of Matthew's proverbial sayings, this one being, "No man can serve two masters: for either he will hate the one, and love the other; or else he will hold to the one, and despise the other. Ye cannot serve God and mammon" (6:24).

Unlike its predecessor, though, this song made an unequivocal commitment to his Lord—and that Lord was Jesus Christ. Whatever Matthew's—and Jesus'—Old Testament source for the sentiment (presumably the one from Joshua), the saying was closely linked to another familiar saying found later in Matthew's exegesis of Messianic prophecies: "He that is not with me is against me" (12:30). Even Dylan's own whimsical description of his conversion experience, at a concert in Syracuse on the fifth day of May 1980, suggested how serious (and simple) he felt the choice had become:

> I know a lot of you never heard of Jesus before. I know I hadn't up till a couple of years ago. [Then] Jesus tapped me on the shoulder, said, "Bob, why are you resisting me?" I said, "I'm not resisting you." He said, "You

gonna follow me?" I said, "Well, I've never thought about that before." He said, "When you're not following me, you're resisting me." John the Baptist baptized with water . . . Jesus baptizes with fire. Fire and the Holy Spirit. So yes, there's been a change in me.

"Gotta Serve Somebody" reflected this change, Dylan taking sides as the End Times finally impinged on him. And yet very little of the song seems inner-directed. "You might be a rock & roll addict prancing on the stage / You might have drugs at your command, women in a cage" might stand as a pretty good description of the mascara'd man who just played sixty-plus arenas across the North American continent. And "you might live in a dome" is surely a dig at himself for building his own Malibu mausoleum. But most of the song's targets are external. And obvious. As Nick Kent wrote, in his *NME* preview of the album, "What strikes me most forcefully . . . is the complete absence of obscure metaphors and the labyrinthine imagery that was once Dylan's premier calling card."

Brooking no such ambiguity, "Gotta Serve Somebody" set the tone for an entire album of judgmentalism, even as he wrapped these words in his most seductive, soulful spoonful of sound, hoping to make the bitter pill go down easy(er). And when the song became a minor hit in its own right, on the back of an impassioned performance on *Saturday Night Live* in October, it seemed it was a message people *were* prepared to take on board in a country founded by Puritans. Opening every one of the 103 shows he played between November 1, 1979, and July 1, 1981, "Gotta Serve Somebody" was the message song to end all message songs.

It also won the man his first Grammy Award, for the Best Vocal Performance of 1979 (evidently voted for by folk who never checked out the rest of the album), Dylan turning up at the Shrine Auditorium on February 27, 1980, to collect his award and perform the definitive version of the song, making the point that his reborn self could pull out these kind of vocal performances at will.

After this defining moment, however, the song seemed to pall in concert, even as Dylan played around with the cast of characters to keep from tiring of the message himself. And though the song hung around in concert long after all other *Slow Train* songs—"I Believe in You" excepted—slipped from their performing berth, the conviction with which this believer once delivered his testament audibly dissipated year on year—as did the sheer vilification that once greeted its sentiments.

In 1979–80, a fired-up Dylan rammed home the message as hard as he could. At some shows in May 1980, he would taunt the audience after this opening sortie, "Gonna talk mostly about the spirit of God. Maybe we can talk about Jesus, too. If you got any demons in you at all you're not gonna like that name." The second night at Earl's Court in 1981, he stalked the stage throughout an extended intro like the Witchfinder General himself. But after that residency, Dylan preferred to harp on about being "Saved" instead.

{380} I BELIEVE IN YOU

Published lyric/s: Lyrics 85; Lyrics 04.
Known studio recordings: Muscle Shoals, Sheffield, AL, May 3, 1979 [STC].
First known performance: Saturday Night Live, NYC, October 20, 1979.

> Unto you it is given in the behalf of Christ, not only to believe on him, but also to suffer for his sake. —Philippians 1:29

By the time Dylan wrote "I Believe in You," he had begun to turn other pages of the New Testament, arriving at Philippians soon enough, where he found out that there would be a price to pay for his newfound faith. Almost immediately, he felt compelled to express his conflicted feelings in song. As he told Robert Hilburn, a dozen years down the line, "I Believe in You" was one of those songs that was largely "just about overcoming hardship." From the first verse, the narrator is depicted as a pariah *because* of his faith:

> They look at me and frown, like to drive me from this town
> They don't want me around, 'cause I believe in you.

In conversation with the same L.A. journalist the year after he wrote the song, Dylan confirmed there was an autobiographical dimension to such expressions of rejection: "I did begin telling a few people [about Christ] after a couple of months and a lot of them got angry at me."

Here was something he had spent his life dealing with—rejection. But rather than believing in himself and his own judgment in the face of such hostility, he believed in Him. And how. Fusing blues commonplaces like "walk out on my own / A thousand miles from home . . . don't mind the pain / Don't mind the driving rain" to express the kind of treatment meted out to many an accidental martyr, he insists such belief cannot be shaken—not even "if white turn to black." At song's end, though "friends forsake" him, he knows he "will sustain."

The song, which in performance rarely wavered in intensity right through 1981, has itself sustained. A new, more muscular musical arrangement at the European shows that summer could not make its singer deviate from a profound conviction. Indeed, the sentiments of this song remained real enough—and personal enough—to transfer success-fully to the Never Ending Tour, where it was reintroduced in July 1989, and where even a fast-failing capacity to hit the high notes could not dissuade Dylan from restating a now decade-old commitment. One likes to imagine that the night he sang it with all the passion—if little of the range—of yesteryear, in Minneapolis on September 3, 1992, he was singing it to his mother and brother, sat in the fifth row, wondering what this good Jewish boy was thinking. Well, he still wasn't gonna go to hell for anybody—not for mother, not for brother.

{381} YE SHALL BE CHANGED

Published lyric/s: Lyrics 04.
Known studio recordings: Muscle Shoals, Sheffield, AL, May 2, 1979 [TBS].

> In a moment, in the twinkling of an eye, at the last trump: for the trumpet shall sound, and the dead shall be raised incorruptible, and we shall be changed. —1 Corinthians 15:52

"Ye Shall Be Changed" appears to be the fourth song he wrote around a precept from the New Testament that winter. As with "I Believe in You," each refrain stuck to its source religiously. And yet in neither song does Dylan pepper his verses with biblical titbits of wisdom, perhaps suggesting he had yet to start his daily Bible classes when he penned them.

It is not only the language of the verses that remains his. So do the targets of his admonishments: "All your loved ones had walked out the door / You're not even sure 'bout your wife and kids no more" feels very close to home. One suspects it is Dylan who had been drinking bitter water and "eating the bread of sorrow," making for yet another instance of "when I used words like 'he' and 'it' and 'they,' and talking about other people, I was really talking about nobody but me."

By addressing such concerns head-on, he was contrasting his former life with that of the born-again Bob. He had been changed, and this song is an out-and-out product of some extracurricular reading—in this case Hal Lindsey's *Late Great Planet Earth*, specifically chapter eleven, "The Ultimate Trip," in which Lindsey interprets the above chapter from Corinthians in a very specific way: "It means He will move out all the Christians—and at that point we shall be changed . . . in essence. . . . In the Rapture, only the Christians see Him—it's a mystery, a secret. When the living believers are taken out, the world is going to be mystified."

It seems incredible that an intelligent man such as Dylan could have decided Lindsey was on to something and that his fantastical explanation of a contentious passage in the Bible made perfect sense. But believe it he did. Not only that, but he seems to have held onto this belief well past the first flush of faith. He told *Rolling Stone*'s Kurt Loder as late as March 1984, "The new kingdom that comes in, people can't even imagine what it's gonna be like. . . . If the new kingdom happened tomorrow and you were sitting there and I was sitting there, you wouldn't even remember me." Also, the opening couplet to 1983's "License to Kill" requires only two additional words to repeat the message of this 1979 outtake: "Man thinks 'cause he rules the earth, he can do with it as he please, / And if things don't change soon, he will . . ."—be changed, that is.

Yet the man hadn't entirely lost his marbles. He knew that releasing such a view into the world at large really would have the men in long white coats beating a path to his door. Although he recorded the song for *Slow Train Coming* in May, not only was it one of two songs left unreleased from these sessions, but also it was the only Muscle Shoals product neither released nor performed in concert that year. Indeed, it is somewhat surprising that he OK'd for the track to be released on the 1991 set, *The Bootleg Series Vols. 1–3*, having already nixed another track with a killer vocal from a more moderate man, "Yonder Comes Sin."

Thankfully, no one was looking to take him to task any longer regarding the meaning of that chorus, when "the dead will arise and burst out of your clothes, and ye shall be changed." Nor question him about why "you don't have to go to Russia or Iran / Just surrender to God, He'll move you where you make a stand." Dylan knew what he meant—or what he had gleaned from Lindsey's ingenious commingling of biblical prophesies and contemporary world events. He spelled it out to one particularly sceptical audience in Tempe, Arizona, six months after the *Slow Train Coming* sessions:

> Jesus Christ is . . . supposed to come two times. He came once already. See, that's the thing, he's been here already. Now, he's coming back again. You gotta be prepared for this. Because, no matter what you read in the newspapers, that's all deceit. The real truth is that he's coming back already. And you just watch your newspapers. You're gonna see, maybe two years, maybe three years, five years from now, you just watch and see. Russia will come down and attack in the Middle East. China's got an army of two hundred million people. They're gonna come down in the Middle East. There's gonna be a war called the Battle of Armageddon, which is like some war you never even dreamed about. And Christ will set up his kingdom. He will set up his kingdom and he'll rule it from Jerusalem. I know, as far out as that might seem, this is what the Bible says. (November 26, 1979)

This was the gospel according to Hal Lindsey, not the gospel truth. It would take Dylan a year and a half to admit, to the ever-attendant Hilburn, "You can find anything you want in the Bible. You can twist it around any way you want." By then, he had been thoroughly immersing himself in the Good Book, not merely relying on the skewed views of the anti-intellectual Mr. Lindsey. But before subsuming himself in the revealed scriptural Word, he still had something he wanted to get off his chest . . .

{382} TROUBLE IN MIND

Published lyric/s: Lyrics 85; Lyrics 04.
Known studio recordings: Muscle Shoals, Sheffield, AL, April 30, 1979—8 takes [45—tk. 7].

A lot of people think that Jesus comes into a person's life . . . when they are either down and out or are miserable or just old and withering away. That's not the way it was for me. I was doing fine. —Dylan, to Robert Hilburn, 1980

Everything about "Trouble in Mind"—as personal a song as "I Believe in You"—demonstrates that Dylan had been in the exact opposite frame of mind when Christ entered his life: wretched, lonely, and afraid. Though he only sings the first and last verses in the first person, the whole song stands as an indictment of his life to date. And it is bookended by two very personal pleas to the Lord: "I got to know, Lord, when to pull back on the reins" and a question that again bears the mark of Philippians: "How long must I suffer, Lord, how long must I be provoked?"

This man has gone back to school, bringing his new textbook, the King James Bible, and disregarding any false knight on the road. A letter to a fellow believer the following April confirmed that he relied on the classic 1611 text as he thanks "Steve" for sending along a newer translation, which he suggests has been "helpful in discerning a few phrases from and shedding more light on what the King James Version reads." When it came to poetics, he stuck with the archly Jacobean language he already knew and loved ("I had always read the Bible, but . . . [previously I] only looked at it as literature." —Dylan, 1980).

Primary sources for this song's troubled imagery come from the Old Testament. The above pleas to the Lord mirror the series of questions King David asks in the Book of Psalms, fearing that he has been abandoned: "How long wilt thou forget me, O Lord? for ever? how long wilt thou hide thy face from me? How long shall I take counsel in my soul, having sorrow in my heart daily?" (13:1–2) Psalms also provides the inspiration for another of the song's more evocative images. "When my life is over, it'll be like a puff of smoke" is a palpably poetic paraphrase of "for my days are consumed like smoke" (102:3), Dylan grafting this idea to the sentiments of that well-known gospel song "Just a Closer Walk with Thee," which sings of "When my feeble life is o'er . . . guide me gently, safely on / To thy shore, dear Lord."

For all its nominal resemblance to a modern-day "Me and the Devil Blues," "Trouble in Mind" is the first *Slow Train Coming*–period song not only to take its impetus from chapter/verse, but also to be replete with references to biblical texts. Ephesians provides the description of Satan as "the prince of the power of the air" (2:2) that provides the impetus for a verse castigating those who "make a law unto yourself [and] deaden your conscience 'til you worship the work of your own hands" (a line culled from an Old Testament prophetic text, Jeremiah 1:16: "I will utter my judgments against them touching all their wickedness, who have forsaken me, and have burned incense unto other gods, and worshipped the works of their own hands").

In "Trouble in Mind" any sorties against the spirit are directly waged by the devil. If Dylan had taken a long time learning to believe in the Lord, he had taken no such convincing when it came to Lucifer. As early as 1962's "Talkin' Devil," the fallen angel had made his presence known to this sinner man. And a year *before* he felt Christ's presence, he was already talking about the devil as a force to fear: "Death's not here to get anybody. It's the appearance of the Devil, and the Devil is a coward, so knowledge will overcome that. . . . The Devil will go as deep as you let the Devil go. You can leave yourself open to that."

He has now realized he had been leaving himself open to this smooth talker, who talks like he'd just emerged from some Skip James or Robert Johnson song: "Well, I don't wanna bore ya / But when ya get tired of that Miss So-and-So / I got another woman for ya." (Dylan derives much of his characterization of the devil in this period from another Hal Lindsey tome, *Satan Is Alive and Well on Planet Earth* (1972), specifically drawing on the section, "Prince of the Power of the Air," pages 65–9.)

"Trouble in Mind" defines an essential part of Dylan's conversion experience, a chilling fear of his own damnation. Even in that final verse, he is praying for the Lord to "keep my blind side covered and see that I don't bleed." However, this part was kept from fans on the song's release in 1979. When it appeared on the B-side of "Gotta Serve Somebody" or

"Precious Angel" (depending on the territory) it was trimmed of that heartfelt conclusion. Quite why the song was treated so unkindly is not clear. Paul Williams suggests in *What Happened?* that it was the song's personal nature which resulted in its exclusion from *Slow Train Coming.* He probably has a point—it could have muddied the salutary message. But Dylan clearly thought the song too important to discard, even if he couldn't find a place for it on the album, or a slot in the all-gospel show he was planning for the fall.

Someone certainly made a point of including the song (with that "missing" sixth verse) in the lyric sheet that accompanied press copies of the album. And the fact that Dylan spent the whole of the first *Slow Train* session in Sheffield, Alabama, working on such a troubling song suggests he always intended to put it out. I guess by the time he did, the Lord had freed him from the pit; and the saved man was not so inclined to remind himself nightly about what it felt like to be lost.

{383} MAN GAVE NAMES TO ALL THE ANIMALS

Published lyric/s: Lyrics 85; Lyrics 04.
Known studio recordings: Muscle Shoals, Sheffield, AL, May 4, 1979—6 takes [STC—tk. 6].
First known performance: Warfield Theatre, San Francisco, November 1, 1979.

And out of the ground the Lord God formed every beast of the field, and every fowl of the air; and brought them unto Adam to see what he would call them: and whatsoever Adam called every living creature, that was the name thereof. And Adam gave names to all cattle, and to the fowl of the air, and to every beast of the field. —Genesis 2:19–20

Dylan's next song about Satan was, at least ostensibly, in a lighter vein. A nursery rhyme about Adam naming the animals in the garden of Eden, it had its own sting in the tail: "an animal as smooth as glass / Slithering his way through the grass / Saw him disappear by a tree near a lake . . ." And though he does not complete the thought—preferring an ominous conclusion to the hitherto childlike song—there is no mistaking the animal's identity, nor its purpose. In concert, he sometimes added his own post-song commentary, as at a May 1980 show in Pittsburgh, explicating the underlying message:

> As everybody has guessed, the animal in the last song was a snake. Same snake that was in the Garden of Eden that deceived Eve and deceived Adam, and still running around loose right now, deceiving the nation. See, Lucifer put his spirit inside that snake. Lucifer was a high angel of God before he became the Devil. Anyway, Adam gave him the keys to this world, and he owns it. He owns everything about it. He owns the newspapers, he owns the political parties, he owns the doctors and he owns the lawyers. He owns the educational system, he owns it all. But Jesus Christ went to the Cross to defeat that power. I know that's a secret that Satan keeps. Jesus went to the Cross not only for forgiveness of sins but to destroy the works of the Devil, and he accomplished just that. Something no man has ever done. (May 16, 1980)

So much for "Man Gave Names" being a kiddies' song. And yet, in those European countries where it was released as a single, the song enjoyed a life independent of its brow-beating brethren, even charting in territories where its religious message slipped by listeners interested in sing-along ska. When Dylan was informed on his 1987 European tour of the song's chart success in France and Belgium, he reintroduced a song abandoned back in 1981. This time, though, his combo couldn't quite manage the same groove as that slick-as-oil 1979 band, with whom he would sometimes get real playful with the lyric live: "Wasn't too small and he wasn't too big / Mmmm, think I'll call it a . . . giraffe." Little did those audiences realize there was a whole slew of songs about the snake in the grass to come.

{384} NO MAN RIGHTEOUS (NO NOT ONE)

Published lyric/s: Telegraph #14; Lyrics 85; Lyrics 04.
Known studio recordings: Muscle Shoals, Sheffield, AL, May 1, 1979—10 takes; May 3, 1979.
First known performance: Warfield Theatre, San Francisco, November 16, 1979.

As it is written, There is none righteous, no, not one. —Romans 3:10

As Dylan told DJ Bruce Heiman, in a December 1979 radio interview, "My ideology now would be coming out of the Scripture ... these things have just been shown to me." And "No Man Righteous" was very much "coming out of the Scripture"; those two favorites the book of Psalms and the gospel according to Matthew again serving to show him the way.

Thus, when Dylan put "your goodness next to God's," only to find "it comes out like a filthy rag," he placed himself in the court of King David. "The Lord looked down from heaven upon the children of men, to see if there were any that did understand, and seek God. They are all gone aside, they are all together become filthy: there is none that doeth good, no, not one" [Psalms 14:2–3]. He continues in a similar vein by singing of "social hypocrites / [Who] like to make rules for others while they do just the opposite," a rephrasing of Jesus' own words when targeting "the scribes and the Pharisees [who] sit in Moses" seat," instructing his disciples, "Whatsoever they bid you observe, that observe and do; but do not ye after their works: for they say, and do not" (Matthew 23:2–3).

Another song which was recorded for but omitted from *Slow Train Coming*, "No Man Righteous" was scheduled to be included on the original 4-CD version of *The Bootleg Series* (1991), before it was trimmed to three CDs. As such, the studio version remains unreleased—and uncirculated. Thankfully, Dylan sang the song at the last Warfield show in November 1979, and that performance was captured by a particularly competent audience taper.

Having grown in confidence throughout the two-week residency, Dylan even cracks a joke prior to the song's live debut, suggesting, "This is a song that nobody knows. Nobody in this band even knows it—that's how I can tell who really wants to stick with me and who doesn't." So energized and spirited is the performance that, at the end of it, he announces "Yes, I'm sure that's going to be on the next album." It wasn't. Indeed, he only ever sang the song live one more time (in Hartford, May 7, 1980), as a (less effective) duet with backing singer Regina Havis.

By then, he had already effectively donated the song to Havis, who occasionally sang it in her solo slot at these shows. It had firmly disappeared from the set by the time Dylan returned to the Warfield the following fall, though Havis and Co. continued to soundcheck it. In the interim it had become a demo for other artists. Reggae artist Jah Malla responded to the call, releasing his own Jah-maican take on his 1981 solo LP. Malla's jaunty version does this unsparingly judgmental song no favors, especially as he abbreviates it, omitting the final verse which returns the song to the first person, expressing born-again Bob's fervent hope that he shall spared (or as he sang it in Hartford, changed):

> When I'm gone, don't wonder where I'll be,
> Just say that I believed in Christ, and Jesus lifted me,
> He defeated the devil and was God's own son,
> And there ain't no man righteous, no not one.[8]

Perhaps Malla never got to hear Dylan's studio version, recorded in the first flush of enthusiasm with the received word of God, and so knew nothing of this verse. Both the live Dylan rendition and Malla's omit the penultimate verse ("God got the power, man has got his vanity"), though the song still contains the odd autobiographical admission of unrighteousness. When he sings in the second bridge, "Done so many evil things in the name of love," he makes it plain that he too once surrendered to sin. Maybe he came to feel "No Man Righteous" was one too many a song addressing human-made imperfection. Or it may simply have suffered from being done too early at the album sessions, an ongoing blind spot in the man's makeup.

{385} GONNA CHANGE MY WAY OF THINKING

Published lyric/s: Lyrics 85; Lyrics 04 x2.
Known studio recordings: Muscle Shoals, Sheffield, AL, May 2, 1979 [STC];
?Sony Studios, NYC, March 4, 2002 [GSoBD].
First known performance: Warfield Theatre, San Francisco, November 1, 1979.

You can't go out and try to save the world. You just say what is available to you to say. —Dylan, to Joel Kotkin, January 1978

With "Gonna Change My Way of Thinking," Dylan finally—and unambiguously—took on the mantle of prophet he had spent the past sixteen years rejecting. This elemental blues—inspired methinks by Taj Mahal's recording of "Done Changed My Way of Living"—was now being requisitioned to browbeat nonbelievers. "Lies that life is black and white" had become the Truth, and Dylan was not only taking sides, he was hurling biblical words of damnation from his side of the barricades:

> Jesus said, Be ready,
> For you know not the hour in which I come, [x2]
> He said, He who is not for Me is against Me,
> Just so you know where He's coming from.

In order to make his polemical point, Dylan was obliged to staple together two separate statements reported in Matthew twelve chapters apart: ("Watch therefore: for ye know not what hour your Lord doth come" [24:42] and "He that is not with me is against me; and he that gathereth not with me scattereth abroad" [12:30]). And he was just as anxious as Matthew to ensure this Messiah ticked all the Old Testament prophecy boxes—particularly those from Isaiah. And so when he sings "Stripes on your shoulders / Stripes on your back and on your hands," he is not merely describing the scourging of the Lord. He is suggesting the treatment meted out at the Crucifixion represents another prophecy fulfilled: "He was wounded for our transgressions, he was bruised for our iniquities: the chastisement of our peace was upon him; and with his stripes we are healed" (Isaiah 53:5).

Unfortunately, however righteous its message may be, "Gonna Change My Way of Thinking" is an ill-conceived mess—and a tuneless one at that. Even that vituperative vocal—usually a cause for celebration with Dylan—cannot save the song from itself. Not sure whether to lambast the faithless, celebrate salvation through suffering, or reassure his "God-fearing woman" of his constancy ("a woman that feareth the Lord, she shall be praised" [Proverbs 31:30], Dylan attempts to conjoin all three in a song that spreads precious little joy. Even in that final verse, which speaks of "a kingdom called Heaven / A place where there is no pain of birth," he adopts the tone of a Father Christmas who is about to recall a child's toy because s/he's been naughty.

Which makes it all the more bizarre that Dylan should select "Gonna Change My Way of Thinking" as the song he wished to revisit when asked to retake a *Slow Train* song for an album of (pretty appalling) cover versions, *Gotta Serve Somebody: The Gospel Songs of Bob Dylan* (2003). Predictably, the 60-year-old Dylan decided the old words needed to be junked and a new set put in their place, having replaced the Queens of Rhythm with the legendary Mavis Staples. The grand old lady arrived at the March 2002 session to find the great man had already started rewriting the song in the studio:

> He'd write a line and show it to me. Then he'd write another line and show me that. But I'd say, "Bobby, you write so little." He said he couldn't help it. When a person writes small like that, they're humble. He'd never heard that before. Then he came up with the line, "I'm so hungry, I could eat a horse." I said, "Which one of us is gonna sing that?" He said we'd figure it out. Bobby could not be satisfied. We were in the studio until one in the morning. He kept rough mixing.

It sounds like they were having fun, but, on the basis of what ended up being released, the engineer never got further than said rough mix, to which Dylan and Staples then tacked on a hokey spoken intro, lifted almost verbatim from a famous recording that the Carter Family and Jimmie Rodgers made in Louisville in June 1931. Said spiel implies the session was in California, though I wouldn't put it past the man to be in Sony's New York studios when delivering these lines.

As for the new lyric, "Sad-Eyed Lady of the Lowlands" it ain't. Every time Dylan got stuck on a line, he simply used some traditional song title to fill in the blank ("Gonna Sit at the Welcome Table," "When God Comes and Gathers His Jewels," "The Sun Is Shining," "The Storms Are on the Ocean"). It was a technique which had been serving him well for the past five years but never applied on quite this scale. It is almost as if he cannot bring himself to sing a single original verse, save the first. He even makes a bad joke out of one of the better original couplets, "You remember only about the brass ring / You forget all about the golden rule." Its replacement—"We['re] living by the golden rule / Whoever got the gold rules"—sounds like a snippet of rejected dialogue from *Masked and Anonymous*.

In the end, the entire performance seems to have been constructed to enable Dylan to insert a punch line with its own biblical connotations: "A brave man will kill you with a sword, a coward with a kiss." Yet even such a drastic rewrite did not prompt an immediate return to the live set for a song he had last performed twenty-two years earlier, when preparing for "that day and hour [of which] knoweth no man, no, not the angels of heaven, but my Father only" (Matthew 24:36). It took until October 4, 2009, for it to reappear, when its 2002 incarnation (minus spoken intro) opened the first show of a new NET leg.

{386} PRECIOUS ANGEL

Published lyric/s: Lyrics 85; Lyrics 04.
Known studio recordings: Muscle Shoals, Sheffield, AL, May 1, 1979 [STC].
First known performance: Warfield Theatre, San Francisco, November 1, 1979.

> Ye are the light of the world. A city that is set on an hill cannot be hid. Neither do men light a candle, and put it under a bushel, but on a candlestick; and it giveth light unto all that are in the house. Let your light so shine before men, that they may see your good works, and glorify your Father which is in heaven. —Matthew 5:14–16

"Precious Angel" revisits personal revelation as a theme, now drawing on the full gamut of scriptural texts to illuminate the lyrics. In one of his more sophisticated uses of biblical imagery, Dylan conveys the Christlike qualities of his own "precious angel" by applying to *her* qualities which the Bible applies to Him. In particular, she is described as "the lamp of my soul, and you torch up the night," compelling evidence that Dylan had not lost the ability to poeticize his path to redemption, or convey desire. This final-verse evocation seals the special bond that now exists between Dylan, Christ, and "her." She is the lesser beacon who has brought Dylan to see "the light of the world." And it is to both of them he sings the song's heartfelt chorus,

"Shine your light, shine your light on me / Ya know, I just couldn't make it by myself / I'm a little too blind to see."

It is again Corinthians which has triggered a song idea, contrasting the light of Christ with the permanent darkness that shall be the fate of all those deluded by the devil: "For God, who commanded the light to shine out of darkness, hath shined in our hearts, to give the light of the knowledge of the glory of God in the face of Jesus Christ . . . In whom the god of this world hath blinded the minds of them which believe not, lest the light of the glorious gospel of Christ, who is the image of God, should shine unto them" (2 Corinthians 4:4, 4:6). Another, direct source provides Dylan with the image of a man "too blind to see": the gospel according to John, in which Christ heals a blind man who proclaims, "Whereas I was blind, now I see" (9:25).

In Dylan's case, it was not a physical blindness but a blindness of the mind from which he was suffering. He communicated his then-frame of mind to Robert Hilburn, in his first post-conversion interview of importance: "Most of the people I know don't believe that Jesus was resurrected, that He is alive. It's like He was just another prophet or something, one of many good people." In "Precious Angel," he continues to voice his concern for those friends who still think this way:

> My so-called friends have fallen under a spell
> They look me squarely in the eye and they say "All is well"
> Can they imagine the darkness that will fall from on high
> When men will beg God to kill them and they won't be able to die?

Not surprisingly, Dylan's depiction of a fate worse than death has a direct scriptural source, Revelation 9:6: "In those days shall men seek death, and shall not find it; and shall desire to die, and death shall flee from them." He also demonstrates a more nuanced reading of the Good Book. "The darkness that will fall from high," is its own commentary on an earlier foretelling of Judgment, "The high places also of Aven, the sin of Israel, shall be destroyed . . . and they shall say to the mountains, Cover us; and to the hills, Fall on us" (Hosea 10:8). Not only is Judgment Day coming, but it has been since the original exodus: all "the way out of Egypt, through Ethiopia, to the judgment hall of Christ." (2 Corinthians 5:10 provides another subtext here: "For we must all appear before the judgment seat of Christ; that every one may receive the things done in his body, according to that he hath done, whether it be good or bad.")

Throughout the lyrics, Dylan brings poetic distillations to bear on his message of salvation. "Now there's spiritual warfare, flesh and blood breaking down," takes a passage from 2 Corinthians, "For though we walk in the flesh, we do not war after the flesh" (10:3), and introduces it to Ephesians 6:12: "For we wrestle not against flesh and blood, but against principalities, against powers, against the rulers of the darkness of this world, against spiritual wickedness in high places." No wonder it was the first *Slow Train Coming* song he leaked to the media.

The lady who had shone on the songwriter was already the subject of much media speculation. Various journalists reported that she was a black girlfriend, Mary Alice Artes—hence, "both our forefathers were slaves." Artes, having been converted by the Vineyard Fellowship herself, subsequently set Dylan on the same path to salvation (all this came *after* he had received his own vision of Christ back in November). Artes remains a shadowy figure biographically, which allowed Dylan to make fun of those fascinated by the minutiae of his life in a rap that preceded "Precious Angel" at a show in snowy Portland in January 1980:

> I was talking with someone last night who . . . was riding in a cab once and . . . it was in a big city. Cab driver turned around in the cab and said, "Did you hear Bob Dylan's a Christian now?" And this girl said, "Oh, I think I have heard that. How does that relate to you? Are you a Christian?" And the driver said, "No, but I been following Bob now for a long time." And the lady said, "Well, what you think of his new thing?" And he said, "Well, I think they're real good [songs]. But I tell you I think that if I could meet that person who brought Bob Dylan to the Lord, I think I might become a Christian, too." And this here song is all about that certain person. (January 14, 1980)

Any sense of gratitude did not ensure the song's retention in the live set beyond fall 1980. Its last performance (November 12, at the Warfield) was hardly typical. Playing harmonica over the girl chorus, Dylan sings the verses in a hard, insistent style, almost forcing himself to believe in the power of the words. The same night he also sang for the first and last time "Caribbean Wind," another valedictory to this precious angel and one of his greatest-ever love songs.

{387} WHEN YOU GONNA WAKE UP?

Published lyric/s: Lyrics 85; Lyrics 04.
Known studio recordings: Muscle Shoals, Sheffield AL, May 2, 1979 [STC].
First known performance: Saturday Night Live, NYC, October 20, 1979.

Be watchful, and strengthen the things which remain, that are ready to die: for I have not found thy works perfect before God.—Revelation 3:2

God's not in the business of dishing out material things to make people happy. He doesn't give you a house in the country and expect you to be content and happy. And if he does, he doesn't give it to you for nothing, anyway. —Dylan, to Charles Kaiser, 1985

"When You Gonna Wake Up?"—another song springing from a New Testament precept—seems to be the last song of self-chastisement Dylan wrote for *Slow Train Coming*. Its title image conveys a man sleep-walking his way to damnation, as per Romans 13:11: "Now it is high time to awake out of sleep: for now is our salvation nearer than when we believed." It is a solid idea, but, save for the first and last verses, he allows the song to become another long, tedious list of all the things wrong with the world—and how material things are a distraction along the way ("the rich seduce the poor," an excellent line, is ruined by its querulous counterpoint, "the old are seduced by the young").

The message is already beginning to get tiresome, which is perhaps why this song was sometimes prefaced in concert by the most haranguing rap with which Dylan testified. Few of these raps, though, addressed the song itself, save in the generic sense that they were concerned with the state of the world. But at the last show of a Santa Monica residency (November, 18–21, 1979), to an audience of mostly fellow believers (the shows being benefits for a nondenominational Christian charity), he used the G-word to spell it out, to whoops of affirmation:

> I don't know what kind of God you believe in, but I believe in a God that can raise the dead. He does it all the time, every day. Now there's certain men, you know, many of them who live right in this town, who seek to lead you astray. You be careful now. The real God, the real God, the one and only God, he don't make promises that he don't keep. That's how you can tell he's the real God.

He made much the same point to Karen Hughes, six months later: "You're not talking about some dead man who had a bunch of good ideas and was nailed to a tree. . . . You're talking about a resurrected Christ who is Lord of your life." Having crossed over to the other side, the sight lines in his rearview mirror had become obscured. Some of the targets in this song are plain bizarre: "Unrighteous doctors / dealing drugs that'll never cure your ills," "Adulterers in church," even Henry Kissinger, are counted among the spiritually somnambulant.

After the endless accusations, the moralizing final verse comes almost as a relief, though it is little more than a straight cantation from 1 Corinthians, "I determined not to know any thing among you, save Jesus Christ, and him crucified . . . And my speech and my preaching was not with enticing words of man's wisdom, but in demonstration of the Spirit and of power" (2:2, 2:4). Or, as Dylan put it:

> There's a man on a cross, and He been crucified for you,
> Believe in His power, that's about all you got to do.

He was soon modifying the message, dropping the "for you" in concert and changing the final line to, "You know who He is, and why He died." And it stayed this way through 1981, even as the song itself was rein-fused at least twice. But when the opportunity arose to restate the same message on the 1984 tour (in which the song sporadically appeared), this final verse was garbled, and rather than strengthening the things that remain, Dylan confined himself to asserting that if you don't wake up now, "you never will." He also stumbled over the song in its one and only post-1984 performance—at a October 1989 show in Poughkeepsie—when he played it at the piano, perhaps because this is where it was written originally. This time, though fumbling in the dark lyrically, the vocal was thankfully the spirited affirmation of a wide-awake believer.

Note: When the song appeared in the 1985 *Lyrics*, that last, unequivocal sentiment had become a question: "Do you have any idea why or for who He died?"

{388} WHEN HE RETURNS

Published lyric/s: Lyrics 85; Lyrics 04.
Known studio recordings: Muscle Shoals, Sheffield, AL, May 4, 1979—9 takes. [STC—tk. 9].
First known performance: Warfield Theatre, San Francisco, November 1, 1979.

For yourselves know perfectly that the day of the Lord so cometh as a thief in the night. —1 Thessalonians 5:2

Though *Slow Train Coming* was not an album written sequentially, Dylan constructed a sequence that told its own story. Opening with three songs betraying a personal dimension to the message of salvation—and damnation—the album slipped into apocalyptic mode from the title track on, building in intensity right up to its dramaturgical finale, "When He Returns," leaving the listener standing at the very threshold of the Judgment Hall. Even Dylan was afraid he might have gone too far. As he told fellow Christian rock star Bono in 1984, discussing these songs, "I didn't like writing them. I didn't want to write them." But write them he did, as he prepared himself for "the day of the Lord," as foretold in Revelation.

Indisputably, he now believed in a literal Judgment Day, and some time soon. As he told one Toronto crowd of potential converts, "In the Bible it tells you specific things and in the Book of Daniel, and in the Book of Revelation, which just might apply to these times here. And it says certain wars are gonna, soon gonna happen. I can't say exactly when, but pretty soon. Anyway . . . I been reading all kinds of books my whole life, magazines, books, whatever I could get my hands on, anywhere, and I never found any truth in any of them . . . But these things in the Bible they seem to uplift me and tell me the Truth" (April 20, 1980).

"When He Returns" again relies on blending elements from the New Testament to construct a compelling litany of what awaits one and all "when He returns." More of a mosaic than the other *Slow Train Coming* songs, the biblical parallels can be found at every turn. Bookended by two allusions to St. John the Divine, it portrays the Messiah as a Davidic avenger, bent on retribution and judgment. When Dylan sings of a rod of iron that no iron hand can match, he is taking Revelation at its judgmental word: "Out of his mouth goeth a sharp sword, that with it he should smite the nations: and he shall rule them with a rod of iron" (19:15).

By the second verse he has resumed leafing through Matthew (perhaps after a quick listen to "Restless Farewell"): "Truth is an arrow, and the gate is narrow, that it passes through / He unleashed his power at an unknown hour that no one knew" is his way of reminding us of "that day and hour [of which] knoweth no man, no, not the angels of heaven, but my Father only" (24:36), knowing full well the path to salvation is not so easy to follow "Because strait is the gate, and narrow is the way, which leadeth unto life, and few there be that find it" (7:14). A contrite Dylan portrays his former self as "drunk on fear out in the wilderness," for he too has known temptation.

In the third and final verse, we are back at the Judgment Hall, where "four and twenty elders fall down before him that sat on the throne, and worship him that liveth for ever and ever, and cast their crowns before the throne" (Revelation 4:10). Dylan transmutes these elders' obeisances into something positively Shakespearean—"Surrender your crown on this blood-stained ground, take off your mask"—before revealing the machinations of Man in all their innate futility: "Of every earthly plan that be known to man, He is unconcerned / He's got plans of His own, to set up His throne / When He returns." It is as stark and uncompromising a message as the one St. John the Divine delivered, nineteen centuries earlier. And just as poetic.

Getting the right setting for such a song, though, proved as much of a challenge as its composition. The *Rolling Stone* review of the album reported producer Jerry Wexler as remembering, "It was Dylan's intention not to sing on the song at all, rather it was to be a lead ensemble by the otherwise backup female singers. [Barry] Beckett's piano track was an ad-lib accompaniment to a vocal Dylan had made as a demo for the singers to use while rehearsing. Ultimately, however, Dylan abandoned his original notion, and after practising overnight, redid his vocal to fit the demo's spontaneous piano track."

The track sheets do not entirely tally with Wexler's account. They confirm that the first take, recorded on May 4, was "w/ band," though whether he had already turned the song over to the girls has not been documented. It seems unlikely that Dylan would have attempted to overdub a vocal to a prerecorded piano track, especially when the pianist in question, doubling as recording engineer, was to hand. More likely, he decided the "band" version did not work, for whatever reason, and elected to replicate the stark demo instead. It still took a few takes for Dylan to warm up the ol' vocal cords; but when he did, the divine spirit made its presence known, Dylan delivering a God-given performance of searing intensity. After all that Shoalsian slickness, it was a welcome reminder of the vocal power that was part and parcel of this higher calling.

Nor was it a fluke, as proven when Dylan performed it night after night between November 1, 1979, and April 20, 1980, invariably to a standing ovation. Its penultimate performance the last night in Toronto, for the benefit of a professional film crew, is no less intense than the first, beads of sweat pouring off the man as he puts mankind's choice in another New Testament nutshell. Yet he then decided to drop such a tour de force; one of those mysterious things. However, it got a single encore eighteen months later in Cincinnati. Unfinished business, perhaps (the religious tour had stopped just short of the city in May 1980). By then, any attempt at "preaching the gospel from place to place" had run its course and the gesture was lost on the arena crowd, mostly there to see the same man they'd seen three years earlier.

{389} SAVING GRACE

Published lyric/s: Lyrics 85; Lyrics 04.
First known performance: Warfield Theatre, San Francisco, November 1, 1979.
Known studio recordings: Muscle Shoals, Sheffield, AL, February 13, 1980—4 takes [SAV].

> For by grace are ye saved through faith; and that not of yourselves: it is the gift of God. —Ephesians 2:8

Normally, one would expect a songwriting respite on Dylan's part after recording an album—even one that came together as quickly as *Slow Train Coming*. But that LP never came close to completing what he now felt inspired to say. In his mind, he had barely begun his Bible-based expositions. Initially, the *Saved* songs took up where two of the more successful songs on *Slow Train*—"I Believe in You" and "Precious Angel"—left off, rejoicing in the radiance of redemption.

The first of the *Saved* songs he composed, "Saving Grace That's Over Me" (as it was originally copyrighted), was written by early September, when it was registered with half a dozen former collaborations with Helena Springs. Given that he was still putting together a touring band, one wonders what recording was used for the purpose of copyrighting. A solo demo, à la "When He Returns"?!

Here was a very personal prayer of gratitude in song and proof he hadn't stopped writing exquisite melodies to assuage the bluntness of his message to mankind. That underlying message had changed little in the passage from the pre-school "I Believe in You" to the more Scriptural material he was now writing. After all, as he told Scott Cohen six years later, "What I learned in Bible school was just another side of an extension of the same thing I believed in all along, but just couldn't verbalize or articulate."

Having become an increasingly articulate advocate for the word of God (and the Vineyard creed), he was becoming quite adept at assimilating the received word into his message songs. A couplet like "The Devil's shining light, it can be most blinding / But to search for love, that ain't no more than vanity" has the authentic Dylan ring (the second line could come straight from a *Street-Legal* song), yet fully reflects its New Testament subtext, that constant bedside companion 2 Corinthians: "For such are false apostles, deceitful workers, transforming themselves into the apostles of Christ. And no marvel; for Satan himself is transformed into an angel of light" (11:13–14).

"Saving Grace" even contains a remarkable passage where Dylan considers his own damnation: "Well, the death of life, then comes the resurrection, / Wherever I am welcome is where I will be, / I put all my confidence in Him, my sole protection / Is the saving grace that's over me." Having been taught to believe in "salvation by faith," presumably at Reseda, Dylan insists he will not take the "gift of God"—eternal life—for granted. A thankful Dylan firmly believed that only "by grace are ye saved," and song was the one way he knew how to truly express the sincerity of his newfound faith.

Singing it with all the grace notes he could muster, he delivered the good news nightly throughout six months' worth of shows beginning November 1, designed to "preach the gospel from place to place." No longer does he sound like a man who believes he will soon "be sleeping in a pine box for all eternity." Sandwiched between "Solid Rock" and the raucous "Saved," "Saving Grace" is the musical equivalent of Jesus' calming of the waters. Sadly, the same cannot be said for the live performances it received a quarter of a century later, in 2003–5, when the symbolism of the gesture was profoundly significant, but the performances themselves were almost uniformly wretched.

{390} STAND BY FAITH

Published lyric/s: [Words Fill My Head]
Known studio recordings: ?Rundown Studios, Santa Monica, CA, September 1979.

> Because of unbelief they were broken off, and thou standest by faith.
> —Romans 11:20

As a prelude to a resumption of performing, now needing enough scripturally sound songs for a full evening's entertainment, Dylan wrote and copyrighted an album's worth of brand new songs that continued down the same path. Of these, five songs were copyrighted in mid-November 1979 (songs #389–93), presumably from rehearsal versions recorded at Rundown.[9.] Two of them were apparently intended simply as performance pieces: "Stand by Faith" and "Blessed Is the Name," though only the latter made it into the set.

And yet Dylan made a number of references to standing by faith at the shows, along the lines of, "When Jesus did go to the cross, he did defeat the devil. We know this. We know this is true, and we believe it, and we stand on that faith" (Santa Monica, November 20, 1979). Six months later, at a show in Hartford, he got worked up when the audience refused to testify: "The Bible says, 'Resist the devil and the devil will flee.' You gotta stand to resist him. How we got to stand? Anybody know how to stand? You listening to me? Do you understand, you gotta stand. Anybody know how? We gotta stand here, and come back tomorrow night. Oh mercy!" He also reiterated this stance to the one radio DJ who got an interview out of him at this troubled time: "These things have just been shown to me and I'll stand on that faith . . . I know they're true." And yet, the song itself—a simplistic call-and-answer affair ("how shall we move/see/love/stand/walk, / By faith, by faith, oh Lord")—steadfastly failed to appear in any of the shows.

{391} BLESSED IS THE NAME

Published lyric/s: In His Own Write [*revised 1980 edition*].
First known performance: Warfield Theatre, San Francisco, November 1, 1979.

> Blessed be the name of God for ever and ever: for wisdom and might are his.
> —Daniel 2:20

"Blessed Is the Name" is the one song Dylan sang nightly at the three months of shows which preceded the *Saved* sessions that was not then recorded in the studio, though it was copyrighted—and to Dylan, not "Trad. Arr. Dylan." Even though there had been a well-known song of the same title and same chorus (the above extract from Daniel versified) since at least the middle of the nineteenth century, when it appeared in a sacred cantata called *Daniel, or the Captivity and Restoration.*

The verses, however, were all Dylan's work. And though they generally abstained from direct biblical quotation, they retained the now familiar element of fire 'n' brimstone, with him singing about the Lord bringing "judgment to all His faithful," just as He once had to Sodom and Gomorrah. The final verse even explicates the nature of the Judgment to come, and the fate of those who disbelieve: "Well, He made a wave on the ocean, and He's got His own timeclock / But he will not sell His glory, and He will not be mocked." It turns out he was only warming up for "Are You Ready?" against which "Blessed Is the Name" comes across as little more than a nursery rhyme.

{392} COVENANT WOMAN

Published lyric/s: Lyrics 85; Lyrics 04.
First known performance: Warfield Theatre, San Francisco, November 1, 1979.
Known studio recordings: Muscle Shoals, Sheffield, AL, February 11, 1980—11
takes; February 15, 1980 [SAV].

> Behold, the days come, saith the Lord, that I will make a new covenant
> with the house of Israel, and with the house of Judah. —Jeremiah 31:31

The covenant Dylan alludes to in the title of this song and on the inner sleeve to *Saved* is not the one made with Moses and his people, "which . . . covenant they brake, although I was an husband to them, saith the Lord" (Jeremiah 31:32). It was a second covenant, after the big J agreed to "forgive their iniquity, and . . . remember their sin no more" (31:34). However, said covenant now had a few strings attached: "I will not turn away from them, to do them good; but I will put my fear in their hearts, that they shall not depart from me" (32:40).

It was this covenant that first drew Dylan to change his way of thinking. By December 1978, he was quoting the above verse in "Tangled Up in Blue." And the fact that it was emblazoned across the inner sleeve of *Saved* bespeaks a quite personal relevance. This covenant provided the specific bond which also tied Dylan to his precious angel. It was a bond he had been looking for long before finding Christ. As he told Julia Orange in January 1978, "Two people who are in love can't be just in love with each other. There has to be a third element, an ideal. They both must love and share the same ideal . . . [Otherwise it's] not love, that's need."

Now both partners had "a contract with the Lord." "Covenant Woman," a reaffirmation of his "Precious Angel," fuses faith to that more familiar terrain, the love song, even as Dylan imbues his righteous gal with Christlike qualities. When he offers "to stay closer than any friend," s/he knows that "there is a friend that sticketh closer than a brother" (Proverbs 18:24)—the Lord. More contentiously, in its original guise Dylan credited the lady with "see[ing] all the invisible things of Him that are hidden from the world." But by the time he recorded the song, he had changed the line to "knows all the secret things of me," losing the sense that they have a relationship with the Lord first and each other second, and diminishing any allusion to the prophetic powers of Daniel, to whom "He revealeth the deep and secret things . . . what is in the darkness, and the light [that] dwelleth with him" (2:22).

One wonders if Dylan had run the song by the pastor, Larry Myers—who, according to Ken Gulliksen, was "often the backboard for Bob to share the lyrics." If the original line credited her with divinatory powers, the rewrite preferred to contrast the two converts" intimacy-in-faith with their perceived relationship to the temporal world. "We are strangers in a land we're passing through" is both a reference to that Carter Family favorite "I Can't Feel at Home in This World Anymore" and to the chapter in Hebrews regarding forefathers who "confessed that they were strangers and pilgrims on the earth" (11:13).

Even more powerful was Dylan's imagery in the second verse. Having "been broken, shattered like an empty cup," he finds himself "just waiting on the Lord to rebuild and fill me up." Conceiving of himself as a mere vessel into which the spirit of the Lord may be poured, he demonstrates an awareness of the symbolism inherent in the true teachings of Christ. And by making the Lord "faithful and . . . true" he reaffirms the nature of the contract.

"Covenant Woman" proved to be a rather delicate flower. Once plucked as a performance piece, its fragile hue began to fade real quick. It was *the* highlight of the November 1979 shows but rapidly wilted upon its removal from its homegrown vineyard. By the time Dylan came to the *Saved* sessions, in mid-February 1980, any sense of intimacy had all but gone. As with the previous album, Dylan spent the whole of the first day at Muscle Shoals working on the most intensely personal of the songs he planned to record. Despite three months spent performing it on the road, "Covenant Woman" required three three-hour sessions before take nine was pulled to the master reel, this version forming part of the original album sequence, only to be removed when Dylan and Wexler decided to resequence the album and rerecord two songs.

On February 15, five days after they began the recording process, Dylan recorded the same song again and somehow managed to remove more layers of subtlety from it. Amid stories in the press that he had been seen buying an engagement ring (presumably) for his spiritual soul mate, he made the contract with "her" song null and void, dropping it from the set. By November 1980, "Covenant Woman" was gone for good, at almost the exact same moment he dispensed with "Precious Angel." In their place were "Caribbean Wind" and "Groom's Still Waiting at the Altar."

{393} IN THE GARDEN

Published lyric/s: Lyrics 85; Lyrics 04.
First known performance: Warfield Theatre, San Francisco, November 1, 1979.
Known studio recordings: Muscle Shoals, Sheffield, AL, February 14, 1980—4 takes [SAV].

> Being born again, not of corruptible seed, but of incorruptible, by the word of God, which liveth and abideth for ever. —1 Peter 1:23

> Being born again is a hard thing . . . We don't like to lose those old attitudes and hang-ups . . . You're reborn, but like a baby. A baby doesn't know anything about this world . . . You're a stranger. You have to learn all over again. —Dylan, to Karen Hughes, May 1980

When Dylan decided to write at entire song around the arrest and execution of Jesus, one might assume he would base it on the account in his favorite gospel, Matthew. In fact, "In the Garden" generally draws its version of events from John, the least historically reliable of the canonical gospels, and the one text not drawn from an otherwise common Aramaic source (the so-called Q). Not that Dylan was very interested in redrafting history. He was writing a parable in song, as a pre-song rap at the penultimate Santa Monica gig in November makes clear:

> You know, when Jesus was in the Garden, [and] they came to get him, Peter, who was one of his men there with him . . . took out his sword and he cut this man's ear off, when he came in to get Jesus, and Jesus says "Hold it Peter . . . Don't you think that if I pray to my father, he would give me twelve legions of angels to take care of this matter. This cup that's coming to me, I must drink it." (November 20, 1979)

These "twelve legions of angels" show that Dylan was still inclined to consult Matthew, in which Jesus reportedly said, "Thinkest thou that I cannot now pray to my father, and he shall presently give me more than twelve legions of angels?" (26:53) In John's account Jesus merely says to Peter, "Put up thy sword into the sheath: the cup which my Father hath given me, shall I not drink it?" (18:11) Where he draws exclusively on John is in Jesus' meeting with a Pharisee called Nicodemus—because it is his gospel alone which uses the expression "born again." Dylan presents his case with all the balladic skill he can muster:

> Nicodemus he came at night, so he wouldn't be seen by men,
> Saying, "Master, tell me why a man must be born again?"

Though Jesus never replies to the question in the song—which is essentially a series of rhetorical questions—he answered it at length in John: "Except a man be born again, he cannot see the kingdom of God . . . I say unto thee, Except a man be born of water and of the Spirit, he cannot enter into the kingdom of God. That which is born of the flesh is flesh; and that which is born of the Spirit is spirit" (3:3, 5–6). Dylan provided his own glossary to this quote when interviewed by Dave Herman in July 1981: "What they mean by [that] saying . . . is that they're born again by the spirit from above. Born once is born with the spirit from below. Which, when you're born, is the spirit that you're born with. Born again is born with the spirit from above, which is a little bit different." (At the time, "In the Garden" was still the set closer at every show, this being the only time Dylan used the expression "born again" in a song of his own.)

His reliance on John's account of Jesus' betrayal and arrest continues through the third verse, when he telescopes ten verses of said gospel into just two lines: "Pick up thy bed and walk, why must you criticize? / Same thing My Father do, I can do likewise." Jesus had in fact directed a cripple to "rise, take up thy bed, and walk" (5:8), prompting a mob to seek "to slay him, because he had done these things on the sabbath day." In response, He provocatively equates Himself with the Father, though not in quite the unequivocal way the singer claims on His behalf. Dylan trims Jesus' retort, "The Son can do nothing of himself, but what he seeth the Father do: for what things soever he doeth, these also doeth the Son likewise" (5:19) down to the nuance-free "Same thing my Father do, I can do likewise."

Then he cleverly segues from one mob wanting to slay Him, to "the multitude want[ing] to make Him king, put a crown upon His Head." As he reminded one April 1980 Albany audience, "When Jesus walked into Jerusalem, all the people there, shouting, went off and broke branches off the trees. 'Hail! Hail! The King is coming.' . . . They worshipped and bowed down. But, you know, it's the same people who did that who shouted to crucify him." Again, it is John who provides the textual backdrop for Jesus' refusal of the proffered crown: "When Jesus therefore perceived that they would come and take him by force, to make him a king, he departed again" (6:15).

Only in the final verse, when Christ rises from the grave, does Dylan return to Matthew for the turn of phrase he requires: "When they saw him, they worshipped him: but some doubted. And Jesus came and spake unto them, saying, All power is given unto me in heaven and in earth" (28:17–18). Thus the song culminates with a thrice-repeated thud of rhetorical righteousness: "When He rose from the dead, did they believe?"

"In the Garden" was not only one of eight new songs Dylan debuted the opening night at San Francisco's Warfield Theatre (November 1, 1979) but proved to be (by a long chalk) the last song preaching salvation to pass from the regular live set. Save for the European 1984 tour, when the conversion era was all but wiped from the record, it would remain a feature on every major tour up to the G. E. Smith era. It was also the song with which Dylan chose to open his 1986 HBO *Hard to Handle* TV special, prefacing it with a pointed pre-song rap, "This last song now is all about my hero. . ."

Of all the songs from this period, "In the Garden" remains the most incontestably inspired by the gospels, providing a crash course in Christ's own teachings not necessarily found in the more apocalyptic songs. Its continued inclusion in concert argued against the slide into apostasy that friends like Allen Ginsberg claimed on his behalf (a point I once made rather forcefully to the great poet). Ironically, it was also a song which Ginsberg himself may have unwittingly inspired, at least melodically. As he told *Goldmine* in 1989, "I think I invented the chord-change in 'In the Garden.' We went around trick-or-treating in Zuma Beach in masks, and I had my harmonium, and I was playing a funny ascending chord thing, where you just move one finger at a time." Sure enough, Dylan ended up using that ascending chord in "In the Garden," which he composed almost two years to the day after their Halloween outing.

{394} PRESSING ON

Published lyric/s: Lyrics 85; Lyrics 04.
First known performance: Warfield Theatre, San Francisco, November 1, 1979.
Known studio recordings: Muscle Shoals, Sheffield, AL, February 13, 1980—9 takes [SAV].

> This one thing I do, forgetting those things which are behind, and reaching forth unto those things which are before, I press toward the mark for the prize of the high calling of God in Christ Jesus. —Philippians 3:13–14

> I believe that ever since Adam and Eve got thrown out of the garden that the whole nature of the planet has been heading in one direction— towards Apocalypse. It's all there in the Book of Revelation. —Dylan, to Mick Brown, 1984

"Pressing On"—on the face of it one of the more straightforward songs of salvation written to counterbalance the *Slow Train Coming* songs in concert—comprises just two verses and a burden which just repeats the song's full title, "Pressing on to the higher calling of my Lord." But again Dylan draws on myriad ideas from both New and Old Testaments.

The first verse is largely built around another confrontation between the Pharisees and Jesus, after they tried to trick Him into an act of blasphemy by asking, "What sign shewest thou then, that we may see [a miracle], and believe thee?" (John 6:30) Dylan for once places himself in Jesus' shoes, knowing full well "many try to stop me, shake me up in my mind." However, he reserves the real mantra for the second verse, where he discourses on "original sin" in terms that take us from Genesis to Revelation, from second- to third- to first-person:

> Shake the dust off of your feet, don't look back,
> Nothing now can hold you down, nothing that you lack,
> Temptation not an easy thing, Adam given the devil reign,
> 'Cause he sinned I got no choice, it run in my vein.

The image with which Dylan opens the second verse alludes to the judgment to come, deriving from Jesus' instructions to his disciples when sent to spread the word, "Whosoever shall not receive you, nor hear you, when ye depart thence, shake off the dust under your feet for a testimony against them. [For] I say unto you, It shall be more tolerable for Sodom and Gomorrah in the day of judgment, than for that city" (Mark 6:11).

Dylan also draws a line from Adam via Satan, the tempter and tormenter of mankind, to Jesus, and then to Christ returned. As he said before singing "Saved," one night in Buffalo, "Satan is called the God of Self. He's the defeated foe. But there really isn't any self, it's just a big bluff. So if you're a descendant of Adam . . . anybody here descended from Adam? Well, Adam gave those keys over you. And Jesus Christ went to the cross and took those keys back" (May 1, 1980). He certainly continued to believe man was born into sin. As late as 1985 he told Bill Flanagan, "People seem to think that because their sins are different from other people's sins, they're not sinners . . . Most people walking around have this strange conception that they're born good . . . I have another point of view." The twin themes of sinfulness and judgment appear also in an additional verse the song had at its first two performances:

> Well, you know them episodes when you meet with the Beast
> He always comes at you at times that you expect it least
> And we know that he is responsible for death and pain and loss
> But we know we have victory by Him going on the cross.

This time it was Romans Dylan had been ransacking, wherein one finds, "By one man [Adam], sin entered into the world, and death by sin; and so death passed upon all men, for that all have sinned . . . [But] as sin hath reigned unto death, even so might grace reign through righteousness unto eternal life by Jesus Christ our Lord" (5:12, 5:21). The song was presumably originally copyrighted with said verse (from a rehearsal recording, I guess), but it was soon deemed surplus to requirements for a second encore that even agnostic members of audiences could hum.

On *Saved* itself, Dylan found a far more convincing way to convey his message, building the song in increments on the bedrock of a bevy of backing singers, who press on all the way to the end. It would be the standout track on the album, opening side two in feverish fashion. But by the time the album appeared he had decided to look back, after all, dropping the song from the live set in favor of an acoustic oldie from a former calling. It did not return.

{395} SAVED

Published lyric/s: Lyrics 85; Lyrics 04.
First known performance: Warfield Theatre, San Francisco, November 1, 1979.
Known studio recordings: Muscle Shoals, Sheffield, AL, February 12, 1980—3 takes; February 15, 1980 [SAV].

> Ye were not redeemed with corruptible things . . . but with the precious blood of Christ, as of a lamb without blemish and without spot. —1 Peter 1:18–19

Though the bulk of the *Saved* songs were copyrighted on November 13, 1979, three songs—"Saved," "Solid Rock," and "What Can I Do for You?"—would not be registered for another fifteen days, suggesting they were actually written during rehearsals for the West Coast tour, to create an entire set comprising songs "given to me by the Lord to sing." Dylan was quite clear about this one thing. As he told a TV interviewer the following spring, "The old stuff's not gonna save them . . . They can boogie all night, but it's not gonna work."

Well, "Saved" continued where "Pressing On" left off, in a state of original sin: "I was blinded by the devil, born already ruined / Stone-cold dead, as I stepped out of the womb," as the songwriter embraces the sentiments of both Psalm 51:5, "Behold, I was shapen in iniquity; and in sin did my mother conceive me" and 2 Corinthians 4:4, "The god of this world hath blinded the minds of them which believe not." New to such intense feelings, Dylan introduced the song at the final Warfield show with a simple profession of faith: "You know Satan's called the God of this world, that's true, and it's such a wonderful feeling when you've been delivered from that." The November 16 version is that glorious gladness personified.

For those who still wondered what Dylan had been saved from, the second verse spelled it out: "He bought me with a price, freed me from the pit / Full of emptiness and wrath, and the fire that burns in it." The pit in question had already been vividly described by St. John the Divine: "And he opened the bottomless pit; and there arose a smoke out of the pit, as the smoke of a great furnace; and the sun and the air were darkened by reason of the smoke of the pit" (Revelation 9:2). Thankfully, the singer himself "by His mercy" had been spared. No wonder he was "glad, so glad."

Just like "Blessed Is the Name" and "Pressing On," "Saved" was another song that worked best in its element, a revivalist meeting disguised as a Bob Dylan concert. Capturing that spirit in the studio was bound to be problematic. Although recorded in a couple of takes (and a false start) on the second day of the *Saved* sessions (February 12), producer Jerry Wexler told *Rolling Stone*, "On the fifth day, we re-examined everything we'd done and wound up recutting two songs . . . 'Covenant Woman' and 'Saved' . . . It was pretty much Bob's instinct to redo them."

It would appear Dylan did "short-list" two versions of "Saved"—as he had with two of the songs on *John Wesley Harding* many moons ago. In the end, the LP version was the one recorded on the fifteenth, as Wexler accurately recalled a matter of months later. Even here, though, Dylan struggled to convey the impact of his own conversion experience with the same immediacy he managed back in San Francisco. The song held its own in the live set until the European 1981 tour, opening most mainland shows before the gladness faded, and the singer resumed his search for a shot of love.

Note: Two versions of the same take were assigned to the eight-track master (yes, they really were still making eight-track cartridges in 1980), but with two distinctly different timings, neither an exact match with the album version (one is 3:42, the other is 4:29, spread across two of the cartridge's four bands—the one on *Saved* clocks in at 4:01), making for one of the oddest anomalies in Dylan's official catalog.

{396} SOLID ROCK

Published lyric/s: Lyrics 85; Lyrics 04.
First known performance: Warfield Theatre, San Francisco, November 1, 1979.
Known studio recordings: Muscle Shoals, Sheffield, AL, February 12, 1980—7 takes [SAV].

> According as he hath chosen us in him before the foundation of the world, that we should be holy and without blame before him in love.
> —Ephesians 1:4

"Hanging on to a Solid Rock"—as it was first copyrighted—was another song conceived only after Dylan knew the kind of band he would have at his disposal in concert. An up-tempo rocker, befitting its title, the song was frequently prefaced in concert by the singer explaining the meaning of the title: "Jesus Christ is that solid rock. He's supposed to come two times. He came once already . . . What you're gonna need is something strong to hang on to. You got drugs to hang on to now. You might have a job to hang on to now. You might have your college education to hang on to now. But you're gonna need something very solid to hang on to when these days come" (November 26, 1979).

Without question, here was another song about the End Times. And this time he was unequivocally stating that the end had been coming since "the foundation of the world," as foretold by Jesus in an account of the Sermon on the Mount unique to Matthew's gospel: "Then shall the King say unto them on his right hand, Come, ye blessed of my Father, inherit the kingdom prepared for you from the foundation of the world" (25:34). By being "rejected by a world that He created," he also fulfilled a prophecy dating back to the book of Isaiah: "Despised and rejected of men; a man of sorrows, and acquainted with grief . . . he hath borne our griefs, and carried our sorrows: yet we did esteem him stricken, smitten of God, and afflicted. But he was wounded for our transgressions, he was bruised for our iniquities" (53:3–5).

But the Son of Man would be returning as an avenging King. This messianic figure, the resurrected Christ, would be the one solid rock in the troubled times to come. Like father, like son, he "is the Rock, his work is perfect: for all his ways are judgment: a God of truth and without iniquity, just and right is he" (Deuteronomy 32:4). And He was coming back to remind us "all things . . . that are in heaven, and that are in earth, visible and invisible, whether they be thrones, or dominions, or principalities, or powers: all things were created by him, and for him" (Colossians 1:16). This carrot and stick approach was also adopted by Dylan the disciple, who occasionally prefaced the song with a warning which was a couple of times longer than the song. Usually, though, he was content to let the song itself spell it out:

> Nations are angry, cursed are some,
> People are expectin' a false peace to come.
> But I'm hanging on to a solid rock.

Again, Revelation served as Dylan's guide when condensing the End Times St. John prophesized into a few haranguing lines of his own. (The original chapter reads: "And the nations were angry, and thy wrath is come, and the time of the dead, that they should be judged, and that thou shouldest give reward unto thy servants the prophets, and to the saints, and them that fear thy name, small and great" [11:18].)

Just a year after he told one American journalist, "Being faithful to an idea . . . it's illusory. You're always grasping [at] it . . . but even when you get hold of it you don't have anything," Dylan felt he had genuinely found something worth hanging on to. Another song that worked especially well in concert—particularly early on, when he allowed it that little breathing space in midsong to build up a head of steam—"Solid Rock" live invariably transcended the anaemic version released on *Saved*. It remained in the set through 1981, though his response to fans just getting off on the music, and not hearing the message, was to slow the song down to a gelatinous groove in the fall of 1981, confirmation that he was losing his grip on such intentionally salutary material.

{397} WHAT CAN I DO FOR YOU?

Published lyric/s: Lyrics 85; Lyrics 04.

First known performance: Warfield Theatre, San Francisco, November 1, 1979.

Known studio recordings: Muscle Shoals, Sheffield, AL, February 12, 1980—2 takes [SAV].

Yet man is born unto trouble, as the sparks fly upward. —Job 5:7

"What Can I Do for You?" necessarily reintroduced the twin themes of humility and supplication to the fall 1979/winter 1980 shows, Dylan working himself up to the redemptive nightly finale of "In the Garden," "Blessed Is the Name," and "Pressing On." And as long as it retained said sense of contrition, it successfully conveyed the passage from belief to grace to gratitude. Since he invariably capped it off with a harmonica solo that soared to the gods, the strength of his conviction was all too plain to hear.

Another seemingly simple incantation to the Lord, "What Can I Do for You?" again demonstrated the care with which Dylan now crafted his Bible-based imagery. The line "I know all about fiery darts" sounds like one of those Dylanesque aphorisms, but Ephesians reveals their true identity: "Above all, taking the shield of faith, wherewith ye shall be able to quench all the fiery darts of the wicked" (6:16). Likewise, the opening lines of verse two, "Soon as a man is born, you know the sparks begin to fly / He gets wise in his own eyes" synthesize the verse from Job above with a warning found in Proverbs, "Be not wise in thine own eyes: fear the Lord, and depart from evil" (3:7). And when he thanks the Lord for opening "up a door no man can shut," it is because he has been trawling Revelation again, to find Christ telling believers, "Behold, I have set before thee an open door, and no man can shut it: for thou . . . hast not denied my name" (3:8).

One can't help but respond to the affecting humility with which Dylan pleads "What can I do for You?" at the end of every verse and chorus, leading up to the moment he sings, "Well, I don't deserve it, but I'm sure to make it through / What can I do for you?" at song's end. However, by the time he reached Muscle Shoals in mid-February 1980, he felt he had already got where he needed to go, changing that sincere supplication into "I don't deserve it, but I sure *did* make it through." As Paul Williams observed, it now read like he made the right bet. And though the song's live self survived to 1981, as of November 1980 he was no longer raising the rafters with a holy harmonica. By July 1981, pride had again put its foot down and another song of salvation bit the dust.

{398} ARE YOU READY?

Published lyric/s: Lyrics 85; Lyrics 04.
First known performance: Charleston, WV, February 8, 1980.
Known studio recordings: Muscle Shoals, Sheffield, AL, February 14, 1980—9 takes [SAV].

> Be ye therefore ready also: for the Son of man cometh at an hour when ye think not. —Luke 12:40

> Preaching would be an extension of what I am and what I do and the music I play. —Dylan, to Denise Worrell, 1985

As Dylan continued preaching about the imminence of Armageddon, he worked himself into quite a lather at some of the fall 1979 shows. On the resumption of touring in the winter of 1980, he transferred these feelings back into the songs, which continued to burn with a righteous fury. However, it took until early February before he wrote the born-again equivalent of "Positively Fourth Street." "Are You Ready?" was a righteous retort to the disbelieving students of Arizona and Albuquerque, New Mexico—an open letter to those who seemed content to "rock & roll all the way down to the pit" (see my account in *Behind the Shades 2*, pages 516–19).

And this time, he drew on just about every apocalyptic text he could lay his hands on. From Isaiah, he took "Therefore shall evil come upon thee; thou shalt not know from whence it riseth: and mischief shall fall upon thee; thou shalt not be able to put it off: and desolation shall come upon thee suddenly, which thou shalt not know" (47:11). In his hands, this became an unanswerable question directed foursquare at America's budding intellectuals: "When destruction cometh swiftly . . . have you decided whether you want to be / in heaven or in hell?" Having already told the faithless folk in Tempe "Every knee shall bow!" he had added to the armory of questions he wanted *them* to answer:

> Are you ready to meet Jesus? Are you where you ought to be?
> Will He know you when He sees you, or will He say, "Depart from Me"?

If it was from Revelation he took the admonishment, "Repent; or else I will come unto thee quickly" (2:16), Joel asked the kind of question which further fueled "Are You Ready?": "The Lord shall utter his voice before his army . . . for the day of the Lord is great and very terrible; and who can abide it?" (2:11) Matthew also continued to provide Dylan with some of Jesus' better lines, including: "I profess unto them, I never knew you: depart from me, ye that work iniquity" (7:23).

Introduced into the set at the last two of the winter shows, "Are You Ready?" transferred easily enough to tape at the penultimate *Saved* session, less than a week later. However, putting it last on *Saved*—as Dylan presumably always intended—only drew unkind comparisons to the previous album closer, the superlative "When He Returns." Though the song stayed as second encore through the spring, its sentiments continued to raise more questions than he could answer. It appeared just once more, at a Halloween 1981 show in Kitchener, Ontario, probably as a request from someone who felt "ready for Armageddon."

{399} BE THAT WAY

Known studio recordings: Muscle Shoals, Sheffield, AL, February 14, 1980.

It may not qualify as "the revelation of [a] mystery . . . kept secret since the world began" (Romans 16:25), but it would still be awfully nice to know the identity of "Be That Way." Clearly listed in the Sony database as the last song recorded at the penultimate *Saved* session, according to Krogsgaard it does not exist. Instead, he lists an unknown song at the end of the previous day's session, which according to the session logs required just a single false start and a single full take to complete. These two may well be one and the same. Whatever the case, there would appear to be an undocumented song from the *Saved* sessions, even if "Be That Way" is not its actual title. (Dylan rehearsed a song called "Show

Me the Way" in October 1980—perhaps a reworking of the spiritual in John Work's *American Negro Songs and Spirituals* [1940].)

{400} I WILL LOVE HIM

First known performance: Massey Hall, Toronto, April 19, 1980.

One of at least three new songs Dylan worked on at the soundchecks to a week's worth of shows in Toronto and Montreal in April 1980,[10] "I Will Love Him" is the last of the expressly devotional songs written while preaching the gospel from place to place. A perfect encore song, it was performed just once, though thankfully it was at a show where a mobile truck and a camera crew were at the ready. Sitting at the piano, Dylan commits himself—and his gaggle of girl singers—to "love Him . . . serve Him . . . glorify His name," during what he calls "the latter days."

This song shows someone who continued seeing Revelation through the prism of Hal Lindsey's eschatological rantings. Taking a leaf from *The Late Great Planet Earth* chapter 4, "Israel O Israel," he sees the reestablishment of Israel on May 14, 1948, as the fulfilment of St. John's prophecies, assuring fellow believers that "when victory is looming, He will be at the gate / ['Cause] He was talking about the state of Israel in 1948." For the first time in song, he is citing the same timetable he had been using in pre-song raps to instruct us that "The time is near." Thankfully, within a matter of months, the apocalypse had been postponed, and although Dylan continued to "glorify His name," he was no longer so convinced the time was nigh.

{401} COVER DOWN BREAK THROUGH
{402} AIN'T GONNA GO TO HELL FOR ANYBODY

Published lyric [#401]: Words Fill My Head.
Published lyric/s [#402]: The Telegraph #5. *[Late 1980 version: Words Fill My Head.]*
First known performance/s: Massey Hall, Toronto, April 17, 1980.

> Press on toward what is ahead. I . . . will pray for strength and more strength for ya—always—in the name of Jesus Christ, Son of God, manifest in the flesh. —letter from Bob Dylan to a fellow believer, late April 1980

If "I Will Love Him" marked the end of one era, then the next two songs (#401–2) mark the transition to a new phase, in which the Bible remained a perpetual lyrical backdrop but any message was expressed in Dylan's words, not the scriptures." Not that either "Cover Down" or "Ain't Gonna Go to Hell" exactly announced imminent apostasy—just a change in the angle of attack. For the length of the spring tour, i.e., thirty days and thirty nights, these two songs took over from "When He Returns," one pushing the listener to "repent and confess," the other insisting "it ain't my goal / To gain the whole world and give up my soul."

"Cover Down (Pray Through)"—copyrighted as "Cover Down Break Through," though this is *not* what Dylan sings—is the first Dylan title since "Slow Train" whose meaning is not revealed by a reading of the Good Book. Indeed, there is nothing in the song (and very little outside it) that serves to explain Dylan's use of the expression. Perhaps a single verse of scripture offers a possible source—when Jeremiah addresses an angry God in the Lamentations and says, "Thou hast covered thyself with a cloud, that our prayer should not pass through" (3:44). Given that the song's opening image describes "Pharaoh's army tramping through the mud," searching for the very Hebrew children Jeremiah is bewailing, Dylan could be singing about the power of prayer to sustain when the world comes tumbling down.

The only onstage explanation he ever gave came on opening night in Toronto (April 17), when he introduced the song as "Cover Down," then added, "Get up in the morning, you got to cover down." At a show in Syracuse, a fortnight later, after the song he inquires, "How many of you out there know what I'm talking about?" When he gets an affirmative response, he retorts, "Used to be nobody knew what I was talking about." Plus ça change, plus c'est la même chose.

The song certainly paints a sorry picture of the state of the world, before suggesting the only protection is "the full armor of the Lord / [For] the word of God is sharper than any double-sided sword." A former sinner himself, the singer knows full well that "Sins you can't even remember / Are always waiting to say hello to you there." At least he recognizes "The same spirit running in you raised Christ from the dead / If you're quick in your mortal body, then let it turn to your head" is an encouragingly Dylanesque way of reiterating the sentiments of Romans 8:11: "If the Spirit of him that raised up Jesus from the dead dwell in you, he that raised up Christ from the dead shall also quicken your mortal bodies by his Spirit that dwelleth in you."

"Cover Down" gave Dylan something to get his teeth into at these spring shows, even if the message was bespattered by all that "trampling through the mud." However, despite its appearance on a list of songs rehearsed for the fall 1980 tour, it made its last live appearance at the final spring show, on May 21, when the good gospel was the only thing on his mind.

"Ain't Gonna Go to Hell," on the other hand, not only stayed alive, but was born again at the fall shows. Having begun life as another Warning Writ Large, the song was rewritten over the summer, returning in a guise so impenetrable it made "Cover Down" read like "Saved." In its unambiguous springtime phase, Dylan sometimes prefaced the song with a crystal-clear commentary: "You know, sometimes an evil man might die, [there'd be] long limousines, on their way to the funeral. And you know the man is evil, you just know. And you know how the Minister always says, "Lord accept this man," but by that time it's too late. They try to preach him into Heaven after he's dead." He told another East Coast crowd:

> Can't let nobody take you there—['cause] misery loves company. I know that right now it's not fashionable to think about heaven and hell. I know that. But God has got no fashion, because He's always fashionable. But it's hard not to go to hell you know, there's so many distractions, so many influences, you start walking right, pretty soon there's someone out there [trying] to drag you down. As soon as you get rid of the enemy on the outside then the enemy comes inside. He got all kinds of ways.

He evidently intended to continue his fulminations against college-town audiences. That they continued to prey on his mind was demonstrated three days after debuting "Ain't Gonna Go to Hell" in Toronto, when he gave a four-minute version of the Tempe confrontation the previous November to another bemused Canadian audience.

His description of hell in the bridge certainly suggested it was a place worth avoiding:

Smoke it rises forever, on a one-way ticket to burn,
A place reserved for the devil, and for all of those who love evil,
A place of darkness and shame from which you never return.

At this juncture, almost every line suggested he had been heading hell-ward himself before seeing the light. And this time he was not hiding behind no second-person narrative when describing a man who "had the visions / but they caused divisions"; who knew full well how to "wine 'em and dine 'em / [to] try to realign 'em"; and always knew "how to do it / I've been all the way through it."

That old devil called love, the root cause of former troubles, remained ever on his mind. "I can make believe I'm in love with almost anybody," he confesses, before admitting "I been down that road, I know where it leads." Ain't gonna go there no more. And yet, for all its finger-pointing, this song does not contain a single direct biblical allusion, from a man already starting to distance himself from the Vineyard Fellowship who led him to the Lord, while still proclaiming, "I ain't gonna go to hell for anybody / Not for father, not for mother, not for sister, not for brother, no way."

By November 9, when he debuted an entirely new version of the song, the healing had begun. But he could still smell the fumes of hell. Indeed, the two elements he kept from the spring original were the chorus and the bridge (sadly, he took away the gorgeous hook he had used to open the song, with the girls singing the title phrase over and over until the message sunk in). Self-examination had gone out the window, replaced by a confused narrative of love and rejection that, could one disentangle it, might well qualify as classic Dylan (one night at the Warfield he actually warns the audience, "I don't know if you can get all the lyrics"). In there are a number of potentially juicy aphorisms: "Can't get bitten by the same thing twice"; "Keep on rolling if you're drugged, beaten or shot"; and, best of all, "I see you walking away with your legs spread apart."

Although he still prefaced the song with a spoken intro at a couple of shows, the rap was now almost as obtuse as the lyrics. In San Diego, he told the audience about a couple of newlyweds who were staying at the same hotel and "had come across all the balconies and walked into my room. With a big bottle of champagne. So I invited them down here tonight . . . I want to do this song for them, hope they have a long and happy marriage. It's called 'I Ain't Gonna Go to Hell for Anybody.'" Some wedding song. The rap probably somehow relates to the new opening, "Snowflakes falling on a crowded room, and the leaves are dying / Pulling on the river, so cold I could shiver / I can feel it on the rooftops, I see two lovers sighing . . ." But even these semi-garbled lyrics ultimately got away from him, and after considering recording the song for *Shot of Love*—it appears on a short list of "possible" songs—he changed his mind. It came from a phase he had passed beyond.

1980–1

{ Shot of Love }

Between May 21, 1980, when Dylan suspended his rolling gospel revue then crossing America, and May 15, 1981, when he concluded the sessions for Shot of Love, the songwriter wrote enough songs to fill at least three albums, while putting aside enough for another LP of instrumentals and covers. It had been half a decade since he had hit such a rich vein of writing, qualitatively as well as quantitatively. Half a dozen of these gems were fully worthy of scooping up whenever God gathered his jewels. "Every Grain of Sand," "Angelina," "Caribbean Wind," "Groom's Still Waiting at the Altar," "Yonder Comes Sin," and "In the Summertime" all showed how his quest to become a better man had made him no less of a songwriter. And yet, just the first and last of these six songs ended up gracing the single album CBS deigned to release in the summer of 1981.

Shot of Love was a pale shadow of what it could, and should, have been, because Dylan had again decided to cut the album live, in part at his own rehearsal studio in downtown Santa Monica. By the time he recognized the error of his ways and revoked his ill-conceived decision, the whole band had already been hard at work on the album for over a month. Although sessions resumed—for a further fortnight—at Clover, a favorite hangout of coproducer Chuck Plotkin, the rot had set in. Every attempt to rework songs formulated in another summertime seemed to diminish, not dimensionalize, them; and the new songs he was furiously penning to replace them—like "Dead Man Dead Man" and "Watered-Down Love"—were not really fit for purpose.

And yet, despite clear reservations about the released results, Dylan toured Europe and America promoting his new songs in concert and interview. Six *more months of rehearsing and touring—June through November—failed to galvanize him to do more than devise performance-only pieces like "Jesus Is the One" and "Thief on the Cross"; and by year's end, he had disbanded his standing band, closed his rehearsal studio, and retired to another country with backing singer Clydie King, awaiting an opportune time when he could rise again.*

{403} PROPERTY OF JESUS

Published lyric/s: Lyrics 85; Lyrics 04.
Known studio recordings: Rundown Studios, Santa Monica, CA, October 1980; Rundown Studios April 3–9, 1981; Clover Studios, LA, April 28, 1981—1 take; May 1, 1981 [SoL].

> When the songs are done right, they're done right, and that's it. They're written in stone when they're done right. —Dylan, to Jon Pareles, 1997

"Property of Jesus"—the working title of which appears to have been "Heart of Stone"—is a song that hung around a long, long time. First worked on during a set of rehearsal recordings at Rundown in late September / early October 1980, it was finally "done right" at the final set of *Shot of Love* sessions in late April 1981. Even at a time when he was scrapping many of the songs written the previous year, it managed to feature in both original and final sequence for the LP, compiled in mid-to-late May. However, it never made it to a single show, either in the fall of 1980 or 1981 (indeed, as of 2008, it remains the only song from the so-called Born Again trilogy of albums not to appear in concert).

The fact that the song does not even appear on the set list for the fall 1980 shows (see *Recording Sessions*, page 148) suggests that even after that initial recording it was still deemed a work in progress. Nor was it copyrighted with the two other songs recorded at the same time—"Caribbean Wind" and "Groom's Still Waiting"—and although the chorus remains intact from the outset ("He's the property of Jesus, resent him to the bone / You got something better, you got a heart of stone"), the lyric would remain in a state of flux. One original couplet that got cut, perhaps because it reflected back on its author, was a genuine loss:

Brag about the knowledge and experience you've [known],
Of the lonesome ways and the wasted days, and hope they'll soon be gone.

He has returned to the same citadel as "Ain't Gonna Go to Hell,"
staying there until at least 1983, when he described his former, fallen
state to a reporter thus: "You turn a deaf ear to all that can save you,
while pursuing a . . . strange mirage." "Property of Jesus" may be
another litany in song, but it is generally more sophisticated than its *Slow
Train Coming* brethren, contrasting the wisdom of the believer ("When
the whip keeping you in line doesn't make him jump") with the superfi-
ciality of many sinners' lives: "You can laugh at salvation, you can play
Olympic Games / You think that when you rest at last, you'll go back
from where you came."

In targeting those who guffawed at the very idea of salvation, Dylan
probably still had in mind "the so-called intellectual students [who]
showed their true monstrous selves" (his 1984 description of those
November 1979 college-town audiences). When asked during the
1980 Warfield residency about earlier reports of his on-stage raps, he
responded somewhat defensively, "I was saying stuff I figured people
needed to know. I thought I was giving people an idea of what was
behind the songs." He would continue to defend born-again Bob for
some time to come. As late as March 1991 he told *Spy*, "People didn't
like those [*Saved*] tunes. They rejected all that stuff. When my show
would be all off the new album people would shout, 'We want to hear
the old songs.'"

"Property of Jesus" dispensed these thoughts in such a concentrated form that he insisted on its inclusion on an album that his record
company desperately tried to market as a movement away from the cata-
strophic *Saved*—proof, were it needed, that Dylan wasn't quite ready to
let go of that fire 'n' brimstone persona just yet. The song seems to have
been attempted at least three times at the *Shot of Love* sessions, one time
in early April at Rundown and twice at Clover at the end of the month
(the second time, on May 1, possibly just for overdubs).

That Clover version proved to be one of the musical highlights of the
album, with a great percussive sound, girl singers hopped up on the Lord,
and Dylan doing his very best "Fourth Street" vocal. But the message

alone ensured the song was condemned by reviewers like Nick Kent as "feebly portray[ing] the loyal keeper of the faith [Bob himself, presumably] being derided by typical agnostic wasters." Feeble, it ain't, brother.

{404} EVERY GRAIN OF SAND

Published lyric/s: Lyrics 85; Lyrics 04.
Known studio recordings: Rundown Studios, Santa Monica, CA, September 23, 1980 [TBS]; April 29, 1981—1 take [SoL].
First known performance: Lakeland, FL, November 21, 1981.

> Sometimes you'll write a song where you'll just stick with it and get it done. You'll feel that it's not coming from any place, but it's for you to do . . . You're in an area where there isn't anybody there, and never was. So you just have to . . . not try to go one way or the other—just stay balanced and finish it. "Every Grain of Sand" is a song like that . . . There's no footnotes around . . . There's no precedent for it . . . All you know is that it's a mood piece, and you try to hold onto the mood and finish. Or . . . just get it to a place where you can let it go. —Dylan, to Bill Flanagan, 1985

The above comment to the editor of *Musician*, part of a wide-ranging conversation about songwriting, is one of Dylan's most revealing reflections on his art. Here was a song that came to him whole, and quick. In 1991, the song having been restored to live duties, he told Robert Hilburn it was a "very painless song to write. It took like twelve seconds—or that's how it felt." So inspired did he feel that it remained almost entirely unchanged, at least lyrically, in its eight-month passage from demo to album closer.

"Every Grain of Sand" was the first song he wanted to work on when he and his standing band reassembled at Rundown toward the end of September 1980, after a summer break had revived spirits and inspired Dylan. Though he had spent much of the summer sailing the Caribbean, one suspects that "Every Grain of Sand" was written on the farm in Minnesota. He had spent the early part of the summer there with his children, even catching a concert or two in the state capital. Here, he had found the same inspiration that engendered *Blood on the Tracks* and *Street-Legal*, and now, as then, he found "peace and quiet," even as his mind was in turmoil.

He alluded to his then state of mind in 1991 when discussing the song with *Songtalk*'s Paul Zollo, at a time when he was again struggling to remember how to "get it done": "['Every Grain of Sand' is] in that area where Keats is. That's a good poem set to music . . . [Yet] the simplicity of it can be . . . deceiving . . . A song like that just may have been written in great turmoil . . . Some songs are better written in peace and quiet and delivered in turmoil. Others are best written in turmoil and delivered in a peaceful, quiet way."

Again, Dylan was prepared to reveal a great deal about his intent in writing such a song, while still playing with his interrogator. Are we seriously supposed to believe that he doesn't know the difference between Keats and Blake; or that the song really comes from "that area where Keats is"? Or is this another of Dylan's famous bum steers? As just about every single commentator has observed, the song-poem is Blakean in a multitude of ways (and not just because it patently derived its title from Blake's famous observation in *Auguries of Innocence*, that he could "see a world in a grain of sand / And a heaven in a wild flower" or took some of its philosophy from *Milton*, where Blake claimed to see "the little winged fly, smaller than a grain of sand / It has a heart like thee . . . open to heaven & hell").

It is also Blakean in the sense that it works as both a song and a poem, Dylan demonstrating once and for all that *he* knows the difference. (Witness his comment to Zollo about it being "a good poem set to music.") And it was as a poem he presented it to critic and *Crawdaddy* founder Paul Williams, reading him the lyric backstage at one of the first two Warfield shows in November 1980. Suffice to say, this was not a practice he ever made into a habit, so he must have genuinely felt this one stood up on the page, no matter how much extra it gained from being set to music.

It was his "Jerusalem," bearing more of a resemblance to the "long poem" published by Blake in a large quarto, in 1804, under the punchy title: *Jerusalem: the Emanation of the Giant Albion*—wherein he suggested "there is a grain of sand . . . that Satan cannot find"—than the famous hymn of that title, itself culled from another work published the same year, *Milton: a poem in Two Books* (it did not acquire said title for another hundred years, when set to music by Sir Hubert Parry). This makes it doubly annoying that Dylan allowed it to be published so unsympathetically in *Lyrics*, where three sixteen-line stanzas have been made into six four-line stanzas, deconstructing a fractured, impressionistic narrative:

> In the time of my confession,
> In the hour of my deepest need,
> When the pool of tears beneath my feet
> Flood every newborn seed . . .

Reflecting the immediacy of its inspiration, this published lyric varies only in a couple of instances from the song demoed on September 23, 1980. One line, though, nagged away at Dylan. "I am hanging in the balance of *a perfect, finished plan*" is the way he sang it that day in September; "the reality of man" is how he sang it the following May. Neither is entirely satisfactory, in part because he is trying to commingle two separate ideas (now that is Keatsian): one, that the past, present and future of mankind had already been predetermined by our Maker; and two, that his own salvation hangs in the balance—a concept profound *and* uncanonical.

Though the book of Daniel contains the admonishment, "Thou art weighed in the balances, and art found wanting" (5:27), Dylan has stepped outside the canonical texts for his essential inspiration here. It is in 2 Esdras, part of the Jewish Apocrypha, that we find the expression, "he hath weighed the world in the balance" (4:36). It is this idea that he aims to express, not the one in Daniel. Esdras, like Revelation, was an apocalyptic text inspired by the fall of Jerusalem in AD 70, in which Ezra the scribe receives seven visions from the archangel Uriel, sent by God to answer his questions about the causes of Israel's suffering. (In concert, he has consistently fluffed this line, singing the two versions interchangeably or even intertwined, "the perfect finished of man.")

The purpose of the demo recorded that September afternoon was apparently to convince Greek chanteuse Nana Mouskouri to record the song (which she eventually did, with this original lyric). Hence, presumably, the simple piano-guitar (and barking dog) accompaniment. And though it pains me to agree with Michael Gray, I have to say that I cannot figure what all the fuss is about regarding this acoustic demo, which sounds like, well, just that.

Also cut the same day was a full band arrangement, which works a whole lot better, even if it does not appear that this version was ever considered for *The Bootleg Series Vols 1–3*, the acoustic demo being the one lodged with the music publisher. The band version represents more of an attempt to work out a full arrangement, trying to get "to a place where you can let it go." Recorded with piano, Fender Rhodes electric piano, acoustic guitar, drums, and bass, the take starts with a simple guitar-piano accompaniment until Dylan reaches that "fury of the moment" line and Keltner kick-starts a full band arrangement.

It was presumably as a full band arrangement that it was added to the provisional setlist for the fall shows. And had Paul Williams asked for the song, instead of "Caribbean Wind," at that November 12 show, we may have heard a live version more than a year before we did (though at what cost!). As it is, Dylan quietly forgot the song for a while, knowing he would return to it in time to rekindle "the fury of the moment." When Arthur Rosato compiled a list of the songs scheduled for album sessions in early April 1981, "Grain of Sand" came immediately after the title track.

If Dylan did tackle the song at the early April 1981 Rundown sessions, then any documentation has been mislaid. The only evidence we have of a *Shot of Love* studio take is from the Clover sessions at the end of April. On April 29—the penultimate of those recording sessions scheduled to complete the album—he supposedly began the day's work by cutting this vocally demanding, musically challenging song in a single take. If the log is accurate—i.e., if this first take really is the one which concludes *Shot of Love*—it only enhances one's appreciation of another extraordinary moment in the studio, fully the equal of the June 16 "Like a Rolling Stone" or the February 1966 "Visions of Johanna."

Unlike the more soulful Rundown rehearsal, the Clover recording relies on a guitar-harmonica-accordion mix that further brings out nuances in that uplifting melody. Dylan too steps up to the plate, singing with the precision of a tambourine man (listen to the way he leans into the line "I have gone from rags to riches in the sorrow of the night"), before gracing the song with two heart-stopping harmonica breaks worth their own set of keys to the kingdom. The song was singled out by almost every reviewer, even those who felt the rest of the album was stuck in the same ol' groove. "Good critic" Paul Nelson, in his *Rolling Stone* review, considered it "both the 'Chimes of Freedom' and 'Mr. Tambourine Man' of Bob Dylan's Christian period."

Typically, Dylan shied away from introducing one of his most perfect songs at the ensuing shows, even though he sometimes almost emulated those Clover harmonica breaks on a newly rearranged "Forever Young." "Every Grain of Sand" remained one of three *Shot of Love* songs he refrained from performing on thirty-date tours of Europe and the U.S., intended though they were to promote his recent (i.e., post-1978) output. Only at the final show of the year, in Lakeland, Florida, when his voice had lost a great deal of the range and power it enjoyed earlier that summer, did he disinter his very own hymn to the silence. But without that heavenly harmonica, and coming from a vocalist more concerned with remembering the words than their meaning, the song that night was little more than a soft-shoe salvation shuffle.

Quite why Dylan felt that the crack band to whom he had taught the song when he was still gazing "into the doorway of temptation's angry flame" was not up to replicating the task on a nightly basis, who can say. But it seems particularly perverse, even for Dylan, that the only occasions he has been prepared to give the song a spin round the odd concert arena have been when he has had only the most basic electric accompaniment to hand—guitar-bass-drums, and maybe organ—and usually when he has left his harmonica back at the shack.

Thus, in 1984 it was treated to a leaden AOR arrangement that seemed more designed to show off Mick Taylor's guitar playing than the masterful song. Only in Barcelona, on a hot stadium night when everything finally clicked, did Dylan rise to the challenge, rattling the keys with a vocal suffused with passion and pain. During and after the G. E. Smith era of the Never Ending Tour (1988–90), it was rarely allowed out with the rasp of a mouth harp to lead the way (a welcome exception, and a rare post-G.E. outing of real power, came at the Minneapolis Orpheum, September 3, 1992, which circulates as a splendiferous soundboard).

The real performing highlight, though, occurred one sultry night (June 28, 1989), near the ancient streets of the Greek capital, the song being returned to base by a Dylan picking up an acoustic guitar and singing the song with only G. E. Smith—in the Fred Tackett role—to accompany him. Presumably, he was doing this as a nod to Nana. And this time you could hear a pin drop.

Note: On the 1980 typescript lyric, Dylan has put, "Through sleet and rain, I behold this chain." On the acoustic demo, though, he sings, "Like Cain, I now behold this chain," a weak (and not entirely convincing) rewrite which was nonetheless retained. Perhaps the original image was too close to one used in "I Believe in You."

{405} CARIBBEAN WIND

Published lyric/s: The Telegraph #1; Lyrics 85; Lyrics 04. *[Special Rider version:* Words Fill My Head*]*

Known studio recordings: Rundown Studios, Santa Monica, CA, October 1980; March 1981; Studio 55, LA, March 31, 1981—8 takes; Rundown Studios, April 7, 1981 [BIO]; April 30, 1981—1 take.

First known performance: Warfield Theatre, San Francisco, November 12, 1980.

The hardest part is when the inspiration dies along the way. Then you spend all your time trying to recapture it. —Dylan, to Neil Hickey, September 1976

I couldn't quite grasp what ["Caribbean Wind"] was about, after I finished it. Sometimes you write something to be very inspired, and you won't quite finish it for one reason or another. Then you'll go back and try and pick it up, and the inspiration is just gone. Either you get it all, and you can leave a few little pieces to fill in, or you're trying always to finish it off. Then it's a struggle. The inspiration's gone and you can't remember why you started it in the first place. Frustration sets in. —Dylan, to Cameron Crowe, *Biograph* notes, 1985

Talk about an exercise in contrasts! If "Every Grain of Sand" seemed to take Dylan twelve seconds to write and was captured in all its iridescent immediacy in a single take, "Caribbean Wind" would prove to be the most frustrating odyssey of his *entire* writing/recording career. At the end of it all, as he told Crowe, "I had to leave it. I just dropped it." He hadn't abandoned a song this good since "She's Your Lover Now," fifteen years earlier.

To add to the mounting ironies, the cause of this conversation with Crowe was to discuss the songs scheduled to appear on a sprawling five-album retrospective set, *Biograph*, which would include some eighteen unreleased performances, marking the official release of such "lost" Dylan classics as "Lay Down Your Weary Tune," "Percy's Song," "I'll Keep It with Mine," "Up to Me," and, yes, "Caribbean Wind." In this context, Dylan's comment to Crowe couldn't be more pertinent, because the version scheduled for inclusion was the one he recorded after the inspiration had withered and died, when it was a denuded husk of a shell of its former self.

And yet *Biograph* compiler Jeff Rosen could have used the version that comes closest to realizing this "Kubla Khan" of a song—its one and only live performance, at San Francisco's Warfield Theatre on November 12, 1980. That version, after all, was recorded from the desk for copyright purposes. This one-off performance—the post-conversion equivalent of the New York version of "Idiot Wind"—came before Dylan made the fateful decision to "go back and try and pick it up." His single greatest in-concert performance, it should have been released aeons ago. Those lucky enough to have witnessed this performance—a list which includes two of America's finer rock critics, Greil Marcus and Paul Williams— assuredly remember the frisson of feelings on hearing a verse like the one below for the very first time:

> Shadows moved closer as we touched on the floor,
> Prodigal son sitting next to the door,
> Preaching resistance, waiting for the night to arrive,
> He was well connected, but her heart was a snare,
> She had left him to die in there.
> But I knew he could get out while he still was alive.

In fact, a general awareness of this seminal song was already perme- ating outward before news traveled of that night in San Francisco. It first came to most fans' attention thanks to a description of a jam session in a hotel room occupied by Dire Straits' Mark Knopfler, two weeks earlier, witnessed by *Melody Maker* journalist Michael Oldfield. Oldfield's description set many a fan drooling: "[He] starts another song, possibly titled 'Caribbean Wind.' This is Dylan at his very best: enigmatic lyrics which seem a lot more gritty than we've been hearing recently, and a simple but beautiful melody."

In all probability, the song was one of those where Dylan "had the idea . . . for a long time, but it just wasn't the right time for it to be written." Hence that paradoxical preface to its one performance, "It's a new song I wrote a while back." One suspects it had been on his mind ever since he lost his grip on "Covenant Woman" back in early spring. He even owned up to a biographical dimension to Cameron Crowe: "I started it in St. Vincent when I woke up from a strange dream in the hot sun. There was a bunch of women working a tobacco field on a high rolling hill . . . I was thinking about living with somebody for all the wrong reasons." Kubla Khan, indeed.

In the original lyrics—though *not* the version included on *Biograph*—there are a number of clues that we are dealing with a true turning point in Dylan's tempestuous life. The line "Would I have married her? I don't know, I suppose . . ." seems to suggest he was thinking about more than just living with somebody—presumably this God-fearing woman was angling for a ring. And, if constancy had not been an overwhelming theme in Dylan's canon to date, the newly galvanized singer had already told one audience that spring about these here "country and western people . . . they sing very often, 'You can put your shoes under my bed any time,' and then they turn around and sing, 'Oh Lord, just a closer walk with thee.' Well, I can't do that."

The song itself seems set within a very particular time reference, Dylan telling us in line one that he "was playing a show at Miami," the very spot at which the 1978 tour had finally run aground. In its one-off performance he reinforces those coordinates by singing about this very wind blowing "from Tokyo to the British Isles," the exact geographical extent of the world tour that ended in Miami. In the original rehearsal take, though, the Caribbean wind blows "from Mexico to Curaçao / From Chinatown to the furnace of desire" in the first two choruses and "from Borneo to the British Isles . . ." in the final chorus. In the accompanying typescript, it blows "from the North Pole to the furnace of desire." (There is both a typescript and a transcript of the 1980 version—the former does not suffer from the mistranscriptions that seem to blight this particular song and should therefore be considered closer to Dylan's intentions.)

We have entered the selfsame "time of my confession / hour of . . . deepest need," as "Every Grain of Sand," so it is no surprise that the concerns—and imagery—of these masterful songs overlap. When he sings in this personal hymn of "the motion of the sea," and how, some times he turns, "there's someone there, other times it's only me," he is making a clear analogy to the image which opens verse five of "Caribbean Wind": "Atlantic City, by the cold grey sea / I hear a voice crying, 'Daddy,' I always think it's for me."

But if "Every Grain of Sand" came to him in a familiar place, "Caribbean Wind" was conjured up from somewhere less familiar, a place Dylan found thanks to an uncharacteristically extravagant gesture on his part, the purchase of a schooner with which to sail the high seas. Docked at Bequia in the West Indies, *The Water Pearl*, as it was named on its November 1979 launch, provided Dylan with new experiences and a release from all he had known, reminding him of the power of nature and his own place in the cosmos. As he informed *Songtalk*, long after he lost the boat, "It's nice to be able to put yourself in an environment where you can completely accept all the unconscious *stuff* that comes to you from your inner workings of your mind. And block yourself off to [a point] where you can control it all, take it down."

In the summer of 1980, sailing this schooner, he resuscitated "those distant ships of liberty / on them iron waves so bold and free" that had presaged a new day coming on 1963's "When the Ship Comes In." Nor were these the only ships now dredged up from the deep of Dylan's past and configured for his new apocalyptic vision. Another liner, doomed to leave "Desolation Row" becomes one of many portents to a pending Armageddon: "And like they say, the ship would sail at dawn." As any Dylan fan knows, only one ship "sails at dawn"—the *Titanic*. In "Caribbean Wind," the street band is already playing "Nearer My God to Thee"—a beautiful touch—suggesting its fate is already sealed. (Another traditional song he had made his own as far back as 1962, "Barbara Allen," is alluded to in the Rundown recording, the Caribbean wind blowing "all the way from Charlotte Town to Mexico.")

On completing the song, Dylan knew he had captured something very special. And like "Every Grain of Sand," he couldn't wait to play the song to his band or make a demo from their mutual discovery of its musical potential. Copyrighted in October 1980, from a Rundown rehearsal version that closely resembles the Warfield rendition a month later, the song seemed signed, sealed, delivered. The only significant change from one to the other—and for the better—sees the narrator going from "paying attention like a rattlesnake does / When he hears footsteps trampling on the flowers" to an altogether more powerful response to perfidy:

> Could I have been used, played as a pawn?
> It certainly was possible as the gay night wore on,
> But victory was mine, and I held it with the help of God's power.

If only Dylan had recorded it there and then. Instead, he gave himself time to tinker further with the song. But now he wasn't necessarily improving it. Rather, he was painstakingly removing autobiographical elements, pin by linchpin, à la "Idiot Wind." Even his opening description of the woman he might have married—"She was from Haiti, fair brown and intense"—made him uncomfortable. He fluffed the line at the Warfield, and next time he plays the song, in the studio, she is "well-rehearsed, fair brown and blonde," a description generic to the point of meaningless. And he knows it, changing it again, to something superficially poetic but equally meaningless: "She was the rose of Sharon from paradise lost."

At the same time he betrays and then forsakes the evangelical connection they once shared by transforming "I told her about Jesus, told her about the rain / She told me about division, she told me about the pain."[11] into something only ostensibly evocative: "Told me of the shadows where they talked in the rain / I could tell she was still feeling the pain" Eventually, he allows the line to become plain incongruous: "She told me about the jungle where her brothers were slain." This process, which took some months, was bisected by at least two attempts to capture the song on tape.

When Dylan entered L.A.'s Studio 55 on the last day in March, he had already given the song its own heart transplant, inadvertently removing its guts. And his inner voice knew it, because when he arrived at Studio 55, it refused to sing for him. Which proved to be the least of the assembled cast's problems. Dylan's assistant, Arthur Rosato, takes up the story: "When we did 'Caribbean Wind' I had the original recording that I did back at [Rundown]. I played that for all the musicians . . . All the musicians loved the song. So Bob finally shows up . . . [and] as soon as the musicians ran through it once, he goes, 'Nah, nah, nah, that's all wrong.' They could see it all coming because they had all worked with him before . . . And instead of that version, he had turned it into this country & western thing." The tortuous process of recording this version, bootlegged on *The Genuine Bootleg Series Vol. 1*, was embellished further by Fred Tackett in an interview for *The Bridge*:

> Jimmy Iovine was producing . . . Bob always liked to just have everybody in a room together and just amps, no baffles, nothing separating, just all the music. Put a couple of mikes up and record it live, a real raw live sound is what he loves, and at that time, the style of recording was to have everything separated so you could control [the sound] . . . but in Bob's style, you couldn't take anything in or out, it was just all in a room . . . So we get there early and Jimmy Iovine puts us all in little boxes. I was literally in a closet with my mandolin playing this "Caribbean Wind' song . . . We cut the song and we go back and listen to the playback, which sounds like a 1980s really slick pop record and, of course, Bob hates it.

On this version the rattlesnake has returned, still hearing footsteps "trampling over the flowers," but the prodigal son had left the building, leaving the lady clairvoyant there:

> She looked into my soul through the clothes that I wore,
> She said, "We got a mutual friend standing at the door,
> Yeah, you know he's got our best interest in mind."

Their secret rendezvous has also been moved. No longer is it "where the mission bells ring"—with all the *Blonde on Blonde* connotations that image brought to bear—but at a place "where we drank from a spring," another phrase filled with what Paul Williams has called "the shadow of greatness." Even the one change retained from that earlier Warfield performance, "She had bells in her braids, and they hung to her toes," was inferior to the copyrighted lyric, "There were bells in her braids and fire in her clothes."

After a dozen takes or so, Dylan realized he should have listened to his inner voice. As Rosato recalls, "Towards the end of the session . . . Bob himself even realized it wasn't working and [said], 'Let's go back and try the original version.'" Rosato remembers them trying to record it with "these backing vocalists singing this like train whoosh and that was really bad. I don't even know how he ended up keeping it." That particular travesty, though, was from a different time and place. What Rosato is remembering (a decade and a half after the fact) is the version on 1985's *Biograph*. That take, cut a week later, was yet another attempt to reignite the song by reconstructing the entire narrative.

This version, dated April 7 on the *Biograph* set, is probably from the same Rundown session as a misdated AFM sheet which includes four other songs recorded at sessions the week before. Misassigned to May 1 because of late filing with the local American Federation of Musicians (an ongoing problem with these sessions, until Debbie Gold was dispatched by Naomi Saltzman to sort out the chaos), the tracks logged for the session ran as follows: "It's All Dangerous to Me," "My Oriental Home," "Caribbean Wind," "Ah Ah Ah," and "Let It Be Me." (An April 7 session would explain "Let It Be Me" appearing on an April 10 reel of "Early Roughs." The released B-side definitely does not correspond to the version recorded at the April 2 session.)

In the interim, Dylan had decided that, rather than "try[ing] the original version," he would move yet further away from that initial, highly personal inspiration. Almost all of the new lines sound fine in isolation, but, pray tell, what the fudge doth *this* couplet mean: "Were we sniper bait, did we follow a star / Through a hole in the wall to where the long arm of the law cannot reach"? The mutual friend has gone and joined the prodigal son, backlit by yet more portents of Apocalypse: "Sea breeze blowin," there's a hellhound loose / Redeemed men who have escaped from the noose / Preaching faith and salvation, waiting for the night to arrive."[12] That long-heralded Judgment Day also provides Dylan with the one new section that *almost* justifies the loss of the Titanic and the girl of color:

> I see the screws breaking loose, see the devil pounding on tin,
> I see a house in the country being torn apart from within.
> I can hear my ancestors calling from the land far beyond.

Unfortunately, what we lose through this substitution is the original final couplet—"I was gonna say, 'Come on with me girl, I got plenty of room,' / But I knew I'd be lying, and besides she had already gone"— taking away any sense that these star-crossed lovers have made different choices and must now learn to live with them. As a result, we lose the lyrical thread that connected it to "Groom's Still Waiting at the Altar" and "Angelina."

Dylan felt the loss keenly. He even made a symbolic, but equally unsuccessful, stab at the song at the last "pre-mix" Clover session (April 30). As late as July he was still talking about the song as a real break-through, to *NME*'s Neil Spencer, at the same time admitting it had no place on the album he ended up with: "We left another [song] off the album, which is quite different to anything I wrote [previously] . . . In a lyric content-way it's interesting: the way the story-line changes from third person to first person and that person becomes you, then these people are there and they're not there. And then the time goes way back and then it's brought up to the present. And I thought it was really effective, but that again is a long song."

Like a true artist, once he had given up on the song, he dismissed it from his thoughts. When the song appeared in the 1985 *Lyrics*, riddled with mistranscriptions ("lone brown eyes" for "chrome brown eyes," "waiting for the night to arise," not "arrive," etc.), it was a warped reflection of the recording released on *Biograph*, not even the one copyrighted the previous October—a lyric which had been good enough to bear comparison with his very best work.

By then, he knew why he had let the song go. As he told Bill Flanagan six months before its appearance on *Biograph*, making a general point, but surely with this ringing example in mind: "The saddest thing about songwriting is when you get something really good and you put it down for a while, and you take it for granted that you'll be able to get back to it with whatever inspired you . . . in the first place—well, whatever inspired you to do it in the first place is never there . . . So then you've got to consciously stir up the inspiration to figure what it was about. Usually you get one good part and one not-so-good part, and the not-so-good part wipes out the good part." He resisted venturing down this path again, telling Paul Zollo, six years later, "When you write a dream . . . you're never quite sure if you're getting it right or not."

Note: The published lyrics to "Caribbean Wind" stand as a mess of titanic proportions. The song was copyrighted two times, first in 1980 and then in 1985. Meanwhile, a transcription sheet was done in 1981—from the March 31 session (i.e., "well-rehearsed, fair-brown and blonde" lyric)—but was never lodged. The 1980 lyric (cf. *Words Fill My Head*) derives from a version recorded at Rundown, probably cross-checked against a typescript. That original typescript does have two minor differences: it is "the judge and the jailer," not "the judge and the jury" who are "meeting with the man of the hour" in verse one, and the opening line of verse two strengthens the two lovers' connection: "Our shadows drew closer 'til they touched on the floor." But it was the April 7, 1981 version—sullied by a series of horrendous mistranscriptions—that was used in the 1985 *Lyrics*. This was "corrected" when the official website published the lyrics online in 1997. Unfortunately, the version used then was apparently one given to Dylan's then-lawyer Naomi Saltzman in 1981, being a composite of the versions recorded on March 31 and April 7, making it neither one thing nor the other. Nonetheless, it is this version that appears in the 2004 *Lyrics*, continuing the sorry saga of this epic song on tape and in print.

{406} GROOM'S STILL WAITING AT THE ALTAR

Published lyric/s: The Telegraph #7 [x2]; Lyrics 85; Lyrics 04.
First known performance: Warfield Theatre, San Francisco, November 13, 1980.
Known studio recordings: Rundown Studios, Santa Monica, CA, October 1980; March 27, 1981—11 takes; Clover Studios, L.A., April 23, 1981; late April 1981 [45/SoL Mk.2].

"Groom's Still Waiting at the Altar" is the second extraordinary song Dylan wrote during the summer of 1980 about (these) star-crossed lovers in a world on the brink. Like "Caribbean Wind," it was a song that Dylan felt ultimately got away from him. In fact, unlike "Caribbean Wind" and its other sister song "Angelina," "Groom" never even featured on any short list for *Shot of Love*. Which makes it all the more remarkable that it has become the song that compilers—well, one well-placed compiler—reach for when representing this period in song. (To date, this one-time B-side has appeared on the expanded, ten-track reissue of *Shot of Love, Biograph, Greatest Hits Vol. 3*, and the three-CD *Dylan* boxed set, making it by far the most anthologized song of the era.)

For this state of affairs, one must thank first and foremost the ever-determined Debbie Gold, who arrived at these sessions as a mere "consultant," but fearlessly cajoled Dylan into releasing the song. Eventually he gave in, agreeing to its inclusion on the B-side of the U.S.-only "Heart of Mine" 45. Needless to say, DJs the country over quickly skipped the so-called A-side, playing the gut-busting B-side for all they were worth. After which, it was but a short step for CBS to reissue the album with "Groom" now opening side two. And it was in this form that *Shot of Love* duly appeared on CD, making "Groom" now a part of an album Dylan sequenced *after* abandoning "Claudette," the woman who left the groom standing at the altar.

Only Dylan could confirm whether the "Groom" that now sits amid *Shot of Love*'s festive fare truly represents the song he wrote the summer before. After all, the lyrical changes he wrought on the song between its debut at the Warfield shows in November 1980 and the Plotkin-produced cut—recorded at the end of April 1981—are almost as profound as those inflicted on "Caribbean Wind." The difference is that he did not lose the spirit of the song in the process.

If "Caribbean Wind" only got a single outing at the Warfield residency, Dylan gave "Groom" a thorough road test, performing it at three consecutive shows, with three guest guitarists imposing their trademark licks on it—a wailin' Carlos Santana on the thirteenth, the immortal Michael Bloomfield on the fifteenth (his last ever live performance!), and that unregenerate doodler Jerry Garcia—who in fairness does a pretty good job—on the sixteenth. At the same time, the lyric was given an equally thorough workout, new lines leaping in at a moment's notice. The original chorus, though, remained gratefully intact:

> Set my affections on things above, let nothing get in the way of that love,
> Not even the rock of Gibraltar.
> If you see her on Fanning Street, tell her I still think she's neat,
> And that the Groom's Still Waiting at the Altar.

Powerful stuff. The image of her on Fanning Street, a notorious thoroughfare in New Orleans frequented by streetwalkers and immortalized by a Lead Belly song, shows that Dylan had yet to resolve his tendency to view women as either Madonnas or whores. Rather than reach resolution, he decided to foreground the apocalyptic element when recording the song for *Shot of Love* at the end of April 1981 (though as of April 23 he was still singing the Fanning Street lyric):

> West of the Jordan,
> East of the rock of Gibraltar,
> Seen the turning of the page, curtain risin' on a new age,
> See the groom still waitin' at the altar.

The other changes wrought on the song were not so significant, though he had started "cleaning up" the song as early as its second performance at the Warfield, when he no longer explicitly sang "World's coming to an end, wise men standing around like furniture"; nor did he continue to suggest he was "Waiting on my Savior, been slandered and humiliated."

By the time the song got a live airing, it was "highwaymen and hitmen pushing women into robbery," not the original "Dream-peddlers" sung of in rehearsal. Otherwise, the Warfield versions largely stuck to the template minted back at Rundown in early October (save for losing the barbed aside "People bringing the Lord's name into every senseless conversation" and turning "obligation" to "obligated"). That Rundown version apparently featured Danny Kortchmar on lead guitar, an honor also accorded him on the *Shot of Love* recording. Though he can't match the sheer chops evident on Bloomfield's fond farewell, he still hits the G-spot when g = groove.

Whether another version recorded at Rundown in late March 1981, with Jimmy Iovine taking notes, matched these other guises remains undocumented. But, suffice to say, it went the same way as March versions of its sister songs "Angelina" and "Caribbean Wind." Though there is no recording date for the released version, it was recorded some time after April 23 but before May 11 when it was mixed.

On this Clover version, Dylan still seems to be hunting for new ways to describe a world to come ("Cities on fire, phones out of order / They're killing nuns and soldiers, there's fighting on the border" was one such solution). Lost in the process is "the overweight dancer," whose vocation and voluptuousness draw no comment on the released version. Instead, he "felt around for the light-switch, felt around for her face / Been treated like a farm animal on a wild goose chase." All the while, the song remained the same beast, and Dylan would have been well advised to stick it in the "Trouble" slot, addressing as it did a whole world of trouble with the words of a poet, not a zealot.

Note: In *Lyrics*, Dylan reverts to rhyming "became nauseated" with "walking down the hallway while the walls deteriorated," rather than fumbling for her face, as he does on the record.

{407} YONDER COMES SIN

Published lyric/s: [Words Fill My Head]
Known studio recordings: Rundown Studios, Santa Monica, CA, October 1980.

That's what sin is, politics . . . The way they take sin and put it in front of people . . . the way that they say this is good and that's bad, you can do this and you can't do that; the way that sin is taken and split up and categorized and put on different levels so it becomes more of a structure of sin. —Dylan, to Neil Spencer, July 1981

"Yonder Comes Sin" seems to be a song Dylan wishes would just go away. Recorded in the full fury of the moment at a Rundown "rehearsal" in October 1980, it seemed at the time like the summation of various strands of millennial fury he had been binding together for the past eighteen months. But the feeling passed—and quickly. The song never even made it to the fall live set, let alone the *Shot of Love* sessions, six months hence. It was also apparently the one song he nixed from the original *Bootleg Series* boxed set, back in 1991.

Despite such distaste, "Yonder Comes Sin" is a mighty important song—and a far better extemporization on the theme of man's iniquities than "Trouble" or "You Changed My Life," both songs hastily conceived at a time when an album *was* imminent. It also represents the first time Dylan explicitly uses "sin" as a cipher for "the blues" (something he later repeated with "Blind Willie McTell"—see John Bauldie's article in *All Across the Telegraph*), even down to the clear allusion to Ma Rainey's "Yonder Comes the Blues" in the song title.

This time, rather than describing all the things that are giving the singer the blues, Dylan catalogs all the things that are driving the world to the brink. And he does so with a full awareness that his words will fall on stony ground. In verse four, he even portrays himself as a modern Jeremiah, a figure who "preached repentance / to those who would turn from hell / But the critics gave him such bad reviews / Put him to the bottom of the well." If the original Jeremiah would never have used a term like hell, Dylan would and did—he'd just spent six months preaching repentance to two thousand-plus fans a night. His identification with Jeremiah was undoubtedly real. In conversation with Martin Keller at the time of *Infidels*, he even addressed his genetic heritage in these highly emotive terms: "Talking about Jewish roots, you want to know more? Check upon Elijah the prophet. He could make rain. Isaiah the prophet, even Jeremiah, see if their brethren didn't want to bust their brains for telling it right like it is—these are my roots."

Stalking through the song's undergrowth is that other figure perennially found in "the blues"—the devil; but it takes until the seventh and final verse for him to make an actual appearance, and it takes the prophetic narrator to point him out: "I'll be down the line when the morning comes / Just remember that I loved you best / And that I pulled the hood up for you / So that you could see real good your uninvited guest."

He made a similar point to *NME*'s editor the following summer, in the best of the 1981 interviews: "You would think the enemy is someone you can strike at, and that would solve the problem. But the real enemy is the Devil . . . [and] he tends to shade himself and hide himself and put it into people's minds that he's not really there and he's really not so bad, and that he's got a lot of good things to offer, too. So there's this conflict going [on], to blind the minds of men."

"Yonder Comes Sin" takes the concerns of "Trouble in Mind" and universalizes them. In the process, he devotes seven eight-line verses to addressing the sins of pride ("Proud like a peacock / Swifter than an eagle / Look at your feet, see where they've been to . . .") and avarice ("You turn your back on the hard truth / Just to fatten up your purse"). He even manages to take a swipe at Macbeth, who "in order to possess that corruptible crown" made "a deal with Mr. Death" (he seems to be confusing the Scottish king with Faust). By the end, he has worked himself into the kind of lather he reached in concert when singing "Are You Ready?" Such a song would hardly have necessitated any further examination of sin if it had appeared on *Shot of Love*. But then, its author was already convinced sin "rules the airwaves / It rules the planet" and that the message would therefore go unheeded.

Note: The circulating tape only includes the first four of the song's seven verses, cutting abruptly in midtake.

{408} LET'S KEEP IT BETWEEN US

Published lyric/s: The Telegraph #10; Lyrics 85; Lyrics 04.
Known studio recordings: Rundown Studios, Santa Monica, CA, October 1980.
First known performance: Warfield Theatre, San Francisco, November 9, 1980.

Of all the original songs Dylan elected to debut at the fall 1980 shows, "Let's Keep It Between Us" is the most surprising omission from the *Shot of Love* sessions the following spring. He sang it at all but one of the fall shows, with an audible vocal commitment there for all to hear. To my mind, it also has the edge on similar-minded songs he did record for said album, like "Need a Woman" and "Don't Ever Take Yourself Away." And though hardly a major song, it does address a perennial preoccupation—rejection by his peers, this time for his newfound faith and/or the color of his girlfriend's skin. He even refers to (former) rules of segregation by singing, in concert, "In the company of fools, we'll fall / So let's just move to the back of (the back of) the bus," just before his feeling of general alienation spills over into the bridge:

I know we ain't perfect. Then again, so what?
Ain't no reason to treat me like a slave and treat you like you was a slut,
And it's just making me angry.[13]

At the Warfield, Dylan comes down hard on every last word—like he is back in Fort Collins raging against the ubiquitous winds of idiocy. Yet such strong feelings faded real fast. By 1981, it was off the checklist and by the time of the 1985 *Lyrics*, he had rewritten the bridge so that this time, "They act like we got to live for them . . . And it's makin' me kind of tired." My oh my. Other lines, too, receive the same mild-mannered makeover, the bite being removed from a line like "Before we wake up and find ourselves in a game that we both have lost" and replaced by "find[ing] ourselves in a daze that's got us out of our minds." Worse still, he finds a substitute for "instant cures and easy answers [telling him] he can't afford the cost," the mid-eighties Dylan preferring to "drop down now and get back behind the lines." All very street, but hardly reet petite.

In fact, the "correct" lyric had already been published back in February 1983 in *The Telegraph* #10, being taken directly from the October 1980 Rundown demo, which served as a spirited guide when Bonnie Raitt cut the song for her 1982 album *Green Light*. Raitt's then producer/husband Rob Fraboni had secured a copy of the demo, which is taken at a much slower tempo than its live incarnation but has a slightly superior melody line. Both are carefully preserved on one of the better cover versions of a "lost" Dylan song. For passion and punch, though, it can't compare with Dylan's performances at the Warfield when—one imagines—there were some uncomfortable so-called friends sitting in the front rows.

{409} MAKIN' A LIAR

Known studio recordings: ?Rundown Studios, Santa Monica, CA, October 1980.

A song with this title is listed as being rehearsed for the fall 1980 shows (see *Recording Sessions*, page 148). It is one of the half a dozen songs ticked (of the sixty songs listed), the others all being recorded at this time. However, unlike some twenty covers on said list, it is *not* asterisked. All in all, probably an original composition Dylan recorded at Rundown that October, before it was not so much saved as lost.

{410} CITY OF GOLD

Published lyric/s: The Telegraph #2; Lyrics 04.

First known performance: Warfield Theatre, San Francisco, November 10, 1980.

"City of Gold," though it came and went without ever apparently testing out the Rundown tape recorder, was no whim on Dylan's part. One of those songs written specifically as a performance piece for the fall 1980 shows, to highlight his ongoing commitment to reaching that *civitas dei*, it lasted until as late as July 5, 1981, when it was an unexpected encore at the last of eight English arena shows, at Birmingham's National Exhibition Center.

It then became a mere footnote to this prolific period until 2003 when a rewritten version—sung by the Dixie Hummingbirds—appeared in Dylan's first movie in a quarter of a century, *Masked and Anonymous*. A year later, it made a belated appearance in the 2004 edition of *Lyrics*, incorrectly assigned to the *Saved* section, rather than sitting in its rightful place with the lost songs from the *Shot of Love* era. Whether the new version was the product of a recent rewrite, à la "Gonna Change My Way of Thinking," or some former version now uncovered, the 2003 copyright does not reveal.

The original copyright, made in December 1980, relied on a live version from the Warfield. Indeed, given that the song is absent from the list of songs rehearsed at Rundown for these shows (see *Recording Sessions*, page 148), it is likely that this was a song Dylan wrote as the second Warfield residency got underway. The straightforward nature of the lyric—"There is a city of gold / a city of hope / a country of love . . ."—allowed him to play with the words on a nightly basis. And he did not let the opportunity go to waste. Some early versions had the following revealing verse:

> There is a city of hope
> Don't need no doctor, don't need no dope,
> I'm ready and willing, throw down a rope,
> There is a city of hope.

Other nights Dylan sang of a "rest from your labor / and the bars that hold" and of "the stuff that dreams are made of / Beyond the sunset /

And stars high above." Imbued with the same spirit as "That Lucky Ol' Sun"—a song regularly performed in 1985–6—it was as straightforward a song of salvation as "Blessed Is the Name" and, as such, a highly effective conclusion to proceedings at these landmark shows.

But it worked just as well as the fitting finale to Dylan's 2003 celluloid vision, *Masked and Anonymous*, with his character, Jack Fate, being led away to jail (again). For this occasion, one surmises, Dylan must have penned at least one new verse: "There is a City of Peace / Where all foul forms of destruction cease / Where the mighty have fallen and there are no police. . ."

{411} SHOT OF LOVE

Published lyric/s: Lyrics 85; Lyrics 04.

Known studio recordings: Rundown Studios, Santa Monica, CA, March 11, 1981; April 6, 1981; Rundown Studios, mid/late April, 1981 [SoL]; Rundown/ Clover Studios, April 23, 1981.

First known performance: Earl's Court, London, July 1, 1981.

> Most people's sensibilities are determined by the newspaper they read in the morning . . . [which] is doing nothing to get you into the world to come . . . To those who care now where Bob Dylan is at, they should listen to "Shot of Love" . . . It's my most perfect song. It defines where I am at spiritually, musically, romantically and whatever else . . . It's all there in that one song. —Dylan, to Martin Keller, July 1983

Right at the top of right-hand man Arthur Rosato's list of songs his boss intended to record for the next album in April 1981 sits the title "Shot of Love." And when the musicians reassembled at Rundown for further rehearsals, on or around March 11, this was apparently the first song Dylan wanted them to work on. Still working out the words, and taking the song at a medium-slow tempo, he spent some time coaxing the girl singers to give their all on the unambiguous chorus, "I need a shot of love."

After a weeklong experiment with studio setups—at a series of sessions from March 27 to April 2—Dylan resumed work at Rundown, on or around April 6, immediately returning to this song. And still, the song was taken at a leisurely pace, relying on a simple percussive backing and a lead vocal that had none of the stridency of the later "Blackwell" version. The version he cut that day was immediately transferred to a reel of "Early Rough (Mix)es" under consideration for the album that would bear its name.

And yet he was still working on the song two and a half weeks later, as sessions transferred from Rundown to Clover, changing the words around in a playful, probably impromptu way, singing couplets like "Use me and abuse me, drop me in a hole / I need a shot of love." And now, rather than "spending time with you," he insists "I don't need no alibi to explain where I been / Seen the kingdoms of the world, [been] into the lion's den." But no finished take seems to have resulted from the lengthy, exploratory April 23 session. Perhaps he had already got where he wanted to be.

The version that ended up opening the album was apparently already in the can, recorded at Rundown (or, as credited on the LP sleeve, Peacock), produced by the legendary Specialty producer "Bumps" Blackwell. Dylan, in awe of Blackwell in a way he never could be with modern producers like Iovine and Plotkin, responded with a performance that was as juiced up as anything on the gospel tours. Howling at the moon goddess, he dismisses Veronica ("not here"), Mavis ("just ain't right"), and, by implication, Angelina and Claudette. He has a different kind of love in mind, one that satisfies "the hurt inside." Though an inordinate amount of time was expended on getting the mix right (and trimming a few seconds off the long fade), the album opener still leapt out of the grooves on its release, as Dylan intended.

This heartfelt testament was meant to set the tone for a whole album addressing similar concerns. As Dylan told Dave Herman for the interview album sent out to radio stations as a promotional tool, "There's enough so-called music out there which is sick music. It's just sick. It's made by sick people and it's played to sick people to further a whole world of sickness . . . It caters to people's sickness. And if I can't do something that is telling people . . . you can be healed . . . I'd as soon be on a boat, you know, [or] off hiking through the woods."

Such preoccupations would not change for a while—hence his

description to Keller, when mixing *Infidels,* of "Shot of Love" as his "most perfect song." Two years later, he was still suggesting he wanted to address in song "such things as ghetto bosses, salvation and sin, lust, murderers going free, and children without hope—messianic kingdom-type stuff," the exact things that preoccupy him on "Shot of Love."

Despite this, "Shot Of Love" struggled to maintain a hold in the live set after 1981—perhaps because he wanted critics to get away from the idea that he was only interested in making "some kind of Methodist record," a label he (said they) attached to *Shot of Love* in the *Biograph* interview. Introduced live at the final Earl's Court show on July 1, 1981, it stayed in the set through the remainder of the year, but was not performed again until the opening show of the 1986 tour, in Wellington, New Zealand, and then it only lasted three shows. And though it enjoyed fleeting favor on the 1987 European tour, and G. E. Smith reinvigorated the riff in 1989, his "most perfect song" has been accorded very little onstage time post *Infidels.*

{412} YOU CHANGED MY LIFE

Published lyric/s: Lyrics 04. *[1982 copyrighted version:* Words Fill My Head*]*
*Known studio recordings: Rundown Studios, Santa Monica, CA, March 11,
1981; Cream Studio, L.A., April 1, 1981; United Western, L.A., April 2, 1981;
Rundown Studios, April 23, 1981—11 takes [TBS].*

> What Jesus does for an ignorant man like myself is to make the character-
> istics and qualities of God more believable to me, 'cause I can't beat the
> devil. Only God can. —Dylan, to Neil Spencer, July 1981

"You Changed My Life" is another song which got lost in the *Shot of Love* shuffle, not even being bootlegged before its appearance on 1991's *Bootleg Series* set. However, unlike some other lost songs written early and rejected late, it simply didn't make the grade. One suspects it was already an old, i.e., 1980, song—though it is absent from the fall 1980 checklist. Lines like "Talk about salvation, people suddenly get tired" and "I was listening to the voices of death on parade / responding to the call of the saints' masquerade"—as he sung it on March 11—suggests a kinship with "Property of Jesus." He is again addressing his "Lord . . . and Savior" in every verse—this time directly and unambiguously.

Indeed, the fact that he wanted to work on the song at the March 11 rehearsal session (when he first worked up "Shot of Love") suggests he was still "responding to the call." He also took the time to try it again at Cream and United Western studios in early April. And yet, when sessions resumed on April 23, he felt like reteaching the song to the band. Starting out with atmospheric piano accompaniment, the song was then transformed over at least eleven takes into the version released in 1991. Even so there is no evidence the song was ever part of the May mixdown sessions.

Further proof that he didn't feel he had realized the song to his satisfaction came the following year when it was copyrighted at the expense of its first two and last two verses—in which he castigated those who do "the work of the devil" and a world that is set against Him: "Your eyes were on fire, Your feet were made of brass / In a world that you made, You were made an outcast" (another allusion to Revelation, 2:18: "These things saith the Son of God, who hath his eyes like unto a flame of fire, and his feet are like fine brass"). In their place was a new last verse that suggested those seeds of doubt had begun to sprout roots, and the power of Woman was to blame:

> Truce makers and partakers of every selfish whim
> Her running to meet me running to her
> And you running back to him
> Their destruction of my confidence was like a sharpness of the tongue
> I said: Make my faith greater, but I was a little high-strung.

If the cryptic second and third lines remain wholly impenetrable, that final line suggests someone identifying with the "Thief on the Cross." It seems unlikely, though, that a recording was made of this song in its reconfigured state.

Note: In the 2004 *Lyrics*, the "orphans of man" dance "to the beat of the palm," whereas the original 1982 transcript and the 1981 recording give the line as "the beat of the balm," which is probably what Dylan intended, however odd such an expression sounds.

{413} ANGELINA

Published lyric/s: Lyrics 04.

Known studio recordings: Rundown Studios, Santa Monica, CA, March 26, 1981—2 takes; Clover Studio, L.A., late April, 1981 [TBS].

> There were some real long songs . . . that we recorded [for the album], a couple of really long songs. Like, there was one I did—do you remember "Visions of Johanna"?—there was one like that. I'd never done anything like it before. [But] it's got that same kind of [vibe] to it. It seems to be very sensitive and gentle on one level, then on another level the lyrics aren't sensitive or gentle at all. We left that off the album. —Dylan, to Neil Spencer, July 1981

According to the Krogsgaard sessionography, "Angelina" was a song recorded in two takes at a Rundown session in late March 1981. If so, it was a misleadingly propitious start to the *Shot of Love* sessions I remain unconvinced that the *Bootleg Series* take comes from that session or was produced by Jimmy Iovine, who receives no credit in the booklet accompanying the official release. One thing is certain: there was a "full-band" version of "Angelina" recorded at one of these sessions, in which the girl singers were mixed very much to the fore and two sections of lyric were quite different to their final form. After the first chorus, he continues describing the angelic-looking Angelina in a way that was neither sensitive nor gentle:

> Her eyes were two slits, make any snake proud,
> With a face any painter would paint, and well-endowed,
> Praising the dead as she rode a donkey through the crowd,
> Or was it a hyena?

Only after serving her with a subpoena does he remember what kind of woman he has been dealing with all along: "A peaceful exchange of ideas for you was always too tame / Inter-tribal warfare was always more your style and your game / Your best friend . . ."

This version was still under consideration for the album in May, when both variants were mixed.[14] But when it came time to sequence the album, on May 12, it was the gentler arrangement on *The Bootleg Series 1–3* that got the vote, presumably to make the counterpoint between arrangement and lyric that much greater.[15] Its position as the album closer in this original sequence, after the slow waltz "Every Grain of Sand," would also have heightened its impact. But in the end the song was cut—at the expense of Dylan's whole original concept for the album.

That Dylan felt the loss keenly is clear from the description of the song to Neil Spencer, above, which he further embellished, "When I came down to putting the songs on the album we had to cut some, so we cut ['Angelina' and 'Caribbean Wind']. Now what we have left is an album which seems to make its kind of general statement, but it's too soon to say what that general statement is." All of which reads like Bobspeak for "I've no idea what album I made, but I know what album I set out to make." The album he planned to make revolved around the first three songs he set out to record at these sessions—"Angelina," "The Groom's Still Waiting," and "Caribbean Wind."

This trilogy set the (one) immortal story against a common backdrop ("I see pieces of men marching, trying to take heaven by force," "Cities on fire . . . there's fighting on the border," and even "Every new messenger brings his evil report, about . . . time that is short"). Having established said vantage point, Dylan could fill in the blanks with a number of songs about the search for love, in both its witchy and its messianic guises.

"Angelina" itself sets out to tell us what happened to the (kind of) woman who, at the end of "Groom's Still Waiting," could be "respectably married, or running a whorehouse in Buenos Aires." (In "Angelina" he specifically asks her minions, "Where would you like to be overthrown / In Jerusalem or Argentina?") If Angelina is not the Claudette in "Groom" "come back to haunt me," they are sisters under the skin. Either would have "left him to die in there" ("Caribbean Wind"), but by the time he wrote "Angelina," everything she has wrought is set to be judged by a higher power. Which is why at the end of the song the author sees "her" beating "a path of retreat up them spiral staircases / Pass the tree of smoke, pass the angel with four faces / Begging God for mercy and weepin' in unholy places." He whispers her name one last time, "Oh Angelina," knowing that her fate had been foretold earlier in the song: "He's surrounded by God's angels, and she's wearin' a blindfold."

It is a beautifully crafted song, and the performance from Dylan—coaxing out the words he offsets with that teasing tune on the piano—is fully up to the task. And yet, "Angelina" seems to leave some commentators cold, offended perhaps by the slightly corny rhymes Dylan devises for the lady's name (concertina, hyena, subpoena, Argentina, and arena). It is as if he is not allowed to have fun with the AAABCCCB rhyme scheme in such a serious song. Something troubled Dylan too, because in the end he decided the reconfigured album could not bear this weight. And when the songwriter decided—reluctantly—to cast aside this lady, the other two followed as a matter of course (even if "Groom's Still Waiting" was later added to the album). Just a single song on capricious females remained on the album, and it was hardly one worthy of Angelina's challenging company.

{414} HEART OF MINE

Published lyric/s: Lyrics 85; Lyrics 04.
Known studio recordings: Rundown Studios, Santa Monica, CA, March 1981; Clover Studios, L.A., April 28—4 takes; April 29; May 15—7 takes [SoL].
First known performance: Earl's Court, London, July 1, 1981.

Our hearts are not good. If your heart's not good, what good does beauty do, that comes through your eyes, going down to your heart, which isn't good anyway? . . . I've spent a lot of time dealing with the man-made beauty, so that sometimes the beauty of God's world has evaded me."
—Dylan, to Dave Herman, July 1981

In Dylan's entire canon, "Heart of Mine" is hardly the odd one out for addressing that familiar concern, "man-made beauty." But on *Shot of Love* it stood alone, save perhaps for a more benign reflection on side two, "In the Summertime." The fact that he should choose the song over the likes of "Let's Keep It Between Us," "Need a Woman," or "Don't Ever Take Yourself Away" seems slightly perverse. That he then chose a half-assed, ill-conceived rehearsal version from a last-minute add-on session, with buddies Ringo Starr and Ron Wood sitting in, over the altogether more engaging, pop-friendly version from April 1981, puts the icing on this particular eskimo pie.

Yet Starr was not at the sticks; producer Chuck Plotkin was. And Fred Tackett describes how "Chuck . . . actually got behind Ringo Starr's drumset and was playing drums; and Ringo's standing over next to me by the wall . . . and he can't believe this guy's playing . . . He's a terrible drummer, but he was like crazy . . . [And] Ringo's playing a tambourine. That's why it said he's playing on percussion." So how come it appeared on the album? Even Dylan admitted it was a perverse decision. In conversation with some post-punk musicians he took to jamming with in the winter of 1984, he opined, "I chose for some reason a particularly funky version of that [song]—and it's really scattered. It's not as good as some of the other versions." Probably, he just wanted to mess with the producer's mind. Plotkin, after all, had just spent countless hours remixing the Clover version myriad ways.

The song itself rambles from cliché to cliché (in a couple of cases, quite literally: "If you can't do the time, don't do the crime" and "Give her an inch and she'll take a mile"), while embracing the odd mixed metaphor ("You can play with fire, but you'll get the bill"), only for its most cogent image to be sacrificed when Starr and Wood are unleashed. "Don't let her pour out her wine" cleverly conveys both religious infatuation and original sin, but, looking to trim the album of excess weight, he commingled two verses—"Go back where you been . . ." and "You know she'll never be true . . ."—on the May 15 version and lost the image in the process. In print, he also couldn't make up his mind, changing this line to the innocuous "Don't let her know she's so fine" in the 1985 edition of Lyrics, and then, in 2004, revising it further: "Don't let her think you think she's fine."

Dylan continued to rate the song—performing it regularly through 1981, and sporadically through 1984, 1986, 1987, and the G. E. Smith era of the Never Ending Tour. He also selected it as the A-side of the first single from the album, thus ensuring that the album had minimum impact on the airwaves or charts. Quite what he heard here, I can't hear myself. I suspect it is the message of the song which he can relate to. As he told Mick Brown in 1984, when the song still sprung up on occasion,

"I still have desires . . . that lead me around once in a while . . . You get to know what line not to step over—usually because you stepped over it before and were lucky to get back."

{415} IS IT WORTH IT?
{416} YES SIR, NO SIR (HALLELUIAH)

Known studio recordings: [#415–16] Rundown Studios, Santa Monica, CA, March 1981; [415] Cream Studio, L.A., April 1, 1981—5 takes; United Western, LA, April 2, 1981—4 takes; [416] United Western, April 2, 1981—13 takes.

In January 1985 Dylan's publishing office copyrighted a tape of some twenty-two songs (including ten instrumentals), under the memorable title *Compilation #2*. Because it came with no information as to the recording date of the material, and not a single one of the songs had been copyrighted or rumored previously, a great deal of debate ensued regarding its source. From day one, I was among those convinced it came from the *Shot of Love* period, simply because of the sound—and so it proved. But the purpose of the material—none of which appeared on *Shot of Love* or even came from known sessions—remained a mystery until a 1995 conversation with Dylan sidekick (and nominal producer of these sessions) Arthur Rosato offered a likely source for much of this "stuff":

> We did like a studio tour and that's where a lot of those outtakes came from. Bob decided that we should check out some studios, so we'd record in people's garage setups and do one song, then we went over to United Western and . . . recorded a bunch of stuff.

The clincher was a tape in Arthur's possession from United Western Studio A, dated April 2, 1981, which contained the copyrighted versions of "Is It Worth It?," "Yes Sir, No Sir," and a song called simply "Ah Ah Ah"—the first three songs on *Compilation #2*, and clearly all derived from the same source. Also among his cassettes was an earlier March 1981 Rundown rehearsal of the first two songs, confirming that, at least in these two instances, *Compilation #2* was not a case of Dylan deciding to "babble into the microphone, then rush into the control room and listen to what he said, and write it down, and then maybe arrange it a little bit, and then maybe rush back out in front and sing it [again]," à la 1965.

When Krogsgaard located fuller track information for the United Western session, as well as details from a session at the mysterious Cream Studio the previous day, it confirmed that Dylan had worked long and hard on both songs. "Is It Worth It?" was tried five times at Cream, and four more times at United Western, while the man was prepared to do thirteen takes (seven complete) of "Yes Sir, No Sir"—which on the track sheet has a bracketed "Halleluiah" in the title—though why he should reuse a Ray Davies song title (from the *Arthur* album) when no such phrase appears in the song eludes me. Despite such endeavors, when it came time to mix the resultant album in May, neither song became part of that process.

And for all the effort expended, at no point does it appear that Dylan gave either song a lyric any more realized than "I'm Not There," or more coherent than "Baby Won't You Be My Baby." Both songs remained skeletal musical outlines onto which Dylan has draped the merest of refrains—"Is it worth it / what you're doing to me" in the first instance, while the rest of the lyrics are hard to discern, though "Cadillac roadster in my pocket / Can't wrong" certainly suggest dummy lyrics from the "Jet Pilot" school. If "Is It Worth It?" also displays an ongoing, unhealthy fixation with reggae riffs on Dylan's part, "Yes Sir, No Sir" has a much more interesting musical structure, with a loping bass, and stop-start arrangement that maintains a good groove, but with any lyric secondary to "feel," man. Whatever their merits, neither song seemed to warrant the second and third thoughts Dylan expended on them, and by the end of the month he had realized that he had no shortage of more realized songs.

{417} IN THE SUMMERTIME

Published lyric/s: Lyrics 85; Lyrics 04.

Known studio recordings: Cream Studio, L.A., April 1, 1981; Clover Studios, L.A., April 27—11 takes [SoL]; May 14, 1981.

First known performance: Earl's Court, London, June 29, 1981.

I love those old piano ballads. In my hometown . . . you would some-
times hear parlor tunes coming out of doorways and open windows . . .
I actually tried to conjure up that feeling once in a song . . . called "In the
Summertime." —Dylan, to Bill Flanagan, 2009

"In the Summertime" is another of those classic cast-iron torch
ballads Dylan is inclined to hide in the grooves of patchy albums for
the diggers to find. He recorded it initially in a single take at the April
1 session, and then returned to it for real at Clover at the end of the
month to confirm it was no mere whim. One listen convinces that this
is a song he had carried with him a while. Not only does it look back to
an idyllic time, before things got too messy, it also shares the concerns
of another song from the period, "Let's Keep It Between Us," notably in
the couplet "Strangers they meddled in our affairs, poverty and shame
was theirs / But all that suffering's not to be compared with the glory
that is to be."

Like Lot's wife, "In the Summertime" can't help but look back. The
time in question probably preceded Dylan's conversion experience—
which he implies by asking rhetorically, "Did I lose my mind when I
tried to get rid of everything you see?" Strangers meddling in his affairs
could easily apply to his relationship with Faridi McFree, his children's
art teacher, the summer after his divorce from Sara (see *Behind the Shades*,
pages 454–5). That summer on his Minnesotan farm certainly seemed
idyllic to McFree, who remembers a man who "was shot emotionally.
The farm was really where he got back on his feet again." Elsewhere in
the song, Dylan suggests his religious epiphany came shortly *after* these
two lovers parted:

> I got the heart and you got the blood.
> We cut through iron and we cut through mud.
> Then came the warning that was before the flood,
> That set everybody free. ·

"The warning" to which Dylan appears to be alluding is the one
given to Noah after God brought the great flood down on Man, to
which Jesus refers when preaching of the judgment to come in

Matthew's gospel: "For as in the days that were before the flood they were eating and drinking, marrying and giving in marriage, until the day that Noe entered into the ark. And knew not until the flood came, and took them all away; so shall also the coming of the Son of man be" (24:38–9).

Actually, in the *Shot of Love* songbook the line reads quite differently: "Then came the morning before the flood / That set everybody free." One might assume that this was a simple mistake in transcription—particularly as the line is given in *Lyrics* the way Dylan sings it—were it not that the typescript made for copyright purposes in 1981 has been hand-corrected from "warning" to "morning," and the legend "OK, per BD 6/4" added. Evidently, said alteration was deliberate.

In concert, Dylan continued to sing of the warning before the flood. And in the period between June 28, 1981, when it debuted, and the end of the European tour, "In the Summertime" continued to whet audiences" appetite for the impending album with its affecting wistfulness—even when it preached of the judgment (and redemption) to come. However, when the song appeared on the August release, it shared the demo-like quality of much of the album. Though this abrasive quality worked on the more rough and ready songs, this song deserved the same care and attention to detail "Every Grain of Sand" received. Instead, after nine distinct mixes and several overdubs, all that changed was Dylan and/ or Plotkin elected to prune a good forty-five seconds of heartbreakin' harmonica, a sin he thankfully stopped short of committing on the other *Shot of Love* song "written in turmoil [but] delivered in a peaceful, quiet way."

{418} NEED A WOMAN

Published lyric/s: The Telegraph #19; Lyrics 85; Lyrics 04. *[Recorded version:* In His Own Words 3.*]*

Known studio recordings: Cream Studio, L.A., April 1, 1981; Clover Studios, L.A., April 27, 1981—4 takes [TBS].

"Need a Woman" is a song that survived almost the entire, tortuous recording process for *Shot of Love*, only falling at the final hurdle, when the album was sequenced in mid-May. Even then, it would appear that

Dylan was not quite ready to give up on the song, providing two quite separate lyrical rewrites to ex–Magic Band guitarist Ry Cooder when he looked to record it for his own 1982 LP, *The Slide Area.*

Having featured on the original "Rosato list" (see #420–4) as a bracketed song, it was hardly a surprise that Dylan made a couple of fitful attempts to record "Need a Woman" as early as the April 1 Cream session. However, he did not make a serious commitment to this muse until the Clover sessions, the last week of April. The version recorded on April 27 is the one that appears on *The Bootleg Series Vols 1–3* (having already circulated from a four-song publishing demo). And that version fully reflects the original "hanging in the balance" conceit underlying most of the initial *Shot of Love* material, combining his search for "a woman drinking from the same cup" of salvation with his own personal quest for redemption:

> Searching for the truth the way God designed it,
> Well, the real truth is I may be afraid to find it . . .
> That which is not permanent don't last,
> Whatever's waiting in the future could be what you're running from in the past.

The April 27 take has the same gnarled gusto as the title track, being hitched to a groove that never lets up. It was subjected to two mixes at the May 4 mix session (the second of which appears on *The Bootleg Series*), along with the likes of "Angelina," "Every Grain of Sand," and "Trouble," before being added to the shortlist for *Shot of Love*—where it stalled. That is, until Dylan's rhythm section—who had evidently enjoyed the whole feel of the track—found themselves working with Ry Cooder. Bassist Tim Drummond suggested they try the song again.

Cooder, talking to Norwegian pop periodical *Puls* at the time of his album's release, recalled the circumstances which led him to record it: "Tim Drummond and Jim Keltner had been on tour with Dylan and . . . he had this song which hadn't got recorded . . . We tried it out and it worked . . . [but] I had to change a good part of the lyrics . . . I had to focus the lyrics. He's so vague, y'know—his words go in all [sorts of] directions . . . I thought, 'I must make a story out of it.' . . . He didn't care. It was all the same to him. I appreciated that a lot. He didn't interfere or stop me from changing the lyrics."

Setting aside for a moment the sheer hubris of a cotton-pickin' slide-guitarist deciding he would "improve" a lyric coming from the pen of his generation's finest songwriter, it severely overstates the case to suggest that Dylan "didn't care" just because he didn't stop Cooder from "changing the lyrics." When the lyric was published in the 1985 edition of *Lyrics*, it was neither the version recorded for *Shot of Love* nor that reproduced on the rear sleeve of Cooder's album.

Rather, it bears all the hallmarks of the lyric Cooder received—and felt lacked focus. They were credited solely to Dylan. Gone was the couplet "Now you don't frighten me / I ain't no defendant" and the dreadful last verse Cooder added to "make a story out of it." So maybe Dylan didn't care a great deal for Cooder's own co-Dylan scenario. (Cooder has the song's protagonists "riding out . . . at midnight like two Spanish desperadoes / Gazing down upon the futile world in her Cadillac Eldorado." Don't give up the day job, Ry.)

This verse of Cooder's—for all its lyrical lapses—raises its own question. The guitarist must have seen more than one set of Dylan lyrics, because the image of "a futile world" has been nabbed not from the version reproduced in *Lyrics,* but from a set that was sent out in typescript with a demo tape of the *Shot of Love* version. This version, which has not been reproduced anywhere else (as far as I'm aware) is the best of the lot. And in the final chorus, Dylan depicts himself as being stuck at "midnight on the desert in the belly of a futile world / In a house that shines on the side of the hill, going up with boys and girls."

Though based on the *Shot of Love* recording, at least half the lyric has been rewritten. This "Need a Woman" represents a halfway house between the April 1981 recording and the 1982 rewrite included in *Lyrics* (which I suspect Dylan gave to an ungrateful Cooder). From the same top drawer as the rewritten "Groom's Still Waiting," this variant contains enough classic Dylan couplets to put Cooder's clumsy composite to shame:

It's been raining on my roof all day, and I'm soaking wet,
My heart feels like it is on fire, but my clothes ain't burning yet.

You can believe anything you want to, long as you don't believe in what's wrong,
That unseen eye is watching you—got to be cool all day long.

I looked into the mirror this morning; I seen a man without a face,
I covered my eyes, I looked back again but all I saw was empty space.

Quite when Dylan reworked the lyric is not clear. Was it before he rerecorded a handful of *Shot of Love* songs in two post-mix, mid-May sessions? Or did he intend to rerecord some of the leftover songs later in the year, as he hinted he might to Neil Spencer? Another 1982 rewrite, of "You Changed My Life," suggests he had not quite given up on the missing songs from the double album that never was.

Whatever the case, he evidently preferred this lyric. Otherwise why send it out with a demo tape that included the original recording (along with "Angelina" and "Yonder Comes Sin")? Quite why Dylan subsequently had a further go at the lyric on Cooder's behalf is less obvious. The version in *Lyrics* has its share of good lines ("It's been raining in the trenches all day long, dripping down to my clothes"), but nothing leaps out at you like the lines quoted above. Perhaps Cooder dared to ask Dylan if *he* could "focus the lyrics," and this is what he came up with. By the 2004 edition of *Lyrics*, the original 1981 version had been released officially on *The Bootleg Series 1–3*, but *Lyrics* continued to include Dylan's Cooderesque rewrite. Whatever the relative merits of Dylan's respective versions, Cooder should have stuck with what he received. Or Dylan should have given it to someone who knew the difference between obtuse and vague.

{419} **ALMOST PERSUADED**

{420} **BORROWED TIME**

{421} **ROCKIN' BOAT**

{422} **I WANT YOU TO KNOW I LOVE YOU**

{423} **GONNA LOVE YOU ANYWAY**

> *Known studio recordings [#419–23]: Cream Studio, L.A. April 1, 1981.*
> *[#419 & ?423: Rundown Studios, Santa Monica, CA, April 3–9, 1981.]*

> I learned how to make records . . . when I recorded for John Hammond.
> And we [still] work the same way, which is, going into the studio and
> making a record. Right then and there. I know the other way, and I
> know a lot of people do it the other way . . . but I'm not interested
> in that aspect of recording: laying down tracks and then coming back
> and perfecting those tracks and then perfecting lyrics which seem
> to wanna go with those tracks—songs [which] are created in the
> recording studio. For me, I'm a live performer. I have to play songs
> which relate to the faces that I'm singing to. And I can't do that if I was
> spending a year in the studio working on a track. —Dylan, to Dave
> Herman, July 1981

On April 1, 1981, Dylan temporarily suspended work on the key
songs intended for his next album—and the irreconcilable demands
of an unsympathetic producer, Jimmy Iovine—to knock out a bunch
of demos at a small demo studio nearby. The exercise—quantitatively,
if not qualitatively—proved that Dylan was more adept at this kind
of recording. Twenty-plus songs were recorded in a single day. And
although fully half of those began as instrumentals, and at least three
were covers, it produced prototypes for at least three songs he then
transferred to the album sessions proper—"Need a Woman," "You
Changed My Life," and "In the Summertime." Also cut were five
songs that were finally copyrighted on the 1985 *Compilation #2* tape
and a single song subsequently pulled to a reel of "Early Roughs."

That last song, "I Wish It Would Rain," remains the most tantalizing of the lot. One's natural inclination is to assume it is the famous
Whitfield-Strong soul classic, covered by Marvin Gaye for the same 1970
album that included "Abraham, Martin, & John" (*That's the Way Love
Is*), a song Dylan had been performing the previous fall. And yet, he
expended far more effort on it than either of the other covers recorded at
Cream—Hank Williams's "Cold Cold Heart" and the traditional "Wild
Mountain Thyme," both dispatched in a single take. Nonetheless, at
least one individual who has heard it says it *is* the soul classic.

Meanwhile, the five fully fledged songs (excluding instrumentals) copyrighted on *Compilation #2* from this session present their own problems
of identification. Firstly, "Gonna Love Her Anyway" *is* an instrumental,

or at least it is on *Compilation #2*. However, at some juncture I suspect it had a lyric, because it was included on the list of "scheduled" songs made by Arthur Rosato in advance of the sessions (then updated to include songs he came up with in the interim).[16] In this list, which groups the instrumentals together irrespective of the session at which they were recorded, "Gonna Love You [*sic*] Anyway" instead comes between "Is It Worth It?" and "The Groom's Still Waiting" as one of eleven bracketed songs that were probably part of a provisional album sequence. A title like "Gonna Love You Anyway" also rather suggests lyrics (as does "It's All Dangerous to Me," another song cut at Cream which he appears to have recut at Rundown).

The other four songs from Cream (#419–22) also appear on Arthur's list—in the case of "I Want You to Know That I Love You," under the more correct title, i.e., what the girls sing throughout, "You Can't Make It on Your Own"—while "Borrowed Time" and "Almost Persuaded" both appear in that initial eleven-song sequence. Again, they were presumably meant to be real songs, "Borrowed Time" being an apposite title for a song that lasts ten minutes before Dylan decides to give up the search.

"Almost Persuaded" may have had the most potential of any among this group of songs, but the version on *Compilation #2* was probably not recorded at Cream. The four other Cream songs pulled to a copyright reel (i.e., *Compilation #2*) at some point in December 1984 are marked thus on the session tape. "Almost Persuaded" is not. And it comes at the end of said compilation cassette, sandwiched between two ramblin' instrumentals, neither of which appear on the Cream track sheet: "All the Way" (not to be confused with "All the Way Down") and "Tune After Almost," while the April 1 log identifies all three versions of "Almost Persuaded" as "false starts." A later Rundown run-through seems likelier.

424} MOVIN' (WAIT & SEE)

425} FUR SLIPPERS

426} SINGING THIS SONG FOR YOU

427} REACH OUT

{428} AH AH AH

Published lyric/s [#425]: Words Fill My Head.
Known studio recordings: United Western, L.A., April 2, 1981 [#425: Rundown Studios, Santa Monica, CA, April 3–9, 1981; #428: Rundown Studios, April 7, 1981].

Again, any picture I construct of the United Western session is bound to be frustratingly incomplete and contradictory. Aside from the three songs definitely included on *Compilation #2*—"Is It Worth It?," "Yes Sir, No Sir," and "Ah, Ah, Ah"—there is at least one other song from this session which appears on said compilation. Listed as "Movin" on the session log, as "Wait & See" on the compilation cassette, and under both titles on Rosato's list, the song is preceded by an "Instrumental—Up Tempo" (in all likelihood, the "Instrumental Calypso" which precedes it on *Compilation #2*).

The session log proves equally unhelpful regarding the other material recorded on this day—which began with multiple takes of two untitled songs. Later on, Dylan records another untitled song, a single take of a song called "Reach Out" and then five takes (three complete) of something called "Singing a Song for You." The latter pair could well be covers, "Reach Out" being either the gospel song "Reach Out to Jesus"—once covered by Elvis—or "Reach Out (I'll Be There)" if he was exploring the Motown catalog. Or a new song. "Singing a Song for You" could also be either. If it is a cover, Leon Russell's "A Song for You" would be a strong candidate (though "I'm singing this song *to* you" is what Russell actually sings). But three complete takes probably argues for an original song (historically, Dylan doesn't tend to redo covers he's already sung complete).

Original or not, Dylan recorded both songs and then promptly forgot about them. The five songs deemed worthy of preservation—copied to cassette by Rosato, presumably from a comp reel—comprised two versions of "Yes Sir, No Sir," a full band version of the Everlys' "Let It Be Me," "Is It Worth It?," "Ah Ah Ah," and an incongruous attempt at a fifties-style R&B single, "Fur Slippers." (Incidentally, if said comp reel *is* the direct source for *Compilation #2*, then "Movin'" was *definitely* rerecorded at Rundown).

"Fur Slippers" is a song Dylan copyrighted a year after *Shot of Love*, three whole years before *Compilation #2*. One of four leftovers from these sessions that were copyrighted in June–July 1982 (as was the live 1981 song "Jesus Is the One"), "Fur Slippers" was either given a lyrical overhaul at the time of its copyrighting (like "You Changed My Life") or was reworked at Rundown after the United Western session, acquiring in the interim a lyric peculiar enough—and awful enough—to have appeared on *Nashville Skyline*: "I sure do miss them fur slippers as much as I miss you."

It would be seventeen long years before anyone took this lyric at face value and covered them, beginning in 1999 when B. B. King, of all people, decided that it expressed his kinda blues. One of a number of old timers bribed to record something for a CBS miniseries called *Shake, Rattle, & Roll*, King gave the song—now cocredited to Dylan and bassist Tim Drummond—a more orthodox setting:

> Ain't got no radio, ain't got no telephone,
> Ain't got no girlfriend, ain't got nowhere to go,
> She was here yesterday, now she's gone away,
> And when she left, she took my fur slippers away.

Those last two lines are Dylan's. The first two remain so mired in the blues lexicon that to give anyone credit would require a lotta nerve. And while there is now a bridge to the song, "They was so soft, they look so fine / They felt so good, they were all mine," Dylan didn't seem to think the song warranted further recognition, omitting it from the 2004 *Lyrics*. Despite which, those other darn fools the Crudup Brothers went and recorded the song in the interim.

429} ALL THE WAY DOWN

430} WIND BLOWIN' ON THE WATER

431} CHILD TO ME

432} THE KING IS ON THE THRONE

Known studio recordings: Rundown Studios, Santa Monica, CA, April 3–9, 1981.

According to our friend Krogsgaard, there was a twenty-one day gap between the United Western session and a resumption of work at Clover Studios. He makes such a claim in the face of a mountain of evidence to the contrary. Collectors have at least six songs—and know of at least one more lost original—from these sessions for which we cannot account unless Dylan undertook at least two further sessions in the interim, and probably more like four or five. We also have two solid dates for sessions from the week after the Cream and United Western sessions—of April 6 and 7—from official sources. A tape box bearing the date April 6 features an early (bootlegged) version of "Shot of Love"; while April 7 is given on the *Biograph* boxed set as the recording date for that version of "Caribbean Wind." (Krogsgaard suggests "this date may refer to the mixing date," unable to hear any fundamental difference between the two studio versions, only one of which can realistically come from the March 31 session.[17])

Another early April session misfiled with the AFM (this time dated April 29) features three more songs written in advance of the Clover sessions: "Property of Jesus," "Fur Slippers," and something called "The King Is on the Throne." This last song appears on the Rosato list (first draft). Its inclusion there strongly suggests it was a Dylan original. One presumes said song was concerned with the Day of the Lord, having possibly been influenced by a gospel blues Blind Willie Johnson recorded back in 1929, "Going to See the King." Said song, by a long-standing favorite of Dylan's (Johnson's "In My Time of Dyin'" appearing on his debut LP), had been rehearsed the previous fall. It later provided Dylan with another song title (its full title being "Bye and Bye Going to See the King").

To further reinforce the suspicion that Dylan and his band did not remain idle the first three weeks in April, there are nine other recordings which cannot (all) be accounted for with the session logs we know about: the three songs from the "Almost Persuaded" tape (mentioned above),three unattributed instrumentals from *Compilation #2* that may or may not be the unnamed instrumentals on the Cream and United Western reels ("More to This than Meets the Eye," "Instrumental Calypso," and "Walking on Eggs"), and the first three songs listed above, all of which have been grouped together on *Compilation #2* ("Child to Me," "Wind Blowing on the Water," and "All the Way Down").

Intriguingly, none of the above trio feature in Rosato's initial list, which suggests they were written (or improvised) later. They probably come from the April 6 session, for which we have just a single song logged. Persuasive evidence that this was no jam session but a pukka album session actually resides in Krogsgaard's sessionography—two of these three songs, "Wind Blowing on the Water" and "All the Way Down," were given proper mixes on May 5, as were two other recordings probably made within twenty-four hours: "Caribbean Wind" and "Property of Jesus."

"Wind Blowing on the Water" and "All the Way Down" exemplify the Dylan uninterested in "perfecting lyrics which seem to wanna go with those tracks," even if both have something going for them musically. The girl singers certainly give Dylan his money's worth vocally, especially on that curious coda to "Ain't Gonna Go to Hell," "All the Way Down," where they chant the one line, "You're going all the way down" throughout. "(You're Just A) Child to Me" sounds half-formed, not to say half-baked, it taking the pooling of these early session tapes as *Compilation #2* for anyone to remember it was even there.

By the time Dylan was working on these songs he had already acquired an impressive stockpile of tracks. And yet at some point— probably around April 10, when that reel of "Early Roughs" was made—he took a break in order to write yet more material for an album whose identity was morphing on a daily basis. When he returned to Rundown (and then Clover), on or around April 23, he had seven more songs to record, and much of what he had cut to date he was inclined to rerecord.

{433} BE CAREFUL

Known studio recordings: Rundown Studio, Santa Monica, CA, April 23, 1981—2 takes.

At some point in late April, or even early May, Arthur Rosato added eight songs to his earlier list of songs for the new Dylan album. Those eight titles were: "Property of Jesus," "Magic," "Don't Take Yourself Away," "Be Careful," "Trouble," "Bolero," "Dead Man, Dead Man," and "Watered-Down Love." "Bolero" is in fact "Heart of Mine" (Rosato amends the title himself). Just about all of the other songs were ones Dylan had written in the interim, though "Heart of Mine" had figured in the March rehearsals. Of the other seven, only "Property of Jesus" had been recorded in real time at Rundown, probably on April 7. Five of them would make the nine-track *Shot of Love*.

Of the three still unreleased songs, only "Be Careful" remains wholly unheard by collectors. According to Krogsgaard's sessionography, the song was cut in two takes at the first Clover session on April 23, between numerous takes of "You Changed My Life." However, it was never shortlisted for the album and disappeared forthwith.

{434} MAGIC

Known studio recordings: Rundown Studios, Santa Monica, CA, April 23, 1981—1 take; April 24—2 takes.

The session logs suggest "Magic" was recorded on consecutive days, in a single take on April 23, and twice more on the twenty-fourth. One of these was copyrighted on the 1985 *Compilation #2*, the only song from the productive Clover sessions to appear on that comp. Indeed, the non-copyrighting of this particular song in 1981–2 seems to have been an oversight, perhaps occasioned by the problem of transcribing a set of lyrics. Whereas "Need a Woman," "You Changed My Life," and "Don't Ever Take Yourself Away" proved straightforward enough to receive full protection in 1982, "Magic" was only copyrighted as part of the 1985 compilation tape.

It is in fact little more than another Rundown groove which Dylan feels like extemporizing over (along the lines of "anything she wants he will give her 'cause it's magic"). And yet, unlike those other songs, "Magic" was a hair's breadth away from making the pukka platter, the real deal, the album itself. Mixed on May 5 at the same session as "Caribbean Wind," "Wind Blowing on the Water," and "All the Way Down," "Magic" was third track on side two of the original May 12 sequence for *Shot of Love*, sandwiched between "In the Summertime" and "Trouble"—presumably intended as boogie-lite relief from stronger fare. And it must be said that among the semi-throwaway *Shot of Love* detritus, it stands tall. Bob and Clydie King build up a real head of steam, even if such enthusiasm only sporadically carried over to the remainder of what proved to be a long and winding session.

It was also a first take. The version slotted onto *Compilation #2*—also the version mixed and sequenced in May (and transferred to a comp. reel on May 18, along with "Caribbean Wind" and "Angelina")—comes from the twenty-third. Also transferred from that session tape were finished takes of "Trouble" and "Heart of Mine," all three making it to the May 12 sequence for *Shot of Love*, though not to the album proper. The two takes of "Magic" listed from the twenty-fourth were presumably unsuccessful attempts to recreate the same groove, leaving Dylan little choice but to go with his initial grab. The mix used for the May 18 comp. reel—which has a slightly different feel to the rougher *Compilation #2* mix—later snuck onto *The Genuine Bootleg Series—Take Two* bootleg collection.

435} DEAD MAN, DEAD MAN

Published lyric/s: Lyrics 85; Lyrics 04.
Known studio recordings: Rundown Studio, Santa Monica, CA, April 23, 1981; Clover Studios, L.A., April 27—3 takes; April 28—3 takes; April 29—2 takes; April 30—6 takes; May 14, 1981 [SoL].
First known performance: Poplar Creek, IL, June 10, 1981.

Rarely has Dylan changed direction in mid-album as radically as he did on April 23, 1981. He arrived at the session, credited to Clover on some listings but quite possibly still held at his own studio off Santa Monica Boulevard, with half a dozen new songs he wanted to record. With these songs, and the others he would add over the following week, *Shot of Love* was transformed from an album of disaffected love set against the End Times into the third instalment in a highly judgmental trilogy. He alluded to the change in conversation with *NME*'s Neil Spencer, suggesting the loss of "Angelina" and "Caribbean Wind" had convinced him to make a quite different, more retrograde album.

By opening side two of the released record with a similar message to the title track, but seen now from the other side of the mirror, Dylan shifted the emphasis 180 degrees. As he told a Birmingham audience the following July, "['Dead Man, Dead Man'] is a song about myself . . . I just recall I wrote this song while looking into the mirror." One couplet might even have come from a draft version of the title track: "What are you trying to overpower me with, the doctrine or the gun / My back's already to the wall—where can I run?"

As a song, "Dead Man, Dead Man" was designed to stand up both scripturally and sonically. Its primary inspiration was a passage in Romans already referred to in concert the previous May, when Dylan prefaced "Slow Train" by reminding any sceptics, "That's why it says, I think it's Romans 8, that same spirit that raised Christ from the dead, dwells in you, and shall quicken your mortal life . . . Lots of dead people walking around today, telling everybody they're alive. Nations are being ruled by dead people, people with no life in them at all." (The passage he refers to is indeed from Romans 8—verse 11.)

He is also drawing on the opening chapter of Romans, taking the phrase "reprobate mind" from a passage that runs, "God gave them over to a reprobate mind . . . being filled with all [forms of] unrighteousness, fornication, wickedness, covetousness, maliciousness; full of envy, murder, debate, deceit, malignity; whisperers, Backbiters, haters of God . . . They which commit such things are worthy of death" (1:28–32). While from Ephesians 5:14—"Awake thou that sleepest, and arise from the dead"—he has drawn the inspiration underlying his query to said dead man, "When will you arise?"

So, here he was again writing glossaries to the Scriptures in song. Elsewhere, though, the lyrics focus on modern manifestations of the spirit of Babel, as he constructs another retinue of losers in the ultimate lottery, arriving at the exact same spot as "I'd Hate to Be You on That Dreadful Day," almost two decades earlier, playing Lazarus to some modern-day Dives: "The tuxedo that you're wearing, the flower in your lapel / Oooh, I can't stand it, I can't stand it—it's taking me down to hell."

Unfortunately, having sprung the song on a slightly bemused band, Dylan failed to fire them up in the same way he had managed earlier with the title track. Despite being attempted at just about every Clover session that last week in April, he was still reworking "Dead Man, Dead Man" after the original May 12 sequence. On May 14, further recording ensued, but still the song's punchy self failed to arise. Only in concert that summer, a nightly occurrence, did Dylan wipe the cobwebs from his mind and the dust of the road from his eyes, delivering the pummeling performance he never quite managed in the studio.

It took until 1989 for him to accept fully the fact that this song was served best by being left as a performance piece. At this juncture, a live version of the song suddenly appeared on the B-side of the *Oh Mercy* single "Everything Is Broken." But this live version came from a New Orleans show in November 1981 (from which the *Biograph* "Heart of Mine" had already been culled). And damn fine it still sounded, even in this peculiar context. As if to reinforce its resurrection, "Dead Man, Dead Man" was then fleetingly restored to live favor, featured on opening night at the Beacon Theatre in New York (October 10, 1989)—as well as the following two nights and at a show later that month in Poughkeepsie—when it came hard on the heels of two other songs that dealt with the dangers of self-deception, "Seeing the Real You at Last" and "What Good Am I?" After which, it fell back to the ground.

{436} TROUBLE

Published lyric/s: Lyrics 85; Lyrics 04.

Known studio recordings: Rundown Studios, Santa Monica, CA, April 23, 1981—3 takes; Clover Studios L.A., May 14, 1981 [SoL].

First known performance: Holmdel, NJ, July 21, 1989.

Trouble—another Dylanesque cipher for sinfulness—was still on the man's mind as he set about reconfiguring the album he was due to release. One supposes a song like this came easily enough—after all, it has no tune, doggerel for the lyric, and the most basic blues structure. How hard can it have been? It certainly came easily in the studio, being cut in just three takes—all complete—at the April 23 session. Two of these were short-listed for the album, as he again hedged his bets. But neither would make the final album as just three days after a provisional sequence had been agreed—on which the April 23 "Trouble" again followed "Magic"—Dylan fiddled with the song some more.

A May 14 session managed to produce an even more tuneless take, despite the presence of some of the finest players on the block, notably ex-Elvis saxophonist Steve Douglas and Heartbreakers organist Benmont Tench. Predictably, this was the one Dylan elected to release. And that was that—for eight years or so. Only in 1989 did it occur to him that he might flay his way through the troubles of the world again. With G. E. Smith doing his very best B. B. King impersonation, Dylan sporadically flirted with these sentiments through a number of summer shows.

{437} DON'T EVER TAKE YOURSELF AWAY

Published lyric/s: Words Fill My Head.
Known studio recordings: Rundown Studio, Santa Monica, CA, April 23, 1981—2 takes.

"Don't Ever Take Yourself Away," one of the new songs that Dylan brought to the mammoth April 23 session, was also one of the few he completed that day to his satisfaction.[18] While it would have been a pleasant diversion on a minor Dylan album, it hardly added a great deal to the tranche of stay-with-me songs penned over the past few months. Largely an exercise in fitting a jerky lyric to a tango backing, it sounds like he was hoping for another radio hit, à la "Baby Stop Crying." At some point, though, he remembered something he had told Paul Vincent the previous November: "I really keep my songs and make 'em happen so they last a while, rather than just be a hit record and gone."

As a result, the song was shuffled sideways, only being copyrighted during a clearing-up exercise in 1982. That transcription did the song few favors, the forced internal rhymes ("Words can't express / [what] my heart would confess") reading particularly badly on the page. The copyrighted lyric also put the first verse he recorded last, while adding an additional verse:

> Dearest you're the _____
> You're perfect for me
> You're the one I hoped for
> The one that I waited my whole life for
> Dearest, I think we've only just begun
> Wherever I [may] be I want you next to me
> At the end, when my race has been run.

Thankfully, the outtake's illicit appearance on *The Genuine Bootleg Series Vol. 1* put the lyric back where it belonged, on a jerkin' boat.

{438} WATERED-DOWN LOVE

Published lyric/s: Lyrics 85; Lyrics 04.

Known studio recordings: Clover Studios, L.A., April 27—1 take; April 28—4 takes [SoL]; May 15—9 takes.

First known performance: Poplar Creek IL, June 10, 1981.

Having discovered this lyric-writing lark to be so much easier when he just gave vent to his despair at the world, Dylan wrote the third in a trilogy designed to replace those epic love songs that had once been the core constituents of his next album. A lot less lame than "Trouble," marginally inferior to "Dead Man, Dead Man," "Watered-Down Love" prefaces the pair on the released album. Ironically, the one place where it would have made sense would have been *after* the likes of "Angelina" and "The Groom's Still Waiting," as a conscious retort to the man-made beauty those songs addressed and which had proven so beguiling.

Again, Dylan came up with this song late in the process, and perhaps it was this urgency that prompted him to grab the first riff that came to him—Betty Wright's "Clean Up Woman" (a point Nick Kent made in his *NME* review of the album). What he does with Wright's Atlantic masterpiece qualifies as a rather canny reinterpretation—the use of the girls making the debt less obvious in concert. But the track still goes on far longer than Wright's hit 45, and with ever-diminishing effect, which is presumably why Dylan edited the song down from 4:50 to 4:10 on the album, deleting the fifth verse in the process:

> Love that's pure is not what you teach me,
> I got to go where it can reach me,
> I got to flee towards patience and meekness,
> You miscalculate me, mistake my kindness for weakness.

In concert, though, this final verse was retained, suggesting the edit had been part of a general trimming down of the album to the forty-minute mark. (Aside from a straight deletion of two songs—"Angelina" and "Magic"—the versions of "Shot of Love," "In the Summertime," and "Watered-Down Love" were all edited.) Dylan seems to have set about recutting the song, spending much of a last-minute session on May 15 trying to capture its soul.

{ Still on the Road }

The endeavor proved unsuccessful, and the master remained as before. By the time this slightly tepid Clover version was released, Dylan had played the song throughout the arenas of Europe, any single perform-ance making the studio incarnation sound decidedly inferior. The song remained its sprightly self throughout the fall U.S. tour, but went the way of most *Shot of Love* songs when the lease expired on his Rundown rehearsal studio at year's end. A perfunctory run-through at last-minute theater rehearsals for the 1984 European tour is the closest it ever came to a latter-day revival.

Note: The published lyric changes the line "Won't hold you back, *won't get in your way*," to "won't mess up your day." It also changes "Capture your soul and hold it for ransom" to "Capture your heart," which is hardly a good way of affirming the song's messianic message.

{439} LENNY BRUCE

Published lyric/s: Lyrics 85; Lyrics 04.

Known studio recordings: Clover Studios, L.A., April 29, 1981—2 takes; April 30—1 take; May 14, 1981 [SoL].

First known performance: Poplar Creek, IL, June 10, 1981.

"Lenny Bruce" stands as the "George Jackson" of Dylan's religious period. Written in a few minutes—and boy does it show—the sole purpose of the song seems to have been to demonstrate that Dylan could still write about something other than the End Times. And protest eulogies had long been a favorite form for the man's song-writing skills. This time, he had even met the man who shared the same hip-speakin' Village milieu. Dylan caught his act at least once, the late show at the Village Theatre on November 30, 1963, when Bruce was still in command of his stagecraft. And as he told Dave Herman on the song's release, "It is true I rode with [Lenny Bruce] once in a taxi cab. I thought it was a little strange after he died that people made such a hero out of him, [but] when he was alive he couldn't even get a break. Certainly now comedy is rank, dirty and vulgar and very unfunny and stupid."

Nor could Dylan have been unaware that a (okay, the) principal target of Bruce's comedy was organized religion (his skit on Jesus returning to earth during a sermon from Cardinal Spellman, who promptly phones up the Pope to ask what he is paying protection money for, being the supreme example). Nor should one necessarily assume that Dylan felt conflicted about this aspect of Bruce's message. As he told one radio interviewer, at the height of his evangelical mission, "Religion is another form of bondage which man invents to get himself to God. But that's why Christ came. Christ didn't preach religion. He preached the Truth, the Way, and the Life."

On some level, Dylan clearly intended to draw an analogy between Bruce and Christ, both of whom were castigated for telling it like it is. He reinforced this goal when he took to prefacing the song with a brief rap—on the Japanese leg of the True Confessions tour in 1986—referencing another artist who died ignominiously: "Here's a song about recognition, or lack of recognition. It was Tennessee Williams who said, 'I don't ask for your pity, just your understanding. Not even that, but just your recognition of me in you and Time, the enemy in us all.' Anyway, Tennessee Williams led a pretty drastic life. He died all by himself in a New York hotel room without a friend in the world. Another man died like that." Dylan, who had just seen Lauren Bacall starring in *Sweet Bird of Youth*, recognized the parallels immediately.

Meanwhile, "Lenny Bruce" continued to exercise a strange fascination on its author, even after most fans and commentators (myself included) dismissed it as trite and simplistic. Performed throughout 1981, it again became a regular in the 1986–7 Heartbreakers sets, hanging on through the early years of the Never Ending Tour, sometimes sung with the same passion, and always set to the same affecting tune—both of which were wasted on such a hastily conceived song.

Perhaps Dylan simply remembered the personal satisfaction he felt when the song came so easily and effortlessly, after months of wrestling with greater works that got away from him. He was already slightly defensive about the song by July 1981, when he informed *NME* editor Neil Spencer, "I wrote that [song] in about five minutes . . . I didn't even know why I was writing it; it just naturally came out." Absent from the Rosato lists, and only recorded when the sessions were winding down, we can be fairly confident "Lenny Bruce" was a last-minute attempt to broaden the nature of the album he sure hoped he'd completed.

{440} JESUS IS THE ONE

Published lyric/s: Words Fill My Head.

First known performance: Oslo, July 9, 1981.

"Jesus Is the One" is definitely one of the odder unreleased Dylan songs, not because of its sentiment—which is pretty much revealed by the title, compounded by a list in verse form of people who ain't Him and therefore can't raise the dead—but because of where and when he introduced it into the set. Having initially decided to meet fans halfway on his first tour of 1981 by dropping the more proselytizing polemics from the set—perhaps at the insistence of European promoters with sheaves of tickets in their hands—barely had Dylan touched down on the European mainland than he introduced this polemic. It was even retained for much of the European leg, before reappearing at the final show of 1981, in Lakeland, Florida, where it continued to hammer home its message. Well, message received.

{441} THIEF ON THE CROSS

Published lyric/s: Words Fill My Head.

First known performance: New Orleans, LA, November 10, 1981.

Here is a song Dylan performed just once, towards the end of the final U.S. tour with a band formed two years earlier to "preach the gospel from place to place." It seems to have been unveiled on this occasion for a specific reason—a possible live album. A multitrack had been brought in to record both New Orleans shows for a historic document of the band he was about to disband, and in this instance Dylan was looking to capture the song on its very first performance. When he scrapped the album, he forgot the song—though it was copyrighted from the live tape in a "cleaning up" exercise the following year, as the lease on Rundown expired and he took a much-needed respite from the road.

As the last song from the so-called gospel years, "Thief on the Cross" perhaps retains a significance at odds with its repetitive lyric and iden-tikit arrangement. His commitment to Christ and an abiding apocalyptic conceit are apparent as he lambasts his fellow man one more time: "Now there's winnin', rulin', and readin' / Everybody goes sinnin' by the rules." As to the thief of the title, one must assume Dylan means the two light-fingered but unnamed men crucified alongside Jesus, as opposed to "the thief in the night" himself. The opening verse certainly implies Our Lord is not the focus here: "Well, everybody's been diverted / Everybody looking the other way." On the other hand, the singer seems to "wanna talk to him," perhaps because he is wondering whether a time might come when he too will be hung as a thief.

{442} LET ME BEGIN TO LOVE

Auctioned manuscript, undated, ?circa 1981–2.

Rarely does a Dylan song present as great a problem with dating composition as "Let Me Begin to Love." There is a simple explanation for this: he never finished the song, nor does he appear to have attempted to record it. It owes its survival to the acquisition of the handwritten manuscript by person/s unknown, who recognized it for what it was, proceeding to sell it at auction in the late eighties.

But unlike "Shirley's Room" (#278), no information came with the sheet in question (though the West Coast auction house kindly reproduced the lyric in their catalog). So only textual clues can come to our aid. The use of the term "unlearn" ("I got so much to unlearn") pretty much declares it to be a product of the post-conversion years, while the couplet "Down yonder sits Maggy and her hip cousin, Bill / She's from Oklahoma City, he's from Brazil" not only alludes to two traditional songs he had or would record ("Little Maggie" and "Tell Ol' Bill") but also uses the kind of geographical counterpointing used extensively in "Caribbean Wind," "Groom's Still Waiting at the Altar," and "Angelina." Finally, the opening line of the song, "The sidewalks are crooked, the (arrows) are straight" has the aroma of "Blind Willie McTell."

All things considered, I'd place it somewhere between *Shot of Love* and *Infidels*—which may explain why the song went unfinished and unused. But plain dissatisfaction with the lyric's direction may also explain its fate. After he portrays Maggie and Bill "crying in their beer, [as] they wipe their faces with a glove" he changes his mind, rewriting it to fit the terser lines that surround it: "There's tears in their eyes which they wipe with a glove / 'Oh Maggy,' says Bill 'let us begin to love.'" Of course, the whole song might just be another writing exercise from a man hoping to see if he'd successfully memorized that rhyming dictionary. The good lines do generally rhyme with the title line: "I kicked over the barrel, 'cause it needed a shove," "I can't get with it and fly like a dove," and, best of all, "How high is the moon, man, is it that far above?" However, after four verses, any decision to henceforth concentrate on unwatered-down love has been abandoned.

1982–3

{ Infidels }

Though the media continued to fixate on Dylan's religious views—suggesting in a number of wholly unfounded reports that he had renounced his Christian faith—the significant changes in direction, on the album it took him eighteen months to get around to recording, came on a couple of wholly nontheological levels. After the abortive Shot of Love *experiment, the 1983 album saw Dylan resume recording original albums of songs—*Empire Burlesque *and* under the red sky *excepted—in single blocks of sessions, using songs old and new, borrowed and unused. At the same time, it marks the beginning of a grudging acceptance of the modern approach to recording, fiercely resisted for the past decade. This means a series of vocal overdubs at the mixing stage, changing the very nature of what he sings, and its coeval relationship to the song's performance.*

Infidels *also coincides with Dylan's disappearance from the world stage for two and a half years—his longest break since 1974—making it considerably more difficult (okay, nigh on impossible) to organize the songs by strict order of composition. If the writing process evidently began in the Caribbean, he seems to have still recorded "trigger" songs early on and to have continued producing new songs throughout the sessions—"Lord Protect My Child" and "Death Is Not the End" both appear to be contemporaneous with sessions at the Power Station.*

For all the positive aspects of these changes, the old problem of what to do when "not-so-great things happen" continued to haunt him. The album he released was another second guess, and all the poorer for it. After a month of solid endeavor, some fifteen songs were short-listed for the album, and nine picked for it—including the magnificent "Foot of Pride" and "Blind Willie McTell"—before Dylan again allowed his own doubting Thomas to reconfigure the album and redo half the vocal tracks. Eight years later, he owned up to his misdeed, admitting that "lots of songs on that album got away from me." Truly, a sign of the times . . .

{443} IT'S RIGHT

Written circa summer 1982, with Bankie Banx.

While sailing the Caribbean in his own schooner, Dylan visited the island of Anguilla, where he heard about a local reggae artist, Bankie Banx, who was considered the "Anguillan Bob Dylan." Interested in an artist who fused reggae with his kind of singer-songwriting, Dylan apparently cowrote a song with Banx called "It's Right," which they recorded together at Banx's own studio with Dylan playing keyboards. This is the last we hear of their collaboration, though Dylan's next album will engage in a discreet flirtation with reggae throughout.

{444} JOKERMAN

Published lyric/s: Lyrics 85; Lyrics 04. [Original version: Words Fill My Head.]
Known studio recordings: Power Station Studios, NYC, April 13, 1983—5 takes; April 14—1 take; June 1983 [vcl overdubs] [INF].
First known performance: Late Night with David Letterman, NYC, March 22, 1984.

> I'm usually either here [in New York], or on the west coast, or down in the Caribbean. Me and another guy have a boat down there. "Jokerman" kinda came to me in the islands. It's very mystical. The shapes there, and shadows, seem to be so ancient. The song was sorta inspired by these spirits they call *jumbis.* —Dylan, to Kurt Loder, March 1984

Though it was not the first song he recorded for *Infidels,* Dylan did not hang about recording "Jokerman." Nor did he seem to entertain any doubts where it belonged—making it the opening song on the album in both its original nine-track guise and the more denuded released artefact. In fact, the song starts where "Caribbean Wind" lets off, with "those distant ships of liberty" now "sailing into the mist," the Apocalypse they foretold temporarily put on hold while a false messiah stalks the earth, bending people to his will: "You're a man on the mountain, you can walk on the clouds / Manipulator of crowds, you're a dream twister."

As a way of setting up an album subtly invoking the End Times, it is masterful. The Jokerman is the prodigal son from "Caribbean Wind," "waiting for the night to arrive," but this time the narrator is stepping back from events to see how the inevitable conflagration between good and evil works out. In the final verse, as the Son of man is born again—"A woman just gave birth to a prince today, and dressed him in scarlet"—the narrator reminds the Jokerman of previous prophecies: "You know what he wants . . . you don't show any response." It will not be the last time he alludes to the revealed word on this richly symbolic album.

And yet plenty of folk saw *Infidels* as an album that abandoned the concerns of the so-called Christian trilogy; needless to say, it was nothing of the sort. The transition to the kind of dense imagery evident in a song like "Jokerman" might have been smoother if *Shot of Love* had been the album he originally intended. He was again writing in the same rich vein as he had on songs like "Angelina" and "Caribbean Wind," with a similar mind-set. He was also finding inspiration from the same vistas, "in the islands" of the Caribbean.

Like those earlier songs, "Jokerman" seems to have been a song he carried with him. Knack drummer Bruce Gary, who jammed with Dylan on some instrumental material in early June 1982—with the tapes rolling—thought they worked on an early version of the song. In New York it became the third song Dylan set about recording for the album, as he started the third session with it, after spending two frustrating days trying to get a grip on "Blind Willie McTell" and "Don't Fall Apart on Me Tonight." He still allowed himself to be distracted from his central purpose, indulging in blues jams and other instrumentals (given titles on the track sheet like "Slow Try Baby" and "Columbus Georgia") between various attempts at "Jokerman." Finally, he decided to try another, lesser song ("License to Kill"), which he got in a single take.

When he returned the following day, he tried the same trick with "Jokerman" itself—cutting it in a single take between versions of "Man of Peace" (its mirror song) and "Clean-Cut Kid"—and presumably it worked, because it is the last time he tried the song at these sessions.

Indeed, a few days later it was copyrighted in the form it would occupy on the first *Infidels* sequence. And that would have been that had Dylan not decided that what worked (commercially) with *Blood on the Tracks* would work again. And so, having reviewed the album some time in late May/early June, he decided to redo a number of vocals, thus reconfiguring, i.e., second-guessing, another potentially important album.

As the opening track, "Jokerman" was ripe for reevaluation, and once Dylan had it explained to him that with digital technology he could keep reworking not only the vocal track but the lyrics themselves, he developed an entirely new methodology, one he brought to bear for most future albums. It was "Idiot Wind" all over again, minus a new set of musicians he was obliged to tutor. To rewrite the song in its entirety with him, could be the work of a moment. And now, if he didn't like the results, he could do it all over again and overdub all over that one too. And though Dylan knew his vocals were best caught early, the lyrics sometimes needed time to mature.

On "Jokerman," he sacrificed one of his sublimer studio vocals from the post-conversion years at the altar of a marginally superior lyrical rewrite. In fairness, some of the rewrites are terrific: "Friend to the martyr, a friend to the woman of shame / You look into the fiery furnace, see the rich man without any name," for one. But then, the original was pretty good, too. And what he gained on the straight, he assuredly lost around the bends. Just to hear Dylan sing "Scratching the world with a fine tooth comb / You're a king among Nations, you're a stranger at home," I would be willing to lose any number of clever rewrites. And sometimes he ended up replacing real concerns with mere catchphrases, which is what happened when he exchanged "Well, the preacherman talking about the deaf and the dumb / And a world to come, that's already been predetermined" for the less arresting, eschatologically uninteresting "Well, the rifleman's stalking the sick and the lame / Preacherman seeks the same, who'll get there first is uncertain." The one time he gains more than he gave up comes in the final verse, as he goes from:

> They'll put priests into pimps and make old men bark,
> Take a woman who could have been Joan of Arc
> And turn her into a harlot . . .

to:

> He'll put the priest in his pocket, put the blade to the heat,
> Take the motherless children off the street,
> And place them at the feet of a harlot.

The latter is more Dylanesque, and terser, too (it surely refers to a passage in Joel, regarding the judgment of those who "have cast lots for my people; and have given a boy for an harlot, and sold a girl for wine" [3:3]). Indulging in digital overdubs gave him the opportunity to prevaricate, allowing him to postpone the finishing end on any project. Only later did he recognize the error of his ways, confessing to Paul Zollo in 1991 that "Jokerman" was "a song that got away from me. Lots of songs on that album got away from me . . . They hung around too long. They were better before they were tampered with." Having continued throughout the eighties to redo vocal tracks like the man who has found an eternal fountain he is determined to drink dry, he began to use the technique more sparingly, post–*red sky*.

And though he never doubted that the new "Jokerman" lyric was better—sticking stoically to it in concert throughout the years when it enjoyed a general favor, i.e., 1984 and 1994—he has tried hard to get back to the original spirit in performance. If the results have been mixed—the 1984 arrangement is particularly stodgy and lugubrious—the song has occasionally risen to former heights: notably the truncated *David Letterman* performance in March 1984, when he found the heart and soul of the song in a form that was closer to "London Calling" than his studio recording. And at Woodstock 1994, having reintroduced the song six months earlier in Japan, he dared to open the biggest show of the whole Never Ending Tour, to a sea of muddy Green Day fans, with a song whose meaning lay entirely in the words, which he enunciated that night with a rare precision, still aiming to keep "one step ahead of the persecutor within."

{ Still on the Road }

{445} I AND I

Published lyric/s: Lyrics 85; Lyrics 04.
Known studio recordings: Power Station Studios, NYC, April 27, 1983—9 takes [INF].
First known performance: Verona, May 28, 1984.

> The thing to do, as soon as you get into [writing], it is to realize you *must get out of it.* And unless you get out of it quickly and effortlessly, there's no use staying in it. It will just drag you down. You could be spending years writing the same song, telling the same story, doing the same thing . . . The best songs to me—my best songs—are songs which were written very quickly . . . Just about as much time as it takes to write it down is about as long as it takes to write it. —Dylan, to Paul Zollo, January 1991

One of the classic anecdotes regarding Dylan the songwriter comes from another poet of performance, Leonard Cohen. Conversing with the man who dissolved any dichotomy between page and performance after a February 1990 Parisian residency, Cohen found that Dylan wanted to know how long he spent writing "Hallelujah" (a song Dylan stripped to the core in devastating fashion at two summer 1988 shows). He said it had taken him about two years, before inquiring of Dylan how long it had taken him to write "I and I." Fifteen minutes.

I doubt this was mere bravado on Dylan's part; he was simply highlighting a key difference between himself and one of the contemporary singer-songwriters he genuinely rated. For, as he informed Zollo, his own "best songs are . . . [usually] written very quickly." And "I and I" falls into this category, being in his words, "one of them Caribbean songs. One year a bunch of songs just came to me hanging around down in the islands."

And yet, at the sessions, it was a song Dylan took his time getting around to recording—perhaps because he was unclear how it should sound. As with another Water Pearl song, this one deals with a "strange woman [who] has slept in my bed," set against the backdrop of a world on the brink—"the world could come to an end tonight, but that's all right." Less clear is the message Dylan is trying to convey with the title phrase, "I and I," a Rasta expression conveying the God within us all. He has added the expression to a chorus that otherwise took for its inspiration the familiar edict from Jehovah to Moses, "Thou canst not see my face: for there shall no man see me, and live" (Exodus 33:20).

Elsewhere in the song, he aspires to be someone who can show himself "approved unto God, a workman that needeth not to be ashamed, rightly dividing the word of truth" (2 Timothy 2:15). Dylan was evidently still trawling through his Bible on a daily basis. He also seems to be trying the same trick previously attempted with "Caribbean Wind," making "the story-line change from third person to first person and that person becomes you, then these people are there and they're not there. And then the time goes way back and then it's brought up to the present."

Here, he transports the dreaming woman to a time when she could be cohort to "some righteous king who wrote psalms besides moonlit streams," presumably a reference to King David. Meanwhile, he has wandered onto a train platform where two men are "waiting for spring to come, smoking down the track."[19] Some unspecified animosity hangs in the air—"one's nature neither honors nor forgives." But still the narrator pushes himself "along the road, the darkest part," perhaps humming "Dark Was the Night" while he does. He ain't going back for her—if he did, "she would still be there sleepin'." But for him, sleep will not come. (As he commented in 1985, "Whatever is truthful haunts you and don't let you sleep at night.")

This sense of unfinished business makes "I and I" something of a spectral presence at the sessions. One suspects it was one of those songs which initially he only could "feel what [it was] about." It would require him to record (and perform) it before he could "*understand* what [it was] about." If it took him a fair while to press record, when he did the song came together easily enough, being cut in just three complete takes at the April 27 session (the second take being the one he ultimately preferred).

That second take stayed part of the album process all the way from April 27 to the first week of July, when a final mix and sequence was duly approved. Which is not to say that "I and I" emerged unscathed from that wholesale *Infidels* rethink. Far from it. The "original mix," which appears on the mid-May comp. reel and the so-called Knopfler sequence for the album, is an altogether subtler, sweeter thing, thanks to guitars that wash in and out of the mix, echoing every ebb in the song.

The three guitars each serve quite distinct functions. Knopfler, playing with real sympathy and restraint, justifies Dylan's description of him as someone who wouldn't "step all over [a song] with fancy licks"—still wholly unaware that he is just days away from being removed from the process by an assertive artist. Dylan's acoustic operates almost like a conductor's baton, punctuating changes of tone and mood with a downward strum or two, while Mick Taylor's dirty rhythm guitar cuts to the chase, like a man tutored in the art of economy by the master we call Keef. But something—and I strongly suspect it was that Straits-esque sound—rubbed Robert the wrong way, and he set about grungifying the mix (after getting shot of its architect). On *Infidels*, the nice stereo echo has been muted—while a (possibly overdubbed) rhythm guitar begins to de-beautify the whole arrangement about halfway through the song.

Dylan has done a "Thin Man" (see #158)—taking out what he deemed to be distractions from the centrality of his own performance; and though the song remains the same, there is a slight diminishing of its audiophonic aura. Which is not to say that "I and I" ain't one of the stand-out songs on the released album—probably second only to "Jokerman." It is just that its impact, already diluted in the mix, lessened further when it lost its counterpoint, the original album closer, "Foot of Pride," which it was scheduled to precede.

Dylan, though, seemed happy enough with the outcome, even as he moved ever further away from the song's mellifluous feel in concert. Over a ten-year period (1984–93), "I and I," a regular favorite in the set, became an entirely different beast, intermittently atmospheric, but often overbearing in its insistence on some suspiciously Grateful groove. Lost in the process were words that once had as much penetrative power as Cohen's own portrait of lust, faith, and folly.

{446} CLEAN CUT KID

Published lyric/s: The Telegraph #18; Lyrics 85; Lyrics 04. [1983 + 1984 lyrics: Words Fill My Head.][*as printed on Textones LP:* In His Own Words 2.]

Known studio recordings: Special Rider demo, New York, winter 1983; Power Station Studios, NYC, April 14, 1983—3 takes; April 15—5 takes; Delta Sound, NYC, July 26, 1984—2 takes [EB].

First known performance: Farm Aid, Champaign, IL, September 22, 1985.

On May 26, 1983, two songs—"Clean Cut Kid" and "Union Sundown"—were copyrighted in Dylan's name, using tape recordings as the basis for their registration under the umbrella heading "1983 Album Compilation #4." This odd pair concluded the registration of songs from these sessions (some fourteen songs had already been copyrighted in the past three weeks). One wonders what took so long. "Clean Cut Kid" was a song Dylan recorded very early in the sessions and, as far as we know, never returned to after the first week.

Unlike the other registered *Infidels* recordings, these two songs sound rough as hell. The word "demo" is written all over their foreheads. And so, despite the fact that they were copyrighted last, I suspect both recordings predate the album sessions, and may even be taken as evidence of a far bluesier conceit at the outset (possibly Knopfler is not even on these songs—the rhythm guitar is scratchy enough to be Dylan and the slide guitar sings of Taylor).

And yet "Clean Cut Kid" was at one point a genuine candidate for the album, as is evident from a comment Dylan made to engineer Neil Dorfsman during the April 18 "Sweetheart" run-through (see later). Between takes, he asks Dorfsman to specifically pull the third take of "Clean Cut Kid," cut earlier, so that he can listen back to it. Only then does he remember to consult his so-called coproducer Knopfler. So much for giving up control of the sessions!

What prompted Dylan to recall the song is unclear. Logged initially as "Brooklyn Anthem," "Clean Cut Kid" had been attempted on the fourteenth and again the following day, when it was the primary focus of the session, with the band trying it in both slow and fast incarnations. But after that, Dylan moved on to other concerns, and the song failed to appear on any known mix tape or provisional sequence (it is one of just two completed originals omitted from the fifteen-song comp. reel made in mid-May, which constitutes the first volume of the *Rough Cuts* two-CD bootleg set).

Gone but not forgotten, it became a rather mystifying choice for the song that broke a nineteen-year-old habit of ring-fencing material to specific albums. After years of refusing to revisit discarded songs at later sessions, he abandoned the practice for 1985's *Empire Burlesque*, an album destined to include two "leftovers" from *Infidels*—"Clean Cut Kid" and a drastically rewritten "Someone's Got a Hold of My Heart." From now on, he forgot all about that once-golden rule.

Initially, this may not have been his intention, even after he recut the song in July 1984. Dylan only remixed the song *after* he had "given" this demo of "Clean Cut Kid" to somebody else. Carla Olson—a protégé of Dylan's on-off girlfriend Carole Childs—was a young, blonde, female Tom Petty, with a cowpunk band of her own, the Textones. She had been given the song for their 1984 album *Midnight Mission* and made a pretty good job of it (adding an extra verse, which may or may not be one of Dylan's: "The last time I seen him, he had a smile on his face / Laughin' at nothin' he wanted to go to my place").

It certainly made a lot more sense on a cowpunk LP than on Dylan's idea of a disco album. Its inclusion on *Empire Burlesque* required a drastic remix of the version he (re-)recorded at the July New York session, barely two weeks after the end of a grueling European tour. Though the bluesy feel of that original 1983 demo was long gone, the lyric changed little in the interim. It was still the tale of a clean-cut kid who was transformed into a killer by his experience in Vietnam: "They sent him to a napalm health spa to shape up . . . They made a killer out of him / that's what they did." Now, though, it had a coda, about taking his head and turning it inside out until he did not "know what it was all about." Twenty years after writing "Ballad of Donald White," Dylan now threw in a lethal dose of Bowie's "Running Gun Blues" for good measure.

"Clean Cut Kid" suggested that if the songs ever dried up, he might make a fine sociologist (sociology being, in P. J. O'Rourke's memorable phrase, one of three disciplines designed to prove nothing is anybody's fault). But he was still not done with the song, using it as set opener at the September 1985 Farm Aid tour de force, which announced his return to (center) stage and screen, and persevering with it as a high-energy performance piece throughout his two-year tenure with the Heartbreakers. Only with the start of the Never Ending Tour did it stutter and stall, barely making it out of the garage before the engine broke down for good.

{447} UNION SUNDOWN

Published lyric/s: Lyrics 85; Lyrics 04. [Demo version: Words Fill My Head.]
Known studio recordings: Special Rider demo, New York, winter 1983; Power
Station Studios, NYC, April 27, 1983—2 takes; May 2, 1983—5 takes [INF].
First known performance: Saratoga Springs, NY, July 13, 1986.

If "Clean Cut Kid" updated the concerns of "Donald White," "Union
Sundown" took as its base point another early song, "North Country Blues"—
specifically the lines, "They say that your ore ain't worth digging / . . . It's much
cheaper down in the South American towns / Where the miners work almost
for nothing." Dylan had clearly not forgotten what happened to his hometown.
The following year, in conversation with *Rolling Stone*'s Kurt Loder, the forty-
two-year-old embellished a point he was making about the global economics
of "Union Sundown" by relating it to the north country he once knew:

> There's a big push on to make a big global country—one big country—
> where you can get all the materials from one place and assemble them
> someplace else and sell 'em in another place . . . Ninety per cent of the
> iron for the Second World War came out of those [Minnesota] mines,
> up where I'm from. [Yet] eventually they said, "Listen, this is costing too
> much money to get this out. We must be able to get it someplace else."

Unlike that youthful valedictory to a lost country, "Union Sundown"
struggles to turn the homilies he has accrued about world economics into
a coherent (or even, cogent) lyric. That he intended to write something on
a grand scale seems clear from the original demo, which runs to six verses,
only two and a half of which (the first two and part of the fifth) would
survive to the released recording. The original third verse makes clear the
root cause of Dylan's concern in a way that the album version rather fudges:

> Some people complainin' that there is no work,
> I say, "Brother, how can that be?"
> When nothing you got is U.S. made,
> It all comes from across the sea.
> They call it religious capitalism,
> Under corporate command,
> It says, "Nobody gets hired to do anything
> That can be done cheaper in some other land."

As an analysis of modern economics, it's a tad simplistic. As an insight into the songwriter's most abiding concern—the dignity of the individual—it is a revealing flashback to a time when his own views and those of the liberal intelligentsia ran along similar lines. Yet Dylan continued to chafe at the idea that he might have gone back to writing so-called political songs. He had grander concerns now, as he told fellow Minnesotan Martin Keller that July, while (de)constructing his 1983 album, taking songs of real vision and insight—like "Blind Willie McTell" and "Foot of Pride"—and replacing them with something as weak as *this*:

> I don't write political songs. Political songs are slogans . . . Politics could be useful if it was used for good purposes. For instance, like feeding the hungry and taking care of the orphans. But it's not. It's like the snake with its tail in its mouth. A merry-go-round of sin. Latin America, for example, is a political issue. All you hear about are U.S. interests in Latin America. But what are those interests? . . . Show me an honest politician and I'll show you a sanctified whore.

On the original demo, Dylan certainly seemed to have it in for the man who might preside over the union's sundown. (I doubt he was specifically targeting Ronald Reagan, the then incumbent.) As he said in 2009, "None of those guys [who become president] are immune to the laws of history. They're going to go up or down and they're going to take their people with them." In "Union Sundown" the man in the White House is someone whom Dylan portrays as a pawn of others— presumably, the Jokerman who has come as a man of peace ("I believe in the Book of Revelation. The leaders of this world are eventually gonna play God, if they're not already playing God and eventually a man will come that everybody will think is God." —Dylan, 1984).

Again, though, he removed much of the circuitry to this apocalyptic undercurrent in its passage from demo to album and, with it, any overt relationship to an earlier song on the economics of Armageddon like "Slow Train." One can only wonder what the reaction to the sixth and final verse would have been if it had been released this way at the time:

See the man in a mask in the White House
Who's got no name or important ties,
Just as long as he understands the shape of things to come
He can stay there till he dies.
Gotta be an invisible man
Not a front man for some diseased cause,
Certainly not a union man, an independent man,
Not a man tied to social laws.

As it is, Dylan did not feel that the song had been "developed fully." Initially, he wasn't even sure it would fit the album. Only as the sessions were winding down did he return to the song, recording it first on April 27—sandwiched between more momentous material, "Foot of Pride" and "I and I." One of the two takes cut that day seems to have found its way onto the mid-May fifteen-track comp. reel mentioned above; and musically it's fully worked out, with some great honky-tonk piano (presumably from Alan Clarke) and some lithe slide guitar, transported straight from Main Street. But Dylan has left his lyric sheet at home. He is bluffing his way through the verses, only ever singing the chorus straight. This tends to suggest that Dylan already knows he is going to redo his vocals on some tracks.

This full-band performance seems to have inspired him to look at the song again—and its relevance to the state of the world. As he told Hilburn on the album's release, "Maybe that's always been the state of affairs, but it seems especially true now. That's why I picked these particular songs for [*Infidels*] . . . I felt I had to do these songs *now*." And so, at what was probably the last band session, on May 2, Dylan pushed himself through five more takes—interrupted by a perfectly serious attempt at "Green, Green Grass of Home"—with his singing partner Clydie King making her presence known for the first time at these sessions. Whether he was still singing the verses on the demo or had already reverted to the released lyric is not clear, but the song was evidently subjected to vocal overdubs in June. Yet the song as released revealed no greater grasp of realpolitik than the rough sketch he recorded before sessions were underway.

Later perhaps Dylan began to suspect this analysis lacked intellectual rigor, even as he sought to memorialize the decayed state of the union. When the song was introduced into the live set, well into the 1986 *True Confessions* tour, the lyric had reverted to its April 27 state from whence it never reemerged. Revived in 1992, when the arrow on the doorpost had fallen into even greater disrepair, Dylan was still gargling his way through most verses, whether in Hawaii or his home state. By then, he had finally got around to releasing an altogether more lucid assessment of the shape of things to come, the very song which "Union Sundown" ended up replacing on the 1983 artefact . . .

{448} BLIND WILLIE McTELL

Published lyric/s: Lyrics 04.
Known studio recordings: Power Station Studios, NYC, April 11, 1983—7 takes; April 18, 1983—2 takes [May 15, 1983] [TBS].
First known performance: Montreal, August 5, 1997.

> To resolve is nothing more than letting go. Do you think Rembrandt ever finished a painting? —Dylan, to Allen Ginsberg, October 1977

For many people, "Blind Willie McTell" is Dylan's one indisputable masterpiece of the early eighties. It has become one of those songs which has taken on a life of its own. Yet for eight years it was another of those bootleg-only must-haves he'd been producing since day one. When it was finally released on *The Bootleg Series,* already a legend in its own lunchtime, it was still not in the form that the artist himself preferred. The acoustic versus electric argument still rages (I have already put my hat firmly in the latter camp—see *Recording Sessions,* page 152). But whatever one's persuasion, one would be hard-pressed to validate the decision to second-guess Dylan himself by utilizing an all-acoustic take previously used for copyright purposes on the 1991 set, after the artist put the *electric* version on the first *Infidels* sequence (and on the mid-May fifteen-track comp. reel).

Not surprisingly, given all the plaudits this "reject" has received, "Blind Willie McTell" is a song about which Dylan gets rather defensive. Asked about it in 1997—when he had finally begun performing it in concert—he retorted, "So many [songs] that people elevate on such a high level were in some sense only first drafts." He went on to say something similar to novelist Jonathan Lethem in their 2006 interview: "['Blind Willie McTell'] was never developed fully; I never got around to completing it. There wouldn't have been any other reason for leaving it off the record."

This latter-day mantra fails to convince. Not only was the tune not his to change, but also he never altered a single word in the month he spent intermittently attempting to "complete" it. He appears to have been altogether more up-front talking to Kurt Loder less than a year after he recorded it, matter-of-factly stating, "I didn't think I recorded it right." All the evidence supports this contemporary statement. The tape logs for the *Infidels* sessions can only tell us part of the story, but they show a pattern similar to the one for "Caribbean Wind" at the *Shot of Love* sessions. Almost the entire first session at Power Station (April 11) was occupied by a preoccupied Dylan trying to get *this* set of sessions off to a propitious start. (Something called "Run Down" was cut fourteen times at the start of the April 11 session, the first thirteen all being marked "instrumental." It is unlikely to be another cover but is probably "Blind Willie McTell" in its pre-lyrical guise. Said "song" is succeeded by a series of attempts at the latter composition.)

It is decidedly unlike Dylan to run down a song thirteen times before getting down to the meat of the matter, especially with tape rolling. He was clearly investing a lot of psychic energy in getting this one right. When that didn't work, he returned to it a week later, at the end of a session designed to produce a usable "Sweetheart Like You," cutting the song twice more. And finally, on May 5, he cut it one last time—this time in an acoustic guise from which it was copyrighted ten days later. (Though Knopfler is credited with second guitar on this take, Taylor is the more logical candidate. Hadn't Knopfler already been summarily fired by Dylan?)

The acoustic version was evidently a last throw of the dice. And the fact that it was the version copyrighted—along with "Tell Me"— suggests it may have been under consideration for album duties. But although "Blind Willie McTell" came very close to making the album— appearing on the first so-called Knopfler sequence—it appeared there in its electric guise (like the *Blood on the Tracks* test pressing, this first

Infidels sequence was circulating *before* the kosher artifact appeared in the shops).

For Dylan to have worked as long and hard on the song as he did, he must have thought very highly of it. He certainly admired, to the point of reverence, Blind Willie McTell (namechecking McTell in interview as early as 1977, as he entered his "New Pony" phase). That he considered him some kind of tortured soul is evidenced by a comment made to Elliott Mintz on the song's eventual release in 1991, when he described the man as "a very smooth operating blues man . . . [whose] vocal style, and his sound seems to fit right in with that lonesome sound . . . You could probably say he was the Van Gogh of the country blues."

It is an odd description, if you ask me. The first part rings true, but in comparison with many blind blues contemporaries, McTell had a long, "successful" career. And he was an entertainer first, a performer second, and a tortured artist a poor third, rather belying the symbolic value Dylan accords the name. Equally curious is the fact that the twelve-string guitarist's standard material was hardly immersed in the Apocalypse the song bearing his name foretells. In fact, Willie Hodges, who often played with McTell outside the Jaekel Hotel in Statesboro, recalled, "We was singing all kinds of blues and ragtime . . . [Whereas,] we [only] sang a spiritual every now and then." This held true even at the end. At his last session, McTell recorded nineteen songs, not one of which was a religious number.

Another blind Willie, though, sang of nothing but redemption and judgment—Blind Willie Johnson—and perfectly fits the sobriquet "the Van Gogh of the country blues." Wouldn't it just be the most deliciously Dylanesque irony if he picked McTell—rather than Johnson—because the name *rhymes* real well (he might have had more problems if McTell had pronounced his surname correctly, as McTear)? It wouldn't be the first time, now would it?

Something ain't quite right. McTell—who now has an entire book to his name, courtesy of a man named Gray—did self-consciously record one song called "Mr. McTell Got the Blues," but precious little of his output really fits the tenor of the song, which reeks of the fumes of hell-fire. McTell tended to like up-tempo pieces, and though he had a small, if growing, number of gospel-type songs in his repertoire—of which the "Motherless Children" on his 1949 Atlantic LP[20] stands tall—his material could be as salacious as the best of 'em (the one McTell song Dylan *has* released, "Broke Down Engine"—a song about impotence—sits very firmly in this camp).

Blind Willie Johnson, on the other hand, was a singer who really could have brought the whole damned curtain down. Unlike his namesake, Johnson enjoyed no thirty-year recording career. He cut a couple of dozen tracks between November 1927 and April 1930, before disappearing into the backwater from whence he came, ultimately dying of pneumonia in the forties after being turned away from a hospital because he was blind. He also knew McTell personally (McTell told John Lomax in 1940 that they had traveled together "from Maine to the Mobile Bay" in the thirties).

Dylan knew Johnson's work well, recording a variant of "Jesus Make Up My Dyin' Bed" (aka "In My Time of Dyin'") in 1961, while in the fall of 1980 he worked up versions of "Bye and Bye I'm Goin' to See the King" and "Nobody's Fault but Mine." Johnson's entire work was explicitly religious. A street-corner singing evangelist, he recorded a "Motherless Children" even more haunting than McTell's, part of a full repertoire of songs about the great day coming, including "Trouble Will Soon Be Over," the aforementioned "Going to See the King," and his real showstopper, "John the Revelator" (the one Johnson song used by Harry Smith on his fabled *Anthology of American Folk Music*).

However, surely Johnson's most haunting recording is "Dark Was the Night," a piece that is nothing more than a series of moans set to a simple six-string accompaniment, yet would have given namesake Robert the willies. In its apposite inarticulacy, it is the perfect valedictory to Man (one of a handful of recordings put on the Voyager spacecraft, it may yet be the one example of "the blues" to survive the End Times, if—as Dylan suggests on another *Infidels* recording—"Man has invented his doom").

Johnson would certainly have shared Dylan's newfound obsession with the sins—and sinfulness—of this world we live in, and would undoubtedly have agreed about the cause—"corruptible seed," as Dylan puts it. Original sin, passed on by the seed of Adam. That it oppresses the rock singer is clear from the context: "Power and greed and corruptible seed seems to be all that there is." Dylan is telling us he still believes he has been "born again, not of corruptible seed, but of incorruptible, by the word of God, which liveth and abideth for ever" (1 Peter 1:23). At the same time, the narrator of "Blind Willie McTell" is consumed by his own mortality, sensing that he is nearing the end of his time on this earth. Reflecting the song's self-conscious setting—the Saint James Infirmary—he can "hear that undertaker's bell."

To reinforce that sense of impending doom, and to give this song *about* the blues the requisite setting, Dylan has gone back to a familiar practice, taking a tune from some traditional "fare thee well." He twice alludes to his debt to "St. James Infirmary" in the song's lyric: first, in the opening couplet, where he suggests the coming darkness will spread "all the way from New Orleans to Jerusalem" (the original St. James Infirmary was in New Orleans). He also sings, in the final couplet, of "gazing out the window of that old St. James Hotel," which shows a knowledge of the song's history—the infirmary often being called a hotel ("hotel" meaning "hospital" in French). He thus emphasizes that the narrator is singing his own version of "St. James Infirmary," a song which looked back on a wasted life:

> When I die, pretty woman, please bury me,
> Six more to sing a song,
> Got my pockets full of moonshine whiskey,
> And I'll drink as the world rolls on.

Dylan may not have known the full history of the original he so recrafts, but he would have recognized the type in an instant. "St. James Infirmary" is a Wild & Wicked Youth song, like the "Newlyn Town" he used to perform and parodied on "I Am a Lonesome Hobo." Its origins date back to an old British-Irish broadside-archetype, "The Unfortunate Rake," which can, with a degree of certainty, be dated to the early nineteenth century, but was probably an old drinking song even then. "Blind Willie McTell" reinvigorates the tradition—and this time the wild and wicked youth is the whole damned world.

The archetype in question spawned so many derivatives it was almost bound to appear in a repertoire as extensive and eclectic as Blind

Willie McTell's. Sure enough, at his 1949 Atlantic session, coproduced by the late great Ahmet Ertegun—which means McTell was recorded by probably the two most important producers of the pre-rock era, the other being Ralph Peer—McTell recorded a song of his own, "Dyin' Crapshooter's Blues," that not only is a spirited adaptation of the "St. James" tune, but also rewrote the single "floating" verse in a devil-may-care way:

> Sixteen real good crapshooters
> Sixteen bootleggers to sing my song
> Sixteen racket-men gamblin'
> Cover [till-bar] while I'm rollin' along.

Yet McTell's "Dyin' Crapshooter's Blues" is no more "St. James Infirmary" than is Dylan's blues.[21] Even if one is a traditional artist working in the idiom and the other is a conscious songwriter of the first water, the notion that this is what Dylan envisages being sung at the world's end beggars belief. "Blind Willie McTell" is mournful. McTell's song is an I-did-it-my-way fuck-you to the world. It is the Clancys' "I've Been a Moonshiner" to Dylan's "Moonshine Blues."

Like that equally fatalistic reinvention of tradition, Dylan was determined to put every ounce of expression into "Blind Willie McTell" in the studio—acoustic or electric—and when he felt he hadn't delivered, he decided the world deserved better. It would take fourteen years, and a cover version from some old friends, to convince him otherwise. As he later admitted, "I started playing ["Blind Willie McTell"] live because I heard The Band doing it." (Their so-so version appeared on their 1993 "comeback" album, *Jericho.*)

Not that The Band were the first rock combo to cover this lost classic. Five years earlier, it had been L.A.-based Paisley Underground darlings Dream Syndicate who thought it worthy of its own vinyl record (their version appearing as a free 45 in the musiczine, *Bucketful of Brains*). And whereas The Band took Dylan's acoustic retake as their template, Steve Wynn's band leaned on the electric original.

Dylan also adopted the electric version as his own template when he finally put the song where it belonged—in his live set during the summer of 1997, awaiting the release of his first original album in seven years. He even made the message of the song marginally more explicit, singing of a land condemned "all the way from New Orleans to *New Jerusalem*." Because he had meant the city of God—not some temporal coordinates on a map—all along. Like Blind Willie Johnson, he could happily quote John the Revelator, who "saw the holy city, new Jerusalem, coming down from God out of heaven" (Revelation 21:2) long after he checked out of the St. James Hotel.

{449} DON'T FALL APART ON ME TONIGHT

Published lyric/s: Lyrics 85; Lyrics 04.
Known studio recordings: Power Station Studios, NYC, April 11, 1983—5 takes; April 12—7 takes; June 1983 [vcl overdubs] [INF].

> There's other things that I would really enjoy doing, besides playing [music] . . . like become a doctor . . . who can save somebody's life on the highway. I mean, that's a man I'm gonna look up to. —Dylan, to Dave Herman, July 1981

It had been five years since Dylan recorded songs like "True Love Tends to Forget" and "Baby Stop Crying" when he made a return to the same potentially rich vein. "Don't Fall Apart on Me Tonight" was one side of a conversation between (ex-)lovers, a sequel to some rumpy-pumpy. And yet he tried to distance himself from such subject matter on the one occasion he talked about it, in 1985, when he insisted: "A lot of times you'll just hear things and you'll know that . . . you want to put [these things] in your song . . . They don't have to be your particular thoughts. They just sound good . . . Half my stuff falls along those lines . . . A song like 'Don't Fall Apart on Me Tonight' falls into that category . . . A guy's getting out of bed saying don't talk to me; it's leaving time. I didn't originate those kind of thoughts."

This is a peculiar and unconvincing form of deflection; "Don't Fall Apart on Me Tonight" clearly provided a specific dimension Dylan wanted on his 1983 album. Hence his determination to cut the song early on in the process. It even carried over from the "Blind Willie McTell" session to the following day's proceedings, after which he was finally happy with the result. He presumably was thinking it might be a single, too, because it was one of two songs recorded early on (along with "License to Kill"), then made into promo videos by miming (extremely badly) during a studio break.

The footage went unused, not just because it was the kind of thing a nascent MTV might pass on, but because Dylan subsequently decided to rerecord the song with a sung vocal on the verses as well as chorus. As a result, he gave the vocal track a slightly supercilious singing tone, before placing it as a most uncharacteristic album closer, an unworthy companion piece to "I and I." If the song's luster faded real quick for its author—who never revisited it in performance—it was given a dose of the right stuff by king of the torch ballads, Aaron Neville, on 1993's *The Grand Tour*.

{450} LICENSE TO KILL

Published lyric/s: Lyrics 85; Lyrics 04.
Known studio recordings: Power Station Studios, NYC, April 13, 1983—1 take [INF].
First known performance: Late Night with David Letterman, NYC, March 22, 1984.

What's the purpose of going to the moon? To me, it doesn't make any sense . . . Is that supposed to be something that a person is supposed to get excited about? Is that progress? —Dylan to Kurt Loder, March 1984

One feature on *Infidels* that came in for particular stick in the press was its abidingly reactionary view of the modern world. Dylan may have stopped Bible bashing, but his views were still colored by an Old Testament view of people's nature and proclivities. And on this point they were destined to stay pretty fixed. As he told a set of European journalists in 1997, "I really don't know what politics are. When I am seriously dealing with something, I find myself to be on the side of the right this time and the next moment I am completely on . . . the left side . . . People haven't changed since Moses." In *Chronicles*, he was equally explicit: "Thucydides' *The Athenian General* . . . was written four hundred years before Christ and it talks about how human nature is always the enemy of anything superior . . . Nothing has changed from his time to mine."

Songs like "Union Sundown," "Neighborhood Bully," and "License to Kill"—all widely interpreted as political songs—were, according to their author, no such thing. For him, they were all infused by "the shape of things to come" and should be viewed in that light. In "License to Kill" he managed to paint an idealized portrait of this peace-loving "woman on my block"—a twentieth-century angel of the hearth—while worrying nightly that the end is coming, because "Man has invented his doom / First step was touching the moon."

Not only is this one of the corniest couplets the man ever wrote, it is hardly an astute analysis. If mankind had indeed acquired the capability to destroy itself, it had done so a quarter of a century before anyone landed on the Moon. Bob, though, had a bee in his bonnet about the space program, and he had decided it was time to start waving his arms and banging his drum. When he asked rhetorically, "Is that progress?" the subtext was clear. When one is living during the countdown to Judgment Day, what kind of person uses their time exploring the cosmos?

His view had changed little three years later, when the plug *was* temporarily pulled on space exploration by the U.S. government, after the space shuttle disaster of January 1986. A couple of weeks later, in Sydney, Australia, Dylan prefaced his first live performance of "License to Kill" in two years with the following, extraordinary rap:

> Here's something I wrote a while back; it's all about the space program. I suppose you heard about this [recent] tragedy, right? I don't need to tell you it really was a tragedy . . . You see, these people had no business going up there. Like, there's not enough problems on Earth to solve? So I wanna dedicate this song to all those poor people, who were fooled into going up there.

The take he had released back in 1983 bore just as many hallmarks of haste in its construction as in its execution. The song was cut in a single take, at the end of the third *Infidels* session. Although Dylan delivers a vocal of rugged resilience, the band seem to be sleepwalking through the live-in-studio performance. The author, though, decided the song was done and dusted, and that neither lyric nor arrangement needed further work.

However, "License to Kill" is one eighties work that successfully demonstrates Dylan's maxim: "Songs need a structure, stratagems, codes and stability, and then you hang lyrics on them . . . [but it is only] when we transfer all that to the stage . . . [that] all those elements come into play." In performance, time and time again, Dylan has transformed this righteous rant into a message-song that compels its audience to sit up and take notice (if not actually adhere to its edicts). And he began its transformation with its first live outing, on *Late Night with David Letterman*, when he plugged into the song with a conviction last seen when he still carried the Good Book on stage with him.

Likewise, on the two occasions in 1986 when he felt prompted to reissue his warning—in Sydney in February and during an ultraloose three-song set at an Amnesty benefit in early June—he struck the requisite match that rendered it anew. Whether he found himself in Turin in September 1987, in Denver in June 1988, or in Louisville in April 1994, he seemed to stamp each and every licence with vigor. But nothing compares (no, nothing compares) to the chilling, slow-burn performance, harmonica in hand, he gave it at the last of those landmark Prague shows in March 1995. Still waiting on the closing curtain, Dylan appropriated all the valedictory quality of "Blind Willie McTell" and applied it to a song that, on the page, really should have been printed in black letter blocks.

Note: The one clever use of wordplay in the song, the title itself, is lost on most English readers of the James Bond novels, for whom "license" and "licence" have entirely different meanings. American English, by losing any distinction between noun and verb through a common spelling ("license"), allows both meanings in a single word.

{451} MAN OF PEACE

Published lyric/s: Lyrics 85; Lyrics 04.
Known studio recordings: Power Station Studios, NYC, April 14, 1983—3 takes [INF].
First known performance: Verona, May 28, 1984.

A saint is . . . the master of his own reality, the voice of simplicity. The trick is to stay away from mirror images. —Dylan, to Ron Rosenbaum, November 1977

The day after he dispatched "License to Kill" in a single take, Dylan did it again. He put "Man of Peace" in its rightful place after just two false starts. He may even have thought he had started to get a handle on all this new material, having "completed" five songs in the first four sessions, more than half the album. (He had yet to become bogged down for *days* on two songs that should have, but didn't, make the album: "Foot of Pride" and "Someone's Got a Hold of My Heart.")

"Jokerman" and "Man of Peace" had already provided him with two belligerent beacons to light the listeners' way. The songs which ended up opening sides one and two—in the days when albums had sides— were both reflections of Narcissus the false messiah, shimmering from the same stagnant pool. Dylan didn't pull his punches about the real subject matter of "Man of Peace" in his 1984 *Rolling Stone* interview, stating without equivocation, "You can't be for peace and be global. It's just like that song 'Man of Peace.' None of this matters, if you believe in another world. [But] if you believe in this world . . . you'll go mad, 'cause you won't see the end of it."

Again, Dylan's concerns remained fixed on the final page, contrasting the mysterious figure who "sometimes comes as a man of peace" with He who had already warned, in the gospel according to Matthew, "Think not that I am come to send peace on earth; I came not to send peace, but a sword" (10:34). In this man's mind, a time was fast approaching when "Satan [shall be] transformed into an angel of light" (2 Corinthians 11:14). In such a climate, many would be deceived by some "great humanitarian . . . [and] philanthropist" who "knows just where to touch you, honey, and how you like to be kissed." Only after they had felt "the tender touch of the Beast" would things start to go pear-shaped, an event which Dylan describes with a terrific amalgam of blues-based and biblical imagery ("Howl, O ye oaks of Bashan; for the forest of the vintage is come down" [Zechariah 11:2]):

> Well, the howling wolf will howl tonight, the king snake will crawl,
> Trees that have stood for a thousand years suddenly will fall.

A bridge between the world visions of "Jokerman" and "License to Kill" via "When the Ship Comes In," Dylan is here suggesting in verse after verse that the "man of peace" will fool the wise, while the poor and neglected shall be redeemed. It was a view he reiterated to Scott Cohen, just a couple of years later: "It's the people who live under tyranny and oppression, the plain, simple people, that count . . . They'll see that God is coming . . . Not some crackpot lawyer or politician with the mark of the beast, but somebody who makes them feel holy . . . People who believe in the coming of the Messiah live their lives right now as if he was here. That's my idea of it, anyway."

So much for *Infidels* demonstrating a lessening faith, even if the world at large was still not ready to hear how to recognize the "mark of the beast." Each attempt to introduce "Man of Peace" into his live set, beginning on the 1984 tour, fell largely on deaf ears. And although he sprang the song on audiences at the first Verona gig in 1984, at the Foxborough gig with the Grateful Dead in 1987, in Jerusalem with the Heartbreakers the same year (after being rehearsed with Petty's band as far back as January 1986), and at the last two Beacon shows in 1989, in each case the song was only imposed on a handful of audiences before it returned to the darkness. Which is a real shame, because it has always been a song Dylan sang with enough sound and fury to signify something.

{452} SWEETHEART LIKE YOU

Published lyric/s: Lyrics 85; Lyrics 04. [Original lyric: Words Fill My Head.]
Known studio recordings: Power Station Studios, NYC, April 14, 1983—2
takes; April 18, 1983—18 takes; June 1983 [vcl overdub] [INF].

> I guess that [song]'s a Byronesque ballad. Sort of like "Childe Harold" in Babylon or Elizabethan rhythm and blues. —Dylan, to Martin Keller, July 1983

In tape terms, "Sweetheart Like You"—initially logged as "By the Way That's a Cute Hat"—is the most well-documented of the songs recorded for *Infidels*. Three complete versions of the song circulate: one, from the mid-May comp. reel; a second, from the original nine-track *Infidels*; and third and last, the released take—which also served as the lead single in the U.S. As well as these finished versions, there is a running tape of

Dylan working the song out in the studio, presumably from the April 18 session, the second time he worked on the song (after making a couple of attempts on the fourteenth).

Although there are only two takes in Krogsgaard's sessionography attributed to the session on the fourteenth, it does not follow that the running tape corresponds to the finished takes logged on the eighteenth. If they are one and the same, they precede the one marked "?take one"(actually, the fifth take). The "rehearsal" is clearly just that, and what we have sounds like a two-track "live" tape of the session, not a mixdown from a multitrack, which was only usually rolling when they were trying for a take (hence, Dylan's comment about how the engineer can "roll over all of this").

Dylan's between-take mention of an "earlier" "Clean Cut Kid" from the "other night" (it was cut on the fourteenth and fifteenth only) and the inclusion of certain key lyrical phrases which appear in the "final" version, yet are absent from the version on the *Rough Cuts* bootleg CD (probably from the fourteenth), argue strongly for this tape coming from the second "Sweetheart" session. In the four days it took him to return to the song, he had evidently cleaned up the lyric, until by the end of the session on the eighteenth he had recorded the version that appeared on the original album sequence (which would be given a new vocal track, and slightly different lyric, at the mixing stage).

The running tape comes in part way through a take. The next take is almost the whole song, though it has several lines that never make it any further, notably a great opening couplet, "The boss ain't here, he gone north, I can't remember where, / He caught the red-eye, it left on time, he's starting a graveyard down there." Other couplets cut by the end of the session include "Y'know, I took my clothes down to the red river to be done, / In a quarter of an hour they're on good terms with everyone" and a rhyme for the title line that sees the singer fighting his own lustful self: "You look to me like a raw-T, it's a thought I just can't resist, / But what's a sweetheart like you doing in a dump like this?" (He pronounces "raw-T" a lot like "royalty," which doesn't work as well.) The version on the mid-May comp. reel has also used these last two couplets, but by the end of the session on the eighteenth they are gone. The opening has also moved on:

Well, the pressure's down, the boss ain't here,
He gone up north for a while,
The very last thing he said was, "See you later,"
He did go out in style.

Dylan continued shuffling this opening image, with the missing boss eventually going "up north, to that lighthouse beyond the bend," while painting a picture of a woman who had learned the hard way "that oppression is a cruel tutor and injustice is a nurse." It took him a while to accept the wisdom of something he told Ron Rosenbaum six years earlier: "I reject a lot of inspiring lines . . . a lot of lines that would be better off just staying on a printed page and finishing up as poems . . . I try not to pay too much attention to those wild, obscure lines."

As it is, the most contentious line of the whole song survived the entire monthlong process of rehearsing, recording, and overdubbing. And yet, if we are to believe a later comment, the line in question—"a woman like you should be at home / that's where you belong"—still didn't come out quite how he wanted it to. He claimed, "I could easily have changed that line . . . but I think the concept still woulda been the same. You see a fine-looking woman walking down the street, you start going, 'Well, what are you doing on the street? You're so fine, what do you need all this for?'" For all its lyrical detours and deviations, the song never fell far from the root idea—saving a woman from herself—an idea which would have been entirely acceptable for a soul singer, but for a former civil rights activist was apparently a no-no.

{453} BACK TO THE WALL
{454} HOW MANY DAYS?
{455} HALF-FINISHED SONG

#453—Known studio recording: Power Station Studios, NYC, April 13, 1983.
#454–5—Known studio recordings: Power Station Studios, NYC, April 14–15, 1983.

There are any number of intriguing song titles found in the *Infidels* studio logs, though those with titles like "Don't Drink No Chevy," "Love You Too Jam," and "Dadada Grateful Dead" can probably be discounted as jams and/or instrumentals.[22] While most other "unknown songs" appear to be cover versions, not everything can be so readily allocated. Some of the song titles logged are just plain weird ("Trees Hannibal Alps" deserves a special award). In all likelihood, at least a couple of these will prove to be either improvisations around a preconceived idea (like "Rock Me Mama" in 1973 or "To Fall in Love with You" in 1986) or original songs that never worked out, and were therefore never copyrighted (we know of at least one such instance—see below). Possible candidates that fall into one of these categories include the three titles above, even though—the self-explanatory "Half-Finished Song" excepted—they could equally be covers or known songs mislabeled.

Some fourteen covers were recorded at these sessions, according to Martin Keller, who interviewed Dylan at the mixing sessions in July. Of these, "Angel Flying Too Close to the Ground" was still under consideration for the album at this late stage. One need not get too creative with the songs logged on the tape boxes to arrive at that number. Besides "Angel Flying Too Close to the Ground" they include the likes of "Over the Rainbow" (or possibly "Rainbow Connection"), "This Was My Love," "Jesus Met a Woman at the Well," "Sixteen Tons," "He's Gone" (presumably either the Grateful Dead song or Bessie Smith's "He's Gone Blues"), "O Susanna," "Green Onions," "Across the Borderline," "Silent Night," something logged as "Glory to the Lord," "Dark as a Dungeon," "Choo Choo Boogie," "Cold, Cold Heart," "I'm Movin' On," and "Green Green Grass of Home." Unfinished versions of "Home on the Range," "Buttons & Buns," and "Gonna Wash That Man" were also all recorded at the end of a long session on April 29.

However, "Back to the Wall" and "How Many Days?" do not fit easily in the cover category. The latter song sure sounds like a blues song title, along the lines of Howlin' Wolf's "How Many More Years?," but nothing exactly fits. The former phrase can be found in a song Dylan covered in both 1980 and 1986, Shel Silverstein's "A Couple More Years": "I just spent more time with my back to the wall." That said, "Back to the Wall" would be a pretty weird guesstimate for Silverstein's song, where the title itself appears a number of times in the song's burden, "I picked up a couple more years on you babe, but that's all." And it is a phrase Dylan liked to use himself. As Mick Taylor commented to one journalist, a few years after the *Infidels* sessions, "When he made *Infidels*, you could see that he was really inspired, and that he's a really great singer when he's relaxed. But when I talked to him recently, he said 'You know me, Mick; I can only write songs when my back is to the wall.'"

{456} PRISON STATION BLUES

Known studio recordings: Power Station Studios, NYC, April 26, 1983—1 take.

We are reliant on Mark Knopfler's memory for confirmation that a song Dylan broke into between "Foot of Pride" and "Someone's Got a Hold of My Heart" at the April 26 *Infidels* session was something more than just another abstract blues. The guitarist-producer told *Musician* editor Bill Flanagan about this Dylan "song called 'Prison Guard' [which was] about a complete skunk," and so, when Flanagan interviewed the man himself in March 1985, he dared to ask him about it.

For once, Dylan didn't shrug his metaphorical shoulders and look blank but admitted that, yes, "Mark heard that song" (presumably, he means before the sessions), before going on to suggest: "I never recorded it. I didn't think I needed to record it. It was a talking thing about this prison guard who's just sort of a rough character. He doesn't mind throwing people off the fourth tier and busting anybody's head in. And then it goes on to describe his family and his town. Then when I got done, I just thought it was pretty pathetic . . . It was . . . one of these things where somebody in a uniform can get away with something that somebody who's not wearing a uniform can't." Sounds like a cross between "Clean Cut Kid" and "Neighborhood Bully," then. And, despite the protestation to the contrary, he did record it. Let's hope he got all the way through it before changing the mood somewhat with a song logged as "Forever My Darling."

{457} SOMEONE'S GOT A HOLD OF MY HEART

Published lyric: Lyrics 04.

= TIGHT CONNECTION TO MY HEART (HAS ANYBODY SEEN MY LOVE)

Published lyric/s: Lyrics 85; Lyrics 04.

Known studio recordings [I]: Power Station Studios, NYC, April 16, 1983—6 takes; April 25—3 takes [TBS]; April 26—3 takes.

{ Still on the Road }

[II] Cherokee Studios, LA, December 22, 1984 [overdubs: Power Station, NYC, January 15, 1985] [EB].
First known performance [II]: Toad's Place, New Haven, CT, January 12, 1990.

> If I wrote a song three years ago, I seldom go back and get that. I just leave 'em alone. —Dylan to Kurt Loder, March 1984

Four months later Dylan abandoned the methodology outlined to Loder, which had selflessly served him for the past two decades. If the transformation from "Someone's Got a Hold of My Heart" to the opening song on *Empire Burlesque*, "Tight Connection," represents the most radical, unexpected example of Dylan reworking an earlier song, the song (or at least, its second half) remained readily identifiable. In fact, the transformation over ten days in April 1983, from its first studio outing to its second, is in one sense as great as from Power Station to Cherokee, eighteen months later.

Attempted first on April 16, "Someone's Got a Hold" was then sidelined for nine days, the first serious attempt to cut the song coming on the twenty-fifth, from where the stuttering take on *The Bootleg Series* comes. The song at this stage is a lyric in need of a tune, the boys in the band merely busking along while the singer reads the autocue. Having revisited the song unsuccessfully on this occasion, Dylan attacked the song again the following day, cutting it twice after a single false start, and nailing it to that masthead marked "performance poet." By the twenty-sixth, Prometheus has come and gone, leaving the song burning with all the passion to which flesh is heir. Copyrighted a fortnight later in this guise, and transferred to the comp. reel, it was placed on a safety reel on May 16, awaiting its transference to the land of *Infidels*. But it did not make it as far as the shore, Dylan preferring to fill the album with "too much information 'bout nothing / too much educated rap."

(The recording date for the version included on the official *Bootleg Series Vols 1–3* is given as April 25, the second of three days when the song was attempted at Power Station—the sixteenth, twenty-fifth, and twenty-sixth. The oft-bootlegged alternate, which was transferred to the mid-May *Infidels* "roughs" tape and was copyrighted on *Album Compilation #2* on May 10, therefore presumably dates from the following day's session. This would mean that the mysterious "?take 5" listed in Krogsgaard's sessionography for April 25 is the *Bootleg Series* take of "Someone's Got a Hold of My Heart"—and not, as he suggests, "Foot of Pride"—the three previous takes all being marked incomplete.)

By the twenty-sixth, Dylan has finally figured out what he wants to say to the lady/ies rescued in "Sweetheart Like You" and then seduced in "I and I": "The moon rising like wild fire, I feel the breath of a storm / Something I got to do tonight, you go inside and stay warm." Torn between achieving grace ("Never could learn to drink that blood and call it wine") and succumbing to more earthly desires ("Never could learn to look at your face and call it mine"), the narrator fears for his very soul. This time around, he sounds like a soul in torment, as he admits that he "can still hear that voice crying in the wilderness," presumably the self-same voice found in Mark 1:3 and Matthew 3:3 and first of all Isaiah 40:3, which once echoed through "Caribbean Wind" and "Every Grain of Sand." Perhaps he wasn't willing to show himself suffused by such doubt, because this majestic song was not even included on the first *Infidels* sequence, joining that choir of lost opportunities already peopled by "Blind Willie McTell," "Clean Cut Kid," and friends.

But things changed between *Infidels* and its successor. Discarded songs were now sometimes revived. Two *Infidels* outtakes made it onto *Empire Burlesque*, while its ramshackle eight-track successor used three leftovers from the 1985 album itself (one of them an eleven-minute epic). And "Someone's Got a Hold of My Heart" was one such survivor, though only after much plastic surgery. In the interim Dylan had decided he really wanted to turn the song into a visual narrative, and in order to achieve this he set about rewriting it in a more "cinematic" fashion. It was a trick he had tried once before, on the 1975 rewrite of "Simple Twist of Fate."

What was entirely unexpected was Dylan's newfound reliance on the dialogue of Hollywood scriptwriters for any lyrical gaps, as he replaced blazingly original lines from "Someone's Got a Hold of My Heart" with excerpts from Humphrey Bogart movie scripts, beginning with the opening couplet of "Tight Connection," lifted verbatim from *Sirocco* ("Well, I had to move fast / And I couldn't with you around my neck"). Also referenced are the likes of *Key Largo*, *Tokyo Joe*, and *The Maltese*

Falcon, from which Dylan has taken the opening couplet of verse two ("You want to talk to me / Go ahead and talk").

Unlike other *Burlesque* songs, he still has something highly original to work around. Indeed, for the second half of the song, Dylan reverts to his "Hold of My Heart" persona, abandoning the video recorder for an old notebook or two. There is just one time in the second half of the song that he reworks a couplet completely, and again he replaces an original thought—"You must first realize / I'm not another man for hire"—with a line from *Sirocco*, "I don't know whether I'm too good for you / Or you're too good for me."

It wasn't just a disinclination to work too hard reworking the lyrics; he was equally unwilling to rework the music from the ground up, preferring to apply layers to a basic track he recorded for *Infidels*. Quite what—or who—prompted Dylan to remember this 1983 recording two years later is another one for the "to live outside the law you must be honest" press conference. But remember it he did, and such was his recall that it was the April 25 "disco" version he chose to reconfigure.

There are a number of clues that the 1983 basic track underlies the released recording of "Tight Connection": one, the song is listed as "Hold of My Heart" at the session in January 1985 when new vocals were applied to the track (ostensibly by the girl singers, but possibly also by Dylan); two, said session was the first *Burlesque* session to be held at Power Station, where the 1983 original had been recorded; and three, the musician credits reveal an *Infidels* outtake (they feature Mick Taylor, who appears on no other *Burlesque* track, as well as Sly Dunbar and Robbie Shakespeare). The Richard Scher synth-wash and Ted Perlman's blippy guitar overdubs do little to disguise the original source.

As Dylan stopped addressing himself, and started addressing the lady he has decided to discard, he addresses the chorus to the listener: "Has anybody seen my love?" Having set the song around noir one-liners, he gave it a promo video with an even odder narrative. After he filmed this clichéd pop video with the respected film director Paul Schrader, he admitted to two British video directors that he had asked for Schrader because he thought it might look like *Mishima*, which Schrader shot in black and white. He also talked about the song in terms of film later in the year, to *Spin*'s Scott Cohen:

"Tight Connection to My Heart" is a very visual song. I want to make a movie out of it. I don't think it's going to get done . . . but of all the songs I've ever written, that might be one of the most visual . . . I can see the people in it. Have you ever heard that song, "I'm a Rambler, I'm a Gambler," "I once had a sweetheart, age was 16, she was the flower of Belton and the Rose of Saline"? Same girl, maybe older. I don't know, maybe it should stay a song.

"Stay a song" it did. But what "Tight Connection" really needed was an injection of adrenaline, and a dose of passion juice, much like its original 1983 incarnation received. When he did work up a live arrangement in the winter of 1990 that stripped away the annoying girl chorus, the click-track, and the overbaked production—to replace it with the same kind of steamy inflection it had on April 26, 1983—the lyric really didn't seem damaged beyond repair. The reinvented song—minus the corny "You got a tight connection to my heart" motif—reemerged again at the 1993 Supper Club shows, when Dylan had a second opportunity to visualize it but chose to let it "stay a song."

{458} NEIGHBORHOOD BULLY

Published lyric/s: Lyrics 85; Lyrics 04.
Known studio recordings: Power Station Studios, NYC, April 19, 1983—6 takes [INF].

"Neighborhood Bully," to me, is not a political song . . . If you listen closely, it really could be about other things . . . You're making it specific to what's going on today. But what's going on today isn't going to last, you know? The battle of Armageddon is specifically spelled out: where it will be fought and, if you wanna get technical, when it will be fought. And the battle of Armageddon definitely will be fought in the Middle East. —Dylan, to Kurt Loder, March 1984

"Neighborhood Bully" provides an excellent example of a song whose qualities have been overlooked simply because of the message it expounds. The above rant came about because Loder accused the man of writing "a strong Zionist political statement" (to which

Dylan caustically counters, "What line is in it that spells *that* out?").
He continued to be dismissive of such a narrow interpretation, telling
Robert Hilburn in the wake of his first ever Israeli concert in September
1987, "I don't know if [that song] was about any one certain thing. You
could use Israel, I guess, as a place to start from, but I'm sure there was
more intended than that."

The song is unquestionably about *an* Israel, if not necessarily the
Israel of 1983 (though it is hard to see how a line like "he destroyed the
bomb factory" can be about anything other than the 1982 bombing of
Iraqi weapons plants). Remarkably, Dylan is still taking history lessons
from Hal Lindsey, specifically the chapter in *The Late Great Planet Earth*
entitled "Israel O Israel." In the sections "Misery in Babylon" and "The
Winds of Rome," Lindsey set out how the Jews were told by Moses, on
their flight from Egypt, that they "would be chastened . . . twice as a
nation, for not believing their God and rejecting His ways" before finally
being allowed to return home. This provides the impetus for at least one
couplet in "Neighborhood Bully": "Every empire that's enslaved him is
gone / Egypt and Rome, even the great Babylon."

Lindsey also suggested "The new State of Israel will be plagued by a
certain pattern of events which has clearly been forecasted." It is these
that concern a Dylan who wails like a male banshee on "Neighborhood
Bully." As with most of *Infidels*, he gives his all vocally to get the song
across. More so than on many a mid-sixties masterpiece, the vocal on
"Neighborhood Bully" transmutes the leaden message into something
that genuinely glistens. Listen to a couplet like "There's a noose at his
neck, and a gun in his back / And a license to kill him given out to ev'ry
maniac" and tell me he ain't testifying, Mr. Jones.

Dylan even wanted to make the song into a promo video—and
apparently had storyboards already worked out—but wiser commercial
counsel prevailed, and we got "Jokerman" instead. Of course, if he had
really wanted to get the message out there, he might have retained the
original sequence of the album, where side one just got progressively
more apocalyptic, culminating in this a sonic portrait of a man "standing
on the hill / Running out the clock, time standing still" (the *Infidels* inner
sleeve features just such a man, the photo being taken by ex-wife Sara on
a family trip to Jerusalem in September). "Jokerman," "License to Kill,"

"Man of Peace," "Neighborhood Bully" in that order—now that really would have had them running for the hills.

{459} **TELL ME**

Published lyric/s: Lyrics 04. *[Original version:* Words Fill My Head.*]*
Known studio recordings: Power Station Studios, NYC, April 21, 1983—8 takes [TBS].

According to the Krogsgaard sessionography, "Tell Me" was a song Dylan worked on for a single day (April 21), after which it was forgotten. I suspect otherwise. Though it seems he cut six complete takes on the day in question, the song was still being worked on in May, as evidenced by the two versions in general circulation: one from a copyright tape registered on May 15, 1983, accompanying the May 5 acoustic "Blind Willie McTell" (*1983 Album Compilation #3*). The other, a previously unknown alternate complete with backing singers (clearly overdubbed, presumably by Full Force) and a slightly different lyric, was included on *The Bootleg Series 1–3*. At least one of these has been reworked in the interim. The question is, when?

A May 8 overdub session includes a song called "Fly Me," which Krogsgaard thinks could be "Angel Flying Too Close to the Ground" (possible) or "Don't Fly Unless It's Safe" (not possible). It is *far* more likely to be "Tell Me," which was transferred to a safety master on May 16. The version copyrighted the day before was the selfsame one included on the mid-May fifteen-track comp. reel, making the official "Tell Me" another second guess on *Bootleg Series* compiler Jeff Rosen's part.

As it happens, both versions work just fine, though the copyrighted version sounds smoother to my ears. The other sounds more stilted, and has the weaker lyric—suggesting it is an earlier take. And yet, the addition of backing singers (on May 18) suggests it had superseded the copyright version. One therefore wonders whether the couplet he changes in the penultimate verse is the start of a "Tight Connection"–like transformation of another *Infidels* song. Certainly, the "original" couplet more accurately reflects the spirit of the 1983 album:

> Do you long to ride on that old ship of Zion,
> What means more to you, a live dog or a dead lion?

The latter line—a direct reference to Ecclesiastes 9:4, "To him that is joined to all the living there is hope: for a living dog is better than a dead lion"—conveys the notion that the female addressed knows not that she "is joined to all the living." The replacement couplet—"Is that a smile I see on your face / Will it lead me to glory or lead me to disgrace?"— would not have been out of place on "When the Night Comes Falling from the Sky." It works less well here. In the 2004 *Lyrics* the line is tweaked again, the transfer into the second person suggesting a later intrusion, "Will it take you to glory or to disgrace?"

Another line troubled him, too. On *The Bootleg Series* take, it appears as "Are those rock 'n' roll dreams in your eyes?" while in the 2004 *Lyrics* it reads, "What's in back of them pretty brown eyes?" Neither achieves the same aural efficacy as the original, copyrighted version: "Do those neon lights blind your eyes?" At least the continuing work on the song suggests it was still a serious contender for the album, two weeks after the band sessions ceased. Its failure to mount this final hurdle is a shame, but not the crying shame the omission of the following song represents . . .

{460} FOOT OF PRIDE

Published lyric/s: Lyrics 85; Lyrics 04. *[Recorded version:* Words Fill My Head.*]*
Known studio recordings: Power Station Studios, NYC, April 22, 1983—9 takes; April 23—17 takes; April 25—9 takes; April 26—3 takes; April 27—5 takes; April 29—1 take [TBS].

> Let not the foot of pride come against me, and let not the hand of the wicked remove me. —Psalms 36:11

Dylan straps on his Jeremiah garb again to deliver a "Yonder Comes the Sin of Pride" to the Greed is Good generation—for whom he reserves a couplet just as apposite in 2009 as it was in 1983: "They like to take all this money from sin, build big universities to study in / Sing 'Amazing Grace' all the way to the Swiss banks." He's definitely still got it in for the kind of education dispensed in college.

"Foot of Pride" remains one of his most unrelenting polemics, and one of his best. This time he wraps what is really one long rant in the language of Kings, while namechecking a number of popular songs coopted by the proud to cover their parasitic tracks: "Danny Boy," "Amazing Grace," and even "Abraham, Martin, and John" (from which he quotes the line "Only the good die young"). The generic "You'll Love Me Till the Morning, Stranger" doesn't really exist, but sounds like it should.

All of these are valedictories one might hear at a wake—which is fitting because "Foot of Pride" is told from the vantage point of a mourner at a funeral, looking down on a man the narrator had known, and looking back on the life he led, as "the earth just opened and swallowed him up." At the end of the song, he even delivers the perfect eulogy to a man killed by his own hubris—as befits a song whose title on the tape logs was "Too Late":[23]

> Yes, I guess I loved him, too,
> I can still see him in my mind, climbing that hill,
> Did he make it to the top, well, he probably did and dropped,
> Struck down by the strength of the will.

(It is hard to resist interpreting these lines as a reference to George Mallory's ill-fated ascent of Everest in 1924. Mallory, a heroic figure to many of Dylan's generation, was indeed sighted "climbing that hill" and has been the subject of eighty-five years of speculation as to whether he made "it to the top" before he dropped.)

It has been suggested that the song was prompted by a real funeral for a friend—Christian singer Keith Green, with whom Dylan recorded back in 1980. If Green, who died in a plane crash in July 1982, is in there, the song is surprisingly unsentimental about his compadre in Christ. Our Savior appears at song's end as the man with no name, to inform the narrator, "Let the dead bury the dead [a direct quote from Jesus, 'Follow me; and let the dead bury their dead' —Matthew 8:22] / Your time will come." Not surprisingly, Christ stalks much of the song, appearing first in verse two:

> He got a brother named James, don't forget faces and names,
> Sunken cheeks and his blood is mixed,
> He looks straight into the sun, and says, "Revenge is mine, hon . . .
> Say one more stupid thing to me, before the final nail is driven in."

{ Still on the Road }

No question, this is the Christ who has come to judge ("Vengeance is mine; I will repay, saith the Lord" [Romans 12:19]), Dylan mocking those who "don't believe in mercy / Judgment on them is something that you'll never see." He was still talking the talk in 1985, when he told *Spin*'s Scott Cohen, "I've never been able to understand . . . the seriousness of pride. People talk, act, live as if they're never gonna die. And what do they leave behind . . .—nothing but a mask." Aiming to depict "pride before the fall" in all its venality, Dylan draws from the full span of history, finding an Old Testament parallel to every modern folly. Just as omnipresent as the one true messiah is the Antichrist, recast as "a retired businessman named Red / Cast down from heaven and he's out of his head." The clock is ticking.

Whether the song ever really "had a bunch of extra verses"—as Dylan suggested to Elliott Mintz—only the other forty-three takes are likely to reveal. There are more than enough words herein. On the released take he somehow manages to deliver one of his most convoluted lyrics without tripping himself up, though he comes damn close in verse four with "How to enter into the gates of paradise; and know / How to carry a burden too heavy to be yours," briefly choking on "and know." (This couplet is rendered nonsensical in the 2004 *Lyrics*, becoming "paradise / No, how to carry . . ." Qué?)

"Foot of Pride" elucidated a feeling he sometimes struggled to articulate on lesser *Infidels* cuts. Placed last on an album, it would have left no one in any doubt that he remained appalled by man's inhumanity to man. But at the last minute the song was pulled. Was this a simple failure of nerve? Dylan claimed not, telling Mintz in 1991, "The reason why it was never used was because the tempo speeded up . . . for some vague and curious reason." Hardly the most convincing of explanations, especially when this was a song he cut more times than any other in his studio career to date. The tape logs reveal he did forty-four takes of the song, across six sessions, of which the sessions on the twenty-second, twenty-third, and twenty-fifth were devoted largely or entirely to this single song.

Having tried the song every which way, including (unbelievably) a bossa nova version—as well as the inevitable reggaefied rendition—one and all failed to satisfy. Even after three solid days working on the song, he refused to give up on it. At the next two sessions (twenty-sixth and twenty-eighth), he tried to put his foot down and, even on the twenty-ninth, with the end nigh, he tried one last version at night's end. But even after forty-three goes at it, the thing still broke down. The song was finally copyrighted on *1983 Album Compilation #2*, around May 2, from the very same version that made the first album sequence (and, eventually, *The Bootleg Series*). So Dylan did succeed in picking a version out, one in which the tempo—and the message—never deviated.

Note: The version in the 2004 *Lyrics* is again full of badly mistranscribed lines. "You'll love me till the morning, stranger" comes out as "ya love me to the moon and the stranger," and instead of "sleeping with your head face down in the plate," one gets "your head face down in a grave." Even more bizarre, the last word of the line "They can exult you up or bring you down *bankrupt*" is given as "main route." See me after class, Ludwig.

{461} JULIUS AND ETHEL

Published lyric: Words Fill My Head.
Known studio recordings: Power Station Studios, NYC, April 27, 1983—2 takes.

> I'm interested in the fact that Jews are Semites, like Babylonians, Hittites, Arabs, Syrians, Ethiopians. But a Jew is different because a lot of people hate Jews. There's something going on here that's hard to explain.
> —Dylan, to Neil Hickey, September 1976

However many Dylan sessions threw up detritus unworthy of expensive two-inch tape, nothing quite prepares one for "Julius and Ethel." Though it never appeared officially, any critic worth their salt is obliged to ask, "What is this *shit*?" And yet it was recorded late on in the *Infidels* sessions, was duly copyrighted on the *1983 Album Compilation #2*, and transferred to the comp. reel in mid-May. All of which suggests it was on the verge of becoming another "Lenny Bruce."

Tackling a contentious court case with underlying issues of race (the treatment of the Rosenbergs was widely regarded as being a manifestation of deep-rooted anti-Semitism), Dylan was yet again hopelessly confused and/or ill-informed about the facts. And again he decided to write a song based entirely on a single source, albeit an esteemed one. It was French existentialist Jean-Paul Sartre who memorably described the outcome—a double execution—as "a legal lynching which smears with blood a whole nation. By killing the Rosenbergs, you have quite simply tried to halt the progress of science by human sacrifice. Magic, witch-hunts, auto-da-fés, sacrifices—we are here getting to the point: your country is sick with fear . . . you are afraid of the shadow of your own bomb."

Dylan himself agrees with Sartre as to the driving force in the country at the time, "Fear had you in a trance," describing the unfortunate pair as "sacrificial lambs in the marketplace sold," while giving his own summation of the fifties mind-set, "As long as you said nothing, you could say anything." But his attempt to sidestep the actual issue ("Some people said there hadn't been any crime") does not diminish the demonstrable guilt of the two scientists. At least one Rosenberg—Julius—certainly *did* (attempt to) give "the secrets of the atom bomb away." Nor does his attempt to portray the Rosenbergs' love for each other assuage their guilt. Still, it proved that the songwriter who once thought Joey Gallo was a Robin Hood figure was alive and well and living in la-la land.

{462} LORD PROTECT MY CHILD

Published lyric/s: Lyrics 04.
Known studio recordings: Power Station Studios, NYC, May 2, 1983—10 takes [TBS].

Of the last three original songs Dylan attempted at these sessions, "Lord Protect My Child" is the only one really worthy of what had come before. Doubtless conceived as a post-conversion "Forever Young," it deserved a slightly better fate than being stuck between "Tell Me" and "Foot of Pride" on *The Bootleg Series*. After all the talk of a world on the brink, this time he comes to terms with his *own* mortality ("If I fall along the way, and can't see another day") and the possibility that he might not live to see the Day of the Lord:

There'll be a time I hear tell, when all will be well,
When God and Man will be reconciled,
But until men lose their chains, and Righteousness reigns,
Lord, protect my child.

The vocal alone warrants its inclusion on a more auspicious artifact, Dylan duetting with Clydie King, who couldn't help but share the sentiments so eloquently expressed. Yet Dylan is deliberately wearing one of his disguises, portraying the "child" in the song as someone who is "young and on fire, full of hopes and desire" at one juncture, only to recall how "seeing him at play makes me smile" at another. Having become a father again for the first time in over a decade, he went to great lengths to imply that the song (only) addressed his teenage sons. It did not. As it happens, he need not have gone to such lengths because, after spending much of the last full *Infidels* session achieving the requisite degree of expressiveness, he decided not to risk the inevitable questions, electing to protect his youngest child from prying eyes / ears.

{463} **DEATH IS NOT THE END**

Published lyric/s: Lyrics 04.

Known studio recordings: Power Station Studios, NYC, May 2, 1983—1 take [DIG].

Dylan is generally known to write album closers late on in the process of assembling a collection. Yet he surely never intended to make this dirge *Infidels*" full stop (leaving the album to end with, "When the cities are on fire with the burning flesh of men"). Recorded in a single take, immediately after the completion of "Lord Protect My Child," "Death Is Not the End" was copyrighted just eight days later, on *1983 Album Compilation #2*. However, it does not appear on the fifteen-song comp. reel, compiled around May 16, which suggests even Dylan realized the song meandered monotonously, wandering from thought to thought. Nontheless, two days later someone was overdubbing backing vocals (wailing the single word "No"), for purpose/s unknown.

Quite what prompted Dylan to remember the song four years after the fact, putting it on that threadbare contract filler *Down in the Groove*, while "Blind Willie McTell" and "Foot of Pride" remained unreleased, he has never explained (a turkey remains a turkey no matter how many times you reheat it). At least we can be grateful that Dylan never had the nerve to inflict it on paying punters, preferring to leave it down among the grooveless detritus. Unfortunately, by 1987, when "Death Is Not the End" was released, the mercurial magnificence of much of the *Infidels* material had become as mysterious to the relapsed amnesiac as it was to his diminishing audience.

1984-6

{ Empire Burlesque; Knocked Out Loaded; Hearts of Fire }

For once, Dylan decided to take his time with the album that would consolidate Infidels' *modest commercial success. Even songs rejected from* Infidels, *or demoed in the garage in Malibu, were fair game, being reworked according to the current template—a self-produced "pop" album recorded over three series of sessions, spanning July 1984 through March 1985. Perhaps surprisingly, Dylan still felt he could afford to overlook several songs he had rehearsed in the lead-up to the summer 1984 tour. But then, the songs were still coming easily enough.*

The problem was largely one of subject matter. Save for two of the better songs recorded in this period—"Something's Burning, Baby" and "When the Night Comes Falling from the Sky"—he now bypassed the apocalyptic concerns which had suffused his work for half a decade. Unsure of which thematic direction he should go in, he admitted to Bill Flanagan during the mixing of the album, "I really don't have any idea what I'm doing. But I'll tell you one thing . . . there's no way I could write anything that would be scripturally incorrect . . . I'm not going to say anything that . . . there's not a law for." Mostly, he returned to bitching about capricious women in a surprisingly charmless way that reflected a worrying decline in discrimination when it came to liaisons with the opposite sex.

A rudderless writer replaced a previous sureness of purpose with plastic platitudes. He also remained uncomfortable with new technology that was supposed to make things easier but merely made the results sound sterile and lifeless.

{ Still on the Road }

Even after the 1985 album failed to reverse a long-term commercial decline, he persevered with a jigsaw puzzle approach that meant released cuts began life as backing tracks, morphing into something else when Dylan decided to add a new vocal (like as not with a new set of lyrics), and/or dollop on the overused (and often overbearing) Queens of Rhythm.

By 1986, even strong song ideas—still evident on Empire Burlesque*—had begun to dry up in an alarming way. After recording another fine "state of the world" song ("It's Hell Time Man!") in Australia that February, he barely had enough ideas left to rustle up an EP of genuinely worthy product. And yet he insisted on recording and releasing a full follow-up to* Empire Burlesque, Knocked Out Loaded, *before fleeing to London, where he recorded another set of songs for the soundtrack to his latest film,* Hearts of Fire. *The results suggested an artist in creative free fall, unable to even recraft the kind of cover song he used to play just to warm-up the band and the ol' vocal cords.*

{464} I ONCE KNEW A MAN
{465} WHO LOVES YOU?

Published lyric [#465]: Words Fill My Head.

Known studio recordings: [#464]: NBC Studio, NYC, March 22, 1984;
[#465]: ?Garage studio, Malibu, CA, March 1984; Delta Sound, NYC, July 26, 1984.

When, in the winter of 1984, Dylan began jamming with wannabe West Coast musicians hungry to make a name for themselves, it had been nine months since he said farewell to the *Infidels* songs. These rehearsals provided a necessary release for the middle-aged icon still searching for spontaneity, as everything he tried on the young guns came as a surprise—whether it was an old song of his, a "real old song," or a new song. (Unfortunately, the recollections of these ill-informed musicians give very little indication of the breadth of material rehearsed/recorded.)

Just one of these rehearsals is known to collectors, and though the recording quality is decent, Dylan seems to be singing off-mike (presumably, this is deliberate). Aside from this one garage session, there is just a single-camera run-through for the March 1984 *Letterman* performance which provides a flavor of the kind of material they had been working on. This run-through includes an otherwise undocumented Dylanesque reworking of an old blues, "I Once Knew a Man," that still defeats attributionists. The lyric, such as it is, revolves around the couplet "I once knew a man / Seemed like only yesterday, he done passed this way / I once knew a man," but the song does not make it to the telecast itself.

And at least one of the previous "garage" jams appears to have led somewhere, mutating into a song recorded at New York's Delta Sound in late July, when studio work began on *Infidels'* successor. "Who Loves You More?," as it is logged on the track sheet, already suggested Dylan's decision to relocate to Tin Pan Alley might be a mistake. He is trying *way* too hard to force platitudes into the lyrical threshing machine ("you're the answer to my every prayer"), hoping they might come out the other side as archetypal expressions. The song's repeated refrain, "Who loves you more, who loves you true / Baby, I do," establishes a worrying pattern he will repeat for the next couple of years.

Mind you, it might have helped if he'd bothered to finish the lyric before they rolled tape. Much of the song is unadulterated gibberish—"I shall fulfill my soul, if you're the one / Face the day and the brightening sun," anyone?—and what isn't, might as well be. All of which merely confirms that Dylan never intended to do more than lay down demos at Delta, secure in the knowledge that a digital vocal overdub was now a ready recourse. At least the head of steam he'd (belatedly) built up in Europe carried over to the end of the month. Despite that lyric, the "Who Loves You More?" vocal almost convinces.

{466} ALMOST DONE (ANGEL OF RAIN)

{467} I SEE YOU ROUND AND ROUND

Known rehearsal recordings [#466–67]: Beverly Theatre, LA, May 23, 1984;
Known rehearsal recordings [#467]: Arena di Verona, May 27, 1984.

In the years 1974–84, Dylan continued his pre-accident practice of debuting songs in concert that he had already recorded but not released or not even yet recorded but felt like trying out live. Less than twelve months after the end of his European 1984 tour, though, he was telling *Musician*'s Bill Flanagan, "When I'm making a record, I'll need some songs and I'll start digging through my pockets and drawers trying to find these songs . . . But regardless of what happens, when I do it in the studio it's the first time I've ever done it." This new credo he has stuck to ever since. In the past twenty-five years, he has simply stopped performing any original songs in concert not already released.

But in May 1984, prepping for a six-week tour of Europe, he was still working on a number of unrecorded originals. And though he only ended up performing one of them—"Enough Is Enough"—he clearly intended to do more. At the Verona press conference, the day after the opening show (cum–dress rehearsal), journalists were given a set list for the tour which included three new song titles: the aforementioned "Enough Is Enough," "Dirty Lie," and something called "Angel of Rain."

As evocative titles for unknown Dylan songs go, "Angel of Rain" is right up there. But no song containing such a line ever revealed itself. Even the emergence of two pre-tour rehearsal tapes—one from L.A. six days before the press conference, the other from Verona itself—failed to yield forth such fruit. Unless, that is, she is wearing a disguise, as I suspect she is.

What *can* be found on these two invaluable recordings are a number of attempts at a rather beautiful original song, which on the evidence of multiple versions from the Verona rehearsal has the repeated refrain, "almost done." Four days earlier, in L.A., it began life as a snatch of melody and a few half-strangled phrases about how "the dawn is gonna shine," and a snatched chorus of "Almost done, you're still the one." Even on the first Verona rehearsal—which is largely devoted to working on all three new songs (and a couple of country covers)—the words are a lot less developed than the melody or the rat-a-tat arrangement. Almost done? Maybe not.

Again, Dylan seems to enjoy a real rapport with Mick Taylor, who still remembered that "Sweetheart Like You" began this way. Though there is no shortage of dummy lyrics, the focus of the song remains: "Trust in me, I'll trust in you." In all likelihood, he continued to work on the lyric over the next couple of days. This would fit former patterns, the song resolving itself around another Rose of Sharon–like figure. By then, though, band rehearsals had transferred to the stages of Europe and, as he quickly discovered, stadium and arena audiences were notoriously reluctant to stand and listen to some slow, semi-defined song they'd never heard before. The slot one imagines this song would have filled he instead devoted to a Willie Nelson cover of a similar hue, "Why Do I Have to Choose?"

By the time Dylan returned to New York, the second week in July, he had already decided that all three songs rehearsed in Verona were surplus to requirements. This gorgeous melody went unused, even as he set about recording four songs with nary a decent tune between them. Also discarded, this time before he even boarded the plane for Italy, was another snatch of a song he was working on at the L.A. rehearsals. "I See You Round and Round," perhaps a leftover from the garage jam sessions, amounted to little more than a riff that went around and around, as the ninety-second fragment from the Beverly Theatre attests.

{468} DIRTY LIE

Published lyric: Isis #28, p6; Words Fill My Head.
Known rehearsal recordings: Arena di Verona, May 27, 1984.

"Dirty Lie," the most worked out of the new songs he spent time rehearsing in an arena where ancient footsteps really were everywhere, is perhaps the most surprising omission from the resultant tour. A great little toe tapper, it slips effortlessly into its own lyrical complaint, "Whoever told ya, told a dirty lie." Again, some poor gal has been on the receiving end of some kinda exploitation until the singer suggests they split: "I want to leave, my feet's soakin' wet / I want to leave, but I ain't found you yet." It's an updated "Let's Keep It Between Us," with Dylan following his own advice.

{469} ENOUGH IS ENOUGH

Published lyric/s: Words Fill My Head.
First known performance: Rome, June 21, 1984.
Known rehearsal recordings: Arena di Verona, May 27, 1984.

The one new song that made the transition from rehearsal to stage, "Enough Is Enough" took its time fixing itself in the 1984 set. Rehearsed in Verona, when the lyric was still up for grabs, the structure was fully up and running. But Dylan was diverted from the task of finishing the lyric by his decision to rewrite two *Blood on the Tracks* songs he would have been hard pressed to improve on ("Tangled Up in Blue" and "Simple Twist of Fate"). At the third show in Rome, he stopped repainting these masterpieces long enough to proclaim this simple statement: "A dollar is a dollar, and the downtown boys sure play rough / Go all the way back, baby, and tell 'em, Enough is enough."

The interjection of a new, up-tempo song into a set mired in mid-tempo rockers was a smart move, and Dylan kept the song in the set long enough to record it for an end-of-the-road "souvenir" album, *Real Live*. However, even though he already knew he wasn't saving it for his next studio album, he passed over the one song that might have got his fans to part with their hard-earned cash for a live album of largely life-less retreads. I guess he really meant it when he sang, "I'd rather be lucky than be rich."

{470} GO 'WAY LITTLE BOY
{471} HONEY, WAIT FOR ME

Published lyric/s: Words Fill My Head.

Known studio recordings: [#470]: Power Station, NYC, July 1984 [w/ Lone Justice]; [#471]: Intergalactic Studio, NYC, July 24, 1984.

Not surprisingly, the Krogsgaard sessionography does not include "Go 'Way Little Boy" in the credits for the July 26, 1984, session at Delta, even though it had circulated with the songs recorded there. Copyrighted a week before the four copyrighted songs attempted there,[24] it was cut at least a couple of days earlier. A negligible addition to the canon, it was perhaps a song he was always looking to give away. As such, when his on-off girlfriend Carole Childs pressed him to provide a song for the latest hot property she was A&Ring at Geffen, he remembered this one.

Uncharacteristically for this period, "Go 'Way Little Boy" is written from the vantage point of a full-grown woman spurning the advances of a young pup, while still looking to let him down gently (one line designed to lessen the pain is ultimately transferred to "something's burning, I don't wanna see you bleed"). As such, Maria McKee, the lead singer of cowpunk combo Lone Justice, was the ideal recipient. All woman, she had already been given the two-edged "Ways to Be Wicked" by Tom Petty, as if limbering up for that role as a gal too hot to handle. The brazen Childs seems to have expected more of her beau, cajoling him into attending the recording session, only to find producer Jimmy Iovine still gumming up the works of the wicked.

The Lone Justice drummer, Don Heffington, recalls, "We did a version with Bob singing so [our singer] Maria could learn it and then we recorded one with Maria singing a scratch vocal which she later replaced . . . and that came out as a B-side." The version copyrighted sure sounds like such a run-through.

Aside from coaching McKee to sing it like *him* (forgetting, for a minute, that nobody sings Dylan like Dylan), the songwriter's contribution—according to the credits on the Lone Justice "best of" anthology, *The World Is Not My Home* (1999)—was confined to rhythm guitar. However, the version on this mixed-bag compilation was *not* the one released back in 1985 as a B-side to the second Lone Justice 45, "Sweet, Sweet Baby (I'm Falling)." On this twelve-inch single, it sure sounds like Dylan wailing away on harp (unless Maria thought any serious Dylan impersonation required her to send up his harp playing, too). According to Heffington, "When it was mixed, somehow the executive decision was made to wipe Bob and Ron Wood off the thing . . . They put them back on when it was remixed later for some sort of compilation."

If "Go 'Way Little Boy" was at least copyrighted, another song from the session was not, probably because Dylan had forgotten his lyric sheet. As Heffington says, "First thing we did was a blues, a slow 12/8 blues . . . Just fooling around really. They weren't really blues changes, if I remember right . . . I think it just hung on one chord. Anyway, Bob and I started playing . . . Benmont [Tench] and Marvin [Etzioni] figured out the key and we played through this tune. 'Baby, oh baby,' he was singing. I never heard it back again after that night."

If that song fell through the cracks, another similar sounding jam turned up on the end of some Live Aid rehearsals (yes, they really did rehearse!). "Honey, Wait For Me" may well be a product of another session that month with the Al Green band. Woody—again along for the ride—says they "did six or seven brand new songs" with Green's band. This stray song is little more than a riff to which Dylan repeatedly adds the plea "Honey, wait, honey wait for me." Working the song out in performance takes up almost five minutes, but he is no nearer improvising a fuller lyric at the end than at the beginning. According to Ron Wood, "All these guys from Memphis couldn't understand [his] chord sequences . . . [and] if we were doing the same song over and over, every time it would be in a different key." Already, it seems, Dylan was recording studio jams with a view to grafting on a lyric at a later date. And he wasn't about to let the musicians in on his little secret.

{472} DRIFTIN' TOO FAR FROM SHORE

Published lyric/s: Lyrics 85; Lyrics 04. *[Original lyric:* Words Fill My Head.*]*
*Known studio recordings: Delta Sound, NYC, July 1984; Skyline Studios,
Topanga, CA, May 1986 [KOL].*
First known performance: Concord, CA, June 7, 1988.

> To me, the machinery is making sound the thing, not the song. I'm
> trying to find a balance . . . Anything raw you put in, it's going to come
> out sterilized. —Dylan to Denise Worrell, November 1985

Two of the songs from the July Delta demo tape would in fact end up being released by Dylan—a rekindled "Clean Cut Kid" and the off-kilter "Driftin' Too Far From Shore." In its original Delta incarnation, the latter is little more than a rhythm track to which someone has applied a synthesizer wash on repeat spin. Yet Ron Wood remembered the song on the day as "a really vibrant rock and roll track." He even asked Dylan, on hearing the *Knocked Out Loaded* cut, "What's happened! What happened to your piano? What happened to the drums?" So I guess it lost something in the transition. The original Delta recording used the same rhythm section as "Clean Cut Kid," with session musician Anton Fig demonstrating the modern way of drumming. In fact, according to Ira Ingber, "Driftin'" was one song where "we put the drums on [at Skyline] 'cause they were recorded awfully [originally] at the guy's studio." So Wood was right—they did tamper with the drum sound, though the album sleeve still credits Fig.

The song took its title, but nothing else, from a Charles E. Moody spiritual, "Drifting Too Far From the Shore," which Dylan almost certainly knew from the 1936 Monroe Brothers 78 (though it was also recorded by Hank Williams). A perfect song for a Dylan/Clydie King duet, one can easily imagine their harmonies wrapping around the sentiment, "Come to Jesus today, let him show you the way / You're drifting too far from the shore." But here it is the twin vocal powers of Dylan and that other sometime partner Carolyn Dennis who grapple with a song so named. Whether Dylan was singing it with Dennis or at her, I speculate not; but the one repeated verse in there, directly dealing with mammon, is the only verse to survive its transference to Skyline Studios, and the *Knocked Out Loaded* damage-limitation exercise:

> I sent you all my money, just like I did before,
> I tried to reach you honey, but you're drifting too far from shore.

The original Delta lyric was left that way for another two years, until it went the way of the original drum and synthesizer tracks, over-dubbed into oblivion by the Skyline machinery. In its place were some lines that got a whole lot more personal. If "I never could guess your weight baby / Never needed to call you my whore" sounds cutting enough, our boy wasn't done. "No gentleman likes making love to a servant / 'Specially when he's in his father's house" suggests a link between easy virtue and easy money that would have had Reverend Moody reaching for the smelling salts. (It turns out that this line was another one purloined from a Bogart movie, *Sabrina*, save for switching mother for father, proving he was still inclined to indulge in such a lyrical ruse.)

The Skyline scrub also dispensed with the handclaps that Dylan had boasted about adding "manually" in a radio interview just days after the Delta session. The 1986 rewrite, though, did not stick in his mind, and when he fleetingly decided to give the song a live dimension—during the first summer of the Never Ending Tour in 1988—he barely got past money matters in his attempt to quicken the already dead. How one wishes it had been Moody's microcosmic masterpiece that Dylan had decided to tackle on the 1986 album.

{473} NEW DANVILLE GIRL (=BROWNSVILLE GIRL)
Published lyric/s: Lyrics 04. *[Danville Girl:* Words Fill My Head.*]*
Known studio recordings: Cherokee Studios, L.A., December 6, 1984; Skyline Studios, Topanga, CA, May, 1986 [KOL].
First known performance: Paso Robles, CA, August 6, 1986.

A movie is something that gives the illusion of stopping time. You go someplace and you sit there for a while. You're looking at something. You're trapped. It's all happening in your brain and it seems like nothing else is going on in the world. Time has stopped. The world could be coming to an end outside, but for you time has stopped. Then someone says, "What was it about?" "Well, I don't know. It was about two guys who were after the same girl." —Dylan to Bill Flanagan, March 1985

The one indisputable masterpiece from Dylan's *Burlesque* years, "New Danville Girl," which he cowrote with the playwright Sam Shepard, is a song of sweeping ambition, as deep and as wide as the fineSt. John Ford western. (It is "New Danville Girl" because there was already a "Danville Girl" which Woody wrote.) And, in keeping with an album littered with cinematic allusions, the song that began the recording of *Empire Burlesque* in earnest takes as its starting point the classic 1950 western *The Gunfighter,* directed by Henry King, with Gregory Peck in the title role.

Of course, this being Dylan, he doesn't tell us this is the film's name. Rather, he claims, "All I remember about it was that it starred Gregory Peck / He was shot down in the back by a hungry kid / Trying to make a name for himself." He then cleverly skews the plot of the film—just as one would if trying to recall a movie, as opposed to directly reexperiencing it. So the lines that the dying gunfighter utters in the song are not quite what Peck says. In the film he merely gasps, "If I was doing you a favor, I would let them hang you right now . . . but I don't want you to get off that light . . . I want you to see what it means to have to live like a big, tough gunnie." Whereas in the song he says, "Turn him loose, let him go, let him say he outdrew me fair and square / I want him to feel what it's like to every moment face his death." What a great rewrite, if not remotely like Bower and Sellers, authors of the original film script.

But then the song is primarily concerned with how the memory plays tricks. As Shepard put it, "It has to do with a guy standing on line and waiting to see an old . . . movie that he can't quite remember—only pieces of it—and then this whole memory thing happens." The way the story unfolds is wondrous to behold, and quite revealing. It seems whenever Dylan gets all cinematic, he can't help showing that he is a darn sight better read than he likes to let on. Or is it his collaborator who shows such a keen understanding of the rudiments of Platonic thought to come up with a line like "We're busy talkin' back and forth to our shadows . . ."?

One of the coauthors also seems to know his Dickens (or maybe he just saw the 1935 movie, directed by Jack Conway). The line "It was the worst of times," seemingly tossed into the narrative ad hoc, tells us we have experienced a real narrative. Threatening to emulate Dickens's fabled introduction to *A Tale of Two Cities* ("It was the best of times, it was the worst of times"), Dylan rejects such a neat summation, leaving the line hanging. The story is all done, as he is back replaying *The Gunfighter* in his mind, except this time he is not sure whether he is watching or appearing in it: "I don't remember who I was, or what part I played." He is "trapped. It's all happening in [his] brain and it seems like nothing else is going on in the world. Time has stopped."

If the Dickens line could have been Shepard's suggestion, plenty of others smack of Dylan. The preceding line, "Tell me about the time that our engine broke down," is at least partly an allusion to Blind Willie McTell's "Broke Down Engine Blues," a song Dylan later covered. The engine in question was, of course, in his pants. (I'm not suggesting Shepard didn't know American music. After all, he had been in Pete Stampfel's Unholy Modal Rounders, a credential which probably far outweighed his screen credits to Dylan's mind.) Likewise, it was probably Dylan who came up with the couplet "You saw my picture in The *Corpus Christi Tribune* / Underneath it said, 'A man with no alibi,'" which in two lines summarizes the entire plot for "Long Black Veil," a longtime personal favorite he once taught to The Band.

This time, the woman does provide the alibi—and so the troubled narrator lives to tell his tale. The rich cross-stitching of sources continues when she delivers her testimony in court. In the original December 1984 recording Dylan sings, "I watched you break down in front of the judge and cry," but by the May 1986 recording he has added two words, "real tears." The line in question—"She broke down and cried real tears"—comes from *To Kill a Mockingbird*, the movie that won Gregory Peck his Best Actor Oscar. Evidently, "this stuff" really did just come "rolling in," blowing through him "like a ball and chain." But what began as a clever way of interweaving dialogue with the lyrical was by 1986 perpetuating his writer's block. The fog of forgetfulness had fully descended, prompting Dylan to self-consciously send up the very thing he began doing on "New Danville Girl" by interjecting, "If there's an original thought out there, I could use it right now."

Back in 1984, he was still looking to condense a complex narrative so that it fit a popular song, albeit a twelve minute one. One suspects he had been yearning to write such a compressed ballad movie ever since "Lily, Rosemary, and the Jack of Hearts" kicked off that set of songs (like that earlier epic, he was soon thinking "about making a movie out of that"; the project remains ongoing[25]). It was a form he loved, partly because it allowed him to address the love of film itself—and a particular kind of film he revered above all others. It took another quarter of a century for some enterprising interviewer to get on to the subject of Hollywood westerns, but when he did Dylan delivered quite a panegyric:

[John Ford]'s films were easy to understand. I like that period of time in American films. I think America has produced the greatest films ever. No other country has ever come close. The great movies that came out of America in the studio system . . . were heroic and visionary, and inspired people in a way that no other country has ever done. If film is the ultimate art form, then you'll need to look no further than those films.

But by 1984 Dylan's boredom threshold, never of exactly Olympian proportions, was already starting to sap away at his songwriting drive, even as a general dissatisfaction with the limitations of popular song was prompting him to explore artistic tangents he was less equipped to make his own. On at least two occasions the following year he referred to an unfinished novel called *Ho Chi Minh in Harlem*, which he admitted to one journalist "excited me there for a minute." He had also started sending assorted hangers-on to go off and research possible story lines for movies.

When he did make a movie, though, it was someone else's: Richard Marquand's cinematic car crash *Hearts of Fire*. Even then, Dylan had his own ideas about *his* character. As Marquand told *San Francisco Chronicle's* Donald Chase: "He contributed ideas about what might have happened in Billy Parker's past. Making it rougher and tougher than what I had been thinking about. There was a very nice thing about how his father might have traveled with him. And Bob felt strongly that Billy's reasons for dropping out should be made clear, and came up with reasons very specific to Billy's life, such as the behavior of his manager." Proof positive he could think cinematically *outside* song.

As the other *Empire Burlesque* songs attest, he had been happily ransacking his local Blockbuster for inspiration. Yet what sparked "New Danville Girl" was not any visual aid but a discussion with his friend Sam Shepard about a recent Lou Reed composition, "Doin' the Things That We Want To." The song in question, released on *New Sensations* at the beginning of October 1984, begins with the author visiting a performance of one of Shepard's plays (*Fool For Love*):

> The other night we went to see Sam's play,
> It was very physical, it held you to the stage,
> The guy's a cowboy from some rodeo,
> The girl had once loved him but now she wants to go.

Reed's song contained at least one line that Dylan would have wholly embraced: "There's not much you hear on the radio, but you can still see a movie or a play." Lou's lyrical review of the play soon changes tack, though, turning into a eulogy on the art of Sam Shepard and Martin Scorsese, prompting the former to respond in kind. And Shepard and Dylan were by now old friends. Recruited as a writer on the first Rolling Thunder Revue in 1975, Shepard ended up playing a part in (the wholly improvised) *Renaldo and Clara*, before publishing his road notes as *Rolling Thunder Logbook* (1977). And though he continued to produce plays with true grit, he also began acting in earnest with 1978's *Days of Heaven*, culminating in the year of their collaboration with an Oscar nomination for his portrayal of Chuck Yeager in *The Right Stuff*.

Just as his prior association with Jacques Levy—his last significant colyricist (sorry, Helena)—allowed Dylan to pretend the other guy was the erudite one, so his single-song association with Sam Shepard gave him the latitude to let all that hidden learning leak out for all to see (this was another trick he learnt from Guthrie, who played the hokey Okie to the hilt while reading voraciously on the quiet).

Without wishing in any way to diminish Shepard's role in the song's lyric or his own gifts for dialogue, it seems that his primary function in the writing process—like Jacques Levy nine years earlier—was to push Dylan to not give up on the idea or settle for second best. According to Shepard, they "spent two days writing the lyrics—Bob had previously composed the melody line." Dylan acknowledged his colyricist's input when talking about their collaboration to a German journalist in 1997: "Working with Sam was not necessarily easier, but it was certainly less meaningless. In every case writing a song is done faster when you got someone like Sam and are not on your own." The once prolific penman had evidently been struggling to motivate himself to, as it were, give the envelope a shove one more time, until Shepard brought along his shovel.

"New Danville Girl" temporarily satiated two impulses which would continue to pull Dylan in opposite directions—the need to find a way to trample the constraints of popular song while presenting his world-view in widescreen. And even though he undoubtedly knew it wouldn't be a breakthrough commensurate with those that came out of similar frustrations in 1963 and 1965, the recording of "New Danville Girl" did return him to the studio and remind him what he did for a living.

As it happens, the process of translating this epic ballad into a releasable recording lasted longer than most film shoots—from December 6, 1984 to May 20, 1986, to be precise, when another bevy of girl singers were applied to the once-sparse backing track. Only then did it become the one and only reason for fans to rush out and buy *Empire Burlesque*'s sorry successor, *Knocked Out Loaded*.

In the interim, Dylan decided that the album "New Danville Girl" jump-started would not be obliged to live in its shadow. Instead, a series of rather samey songs directed at Danvillesque heartbreakers past and present poured out of him, while what should have been the narrative core of *Empire Burlesque* became a victim of another willful act of artistic self-destruction. A reheated leftover from *Infidels*, "Tight Connection to My Heart," was allowed to set the album's tone instead.

Unlike the equally important songs cut from the two previous long-players, "New Danville Girl" had been recorded with relative ease, using a rock quartet of young L.A. guns—guitarist Ira Ingber, drummer Don Heffington, organist Vince Melamed, and bassist Carl Sealove. Even after he allowed Madelyn Quebec to impose that voice without restraint, the song sat up and demanded attention. Indeed, Ira Ingber remembers, "When we first recorded it . . . we made a cassette. And he took it out and started playing it. He came back the next day we were working and said, 'Yeah, a lot of people like this thing.'"

And still, for the third time running, Dylan chose to omit the central song from a record he was seeking to make. Nor was "New Danville Girl" alone. It was just one of four songs Dylan admitted to leaving off the album to *Time* correspondent Denise Worrell, though he was quick to add: "When I go back in the studio next time, I'll look at that stuff." Sure enough, within hours of arriving at Skyline Studios in April 1986, he was calling up those Cherokee (and Delta Sound) tapes.

At least six *Knocked Out Loaded* sessions were partly devoted to over-dubbing "New Danville Girl," without ever doing anything to the basic track, which he never improved on. Dylan concentrated instead on adding some sympathetic sax and omnipresent western-style trumpet—courtesy of Stevie Douglas and Madaio—before imposing a new vocal of his own (with the inevitable rewrites). He then almost undid all this good work by letting the Queens of Rhythm loose. (If anyone has an old-style studio fader, I could use it right now.)

So what about Dylan's own vocal performance? After all, he hadn't much of a track record when it came to enhancing one of his own songs in "postproduction." The 1986 vocal is actually pretty dynamic, and most of the lyric he leaves well alone. However, in that fine Hollywood tradition, he decided at some point to rewrite the entire ending. (Assistant engineer at the *Knocked Out Loaded* sessions, Dave Garfield, remembers "Brownsville Girl"—as the song was now known—being "one of the ones he would stop in the middle of things . . . and start penning some new lyrics.") In burying evidence of a seismic change in worldview—from 1979's "He's got plans of His own" to "Nothing happens on purpose"—he sacrifices some of his most poignant lines:

> Nothin' happens on purpose, it's an accident if it happens at all,
> And everything that's happening to us seems like it's happening without
> our consent,
> While we're busy talking back and forth to our shadows on the old stone wall.
> Oh, you got to talk to me now, baby, tell me about the man that you used
> to love,
> And tell me about your dreams just before the time you passed out.
> Tell me about the time that our engine broke down, and it was the worst
> of times,
> Tell me about all the things I couldn't do nothing about.
> There was a movie I seen one time . . .

And yet, the above verse excepted, the few rewrites were neither as drastic nor as deleterious as on "Driftin' Too Far From Shore" or "Tight Connection" (though I personally miss the great rhyme lost by replacing "fell out under the stars . . . whole place started feelin' like Mars" with "tender and soft . . . my head get blown off," good as the substitute lines are).

After all the changes, "Brownsville Girl" still justified every single plaudit that came its way, a marked contrast to the crescendo of criticism that greeted the remainder of an awful album. But Dylan never tackled the track live—save for a half-assed interpolation of the chorus at the final summer 1986 show at a county fair in Paso Robles. I guess he thought that if he did try to recall the whole thing, his memory would play tricks.

{474} SOMETHING'S BURNING, BABY

Published lyric/s: Lyrics 85; Lyrics 04. *[Original lyric:* Words Fill My Head.*]*
Known studio recordings: Cherokee Studios, L.A., December [13–]14, 1984 [EB]; Power Station, NYC, February 21, 1985.

According to the tape logs listed by Krogsgaard, there were two entirely separate attempts to record this overlooked gem. Dylan certainly spent some time working on the song, which is almost a spiritual version of a song he performed magnetically in 1980 (and then recorded for his 1986 film), "A Couple More Years." But whereas Shel Silverstein just wanted to ease her worried mind—"It ain't that I'm wiser, I just spent more time with my back to the wall"—Dylan is concerned for the woman's very soul: "I don't wanna see you bleed, I know what you need / But it ain't what you deserve."

However, the versions in said sessionography cannot be reconciled with either the version Dylan released or the one he copyrighted (from which the released version was partly constructed). The version copyrighted—and in general circulation—is another Ingber–Melamed–Heffington concoction, onto which Madelyn Quebec has added her voice, without being in any way prepped ("Maddy did not know the words when they did the vocal, 'cause I watched her . . . She was trying to sing harmonies with him live" —Ira Ingber). It probably dates from the December 13 session, for which we have no details. Heffington remembers that "Dylan kept working on it even as we cut it. He had scraps of paper and he was writing things on paper bags . . . whatever was around. It was amazing how he'd change things up. I put a bunch of percussion on it but it's not listed on the album . . . a big bass drum, some toms, a tambourine. Later they took it to NY and reworked it."

When work did resume on the song, in New York the following February, Dylan had decided to bring the full weight of the Power Station wrecking crew to bear on the original Cherokee basic track. With the basic rhythmic bedrock supplied by the inestimable Sly 'n' Robbie, Dylan set about recording what is logged as "Something Is Burning (recut)" with a gaggle of backing singers, Stuart Kimball and old friend Al Kooper on guitars, and Richard Stevenson (né Scher) providing the old synth wash.

Dylan must have liked what he heard, because he used the exact same combination two days later to suck an entire whirlpool of life out of "When the Night Comes Falling." With "Something's Burning," though, he went back to the original, transcontinental basic track. He presumably decided that the recut had crushed the life out of this funereal march because he returned to the Cherokee reel, aside from imposing the New York bassline on it (courtesy of Robbie S.) and some blips and beeps from Scher.

A new vocal to the second half of the song also appeared when the song was recopyrighted, which showed him still messing with the narrative (from where her eyes are "staring off in the night"). This time he was looking to amplify the biblical subtext to make it crystal clear that the smell of burning is coming from down below, where they're having another barbecue of men's souls. The fumes of hellfire, which have been flicking around this femme fatale a while ("Something is the matter, baby, there's smoke in your hair"), have begun to consume her (just like Wentworth in Charles Williams' penultimate novel, *Descent Into Hell).* If the original final verse suggested her fate was hanging in the balance, the new version spelled it out:

Original take: Somebody bigger than me is gonna know what you're about,
Somebody parked in a truck in the shade is gonna figure you out,
Ring down when you're ready, baby, I'm waiting alone,
The life you're saving just might be your own.

Final take: Something is burning, baby, something's in flames,
There's a man going round calling names,
Ring down when you're ready, baby, I'm waiting for you,
I believe in the impossible, you know that I do.

The "man going round calling names" is clearly the Big Cheese who "the dead, small and great, [shall] stand before . . . [and be] judged . . . according to their works" (Revelation 20:12). The final line is as explicit a commitment to Christ as any made in the past four years, recalling the verse in Matthew where Jesus says unto his disciples, "If ye have faith . . . nothing shall be impossible unto you" (17:20). Nor are these the only biblical allusions introduced at this late stage. Replacing a corny attempt to rhyme "taking flight" and "white skin-tight," he introduces two references to the Christian Messiah and his message of hope: "You can't live by bread alone, you won't be satisfied / You can't roll away the stone if your hands are tied." While the latter line immediately conjures up an image of the stone which sealed the door to Jesus' tomb (see Mark

16:1–4), the former line paraphrases in street lingo Christ's retort to the devil when the latter suggested he turn stones to bread: "It is written, Man shall not live by bread alone, but by every word that proceedeth out of the mouth of God" (Matthew 4:4).

By the time Dylan added the new lyrics, he had probably already written its sister song, "When the Night Comes Falling," about a lass who *had* fallen by the wayside. An album that could have creaked to its clichéd conclusion would now end with "When the Night Comes Falling," "Something's Burning," and "Dark Eyes"—as ominous an ending as anything on the man's "Christian" trilogy. These apocalyptic incursions also demonstrated that the man's songwriting had not diminished to nothing just because he thought he could croon a tune.

Such was Dylan's determination to get "Something's Burning" right that he even punched in two last-minute lyrical tweaks, changing "on bread" to "by bread," to make it fit its biblical source, while "the outskirts of town," in place of "shaking ground," attaches a Louis Jordan sound track to his *Mexico City Blues*. But for all of this fully warranted attention to detail, the song was never imposed on live audiences, though it was apparently rehearsed in the summer of 1990.

{475} LOOK YONDER

{476} GRAVITY SONG

{477} PRINCE OF PLUNDER (= MAYBE SOMEDAY)

Published lyric/s: Lyrics 04. *[Maybe Someday]*

Known studio recordings: Cherokee Studios, L.A., December 7, 1984 and ?February 17, 1985 [#475]; December 9, 1984 [#476]; January 28, 1985 [#477]; [Maybe Someday]: Skyline Studios, Topanga, CA, May 14, 1986 [KOL].

Though Dylan seemed happy to copyright material left over from the Delta Sound sessions the previous July, or the Power Station sessions the following February, the songs from the December 1984 Cherokee sessions he discarded received no such recognition. Yet the fact that he devoted a session each to "Look Yonder" and the "Gravity Song," using the same combination who executed "New Danville Girl" with such aplomb (Ingber, Melamed, Sealove, and Heffington) suggests he was not just killing time.

I doubt that the former is Elmore James's "Look On Yonder Wall"—though it is possible. He did subsequently record the James song with Dave Alvin, probably at an undocumented *Knocked Out Loaded* session. (The Isis Misinformation Service thinks it was at the "Driftin' Too Far From Shore" session on April 28. I think not.) These December 1984 sessions are clearly designed to produce an all-original album, and the fact that the song was subject to overdubs/reworking at a later session argues against an impromptu jam of an old blues standard.

"Prince of Plunder" was a song Dylan recorded alongside early versions of "I'll Remember You" and "Seeing the Real You at Last."[26] This time, Dylan relied on the Heartbreaker combination of Mike Campbell and Howie Epstein. Lone Justice drummer Don Heffington also continued to enjoy Dylan's largesse. Unlike those other two songs, it was not worked on further in New York. However, it was not entirely forgotten, reappearing as "Maybe Someday" at the May 1986 Skyline sessions, having acquired an entirely new lyric for the *Knocked Out Loaded* sessions. (Heffington recalls that the basic track "was cut at Cherokee, with the personnel that's listed. Dylan just started playing these chords and we played along. He put the lyrics on later.")

Beneath layers of technogunk and a snarling vocal that does the song precious few favors hides a decent little ditty, even if only the musician credits on the *Knocked Out Loaded* inner sleeve tell us the song had begun life as another "lost" *Empire Burlesque* track. Those credits give a basic lineup of Don Heffington on drums, Mike Campbell on guitar, and Howie Epstein on bass; the only occasion that combination shared a studio with his irascible self was on January 28, 1985, when the musicians cut three songs: "I'll Remember You," "Seeing the Real You At Last," and the otherwise unheard "Prince of Plunder." (For the February 1985 Cherokee sessions Dylan used Jim Keltner on drums, as both Debbie Gold—who A&R'd the session—and Don Heffington have confirmed to me. The Krogsgaard sessionography is therefore not only incomplete but incorrect in essential details regarding these sessions.)

Despite being recorded at a session which resulted in two album cuts, "Prince of Plunder" was not one of the twelve songs copyrighted as part of the *1985 Album Compilation #1*. Dylan told Denise Worrell that of the four songs nixed from the album at the last minute, one song was specifically left off because it "didn't get finished," which would explain both the failure to copyright the song in 1985 and its reinvention on *Knocked Out Loaded*. It is not clear at what point he changed tack and scribbled the words that came out as "Maybe Someday," but it would appear to have been late on in the *KOL* process. It was not until May 14, 1986, that the song was added to the album, which Dylan was now describing as compiled from "all sorts of stuff . . . not really hav[ing] a theme or a purpose."

Over the next ten days, any available kitchen sink was added to an already overbearing backing track. The eighties-style production and deadpan delivery took care of anyone ever paying attention to some great little one-liners tucked away here, whether it be the double-edged "Always was a sucker for the right cross" or the quintessential contrariness of "Maybe someday, when you're by yourself alone / You'll know the love that I had for you was never my own." Dylan was one of those who overlooked it, unwilling to be reminded what this prince of plunder had done to him.

{478} SEEING THE REAL YOU AT LAST

Published lyric/s: Lyrics 85; Lyrics 04. *[Extra verses: Words Fill My Head.]*
Known studio recordings: Cherokee Studios, L.A., [December 22, 1984;]
January 28, 1985 [EB].
First known performance: Wellington, New Zealand, February 5, 1986.

> What I got out of Buddy [Holly] was that you can take influences from anywhere. Like his "That'll Be the Day." I read somewhere that it was a line he heard in a movie, and I started realizing you can take things from everyday life that you hear people say. I still find that true. You can go anywhere in daily life and have your ears open and hear something . . . If it has resonance, you can use it in a song. —Dylan, to Robert Hilburn, 2004

By the time Dylan made the above comment, this was becoming a familiar mantra for him. In reality, most of the dialogue self-consciously introduced into mid-eighties songs was at least one step removed from reality, having been beamed direct to Dylan's TV remote from the hills of

Hollywood. Like Hollywood, he was much more likely to use "a line he heard in a movie" than "go somewhere and sit around . . . where you're going to throw yourself into the atmosphere of overhearing a lot of people talking to . . . other people" (something he claimed he had tried in one latter-day conversation). It was symptomatic of his increasing sense of isolation from humanity that he drew on film dialogue from Tinseltown. He talked at length about this sense of detachment the following year to *Omnibus* producer Christopher Sykes, on a film set of all places: "I don't know what people think . . . I only know about what . . . people who want you to do things say."

"Seeing the Real You At Last" (and the rewritten parts of "Someone's Got a Hold of My Heart" aka "Tight Connection," which he reworked at the same juncture, and clearly under the same influence) was almost entirely a composite from the movies of Hollywood's heyday—the forties and fifties. The song *literally* took its cue from a line delivered by Edward G. Robinson in the John Huston classic noir thriller *Key Largo*, "Think this rain would cool things off, but it don't."

It seems that Bogie box set was getting a lot of wear and tear. Bogart's Sam Spade in *The Maltese Falcon* provided Dylan with another line, "I'll have some rotten nights after I've sent you over—but that'll pass," which became "Well, I have had some rotten nights / Didn't think that they would pass"; while the last two lines of *The Big Sleep* film—though not the novel—gave Dylan the elements needed for the line, "At one time there was nothing wrong with me that you could not fix." (The profound debt that "Seeing the Real You At Last" and *Empire Burlesque* as a whole owe to Humphrey Bogart movies was first pointed out in an article by my fellow Wanted Man, John Lindley, in issue 25 of *The Telegraph*.)

However, Dylan wasn't just revisiting noir thrillers—usually the best source for great cinematic one-liners—when penning this song. From *The Hustler*, he took a line delivered by Paul Newman's title character: "I got troubles, I think maybe you got troubles. I think we'd better leave each other alone." From Clint Eastwood's *Bronco Billy*, he took the line, delivered by Clint himself when Sandra Locke asked him what kind of woman he was looking for, "One who can ride like Annie Oakley and shoot like Belle Starr." Indeed, Lindley's article resulted in something of a contest among Wanted Man subscribers to find the most left-field debt derived from a movie or TV program on *Empire Burlesque* (a contest I personally consider I won by pointing out that he had taken two lines from a *Star Trek* episode—"The Squire of Gothos"—in the "new" part of "Tight Connection").

To give Dylan the benefit of the doubt—for this song, anyway—it was all part of the gag: using "seeing the real you" as the title of a song *about* the artifice of women who use their feminine wiles to ensnare a mate. Nor is he bound to the silver screen, resorting to the more classical image of Ulysses "strapped to the mast" while the sirens send him crazy trying to entice him onto the rocks, to make one tight connection. In "Seeing the Real You At Last," we aren't *supposed* to see the real I. He—the narrator—remains another.

And taken on this level, the song works well. Unfortunately for Dylan's ongoing artistry, he turned a one-time ruse into a regular recourse in his bag of tricks. Equally unfortunately, the released recording added extraneous layers of artifice (percussion, horns, and even a sax solo) to a decent basic track, recorded at Cherokee in late January 1985 with Howie Epstein, Mike Campbell, Don Heffington, Bob Glaub, and Benmont Tench.[27] The song as originally revealed even had an extra verse, which Dylan presumably trimmed because it made the song overlong, though it was a good 'un:

Say goodbye to Frank Riley, say goodbye to Frances Jordan too,
Funny how I never did know how they were so tied up with you,
It just never ceases to amaze me, all these surprises they come to pass,
Well, it's all over now, I'm seeing the real you at last.

Frank Riley and Frances Jordan sound like two friends of Henry Porter. They may even have once belonged to "New Danville Girl," though. In the end, Dylan decided they didn't belong in either place. Even without them, the song survived into the *True Confessions* set where the Heartbreakers reclaimed it. Indeed, the song endured beyond the G. E. Smith era, though its last memorable incarnation was as the nightly opener at the 1989 New York Beacon residency, when Dylan reconnected with his performing self at last.

{479} I'LL REMEMBER YOU

Published lyric/s: Lyrics 85; Lyrics 04.

Known studio recordings: Cherokee Studios, L.A., January 28, 30; February 5, 1985 [EB].

First known performance: Farm Aid, Champaign, IL, September 22, 1985.

By the time Dylan resumed work on *Empire Burlesque* in late January 1985—after taking his usual Christmas break—he had presumably decided to make the kind of album he ended up releasing. With the likes of "I'll Remember You," "Seeing the Real You At Last," and "Trust Yourself" all recorded on his return to Cherokee, he was again writing songs from scraps. He talked about the experience of writing such songs later in the year, when he told *Time*, "I go through . . . long spells where I don't really write anything. I just jot down little phrases and things I overhear, people talking to me, stuff like that . . . [But] when I do work . . . I'll work for, like twenty-four hours at a time, and then readjust after that."

"I'll Remember You" needed more than twenty-four hours. And got it—Dylan apparently attempting the song at a session with Don Heffington and then with Jim Keltner applying the beat. Conceived to resemble something from the forties, it was his first overt attempt to write a song that could fit in a black and white movie sung by the romantic lead "at the end of the trail." Using his newfound lyric prompt—classic noir movies—he changed exactly one word from a line found in the greatest noir movie of them all, *The Big Sleep*: "There's some people that you don't forget even if you've only seen them once." But coming across more like Jerome Kern's dim-witted cousin than Raymond Chandler, "I'll Remember You" falls crucially short in the wordsmith department. "You to me were true / You to me were the best" is the kind of cliché he used to eye up with a machete. No more.

Whereas the likes of Gershwin or Berlin never allowed lyrical joins to show, "I'll Remember You" was stitched together by a songwriter who was all thumbs when it came to composing a crooner's ballad. A song he worked on long, it was best forgotten; as such, it was bound to be one song he consistently performed throughout the entire Heartbreakers era, Madelyn Quebec often gamely struggling to make a duet of it. Dylan even allowed those plangent chords to infect the Never Ending Tour long after he'd forgotten everything else Cherokee had had to offer.

{480} QUEEN OF ROCK AND ROLL

Known studio recordings: Cherokee Studios, L.A., February 5, 1985 [possible overdubs: February 17, 1985].

One of three songs recorded at a February 1985 Cherokee session that continued to utilize key components of Tom Petty's Heartbreakers, but with a drummer other than Stan Lynch—in this case the inestimable Jim Keltner—"Queen of Rock and Roll" was not one of the songs copyrighted on the *1985 Album Compilation #1* tape, rather suggesting that it was recorded and then forgotten. However, the story of this royal tune did not end when the engineer pressed stop. A song bearing said title was one of three titles seemingly subjected to overdubs at an undated session: "New Danville Girl," "Queen of Rock and Roll," and "Look Yonder."

According to Krogsgaard's sessionography, this session took place the same day they recorded "New Danville Girl," i.e., December 6, even though two of the three songs had yet to be recorded and despite using three members of the Heartbreakers (Campbell, Tench, and Epstein). Both Gold and Heffington have confirmed that none of Petty's band were involved in any sessions before the new year. Much more likely is that these overdubs were done at either the last Cherokee session, on February 17, for which we have no track information, or conceivably at sessions the previous week (on twelfth and fourteenth) when Dylan continued working with the trio of Heartbreakers on new material. Either way, such work suggests the song warranted consideration for the album Dylan was about to travel to New York to complete.

{481} TRUST YOURSELF

Published lyric/s: Lyrics 85; Lyrics 04.
Known studio recordings: Cherokee Studios, L.A., February 5, 1985 [EB]; Winter 1993, L.A., w/ Carlene Carter [Hindsight 20/20].
First known performance: Farm Aid, Champaign, IL, September 22, 1985.

Being faithful to oneself is more worthy than being faithful to an idea.
—Dylan to Matt Damsker, September 1978

As Dylan proved when he took this ditty for its first spin at the Farm Aid telecast, "Trust Yourself" was always a terrific little song, with a simple, if didactic, message: "If you want somebody you can trust, trust yourself." He'd said it before—most notably on "I Am a Lonesome Hobo" ("live by no man's code")—but it was nonetheless an invigorating counterpoint to the kind of proselytizing he had indulged in a few years earlier. Nor does it seem to be a song he particularly struggled to record, or one that executive producer Arthur Baker could do a great deal to undo (try as he might). Recorded at one of the last Cherokee sessions, with a set of musos fully familiar with the man's methodology (Jim Keltner, Mike Campbell, Howie Epstein, Benmont Tench), it was copyrighted in its pre-Bakerized form, which is how it really should be heard.

In this form it stands revealed as a familiar Dylan declamation, set to a live-in-the-studio groove of which the *Shot of Love* band would have been proud. Its transition to the live Dylan/Heartbreakers set was equally painless, as just one replay of the Farm Aid telecast confirms. But it would appear that the song became so inextricably associated in Dylan's mind with those guys that when their association came to an end on October 17, 1987, he simply set it aside. However, it was not entirely forgotten. When Johnny Cash's daughter, Carlene Carter, whom Dylan had known since she was a pup, decided to record it for her 1993 album *Little Love Letters* (though it initially appeared only as a B-side), guess who was on hand to add his own gruff backing vocal to the track.

{482} EMOTIONALLY YOURS

Published lyric/s: Lyrics 85; Lyrics 04.
Known studio recordings: Cherokee Studios, L.A., February 12 and 14, 1985 [EB].
First known performance: Sydney, February 11, 1986.

The Dylan of yore may have believed one never repeated oneself, but *Burlesque* Bob no longer clung to such a credo. "Emotionally Yours," apparently written immediately after "I'll Remember You," suggested he needed to relearn this lesson. And yet, he has continued to return regularly to this kind of song, with little of the facility one might expect from a member of the Songwriters Hall of Fame (into which he was inaugurated in March 1982, all the while protesting that he couldn't "read or write a note of music").

He had however picked up one useful technique on his recent travels through the American songbook—pick a title phrase that on the surface seems replete with romantic connotations but means absolutely nothing (in this instance it wasn't even grammatically correct). Convinced he now had what it once took, he demoed "Emotionally Yours" on February 12, then firmly wrung its neck two days later while his studio band looked on askance. Seeing the song as giving the girls something to do in concert, Dylan alternated it with the equally forgettable "I'll Remember You" throughout 1986. What no one expected—or particularly asked for—was that he should revive it in September 1993 on a brief joint Dylan/Santana tour, when he was even less equipped vocally to tackle its mawkish tune.

{483} STRAIGHT AS IN LOVE
{484} THE VERY THOUGHT OF YOU
{485} WAITING TO GET BEAT

Published lyric/s: Words Fill My Head; *[#483]* In His Own Words 2 *[printed on LP sleeve].*

Known studio recordings: Cherokee Studios, L.A., February 14, 1985 [#483 2 tks + 5 tks. ?February 12].[28]

The songs Dylan recorded at Cherokee on February 14 smack of someone looking to fill up an album. One assumes that these songs comprise three of the four titles Dylan later told *Time* almost made the album. They certainly all ended up on the *1985 Album Compilation #1* copyright tape (placed at the end, presumably because they were already deemed surplus to requirements). In each case, they exemplify a Dylan who starts with a title, embroidering the idea till he runs out of cloth. For the first two, the song title in question was not even his own, but came from his extensive album collection.

The original "Straight as in Love," a Johnny Cash original the man in black cut for Sun back in 1956, was a song he knew extremely well ("I tell people . . . they should listen to Johnny on his Sun records and reject all that notorious low-grade stuff he did in his later years" —Dylan, 2009).

However, whereas the Cash song is a piece of bravado from a man who underachieved at school save when it came to wooing the gals, Dylan puts the song in the second person, making it about a girl who "ain't so good at arithmetic / you don't know how to count . . . but in love, crazy love, you get straight As." In fairness, the whole song sounds like it is *meant* to be a pastiche of a fifties prom song, in the manner (but minus the manic disposition) of "I'm Your Teenage Prayer." The two complete takes in circulation share a certain good humor, which the Williams Brothers only partially transferred to their 1987 version (on *Two Stories*).

"The Very Thought of You" set the bar somewhat higher. Originally the title to a twenty-four-carat classic written by Ray Noble in 1934 for his orchestra (fronted by the great Al Bowlly), it was covered by just about every grade-A crooner (Bing Crosby, Tony Bennett, Frank Sinatra) or jazz diva (Ella Fitzgerald, Billie Holiday) known to the U.S. male. Dylan's lyric—"So deep in my mind / I'm so intertwined / With the very thought of you"—are no worse than Noble's, but he falls well short of the exquisite original melody. Nor was the forty-three-year-old Dylan equipped to hit all those notes, no matter how long he could hold his breath. "Waiting to Get Beat" made a poor joke of the idea that the song has a ska beat, while the singer himself has been beat up. I almost split my side, first time around.

{486} WHEN THE NIGHT COMES FALLING FROM THE SKY

Published lyric/s: Lyrics 85; Lyrics 04. *[Van Zandt version:* Words Fill My Head.*]*
Known studio recordings: Power Station, NYC, February 19, 1985—4 takes [TBS]; February 23, 1985 [EB].
First known performance: Wellington, New Zealand, February 5, 1986.

If "New Danville Girl" was the one really major song to come from the Cherokee sessions, Dylan rustled up another magnum opus as the deadline loomed over the Power Station sessions concluding the *Empire Burlesque* experiment. Like its powerful predecessor, "When the Night Comes Falling from the Sky" was a song Dylan was prepared to work on. He may even have given it a trial spin at the last Cherokee session. A single take of a song called "I See Fire in Your Eyes" was logged on February 14, but is never heard of again. Five days later, in New York,

Dylan made his first attempt to record "When the Night Comes Falling," which contains the line "Smoke is in your eyes, you draw a smile."

The phrase "smoke is in your eyes" was both a well-known MOR tune and another snip of movie dialogue, from the Astaire-Rogers musical *Roberta*. (Irene Dunne introduces the famous croon-tune "Smoke Gets in Your Eyes" with a belabored scene in which smoke gets in her eyes.) Again, the one time Dylan talked about this important song "on the record," for a radio special about *The Bootleg Series 1–3*, he claimed it comprised "lines overheard here and there, you know, strung together over a long period of time." Yeah, right.

"When the Night Comes Falling" finds Dylan in full-on haranguing mode, looking to reiterate that all-important message for humanity— prepare for the Day of the Lord—because "it don't matter who loves who . . . when the night comes falling from the sky." On the album take, he even slipped in just enough of the 1978 arrangement of "All Along the Watchtower" to remind listeners of Isaiah ("Prepare the table, watch in the watchtower " [21:5]).

The opening line could well be intended as the rebuke of a returning Christ. "Look out across the fields, see me returning" echoes a phrase from Jesus to His disciples: "Lift up your eyes and look on the fields; for they are . . . ready to harvest" (John 4:35). Dylan was certainly still agitating for Armageddon, affirming as much to Scott Cohen later that year: "This world is scheduled to go for 7,000 years. Six thousand years of this, where man has his way, and 1,000 years when God has His way . . . The last thousand years is called the Messianic Age. Messiah will rule."

While Judgment Day remained on the agenda, on the two occasions Dylan introduced the song in concert—on consecutive nights in Melbourne the following February—he told ticket holders he actually wrote it to take to task those people who judge others (as in, "Judge not, that ye be not judged" [Matthew 7:1]), proclaiming, "This is a song I wrote about people sitting in judgment on other people. I can't stand this kind of people." Yet in the song, he appears to chastise himself for abandoning his mission, describing how he "saw thousands who could have overcome the darkness / For the love of a lousy buck, I watched them die."[29]

These were not lines given to him by Jerome Kern's third cousin. Even under "some kind of deadline pressure," he was prepared to apply some craft to this one. Any readjustment in the lyric came after he had spent February 19 at New York's Power Station trying to capture the birth pangs of the Messiah in a five-and-a-half-minute song. Along for this highly charged ride were two key elements from the E Street Band, "Miami" Steve Van Zandt and Roy Bittan, and a rhythm section straight from Jah, Sly 'n' Robbie. According to the track sheet, they began by attempting a slow version, building up to a fast version or two.

One presumes it is the latter which appears on 1991's *Bootleg Series Vols 1–3*, though it takes its own sweet time picking up the requisite steam. Beginning on low simmer, Dylan doesn't start cooking until the band joins in—on "I can see through your walls." However, once he sits full square on the hot plate, he bellows like a wild wolf. This time he may have got another Angelina in his sights, but he has already given up trying to save her from herself. On the February 19 take, there is no mistaking the separation in ideals of the two protagonists:

> Well, I gave to you my heart like buried treasure
> When suffering seemed to fit you like a glove,
> I'm so tired of those who use you for their own pleasure,
> Who think they've got the monopoly on love.
> This time I'm asking for freedom, freedom from a world that you deny . . .

Again, though, Dylan decided the song needed filling out, lyrically and musically, retiring it for four days while he set about reworking that other endgame song, "Something's Burning." When he returned, he had evidently been listening to some half-witted engineer/producer who thought that what the song needed was more clutter, less intensity. Having gone along with the scheme, he would complain at the end of the year about how he was expected "to fill up the space on a record now because the space has a noise of its own . . . So therefore you have to fill up the space. People's ears have become accustomed to hearing every space filled up, and they're throwing everything in. More is there to make you think less." Sounds like someone who just learned the hard way, trust yourself.

Yet anyone looking to name the guilty men would have to rope in the man from Minnesota, who not only went along with adding synthesizer, percussion and horns, but also removed much of the passion, as well as perhaps the best line in the whole damn song, "You'll know everything, my love, down below and up above / When the night comes falling . . ." Fittingly, one of those artificial, empty phrases took its place— "You'll know all about it, love, it'll fit you like a glove." Thus, instead of conveying with awe-inspiring immediacy the realization that shall dawn on one and all—the blessed *and* the damned—come that dreadful day, he chose to tone down such biblical connotations.

It is primarily a loss of momentum in the February 23 performance—which takes the song at a uniform, staid tempo, as opposed to the increasingly frenetic feel it had four days earlier—that does for the song. Rather than hurling the listener into the maelstrom, the album version gently leads him/her by the hand, the deficit being writ large in the way Dylan sings the penultimate line, "You'll give it to me now, I'll take it anyhow" like, well, any other line.

Perhaps he sensed the loss the minute he started playing it live, because although he started out performing the song in 1986 with the stately but sedate *Empire Burlesque* arrangement, by the time he crossed the U.S. borderline, he was attempting something akin to that original slow-burn performance. And gradually it began to exceed room temperature again. The following September on the *Temple in Flames* tour, he opened his first (and last) show behind the Iron Curtain, to a hundred thousand East Berliners, with a performance that really did "overcome the darkness."

{487} WHEN THE LINE FORMS

Known studio recordings: Power Station, NYC, February 19, 1985.

Though Dylan spent most of the February 19 session working on "When the Night Comes Falling," he took time out to record two "rough demos" (so marked on the tape log), one of which he reworked as a bona fide studio cut the following day ("Never Gonna Be the Same Again"). The other—"When the Line Forms"—is never heard of again, though it is marked "complete" and appears to have received the full Sly & Robbie/E Street Band treatment.

{488} NEVER GONNA BE THE SAME AGAIN

Published lyric/s: Lyrics 85; Lyrics 04.

Known studio recordings: Power Station, NYC, February 19, 1985; February 20, 1985—9 takes [EB].

First known performance: Melbourne, February 21, 1986.

After the turgid "Emotionally Yours," one might have imagined Dylan would accept that his abiding appreciation for that U.S. pantheon of stage and screen songwriters versed in musical theater and film was not going to result in emulation, let alone reinvention of this genre. Instead, he wrote his worst excuse for a love song this side of Nashville. Though he does plenty of apologizing in the song ("Sorry if I hurt you baby, sorry if I did/ Sorry if I touched the place where your secrets are hid"), he does very little to salvage this sorry apology for a song. The best line in the construct, "I don't mind leaving, I'd just like it to be my idea," is another one purloined, this time from his favorite western, *Shane*. And even then, he delivers the line like it was the first read-through.

Nor does he do the song any favors by letting the Queens of Rhythm get their maws on it. Maybe the demo preserved the kernel of a half-decent song, but after the girls do their thing, it is all over bar the screeching. Even Dylan tired of the song with decent haste, trying it at a single show in Melbourne on the first leg of the *True Confessions* tour and leaving it at that. Or rather, he left it to mature into a fine wine. Nine years later he decanted it again, at a series of spring shows on the West Coast, and this time there were no girls getting in the way. He had even reworked the tune—so unrecognizably that few fans responded to its opening bars—as he again reminded fans that he had continued making albums in the eighties. Despite the musical revamp, and a certain vocal commitment, "Never Gonna Be the Same Again" should have stayed in the cellar, however much he still harbored a desire to be that "hot-blooded singer on a bandstand croon."

{489} DARK EYES

Published lyric/s: Lyrics 85; Lyrics 04.

Known studio recordings: Power Station, NYC, March 3, 1985—6 takes [EB].

First known performance: Sydney, February 25, 1986.

I think my next album is probably gonna just be me and my guitar and harmonica. I'm not saying all of it will be that way, but I'm sure a few songs will be. —Dylan, to Kurt Loder, March 1984

Even if Dylan really was thinking along these lines, he curtailed such instincts for almost the entire *Empire Burlesque* recording process. Only after Arthur Baker had applied layer after layer of morning gunk over the raw tracks recorded at Cherokee and Delta did Dylan decide to include something with just guitar and harmonica, after all. As he revealed later the same year to Denise Worrell, "Dark Eyes" was intended as necessary sonic relief at the end of an album's worth of technopop, being written to order: "This last record I just did, *Empire Burlesque*, there were nine songs I knew belonged on it, and I needed a tenth. I had about four songs, and one of those was going to be the tenth song. I finally figured out that the tenth song needed to be acoustic, so I just wrote it . . . because none of the other songs fit that slot, that certain place."

In *Chronicles*, though, he gives the main credit to that arch-nemesis of natural-sounding production, Arthur Baker:

[Arthur] Baker kept suggesting that we should have an acoustic song at the end of the record, that it would bring everything to the right conclusion. I thought about it and I knew he was right, but I didn't have anything. The night the album was being completed, I told him I'd see what I could come up with, saw the importance of it. I was staying at the Plaza Hotel on 59th Street and had come back after midnight, went through the lobby and headed upstairs. As I stepped out of the elevator, a call girl was coming towards me in the hallway . . . She had blue circles around her eyes, black eyeliner, dark eyes . . . She had a beautifulness, but not for this kind of world. Poor wretch, doomed to walk this hallway for a thousand years.

It is fair to say that "Dark Eyes" divides Dylan fans. Though I'm not convinced he quite pulls it off, at least it sounds like he has a sense of what he wants to do. He even alludes to the first restless farewell in that final couplet: "Oh, time is short and the days are sweet, and passion rules the arrow that flies / A million faces at my feet but all I see are dark eyes." Like that song, there remains a nagging sense phrases have been strung together to create an effect, some of which *are* highly effective ("I can hear a drum beating for the dead that rise"), some of which stop short ("They tell me to be discreet for all intended purposes"). All are secondary to the song's final destination: arrival at that image of a million faces at his feet.

The released recording also presents its own problems. As with "Restless Farewell," Dylan had booked a session to cut this one song but, unlike on that occasion, it had been a long time since he had picked up an acoustic guitar to record solo. Even after six takes his playing lacks any real fluidity. This uncertainty seems to have held him back from playing the song live, too, even though it was one of the more memorable cuts on the album. The one time he attempted the song on the *True Confessions* tour, at the final show in Sydney, he was forced to abandon the performance, apologizing to the crowd, "I don't know what key to do that in. I'd like to do it later. If I knew what key I was in. I can play it, but I can't sing it."

It would be another decade before he was cajoled into trying it again, as a duet with Patti Smith, who had been playing it in her own acoustic sets for a few months. And after a disastrous first go in Boston (December 10, 1995), Dylan dutifully (re)learned the lyric, and the nightly visitations got better and better, even if these two untutored singers were destined to remain surely the most idiosyncratic harmonizers in the history of popular song.

{490} AS TIME PASSES BY
{491} TOO HOT TO DRIVE

Known studio recordings: Cherokee Studios, L.A., April 17, 1985.

> What would happen is we would just record something and we'd be in the room, and we'd go on for a while with the tapes rolling and he'd either say, "Let's work on that more," or, . . . "Remember that one." . . . We'd say, "What do you wanna call it?" and he'd come up with a funny title. —Ira Ingber, to author, 1987

One of the more intriguing session entries from this period came in mid-April 1985, when Dylan returned to Cherokee to record a couple of tunes with the kind of stripped-down lineup he had invited to his

Malibu garage the winter before. Of the three accompanying musicians, drummer Charlie Quintana and Ira Ingber had both recorded with
him before and had proven they could combine great instincts with the
passion of youth. The other musician, Nedra Wheeler, was not only
young, black, and female, but was a classically trained stand-up bassist
more used to the jazz idiom (in fact, she would end up teaching at the
Thelonius Monk Institute of Jazz).

Two songs would end up being logged from the session: "As Time
Passes By" and "Too Hot To Drive." The former could I suppose be
a mis-logged cover version of "As Time Goes By"—but such a choice
would leave one struggling to glean the logic of setting up a session to
record covers at a time when he had only just finished making an original
album. It would also fail to explain the other track, which rings no bells
in the pantheon of popular song.

It seems more likely that Dylan was looking to demo some material
for the follow-up to *Empire Burlesque* and was using favorite old song titles
as a form of inspiration (à la "Drifting Too Far from the Shore," "Straight
as in Love," and "The Very Thought of You"). It was a working practice
he would carry over to the next album, and it would explain the rather
basic nature of the lineup. The material was presumably added to the
stockpile then demoed at sessions in L.A. in October and a chilly London
in November.

{492} SHAKE

First known performance: Farm Aid, Champaign, IL, September 22, 1985.
Known studio recordings: Universal Studios, L.A., September 19, 1985.

In the post–*Empire Burlesque* haze, while Dylan struggled to resolve
another way of moving onward and upward, he decided to further blur
the boundaries between his own songs and any inspiration which infused
and informed them. A series of jam sessions in the summer and fall of
1985 saw him work on stock-in-trade riffs until something happened or
the band ran out of steam, a methodology he admitted to a couple of
months later, when discussing songwriting with a concerned female
journalist: "Sometimes I'll be able to hear the melody and everything
right in my head, sometimes I'll play on the guitar or piano or something, and some kind of thing will come. Other times I'll just go into

the studio and play riffs with other people and then later on listen to the tapes and see what that wants to be."

One of these sessions was filmed as a by-product of a "staged" promo video of "When the Night Comes Falling." Having insisted on filming with live equipment and a real band, Dylan took the opportunity to jam between badly mimed versions of the *Empire Burlesque* song. Those jams occasionally slipped into (and out of) something familiar, as musicians are wont to do. But the front man was clearly looking to do something more than just kill time.

And though any ideas from said jam session faded away when the film crew packed up, Dylan continued working up R&B templates at a series of September rehearsal sessions with his new backing band, Tom Petty and the Heartbreakers—much to the mystification of their ostensible bandleader, who admitted he never knew what was coming next. Most of these songs turned out to be straight covers of Sun and Chess-era 45s. But at least one seems to have come away from its original berth: Roy Head's "Treat Her Right," a song Dylan had been working on back in March 1984, when it was captured by a *David Letterman* cameraman who ran tape on a pre-show run-through he undertook with his favorite post-punk colts.

By the time it docked at the Memorial Stadium in Champaign, Illinois—in preparation for the live debut of Bob Dylan and Tom Petty's Heartbreakers—Head's riff had become part of a Dylanesque hybrid called "Shake." The second song in the Farm Aid set, "Shake" was the first song that night broadcast to a prime-time U.S. TV audience, and around the world.

For the first time in a while, Dylan was clearly reveling in the joys of performance. But the new lyrics clearly still needed work—"Shake like you know you can / Prove to me you're my woman, just like I'm your man" being a good start, before it veers off track with the couplet "Shake baby, like you know you will / Shake for half a million, get somebody killed." But the groove was good, and the song was performed twice on the Australian leg of a Far East tour in February, still without transcending its status as a live reworking of a Roy Head original. This "performance" piece, though, introduced a technique tentatively adopted in the months leading up to the Far East 1986 tour, and one Dylan would intermittently use (and abuse) on future albums.

{493} UNDER YOUR SPELL

Published lyric/s: Lyrics 04.

Known studio recordings: The Church, Crouch End, London, November 22, 1985; Skyline Studio, May 1986 [KOL].

> You might write a song because you feel a certain way about a certain thing . . . I've done that, and then I've done the other way where the song is not really about any certain thing but it all seems focused in on a feeling. —Dylan, to Denise Worrell, November 1985

The greatest mystery surrounding "Under Your Spell," the ever so slightly sickly closer to *Knocked Out Loaded*, is the role of Carole Bayer Sager, Dylan's colyricist on the song. Sager, though once a well-known (if hardly legendary) songwriting partner and former wife of Burt Bacharach, was by 1985 largely known for her movie sound tracks and songs with a sticky sweet center (that cloying theme tune for the *Arthur* movie, which got her an Oscar in 1981, exemplifying both). One must therefore assume that Dylan knew what he would get when suggesting that they collaborate. And she did not disappoint. The middle eight alone would send most Dylan fans reaching for the sick bag:

> Everywhere you go, it's enough to break hearts,
> Someone always gets hurt, a fire always starts,
> You were too hot to handle, you were breaking every vow,
> I trusted you baby, you can trust me now.

What is not clear is *when* the pair wrote this lyric. The basic track for "Under Your Spell," though embellished at Skyline in May 1986, had been recorded during a two-day jam session the previous November, organized by Eurhythmic Dave Stewart using his own studio, a converted church in Crouch End, London. As Dylan described the sessions a couple of months later: "[We] just did a bunch of tracks with . . . no lyrics on 'em . . . just different chord patterns that seem to make up a melody." The footage shot for BBC2's *Whistle Test* from these sessions fully bears out his description.

Presumably, Dylan wrote the lyric with Sager *after* this session, the melody resounding in his head, and maybe with a first line and last couplet already writ. And that opening line—"Something about you that I can't shake"—directs us back to that Brownsville girl, to whom he may be asking "Pray that I don't die of thirst, baby, two feet from the well" at song's end.

{494} BAND OF THE HAND (IT'S HELL TIME MAN!)

Published lyric/s: Lyrics 04.
Known studio recordings: Festival Studios, Sydney, February 8, 1986 [45].
First known performance: Inglewood Forum, L.A., June 6, 1986.

> There's a bunch of songs that I want to write that I haven't been able to get close to at the moment. There'[re] songs I almost have to go out and . . . get, . . . and I haven't done that. I expected to have a little bit more [of] that on *Empire Burlesque* but I just didn't do it. There's a type of song, . . . real things that have happened, where I would like to comment on these things. —Dylan, to Toby Creswell, January 1986

Though it was released as the title track of the tiresome punks-with-guns B-movie, *Band of the Hand*, this song's real title (and message) could be found in brackets, a not uncommon practice for the man ("I Don't Believe You," "Señor," "Tight Connection," and "Floater," to name four other examples). One presumes Dylan had been given only the sketchiest outline of the film's narrative when he agreed to pen his own punk anthem for the new middle ages. The result, hastily thrown together, showed that a working method he talked to Creswell about only a couple of weeks before still worked for him.

Recorded in a single day in a strange studio in an unfamiliar city at the start of six solid months of recording and touring, "Band of the Hand" betrayed an age-old methodology to which he remained addicted. He barely had time to reconfigure R&B Tune D and prep the band before he began recording (according to the session engineer, rewriting as he went). He had always liked recording this way, and it sounds like it. From the first line, "Down these streets the fools rule," he sets the tenor for another "state of the union" song, this one from the vantage point of youths who are not "pimps on the make, [or] politicians on the take" but would rather "blow up your home of voodoo, and watch it burn without regret." Dylan evidently rated the results, or just enjoyed singing the song, because he put it in the set from the very first American show the first week in June, all the while ignoring the entire album he had just spent the last month recording.

{495} ROCK 'EM DEAD
{496} YOU WANNA RAMBLE

First known performance [#495]: Sydney Entertainment Center, February 10, 1986.

Published lyric/s [#496]: Words Fill My Head.

Known studio recordings [#496]: Skyline Studios, CA, May 5 and 14, 1986 [KOL].

> I can't remember any of the words, but we're gonna play it anyway.
> —Dylan's introduction to "Sukiyaki," Osaka, March 6, 1986

Throughout the Far East tour with the Heartbreakers, Dylan seemed determined to challenge his audience to go along with some rather off-the-wall set choices. Aside from nightly versions of country standards like "That Lucky Ol' Sun," "I'm Moving On," and "I Forgot More Than You'll Ever Know" (an unwise choice for a Dylan-Petty duet), he would invariably open the show with an R&B tune from some ill-defined vintage; and before crowds could reach for their lighters, come encore time, he would revisit the same territory, leaving many bemused and bewildered.

Initially he opened shows in New Zealand with an instrumental jam (later known as "Train of Pain," after the girls sang this repeated refrain on the one occasion it gained a lyric, making for a modern "All the Tired Horses"). But by Sydney, said jam was giving way to a Don & Dewey song, "Justine," once covered by the Righteous Brothers. And he wasn't done yet.

Determined to continue the pub quiz on obscure rockabilly and R&B, Dylan included in the encore a song with the refrain "Roll on over and rock 'em dead." Intrepid attributionists, who soon identified it as a version of Warren Smith's "Uranium Rock," proved somewhat hasty in their attribution. Though the debt to Smith's Sun original was obvious enough, the only words Dylan kept from Smith's song were "Money, money, money." Whereas Smith was sending up the whole nuclear debate by suggesting he was going to get a Geiger counter and start digging for "that big uranium rock"—which he would then sell to buy himself a Cadillac—the author of "Talkin' World War III Blues" failed to demonstrate any such wit in his rewrite, which was set instead in a diamond mine.

He doesn't even adhere to the 1958 original in the chorus. Smith's chorus runs as follows: "Money-money honey, the kind you fold / Money-money honey, rock 'n' roll / Rake it in, bale it up like hay / Have a rockin' good time and throw it all away," while Dylan sings "Money, money, money, it's hard to get / Money, money, money, it's faster spent / [unintelligible], keep a hat on your head/ Roll on over and rock 'em dead." Evidently, he felt like continuing his "Shake" experiment, demonstrating an abiding love for old-style rockabilly and messing with the minds of his fans into the bargain. And though he did not record his Warren Smith reworking at the May sessions, he did record Smith's "Red Cadillac and a Black Moustache."

Not that this convinced him to abandon the technique. One can't help but wonder what exactly Dylan had in mind when he started playing Herman "Junior" Parker's "I Wanna Ramble" at one of the early Skyline sessions (Parker remains best known for writing "Mystery Train," a song Dylan already covered at the *Shot of Love* sessions). The sessions to date had largely confined themselves to covers of a more sentimental hue: "You'll Never Walk Alone," "Unchain My Heart," "Lonely Avenue," and, at the same session, "Without Love" (presumably the gospel song Elvis sang the soul out of at the fabled Memphis 1969 sessions)—all part of the "set of Tin Pan Alley covers" which *Rolling Stone*'s Mikal Gilmore suggests initially emerged from these sessions.

Perhaps on the first occasion he tried it, Dylan sang "I Wanna Ramble" straight (May 5) or—not knowing the words quite as well as the tune— simply began to improvise and felt faint flickers of some old flame. Either way, for only the second time on record, Dylan took a cocredit with the original author of a song he was more emulating in spirit than covering in fact. "You Wanna Ramble" shares exactly one phrase with Parker's 1955 original: "You wanna ramble to the break of dawn."

However, unlike his take on "Uranium Rock" (and, indeed, "Honey, Just Allow Me One More Chance"), "You Wanna Ramble" is taken at almost the exact same tempo as the Parker 45. Dylan's vision, though, is a lot darker. Whereas Parker is ready for some fun ("I wanna get me some wine and ramble some more"), Dylan is staring into the abyss, afraid to ramble any "further down the line," distinctly aware that "The night is so empty, so quiet and still / For fifteen hundred dollars, you can have anybody killed."

Generously, the only credit that Dylan took for the song when it was re-copyrighted, in October 1986, was for "additional lyrics." Parker, though, did not stand to benefit a jot as he had died fifteen years earlier from a brain tumor, aged just forty-nine. And rather than continuing to "refine" some of his favorite rockabilly, Dylan went back to doing them straight—revisiting the genre at a number of summer shows.

{497} GOT MY MIND MADE UP
{498} JAMMIN' ME

Known studio recordings: Sound City Studios, L.A., May 19, 1986 [KOL].
First known performance [#497]: San Diego, CA, June 9, 1986.

Thanks to the 1995 release of the original Tom Petty and the Heartbreakers' recording of "Got My Mind Made Up," on the positively hubristic six-CD Heartbreakers boxed set, *Playback 1973–93*, we have a fair gauge as to Dylan's contribution to the song *he* released on *Knocked Out Loaded*. It turns out his input was considerable—all three verses, in fact—which makes its exclusion from the 2004 *Lyrics* both inexplicable and inexcusable. The one lyrical contribution of Petty's would appear to be the title phrase (even if Michael Gray goes to some length to attach some significance to this stock phrase's fourfold appearance in *The Gunfighter*).

But even a cursory scan of the *Knocked Out Loaded* songbook (yes, there really is one!) would have told any eagle-eyed fan that Dylan had put his thumbprint here. "I'm going off to Libya, there's a guy I gotta see / He's been living there three years now, in an oil refinery" is not a line someone with a southern accent would likely deliver. As with "Band of the Hand," Dylan had chosen to write "a type of song . . . [about] real things that have happened, where I . . . comment on these things."

When tackled about the subject of "Got My Mind Made Up" by Mikal Gilmore during the studio playback, he insisted, "I'm opposed to whatever oppresses people's intelligence . . . But that's not a fight for one man, that's everybody's fight."

As per the single made in Sydney, it would appear that he managed to rework the lyric and record the song "Got My Mind Made Up" in a single day, working with a self-contained band who knew the rudiments of anything rock and roll. Back on Hell time, Dylan knows full well he's gonna travel on. This Love Henry ain't staying around to be poisoned or stabbed, having found the perfect way to say so long, good luck, and good-bye: "Well, if you don't want to see me, look the other way / You don't have to feed me, I ain't your dog that's gone astray." He even found the vocal he'd been keeping in reserve ever since he started jamming with these guys, pre–Farm Aid.

So inspired was Dylan that in a single day at Sound City he managed to say more than he had in a month at Skyline. He even found time to lend a hand with another Petty lyric that had not gotten much further than a chorus and a riff. Yet such was the sense of urgency with which Dylan wished to wash his hands of the album he had (knowingly) cobbled together, he donated "Jammin' Me" to the Heartbreakers—who promptly cut it for *Let Me Up (I've Had Enough)*. It seems he still had a few good couplets he'd not managed to jam into "Got My Mind Made Up," and which Petty was more than happy to relocate. Candidates for Dylan's imprimatur include "Take back your acid rain / Let your TV bleed" and the sustained non sequitur "Take back your Iranian torture, and the apple in young Steve's eye / Yeah, take back your losing streak, check your front-wheel drive."

The fact that Dylan did not take his cue from the two experiences of recording with the Heartbreakers (most of whom had already contributed to *Shot of Love* and / or *Empire Burlesque*) and begin work on something worthy of *either* him or them suggests he had already begun to see the "Skyline" album as just one more on the pile. The pressure to which he was being subjected, in order for Sony to have new product to push while his profile was at an eight-year high, made him deliberately deliver the very epitome of Product. As he informed Australian journalist Toby Creswell as far back as January, "I've got to have another record out by June." Interesting choice of phrase.

He certainly seemed to be making a typically Dylanesque point when he played "Got My Mind Made Up" as an encore at the opening show of the U.S. summer tour, because he never played it again—or any other *Knocked Out Loaded* song—at any of the forty-plus shows to come on his first stateside tour in five years. Shame, shame, shame.[30]

{499} HAD A DREAM ABOUT YOU, BABY

Published lyric/s: Lyrics 04.
Known studio recordings: Townhouse Studio, London August 27[-28], 1986— [10 takes] [HoF/DitG].
First known performance: Sacramento, CA, June 9, 1988.

This is desperate stuff—and I'm guessing that Dylan *was* desperate. Having signed up to not only act a part in that risible rom-com *Hearts of Fire*, but to provide it with a soundtrack, à la *Pat Garrett*, he arrived in London, ten days ahead of schedule, with his notebook still bare. Asked about the six songs he was contributing to the film at a London press conference on August 18 he admitted he hadn't actually written, er, any of them. Evidently, he believed something he had stated the previous November still held true: "Usually, when I have some kind of deadline pressure, I'll get prolific." He'd said this before the desultory series of sessions for his latest long-player.

In the few days he allowed himself before he was expected to record these songs, he continued to draw a great big blank. The one song he seems to have brought to the Townhouse in a semi-recordable state was "Had a Dream About You Baby," and even this effort made "Emotionally Yours" sound like "Simple Twist of Fate." The runt of a very thin litter for which Dylan hoped to find some immortal spark in the studio, he spent much of the first session trying to get the right groove, and maybe a hook. One suspects he had a bunch of verses, all much the same, that he planned to shuffle around and see which fit best. Hence why they move around, dropping in and out from take to take.

Inevitably, in the selection process the odd half-decent line got tossed ("Must be an evil moon, I don't know / You're telling someone that you love me so"). Two whole verses included in the "extras handout" (see #503) also failed to make either the film or its sound-track CD. One of these directly related to the song title: "I saw you in a dream, I began to shout / You were sitting in a tub with the water running out." (I wonder what Jung would have made of that one?) The other verse printed for the handout—"Come to see me, baby, tell your driver to wait / There's just a few little things that we've got to get straight"—is not quite what Dylan sings at the session. The second line at the Townhouse is more *Burlesque* in spirit: "Knock me out baby, get me straight."

By the time Dylan took a break from his 498th dream—to run through Billy Joe Shaver's "Old Five and Dimers Like Me," one of three "substitute" covers with which he planned to pad out his contribution to the sound track—he still had not nailed "Had a Dream About You Baby." Two more takes followed, neither of which suggested any great advance. (He is still singing "Had a dream about you baby, all night long / through" rather than the chorus that appears on the sound track, "I had a dream about you baby / Last night you came rollin' across my mind," confirming he still had work to do when the session ends.)

The released version suggests he never did find even a three-amp fuse, let alone that immortal spark. A handful of performances during the first summer of the Never Ending Tour confirmed his muse was getting lazy. Even with a rhythm section who could add swing to the most staid of moonstomps, "Had a Dream About You Baby" continued to have a beat like a cop.

{500} RIDE THIS TRAIN

{501} TO FALL IN LOVE WITH YOU

Known studio recordings: Townhouse Studio, London, August 27[–28], 1986.

Indicative of an ongoing dearth of decent ditties—and maybe too much time spent listening to the Dead—Dylan clung to an ongoing belief, expressed nine months earlier, that as a last resort he could always jam away in the studio until a song or two came through: "[I] go into the studio and play riffs with other people, and then later on listen to the tapes and see what that wants to be." "Ride This Train" and "To Fall in Love with You" both exemplify this technique, to which an increasingly desperate man (re)turned whenever the well at the old homestead ran dry.

Given that both cuts are in many ways superior to the two full-blown originals recorded at these sessions, maybe Dylan knew more than he was letting on. If he did "later on listen to the tapes," it is curious that he didn't do something with "To Fall in Love with You," the best thing to come out of this half-assed project. It had a tune and a vocal that the songs used on the sound track could only dream about, night after desperate night. Dylan has a tune and a few half-formed images already in his head, leaving the assembled musicians to fumble for their respective light switches. It is Ron Wood, reverting to bass duties, who first flicks on the light, responding to Dylan's tentative guitar noodle in a matter of seconds.

The lyric threatens but never quite becomes another "I'm Not There." Expressions of tender regret occasionally reference the attendant film script ("I feel your love and I feel no shame"), but more often just grasp at half-formed phrases in the night—candidates include "Where ages roll, where ages fly, I hear your name where angels lie" and "I see it in your lips / I knew it in your eyes"—Dylan always returning to the one phrase he seems intent on repeating: "To fall in love with you." Though that rusty analogue cable to Inspiration is only working intermittently, we can at least hear Dylan *trying* to make a connection here. After five minutes, though, he gives up and goes home.

"Ride This Train" has none of that sense of grasping at something and finding thin air, but it does manage to find a nice truckin' groove long enough for Dylan to get that train motif out of his system. The tape begins with the boys already well into their journey, as if the engineer just realized he was supposed to be rolling tape. Unfortunately, drummer Henry Spinetti sounds as he does on every one of these Townhouse tracks, like he is clocking in for another day at the hit and miss factory. Lacking the dynamics that a Don Heffington could have brought to the process, this train runs out of steam long before it finds glory (though Dylan, hedging his bets, still requests at song's end, "Just mark that in some kind of way").

{502} NIGHT AFTER NIGHT
{503} FEAR, HATE, ENVY, AND JEALOUSY

> [#502] Published lyric: Lyrics 04. [Recorded version: In His Own Words 2.]
> [#503] Published lyric: Words Fill My Head
> Known studio recordings: Townhouse Studio, London, August [27–]28, 1986
> [#501: HoF].

Though the tape of a session featuring the three previous songs (#499–501) is in general circulation, the "other" *Hearts of Fire* session/s remains undocumented save for the versions of "Night After Night" and "Had a Dream About You Baby" on the sound-track CD and the acoustic "cover" of "A Couple More Years" in the film. However painful a listening experience the finished song might be, I doubt that "Night After Night" was done in a single take. Rather, it probably meandered to its unremarkable destination à la "Had a Dream About You Baby," only for some sonic sadist to apply "do the tango" trumpets for its last rites.

At least the "Night After Night" lyric suggested Dylan had read his shooting script, summing up the entire ninety minutes in a single line, "Night after night, another old man kissing some young girl." Less relevant, but more intriguing, is another song from the project for which we have a set of lyrics, but no recording. "Fear, Hate, Envy, and Jealousy"— chorus line, "I'm talking about fear, hate, envy, and jealousy / It's like a fire all over the world"—was the catchy title of a four-verse humdinger, the lyric of which was handed out to movie extras employed to add some atmosphere to a live concert sequence shot at Bristol's Colston Hall on September 19.

According to the *Hearts of Fire* shooting schedule, they were supposed to shoot two scenes on the Friday at Colston Hall, one of which would feature Pepper Ward—*not* Parker—singing "Fear, Hate." Hence, presumably, why no Dylan version has emerged from the Townhouse sessions. In fact, no such sequence appears in the film, but the fact that the extras were expected to bay along with a prerecorded track to which the "action" would later be synched suggests that this song had been recorded. Other songs also mentioned in the schedule but omitted from the film include "Mile High" and "Punk Song," presumably working titles to songs Dylan never wrote. However, "Fear, Hate" is different. We have a set of lyrics. It was presumably discarded when the scene itself was cut. At least the lyric suggests Dylan had tapped in to the same spirit that infused his last sound-track contribution:

> You know the wicked have sold their souls for gold
> And everybody knows their wealth is in the sky,
> And the very, very, very sad part about it all,
> There ain't nothing [?nor] nobody gonna survive.

The song, though, was not stored away for the next album because Dylan, it seems, had already decided he was going to make that not so eagerly awaited sequel to *Self Portrait*.

1987–9

{ Traveling Wilburys Vol. One; Oh Mercy }

After nine months spent cobbling together the execrable Down in the Groove *from tapes even bootleggers would have passed on, interrupted by his worst-ever concert tour (the Grateful Dead's own sets have the edge on their joint set—that's how bad it got!), Dylan began his rehabilitation in September 1987 with an edgy tour of Europe with the Heartbreakers and special guest Roger McGuinn. Forced to put further tour plans on hold after a freak accident to his hand, Dylan found himself at a loose end through early April 1988, when ex-Beatle George Harrison asked to borrow his home studio for a day. The result was a burst of new songs which again questioned the world he lived in.*

With his hand on the mend, he got that call from old friend Harrison, who wondered if he might use Bob's garage studio. From such a happenstance the Traveling Wilburys were born, and Dylan's creative juices flowed again in the mutually supportive climate of musician friends riffing on ideas and swapping tall stories. By the time Dylan left Dave Stewart's Bel Air home in mid-May, to fly to New York for last-minute tour rehearsals, he was back in the driving seat. It would be another year, though, before he began recording the set of songs he had begun at home the previous winter.

Thanks to the 2004 publication of Chronicles and the 2008 release of Tell Tale Signs (The Bootleg Series Vol. 8), these songs and the resultant sessions are among the better-documented eras of Dylan's post-accident career. Not that the eighty-page section in Chronicles on the writing and recording of his 1989 album is unproblematic. As when authoring "My Life in *a Stolen Moment,"* Dylan *as self-chronicler cannot be entirely trusted. Though he seems to be drawing on some contemporary notes for this fulsome section, the distortions of chronology and interjections of fiction (the whole Sun Pie saga) make it impossible to take at face value. Nonetheless, the* Chronicles *account provides an invaluable insight, even when no aide-memoire. And thankfully there is enough solid recording information, plus around twenty known alternate takes and outtakes from the sessions, to enable a reasonably accurate chronology of songs.*

{504} LOVE RESCUE ME

Published lyric/s: Words Fill My Head.
Known studio recordings: Sun Studios, Memphis, TN, mid-April 1987 [R&H].

Some time between April 11, 1987, when he was at Sunset Sound massacring other folks' masterpieces (including the Stanley Brothers' prophetic "The Darkest Hour Is Just Before the Dawn"), and April 20, when he was back in L.A. helping Bono's band butcher a couple of his own late sixties classics at the Sports Arena, Dylan spent a few days in Memphis recording with Ringo Starr and U2 (separately) and visiting Graceland. The U2 session, at the historic Sun studios (an empty gesture given that Sam Phillips's innovative setup was long gone), was set up by Debbie Gold to record a song Dylan and Bono had written together. They had evidently been working on more than one song, as an *NME* interview by Bono later that year confirmed:

> He's very hung up on actually being Bob Dylan. He feels he's trapped in his past . . . Like, we were trading lines and verses off the top of our heads and Dylan comes out with this absolute classic—"I was listening to the Neville Brothers, it was a quarter to eight / I had an appointment with destiny, but I knew she'd come late/ She tricked me, she addicted me, she turned me on [my] head / Now I can't sleep with these secrets that leave me cold and alone in my bed." Then he goes, "Nah, cancel that." . . . He thought it was too close to what people expect of Bob Dylan.

Dispiritingly, the song they did end up recording, "Love Rescue Me," displayed no such grasp of what had made the older man the preeminent songwriter of his day. At least he voices his concerns—*if* the line "I see

325

the dark shades of what I used to be" is one of his. More worrying, from a man who had just recorded the Stanleys' song of hope and redemption, is the despairing tone of the penultimate verse: "I have cursed thy rod and staff / They no longer comfort me." I guess he knew he had many more miles to go before hearing the cock crow.

(Yet, however badly lit the road he traveled with Ireland's most fortunate sons, it was as nothing to the darkness that descended when he chose to collaborate with Marin County's luckiest soul, Grateful Dead lyricist Robert Hunter. Though Hunter had written a handful of lyrics worthy of, say, Bernie Taupin, "Ugliest Girl in the World" and "Silvio" were not among them. The fact that the Dead had passed on both songs should have been all Dylan needed to know. And yet, he brought them back with him when returning to Los Angeles after a few days in early June spent rehearsing in San Rafael with the Dead.

Less than a fortnight later, he had put music to the Hunter lyrics, prompting the lyricist to enthuse, "I'm very, very pleased with what he did." Alone in his enthusiasm, Hunter stood guilty by association when the songs appeared the following spring on the unredeemable *Down in the Groove*. What has never been satisfactorily resolved is whether Dylan "tampered" with the lyrics he received. The original August 1987 copyright suggests not, the lyrics being wholly credited to Hunter. But by November 1988, with the *Down in the Groove* songbook in the works, the credits read, "Words and music Bob Dylan and Robert Hunter." The subsequent favor "Silvio" has enjoyed in concert rather suggests Dylan sees it as one of his, though as long as the pair stay absent from *Lyrics*, I cling to the belief that they are wholly Hunter's parodic idea of poesy.)

{505} CONGRATULATIONS

Published lyric/s: Words Fill My Head.
Known studio recordings: Dave Stewart's Studio, L.A., May 8–21, 1988 [TW1]; 1305 Soniat, New Orleans, LA, March 21–22, 1989.
First known performance: Glasgow, Scotland, June 6, 1989.

Once in a while, the odd song will come to me like a bulldog at the garden gate and demand to be written. But most of them are rejected out of my mind right away. You get caught up in wondering if anyone really needs to hear it. —Dylan, to Robert Hilburn, November 1991

Dylan makes no mention of "Congratulations" in his autobiographical account of the songs written in the months leading up to the start of the Never Ending Tour, concentrating on those that would end up on *Oh Mercy*, which is not entirely surprising if—as has been rumored—section four of *Chronicles* began life as projected sleeve notes for a deluxe edition of the 1989 album. Yet of all the songs on the first Traveling Wilburys installment, this is the one that seems to belong least to the project. One of three songs from *Volume One* administered by Dylan's music publisher, and sung as a solo vocal by Dylan (save for the hammy communal chorus), "Congratulations" remains the only Wilburys song to ever feature in Dylan's live set, being performed twice in Britain in June 1989 (complete with harmonica break on its debut in Glasgow) and once, as a request from a Chicago coke dealer, at the Toad's four-setter in January 1990.

George Harrison and Jeff Lynne, the two masterminds behind the whole Wilburys project, also spoke of the song as Dylan's on Roger Scott's BBC Radio One Wilburys' special. According to Harrison, "Bob basically had the idea for 'Congratulations,'" with Lynne chipping in, "Those are mostly Bob Dylan's lyrics." I think we can take this as Wilburyspeak for "OK, Bob brought that one to the sessions in May."

Perhaps inspired by the vibe of the initial Wilbury session in early April, he may have penned this torch ballad in the interim. But I suspect he was finishing up a song he'd already started (but otherwise wouldn't have finished), one last reminder of the type of material he'd been gamely attempting to write for the past three years. That he still felt he had possession over "Congratulations," even after the Wilburys album went triple-platinum, was demonstrated when he broke into the song at one of the *Oh Mercy* sessions, when Rockin' Dopsie and His Cajun Band were contributing to the instrumental mix. But it had already served its purpose, and he quickly returned to the matter at hand, which was trying to make "Where Teardrops Fall" sound half as good, and twice as sincere.

{ Still on the Road }

Published lyric/s: Lyrics 04. *[Complete version: "Writings"]*
Known studio recordings: 1305 Soniat, New Orleans, LA, March 8, 1989—2 takes; March 28 [new vocal—2 takes] [OM].
First known performance: Toad's Place, New Haven, CT, January 12, 1990.

> Songs should really be written out of thin air. They should come to you. You shouldn't have to sit down and think, "What should I write a song about?" If you don't have anything in your mind at the moment, you can always look in your notebook and find something. That usually works. I just jot down a bunch of stuff and throw it in a drawer and drag it out and look at it [when I need to]. —Dylan, to Edna Gundersen, September 1989

Though "Political World" is a nothing song, in the Fugsian sense, the author of *Chronicles* asserts that it was the true starting point for his 1989 return to form (and who am I to doubt him?)—which is perhaps why it remained the opening track on every provisional sequence the album underwent from early May to July 1989. Dylan also claims in *Chronicles* that in writing the song he thought he "might have broken through to something, . . . like . . . wak[ing] up from a deep and drugged slumber" and that "there were about twice as many verses as were later recorded."

The latter observation is quite true (though the outtake verse he quotes in his book, like four other examples in the same section, has the resounding ring of artifice). The full version of the song, bootlegged extensively, has sixteen verses—all using almost a limerick style of rhyme, ABCCB—and clocks in at 5:04. The released version has only eleven verses (losing verses four, five, seven, eleven, thirteen, and fifteen). Dylan claimed he realized in midsession "that the lyrics might work better in fragmented rhythms" and so cut the song up. Among the lost verses is the summation of his "whole vision of life," which he insists "all these songs added together doesn't even come close" to revealing:

> We live in a political world,
> World of wine, women and song,
> You could make it through without the first two,
> Boy, without the third, you wouldn't last long.

Such extensive reworking will remain the pattern throughout the sessions. Almost all of the songs on *Oh Mercy*, whenever the basic track was recorded, received vocal overdubs in late March/early April. And in the protracted overdubbing process, Dylan usually took the opportunity to work on the lyrics further, even when the song itself was well over a year old, as was apparently the case with "Political World." So the album version is not merely an edit of the fuller version. One verse is unique to it ("where peace is not welcome at all"), confirming that someone "punched in" at least part of an alternative vocal. According to the Krogsgaard sessionography the song was worked on twice, initially at a highly productive session in early March (the eighth), and then at a session at month's end (March 28).[31]

Though Krogsgaard suggests two versions on the twenty-eighth were actual takes, it seems more likely that they were devoted to fix-ups, vocally and instrumentally. Certainly, the full five-minute version sounds like the same basic track as the released cut, and there is no evidence Dylan recut his vocal after March 28. But even after all this refining and reducing, he was dissatisfied with the reception the song received, insisting a month after the album's release that he had intended a wider target than the politicians of the world: "Just because it's called 'Political World' doesn't necessarily mean it's a political song. You can extract any line from any song you know, and make it into what you want it to be. You could do that with 'White Christmas' . . . You could make a political statement out of that if you cared to."

In *Chronicles*, he continued to make grander claims for the song than it warranted, insisting its subject matter was "more of an underworld, not the world where men live, toil, and die like men." He might have had a stronger argument if he hadn't shot a promo video of the song which was set at a banquet of politicians, indulging in every deadly sin, while Dylan and the lads played the house band—a prototype for that grander visual Bobfest *Masked and Anonymous*, where wisdom really "is thrown into jail [and] rots in a cell, misguided as hell." His archly cynical view of this breed of men underwent little modification in the next two decades. In 2009 he was still insisting, "Politics is entertainment. It's a sport. It's for the well groomed and well heeled. The impeccably dressed . . . The real power is in the hands of small groups of people and I don't think they have titles."

{ Still on the Road }

Despite providing the initial spark for the album, "Political World" was one of the last *Oh Mercy* songs to pass into the live set, not appearing until the famous four-hour, quadruple-set warm-up at Toad's in January 1990. Replacing all those ambient, miked-up guitars with a nice a cappella intro, Dylan was soon singing it like someone who really did despair of the shape of things to come.

{507} WHAT GOOD AM I?

Published lyric/s: Lyrics 04.
Known studio recordings: 1305 Soniat, New Orleans, LA, March 7, 1989—8 takes [OM—tk. 7]; March 29, 1989—2 takes; April 7, 1989 [new vocal][OM].
First known performance: Beacon Theatre, NYC, October 10, 1989.

> I sure would like to be spared of the burden to muse about what my fans think about me or my songs. But . . . I seem to be one of the few artists who attract that kind of people. —Dylan, to *Der Spiegel*, 1997

"What Good Am I?" represents a welcome return for that ostensibly autobiographical persona present in so many great Dylan songs and is the first of three songs of self-examination on *Oh Mercy* ("Most of the Time" and "What Was It You Wanted" being the others). In *Chronicles*, Dylan claims the song came to him "all at once," when he was sitting alone in the art studio on his Malibu estate, and here there is no reason to doubt him.

Less convincing is his assertion that he didn't "know what could have brought it on." The song could as easily have been called "How Good Am I?," for it is as concerned with his artistic worth as his self-worth. He knows just how long it has been since he turned an ear to the thunder in the sky—just as he has always known that he really isn't "like the rest who don't try." Just writing a song like this dispelled some of these doubts, propelling him forward.

But when he returned to the song fifteen months later in N'Orleans, he found himself "hunt[ing] for a melody," having written it as a lyric back in the winter of 1988 (matching the modus operandi of *Street-Legal*, a decade earlier). In the end, he allowed Lanois to make it into another mood piece, even though he realized that "the melody wasn't quite special enough." The resultant track exemplified everything that was good and bad about the production values on *Oh Mercy*. Though there is something instantly enticing about the whole sound of the thing, all that needless noodling is a constant distraction from the central performer's concerns.

An overdubbed vocal tried and failed to make the listener focus in the right place, and it was only when it left Lanois's clutches that the song really sprung to life. Dylan clearly thought he might find the answer on stage, playing the song at the first (post-release) opportunity, opening night at the Beacon Theatre in October 1989, with a passion and intensity only hinted at on the record. For the next ten years, it was a regular feature of the Never Ending Tour, with Dylan often whipping out the harmonica when he felt a need to further express in musical terms what these words already addressed in kind. Since 1999, however, he has stopped interrogating himself.

{508} DIGNITY

Published lyric/s: Lyrics 04. *[Recorded version:* In His Own Words 3.*]*
Known studio recordings: Emlah Court, New Orleans, LA, ?late February, 1989 [CHR][TTS 1]; 1305 Soniat, March 13, 1989; mid-March 1989; April 11, 1989 [new vocal—3 takes] [GH3/BoB2—1 take] [TTS 2—1 take].
First known performance: Unplugged, Sony Studios, NYC, November 17, 1994 [UN].

> Of the virtues, I suppose I think integrity is the most essential. Not dignity—a thief can have dignity. —Dylan, to Barbara Kerr, February 1978

It could be argued that the one song which defined the general artistic direction on all four of Dylan's all-original eighties albums ended up being discarded—leaving a gaping hole at the heart of each released artifact. After omitting "Caribbean Wind" in 1981, "Foot of Pride" in 1983, and "New Danville Girl" in 1985, Dylan completed the set in 1989 with a fourth ace in the hole—"Dignity." And, as with those other songs, he continued to claim "Dignity" was one he never quite finished even if, like "New Danville Girl," it was never entirely forgotten.

In one of the more vivid passages in *Chronicles*, he describes both the song's remarkably painless birth in January 1988 ("I started writing it in the early afternoon . . . and it took me the rest of the day and into the night") and the series of near-death experiences (pages 186–91) it suffered at the New Orleans sessions in March 1989. He dates the actual composition remarkably precisely, telling us he wrote it the day he heard about the death of ex–basketball player Pete Maravich. He doesn't tell us when this was, but Maravich died on January 5, 1988. The death of this peripheral figure who fleetingly crossed the singer's radar here triggers another song about Man's conceits. Maravich's final words, before dropping dead of a congenital heart condition, aged just forty, suggest he found little dignity in death: "I feel great."

And, as with "Political World," it would appear that Dylan just kept writing verse after verse around this simple idea, personifying Dignity in much the way evil had been personified through the ages under a number of monikers. Like Old Nick, no one actually knows what this figure looks like because "Dignity [has] never been photographed." He soon realized that "on a song like this, there's no end to things." And so it proved. He was riffing on the conceit, like a latter-day Lord Buckley.

In one of those rare candid sections in his autobiography, Dylan admits that if he'd written "Dignity" ten years earlier, he'd "have gone immediately to the recording studio. But a lot had changed and I . . . didn't feel the urge and necessity of it." He didn't feel that uncontrollable urge for another fourteen months. Only in late February 1989 did Dylan and his producer Daniel Lanois convene at Lanois's Studio on the Move in New Orleans. Almost immediately they cut a couple of demos to be going along with, of which "Dignity" was one. An eight-verse piano demo mirrored a similar solo recording of "Ring Them Bells" and demonstrated that he really could shuffle this lyric any which way he wanted. Two verses sung here had disappeared entirely from the song by the next time he cut it:

> Stranger stares down into the light,
> From a platinum window in the Mexican night,
> Searching every blood-sucking thing in sight, for dignity.

The soul of a nation is under the knife,
Death is standing in the doorway of life,
In the next room a man fighting with his wife, over dignity.

Unlike "Ring Them Bells," though, the "Dignity" demo is incomplete, breaking down around the two and a half minute mark, as Dylan blows the line when Mary Lou says "she could get killed if anyone saw her talking to me." Already Dylan has asked of the engineer, "Is this anything?" before complaining at the end, "It just don't feel right." A two-minute edit of this demo appeared initially as a promo CD for *Chronicles*, then on *Tell Tale Signs*.

From now on the recording history gets messy. Krogsgaard gives just a single date for the recorded version (March 13), to which overdubs were then applied on March 28 and April 11, but even he admits this section of his sessionography is "incomplete as to the rough tapes. That is: much more was recorded than what is listed [here]. On the other hand, information about the released tracks is quite precise, including dates for overdubbing."

What our Danish friend perhaps means to say is that although he had access to multitrack sheets for the known songs, like the one previously reproduced in *Recording Sessions* for "Broken Days" (aka "Everything is Broken"), he had not found all (or most) of the session tapes and generally relied on the track sheets even when they were contradicted by other resources. To render the results even more problematic, Lanois ran a live two-track throughout the sessions, which recorded various important performances that went undocumented on multitrack.

At least we should be grateful a fastidious engineer not only indicated any overdubs to the multitrack but generally—at least in Dylan's case—dated them. Because of the relevant track sheet, we know that Dylan recorded a "live vocal" for "Dignity," and that there were at least three subsequent attempts to overdub a new vocal, two of which came on April 11 (there was also a "Repair Voc[al] Piano #1," presumably to repair some deficiency in the original live vocal/piano tracks). Of these later overdubs, one has been cryptically identified as "woman lyrics," a mystery the release of *Tell Tale Signs* resolved by the simple expedient of releasing this version (so indicated in the production notes). Of the nine/ten new verses, three are devoted to yet more angels of the hearth:

Dignity is a woman that knows,
Dignity moves like a tropical wind that blows,
Into the cities, into the towns, into the land of the midnight sun . . .

Dignity is a woman unspoiled
By fame and greed, and snakes that're coiled,
In the damp woods, on the river's edge, near the green, green grass of
  home . . .

Dignity is a woman that's light,
She don't tease, she don't travel at night,
Dignity is a woman that bleeds like the hot Egyptian sun.

These do not sound like spontaneous outpourings even of an inspired poet. They are alternative lines, and not necessarily ones which were there from the outset. He is trying to impose them at this late date (April 11) because he wants to see if they might help put the song back on track. It was a trick he tried a number of times at these sessions. The long gestation period these songs enjoyed drove Dylan to revisit some of them repeatedly, even after the sessions were well underway. As *Oh Mercy*'s coengineer Mark Howard recently told *Uncut*: "He would *always* be working on his lyrics. He'd have a piece of paper with thousands of words on it, all different ways, you couldn't even *read* it. Words going upside-down, sideways, all over this page. I never saw him eat. He drank coffee and smoked cigarettes, and he'd sit chipping away at the words, pulling in [lines] from other songs."

Rewriting the song was not the only way Dylan had of helping "Dignity" return to a state of grace during these long and arduous sessions. Having demoed it solo, probably at Emlah Court where the sessions began, he tells us he cut it next with "only" guitarist Brian Stoltz and drummer Willie Green. According to Dylan the chronicler, "This was the first song we did that *delivered* [my italics]." Even though he felt the song was fine "the way we had just cut it, with a minimum of instruments and the vocal up front," Lanois convinced him to cut the song again, "the next night," with Rockin' Dopsie and His Cajun Band.

Dylan, not for the first time, went along with Lanois. It didn't work. But it was already a raison d'être of these sessions to try songs every conceivable way. As guitarist Mason Ruffner told Damien Love, "Seems like we were cutting these songs all kinds of ways. Rock groove, slow groove, a funk or folk kind of groove, just trying different grooves and different tempos to this stuff. He didn't say much about what he was after . . . It just seemed like it was all a big experiment, try the song twenty different ways."

This was hardly the first time Dylan embraced such an approach. As early as December 1977, when his first standing band was rehearsing at Rundown, he was doing something similar, as guitar-tech/sidekick Joel Bernstein recalls: "Once it was reasonably together, he got them to play certain songs in different ways, in one key and then another key and then half-time, then country, then reggae, then rocked up. It was a real experimental thing . . . but he had his own idea about what was the best one to do."

In the case of an important song like "Dignity," though, such an approach went against the grain. The Rockin' Dopsie session— at which they also cut "Where Teardrops Fall" and an impromptu "Congratulations"—became one sustained exercise in deconstructing "Dignity." Whatever they did, it seemed to Dylan that "every perform-ance was stealing more energy. [We] recorded a lot, varying the tempos and even the keys." He knew it was time to go back to "the demo with Willie and Brian," which "had sounded effortless." But before he did that, he and Lanois spent an evening listening to every take of "Dignity." Immediately Dylan realized, "Where[ever] we had started from, we'd never gotten back to . . . In no take did we ever turn back the clock."

They decided to shelve the song. Indeed, according to our would-be chronicler, they "never did go back to it." They definitely did. The track sheet tells us that he was still working on the song as late as April 11, at one of the last sessions where he sought to impose new vocal personae on the songs. The April 11 versions took as their template that "demo with Willie and Brian"—which also evidently featured Tony Hall on bass. What drives this (March 13) version is Dylan's piano, which rides the song like a long-haired mule, applying the odd kick when it lags, before steering it through the gates of the city.

In the past, Dylan's vocal would have played off his piano playing (cf. "Dear Landlord" or "Sign on the Window") in a way no overdub ever could. But for all the overdubbing, it was what Lanois left in from that original three-piece recording that provided a most annoying backdrop. The persistent tap-tap-tap of a snare drum is there on both channels throughout the entire song, like a buzzing mosquito that won't go away. On the track sheet, it even says "transfer [to both channels?] and boost," like it *needed* highlighting. It was symptomatic of Lanois's tendency to clutter tracks. The full track sheet shows the residue of Rockin' Dopsie's input. "Rockabilly dobro," "Up-beat acc[ordion]," and "Ba Da Ba Da Horns—Fats Domino style" are all there spread across the twenty-four tracks, but are absent from the versions on *The Best of Bob Dylan Vol. 2* and *Tell Tale Signs*.

As the original solo piano demo proves, every sound not tethered to that relentless riff acts as a distraction from the vocal and lyric. And Dylan knew he had some really good lines here—even if he seems to be evincing little solace from the faith that had sustained him for the past decade. The couplet "Heard the tongues of angels and the tongues of men / Wasn't any difference to me" directly references 1 Corinthians, "Though I speak with the tongues of men and of angels, and have not charity, I am become as sounding brass" (13:1), a statement intended to convey the idea that without a spirit of charity all gifts are valueless. Elsewhere, he probably references Rimbaud's "Le bateau ivre" for the first time in twenty-five years ("I'm on a rollin' river in a jerkin' boat"). A collage of all he had been through, the song traveled many roads before it was fixed in its "final" form. In all of them, though, our narrator finds himself at song's end "at the edge of the lake"—of Galilee?—wondering "what it's gonna take to find dignity."

After the "Dignity" vocal overdub session (April 11), Dylan reworked just two more songs from the sessions—"Born in Time" and "Where Teardrops Fall." And yet, when a rough first sequence for the album was put forward by Dylan (dated May 2), it featured neither "Dignity" nor "Where Teardrops Fall." The latter made it in the end, but "Dignity" never did, despite Dylan's chronicling claim that this was a song he'd "always be able to remember."

In fact, when he did resurrect it as a performance piece, specifically for the November 1994 *Unplugged* shows, he failed to get all the way through without tripping over words. The song's belated restoration to favor seems to have come about because—like "Blind Willie McTell"— demand for the song had been growing consistently since it leaked into collecting circles in the early nineties.

Dylan later complained at a 2001 press conference that "with all of my records, there's an abundance of material left off—stuff that, for a variety of reasons, doesn't make the final cut. And other people seem to think they have some kind of right to it . . . [Well,] once it gets out, or is recorded by someone else, I'm not keen on going in and re-recording it. It's already been contaminated for me." So how come he had not taken the opportunity to rework "Dignity" for *under the red sky*, with its three other *Oh Mercy* "rejects," when it was still safely under wraps?

"Contaminated" or not, a dissatisfaction with the original recording of "Dignity" continued to needle him, and so when it was suggested that it might be included as a bonus track on an ill-conceived third *Greatest Hits* set, the original multitrack was turned over to Pearl Jam producer Brendan O'Brien, who promptly dispensed with everyone but Dylan, then mixed the singer's piano low enough for us all to gasp in amazement at O'Brien's own unerringly Kooperesque organ work. The results made Alan Douglas's work on Jimi Hendrix's studio tapes sound sympathetic. O'Brien, for his sins, got to reprise his newfound role at the two *Unplugged* performances in November 1994, when Dylan tried to inject half the life the song formerly had for the benefit of the TV cameras, but with only limited success. Either O'Brien was cramping Dylan's style, or the song was still contaminated.

It was only when Dylan persevered with the song at a handful of shows in March 1995, with just the Never Ending Tour band to bolster it, and not a mobile truck in sight, that he found what he'd been looking for all along. On March 29, at a show in Brixton, London, he delivered the definitive "Dignity" vocal (after whimsically introducing it as "a new song—well, pretty new, it's only ten years old"). Though he continued to stumble over the intro and outro, it mattered not. Here was the clear proof that his voice was still searching high and low, while J. J. Jackson brought four years of onstage experience to bear, turning the song inside out without ever once getting in an inspired vocalist's way. It was tried once more on the English leg that spring, but Dylan knew he had finally dived in where Prince Philip feared to tread.

{509} HANDLE WITH CARE

Published lyric: Words Fill My Head.

Known studio recordings: Dylan's home studio, Malibu, CA, April 3, 1988 [TW1].

The story of how the Traveling Wilburys came about has been well and truly told. Initially, they were the product of a series of serendipities when George Harrison was trying to record a single track with his then-producer Jeff Lynne of Idle Race (okay, ELO) fame. They needed a studio—Dylan had one in his garage. They needed a guitar—Tom Petty had one (of theirs) at his house. Roy Orbison was just hanging loose that day, so tagged along. Voilà—one supergroup.

The song they wrote that day in early April started with the title—taken from a sticker on one of the carrying cases that contained their guitars. It was a cute idea—think up a title, throw lines around like a game of Chinese Whispers, strum guitars, hum a tune. The song itself, which should really be called "Handle Me With Care," because *that* is what Harrison actually sings, is a surprisingly sprightly affair with a good hook, a nice blend of voices, and someone's trademark harmonica. Harrison quickly realized it was too good to waste on the B-side of some European twelve-inch. However, it took him some weeks (and a meeting with Warners) to decide what to do next . . .

{510} DIRTY WORLD

{511} END OF THE LINE

{512} HEADING FOR THE LIGHT

{513} LAST NIGHT

{514} MARGARITA

{515} NOT ALONE ANYMORE

{516} RATTLED

Published lyrics: Words Fill My Head.

Known studio recordings: Dave Stewart's Studio, LA, May 8–21, 1988 [TW1].

I liked ["Handle With Care"] and the way it had turned out, with all these people on it, so much I just carried it around in my pocket for ages, thinking, "Well, what can I do with this thing?" And the only thing I could think of was to do another nine—to make an album. And . . . [the others] all loved the idea. It was just a question of timing, 'cause Bob had to go on the road at the end of May . . . so we just said, "Okay, we'll meet on—I think it was the 7th May or something," and we had nine or ten days that we knew we could get Bob for . . . So we just said, "Let's do it . . . We'll write a tune a day and do it that way." And that's what happened.

—George Harrison, to Roger Scott, 1989

Twenty-one years after he last attempted to cut a song a day with friendly musicians in a home-studio setup, Dylan joined the other Wilburys (and honorary Wilbury Jim Keltner) at Dave Stewart's home in Bel Air to help turn the B-side of a European George Harrison twelve-inch single into a fully fledged supergroup album. As Keltner joked one day by the pool, this really was what every music-loving kid imagined happened every day in L.A. As to whether the unique chemistry fleet-ingly found five weeks earlier in Dylan's garage could be re-created when there was a whole album to do, a film-crew in attendance (at Harrison's behest), and a deadline to meet, no one really knew.

Footage in the recent DVD documentary of the five Wilburys sitting around in Stewart's house, notepads in hand, throwing out lines, shows how the process worked on most songs. We even see a heavily bearded Dylan suggesting a line to the others. Like all the footage in this disap-pointing film, the excerpt is frustratingly brief, but for most of the songs, one must assume this was the extent of everyone's contribution. There is certainly very little Dylanesque about the seven songs on *Volume One* where he contributes only backing vocals. The one song from these in-house writing sessions that evidently came from an idea of Dylan's was "Dirty World," about which Harrison offered the following history:

Bob's very funny—I mean, a lot of people take him [too] seriously. And yet if you know Dylan and his songs, he's such a joker really. And Jeff just sat down and said, "OK, what are we gonna do?" and Bob said, "Let's do one like Prince! hahaha." And he just started banging away, "Love your sexy body! Oooh-oooh-oooh-oooh bay-bee!" And it just turned into that tune.

The result bears a lot more resemblance lyrically to Robert Johnson's "Terraplane Blues" than Prince's "Little Red Corvette." No matter. The best part of "Dirty World" is Dylan's delivery. Who would have imagined that the mischievous pervert who sang "I'm Your Teenage Prayer" in another garage, in another lifetime, was alive and kicking, whooping it up in Bel Air with his new buddies and their trembling wilburys. Having rediscovered his sense of humor in song, Dylan felt prepped to tell the story of the comeuppance of a transsexual, drug-dealing, Viet vet called Tweeter . . .

{517} TWEETER AND THE MONKEY MAN

Published lyric: Words Fill My Head.

Known studio recordings: Dave Stewart's Studio, LA, May 8–21, 1988 [TW1].

"Tweeter and the Monkey Man" was Tom Petty and Bob sitting in the kitchen, Jeff and I were there too, but they were talking about all this stuff which didn't make sense to me—Americana kind of stuff. And we got a tape cassette and put it on and transcribed everything they were saying and wrote it down. And then Bob sort of changed it, anyway. That for me was just amazing to watch 'cause I had very little to do with writing that [song] at all—except Jeff and I remembered a little bit that [Bob] did that he'd forgotten—which became that chorus part. It was just fantastic watching him do it because . . . he had one take warming himself up and then he did it for real on take two. The rest of us had more time but Bob had to go on the road and we knew he couldn't do any more vocals again, so we had to get his vocals immediately. And on take two he sang [it] right through, and then what he did was he changed some of the lyrics—maybe in about four places he changed a couple of lines and improved them, and dropped these lines in and that's it—just as it was done and written. And the way he writes the words down! Very tiny, like a spider's written it . . . It's just unbelievable seeing how he does it. —George Harrison, to Roger Scott, 1989

Harrison's above explanation makes it clear that "Tweeter and the Monkey Man" was both the last song recorded for the album—or at least, the last one to benefit from Dylan's direct involvement—and the real heavyweight the album had been missing. Not surprisingly, it was the one time that the other Wilburys stepped back and deferred to Dylan's instincts. If the song began as a conversation between Petty and Dylan, it would seem that it was Dylan who ran with the idea, writing another of his compressed, cinematic narratives in ballad form. (As Petty once said, regarding another of their collaborations, "Jammin' Me," "[It] always seems to me that he writes a lot of verses. Long after you think he's done, he's still writing . . . and then he gets convinced, 'I don't like this,' and then something better shows up in that ninth or tenth verse.")

As with a number of the other songs in the Wilburys experiment, "Tweeter" began life as a pastiche of sorts, albeit a generic one revolving around "Americana kind of stuff," straddling film, TV, and song ("The Monkey Man was on the river bridge, using Tweeter as a shield" rather evokes the climax to Orson Welles's noir classic *Touch of Evil*). Petty and Dylan set out by trying to imagine what would happen if "Pancho and Lefty," a country classic famously covered by both Willie Nelson and Emmylou Harris, turned out to have been written not by Townes Van Zandt but by Bruce Springsteen's inbred first cousin from "Joisy."

All the references to Springsteen songs are beautifully integrated, Dylan summing up all those anti-Vietnam anthems in a single withering couplet: "Tweeter was a Boy Scout 'fore she went to Vietnam / And found out the hard way, nobody gives a damn." And yet when one interviewer tried to draw Dylan about these allusions, citing the line about "secret calls . . . from a mansion on the hill," he simply pointed out that "Mansion on the Hill" was (also) a Hank Williams song. Did Broooce complain?

The results are both very funny and very dark—the kind of balancing act which Dylan had rarely indulged in since the Big Pink days. The repeated refrain, a gratuitously communal incursion, reads like a broadside ballad but acts like a Greek chorus: "And the walls came down, all the way from hell / Never saw them when they're standing, they never saw them when they fell." Harrison later revealed they were lines from an early draft of the song which Dylan had promptly discarded, until the Beatle suggested they be made a burden to each verse, providing a commentary track to the whole minimovie. It was a perfect way of making what would otherwise be a big Bob ballad an integral part of the Wilburys project.

Unfortunately, because of the nature of the sessions, Dylan didn't live with the song long enough to remember to make it his own. Even the way he recorded the vocal in two takes (a frustratingly brief snippet of take one appears in the DVD documentary which accompanies the 2007 CD reissue) suggests he thought he was back at Big Pink, and it was time to stop writing and recording seat-of-the-pants masterpieces and travel on. It is little short of criminal that "Tweeter and the Monkey Man" has never appeared in the live set. Nor would it be included in the 2004 *Lyrics*, despite featuring on one of Dylan's bestselling artifacts of all time, the one truly significant outcome from offering a little help to his friend/s.

{518} BORN IN TIME

Published lyric/s: Lyrics 04. *[Recorded version: In His Own Words 2.]*
Known studio recordings: Emlah Court, New Orleans, LA, 28 February, 1989 [TTS1][new vocal—March 7][TTS3][new vocal—April 13]; The Complex, L.A., March 1990—3 takes [UTRS—tk. 3].
First known performance: Belfast, February 25, 1993

"Born in Time" is one of two songs written for *Oh Mercy* of which Dylan makes no mention in *Chronicles* (the other being "God Knows"). Both tracks would end up on his next album in radically different guises, having undergone a great deal of reconstructive surgery in their passage from New Orleans to Los Angeles. Discounting any solo demos, the February 28 "Born in Time" was the first song definitely recorded for the 1989 LP, which usually means an important song written early in the process. "Born in Time" was both.

And although Dylan discounts the song in his (first) autobiography, the recorded history of the song is well documented, there being six versions in circulation, three each from the *Oh Mercy* and *under the red sky* sessions respectively. Three of these have now been released, one on the 1990 album and two more on *Tell Tale Signs*. Three have not, including the real pearl in the collection—the one that Dylan completed on April 13, 1989, and put on his provisional sequence for *Oh Mercy* on May 2, before returning to the road. (That May 2 sequence read as follows: Side 1—Political World. What Was It You Wanted. Ring Them Bells. Most of the Time. Everything's Broken; Side 2—Man in the Long Black Coat. Disease of Conceit. Born in Time. What Good Am I? Shooting Star.)

Tell Tale Signs gives us two more signposts along the way, though not the ultimate destination. The two versions on this official *Bootleg Series* have quite different backing tracks, as well as distinct vocals (and lyrics). Both basic tracks may well come from the February 28 session, as may the vocal on the first disk of *Tell Tale Signs*. It sounds provisional, and live—though that could just be a by-product of a deliberate (and wholly worthy) attempt to lessen the Lanois ambience when remixing the multis, nineteen years after the fact. (According to Krogsgaard, there were vocal overdubs added to the February 28 basic track on March 7 and April 13—as well as guitar and twelve-string overdubs on April 7 and March 29.)

On the other hand, the version on disk three of the 2008 set—marked as the "post apocalypse" version in the *TTS* production notes—closely relates to the oft-bootlegged version included on Dylan's May 2 sequence. The vocal, though, has less of that acutely measured tenderness, because he has yet to decide how much forgiveness she is due. Hence the rhetorical question on the initial take, "Oh babe, can it be that you been scheming?," which, after the apocalypse, is no longer being asked. Dylan instead settles for the non sequitur, "Oh babe, truer words have not been spoken, or broken."

The lyrical differences between the two takes documented on the eighth *Bootleg Series* illustrate how Dylan continued tinkering with the words. Though this could have been done midsession on the twenty-eighth, it seems unlikely (all the significant changes survive on the definitive vocal on April 13). Whichever the case, it was the two bridges that continued to perturb our penman (even unto the following spring, the *under the red sky* bridges becoming almost unrecognizable). The first bridge from the February 28 version (*TTS* disk one) was soon overhauled:

> Just when I thought you were gone, you came back,
> Just when I was ready to receive you.
> You were smooth, you were rough,
> You were more than enough,
> Oh babe, why did I ever leave you—or grieve you?

Before the next vocal take, the second bridge lost the rhetorical question, replacing "Just when the firelight was gleaming" with the altogether more evocative "Just when the homefires start smoking." But the fact that Dylan then changes only one more line before that final *Oh Mercy* vocal—the penultimate line goes from "You're still so deep inside of me" to the less clichéd "I think of you from deep inside of me"—suggests that the two latter vocals (*Tell Tale Signs* disk three and the bootleg version) were cut the same day.

And yet, the difference between the two performances is night and day, snow and rain. It seems Dylan still had a tendency to worry lest a song might be deemed "too sentimental," and so in the *Tell Tale Signs* take two, he puts some distance between himself and the experience. If the February 28 vocal was recorded before he locked onto what really makes the song tick, the intermediate version fails because he is holding back. It is all technique (and in stark isolation, one would have to say he sings it beautifully); whereas the superior April 13 vocal sacrifices technique at the altar of expressiveness. While recognizing he was lucky to survive the experience ("You took me in, I got what I deserved" is a line he could have used in "Fourth Time Around"), it yearns for the moment again. All six takes of "Born in Time" are gorgeous, but this is the only one that is heartbreaking.

Initially Dylan seems to have recognized this, putting the song where it belonged, at the heart of *Oh Mercy's* second side. But he again allowed his feelings about the ease with which he achieved a particular performance, and the novelty of another recently composed song, to color his judgment. As a result, he replaced "Born in Time" with the vastly inferior "Where Teardrops Fall" at the mixing stage.

However, this being the post-*Infidels* era, "Born in Time" was not necessarily lost for good. Sure enough, when he needed a torch ballad to light up all that boogie-woogie at the March 1990 *under the red sky* sessions, he rekindled the ashes of another fine song of experience. The results were, well, predictable. Firstly, he had been gnawing away at those two bridges that held the song together, moving it still further away from that confessional framework, making it instead a song of recrimination:

> Not one more night, not one more kiss,
> Not this time baby, no more of this,
> Takes too much skill, takes too much will,
> It's too revealing . . .
> You pressed me once, you pressed me twice,
> You hang the flame, you'll pay the price,
> Oh babe, that fire is still smokin."

He then cut the song three times, using the same unvarying lyrical template, before picking the least convincing vocal of the lot. One can almost hear him getting further and further away from that former flame with each take. By the end, he may have stripped her bare, but his own once-bared soul is tucked up snugly in bed. The vocal on the album sounds like it was phoned in as Dylan again demonstrates that—when it comes to recording the moment—you generally can't go back all the way. It took until 1993 before he delved into the song again in performance, and until 1995 before he really (re-)found that inner voice, at a couple of spring shows.

{519} GOD KNOWS

Published lyric/s: Lyrics 04. [Recorded version: In His Own Words 3.]
Known studio recordings: 1305 Soniat, New Orleans, LA, March 8, 1989
[TTS]; March 9, 1989 [new vocals—March 16 and April 10]; March 12,
1989—2 takes [new vocals—March 16 and April 10]; Oceanway Studios, LA,
January 6, 1990 [UTRS].
First known performance: Zurich, January 28, 1991.

"God Knows" is the exception to my just-established rule for post-*Infidels* recorded performances. Here is a song that Dylan began recording on March 8, 1989 (assuming "rough 3/8" in the *TTS* production notes means rough mix, March 8), and finished on January 6, 1990, going through at least three distinct incarnations before it arrived at its proper berth. The song is built around a simple idea—that "God knows" is used in the vernacular as shorthand for "God alone knows," yet God really does know everything. Indeed, he inserts that very line into the 1990 take, while ratcheting up the apocalyptic language by paraphrasing the warning God was said to have given Noah after the flood in a number of modern spirituals: "There's gonna be no more water / But fire next time."

However, its conceptual simplicity hardly kept Dylan in check when it came to writing more verses than he needed to make his point. Of the seven verses on the *Oh Mercy* version (now released on *Tell Tale Signs*), just one survived to the January 1990 outing, and that is there for a reason, to remind us "God knows there a purpose . . ." Of the others, perhaps the most revealing is verse three:

> God knows there's an answer,
> God knows it's all in place,
> God knows it might be workin' right now
> Lookin' at us right straight in the face.

And those seven verses probably have cousins we don't know about. After all, Dylan tackled the song a couple of times in N'Orleans. In his monomania to avoid using *Recording Sessions 1960–1994* as a resource, Krogsgaard simply disregards a track sheet dated March 9, reproduced in that book, which reveals a quite different version to the one he attributes to March 12, 1989. The purpose of a March 12 version—when there were apparently two takes done—is hard to explain if the *TTS* version, which was already circulating on bootleg, is from the eighth, and Dylan then returned to it the following day.

The version recorded on the ninth does not appear to circulate. It is timed at four minutes eighteen seconds, which is a good seventy seconds longer than any later version. It also specifically featured Dylan on harmonica—the relevant track is marked "Bobs harp intro + solo + outro." Dylan also continued working on this take, because there are two distinct vocal overdubs indicated on the track sheet, one for March 16, and another—marked "The King," "regular pitch," and asterisked—dated April 10. These are also the dates on which, according to Krogsgaard, Dylan did overdubs to the version cut on the twelfth, throwing further doubt as to the status of this later take.

In fact, the punchy new mix on *Tell Tale Signs*, which gives the song a spring clean, and proves the Lanois sound is singularly unsuited to anything remotely grungy, suggests he already had the song down four days earlier. But it was never going to make it onto a Lanois-produced LP, and Dylan evidently recognized this. "God Knows" never made it onto *Oh Mercy*, not because Dylan didn't rate the song, but because someone else didn't rate the results achieved in New Orleans.

Unusually for Dylan, he actually set up a session in L.A. nine months after he finished working with Lanois, to record this song *right*. The producer on that L.A. session, Don Was, remembers, "He was troubled by ['God Knows']. He was never ever able to get it quite right and I thought I saw a way to get it right. So . . . we went in and cut it." Was had been given a demo of the song—which I think we can assume was one of those recorded by Lanois. His immediate idea was to assemble a shit-hot band—recruiting those guitarist-siblings Stevie Ray and Jimmie Vaughan, the ultraversatile David Lindley, and that rock of ages Kenny Aronoff, putting himself on bass (which Dylan played on the *Oh Mercy* recording!). Everyone there knew that Dylan liked to get things quickly, to retain that live feel. And everyone this time went with the flow. As Was told *Uncut*:

> "God Knows" was our audition . . . Bob played it on the piano for us, once through, and then we cut it. The modus operandi for all subsequent [*red sky*] sessions was immediately established: listen to Bob and respond sympathetically . . . The first take was a mess—too many musicians. For take two, we began with just Bob and Stevie Ray and built up the arrangement very, very slowly . . . It was a keeper take.

The version they cut that day inspired Dylan to persevere with the Was sound, as he was fully justified in doing. The chemistry on this occasion resulted in one of Dylan's most productive sessions in a decade or more. One can just hear the song build and build. Or one could if Dylan hadn't allowed one of the most premature fade-outs in pop history to apply the brakes just as the song was steaming to its conclusion. The penultimate verse ("God knows there's a heaven . . .") is almost completely lost on the CD, and the final verse is entirely lost, save for its barely audible opening line, "God knows there's an answer," which tells us he has transposed the original verse three to a more suitable spot. No longer concerned with finding that "someone in the world," the forty-nine-year-old singer would rather "walk a million miles by candlelight," trying to get to heaven.

In concert in the winter of 1991—when he acknowledged the song's musical debt to "In the Garden" with an intro that could go either way—Dylan muddled up verses, looking for a place to put the sentiments "God knows there's a reason" and "God knows there's an answer," lines left over from its 1989 incarnation. By 1993, he had reverted to "God knows I love you,"[32] dropping the unnecessary misogyny of "God knows you ain't pretty . . ." Otherwise, the millennial message evident on its official incarnation remained a welcome reminder that this was someone still "walking towards the sun."

{520} DISEASE OF CONCEIT

Published lyric/s: Lyrics 04.
Known studio recordings: 1305 Soniat, New Orleans, LA, March 8, 1989—4 takes; March 28 [overdubs]; March 30, April 3, April 8 [new vocal] [OM].
First known performance: Albany, NY, October 27, 1989.

By Dylan's own autobiographical admission, "Disease of Conceit" was a song that came easily enough ("I didn't have to hunt far for it"). It was another one written in his little studio in Malibu, probably during downtime between bouts of the Never Ending Tour—though he implies otherwise. He also claims this was another one where "there were a few verses left behind." If so, they were left behind when he traveled to New Orleans, as even the first version on tape (March 8) is the exact equivalent of what he ended up releasing.

On this unadulterated version, we get to hear Dylan applying some tonal breath control to both his vocal and piano playing. The vocal he ends up using on *Oh Mercy*—after a series of overdubs had added the kind of guitar fills that used to get in the way (and still do)—can't be said to add a great deal. But then, the song itself doesn't have a great deal to offer. If, as Dylan claims, the song aims to show how "a conceited person has a fake sense of self-worth," it was presumably meant to juxtapose with the songs either side of it, "What Good Am I?" and "What Was It You Wanted." The point is not well made. A couplet like "Well, they've done a lot of research on it / But what it is they're still not sure" demonstrates that first drafts should not *always* be left untouched.

And yet, in concert, the song could be a real highlight—perhaps because as long as Dylan believed it was making some edifyingly original point he continued to invest himself in the song. But it also gave fans an extremely rare sight of the man pounding on the (high school) piano. From October 1989 through to the final night of the February 1990 Hammersmith residency, fans waited eagerly for the moment when he *might* walk over to the piano and plonk away. Even when the piano removers moved in, and Dylan changed to doing the song on guitar, it could still be one of the finer outlets for finger-pointing in performance—as it was on November 12, 1992, at a show in Orlando, when he again seemed to be directing his venom at an uncomprehending audience.

{521} WHAT WAS IT YOU WANTED

Published lyric/s: Lyrics 04.

Known studio recordings: 1305 Soniat, New Orleans, LA, March 8, 1989—2 takes; March 21, 1989—4 takes; March 24 [new vocal]; [? March 28]; April 10 [new vocal] [OM].

First known performance: Toad's Place, New Haven, CT, January 12, 1990.

> Most of [the *Oh Mercy* songs] are stream-of-consciousness songs, the kind that come to you in the middle of the night, when you just want to go back to bed. —Dylan, to Edna Gundersen, September 1989

"What Was It You Wanted," a companion piece to "What Good Am I?" and "Most of the Time," is one of those rare recent songs where Dylan got the tune and the lyric at the same time: "I heard the lyric and melody together in my head and it played itself in a minor key." It had been a while since he had directly addressed (elements of) his audience in song, but the subject matter—the draining effect of others on one's psychic energies—was certainly one that lent itself to the minirant (at himself as much as "her"). As he adroitly expressed it in *Chronicles*, "If you've ever been the object of curiosity, then you [will] know what this song is about."

Another song that "almost wrote itself," it was proof positive that his decision to "come up with a bunch of songs that were original and pay attention to them" was starting to pay dividends. And, according to his own account of the sessions, this song was one of the rare instances where his and Lanois's "interests coincided." The recorded version, as described by Dylan, was "texturally rich, jet lagged and loaded," with Lanois's "sonic atmosphere mak[ing] it sound like [it was] coming out of some mysterious, silent land."

More surprising is his assertion that "Everything was pretty much live the way you hear it." Not the way I hear it, it isn't. To my ears, the whole thing sounds to have been worked on, worked up, worked over. And the track sheets are with me on this. According to these the song, first attempted on March 8, was recut thirteen days later, and then worked on at great length over at least three sessions, acquiring a new vocal (or three) and assorted guitar counterpoints. The results don't quite warrant the fulsome praise Dylan dispenses, but as a prelude to the magnificent "Shooting Star" it kills time effectively enough.

However, Dylan didn't assign it a slot in the fall 1989 five-song *Oh Mercy* suite of songs at a series of U.S. shows. It wasn't until he got to New Haven in early January that he decided the song might benefit from being hauled out of Lanois's sonic swamp and put on stage. Prepping another song that could have benefited from the Was Not Was treatment, he let G.E. and co. loose on it and suddenly found a vocal which added another dimension, making the words jump off the page and into the groove kicked up by an enthused Christopher Parker. And for a while there in 1990, he got what he wanted, before the song slipped out of his mind for good.

{522} BROKEN DAYS

[= EVERYTHING IS BROKEN]

Published lyric/s: Lyrics 04. *["Broken Days" lyric:* "Words fill my head'*]*
Known studio recordings: 1305 Soniat, New Orleans, LA, March 14, 1989—3
takes [TTS]; April 3, 1989—1 take [OM].
First known performance: Beacon Theatre, NYC, October 10, 1989.

Whatever his never fully resolved sequencing issues re *Oh Mercy*, at least Dylan usually managed to break the one habit that had diluted the impact of artifacts earlier in the eighties—his tendency to select inferior versions of superior songs ("Covenant Woman," "Jokerman," "When the Night Comes," etc.—the list goes on). Of the actual takes Lanois and Dylan chose for the 1989 LP, only one was so deficient in merit that it made a once decent song throwaway. "Broken Days," as it is listed on the track sheet, was first recorded on March 14, having been one of those songs Dylan had penned the previous year and "kept . . . in a drawer, but . . . could [always] sense their presence." It is this version that appears—at last—on *Tell Tale Signs* (listed, incorrectly, as "Everything Is Broken").

Dylan the chronicler tells us Lanois thought the song "was a throwaway." (Not yet, it wasn't.) Thankfully, the singer was determined "to cut it—one style and with plenty of tremolo." And after cutting it "with the full band on the floor," Dylan "thought the song did just what it had to do, [and he] wouldn't have to seriously change a thing about it . . . it was already swamped up pretty good."

Unfortunately, his positive mood about the March 14 recording didn't last long enough for it to survive the second-guessing of a revisionist artist who was "*always . . .* working on his lyrics . . . chipping away at the words, pulling in words from other songs." All claims in *Chronicles* notwithstanding, Dylan decided "Broken Days" did need a fair bit of work. Not only did he OK dubbing on additional instruments, but once he started redoing his vocals at the April 3 sessions, he seemed quite unable to stop himself. As Malcolm Burn told Damien Love, "The only thing that made any real difference to him was whether what he was saying was in place. Quite often, he would rewrite even one line. Even when we were mixing the record, I'd be in the middle of the mix and he'd suddenly say, 'Y'know what, I've just rewritten that line, can I resing it?' . . . So I'd be cutting out one line of a mix and editing in the new one to accommodate the rewrite."

The track sheet for "Broken Days" / "Everything Is Broken" attributes one new vocal take and two vocal comps. to the April 3 session. Two of these bear the mark "(new words)." The session also saw Lanois add electric guitar and dobro, as well as some harmonica interjections and Telecaster work from Bob (which he redid three days later). So much for the song being already "swamped up" enough.

It is the lyric that suffers most. "Broken nights, broken days, broken leaves on broken trees / Broken treaties, broken vows, broken hands on broken ploughs" conveys in a swift rat-a-tat of images the sense of a world in pieces, each image part of the same shattered mosaic, whereas "broken lines, broken strings, broken threads, broken springs / Broken idols, broken heads, people sleeping in broken beds" falls strategically short of the same goal. Likewise, "Broken lives hangin' by a thread," the opening line to the second verse, says it all, tied as it is to the original bridge, where we come to realize that his relationship, too, is broken:

> I sent you roses once from a heart that truly grieved,
> Sent you roses once, someone else must have received.

After its transmutation into a list song, the two bridges barely modify the mind-set of the verses, save for one really good line he saves to the end: "Things fall to pieces in my face." Even a last verse that takes elements from the first and last verses of "Broken Days" cannot save the song from itself. And when it was moved from the end of side one—where it served as a counterbalance to album opener "Political World"—to track three, it had at last become what Lanois thought it was all along, a throwaway song. Subsequent live versions did not even benefit from the nice little rasps of harmonica imposed on this April 3 revamp, Dylan being too busy concentrating on getting his Telecaster to play that R&B riff. This didn't stop the song clocking up a disturbingly high number of performances (284 to date).

{523} RING THEM BELLS

Published lyric/s: Lyrics 04.

Known studio recordings: Emlah Court, New Orleans, LA, ?28 February, 1989 [TTS]; 1305 Soniat, March 7, 1989 [OM].

First known performance: Poughkeepsie, NY, October 20, 1989.

["Ring Them Bells"] stands up when you hear it played by me. —Dylan, to Paul Zollo, January 1991

Save for those lucky few (thousand) in the audience at a theater show in Poughkeepsie on October 20, 1989, when Dylan performed the only live version to ever resemble its original Louisiana self, no paying customer has had the privilege of hearing "Ring Them Bells" played solo by the big D, though this it is how it should be heard. And how it should have been released originally (as opposed to on a three-CD set, twenty years late). It was certainly how he started doing it in New Orleans; and this time he found New Jerusalem without the slightest need for ancillary atmospherics.

The solo version issued on disk three of *Tell Tale Signs*—"solo vocal; 2" edit from piano trks 1 & 2," as it is listed in the *TTS* production notes—combines the directness of "When He Returns" with the relentlessness of "Dirge." It also made Lanois a mere engineer, not a creative cohort, before he set about imposing himself on the twenty-two tracks left spare by Dylan's piano/vocal tour de force. When the song was cut on (or around) March 7[33]—according to Krogsgaard in a single take, at the end of a session spent working on "What Good Am I?"—engineers Burn and Lanois were on hand, though one doubts they contributed much that day. All those instruments on the LP appear to have been added to the multitrack after the fact.

Dylan did his bit with all the confidence of yore. The multitrack sheet clearly states "Vocal (Live)," and the piano playing is just as assured as on the earlier solo demo. The singer apparently asked Malcolm Burn to play keyboard bass, after having "talked quite a bit about trying to get a piano-bass . . . [though] none of us really knew what [it] was." Burn also subsequently added some Les Paul guitar, while Lanois added dobro, acoustic guitar, and something called "Ghosts." Assuming that the swirling synth sound on the album cut is "Ghosts," the credits should show Burn on guitar and piano-bass and Lanois on synthesizer. The dobro and acoustic guitar were deemed surplus to requirements. Indeed, Dylan felt none of these overdubs served any real purpose. As he tellingly observed in his written account of the experience, "I felt I could have done it unaccompanied."

Even here, though, on what was clearly a song dear to Dylan, Lanois partly got his way. At least the lyric, honed in a way so many *Oh Mercy* songs were not, never varied in the studio. And, like "Dignity," it remained a piano song in conception and execution, its message ringing loud and clear. For there is no mistaking where "the lines are long, and the fighting is strong / And they're breaking down the distance between right and wrong"—the final battle between good and evil (revealingly, Dylan suggests in *Chronicles* that he was dissatisfied with that last phrase, for fudging the sentiment he had in mind).

Not surprisingly, the song contains its fair share of biblical allusions, all of which suggest someone who continued to await the End Times, when the godless shall have (temporary) dominion. Dylan cleverly uses the ringing of church bells, usually rung to summon believers to prayer or signifying great danger, to indicate the death knell of this world of sinners. "Ring them bells so the world will know that God is one" clearly alludes to the part of Deuteronomy where Moses lays down the Lord's commandments with the specific admonishment, "Hear O Israel: The Lord our God is one Lord" (6:4), itself a comment on the commandment, "Thou shall have none other gods before me" (5:7). Dylan's portrayal of "the mountains . . . filled with lost sheep," also demonstrates a continuing grasp of biblical prophecy. This time he is drawing on Ezekiel 34:6, "My flock was scattered upon all the face of the earth, and none did search or seek after them."

Another song voicing something which needed to be said, "Ring Them Bells" was a surprising omission (Poughkeepsie excepted) from the year he spent promoting *Oh Mercy* with G. E. Smith and co. And aside from being done twice in South America in 1991, it would be November 1993 before these words of warning rang out again. Over four landmark Supper Club performances (November 16–17, 1993), Dylan began by giving the song a full service before really putting it through its paces at the final two shows, testing the brakes at the bridge and roaring through the verses. The early show performance—deservedly released on *Tell Tale Signs* (though I am not wild about the mix, preferring the live mix on the bootlegs)—may well be the single finest moment on the Never Ending Tour.

And the song still had some juice left in it. The following May he set it to a full orchestral arrangement. The Tokyo New Philharmonic Orchestra, relocated to Nara City for the Great Music Experience, found themselves supplemented by drummer Jim Keltner and an energized Dylan, who proved that the song was more than robust enough to be done in such a grandiose way. Dylan even shared the moment with the very world he was calling out to, via a worldwide TV broadcast, still hoping to reach "the chosen few" who got the good news.

{524} SERIES OF DREAMS

Published lyric/s: Lyrics 04. *[Recorded versions:* In His Own Words 3/'Writings']

Known studio recordings: 1305 Soniat, New Orleans, LA, March 23, 1989 *[TTS]; March 30 [new vocal] [TBS].*

First known performance: Wolf Trap, Vienna, VA, September 8, 1993.

> Dreams can tell us a lot about ourselves, if we can remember them. We can see what's coming around the corner sometimes without actually going to the corner. —Dylan, to Bill Flanagan, 2009

"Series of Dreams" was the one *Oh Mercy* song that lent itself to Lanois's sonic solutions. Not surprisingly, it was a song both Lanois and his assistant, Malcolm Burn, continually canvassed Dylan to include on the final artifact until finally he snapped, "Look, I don't think the lyrics are finished; I'm not happy with them. The song's too long. But I don't wanna cut out any of the lyrics." This apparently ended all discussion, the song being omitted from *Oh Mercy*, though it was repeatedly mentioned in interviews at the time by Lanois who, fully recognizing its considerable worth, never gave up on it seeing the light of day.

Sure enough, just eighteen months later it was the final track on the three-volume *Bootleg Series Vols 1–3*, a scattershot sampler of what Sony and/or Dylan had lying around in their vaults. And aside from some supplemental guitar and more ghost-in-the-machine organ, it was the raw *Oh Mercy* version which was now served up on this triple platter. However, the song *had* been tampered with, and in seeming disregard of Dylan's admonishment that they don't "cut out any of the lyrics." A whole verse (the second) had been snipped away:

> Thinking of a series of dreams
> Where the middle and the bottom drop out,
> And you're walking out of the darkness
> And into the shadows of doubt.
> Wasn't going to any great trouble
> To believe in, "It's whatever it seems."
> Nothin' too heavy to burst the bubble
> Just thinkin' of a series of dreams.

The bridge which in the original N'Orleans recording came between verses three and four also now appeared at song's end, giving it a significance not previously enjoyed. Perhaps such a radical reconstruction (turning "verses one, two, three, bridge, four" into "verses one, three, bridge, four, bridge") was Dylan's way of addressing his concern that "the song's too long" (in its March 23, 1989, guise, it runs over six minutes), but I somehow doubt it. It smacks more of Lanois imposing himself on the song. Indeed, in *Chronicles* Dylan baldly states that their disagreement about the song stemmed from the fact that "although Lanois liked the song, he liked the bridge better, [and] wanted the whole song to be like that . . .—[but] thinking about the song this way wasn't healthy. I felt like it was fine the way it was."

So the version released in 1991 is more how Lanois wanted it. This prompts the question: was the edit which appears on the 1991 set actually done at the postproduction sessions in April 1989 as an attempt to make the song work for both writer and producer? The song was definitely worked on after the original four-verse version was recorded on March 23. Not only does Krogsgaard specifically state that a new vocal was recorded a week later, but there are lyrical differences between the basic track used for the 1991 *Bootleg Series 1–3* and the "original" version (issued on a further volume in the Bootleg Series,

Tell Tale Signs). On the former, "the surface was frozen"; on the latter, "numbers were running."

However, the most significant change comes at the start of verse three, where Dylan changes his mind entirely. On the March 23 take he sings, "Where the time and the tempo drag / Suddenly the gate is thrown open, and you're left holding the bag." On the later vocal, it has become "Where the time and the tempo fly / And there's no exit in any direction, 'cept the one that you can't see with your eye." In classic Sony fashion, no one noticed that the version issued in 1991 used an edit from both vocals so that "drag" now rhymed with, er, "eye."

Confirmation it was a cock-up quickly came when they issued an advance five-track promo sampler where the rhyme was correct (i.e., "fly" rhymed with "eye"). This sampler appears to contain the *correct* postproduction version Dylan and Lanois worked on in late March/April 1989 (without the annoying cross-fade used on the commercially released three-CD set). It also provides the template for the handful of live performances the song received: one in the fall of 1993 and nine in early 1994. Rehearsed at several soundchecks before its live debut at the Wolf Trap in September 1993, the song was ecstatically received by the hardcore fans down front. And though Dylan is hardly word-perfect, it is a highly creditable live debut. He even has a go at rewriting that troublesome last verse: "In one, the surface was frozen / In another, they were bargaining for time, / And in another, doors were opening and closing . . ." (Its now also meant he was doing more *Oh Mercy* outtakes at these shows—"Born in Time," "God Knows," and "Series of Dreams"—than songs from the album.)

The Wolf Trap performance, by cutting the second verse and sticking to the lyrical rewrites, suggested Dylan had come to terms with losing a verse for the sake of the song. An even more modulated arrangement was transferred to shows in Japan the following February, where the Far East fans were more bemused than bowled over. But at least it proved Dylan meant it when he stated at a 1986 press conference in Sydney, "I used to pull a lot of [songs] out [of my subconscious]. I [still] pull some . . . out once in a while, but not too often."

{525} MOST OF THE TIME

Published lyric/s: Lyrics 04.

Known studio recordings: 1305 Soniat, New Orleans, LA, March 8, 1989—2 takes [TTS 1]; March 12—6 takes; March 16 [new vocal][TTS 3]; April 12 [new vocal]. [OM]; Culver City Studios, L.A., March 2, 1990 [MotT].

First known performance: Beacon Theatre, NYC, October 10, 1989.

Most of the time I do feel like an amnesiac. It's good for me to feel that way so I can block out the past. —Dylan, to Pete Oppel, October 1978

I don't know who I am most of the time. It doesn't even matter to me. —Dylan, to David Gates, September 1997

A candidate for the most personally revealing thing Dylan *ever* said in an interview is contained in a *Saturday Evening Post* profile compiled by Jules Siegel, during the winter 1966 tour of North America: "I see things that other people don't see. I feel things other people don't feel. It's terrible. They laugh. I felt like that my whole life." "Most of the Time" provides a glossary-in-song on this acute insight into what it is like to be Bob Dylan—most of the time.

The result proved almost too painful to bear—hence why, one March day, he sent it up by doing almost a pastiche of *Blood on the Tracks*–Dylan for the benefit of the small studio crew. This solo performance, assured, right on target, and so direct, appears on *Tell Tale Signs* and is as dramatic a contrast to its "final" self as the solo piano "She's Your Lover Now." But it is also a sham. He does not inhabit the song; he presents it. According to engineer Malcolm Burn, after finishing this impromptu acoustic guitar-harmonica performance, Dylan simply said, "That would be a typical Bob Dylan way of doing it." At least it genuinely was a one-off (the production notes indicate it was "Take 1 Roll 17").

It is probably significant that Dylan does not talk about the song's composition in his published chronicle. Methinks, it came to him late. Indeed, even as he prepared to start recording, he had not acquired the necessary conviction to be done with it. Burn recalls how "Every night, he would come in with a rolled-up bundle of paper, wrapped up with a rubber band, his lyrics that he was in the process of working on. And

[so], when we were working on something like "Most of the Time," he'd be sort of finishing the lyrics." He was still working on the lyric when he cut this solo version. Verse two in particular presents the cocksure side of Dylan:

> Most of the time I'm cool underneath,
> Most of the time I can keep it right between my teeth,
> I can solve any riddle, I can hold my own,
> Deal with the situation right down to the bone.
> I can survive, I can endure . . .

Yet this solo version was not an early attempt at the song—rather, it was a way of expressing his frustrations at his inability to find the apposite arrangement in situ. Hence in *Chronicles* he complains that the song had no melody when he wrote it, and that he "never did come up with any definite melody." And yet both band versions in circulation (from the twelfth) adopt the same basic tune.

It might be revealing to hear one of the versions from four days earlier. One of these could well be the take used on disk three of *Tell Tale Signs*, which, although lyrically very similar to the finished version (thus contradicting Burn), has a nice loping feel to it. The *TTS* production notes designate it "evolution mix Mix DAT 12 track 16"—so it was evidently also the beneficiary of some postproduction, but someone has stripped away all the "layers of parts" added by Lanois (hurrah!), who, even Dylan admitted "put as much ambiance in this song as he could."

Dylan was still uncertain about the lyric, which "w[as]n't putting me in there, where I wanted to be." Even after they recorded the song in the uphill crawl style in which it later appeared, the songwriter says he felt the song "just [became] more unfinished as we rolled along." And yet, for all his talk of surrendering "five or six lines," the lyric went unchanged. Even when he overdubbed a new vocal—as he did on April 12—the words changed very little, perhaps because he was telling the truth when he says he "didn't have the will to work on it. The lyrics were so full of cloudy meaning." (Although Krogsgaard fails to tell us when this overdub was done, the track sheet clearly indicates both a "Vocal Comp" and the April 12 overdub.)

According to the Dane's sessionography, "Most of the Time" was cut six times on March 12. However, he fails to give the track sheet information, or to credit it as the version used on the album. On said track sheet, the song is clearly timed at 4:33; while the delay effect on the guitar track, clearly marked, suggests it *must* be the album version, which audibly uses that aural trick. Aside from the vocal overdub on April 12, a great deal of work was done on the track that month, presumably without Dylan's direct input. This version comes from Roll 16, which confirms that the acoustic solo version on Roll 17 was the last time Dylan attempted it, not the first. That he did not use it suggests that this final roll of the dice was a bust to his mind.

Something left him unsatisfied with the results. Quite possibly, he already knew the song had the potential to be a real classic—and, in the fullness of time, would become one. Such was his sense there was more to it than Lanois ever managed to bring out that, in March 1990, he decided to give it the same treatment he had already given another unrealized song from these sessions, "God Knows." The difference was that he had already released "Most of the Time."

A solution presented itself because Sony wanted him to record a promo video of the song to help their ongoing attempts to promote an album that had been (correctly) received as a real return to form. And Dylan, being Dylan, duly obliged by rerecording the song with the musicians destined to feature on his next album, *under the red sky*, and letting his son Jesse film the results. The resultant thudding threnody was as unambient as it gets. Yet Dylan dug it enough to allow promo CDs of this new version to be released, even though after a month off the road his voice was not in great shape, and the song suffers accordingly.

In many ways, the gesture was unnecessary. The song had been a consistent feature of the shows ever since he debuted *Oh Mercy* material at the first Beacon Theatre residency (October 10–13, 1989). And some of those early live performances were breathtaking. Enough of the amnesia had lifted for Dylan to sing the lines "I can survive, I can endure" in a way that invariably generated whoops of validation from audiences. The song was that rare breed of song that could be sung a number of different ways, depending on its author's moods: as a genuine statement of affirmation (Hammersmith Odeon, February 7, 1990); as a yearning paean to possibilities (Beacon Theatre, October 12, 1989); or as a song of quiet desperation (San Jose, May 12, 1992). That last-named performance would prove to be the *last* live performance, perhaps because every shade of feeling this beguiling lyric ever contained were now nuanced into the night air. The pain, and the glory, was there for all to see—and Dylan knew it. He could now let it rest in peace.

Note: Dylan appears to always sing "She's not far behind," not "She's that far behind," which is how the line appears in *Lyrics*. I personally prefer the former. It sows a necessary seed of doubt about his previous protestation, "Most of the time she ain't even in my mind."

{526} THREE OF US

Known Studio recording: 1305 Soniat, New Orleans, LA, March 14, 1989—2 takes.

The multitrack sheet for "Broken Days" lists what appears, on the face of it, to be just an alternative title for that song, "Three of Us." Not so. The session log for March 14 gives three takes of "Broken Days," a non-specific jam, and two takes of something listed as "Three of Us Be Free." But despite the various tapes to have emerged from the sessions, and the recent trawl through this material for *Tell Tale Signs*, the song remains unheard outside the confines of 1305 Soniat.

{527} TV TALKIN' SONG

Published lyric/s: Lyrics 04.

Known studio recordings: 1305 Soniat, New Orleans, LA, March 14, 1989—5 takes; The Complex, L.A., March 1990; The Complex, ?April 20, 1990 [new vocal] [UTRS].

First known performance: C.W. Post College, NY, October 11, 1990.

TV is so super-powerful. It forms people's opinions. When I was growing up, and even in the sixties, that never was the case. You had to go out and experience things to form opinions. Now you don't have to move. You get knowledge brought into you, without the experience of it . . . I think there's something really dangerous in that. —Dylan, to Charles Kaiser, December 1985

> You've just gotta turn [the bombardment of images] off . . . If all we can
> do is just complain about it and it's destroying the fabric of our minds,
> then we just have to shut it off. —Dylan, to Toby Creswell, January 1986

Of all the songs on *under the red sky*, undoubtedly the one with the longest gestation was "TV Talkin' Song." The two quotes above, made only a few weeks apart in the winter of 1985–6, make it clear how long the deleterious influence of TV had been preying on Dylan's mind. In fact, he had been alluding to its pernicious effect for as long as he had been banging on about the space program.

As early as 1981, he was expressing concern about the fact that "television now goes into every home, [and] there's not much you can do about it." By 1984, he was already talking like the preacher-man at Speakers' Corner in "TV Talkin' Song." Discussing the "commercials on TV" with *Rolling Stone*'s Kurt Loder that spring, he gets scarily close to becoming the man on the soapbox: "They look like they're pushing sex in some kinda way . . . It's to stick the idea in your brain . . . If you start makin' laws against porno magazines and that kinda stuff . . . you gotta stop the prime-time television shows too." It hardly required a leap of faith to get from here to someone "talking to some folks / About TV being evil, and he wasn't telling jokes."

Hard evidence that Dylan had been sketching out the song in his mind for a while is found on a "live" two-track recording of the song made not in L.A. but in New Orleans, back in March 1989, that was under consideration for *Tell Tale Signs*. Though there is no version of the song on the *Oh Mercy* multitracks, this prototype "TV Talkin' Song" was no impromptu improvisation. Dylan worked on the song long enough to get a full version, and the vocal he unleashes is probably his scariest since "Black Cross" in 1961. What is entirely absent is the Speakers' Corner setting, which may be the result of Dylan's time in London in February 1990. In 1989, the man "on a platform" resembles the figure in *Renaldo and Clara* declaiming about how "everything you say to a man of God you say direct to God." A number of lines, however, do survive to the *red sky* sessions, including the image of shooting the TV out, à la Elvis, and something proximate to the damning couplet in the initial *red sky* version, "Puts a [brain] inside your eye, and penetrates your skull / Lays an egg inside your head, and makes you dull."

And "TV Talkin' Song" may not be the only song from New Orleans he was holding over for the next album. Dylan apparently told Lanois he wanted to save "Series of Dreams"; as Mason Ruffner recalls, "I remember [one time] doodling with half of the songs that wound up on his next record, *under the red sky.*" This is a fascinating notion, partly validated by this previously undocumented "TV Talkin' Song" from the swamplands of Louisiana.

When he got around to recording the song for *red sky*, the following March, it was at the same session that he recorded the basic track for another *Oh Mercy* outtake, "Born in Time." However, if that other leftover had been lyrically and musically refined before they rolled tape again, "TV Talkin' Song" was nothing of the sort. At least he had found the right setting this time: the talkin' song, a genre with which he had made his name, but had not revisited since April 1963.

"TV Talkin' Song" had another, more contemporaneous influence, one which is starkly obvious on both *Oh Mercy* and *red sky* outtakes—rap music. An oral art form that began as a way to articulate valid concerns, it had already devolved into a posturing pissing contest in song when "TV Talkin' Song" temporarily reclaimed such territory for the author of "Subterranean Homesick Blues," Dylan taking a song which was "just a riff" and spilling the beans to a rudimentary rhythmic backdrop. As a methodology, it threw at least one musician that day for a loop, guitarist Robben Ford:

> When we started recording, Dylan . . . would just start some kind of a vamp going on the guitar. The whole band was out in the room, in contact with each other—there wasn't a lot of separation. And Bob has a table in front of him, with pages and pages and pages of lyrics, and he would just start some kind of a thing going on the guitar, and we'd all fall in behind him, and just start jamming. And as soon as he kinda liked what was happening, he'd start picking up lyrics, going through the pages, and just start trying to sing it over whatever we were doing.

The two known outtakes, clearly from the same session, confirm the veracity of Ford's recollection. Both start with a scudding bass riff which sounds like it has been building for a while before Dylan launches into this fulminating screed. The lyric at this stage is genuinely creepy. The

first take features two verses in midsong which would have made that
other old-time preacher Hal Lindsey proud:

> Tear the screen apart he said, and climb up on the knobs,
> You can have another life with all the time you've lost,
> Raises little puppets, spins your brain about,
> Sometimes you gotta do like Elvis did, and blow the damn thing out.
>
> TV judges and TV clerks, TV repairmen to fix it so it works,
> TV dads and TV mums, living in TV cities, under bombs.

The second verse above is gone by the next take, Dylan having leafed
through a different set of pages, though still reading from the same black
book. The fate of the man on Speakers' Corner remains severe. After
"the crowd began to riot, they grabbed hold of the man / Hung him
from a lamppost, then they ran," while the narrator walks back to his
hotel just in time to see the incident on TV.

By the time he rerecorded his vocal, probably on April 20, the speaker—
like the drifter—did escape, making for a less interesting news story. It was
part of a series of wholesale changes—and, according to the mix tape dated
April 20, further "edits"—to the song at the dubbing stage, symptomatic
of a newfound belief from Dylan that he could constantly improve a song
by honing the words, even after the album was well into postproduction.
This was the one instance where he was entirely wrong, for which Don
Was nobly assumed some of the blame in conversation with Peter Doggett:

> There are . . . lyrics [on the record] that he just threw on. And then
> as we were mixing the record, the album went by so quickly, he was
> sitting there rewriting the songs. And when each song was mixed, he
> asked for a microphone to be set up, and he went out there and redid
> his vocals—not necessarily to improve the vocals—because I don't think
> he did—but because he was rewriting the songs. And in some cases, the
> songs improved, and in some cases, he should not have second-guessed
> his first instincts. "TV Talkin' Song" is one of [the latter]. In retrospect,
> maybe I should have said, "Let's not start recording [this] until we know
> what we're going to do."

The one lyrical improvement comes when Dylan actually had a good reason to change things. In the original version, the third verse described "The man saying something 'bout children when they're young / Whoever puts their face in it, he said, they should be hung," a fate reserved for him. By the album that second line has become "Being sacrificed to it while lullabies are being sung," which both projects the tender age at which such brainwashing starts and aligns the song—which otherwise sticks out like a sore digit—with the nursery-song imagery surrounding it on *red sky*.

The greatest loss the rerecording brought was the brooding quality of the original track, on which Dylan's deadpan delivery was wholly simpatico with its sparse accompaniment. Though more melodically interesting, the released cut relaxes its magnetic grip. Any vestiges of that melody were finally stripped away on its live debut in October 1990. At least Dylan, to his credit, attacked the song with renewed vigor at the Beacon shows that month; but before the year was out the narrative had become increasingly confused. He continued shedding verses from the song until there was little left to say, and what there was might have been better left unsaid.

{528} WHERE TEARDROPS FALL

Published lyric/s: Lyrics 04.
Known studio recordings: 1305 Soniat, New Orleans, LA, March 21–22, 1989—3 takes; April 15–16 [new vocal] [OM—tk. 2].
First known performance: Toad's Place, New Haven, CT, January 12, 1990.

According to Lanois, interviewed at the time of *Oh Mercy*'s release, Dylan had come in with almost all the necessary songs—"though three were finished off in the studio." Well, there were certainly more than three songs "finished off" in New Orleans. But three songs, it seems, *were* written (down) during Dylan's time in Louisiana: "Where Teardrops Fall," "Shooting Star," and "Man in the Long Black Coat"—all of which, inevitably, ended up on the album.

Of the three, "Where Teardrops Fall" is the least worthy, and the one that worried him the most. A song which he may have been carrying around in sketch form in his head, it is not a composition Dylan discusses in *Chronicles*, though he details its recording history at length. This presumably reflects both the ease with which the song came to him, and the difficulty he had deciding where such a song fit in the scheme of things.

Unfortunately, Dylan's account is nigh on impossible to tally with the great Dane's (increasingly sketchy) sessionography. According to our discographer, the song was recorded three times on March 21–22, new vocals were overdubbed on April 15, 15 [*sic*], and 16, take two then being released on *Oh Mercy*. The song was then cut on March 28, again resulting in three takes—of which the second take was preferred, with new vocals overdubbed on March 30, April 3, and April 8. This version, too, was apparently released on *Oh Mercy*.

These contradictory details do not tally with Dylan's version of events, either. According to *Chronicles*, they cut the song in a single take at the end of a marathon session with Rockin' Dopsie and his Cajun Band, and although "it was just a three-minute ballad . . . it made you stand straight up and stay right where you were. The song was . . . upbeat, and it was complete." The following night they were listening to a playback of the session. And the song came on and blew Dylan away, "but"—and it was a big "but"—"[Lanois] said we could do it better." As such, another session was expended cutting the song again, even though Dylan insists he was constantly thinking, "Why aren't we using the other one? . . . There was no reason to interfere with it, the way it was." Eventually, Dylan prevailed and "Danny . . . went back . . . to Dopsie's version and used it."

Overdubs by Burn and Lanois were then imposed on the version from March 21–22, which would appear to be the version they actually did release. The ghost version from March 28 is almost certainly not "Where Teardrops Fall," but rather a misassigned "What Was It You Wanted."[34] But even with this caveat, Dylan's account fails to add up. I suspect the versions credited to March 21–22 are probably already in postproduction, working with a basic track Dylan already recorded with Rockin' Dopsie. The Dopsie session is not one Krogsgaard got to detail, but it was here that they cut the song first and, in Dylan's mind, foremost. Lanois still managed to mess with the essence of this original take by convincing Dylan to overdub a new vocal (or three) and tinkering with the take even unto a set of early July sessions, when he added his own, superfluous, guitar.

Dylan's defence of the song, and his self-evident commitment to it, detailed in *Chronicles*, gives a real sense of the battle of wills that went on that spring. It is a shame he wasted such energy on this piece of fluff, when he had such an embarrassment of riches. As per usual, his first instinct—which was to prefer "Born in Time"—was the better one. But "Where Teardrops Fall" got the final nod, and it was soon getting the nod in concert, too, one of a number of *Oh Mercy* cuts debuted at Toad's in January 1990. Sporadically in the set until 2001, the one time he came close to capturing the spirit of spontaneity he found with ol' Dopsie was at a show in Kingston, Ontario (May 30, 1990), when he decided to do it at the piano, in a slot usually reserved for "Disease of Conceit." For that one moment, one could envision Dylan sitting at the studio piano, wondering whether George Gershwin really died in vain.

{529} SHOOTING STAR

Published lyric/s: Lyrics 04. *[Outtake lyric: "Writings"]*
Known studio recordings: 1305 Soniat, New Orleans, LA, March 14, 1989—8 takes; April 1+3 [new vocals] [OM—tk. 7 + vcl].
First known performance: Alpine Valley, WI, June 9, 1990.

> I don't much listen to radio. Every time I hear it, it's depressing . . . The stuff you hear on the radio would make it seem like everything's all right everywhere. You really have to seek your salvation in some other place than the popular radio. —Dylan, to Denise Worrell, November 1985

If "Where Teardrops Fall" was last-minute padding, the two songs that completed the 1989 album—closing out sides one and two—were both major additions to the latter-day Dylan canon. "Shooting Star" was his first album closer since "Every Grain of Sand" to share that slightly somnambulant feel, a gorgeous melody, caressed vocal, and an abiding conviction that there are two kinds of people, good (i.e., saved) people and lost people. And one suspects it was that apocalyptic bridge which came first, before there was a song to which it fit:

> Listen to the engine, listen to the bell,
> As the last firetruck from hell goes rollin' by,
> All good people are prayin'."
> It's the last temptation, the last account,
> The last time you might hear the Sermon on the Mount,
> The last radio is playin'."

On both known outtakes—apparently from the March 14–15 session—as Dylan uncharacteristically recorded eight full takes of a song he had not yet tuned into, this bridge is fully intact. He probably felt he should capture it while he could. Describing the inspiration for a song that descended "underneath the . . . magnolia" by the great Mississippi river, he says he "started feeling something about a song called 'Shooting Star' . . . I could vaguely hear it in my mind . . . I didn't want to forget this." Later on, he claimed, "The song came to me complete, full in the eyes like I'd . . . just found it. It was illuminated."

By which I'm obliged to conclude he meant the architecture of the song came to him whole. The lyric certainly didn't. The vocals to the two circulating outtakes, both of which feature distinctly different basic tracks, stick with the same lyrical template. But the only parts that survive to the released version reside with the bridge and that opening (and closing) line that immediately illuminates the song's trajectory, "Seen a shooting star tonight, and I thought of you."

One must assume that Dylan's decision to redo the vocal on April 1 was partially dictated by the fact that he had rewritten all three verses; and, it must be said, to great effect. In place of something impressionistic but only intermittently effective (I personally love "Seen a shooting star tonight against the grain / Up in the hot-rod sky, 'cross the prairies of Maine"), he tightens the nuts and bolts to every verse. As such, verse one now concerns *her* attempt to "break into another world," the second verse addresses his own failings, while the final verse no longer places him "a thousand miles away from when the end of time explodes," but rather on the set of *Gone with the Wind*, uttering (and slightly altering) that famous last line, "Tomorrow will be / Another day."

It is a highly effective send-off to another classic song about star-crossed lovers caught in interesting times (possibly influenced by Chekhov's short story "The House with an Attic," which has a strong shooting star motif) and a perfect way to affirm the restoration of full faculties. Back in 1985, he had openly confessed, "I find it harder [and harder] to hold on and develop a certain idea . . . and explore all the possibilities of it. I haven't really done that as much as maybe I . . . could." If Lanois's pushing and prodding had one immediate purpose, it was to ensure that Dylan did not keep settling for second best. The chronicling crooner himself admits that "Shooting Star" was a song written because he "thought it might be something Lanois was looking for." Praise be.

But in keeping with almost all of the songs cut at Lanois's Studio on the Move, it was not until Dylan started moving "Shooting Star" into his live set that it really came into its own (and lost all those little stereophonic doodles). More surprising, it was the last *Oh Mercy* song to enter the arena, not appearing until a June 1990 show at the open-air Alpine Valley, in Wisconsin; but it was worth the wait. Blowing away the last vestiges of Lanois's swampland with a single flick of his Fender, G. E. Smith led the song a merry march, Dylan's breathless vocal barely keeping up. That is, until they got to the bridge, when the man at the mike took over, singing the final verse with real passion and then driving the band through the bridge a second time, reiterating the real message of the song, "The last radio is playing . . ."

The double-bridge arrangement became the standard way Dylan tackled "Shooting Star" in concert, and added greatly to its power. But what it lacked, on each and every occasion he tackled it live, was the harmonica coda that should have been coming through that last radio set (which even on record he stopped short of delivering). As late as the second *Unplugged* show, in November 1994, he has barely put the harp to his mouth when he decides to pull back, leaving the nonplussed band to play the world's last funeral march. Even the last time the song meant a great deal in performance—when Dylan's delivery burned the bridge down at the Manchester Apollo on April 4, 1995—he stopped short of lifting the rafters with another mouth harp from heaven. Oh well.

{530} MAN IN THE LONG BLACK COAT

Published lyric/s: Lyrics 04.

Known studio recordings: 1305 Soniat, New Orleans, LA, March 29, 1989—2 takes; April 4, 1989 [new vocal] [OM].

First known performance: Beacon Theatre, NYC, October 13, 1989.

> When he first started doing ["Man in the Long Black Coat"], he was singing it maybe an octave higher. And it didn't sound very good. It sounded pretty awful, in fact. And it might have been Bob or it might have been Dan, but someone recognized it wasn't really working, and suggested singing it an octave lower, and that's when he got that "Crickets—a-chirpin—water is high." Suddenly the phrasing came and I was like, "Fuck, this is really good." —Malcolm Burn, to Damien Love, 2008

On March 29, 1989, Dylan completed recording the basic tracks for his first strong album in six years. He had come to the session with a brand-new song he had written after taking a couple of days off to clear his head and a day after he began fixing up what he already had. It was a familiar pattern (though according to *Chronicles* he'd only ever done it once before: "Dark Eyes"). Although "Man in the Long Black Coat" may have had more in common with "Dark Eyes" than, say, "Dirge"—another song he added when already in the midst of mixing and fixing—it was not an album closer. On Dylan's May 2 sequence, it opened the second side, a position to which it would have been more suited, simply because of all those soundtracky atmospherics with which it begins, and which, according to engineer Mark Howard, were played live as the locusts sang way off in the distance:

> Malcolm was playing a Yamaha DX7 that Brian Eno had mastered—he had all these sounds built in . . . and one of the sounds was this crickets sound. Actually, on the Neville Brothers' *Yellow Moon* record . . . when Brian came in with his cricket sounds, he would play this melody, and then these cicada bugs [outside] would repeat it back. It became really creepy.

One doubts the effect was anywhere near as creepy as "Man in the Long Black Coat," once Dylan began doing his best Tom Waits impersonation. At last he and Lanois were reaching for the same vibe. As Dylan writes, "The production [on this song] sounds deserted . . . cut out from the abyss of blackness . . . Something menacing and terrible." Dylan claims he thought of it as his version of Johnny Cash's "I Walk the Line," but it is no such thing. Rather, as I have written elsewhere, it is an updated "The House Carpenter," aka "The Daemon Lover"—where the devil returns, disguised as a long lost love, and entices a carpenter's wife to abandon her husband and children with promises of gold before leading her down to hell ("There was nothing she wrote / She's gone with the man in the long black coat").

If Dylan captured the essence of "The Daemon Lover" in a single take back in 1961, "Man in the Long Black Coat" did not come so easily. According to guitarist Mason Ruffner, they first "tried that [song] with the band, and then Bob, Dan, and Malcolm did it themselves after we left; and they used that version on the record, without the drums." The memories of this musician argue against the song being done in the two takes assigned it in Krogsgaard's sessionography, but it could be that much of the working out was done only to live two-track DAT.

The album vocal, yet again, was added at a later date—April 4— in keeping with almost all of the album;[35] and it may be that in the interim the lyric was also tweaked. Though no outtake with the live vocal circulates, Ruffner remembers he was still "doodling a lot with the lyrics . . . it was like he was always making changes and additions and subtractions as he went." In one of just two interviews he gave to promote the album, Dylan claimed that the line "People don't live or die, people just float" was originally more existential than this: "'People don't live or die / People just are,' that was the line in that song for the longest period of time . . . It was tough trying to come up with a rhyme for that, and then finally [I] gotta just give in and make it rhyme." Now he tells us!

As one of the songs Dylan admits he tailored to what he thought Lanois wanted, "Man in the Long Black Coat" might have become one of the less effective songs when transferred to the bar-band sound of the Never Ending Tour, but such was not the case. The song was introduced as a first encore at the last show of the 1989 Beacon Theatre residency, and it just grew in stature every time Dylan lost another note from his vocal range, and compensated with ever longer harmonica breaks, or by slowing the whole thing down another notch. By the Prague residency of March 1995, one really did begin to believe that this was *the* song that defined an album which became, in Lanois's choice phrase, "something to do with the pushing and pulling of the moon. At nighttime we're ready to be more mysterious and dark. *Oh Mercy*'s about that." Amen.

1990–5:

{ Traveling Wilburys Vol. Three; under the red sky}

under the red sky *seems to oppress an awful lot of Dylan fans. Some particularly infantile criticism has been directed at its self-conscious use of nursery rhyme–like constructions, largely from people entirely ignorant of nursery rhymes' centuries-old role in the folk tradition. Dylan certainly received little credit for daring to make a gut-bustin' R&B record less than a year after leaving the swamplands of Lanoisville. Whatever its failings, the album conveys a real unity of purpose. What it lacked was one song that raised things to a higher plane, preferably at the expense of an album opener that went, "Wiggle wiggle wiggle, like a bowl of soup."*

At least under the red sky *sounded—in session, anyway—like an album from the guy responsible for* Highway 61 Revisited—*which is more than could be said for the second Wilburys instalment,* Volume Three, *an overcooked turkey for which few gave thanks. Written and recorded in another spring burst by the four surviving Wilburys (Orbison having passed away unexpectedly), the album was subjected to the kind of postproduction usually inflicted by Hollywood hackers. This time it was perpetrated by Jeff Lynne and George Harrison, who managed to dilute the essence of just about every track recorded. The results did the legend, and the Wilburys' bank balances, few favors. It also closed the book on a three-year period when Dylan had rediscovered both his lyrical and performing muses. G. E. Smith's departure from the band in October marked the start of a five-year period which made previous bouts of artistic amnesia seem like an afternoon picnic . . .*

{531} HANDY DANDY

Published lyric/s: Lyrics 04 [inc. draft lyric]
*Known studio recordings: Oceanway Studio, L.A., January 6, 1990; The
Complex, LA, ?April 19, 1990 [new vocal] [UTRS].*
First known performance: Recinto Festival, Vigo, Spain, June 27, 2008.

> There's two kinds of thoughts in your mind: there's good thoughts and
> evil thoughts. Both come through your mind . . . And you have to be able
> to sort them out, if you want to be a songwriter. —Dylan, to Paul Zollo,
> January 1991

That single Oceanway session the first week in January 1990—six days
before Dylan again resumed his never-ending touring—proved to be one
of his more remarkable days in the studio. Having entered the session
wondering if coproducers David and Don Was could reheat an *Oh Mercy*
leftover ("God Knows"), he ended up cutting three more songs. All four
results would appear on his next album in something resembling their
Oceanway guises.

According to Don Was, "The ['God Knows'] rough mix from that
moment is the mix that appears on the album." "10,000 Men" was also
left essentially untainted by postproduction "fix-ups." "Handy Dandy"
was not so fortunate. The Oceanway original of "Handy Dandy" has
appeared (albeit illicitly) on *The Genuine Bootleg Series Vol. 3*, and runs to
almost exactly the same time as the released take. It is missing the superimposed, parodic organ work from a recalled Al Kooper and unnecessary
percussion and backing vocals, while retaining Dylan's delicious delivery
on the day, and a full serving of Stevie Ray Vaughan's slippin' and slidin'
guitar.

In fact, Was recently claimed that "Before 'Handy Dandy,' Bob
remarked how, years earlier, he'd been to a Miles Davis session. The
band improvised for an hour and then the producer cut it into a coherent
five-minute piece. We decided to try something similar. 'Handy Dandy'
was originally 34 minutes long." This fanciful, half-hour "Handy Dandy"
rather reminds me of the Beatles' fabled (and still unheard) twenty-seven
minute version of "Helter Skelter," another song which lasted just four
minutes on its release. But for all of Vaughan's fretwork, this is no *Bitches*

Brew—they are doing a Dylan song he brought along, not one he hoped might magically appear out of thin air.

Lyrically, too, the song had already been stripped to its core, which we know because "Handy Dandy" is one of only two latter-day songs where we have recourse to an original typescript of the lyric, courtesy of that most unlikely source, the 2004 edition of *Lyrics*. This original typescript is quite different. Even the opening verse, the only one that resembles its final self, goes off at quite a tangent: "handy dandy contr[o]versy always surrounds him / wherefer he goes[,] too bad for him[,] something back there always hounds him."

The essential character of the song's eponymous subject is further filled in on five "lost" verses. He is a "tower of strength & stability / he does it with mirrors" in verse two; and "compulsive & healt[h]y, plausible obses[s]ive automatic / blo[w]in his horn for the girls & bringing them up to the attic" in verse four. Finally, in verse six, he finds himself "in a ro[o]m full o[f] people and sudden[l]y there's nobody cheering." In their place by the time of the session was "an all-girl orchestra"— thus starting a wholly unsubstantiated legend that the song was "about Prince"—and two bridges, the second of which rejigged the following traditional riddle (the answer, incidentally, is an egg):

> In marble walls as white as milk,
> Lined with a skin as soft as silk,
> With a fountain crystal clear,
> A golden apple does appear.
> No doors there are to this stronghold,
> Yet thieves break in and steal the gold.

Evidently, plundering any arcana that involved riddling rhymes and nonsense songs was a modus operandi from the very start of sessions. But more literary sources may have imposed their presence on Dylan's portrait. It is King Lear who tells the Fool, "Change places, and handy-dandy, which is the justice, which is the thief?" This song's handy-dandy character seems content to play the fool throughout (prompting the girl Nancy to say, "Boy, you talking crazy"), having perhaps been born with an antic disposition, or just discovering that "something in the moonlight still hounds him."

How much of the finished lyric was put there for effect, as opposed to genuinely saying something, is a matter of ongoing dispute. But Dylan dispensed with the song as soon as he left the studio, not playing it again for another eighteen years. Having "been around the world and back again" time after time, he finally murdered "Handy Dandy" without remorse in June 2008, thus putting the last live *red sky* song to bed.

{532} CAT'S IN THE WELL

Published lyric/s: Lyrics 04.
Known studio recordings: Oceanway Studio, L.A., January 6, 1990 [UTRS].
First known performance: Perth, Australia, March 18, 1992.

> Anyway, Lead Belly . . . had been out of prison for some time when he decided to do children's songs and people said, "Oh why did Lead Belly change?" Some people liked the old ones, some people liked the new ones. Some people liked both songs. But he didn't change, he was the same man! —Preface to "Caribbean Wind," Warfield Theatre, San Francisco, November 12, 1980

A jump blues for the Apocalypse, "Cat's in the Well" was the most effective song recorded at the January 6, 1990, session. Its inclusion at this early stage in proceedings suggests that for once Dylan was writing an album in reverse. (Not only would the first one now later be last, but the last first. After recording four-fifths of *red sky*'s second side at this first session, the opening song, "Wiggle Wiggle," would be cut at the last session.)

"Cat's in the Well" served as both a template for the nursery songs of Apocalypse that bestrew the album and the ecological theme that ripples across the red sky ("The world's being slaughtered, it's such a bloody disgrace"). And yet it was the title track, and not this militaristic march, that journalists thought previewed the next crisis in world affairs—the Gulf War. Dylan's response, as reported in a Mexican paper, was that although the album "was released before hostilities [in the Gulf] began . . . it's relevant, I'd say. But so are the songs I wrote thirty years ago."

Considering how many unambiguous songs about the End Times

the man had written in the past decade, he must have been wondering what he had to do in order for the message to sink in. Even surrounding the message with a superficial shell of childlike riddles left a number of listeners unable to recognize he was still preaching the word of God, knowing that the next Gulf War would involve Gog and Magog.

Though much has been made of this song's debt to the familiar Mother Goose rhyme "Ding dong bell / Pussy's in the well," this evocative expression is there merely to set up the punchline. The meaty part of the message is in the final verse, which, save for the title phrase, betrays precious little debt to Mother Goose and her gaggle. However it does reference an earlier song of Dylan's, "The Wicked Messenger" ("the leaves began to fallin'"), a traditional fare-thee-well he would record three years later ("Goodnight my love"), and, most pertinent of all, Psalms 123:3–4 ("Have mercy upon us, O Lord, have mercy upon us: for . . . our soul is exceedingly filled with the scorning of those that are at ease, and with the contempt of the proud"), all of which Dylan condenses down to:

> Cat's in the well, the leaves are starting to fall [x2]
> Goodnight my love, may the Lord have mercy on us all.

The wolf who is looking down the well—not a feature of the pussy fable—is surely one foretold by Jeremiah (5:6), in cahoots with (the lion and) the leopard: "A wolf of the evenings shall spoil them, a leopard shall watch over their cities: every one that goeth out thence shall be torn in pieces: because their transgressions are many, and their backslidings are increased." "The servant . . . at the door" could be a reference to the Last Supper—when Jesus waited on His own disciples—but more likely alludes to another apocalyptic text (Isaiah), via "All Along the Watchtower," where "barefoot servants . . . came and went" (or, as here, "all of his daughters need shoes").

"Cat's in the Well" took its bittersweet time working its way into the live set, only appearing in the winter of 1992 on another Antipodean tour. But once it established itself as an apposite precursor to the "Idiot Wind" blowing through the sets nightly, its ominous presence felt the collars of every sinner man in those auditoriums.

{533} 10,000 MEN

Published lyric/s: Lyrics 04.

Known studio recordings: Oceanway Studio, L.A., January 6, 1990 [UTRS].

First known performance: South Kingston, RI, November 12, 2000.

> ["10,000 Men"] wasn't a planned thing, he just started playing it . . . We finished the take on, I think, "Cat's in the Well" and all of a sudden he started playing [it] . . . The engineer was hip to what was going on and he stopped the playback of the other thing, threw on some new tape and started recording a minute into it . . . That one starts real abrupt . . . you just feel like someone turned a tape recorder on at just that moment.
> —Don Was, to Reid Kopel, October 1990

However much Dylan fondly imagined he could be another Miles, able to spontaneously create form from musical chaos, any attempt throughout the mid- to late-eighties to turn the odd jam into a usable composition had generally crashed and burned. But one *red sky* song cut at Oceanway—a studio he had last used back in 1984, when exclusively recording such jams—caught everyone unawares. It was "10,000 Men," a song of mystery and madness dredged up from the id that seems to take its title—and opening image, "Ten thousand men on a hill"—from the famous nursery rhyme about the Duke of York and his ten thousand men, whom he marched up and down the hill to no obvious purpose.

Like many a nursery rhyme, "10,000 Men" is written in a code so impenetrable it appears to be mere doggerel, or nonsense (its working title, "Hat Pin," isn't about to turn the key, unless our man is telling us how he arrived at the various images). Verses like "Ten thousand women, all sweepin' my room [x2] / Spilling my buttermilk, sweeping it up with a broom" may well have some underlying meaning, but it just seems easier to believe he had written (or improvised) such lines entirely for effect. Any precedent can best be found in "Nottamun Town," which fully demonstrated "mystery is a traditional fact" (and, as Andrew Muir points out in *Troubadour*, "Nottamun Town" not only uses the same kind of riddle-like incongruities but also refers to ten thousand souls, twice: "Ten thousand stood round me yet I was alone" and "Ten thousand got drowned that never were born").

An experiment in both wordplay and improvisation, "10,000 Men" baffled just about every critic instructed to review the record. Dylan, I suspect, just liked how it felt, leaving the song pretty much alone. As Don Was informed Reid Kopel, "The point is feeling. You know, he's not going to go back 'cause someone was a little out of tune or something like that. [But] if it doesn't feel right, he's not going to let it out. If the feeling is good, if the vibe is good, then it's done and he's ready to get on with the next song."

Dylan wasn't so sure whether to unleash the song on audiences and, although he and the G. E. Smith band rehearsed it at New York's Montana Studios before the fall 1990 shows, it would take another ten years before he actually tested his fans' knowledge of his recent output by performing the song at a November 2000 show in Rhode Island (sandwiched between two *Nashville Skyline* songs!). Remarkably, the performance in question proves quite revelatory—Dylan is word-perfect (more so than the original *red sky* recording, where he bluffs a few lines) and the band is wound real tight. With an arrangement ripped clean from the *Time Out of Mind* lexicon of head-in-Mississippi blues, the song no longer seems quite so incongruous set alongside a song like "Cold Irons Bound." Satisfied that it still stood up, Dylan decided it was high time he made a whole album the same way.

{534} NIGHT OF THE LIVING DREAD

Known studio recordings: The Complex, L.A., ?early March 1990; The Complex, ?April 19, 1990 [new vocal].

The basic tracks for *under the red sky* were cut in double-quick time at just four sessions—a marked contrast to the water-torture approach Lanois had demanded of Dylan the previous spring. But there was another, unproductive, session—and, according to Don Was, it preceded all of the other Complex sessions in early March. Continuing their prior agreement that Was pick the band for Dylan, who would receive no advance warning, this second *red sky* session represented the one and only time he recorded with an extant band. Yet Dylan would later pooh-pooh their agreed methodology, in conversation with author Jonathan Lethem:

He'd have a different band for me to play with every day, a lot of *all-stars*, for no particular purpose. Back then I wasn't bringing anything at all into the studio, I was completely disillusioned. I'd let someone else take control of it all and [would] just come up with lyrics to the melody of the song . . . Too many people in the room, too many musicians, too many egos, ego-driven musicians that just wanted to play their thing, and it definitely wasn't my cup of tea.

NRBQ, short for the New Rhythm & Blues Quartet, had been formed in 1967, and had hung in there through thick and thin. They should have had plenty to talk with Dylan about, having been prevented from recording for six years in the eighties thanks to a contractual dispute with one Albert Grossman. They were also known for their spontaneity and willingness to fuse musical forms. The session, though, was a bust.

Maybe Was slightly jumped the gun with the NRBQ session, Dylan not being quite ready with the songs he wanted to record. Having just returned from a triumphant London residency, it would appear that this was one instance when he didn't bring "anything at all into the studio." As Was says, "The tracks from that day didn't make it onto the record . . . because he never finished writing those particular songs." Annoyingly, no one has been forthcoming as to what these unfinished works were, though Was did on one occasion say that there were three songs recorded, one of which was called simply "The Tango."

One potential candidate *is* listed on a rough mix tape dated April 19, reproduced in the final instalment of Krogsgaard's sessionography in *The Bridge* (the online version fails to reproduce such "ephemera"). It is listed as "Night of the Living Dread," his second play on the title of the 1968 horror classic (having namechecked it in "Brownsville Girl," "Welcome to the land of the living dead"). This could be the same song that a member of NRBQ remembered recording under the (presumably sarcastic) title "Some Enchanted Evening." Its inclusion on the April 19 mix tape suggests it was deemed worthy of consideration for the finished album.

{535} UNBELIEVABLE

Published lyric/s: Lyrics 04.

Known studio recordings: The Complex, L.A., March 1990; The Complex, L.A., ?April 20, 1990 [new vocal x2] [UTRS].

First known performance: Ottawa, August 22, 1992.

> If you're singing a line three seconds after you wrote it, your perform-
> ance isn't going to have the confidence that living inside a song will
> allow you. That's a problem on the album we did. —Don Was, to Peter
> Doggett, July 1997

If "Unbelievable" temporarily abandoned the nursery-rhyme lingo of
"Cat's in the Well" and "10,000 Men," it continued the warnings about
a world on the brink. Another catalog of iniquity set to a two-word
exclamation, "It's unbelievable," the song relies on a gradually modifying refrain. First time around that refrain is "It would go this far" (or,
originally, "You let it go this far"), followed by "You can get this rich
this quick" (the superior original of which was, "It would get this close
this quick"). Things get more and more serious, "The day would finally
come" leading to "It would go down this way."

Dylan was still playing around with the words when he began
recording the song, at the same session as "Under the Red Sky." In fact,
the lyrics on the two known outtakes are both quite different from its
final form, and in several significant instances, from each other. It took
him the whole evening to get from "Every seat's been occupied, every
eye is crucified" to the exemplary "Every mouth is open wide, every eye
is occupied." But then he detours into obscurity with "Every head is so
dignified, every moon is so sanctified."

Likewise, during the initial (first) bridge he gets it spot-on, describing
the dreamers of avarice thus: "All the silver, all the gold, all the jelly that
can be rolled / All the sweethearts that you can hold, all hanging on
a tree." But the overdubbed vocal on the album substitutes something
which reads like it was sung "three seconds after [he] wrote it": "All the
silver, all the gold, all the sweethearts you can hold / That don't come
back with stories untold, are hanging on a tree." Plain clumsy.

Throughout the final lyric—apparently dubbed during the April 20 session, when the song was subjected to at least two vocal overdubs (the mix tape credits one take as "after harp and vocal overdubs," the other as "after lyric change")—Dylan prefers to rely on heavy sarcasm to make lines work. He also makes a habit—also carried over to "2 X 2," the next song overdubbed on the twentieth with "new lyrics"—of changing everything from second to third person, depersonalizing the target/s of his invective. Thus, in the second verse, he changes "Too expensive to be built, too well-built to ever melt / Whoever thought you could make it stick" into something a lot less direct: "They said it was the land of milk and honey, now they say it's the land of money / Whoever thought they could ever make that stick."

Warming to the theme of money being the root of all evil, the tinkerer just kept tinkering. He makes a weak pun out of the familiar "Saddle up the horse and beat the drum" by spoonerizing the phrase, "Feed that horse and saddle up the drum." In the last verse, only the final line survives all the rewriting as platitudes again vie for dominion over the compact, evocative phrases of the original, almost all of which do the job better:

> It's unbelievable, just got to be,
> Indestructible, way beyond me,
> Turn the thread, and stretch the hide,
> Do what you're told and come inside,
> Every dog will have its day.
> It's unbelievable that it would go down this way.

As if the song had not suffered enough, Dylan then reached for the fader (again!), trimming the song of a nice little instrumental coda in which his harp plays off some fine piano (probably by Bruce Hornsby), before being buried beneath Al Kooper's over-familiar organ. At least those between-verse harmonica bursts survived intact, as did that great little guitar intro.

The narrative got no clearer after Dylan agreed to film a promotional video for the song, and cajoled part-time squeeze Sally Kirkland and that other fine actress Molly Ringwald into participating in a surreal dry run for his next movie but one. In the video, Dylan plays the Homeric observer witnessing a young lad being beaten up in a bar, before being saved, seduced, and then fleeced by the rapacious Ringwald. After losing his car and his money, the youth is picked up hitchhiking by a grizzled old chauffeur in a stretch limo (Dylan), who appears to be in the employ of a pig with a gold ring in his snout (a reference to Proverbs 11:22—"As a jewel of gold in a swine's snout, so is a fair woman [who] is without discretion"). Personally, I find the whole video a hoot, though any relationship to the song's message is a tad circuitous for me. For all I know, he may be knowingly sending up the whole idea of the story-line promo video.

The song itself lived to fight another day, Dylan proving that it still had legs as an updated "Band of the Hand" in the summer of 1992, when it entered the set at the expense of "Cat's in the Well." The live performances, in that small window when it enjoyed the Never Ending Tour's hospitality, fully justified Was's suspicion that what these songs really needed was "the confidence that living inside a song will allow you." At a five-night residency in Minneapolis at the end of that productive summer, Dylan found that confidence in spades. Strange but true.

{536} UNDER THE RED SKY

Published lyric/s: Lyrics 04.
Known studio recordings: The Complex, L.A., March 1990; The Complex, ?April 20, 1990 [new vocal] [UTRS].
First known performance: C.W. Post College, NY, October 11, 1990.

> The Pharisees also with the Sadducees came, and tempting desired [Jesus] that he would shew them a sign from heaven. He answered and said unto them, When it is evening, ye say, It will be fair weather: for the sky is red. And in the morning, It will be foul weather today: for the sky is red and lowering. O ye hypocrites, ye can discern the face of the sky: but can ye not discern the signs of the times? —Matthew 16:1–3

Though its position in Dylan's latter-day canon remains tainted by its title-track status on an album still dismissed by the critical fraternity at large, "Under the Red Sky" is an important song, as its continued presence in the live set (as of 2009) affirms. Predictably, it is another song of warning, a "Down in the Flood" for postmodern times. Again couched in the language of the nursery, it has been dismissed as a song of minor import. But producer Don Was realized it was something special:

> He wrote it like a little Biblical song . . . It was actually a very moving night when he put the vocal on it. It was about six in the morning, we'd been working all day and he went out there . . . There was something real special to that thing. I could tell from the minute we started playing that this was just coalescing fast, and it had a lot of heart, a lot of feeling . . . I misunderstood [it]. I thought . . . it's about ecology, . . . and he looked at me like I was a total asshole and he said, "Well, it's not about ecology." . . . and he walked out of the room. So I followed him out and I explained why I thought that. And he just shook his head. He said, "I can't believe people read *this* much into it." [But] that's the only time I really ever asked him about a lyric and he told me . . . it's about people who got trapped in his home town.

The town where a "blind horse . . . leads you around" could easily be Dylan's home town, Hibbing—ever on his mind—particularly as the rust-colored iron ore which lines the empty open-cast mines still gives the sky a red luster. But this was no mere north country blues. As Dylan told Edna Gundersen on the album's release, the title track was "intentionally broad and short, so you can draw all kinds of conclusions." This is Dylanspeak for "Can ye not discern the signs of the times?" And if those signs were not stark enough in themselves, Dylan even sang about them twice: "Let the bird sing, let the bird fly / The man in the moon went home and the river went dry." "The man in the moon," once the symbol of hope and promise who prophesied a time when "everything . . . is gonna be new," leaves town for good, thus sealing the fate of the boy and the girl who "lived in an alley under the red sky."

The fact he could invest such layers of meaning in a song which, taken at its "white face value," was simply an amalgam of half-remembered lullabies, suggested he was fully aware that poetic sophistication sometimes hides behind seemingly simple homilies. I doubt it was coincidence when he admitted to an Australian journalist, a coupla years later, that he had been getting "back into reading the William Blake poems again. It seems like when you're young and you read 'em they don't have the effect on you that they do when you get older." The depths of experience had by then rekindled songs of seeming innocence.

The words to "Under the Red Sky," once he had them down, stayed put. This was not a song Dylan wanted to tamper with once captured in the wee hours of a March morning. Recorded in a single take, even the April 20 vocal overdub resulted in just a single lyrical change—rather than repeat "Let the winds blow low," he transplanted the singing bird who flies in judgment from the "Love Henry" ballad: "Let the bird sing, let the bird fly." The song remained both "broad and short" even after the overdubbing process, George Harrison being permitted just two goes at superimposing his fine guitar solo.

G. E. Smith was also given barely a handful of shows to demonstrate what Dylan kept missing by refusing to make him part of the recording process, leaving the bandleader's well-traveled road for good a week after its live debut. "Under the Red Sky," meanwhile, held its own in the live set, even as all other songs cut at the behest of Was have come and gone. All the while, followers of that blind horse continue to circle the key to the kingdom.

{537} HEARTLAND

Published lyric/s: Across The Borderline CD.
First known performance: CBS Studios, Nashville, TN, January 13, 1993.
Known studio recordings: The Complex, L.A., March 1990; Power Station, NYC, October 19, 1992. [ATB]

> I'm sure there are . . . tracks laying around . . . fragments of other things. There is some nice stuff that we begged him to put on [*under the red sky*] . . . [which] we just didn't finish. —Don Was, to Reid Kopel, October 1990

If Dylan had no use for the fragments he "didn't finish," Don Was did. Aside from one song he subsequently donated to Was Not Was (#540), there was a song called "Heartland," which according to Was was recorded the same day as "Under the Red Sky" and "Unbelievable." He told *Record Collector*'s Peter Doggett that it "was a cut we started . . . that Bob never wrote lyrics to. He was holding that one back, I don't know why. We'd cut some other song, and while the band came in to hear the playback, Bob stayed out there and the assistant engineer was smart enough to observe him playing, and turned the recorder on. We were listening to what was going on, and when Bob started humming this song Kenny Aronoff ran out and joined in on drums, and then the rest of the band followed suit. It was a very cool track . . . So when I was doing [Willie Nelson's 1992 album] *Across the Borderline*, I . . . asked Bob if he would mind if Willie finished it."

Nelson told a similar tale to *NME* at the time of his album's release: "Don Was . . . brought me a tape of the melody [Dylan] had recorded, just him humming the tune, with the word 'heartland' every now and then. So I took the word and the melody and wrote a song around it." Responding to the rumor that these old friends had coauthored the song "by fax," Nelson went to some pains to take credit for the lyric. The original March 1993 copyright registration, which assigns music to Dylan and words to Nelson, appears to bear his recollection out.

However, I just don't buy it. Firstly, compare the verse that Dylan sings on the Nelson album with the two that Nelson contributes. Whereas Nelson uses a simple ABCB or ABAB rhyme scheme on both verses, Dylan employs a trick every folksinger learned before venturing to write their modern broadside ballads—putting an internal rhyme in the third and/or fourth lines of a verse:

> There's a home place under fire tonight in the Heartland,
> There's a well with water so bitter nobody can drink,
> Ain't no way to get high, and my mouth is so dry, that I can't speak,
> Don't they know that I'm dyin'," why ain't nobody cryin' for me?

Not convinced? Consider the theme of the song. Does it remind you of any title track to a recent Dylan collection? And not just "Under the Red Sky," but "God Knows" too ("There's a river / God knows how to make it flow") and "2 X 2" ("How much poison did they inhale?"). Similar ecological concerns also spilled over into another set of super-sessions that spring. A second Wilburys album included the likes of "Inside Out" ("Look out your window, the grass ain't green / It's kinda yellow . . .") and "The Devil's Been Busy" ("While you're strolling down the freeway, showing no remorse / Glowing from the poisons they've sprayed on your golf course"), two songs bearing Dylan's indelible thumbprint.

I simply don't believe that Dylan just humming the word "heartland" would have caused the other musicians to start running into the studio to lend a hand. Methinks he was singing the line that gave the song its title, "There's a home place under fire tonight in the Heartland." Or something similar. The other lines he may have written at a later date, in the spirit of those Nelson came up with, but, if so, he upped the ante on Nelson's rather obvious rant against all these bankers "takin' . . . my land from me" (yet not a land he proved willing to finance through direct taxes). The line about the well certainly seems like a residue from *red sky*—as do the entire song's concerns.

Note: The booklet accompanying *Across the Borderline* lists "Heartland" as "Music & Lyrics by Bob Dylan and Willie Nelson." No other song is credited in such a precise way.

{538} WIGGLE WIGGLE

Published lyric/s: Lyrics 04.

First known performance: Toad's Place, New Haven, CT, January 12, 1990 [version 1]; C.W. Post College, NY, October 11, 1990 [Version 2].

Known studio recordings: The Complex, L.A., March 1990; The Complex, ?April 19, 1990 [new vocal] [UTRS].

Don Was thought that "Wiggle Wiggle" was Dylan's way of living out his adolescent fantasy of writing "Tutti Frutti," but if that song was a coded message from the backdoor man, "Wiggle Wiggle" was one delivered by the Man with No Name. It began life at two warm-up shows for another year on the road, as a half-remembered "cover" of a fifties favorite or two (possible templates include 45s by the Accents and Don Lang & the Twisters), crossbred with every frat song he ever knew. The lyric at this stage, when not simply garbled, was exactly what one would expect from a song with such a title, Dylan indulging in one of his "Shake"-like extemporizations.

It seems unlikely that at this stage he envisaged cutting the song in the studio, given that ever since 1986 he had religiously refrained from previewing new material in concert, adhering to the philosophy that "when I do it in the studio, it's the first time I've ever done it." But having passed over "Wiggle Wiggle" at Oceanway, as the *red sky* sessions became Complex he began to rethink his view of this song, beginning to believe it would be the perfect way to set up an album of ostensible nonsense. When he sang, "Wiggle, wiggle, wiggle, all night" at Toad's, I doubt he realized that the night in question was the one which comes falling from the sky. By the time he cut it in March, the song was ready for such a transition, now having a bridge whose message was decidedly at odds with earlier hedonistic sentiments:

> Wiggle till it roars, wiggle till it flies,
> Wiggle till it pours down out of the skies.
> Wiggle till it bites, wiggle till it burns . . .

It was Tempe time again; when, in response to repeated shouts of "rock and roll," the born-again Bob spat out the judgment of a modern-day Jeremiah, "You can rock and roll all the way down to the pit!" And such a message could have set up the 1990 album perfectly. But second-guess Bob intervened. When the day came to overdub a new vocal for this two-minute track, he toned it down a notch, singing, "Wiggle till you're high, wiggle till you're higher / Wiggle till you vomit fire." The image of a reveler vomiting fire still suggested something satanic—especially when combined with the last line of the song, admonishing one and all to "wiggle like a big fat snake"—but it failed to convey the same sense of mankind dancing to its destruction originally evoked. It was quickly dismissed as a song of slight purpose, even when used as a companion piece to "Under the Red Sky" in concert. Perhaps it was an unwise lyricist who decided that "wiggle, wiggle, wiggle, like a bowl of soup" could convey a deeper message.

{539} 2 X 2

Published lyric/s: Lyrics 04.

*Known studio recordings: The Complex, L.A., March 1990; The Complex,
?April 20, 1990 [new vocal] [UTRS].*

First known performance: Correggio, Italy, July 5, 1992.

Not the most complex song recorded at these sessions, "2 X 2"
was nevertheless worked on long after the basic track was done, with
Dylan again distancing himself from the song's concerns by changing
its two bridges from first-person plural to third-person plural. No
longer did he wonder why his own "brothers and sisters still linger
in jail" or "How much poison can *we* inhale?" The most peculiar
rewrite, though, came at song's end, when he anxiously reverted to
the opening line, "One by one, they follow the sun," even as the fader
once again brought down the curtain with a resounding thud. On
the original takes recorded in March, he was less anxious to end the
procession and keener to invoke the Lord's name while this circular
song faded away:

> One by one, they step into the ark
> Two by two, they live in the dark,
> Three by three, what will be will be,
> Four by four, you can tell it some more.
>
> One by one, Thy will be done,
> Two by two, I'm telling it true,
> Three by three, why can't you see?
> Four by four, you've seen it before.

Quite what Dylan added with the new closing couplet, "They follow
the sun . . . to another rendezvous," defeats me. The last verse quoted
above is much more in keeping with the album's tenor, setting up the
last three songs, much as "The Wicked Messenger" set up *John Wesley
Harding's* final pairing. At least the overdubbed vocal puts in more of the
man, though it took until 1992 for the song to find its live feet as a set
opener at four summer shows. This time, he really did emphasize the
fact that this was a circular song, repeatedly singing "One by one, until

there were none," until it segued into the next song of the set (which, first time around, was "I Believe in You").

{540} SHIRLEY TEMPLE DON'T LIVE HERE ANYMORE

Known studio recordings: The Complex, L.A., ?April 19–20, 1990.

> One night, when we were mixing [*under the red sky*], we were sitting around, David Was, myself, and Bob, watching a rerun of *Bewitched*. I was aware this wasn't the smartest thing we could be doing . . . so I half-sarcastically said, "Let's write a song for Paula Abdul." So we shut the TV off, and wrote this . . .[]. . . little song called "Shirley Temple Doesn't Live Here Anymore." It struck me as a companion piece to *The Last Picture Show*, conjuring up images of a dying town and a disappearing way of life. We made a wistful sounding demo that, in all probability, was better suited to a singer like Richard Manuel than poor little Paula. She subsequently passed on the song. A couple years later, we thought we'd funk it up and try it as a Was (Not Was) song. Bob was cool with the idea but wanted to change a few lyrics. We downed a few shots of bourbon, Bob scribbled some new words on the page, and "Mr. Alice Doesn't Live Here Anymore" was ready for the world. We put it on our very next album . . . which was released 16 years later. —Don Was, to Peter Doggett / Rob Hughes

What Was fails to state in his two-part exposition on the history of this "lost" song was whether Dylan ever recorded the song properly himself. The implication is that he did not. After all, they were mixing the album, not recording it. The "wistful sounding demo . . . we made" probably failed to contain a Dylan vocal. Certainly, the version Was Not Was recorded in 1992—presumably around the time Was also produced *Across the Borderline*—fails to feature the song's coauthor, who had already "had it" with the recording process (only to then work with Was again in 1994). Lyrically, though, its concerns are as covered in red dirt as anything recorded in the spring of 1990, with the young going off to war while the town itself is shutting down for good—"The windows are boarded, they pulled down the shade / Even the dog just ran away." Hey Paula, got the perfect song for ya . . .

{541} THE DEVIL'S BEEN BUSY

{542} IF YOU BELONGED TO ME

{543} INSIDE OUT

{544} LIKE A SHIP*

{545} SEVEN DEADLY SINS

{546} SHE'S MY BABY

{547} WHERE WERE YOU LAST NIGHT?

{548} NEW BLUE MOON

{549} WILBURY TWIST

{550} POOR HOUSE

{551} COOL, DRY PLACE

{552} YOU TOOK MY BREATH AWAY

Published lyrics: Words Fill My Head.

Known studio recordings: Camp Wilbury, Bel Air, L.A., April 27–May 15, 1990 [TW3, except *: TWC].

In recent years, Dylan has indulged in a little mischievous myth-making when talking about how he ended up recording *under the red sky* and *Volume Three* so close together. In 2001, he told Mikal Gilmore that he "would leave the Wilburys [sessions] and go down to Sunset Sound and record *under the red sky* simultaneously, all within a set schedule . . . And then both records . . . I'd just leave them hanging and see the finished product later." Warming to his theme, he told Jonathan Lethem five years on, "I worked with George [Harrison] and Jeff [Lynne] during the day—everything had to be done in one day, the track and the song had to be written in one day, and then I'd go down and see Don Was, and I felt like I was walking into a *wall.*"

In fact, the basic-track sessions for *red sky* were done and dusted by mid-March, whereas work on the Wilburys' next instalment did not begin until April 27 (although the reconstituted quartet apparently convened their first informal meeting on March 26). So although the Lethem quote contains a scintilla of truth—he *was* going down to see Was during the recording of the Wilburys' second album, as Was spent at least nine evenings working on overdubs for this all-original album—it is disingenuously expressed.[36] Even the vocal overdubs Dylan imposed predate the Wilburys sessions by at least a week, and it was Dylan's decision to second-guess his lyrics at this stage, casting doubt on his claim that he left both albums "hanging."

It was *Volume Three* he left hanging, just as he had with *Volume One.* Doubtless he expected to be similarly pleased with what Lynne and Harrison ended up producing. As with that earlier experiment, Dylan was due back on the road some time soon (May 29, to be exact), and anything he could bring to the project he needed to produce there and then. Indeed, according to close friend George Harrison, he always knew the score, going along with the plan willingly: "I think everyone, particularly Bob, was more willing to do it this time . . . This time we knew what to expect. Bob was keen to do this one. We said we'll get him to put a vocal on everything and decide later where the rest of us should fit in. But once Bob's vocal is there, it's hard to wipe off, he's got such an exceptional voice."

Well, the evidence is against Harrison. Far from finding it "hard to wipe off" Dylan's vocals—which appear to have been applied to just about everything they recorded for *Volume Three*—Lynne and/or Harrison set about removing His Gruffness with something approaching gusto. The survival—and wholesale bootlegging—of a preproduction rough mix of the material they cut this time around demonstrates that of the six songs where Dylan recorded the entire lead vocal (and in all likelihood wrote the bulk of the lyrics), three were heavily Wilburyized after the fact.

"Where Were You Last Night?," "Seven Deadly Sins," and "She's My Baby" had all been (partly) transformed into communal sing-alongs when all the original Dylan vocals needed was a sprinkling of backing vocals, and maybe a solo or three. The problem was that, in the Orbison-less Wilburys, Dylan was not only the preeminent talent, but also the fastest and most productive worker. As the ex-ELO man told *USA Today* on the album's release, "Word-wise, Bob is a great person to have in the group because he comes up with lyrics in amazing speed."

Initially, this may have made him an ideal partner in a project to which the man devoted barely three weeks of his time, but it also made the others look like little more than backing musicians at times. Lynne's solution was to make Dylan's principal contribution seem slighter and the resultant product more egalitarian. (Harrison, who remained on hand throughout the July postproduction work in Surrey, England, was presumably complicit.) They even omitted one of the best things recorded at the sessions—"Like a Ship"—presumably because it was one too many Dylan songs. It can't have been removed because of any concern about its merit, considering that dregs like "Wilbury Twist" and "New Blue Moon" made the thirty-five-minute album.

The song in question was finally released on the 2007 Deluxe Wilburys set, but it had been subjected to the same postproduction as other Dylan vocals on *Volume Three*, a Harrison harmony vocal being the least vexing of the impositions. By 2007 the familiar feel of the original rough mix had been known to Beatles and Dylan bootleg collectors for some seventeen years, so the track was little more than a curio (rendered more curious still by its inclusion at the end of *Volume One*). The song was as much Dylan's as the other *Volume One* bonus track was Harrison's ("Maxine"). The lyric comes across as almost all Zimmerman:

> Like a ship on the sea, her love rolls over me [x2]
> Like a weeping willow tree, her love hangs over me [x2]
> Go away, go away, let me be.

It was the injuries done to songs like this that drew Dylan's ire. To Gilmore he stated, "That was when I found I'd really had it" (with making records). It signaled the end for the Wilburys, too. And yet, as Harrison told an enquiring Edna Gundersen, Dylan had originally been *"more* willing to do it this time." What went wrong? Well, firstly, the others seemed almost bereft of ideas. Of the thirteen originals recorded at these sessions, seven appear to be largely or wholly Dylan's work—the aforementioned "Like a Ship," "She's My Baby," "Where Were You Last Night?," "If You Belonged to Me," "Inside Out," "Seven Deadly Sins," and "The Devil's Been Busy"—while the other six provided slim pickings indeed.

On the first six titles listed above, Dylan sings the lead vocal on the rough mix, the first four being formulaic pop songs of the broken-hearted variety. Of this quartet, "She's My Baby" was an especially curious choice for the lead single, having neither a great hook nor a great sound. And the whomping drums and close-miked chorus do the song few favors. The other postings from heartbreak hotel at least hint at some of the good-time feel of the 1988 record, even if Dylan's vocals sound far worse than they did on the last leg on the Never Ending Tour. The best of the bunch—"Like a Ship" excepted—is probably "Inside Out," a song which would have slotted easily enough between the title track and "Unbelievable" on his own fab platter. He demonstrated a real concern for the state of the planet and a future that may never be written:

> Take care when you are breathing,
> Something's funny in the air.
> There's something they're not saying,
> 'Bout what's happening out there . . .

> Look into the future, with your mystic crystal ball,
> See if it ain't yellow, see if it's there at all.

The final Dylanesque contribution, "The Devil's Been Busy," though largely sung by Petty, is another song which lyrically reflected current preoccupations: the personification of that ol' prince of the power of the air; the space program; and man's abuse of the planet, to name but three. All are combined in a classical Dylanesque couplet, "Steaming down the highway with your trucks of toxic waste / Where you gonna hide it? Maybe outer space." Interestingly, it is the one song on the released album to feature more of Dylan's vocals than on the so-called rough mix. And not just more vocals, but more lyrics. The released second bridge, which on the rough mix merely repeats the first, embellishes the self-delusion of the song's target:

> Sometimes they say you're wicked, but you know that can't be bad,
> Sometimes you're better off not knowing, it'll only make you sad.

Evidently, Harrison's claim that they got Dylan "to put a vocal on everything, and [we would then] decide later where the rest of us should fit in," had some basis in fact. It is a shame that they couldn't have found somewhere on the deluxe 2007 reissue (say, on the seventy-five minutes they left unused across the two CDs) to put Dylan's original vocal track for "The Devil's Been Busy." He still manages to leave a little clue that this is his work, referencing "Brownsville Girl" in the one verse he sings on the album: "You're in a western movie, playing a little part." Discounting "Maxine" as wholly Harrison's work, this leaves five songs over which Dylan exercised very little perceptible influence: the one potential ELO outtake ("You Take My Breath Away"), Petty's two picks, "Poor House" and "Cool Dry Place," and a pair of flippant fifties pastiches, "Wilbury Twist" and "New Blue Moon"—to which one imagines everyone contributed the first thought that entered their head, Dylan included, even if that first idea wasn't a doozie. Here's hoping that the "New Blue Moon" bridge, which Dylan sings on both occasions, was one of his, left over from some lost Big Pink reel:

> So many moons have come and gone,
> And none of them were blue,
> Too many times the sun came up,
> But it came up without you.

After all the energy Dylan invested in trying to recapture that 1988 lightning strike, he must have felt the whole exercise to be unrewarding. For sure, he never played any of the songs in performance, even those he could have rightfully (re)claimed. Rather, he returned to the preoccupations he had been working on with Was—before he hit that wall. It would take him a while, but in the end he would give every song on *under the red sky* the live outing it deserved. Meanwhile, he barely acknowledged the existence of *Volume Three*, and within a few years it was quietly deleted from the Warners catalog, awaiting its 2007 excavation, itself another wasted opportunity.

{553} STEEL BARS

Published lyric: In His Own Words 3.

> He's kind of hungry to get back out there and wants to work with a few contemporary hit songwriters. Someone who works [for] Dylan called me up and said, "Bob Dylan would like to write with you." I was awed.

I told him, "I don't even know how I could write a lyric when working with you . . . I'm too intimidated." But then we started messing around with some chords and wrote "Steel Bars," a song about obsession. It took two sessions to write. —Michael Bolton, April 1991

Everything went from bad to worst in the winter of 1991, the Never Ending Tour skidding off the rails while Dylan himself fell off the wagon. But the low spot of a very bleak midwinter was surely the couple of afternoons he wasted in the company of a songwriter who made Barry McGuire look cutting-edge. It wouldn't take an archcynic like myself to suspect that this was a meeting hatched more by managers than by the artists concerned. Bolton acquired a certain kudos by writing a song with someone for whom he was not fit to sharpen pencils, and Dylan gained a small but lucrative stake in the Bolton stock, a gilt-edged security in the world of popular songwriting (thus demonstrating the truth of the maxim, "No one ever lost money underestimating the tastes of the public"). Of the actual result, the least said the better, though a quartet of lines in the chorus use two of Dylan's favorite rhymes, probably revealing the man's handiwork, albeit while on cruise control:

> I'm bound forever, till the end of time,
> Steel bars wrapped around this heart of mine.
> Trying hard to recognize,
> See the face behind the eyes.

{554} WELL, WELL, WELL

{555} HOWLIN' AT YOUR WINDOW

{556} TRAGEDY OF THE TRADE

{557} TIME TO END THIS MASQUERADE

Known studio recording [#557]: The Church, London, November 22, 1985 [basic track].

#556–7 Issued on Backroom Blood *(May 7, 1996)—Gerry Goffin. #556 cowritten with Goffin; #557 cowritten with Goffin and Barry Goldberg.*

The process of writing music is inspiration, receiving. An important thing is the environment and songs [then] quietly come to me. If anything disturbs that situation the songs don't come to me, they go somewhere else. Then the songs die. —Dylan, to Akihiko Yamamoto, February 1994

If Michael Bolton was hardly the kind of inspirational figure who might trigger a new spurt of songwriting from the history man, he was not the only cocomposer to whom Dylan placed a call while his own "receiver" was broken. At some juncture, he offered Carole King's ex, Gerry Goffin, a hand writing some songs for Goffin's first solo album in twenty-two years. Two of these appeared on the halfway decent *Backroom Blood* in 1996. Their association dated back to at least 1994, both songs being copyrighted initially in March 1995, the latter under its full title, "Time to End This Masquerade," not the one-word title given to it on the album.

One imagines the collaboration had its own therapeutic value for both these old hands, who had a great deal of fun writing these two sarcastic slices of life on the wrong side of the tracks (and fifty). "Time to End This Masquerade," which Dylan also coproduced, is a hoot and a half. The coproduction credit he received turns out to be fully warranted because underneath the vocal, Wurlitzer, etc., lies a basic track from the same 1985 London session at which he once recorded "Under Your Spell," as can clearly be heard on the fade-out. As the other accoutrements fade away, one can hear the same thudding track partly broadcast on *The Whistle Test* a decade earlier, then called simply "Pipe Organ Ska."

Here it becomes a great little polka tune, made to sound like the carnival carousel just curdled. Some of the lines—"Well, life was sweet till they called the heat / The county jail has just reserved a two-room suite" for two—are laugh-out-loud funny. And when Goffin sings "I forgot to milk the cow, but I don't wanna do it now / I'd like to sleep for a hundred years, till this old world just disappears," the world-weariness may be affected, but it is also affecting. And how about this for eloquently expressing how Dylan probably feels after a particularly bad show on a winter's day in Davenport, Iowa:

> I'm at a loss to entertain
> You see, the cells are paralyzed inside my brain,
> I bid adieu to all of you,
> I think it's time to end this masquerade.

"Tragedy of the Trade" may be more run-of-the-mill doom-mongering, but as another disquisition on a world gone wrong, it has its moments. The one which provides the title for Goffin's album sure sounds like a Dylan lyric: "The world's been run with backroom blood, long before the time of the flood / And it's you who are betrayed [by] the tragedy of the trade." Other couplets also jump out ("If you still have innocence, better lock it in a vault / Once it was a virtue, but now it's a fault"). Sadly, the song is let down by a nondescript arrangement (possibly coauthor Barry Goldberg's contribution) and Goffin's vocals. Though he is putting his whole soul into the song, the guy just can't sing. There's a reason why he was part of a great songwriting team, not fronting a shit-hot band—he makes Tom Waits sound like Caruso.

Two other songs were also copyrighted by Dylan's office during this extended period in the creative wilderness. "Well, Well, Well" was a song cowritten with Danny O'Keefe, which was eventually recorded for Maria Muldaur's 1996 album, *Fanning the Flames*. The first documented performance, though, was by ex-Eagle Don Henley, in September 1993, so the song dates from a similar period to the two Goffin collaborations. "Howlin' at Your Window" was a song he cocomposed in 1993, with female Texan country artist Jude Johnstone, presumably while Dylan was in Austin filming a TV special for Willie Nelson's sixtieth birthday at the end of April. Though demoed by Johnstone at the time, and copyrighted in 2005, the song remains unreleased.

But times weren't what they used to be, and Dylan knew it. Though he spent most of the first half of the nineties ducking interviewers, on those rare occasions when he was tracked down and the tape recorder was running, he admitted he had stopped forcing the issue when it came to songwriting. Even when the performance artist came back off the ropes swinging, as he did in the fall of 1991, he would tell Robert Hilburn: "Part of the secret of being a songwriter is to have an audacious attitude. There was a time when the songs would come three or four at the same time, but those days are long gone." Four months later, he gave an equally dismal account of the current state of creative affairs to Australian journalist Stuart Coupe, revealing how the songs come "natural if they come at all . . . When it's not coming, there's really no inclination on my part to make it happen."

That disinclination had, by the spring of 1992, ossified into full-on writer's block. What finally seems to have convinced him to call up his muse was another abortive attempt at collaborating his way out of this hole. In the summer of 1995, in the wake of Jerry Garcia's wake, Dylan spent a few days at the home of Robert Hunter, a lyricist whose songs had featured often enough on the Never Ending Tour. One must presume that any results more closely resembled "Ugliest Girl in the World" than "Friend of the Devil," "Black Muddy River," and "West L.A. Fadeaway"—all Hunter songs he covered in the post–*red sky* years—because nothing was ever used or copyrighted by either party. However, it reminded him that no one did it quite like him and when, the following winter, his muse finally returned from her lengthy travels, he stopped looking for outside help and let her songs come again . . .

1996–9

{ Time Out of Mind }

As of September 1996, it had been six long years since Dylan released an album of original songs. Even the hints of new songs in interviews and collaborations on others' records had ceased. It seemed like this bout of amnesia had settled in for good. In my own review of Dylan's recording career, published the previous fall, I suggested at book's end that "the commitment required to work on an album of original songs, to bend and twist them to his peculiar vision, in a modern studio, with a band of unfamiliar musicians, is such that only a truly exceptional collection of new songs . . . is likely to drive his weary bones into those narrow confines once more."

Dylan would only confirm he had begun to feel this way some six years later, speaking of these troubled times to Mikal Gilmore: "I didn't feel the need to announce that . . . I'd really had my fill, . . . but I had come to that conclusion. I didn't care to record no more . . . But then you go out and play live shows, and you do get thoughts, and you do get an inspiration here and there. So I just reluctantly started writing things down." By the summer of 1996, he wanted to try some ideas out with his now-settled touring band. But he was still a way off having an album. What began in earnest with demo sessions at Lanois's studio in Oxnard, California, in September 1996 would not be completed until late March 1997, when Dylan added some last-minute vocal overdubs to the album he ended up largely recording in a monthlong stint at Florida's fabled Criteria Studios at the turn of the year.

When the results were released the following September, the evidence suggested he had fallen short of delivering that "truly exceptional collection *of new songs."* Time Out of Mind *merely hinted at such a collection. But then, as one key musical collaborator on the album (Duke Robillard) observed at the time of its release, "I'm told that Dylan always leaves his best song off the album." Already, there were whispers he had done the same here. Two songs in particular—"Mississippi" and "The Girl from the Red River Shore"—eulogized by the session musicians, were cut at the last minute to fit an overlong and over-padded record onto a single CD. It would take another eleven years—with the release of* Tell Tale Signs (The Bootleg Series Vol. 8)—*before Dylan OK'd the release of fulsome evidence that he had had that "truly exceptional collection of new songs" all along . . .*

{558} DIRT ROAD BLUES

Published lyric/s: Lyrics 04.

Known studio recordings: Jam session, ?Malibu, CA, August–September 1996; Real Music Studios, Oxnard, CA, September–October 1996; Criteria Studios, Miami, FL, January 20, 1997 [vcl—March 14, 1997] [TOOM].

> The blues stems from the countryside, from the cotton fields in the south. And they dragged it to the big cities and charged it with electricity. Today this has turned into electronics. One does not perceive that, out there, there is a person that breathes, or that there is still a heart out there. And the more people get away from this, the less they are connected with what I call the blues. —Dylan, to *Der Spiegel*, 1997

"Dirt Road Blues," the second track on Dylan's 1997 album and the only *Time Out of Mind* song never featured in the live set, seems on the face of it an incongruous starting point for such an eagerly awaited set. And yet its appearance at every stage of the six-month-plus production process indicates that Dylan was absolutely determined to use the song, maybe to make a point to producer Daniel Lanois, if not to his audience: this is what I really had in mind before things got immersed in "the muck and the mire of this syrupy mix" (guitarist Jim Dickinson's acute portrayal of the remaining released results).

He insisted on including "Dirt Road Blues" even though by sessions' end it stuck out like a swollen opposable digit, *Dylan* deciding in this one instance to use digital technology to some purpose other than to swamp the musicality of the moment. As Daniel Lanois admitted to the *Irish Times* on the album's release, "With 'Dirt Road Blues,' he made me pull out the original cassette, sample sixteen bars and we all played over that." That original cassette was not made at the Miami sessions, but *before* the sessions, and it was not the band Lanois and Dylan assembled. Rather it involved some hardy musicians with whom Dylan had been plying his trade for the past four years.

Playing on that "original cassette" was drummer Winston Watson, who had been the mainstay of Dylan's rhythm section between September 1992, when he took over the slot from old friend Charlie Quintana, and August 1996, when he played his final shows at the L.A. House of the Blues. And though Watson's enthusiasm sometimes got the better of him (and ultimately required a plastic screen to be erected around his kit, so hard did he hit those skins), he had a way of playing unselfconsciously that his boss genuinely liked. And there was something about that original cassette recording that all the crack musicians at Criteria could not replicate.

As Dylan informed his favorite Gilmore brother, "We worked with a track that I had done at a sound check once in some hall. The assembled group of musicians . . . just couldn't get it, so I said, 'Just use that original track, and I'll sing over it.' It was just some old blues song I always wanted to use, and I felt that once I was able to control it, I could've written about anything with it." Erecting a classic smoke screen, Dylan purports to be talking about the *Time Out of Mind* recording of "Highlands." But "Highlands" was not recorded that way. It was "Dirt Road Blues" that was—as the track sheet confirms.

That track sheet—an oddball incursion within the tantalizing assemblage of tape boxes and track sheets reproduced in the *Tell Tale Signs* booklet[37]—reveals that this is one instance where Dylan sang over a rehearsal take, cryptically listed as "DAT of Dirt Road." So, not quite a cassette of some sound check, but rather a two-track digital audio tape of a jam session at which Dylan tried out musical ideas with some familiar compadres. Jim Dickinson confirms that "before the trio thing [at Oxnard] . . . they tried to do a just-sit-around-and-strum kind of thing," suggesting that he probably got to hear more of this DAT session than this single track.

Though Lanois may not have been party to the impromptu sessions, which presumably took place shortly before Watson handed in his splintered sticks, it was he who taught Dylan the virtues of documenting any and all ideas in this way, having run an open mike DAT at the *Oh Mercy* sessions. But the producer still envisaged building "Dirt Road Blues" up from that buskin' blues. Using the remaining twenty-two tracks to gerrymander a more grandiose statement, he added "group drummers," "clappers," bass, Vox organ, and a series of vocal overdubs to the song at Criteria. (The song had already been worked on at Lanois's own Californian studio the previous fall. The track sheet includes a "BD Vocal—Oxnard.")

Assuming previous patterns played out again, the final vocal—which was not recorded until mid-March 1997, when the album was in post-production—was likely lyrically different from the vocal recorded five months earlier in Oxnard. By March, Dylan knew he was making an album out of ideas that had lingered "time out of mind," and may well have tailored the lyric to fit the tenor of the album. Yet, in its finished form, it is largely free of lines hijacked from the traditional lexicon—which is all the more surprising given the song's title, which self-consciously name-checks recordings by two figures whose ghosts bestride Dylan's entire post-*TOOM* output: Charlie Patton and Arthur "Big Boy" Crudup.

Patton was another of those mythical Mississippi bluesmen who said almost everything worth saying in two sets of sessions (in his case, in the years 1929–30), before fading into obscurity and a premature death (in 1934). Among those classic 1929 tracks was one called "Down the Dirt Road Blues," promoted by his record label with a picture of a man and a donkey sharing hangdog expressions, traipsing down a dirt track. And Patton, in particular, seems to have been increasingly on Dylan's mind. Not only did he claim that he wrote "Highlands" around "the guitar run off an old Charlie Patton record"—though the evidence remains against him—but he would dedicate a song on his next album to the mysterious bluesman ("High Water").

Rather than merely reproducing a series of Patton guitar runs, Dylan was hoping to find a way of replicating the feel of those old-timey recordings with modern technology. And he somehow thought musical magpie Lanois might be the ideal little helper, so he steered him in the direction of the primitive originals. According to Lanois, he made himself listen "to a lot of old records Bob recommended—Charlie Patton, dusty old rock 'n' roll, blues—Tony [Mangurian] and I played along to those, then I built loops of what we did . . . [and] brought these loops to Bob." Sure sounds like a complicated way of lifting something already in the public domain.

Another recording that Dylan may have given Lanois to hear was Arthur Crudup's "Dirt Road Blues," a 1945 prototype for his world-changing 1946 recording of "That's Alright Mama" and one of those "old records from the 1950s [sic]" that Lanois was told to investigate because "Bob really likes [them] . . . . They had a natural depth of field . . . [so] you get the sense that somebody is in the front singing, a couple of other people are further behind and somebody else is way in the back of the room." In the case of "Dirt Road Blues," though, it was Dylan's DAT that they built upon, not its mythopoeic source.

The results would have had Patton and Crudup spinning in their cotton-pickin' graves. But if the recording lacked the feel of those archetypal recordings that set Dylan atwitter, he made a better fist of the lyric. Even if he probably intended to do another "You Wanna Ramble' / "Shake" rejig, the 1997 "Dirt Road Blues" goes off at the kind of tangent from tradition he had made a trademark decades before reimmersing himself in the "only true valid death you can feel today" with the two albums of traditional covers he made with Debbie Gold in 1992–3.

Though the *Time Out of Mind* song has a few lines coopted from that ol' lyrical lexicon (and at least one song title, Mose Allison's "One Room Country Shack"), he has not yet started slavishly sticking to(gether) the original sources. Thus, a line like "Rolling through the rain and hail, looking for the sunny side of love" manages to connect Robert Johnson's "Hellhound on My Trail" and the Carter Family's "Keep On the Sunny Side," without suggesting someone compensating for a paucity of imagination. If Dylan had stuck to this approach throughout the album, or held over "Dirt Road Blues" for his next album, à la "Mississippi," it may have found a setting where it could shine. As it is, it became an oddity *and* a memento of what might have been.

{559} CAN'T WAIT

Published lyric/s: Lyrics 04; *[Alt takes x2]* Words Fill My Head
*Known studio recordings: Jam session, ?Malibu, CA, August–September 1996;
Real Music Studios, Oxnard, CA, September–October 1996 [TTS 1]; Criteria
Studios, Miami, FL, January 21, 1997 [TTS 3]; January 1997 [TOOM].*
*First known performance: Mississippi State University, Starkville, MS, October
24, 1997.*

> [*Time Out of Mind*] is the first album I've done in a while where I've protected
> the songs for a long time. —Dylan, to Nick Krewen, August 1997

Aside from "Dirt Road Blues," the only other song Watson could recall
working on at the sit 'n' strum session was "Can't Wait." ("Highlands"
may also have been worked on, too, as Dylan implies—if so, the results
were *not* used as the basis for the released recording.) Taking the *Time
Out of Mind* versions at "white face value," this was hardly an auspicious
start to such an eagerly awaited set of songs. However, the 2008 release
of *Tell Tale Signs (The Bootleg Series Vol. 8)* reveals "Can't Wait' to be a
song only captured on CD after it had (long) exceeded its "best by" date.
On this expansive overview of the "detritus" from Dylan's 1989–2006
output, fans were given two alternate visions of the song, both radically
different from—and markedly superior to—the one on the 1997 album.
The first came from the fall 1996 Oxnard sessions, the second from
Criteria, at a time when the song was already threatening to defeat the
man (the latter is dubbed "psychedelic mix" in the *TTS* notes).

The release of these two highly revealing recordings, coinciding as
they did with detailed accounts of these sessions by a number of participants (in the November 2008 issue of *Uncut* and its online spin-off), made
it abundantly clear it was this song—along with "Mississippi"—that
provided the real battleground for a conflict between Lanois and Dylan,
which on one occasion even spilled over into the parking lot. To the
victor would go the credit and/or blame for the new album's identity. In
this instance, it was Dylan who made the wrong artistic call, misreading
the producer's motives for pushing the singer to return to the version cut
at Oxnard. Indeed, it would appear that he had developed a complete
mental block regarding that material. According to the ever forthright

Jim Dickinson, "Dylan didn't have *anything* favorable to say about the earlier versions of the songs."

So what exactly was Dylan's problem with the Oxnard arrangement of "Can't Wait"? According to engineer Mark Howard, Dickinson himself could have been the problem: "We had recorded three other versions of 'Can't Wait' . . . One . . . called 'Ragdoll,' another . . . named 'The psychedelic version,' and so on—and those were all us trying to get back to that original [Oxnard] version. But Dylan wouldn't go back to the piano, because we had Dickinson there and Bob wanted his vibe on it." Having point-blank refused to go back to the Oxnard version, he instead tried to replicate its essential vibe in this Floridian setting. Something about those sessions had rubbed him the wrong way, resulting in the decisive move to Criteria, as Howard recalls:

> We're all ready to do [the album with this] computer-based stuff, and one day Bob comes in, sits at the piano, and plays this song, "Can't Wait." And this is a *gospel* version. Tony starts playing this real sexy groove with him, and Bob is hammering out this gospel piano and really singing. The hair on my arms went up. It was stunning. Luckily, I was recording. We were thinking, "If this is going to be anything like this, this record is going to be unbelievable." . . . Then, just as we're all set to make the record in Oxnard, Bob says, "I can't work this close to home. I wanna do it in Miami."

The possibility of him recording at Criteria had been reported in the music press as far back as 1971 (having been Clapton's studio of choice for the *Layla* album). Lanois, who also felt the Oxnard versions—especially "Can't Wait"—were heading in the right direction, lamented Dylan's decision to dispense with several weeks of productive work. For him, those weeks had been a special time:

> I was renting a theater at the time in a place called Oxnard. I had my shop set up there for a while. So Bob Dylan would roll down to the teatro . . . That's where we did the demos for *Time Out of Mind*, and out of that [series of] demo session[s] came some lovely things, including that version of "I Can't Wait," which I feel has a lot of thunder in it. It's very stripped down 'cause it's piano—Bob on my lovely turn of the century Steinway . . . me on my goldtop 1956 Les Paul, through a Vox, and Pretty Tony on the drums."

It may well have been this very recording that convinced Dylan to go in a different direction. The spontaneity of that moment when he suggests they try it in the key of B-flat and begins plonking away at the piano, leaving Mangurian to pick up the beat, went against the whole idea of drum and guitar loops. When the vocal plays off the piano and caresses the words, there are whole layers of feeling that the grind of the road had still to sandpaper away.

The vocal approach on the Oxnard "Can't Wait" is certainly quite different from the one Dylan adopted at Criteria. As Jim Dickinson realized, "All the songs [recorded in Miami] are . . . all low in his vocal register. [Whereas,] apparently, . . . when they were [at Oxnard] doing the trio, or when he was just playing acoustic guitar, he had some of the songs pitched in a higher register." Nothing on the album itself captures the same fragile frisson he injects into the Oxnard couplet "Well, my back is to the sun because the light is too intense / I can see what everybody in the world is up against," lines so precise in their oppressiveness that Dylan hung onto them for a further five years before writing an entire song around them ("Sugar Baby").

As soon as he got to Miami, "Can't Wait" suffered from the pencil in his hand, as he again went to work on this spidery lyric. Dickinson was surprised when Dylan told him "he'd been working on some of the songs five or six years," as he witnessed the wordsmith "lean over this steamer chest and work on his lyrics. With a pencil—because he was erasing stuff." In this instance, he was in "Born in Time" mode, erasing the hurt and replacing it with a rank Xerox. The withering self-analysis of "I been drinking forbidden juices / I been living on lame excuses" has been sold to the junkman, leaving him mystified by how everything went down:

> Well, your loveliness has wounded me, I'm reeling from the blow
> I wish I knew what it was keeps me loving you so.

In Oxnard, he flagellates himself for his former behavior, finding that even a bout of onanism can't shake her from his mind ("I can't wait, waiting just making me go blind / Do you ever lay awake at night, your face turned to the wall / Drowning in your thoughtlessness, and cut off from it all?").

{ Still on the Road }

By the time he arrives in Miami, he has decided it is she who needs the lesson in humility: "I can't wait for you to walk the line / You ever feel just like your brain been bolted to the wall / That you're drowning in your thoughtlessness and cut off from it all?" What began as a lyric about desperately waiting has become a bad-tempered, clock-watching song of complaynt. If the edge of desperation is still there on the painfully drawn-out "psychedelic mix" on disk three of *Tell Tale Signs*, the version he finally went with on *Time Out of Mind* makes a pig's ear out of a prize-winning sow.

At least Dylan managed to hint at what he had been reaching for when he turned the temperature back up during live performances that autumn. Having been dismissed as a lesser song by us fans/critics—ignorant of how it had paled in the process—it roared out its credentials in performance as Dylan raised his game, and the register he sang the song in, to beat his breast and proclaim his angst. But no sooner had he stripped all those Lanois layers away than he decided it worked best as a rave-up in the "so long, good luck, and good-bye" mold. One hundred and sixty-five live performances later, it looked as if he had finally accepted he'd been making lame excuses for not sticking at it.

{560} MISSISSIPPI

Published lyric/s: Lyrics 04; *[Alt take]* Words Fill My Head.
Known studio recordings: Real Music Studios, Oxnard, CA, September–October 1996 [TTS 3]; Criteria Studios, Miami, FL, January 17, 1997 [TTS 1&2]; Sony Studios, NYC, May 21, 2001—4 takes [L+T—tk. 4].
First known performance: Jackson County Fairgrounds, OR, October 9, 2001.

I've been criticized for not putting my best songs on certain albums, but it is because I consider that the song isn't ready yet. It's not been recorded right . . . I turn my back and move on to something else . . . We recut the song "Mississippi" [for *"Love and Theft"*]. We had [done] that on the *Time Out of Mind* [sessions]. It wasn't recorded very well but thank God, it never got out, so we recorded it again. But something like that would never have happened ten years ago. You'd have probably all heard the

By postponing the release of "Mississippi" to 2001's *Love and Theft*," Dylan continued his habit of omitting key songs from released artifacts, a practice which had adversely affected almost every all-original long-player since 1981's *Shot of Love*. If neither "Dirt Road Blues" nor "Can't Wait" could have been said to *define* the album on which they both appear, the inclusion of "Mississippi" would have explicated a working method which unblocked a seven-year logjam of inspiration.

Having spent a great deal of his downtime on and off tour reimmersing himself in the stream of tradition and/or compulsively reworking old blues riffs on the nearest guitar (or piano), Dylan reverted to a methodology he had not really attempted since he was a callow youth imbued with the big city blues: take the kernel of a traditional song and make a new song out of it. Of course, he was an immeasurably more knowledgeable, skilled songwriter than when he was just a po' boy scuffling through the Village. He was hardly going to merely invert a song like "This Train" so it cataloged those hellbound rather than those bound for glory—though that *is* pretty much what he did with "Dirt Road Blues."

Such songs were no longer just a benchmark, they were the backdrop to all the songs to come, a hook on which to hang an idea, as if it were the problem of finding an "original" framework that had been at the root of his recent writer's block. Because, as recently as May 1995, he had told the ever-curious Edna Gundersen, "I get thoughts during the day that I just can't get to. I'll write a verse down and never complete it. It's hard to be vigilant over the whole thing . . . If your mind is intellectually in the way, it will stop you. You've got to program your brain not to think too much."

Writing self-consciously in the traditional idiom—a once common ruse for favorites of Dylan's like Burns, Coleridge, and Keats—was for him a way of deprogramming his brain. Allowing some fragment of Elizabeth Cotton or Sarah Ogan Gunning left behind to trigger something he could call his own is what Fred Neil had done when he rewrote Cotton's "Shake Sugaree" as "I've Got a Secret (Didn't We Shake Sugaree)" on his eponymous 1967 LP, retaining the evocative lines "Didn't I shake sugaree /

Everything I got is done and pawned." I doubt it is a coincidence that Dylan began performing Neil's song in the summer of 1996, playing it for the TV cameras at a House of Blues show in early August, just before the band took a break and he started demoing his new album.

In the case of "Mississippi," Dylan's starting point was an old prison holler, "Rosie," collected by John and Alan Lomax in the early thirties and published in their seminal 1934 anthology, *American Ballads & Folk Songs*. According to the Lomaxes' introduction, "This song, shouted out all day long under the 'hot boiling sun' of Parchman, Mississippi, [was] filled full of a fierce and bitter despair." Composed in performance by the prisoners who improvised variations of commonplace couplets, it was set to a communal chorus, which ran thus: "Ain' but de one thing I done wrong [x3] / Stayed in Miss'ippi jes' a day too long / Day too long, Lawdy, day too long, / Stayed in Miss'ippi jes' a day too long, / Oh Rosie, Oh Rosie, Oh Lawd, gal."

It was just such an expression of "fierce and bitter despair" which Dylan set out to capture in his own account of someone "all boxed in, nowhere to escape." At this juncture he is still inclined to tip a wink to his source in the working title, "Stayed in Mississippi," and in a couplet of his own, "I was thinking about the things that Rosie said / I was dreaming I was sleeping in Rosie's bed," which is exactly the kind of couplet a chain-gang-bound convict might have sung when fixating on a Rosie who served as "the prison counterpart of Mademoiselle from Armentières . . . during the last war." In Dylan's song, the narrator has already served his time but, faced with trying to keep his head above water, can't help but recall the old chain-gang holler and his old partners in crime:

> Well my ship's been split to splinters and it's sinking fast,
> I'm drowning in the poison, got no future, got no past,
> But my heart is not weary, it's light and it's free,
> I got nothing but affection for those who have sailed with me.

Maybe it's me, but the opening reminds me of "The House Carpenter" aka "The Daemon Lover," which in Sir Walter Scott's memorable version ends with the devil striking "the tapmast wi' his hand, the foremast wi' his knee / And he brak that gallant ship in twain, and sank her in the sea." Dylan even gave "Mississippi" its own supernatural dimension in its earliest studio guise—the Oxnard version on disk three of *Tell Tale Signs*—"Winter goes into summer, summer goes into fall / I look into the mirror, don't see anything at all."

The fatalism in the final verse of "Mississippi" is, if anything, even more profound than in that old, old song—"The emptiness is endless, cold as the clay" (and what could be more "trad." than the latter expression). Thus the song ends with him staring his own mortality in the face. Not that Dylan saw it that way, insisting to Gilmore that reviewers and critics were looking at things the wrong way round: "People say the record deals with . . . *my* mortality . . . Well, it *doesn't* deal with my mortality. It maybe just deals with mortality in general . . . But I didn't see any one critic say, 'It deals with my mortality'—you know, his *own* . . . like whoever's writing about the record has got eternal life, and the singer doesn't."

As it happens, "Mississippi" didn't feature on the record coeval with its composition, even as it cast a shadow over it. Dylan had decided that the song was "not ready yet." But it had made its presence felt at every turn, beginning at Oxnard where Lanois used it as a vehicle for his own blinkered ideas about how the album should sound, which, according to Mark Howard, was drum "loop-based, and [then] playing on top of them . . . The original idea was we'd do all this cut-and-paste."

Dylan was never entirely sold on the idea, as became apparent the minute he moved the sessions to Miami, using just four of the rhythm tracks from Oxnard—all overdubbed extensively at Criteria—on the finished album.[38] And yet he refrained from venting his true feelings regarding Lanois's acoustic theories until 2001, during a highly uncharacteristic outburst to *Rolling Stone*'s David Fricke, assigned to write a news story about *Time Out of Mind's* successor:

["Mississippi'] was pretty much laid out intact melodically, lyrically and structurally, but Lanois didn't see it. Thought it was pedestrian. Took it down the Afro-poly-rhythm route—multi-rhythm drumming, that sort of thing. Poly-rhythm has its place, but it doesn't work for knifelike lyrics trying to convey majesty and heroism. Maybe we had worked too hard on other things—I can't remember—but . . . things got contentious once in the parking lot. He tried to convince me that the song had to be "sexy, sexy and more sexy." I know about sexy, too . . . I tried to explain that the song had more to do with the Declaration of Independence, the Constitution and the Bill of Rights than witch doctors, and just couldn't be thought of as some kind of ideological voodoo thing. But he had his own way of looking at things, and in the end I had to reject this because I thought too highly of the expressive meaning behind the lyrics to bury them in some steamy cauldron of drum-theory.

Taken in tandem with his comments at the Rome press conference a few weeks later (see heading), it is clear Dylan had not been prepared to have this particular song put through Lanois's patented threshing machine—he "thought too highly of the expressive meaning behind the lyrics." And this time he held firm. The lyric, even on the Oxnard version, is essentially the same as the two Criteria takes on *Tell Tale Signs* and the one on *"Love and Theft,"* save for a quite different opening verse—"I'm standing in the shadows with an aching heart / I'm looking at the world tear itself apart / Minutes turn to hours, hours turn to days / I'm still loving you in a million ways."

So, lyrically at least, the song was already "pretty much laid out" by the time he landed in Miami. Structurally, though, he was still obliged to fight Lanois all the way—and then some. As Jim Dickinson recalls, "'Mississippi' . . . represented the most conflict in the studio between Dylan and Lanois . . . There was a cut of 'Mississippi' that was very swampy . . . It just wasn't the direction Dylan wanted to go. The two of them really got into it over that one." This "swampy" version is probably the one that opens *Tell Tale Signs*. Set to slow simmer for seven whole minutes, it never quite catches fire. Not that it needed to. The sense of living life on the brink of catastrophe is what makes the song. This *TTS* version—which Larry Sloman's album notes suggest was "probably the first recorded"—is nothing of the sort. It does, however, sound like an attempt to get back to that Oxnard prototype, relying on the sparsest of settings to convey true turmoil.

Whether it came before or after the version on disk two, with its more full-blown arrangement, is mere conjecture. The track sheet reproduced in the *TTS* booklet suggests one or more of them was recorded on January 17, though there were at least two sets of over-dubs the following week at Criteria, suggesting that Dylan and Lanois never did get to agree on the right setting. Nor could Lanois get the musicians to cooperate. After cutting a version of the song with David Kempner on drums early in the Criteria sessions, he called Kempner up and told him, "You can't play pedestrian, we gotta play strange." Since Kempner had been playing with Dylan for the past three months, and was just about done with his contribution to the album, he wasn't about to second-guess his boss.

It proved a smart move. Kempner stuck around long enough to complete the track to Dylan's satisfaction, being at the drum kit four years later at the New York *"Love and Theft"* sessions when Dylan was once again nudged in the direction of "Mississippi." And this time the song stuck. According to Kempner, the sessions were just about done and dusted—a fact confirmed by the tape logs—when "a friend of Bob's passed him a note, and he said, oh, yeah, I forgot about this: 'Mississippi.'" The friend was probably Jeff Rosen, acting as a kind of executive producer to proceedings, and a long-standing advocate of the song (hence, the three versions on *Tell Tale Signs*).

Having allowed Sheryl Crow to release her version of the song ahead of his, Dylan decided it was high time he reclaimed it. The new arrangement prompted him to claim to Fricke that "on the [*"Love and Theft"*] performance, the bass is playing a triplet beat, and that adds up to all the multirhythm you need, even in a slow tempo song." What he no longer had was a voice he could command at will. The *"Love and Theft"* version, and the live counterparts he introduced in 2001, benefit from an arrangement which left any dirge-like element in the dust. But that vocal timbre had not so much diminished as disappeared beneath its crag-like remains. "Mississippi" had stayed in his closet half a decade too long.

561} HIGHLANDS

Published lyric/s: Lyrics 04.

Known studio recordings: Real Music Studios, Oxnard, CA, September–October 1996; Criteria Studios, Miami, FL, January 1997 [TOOM].

First known performance: Coors Amphitheater, Chula Vista, CA, June 25, 1999.

I had the guitar run off an old Charlie Patton record for years and always wanted to do something with that. I was sitting around . . . in some unthinkable trench somewhere, with that sound in my mind and the dichotomy of the highlands . . . The riff was just going repeatedly, hypnotically in my head, then the words eventually come along . . . Every song on the album came that way. —Dylan, to Robert Hilburn, December 1997.

Yup, here goes another of Bob's bum steers. A determined trawl through all the Patton recordings available to Dylan in 1996 failed to yield any guitar run that even resembles "Highlands." The real "dichotomy of the highlands" for him is what it was for Robert Burns, two centuries earlier—the key that flicked the latch. What he does with it is intended to make it his own. Or, as he told a 2001 press conference, "I'm using musical structures, [whether] 12-bar blues or Elizabethan ballads, that I change or dismantle from the inside. I use them as a blueprint, as departure points."

His description of the "Highlands" composition is him readopting that well-tailored disguise, the unconscious artist. But it requires us to believe that by 1996 he still had not learned to do *self*-consciously what he used to do (un)consciously. It also requires us to assume that his appropriation of Burns is aesthetically different from his appropriation of Lomax's prison holler for "Mississippi"—oh, and that it is mere coincidence the album title uses the exact same phrase Scotland's most famous appropriator of tradition had used, three centuries earlier, to describe the kind of songs the poet in question used "as a blueprint, as departure points."

That appropriator was a popular poet, too. His name was Allan Ramsay. In 1725—hard on the heels of editing the most important sixteenth-century manuscript of popular Scottish poetry—Ramsay published a two-volume set of largely Scottish songs, *The Tea-Table Miscellany*, purporting to be "A Collection of Choice Songs, Scots and English." And in his introduction, he explained how it largely comprised "such old verses as have been done *time out of mind*" (my italics), save for "above sixty" songs that Ramsay rewrote according to his own particular brief, having been "well assured how acceptable new words to known good tunes would prove." Ramsay thus set a fashion for reforging tradition that seventy years later was adopted by Robert Burns, and 270 years later, Dylan. Hence, methinks, the title of Dylan's 1997 collection.

If Dylan had indeed been reading his Ramsay—and his Burns—it seems unlikely he did not learn that the Burns song "My Heart's in the Highlands"—the "departure point" for his own set of words—was itself a recrafting of a traditional song, known either as the "The Strong Walls of Derry" or "Bonny Portmore." Burns himself, in a friend's annotated copy of James Johnson's *Scots Musical Museum* (in which his rewrite first appeared), admitted that "the first half-stanza of this song is old; the rest is mine." The "lost" traditional original was not itself published in book form until thirty years after Burns's death (in Peter Buchan's *Ancient Ballads & Songs*). Burns's own take on tradition almost succeeded in overwriting the original—as some of Ramsay's rewrites already had, and Burns's own "Auld Lang Syne" was destined to do. The one verse both shared was the starting point for Dylan, too:

> My heart's in the Highlands, my heart is not here,
> My heart's in the Highlands a-chasing the deer;
> A-chasing the wild deer, and catching the roe,
> My heart's in the Highlands, wherever I go.

Our modern folksinger fancifully imagined he might find Robin Hood there, as well:

> With the twang of the arrow and the snap of the bow,
> My heart's in the Highlands, can't see any other way to go.

Dylan also alludes to a more ancient Scottish ballad, "The Wind has blown my plaid away," placing his own highlands "over the hill and far away," perhaps the most famous refrain in British folksong. "Highlands" perfectly exemplifies a new modus operandi, stitching together myriad couplets from his copious imagination and tying them to some quasi-traditional framework. Which explains why he told *Rolling Stone*, about the album in toto, "I'd been writing down couplets and verses and things, and then putting them together at later times. I had a lot of that—it was starting to pile up."

Lanois confirms Dylan's account. When they first met in New York to discuss what to do with all this raw material, Lanois was introduced to a pile of "couplets and verses," which was pretty much all the singer-songwriter had: "We didn't even have any instruments or any songs to listen to really. He just had a stack of lyrics." Lanois and Howard meanwhile began to advocate making a record that was "loop-based, and [then] playing on top of them." If the idea of applying said technique on any song where "knifelike lyrics [are] trying to convey majesty and heroism" went against the grain, Dylan thought it might work on a song like "Highlands," which, in his own words, brought together "many ideas [that] were connected in a different way than they were written down."

"Actually," as the man said, "it's just a simple blues which can go either this way or that way." In fact, it went all the way. On the album, it clocks in at almost seventeen minutes. Just finding a place for it was bound to be a problem, prompting one of those ubiquitous right-hand men to inquire, after they recorded the finished version at Criteria, "Well, Bob, have you got a short version of that song?" to which Dylan drily replied, "That *was* the short version."

By then, Dylan had inserted a section of dialogue into the song—in which a series of verbal non sequiturs depict a run-in with a waitress in a New England bar-restaurant, stretching the song out while distancing it from its ostensible source. I seem to be in the minority in thinking that this act of self-regarding sabotage ruins an otherwise memorable song. Not that Dylan hadn't written fine dialogue in song—"Isis," for one, springs to mind. And his interest in writing situations of conversational conflict dates back to at least the winter of 1964, when he was working on a play, a seventeen-page draft of which survives among the Margolis and Moss papers. This time the setting is "a combination bar-room—church—part of hotel," and the contretemps is between a "whore" and a "liberal thinker":

Annastasia: . . . if my voice bothered you, then you'd say "shut up" the same as me.

Mr. Sellowth: No young lady I don't think I would. I don't think I would at all. I'd just leave the room if your voice bothered me.

Anna: an that aint sayin' "shut up"?

Sellowth: no it's called leavin, that's what it's called . . .

Anna: my feet dont talk for me, Mr. My mouth talks for me. My mouth says more.

Sellowth: an it's just as rotten as you probably.

Anna: Yeah probably.

Sellowth an it'd do yuh good t use your feet.

The impulse hadn't entirely gone away. He had been threatening to (co-)write a movie script since at least the mid-eighties. And the new vignette would hardly seem out of place in *Masked and Anonymous*, the movie Dylan would cowrite between *Time Out of Mind* and its CD successor. In this conversation between a waitress and an artist, the characters fit Dylan's notional idea of archetypes (as he duly observed of some characters in later songs, "They might not think of themselves like that, but they are. They represent an idea"). On "Highlands," though, the whole story reminds me of all that annoying bleating about the impositions of fame found on Van Morrison albums. It has much of the feel but little of the wit of the scene between Dylan's character, Jack Fate, and "a beautiful but tarted up, vulgarly attired woman" in a bus station that appeared in the *Masked and Anonymous* shooting script (it was not in the released film, but appears as a bonus scene on the DVD):

Woman: Do you remember me?

Jack Fate: I don't know, my memory's blocked.

Woman: Down on Coliseum Street, the Inferno club? I was the lady in red, you made up a song for me.

Jack Fate: Oh yeah. Lady in red. Slow, dreamy ballad.

Woman: The Inferno club burned down. You were there that night.

Jack Fate: Oh was I?

Woman: Would you like to go out? Sensuality is my speciality.

Jack Fate: I got a radical hostility towards sensuality.

Woman: Oh, do you. How do you feel about bikinis?

Jack Fate: Bikinis infuriate me.

Woman: Oh, you sound like a bad man. You got any more songs in you?

Jack Fate: I don't know.

At least "Highlands" shows that Dylan got the hang of recording over a looped drum track remarkably quickly, switching almost seamlessly to the Boston bar and back to the rustic retreat where he feels most at home ("The streams, the forests, the vast emptiness. The land created me . . . Even as I travel the cities, I'm more at home in the vacant lots." —Dylan, 2009). Presumably, this bar scene is intended to intimate why he longs for the highlands, all the while failing to tell us *why* his heart is there or where these highlands might be. However, his description of the Midwest to a *Rolling Stone* reporter in 2009 suggests that his heart is back home in Hibbing: "The air is so pure [there]. And the brooks and rivers are still running. The forests are thick, and the landscape is brutal. And the sky is still blue up there. It is still pretty untarnished."

Such a languorous, looped track, thanks to the inserted verses, made for his longest studio recording to date. In this guise, it hardly lent itself to live performance; as such, for the next eighteen months, Dylan concentrated on reinventing the lesser songs on the new collection, while "Highlands" didn't trouble the NET track listers. But at a June 1999 show in California, he proved that the song need not be quite such a drag, telling the story with remorseless energy and intonation, completing the entire narrative in just eleven inspired minutes. The 1999 "Highlands," word-perfect and sung with a now-rare precision, bent every line to the metronomic beat, again confirming that Lanois's input ruined almost as many things as he improved.

The experiment could have ended there, but even Dylan seems to have been amazed to find it worked so well live. So, although it was never going to be a regular in the set, he pulled it out of his hat a handful of times more: notably in New York (July 27), in California (March 16, 2000), and then in Glasgow the following September (17). He even OK'd the release of the March 16 version on a bonus CD EP accompanying the otherwise pointless *The Best of Bob Dylan Volume 2*. It's another spirited rendition, but Dylan is content to half-speak, half-sing the song, as if auditioning for the role. By the time he unfurled it for the Scots, six months later (and a day after being within spitting distance of the real Highlands), the spirit of Burns was o'er the hills and far away.

{562} ALL I EVER LOVED IS YOU

Known studio recordings: Real Music Studios, Oxnard, CA, September 26, 1996.

After issuing a seventy-two minute album in 1997 and a CD's worth of outtakes in 2008, one might assume the *Time Out of Mind* sessions have been cleansed of all their mysteries. But, ever the tease, Dylan has apparently left at least one *TOOM* outtake up his sleeve. In the insert to the two-disk version of *Tell Tale Signs* (but not the three-disk . . .), there is a track sheet for a song called "All I Ever Loved Is You." Knowledgeable fans were quick to point out the existence of a Stanley Brothers song called "All I Ever Loved Was You." Given that Dylan peppered a fair number of shows in the late nineties with a Stanley Brothers busk or two, it was assumed by many to be another cover tune.

However, it strikes me as unlikely that Dylan would go to the trouble of demoing a cover, whatever its source, for an album that reused old song titles with élan. The slight difference in title, and the fact that it took Dylan three and a half minutes to sing what would be a two-verse song, makes me inclined to think it might be a lost original. Talking of lost originals, another song title mentioned by the Criteria session musicians has singularly failed to appear: "No Turning Back." This may have been turned into something else—as "Doin' Alright" became "Til I Fell in Love with You." Or maybe not.

{563} DREAMIN' OF YOU

Published lyric/s: Words Fill My Head.
Known studio recordings: Real Music Studios, Oxnard, CA, October 1, 1996; Criteria Studios, Miami, FL, January 1997. [TTS]

> We actually had twice as many songs as we needed and had to lose some. Those you hear on the album just naturally hung together, because they share a certain skepticism. They're more concerned with the dread realities of life than the bright and rosy idealism popular today. —Dylan, to Alan Jackson, November 1997

"Dreamin' of You" was one of those songs that fell through the cracks when Dylan recalibrated the album's focus, removing songs of heartache and regret like "Mississippi," "Red River Shore," and the original "Can't Wait." Sloman in his notes to *Tell Tale Signs* confidently asserts that the version of "Dreamin' of You" therein included "is the only take ever recorded," a statement somewhat contradicted by the Criteria status of the released take, while the track sheet reproduced in the booklet details a version from an October 1 Oxnard session (they probably built the Criteria version up from an Oxnard prototype, as with a number of *TOOM* tracks). Engineer Chris Shaw, who worked on the tapes for the 2008 set, has also stated that there were at least two versions of the song.

Sloman is on similarly dodgy ground when he asserts that the "song might have been rejected [because] many of the lyrics later get developed more fully in different songs." This seems to me a misunderstanding of the nature of the *TOOM* material, and the way it was manipulated by its overseer across a six-month period. Dylan himself talked about how he began by "writing down couplets and verses and things" without a specific song in mind, only "putting them together at later times." Much like the folk process itself.

Thus, a line from "Dreamin' of You" like "Well, I eat when I'm hungry, drink when I'm dry, live my life on the square"—itself a tweaking of traditional sources[39]—reappears in "Standing in the Doorway." But then, the line in question fits "Dreamin' of You" far better than the latter. Nor was "Standing in the Doorway" necessarily improved by coopting such a lyric. All in all, it would be unfair to portray "Dreamin' of You" as some kind of prototype for a later, better song, especially as we are talking within the context of an album that would feature "Til I Fell in Love with You" and "To Make Me Feel Your Love," songs bad enough to have been cowritten in the mid-eighties.

At some point, though, Dylan decided that the song lacked "a certain skepticism," transferring some of its sentiments to other songs "more concerned with the dread realities of life." One of those songs where Lanois had "built some loops [out] of what Tony [Mangurian] . . . did, and then abandoned these sources; . . . and built a lot of demos around them," "Dreamin' of You" is another song of regret ("Somewhere dawn is breaking / Light is streaking across the floor. / Church-bells are ringing / I wonder who they're ringing for")[40] and as such was always vying for a place with at least four or five other claimants.

It does include one great little couplet that wouldn't have been out of place on "Time to End This Masquerade," or as a line of dialogue in *The Elephant Man*: "For years they had me locked in a cage / Then they threw me onto the stage." However, its nondescript tune and slightly pedestrian delivery probably did for it in the end, even if sandwiched between "Broken Days" and "Huck's Tune" on *Tell Tale Signs* it sounds sprightly enough. A promo video for the song, featuring Harry Dean Stanton as a traveling bootlegger, proved only that these promo people, they make some pretty bad stuff.

{564} MARCHING TO THE CITY

[= DOING ALRIGHT]

Published lyric/s: Words Fill My Head.

Known studio recordings: Criteria Studios, Miami, FL, January 16, 1997 [TTS 3]; January 1997 [TTS 1].

Sloman again overstates the similarities, real as they are, between "Marching to the City" and the *TOOM* cut "Til I Fell in Love with You" in his *TTS* album notes, describing the former as a song that "eventually became" "Til I Fell in Love with You." What he fails to address is the interim process, from "Marching to the City" into "Doing Alright," a song referred to by musicians at the time and subsequently mistakenly referred to as an alternate title for "Til I Fell in Love with You." The production notes for *Tell Tale Signs* clearly indicate that the so-called alternate take of "Marching to the City" on disk three is actually "Doing Alright," presumably the one recorded on January 16, 1997, the track sheet of which appears in the set's booklet.

In this version of the song the phrase "Til I Fell in Love with You" first appears. However, of the three couplets "Marching to the City" and "Tell I Fell In Love With You" share, neither "Boys in the street beginning to play / Girls like birds flying away" nor "I been hit too hard, seen too much / Nothing can heal me now but your touch" appear in "Doing Alright." This halfway house, which was included on the world's most expensive bonus disk (at a $125 premium) to the three-CD *Tell Tale Signs*, has an entirely different setting, rhythmically and lyrically. And though both melodies are rather similar, they are not identical. "Doing Alright," what with all that moving around, seems to have shed at least three verses, including the following:

> Go over to London, maybe gay Paris
> Follow the river you get to the sea
> I was hoping we could drink from life's clear streams
> I was hoping we could dream life's pleasant dreams.

The first couplet would be transplanted to "Not Dark Yet"—another song "Marching to the City" did not become, while another line from "Doing Alright" makes it into the selfsame song: "I'm not looking for nothing in anyone's eyes." Nothing more perfectly illustrates the patchwork nature of the *Time Out of Mind* lyrics, or their interchangeability when any particular song was required to reflect the themes of the whole album—loneliness, the perfidy of women, mortality ("I'm marching to the city and the road ain't long" is an old man's line, albeit from someone still walking towards the sun). Characteristically, Dylan drew on elements from both "Marching to the City" and "Doing Alright" in order to arrive at the 1997 album's own "Tight Connection," "Til I Fell in Love with You." And not for the first time, leaves me wondering: what was he thinking?

{565} MILLION MILES

Published lyric/s: Lyrics 04.

Known studio recordings: Real Music Studios, Oxnard, CA, September–October 1996; Criteria Studios, Miami, FL, January 1997 [TOOM].

First known performance: Garde Arts Center, New London, CT, January 14, 1998.

"Million Miles" is another *TOOM* song which began as a drum-guitar loop, to which Dylan was soon adding parts at Oxnard, before becoming one of those "ultimate productions" which was part product of California and part product of Criteria. Like "Highlands," it was originally a long song for which the demo was only a draft. By the time it left Criteria, very little residue of its Real Music origins remained, while the lyric had been reduced to its bare bones ("I'm still a million miles from you"). Another song of dislocation and frustrated love that he fondly imagined replicated some "dusty old rock 'n' roll record," "Million Miles" struggled to rise above "the muck and the mire."

Indeed, like a number of the album's lesser songs, it took an injection of onstage adrenaline to raise it up. Debuted at a series of winter 1998 shows Dylan shared with the equally disaffected Van the Man, "Million Miles" was one of four *TOOM* songs issued in a live guise on the widely available 1999 promo CD EP *Million Miles, Live Recordings 1997–1999*. The fact that this February 1999 performance from Binghamton, New York—in keeping with all four cuts on the EP—stripped layers of gunk from the song, demonstrated how the lesser songs on the album suffered most from Lanois's "ideological voodoo thing." One imagines this EP (and its companion CD, *Things Have Changed: Live & Unreleased*) was someone's idea of a riposte.

{566} NOT DARK YET

Published lyric/s: Lyrics 04.

Known studio recordings: Real Music Studios, Oxnard, CA, September–October 1996; Criteria Studios, Miami, FL, January 1997 [TOOM].

First known performance: Columbus Civic Center, Columbus, GA, October 30, 1997.

A lot of the songs [on *Time Out of Mind*] were written after the sun went down . . . This one phrase was going through my head: "Work while the day lasts, because the night of death cometh when no man can work" . . . It wouldn't let me go. I was, like, what does that phrase mean? . . . It was at the forefront of my mind for a long period of time, and I think a lot of that is instilled into this record. —Dylan, to Jon Pareles, 1997

"Not Dark Yet" is many folks' favorite song on Dylan's 1997 album, and for sure it pushes all the right buttons: a gorgeous vocal, a brooding melody, the darkling worldview, and that seemingly effortless way he captured the dusk in his veins. A long-standing fascination with the night had served to make it a key motif in his work, prompting him to write in *Chronicles*, "I like the night. Things grow at night. My imagination is available to me at night." As a man who does most of his work at night,

Dylan has always been a man who lives in the shadows. And it was probably those lengthening shadows that prompted him to give this song such a "Southern" torpor: "Shadows are falling [*sic*], and I been here all day / It's too hot to move, and time is running away . . . It's not dark yet, but it's getting there."

With such a mood piece, the key issue was always going to be how successfully they got the same vibe on tape. As one of those songs Dylan had been carrying around for a while, it definitely demanded a degree of respect from all concerned. Indeed, it required a communal effort to keep Dylan from losing the song altogether. Initially, the demo he cut at Oxnard—which remains unreleased—drew a number of participants to embrace it. And their descriptions do rather whet the appetite. According to Lanois, "'Not Dark Yet' had a radically different feel in the demo we did, which I loved and still miss. It was quicker and more stripped down and then in the studio he changed it into a civil war ballad."

Guitarist Duke Robillard, who (although not credited) plays on the released cut, was also privy to how it sounded in California, endorsing Lanois's assessment: "The tracks on the original [Oxnard] tape were more basic than those at Criteria. I don't mean basic as in demo, but basic as in the feel of the songs, more acoustic. One song that comes to mind is 'Not Dark Yet'; there was a beautiful take of that song on the tape. The version we recorded in Miami was slowed down, nice mood, great take, but I liked the demo a lot."

Unfortunately, this was not one of the Oxnard recordings recovered during the selection process for *Tell Tale Signs*, and so the album cut will have to suffice, for now. Not that "Not Dark Yet" qualifies as another "Can't Wait" scenario. The released version wholly succeeds in its brief, which is to elucidate in seven minutes what Dylan said to Robert Hilburn a few months later in two sentences: "I try to live within that line between despondency and hope. I'm suited to walk that line, right between the fire." Naturally, it defined the album for many people, sitting squat still at the center of this curmudgeonly collection of original colloquies and borrowed chords, prompting Dylan to insist that them thar critics got it wrong for describing the album as "dark and foreboding [just] because we locked into that one dimension in the sound . . . In my mind, there's nothing dark about it. It's not like [it's] Dante's *Inferno*."

But it cannot be mere coincidence that the inexorable process of making the album into a statement prompted him to slow down all of *TOOM*'s major works ("Not Dark Yet," "Standing in the Doorway," and "Tryin' to Get to Heaven"), while speeding up its lesser lights ("Million Miles," "Can't Wait," "Cold Irons Bound"). The former trio suited his bruised vocal cords better, even if Dylan needed a little help here in getting the right one on the record. Engineer Mark Howard specifically remembers "working quite hands-on with Dylan for a while, doing the vocals. Say on . . . 'Not Dark Yet' he'd say, 'I wanna change this one line,' and I'd say, 'Bob, I really love that line, that's my favorite line, please don't change it—but if you are, I'll put it on another track and kind of save it, because you might want to put it back.' And he said, 'Really? Well, OK, don't worry about it.'" (Howard is presumably referring to sessions in March 1997 when Dylan redid a number of vocals on the album, before it went off to the pressing plant and he almost met his Maker.)

The outer darkness would continue to filter through the blinds. In the case of "Not Dark Yet" this was enough to illuminate [*sic*] it in performance. "Not Dark Yet" was one song that Dylan seemed to connect with in concert long after the first flush of enthusiasm for the bulk of *TOOM* songs began to fade. Indeed, I would go as far as to suggest that it did not really come into its own until 1999, when it received some stunning performances on a series of joint summer shows with Paul Simon. He even cracked its kernel in 2002, coaxing a rare moment of artistic calm out of the general hubbub at a show in Bournemouth on the fifth day of May, when he was so much reminded of the Criteria vibe by the presence of Jim Keltner that he raised a harmonica to his lips, to rasp against the dying of the light.

{567} RED RIVER SHORE

Published lyric/s: Words Fill My Head.
Known studio recordings: Real Music Studios, Oxnard, CA, September–October 1996; Criteria Studios, Miami, FL, January 11 and 19, 1997 [TTS x2].

There was one song that I'm not sure will make the cut, that when I first heard Bob do it, right away I thought it was a Jimmie Rodgers thing circa 1929, it was that genuine. I was mesmerized by it, completely blown away

> ... Lanois and Dylan talked about [how the album] was all designed to
> create a mood. The record is set in another time ... it's steamboat, civil
> war, very Mark Twain. —Duke Robillard, *Isis* #73

"Red River Shore," the song Robillard is describing, occupied a great
deal of time at Criteria as Dylan grappled with another original song
he hoped would feel like one written "time out of mind." According
to Chris Shaw, there were at least four versions referenced when
compiling the 2008 set. Of these, at least one came from Oxnard (the
version on *TTS* disk three is probably another Criteria superimposition
over an Oxnard original). All apparently used the same sixteen-verse
narrative to tell a story of lost love that was quite different from the
song alluded to in the full title, the traditional "Girl on the Green Briar
Shore," which he played twice in 1992, having learned it from Tom
Paley's Elektra recording.

The traditional archetype Dylan draws on here has ancient roots
(though nothing as ancient as the ones it is accorded by Sloman, who
fancifully claims a lineage with the medieval "Earl Brand" ballad), being
part of the "Girl I Left Behind" family of songs that includes "The Lakes
of Pontchartrain," another gorgeous trad ballad Dylan had been reinvig-
orating with Never Ending Tour blood. (The other reference in the song
title, Sonny Terry and Brownie McGhee's "Red River Blues," provides
another false trail.)

There is no shortage of lines in "Red River Shore" peeled from the
pages of the lexicon, though most are what would be termed commonplace phrases lifted from so-called floating verses, which, as the name
implies, wander from song to song. Phrases like "pretty maids all in
a row" and "Well, I been to the east and I been to the west" are part
of a language of song, not the property of one songsmith. On several
occasions he succeeds in rifling the repertoire and renewing his craft;
witness:

> Well I'm a stranger here in a strange land
> But I know this is where I belong
> I'll ramble and gamble for the one I love
> And the hills will give me a song.

The reference to ramblin' and gamblin' he has lifted from "The Girl I Left Behind," a traditional song he had cut at least twice, while the first line can't help but recall "We're strangers in a land we're passing through" ("Covenant Woman"), itself a nod to Carter Family classic "I Can't Feel at Home in This World." It is this ever-apposite cross-weaving that makes "Red River Shore" so much more satisfying than the songs which overuse the same approach on *Love and Theft*." Dylan also appears to be alluding to one of his earliest songs, "Long Ago Far Away," when making his first *direct* reference to Christ in a decade:

> Now I heard of a guy who lived a long time ago
> A man full of sorrow and strife
> That if someone around him died—and was dead—
> He knew how to bring 'em on back to life.

"Red River Shore" was another song Dylan didn't want to give up on, which is why he tried it out with all three sets of musicians who passed through Criteria that January. But by the time he got to working with the two Jims, Dickinson and Keltner, he was beginning to despair of ever finding the right peg. As Dickinson recalls, "I personally felt 'Girl from the Red River Shore' was the best thing we recorded, but as we walked in to hear the playback, Dylan was in front of me, and he said, 'Well, we've done everything on *that* one except call the symphony orchestra.' Which indicated to me they'd tried to cut it before." Such a comment rather suggests he had decided it was another one that had stayed in the studio too long.

{568} STANDING IN THE DOORWAY

Published lyric/s: Lyrics 04.
Known studio recordings: Real Music Studios, Oxnard, CA, September–October 1996; Criteria Studios, Miami, FL, January 1997 [TOOM].
First known performance: Roseland Theater, Portland, OR, June 15, 2000.

"Standing in the Doorway," one of the outstanding songs on Dylan's 1997 "comeback," was another song demoed in Oxnard with one version of the tune and reworked at Criteria with another (sidling to within a hairsbreadth of breaking into the Elvis version of "Can't Help Falling in Love," itself a public domain tune). Something about the song clearly bothered him because it would take him three and a half years to debut it in performance, and when he did, it had undergone another tune-tweak (perhaps because he could no longer do justice to the original with his contracting vocal range).

Even if Dylan felt the melody needed further refining, it was not really this that prompted him to work on the song so. Rather, as Duke Robillard relates, "We almost never did another take because the previous one was wrong in any technical sense. It was all to do with mood. If we did three different takes we would get three different songs!" And though "Standing in the Doorway" was set to torch-ballad mode from the start, Dylan continued playing with the words and tempo throughout. One spine-tingling line, contrasting a life (hers) spent around "silver spoons" with his own condition ("too much salt in my wounds"), was only sacrificed at the last minute; and although the album cut runs for more than seven minutes, on at least one occasion Dylan took eight and a half minutes to extract every last ounce of meaning from these wounded words.

The title, if it was another case of Dylan co-opting someone else's idea, did not come from the folk-song canon. But it could conceivably have been something he heard standing at the side of the stage at Minneapolis's Orpheum Theatre in September 1992, when Soul Asylum played their own "Standing in the Doorway" in the support slot at Dylan's five-night residency. But whereas David Pirner was "wonderin' if it's safe to go outside," Dylan was "left . . . standing in the doorway, crying." Again, he tips his hat to a favorite movie genre, painting the man in the song as an outlaw on the run ("Maybe they'll get me and maybe they won't / But not tonight, and it won't be here"); perhaps the selfsame man who in the next song finds himself on the way to the penitentiary, still wondering why his "love for her is taking such a long time to die . . ."

{569} COLD IRONS BOUND

Published lyric/s: Lyrics 04.

Known studio recordings: Criteria Studios, Miami, FL, January 1997 [TOOM].

First known performance: Mississippi State University, Starkville, MS, October 24, 1997.

I felt extremely frustrated because I couldn't get any of the up-tempo songs that I wanted . . . There's a real drive to [*Time Out of Mind*], but it isn't even close to the way I had it envisioned . . . There were things I had to throw out because this assortment of people just couldn't lock in on riffs and rhythms . . . I didn't really dimensionalize the songs . . . I just wish I'd been able to get more of a legitimate rhythm-oriented sense into it. I didn't feel there was any *mathematical* thing about that record at all.

—Dylan, to Mikal Gilmore, October 2001

As with much of the *TOOM* material, he seems to have begun "Cold Irons Bound" with a single, appropriated image—according to Brian Hinton, "bound down by strong irons, their sins to prevail," from the "Irish" ballad, "The Constant Farmer's Wife." I'm not so sure this is Dylan's immediate source, but said broadside is certainly another song known since "time out of mind." Whatever his source, he was still using such images as departure points, not as a necessary lyrical crutch, the mental picture of the singer "twenty miles out of town, in cold irons bound" being graphic enough to sustain the whole song. To this, he dropped in other lexicon-based references ("the road is rocky" comes from one of his, "Paths of Victory"; while "the winds in Chicago" namechecks the home of Chess, nay, electric blues). But the real debt is to a musical subgenre: songs like "Rosie," sung from inside prison, thinking of a woman on the outside. It was a form Dylan had flirted with as far back as *Self Portrait* ("Take a Letter to Mary"), but dates back at least another 350 years, cf. "To Althea from Prison."

"Cold Irons Bound" was another case of Dylan trying to throw off the shackles of sound Lanois was ever seeking to impose. Unhappy with anything up-tempo, Lanois sought to dissuade Dylan from recreating his live sound, leaving "Cold Irons Bound" as the one occasion when core elements of that live sound were allowed into Criteria. It is not known if "Cold Irons Bound" was something he demoed at Oxnard, but if so no part of said demo remains. The album track seems to have been recorded at the very start of the Criteria sessions.

Dylan had brought along three parts of the band he had been playing with since late October (drummer Dave Kempner, the omnipresent Tony Garnier, and multi-instrumentalist Bucky Baxter), to see if they could "lock in on riffs and rhythms" and help him "really dimensionalize the songs." He implied that the experiment did not work, telling Gilmore, "I was kind of auditioning players here and there for a [touring] band, but I didn't feel like I could trust them man-to-man in the studio with unrecorded songs. So we started to use some musicians that Lanois would choose and a couple that I had in mind: Jim Dickinson, Jim Keltner, Duke Robillard."

Given that Dylan was talking in the context of his next album—which he recorded with the selfsame touring band, and completed in a fortnight—maybe he ultimately decided it was his judgment, not their musicianship, which went awry in the winter of 1997. When Duke Robillard turned up to find "Cold Irons Bound" "was finished," Never Ending Tour drummer Kempner was heading the other way: "[After] we got 'Cold Irons Bound' . . . they brought in a whole other crew."

In all likelihood, it was his touring band's failure to capture "Mississippi" which persuaded Dylan to defer to Lanois's instincts. Yet it was the sound of the studio "Cold Irons Bound" that Dylan then took around the world as, for a second time, he took a set of songs bequeathed to Lanois in the studio and in concert imposed the "legitimate rhythm-oriented sense" they had been missing. "Cold Irons Bound," in particular, seemed a mere prototype on the record, whereas the live version reproduced the sound of a man walking down the road, leaving his clanking chains behind. Hence its appearance on a number of releases (the *Live 1961–2000* CD anthology, the *Million Miles Live Recordings 1997–99*, and "Love Sick" CD EPs) in the form he performed that fall, from a residency at the El Rey in L.A. On at least one level, the live sound of "Cold Irons Bound" would inform the whole of the next album, when Dylan would make another attempt to capture that elusive *"mathematical* thing."

{570} TRYIN' TO GET TO HEAVEN

Published lyric/s: Lyrics 04.
Known studio recordings: Criteria Studios, Miami, FL, January 1997 [TOOM].
First known performance: Lisbon, Portugal, April 7, 1999.

> I like storms. I like to stay up during a storm. I get very meditative sometimes. —Dylan, to Jon Pareles, September 1997

If *Time Out of Mind* proved a somewhat convoluted journey, the composition of "Tryin' to Get to Heaven" suggests Dylan had arrived at his destination. Whereas in other lifetimes he had preferred to work out his conceit early, producing the defining template—a "Visions," a "Tangled," a "Caribbean Wind"—*before* spinning off in a series of coded commentaries, he broke the habits of those lifetimes in Miami. A song he appears to have written *after* the likes of "Mississippi" and "Red River Shore" had shown him the way, "Tryin' to Get to Heaven" stood out on the album as the paradigm of this "new" Dylan (partly because he avoided comparisons by leaving those two tracks off). The resultant song contained more wit, imagination, and insight than the whole of the album it ultimately inspired and informed, his 2001 successor, *"Love and Theft."*

Once again it was a song which had existed "time out of mind" that gave Dylan the key to this particular kingdom. After closing out his last album with Doc Watson's "Lone Pilgrim," a song in which "salvation and the needs of mankind are [again] prominent," he rediscovered the spirituals which had been infusing his songwriting soul since he was a nineteen-year-old Guthrie wannabe. As he memorably revealed to *Newsweek*'s David Gates on *Time Out of Mind*'s release, "I find [all] the religiosity and philosophy in the music . . . Songs like 'Let Me Rest on a Peaceful Mountain' or 'I Saw the Light'—that's my religion . . . The songs are my lexicon. I believe the songs."

What provided him with an initial impetus on this occasion was another old Baptist hymn that gave him religion, "The Old Ark's A-Movering," which in certain incarnations contained the following couplet: "Look at that sister coming so slow / She's tryin' to get to heaven fo' they close the do'." Equally apposite to his quest were the lines, "T'ain't but the one thing grieves my mind / Sister's gone to Heav'n and left a-me behind." Dylan even tells us he's "been walking that lonesome valley," reaffirming his view that the road to salvation is a lonely one (or, as the traditional "Lonesome Valley" puts it, "You got to walk that lonesome valley / You got to go there by yourself").

At times it seems like the entire song has been dipped in the lexicon of gospel and blues, thanks to Dylan's penchant for forming whole lines out of well-known traditional song titles like "Going Down to New

Orleans," "I Been All Around This World," and "Going Down the Road Feeling Bad." He also rather brazenly ends the song with a tip of the hat to both Elizabeth Cotton's variant of "Shake Sugaree" (the album's starting point) and Woody Guthrie's rendition of "This Train (Is Bound For Glory)" (*his* starting point):

> Some trains don't pull no gamblers, no midnight ramblers,
> Like they did before.
> I been to Sugartown, I shook the sugar down,
> Now I'm trying to get to heaven before they close the door.

But as with all the very best Dylan songs, the whole of "Tryin' to Get to Heaven" is so much greater than the sum of its purloined parts. And while it may be overstating the case to suggest, as Dylan did to David Gates, that "There's no line that has to be there to get to another line," the listener never wonders whether this is so (at least, not until s/he starts reading the lyric). Unlike many of the songs written in its wake, there is no sense that this one was slung together. He worked on the song so painstakingly throughout the sessions, probably because he had only just finished drafting it when the sessions began. This meant the song ended up being recut two or three times, not because the first take didn't work, but because he wanted to work on the words some more. Duke Robillard thought some of the lines lost were as good as the ones Dylan found to replace them:

> I never got a chance to see what he was writing, he just scribbled away with a pencil between takes and when you did a second or a third take what seemed like perfectly good lyrics were dropped for new ones . . . "Tryin' to Get to Heaven" was another case in question, we did that twice and in between takes he had rewritten the lyrics . . .[]. . . [It] was one of the songs where he'd change a line and you'd think the new words were great, but then you thought back at the old line because the change was so interesting that I'd find myself wanting to listen back to both versions, so I could try and figure out what he was trying to say.

Needless to say, Duke never heard those lost lines again. And nor did the fans. Though other studio takes were considered for *Tell Tale*

Signs, none of them made the cut. Instead, an antiseptic version from an October 2000 show at London's Wembley Arena was chosen, the most baffling inclusion on a generally well-conceived set. If one was trying to find a setting which would make the song slot effortlessly onto *Empire Burlesque*, then that night's performance (which, I hasten to add, I suffered through in person) was a triumph. As for Sloman's sleeve-note assertion that this is "one of Bob's most soulful vocals," well, only if he means Bob the narcoleptic. Other performances with the same reined-in melody—say, the one from Portsmouth ten days earlier, which had already provided *Live 1961–2000* with two terrific signposts from a good year on the road—do at least demonstrate that Dylan was still connected to the song.

Nothing from the autumn 2000 shows, though, comes close to the debut live performance of the song, eighteen months earlier, in the port of Lisbon. Dylan, for once, is not content simply to strum along behind the band. Scratching out a highly effective acoustic guitar lead, he completely reinvents the song, all the while retaining its spiritual core and plaintive tune. Providing an utterly magnetic way to kick off one of the finer latter-day legs from the Never Ending Tour, the vocal has that gospel quality he was already bringing to songs of salvation like "Satisfied Mind" and "Halleluiah I'm Ready to Go" (both recently introduced into the set), proving yet again that you can make it if you try.

{571} MAKE YOU FEEL MY LOVE

Published lyric/s: Lyrics 04.
Known studio recordings: Criteria Studios, Miami, FL, January 1997 [TOOM].
First known performance: Garde Arts Center, New London, CT, January 13, 1998.

Perhaps we should be grateful that it was "Make You Feel My Love" which was given the *Knocked Out Loaded* treatment at the *TOOM* sessions (and was then donated to a Billy Joel album, where it truly belonged). Written, one suspects, as a counterbalance to all the songs of betrayal and lost love that occupied most of the work to date, the song merely reinforces a growing suspicion that, for all his lyrical genius, emulating the songsmiths of Tin Pan Alley was always going to be beyond this former folksinger. Live performances in the winter of 2000 failed to reveal any hidden depths either, though one of them still popped up on the *Things Have Changed: Live & Unreleased* CD EP.

{572} TIL I FELL IN LOVE WITH YOU

Published lyric/s: Lyrics 04.
Known studio recordings: Criteria Studios, Miami, FL, January 1997 [TOOM].
First known performance: Mississippi State University, Starkville, MS,
October 24, 1997.

> I didn't go into it with the idea that this was going to be a finished album.
> It got off the tracks more than a few times, and people got frustrated. I
> know I did. —Dylan, to Mikal Gilmore, October 2001

"Til I Fell in Love with You" was one instance of Dylan going "off the tracks," if not the rails, taking as his departure point not some gnarly ol' blues tune but rather a song of his own he had been gamely trying to complete, "Marching to the City" aka "Doing Alright." The transition from the journey-song "Marching to the City" to the brighter, poppier "Doing Alright" continued its downward arc to "Til I Fell in Love with You," only docking in its pop ballad berth after Dylan despaired of making a grander statement.

The studio version certainly sticks to its own groove, like a demo he was looking to turn over to the Blues Project, but it was still a song whose "structure, stratagems, codes, and stability" remained barely formed when recorded, not coming "into play on [the] record, 'cause my cohorts at the time never really [got to] develop any of that stuff." This reflected its last-minute change of identity. Only when he transferred the song to the stage did "all those elements come into play"—which was how Dylan detailed the difference between his songs live and on record at a 2001 press conference.

Like "Cold Irons Bound" and "Can't Wait," "Til I Fell in Love with You" sprung new limbs when introduced into the set in fall 1997, Dylan finding a vocal furious enough to fit the tenor of what is actually a pretty nasty song. Hence, presumably, why in the four years between albums he (re)issued most of the 1997 album in live instalments. Six *Time Out of Mind* songs would be released in live guises in this period, all of which can be found on either the *Million Miles: Live Recordings 1997–1999* CD EP (1999) or the *Things Have Changed: Live & Unreleased* CD EP (2000)— issued on the back of that song's Oscar triumph. Between them, they (sought to) provide a quite different version of this material to the one Lanois imposed.

{573} LOVE SICK

Published lyric/s: Lyrics 04.
Known studio recordings: Criteria Studios, Miami, FL, January 1997 [TOOM].
First known performance: BIC, Bournemouth, October 1, 1997.

> When we did *Time Out of Mind*, there were some demos of the songs that we listened to . . . that they wanted to do again and flesh out another way. And there were other songs Bob would just go out and begin to play.
> —Jim Keltner, *Uncut*, November 2008

It seems like "Love Sick" was written at the end of the process, as a way of spewing out all that poison in his guts, before becoming one of "those songs Bob would just go out and begin to play." This time Dylan decided to put the song that summed up his ongoing disaffection with the world and his wives not at album's end, but at the beginning. It was an odd way to introduce another side. And as the introduction to his first set of original songs in seven years, it was as ineffective as the equally anodyne "On a Night Like This," a quarter-century earlier. Yet a certain attachment was in evidence from the very night in early October 1997 when he returned to the stage for a second encore at the English seaside resort of Bournemouth and made it the first brand-new original to be performed since 1990, pouring himself into the song to the kind of ecstatic response that used to greet only the most left-field live debut.

Four hundred performances later, the song has still to reveal any hidden layers, though it tended to stay put in the encore slot, still generating a bewildering number of whoops from an audience for whom this was the song from the album that won the man a Grammy. Even on the night he performed it live to a highly sympathetic audience at the 1998 Grammy Awards ceremony in New York, prior to scooping the coveted Best Album award, the song must have left the disengaged wondering what all the fuss was about. About as profound as his last opener to an all-original album ("Wiggle Wiggle"), the song operates as a prologue to an album preoccupied with love, the sicker the better. "I'm sick of love—I wish I'd never met you" provides the theme to many a song at the sessions, and on the album. But this was written long after he had exhausted any insights about his once wretched condition.

{574} THINGS HAVE CHANGED

Published lyric/s: Lyrics 04.
Known studio recordings: Sony Studios, NYC, July ?25–26, 1999 [WB].
First known performance: Sun Theatre, Anaheim, CA, March 10, 2000.

> There wasn't any wasted effort on *Time Out of Mind*, and I don't think there will be on any more of my records. —Dylan, to Murray Engleheart, January 1999

At some point, somebody sat down and explained the attractive economics of a hit movie song to the ever-astute Mr. D, because at some point in the second half of the nineties he began dispensing unreleased originals ("Things Have Changed"), covers ("You Belong to Me"), and plain ol' studio outtakes ("Shelter from the Storm") to the strange creatures of the Hollywood Hills.

In the case of "Things Have Changed," its closest kin was not the album he had recorded thirty months earlier (yes, it had been that long), but another state-of-the-world song he bequeathed to an underachieving movie some thirteen years previously, *Band of the Hand*. Like that straight-to-video title track, "Things Have Changed" recognized that it was "countdown time now." But in this case, rather than coming from street punks, it was an older, wiser man who was "walking forty miles of bad road," wondering whether the Bible was right, i.e., "the world will explode."

The one song on *Time Out of Mind* to which "Things Have Changed" tipped its hat was "Not Dark Yet" (along with that other Lanois leftover, "Dignity"). This was altogether fitting as that was a Dylan song director Curtis Hanson already planned to incorporate into the film, *Wonder Boys*, even before "Things Have Changed" appeared over the opening credits, allowing Dylan to achieve a lifelong ambition of winning an Oscar (though, sadly, not for best movie). The second verse even suggested he had given the shooting script a cursory scan, summarizing the film's raison d'être in six lines, just as he had done twenty-four years before:

> This place ain't doing me any good,
> I'm in the wrong town, I should be in Hollywood,
> Just for a second there I thought I saw something move.
> Gonna take dancing lessons, do the jitterbug rag,
> Ain't no shortcuts, gonna dress in drag,
> Only a fool in here would think he's got anything to prove.

Both the "dancing lessons," slyly sent up by the promo video where Dylan gets up to "do the jitterbug rag" with the perky Katie Holmes, and the reference to dressing "in drag"—just like a character Robert Downey Jr. picks up on the plane—confirm that Dylan was more engaged with this film than he had been with more reliable moneymakers like *Natural Born Killers* and *Jerry McGuire*, to which he had previously contributed kudos in kind.

Director Hanson confirms that there was real contact prior to Dylan writing the song, in his commentary for the DVD release: "I learned that Dylan might be interested in contributing an original song . . . [So] when I came back from [filming in] Pittsburgh, Bob came by the editing room to see some rough cut footage. I told him the story and introduced him to the characters. We talked about Grady Tripp and where he was in life, creatively and emotionally . . . Weeks later, a CD arrived in the mail."

Perhaps it was the seven-year writing block that the lead character (a college professor, beautifully played by Michael Douglas) appears to be suffering which drew Dylan to the script. Or maybe he just recognized it as one of Hollywood's more adult attempts to tell an affirmative story dealing with the kind of real emotions and tangled lives found in his own songs. Certainly, the way the promo video intercuts Dylan and Douglas mouthing the lines of that memorable chorus makes a movie motif out of what might have just another Dylanesque rant at a world going to hell in a handbasket: "People are crazy, times are strange . . . I used to care but things have changed."

Some years later, Dylan told novelist Jonathan Lethem, "*Time Out of Mind* was me getting back in and fighting my way out of the corner." Well, "Things Have Changed" was Dylan's way of announcing he "was out of the corner." The song also proved to him that he could still cut a new original quickly, with just the tools he had to hand. As Chris Shaw recalled, "We did 'Things Have Changed' in one afternoon, and when we were done we did a very quick mix of it . . . it turned out that that rough mix ended up being the final mix."

David Kempner, now encamped at the drum kit, affirms the basics of Shaw's recollection, while elucidating just how impromptu the whole session had been: "We were touring and had a day off in New York. Bob said, 'Tomorrow let's go in the studio. I got a song I want to record.' We went in and he played 'Things Have Changed,' with only an engineer . . . We did two takes. The first was a New Orleans thing. The second was what you hear . . . So in about five hours, we learned it, recorded it, mixed it."

Shaw confirms that there was "one [other version] that . . . was really great [which] had a kind of New Orleans shuffle to it." He was hoping to include this "New Orleans shuffle" on *Tell Tale Signs*, but when the studio multitracks proved elusive (!), the decision was made to use a mediocre June 2000 live performance instead. This choice would have been more understandable if there were a shortage of good live versions, but there wasn't. In fact, the closing cut on the *Live 1961–2000* CD (2001) is a stupendous performance from Portsmouth, just three months later, Dylan intonating every line like it was his life going down the can, not Michael Douglas's character.

Even the prerecorded performance he gave to the assembled academy, broadcast as part of the 2001 Oscar ceremony, would have been a better call, not just because of its historic significance but also because of the way he almost busks his way through a song that requires him to stay "locked in tight." Also worthy of inclusion would have been Dylan's acceptance speech, which, in marked contrast to his 1991 Grammy acceptance speech, got pithily to the point, with him thanking the Academy for being "bold enough to give me this award for this song, which is obviously a song which doesn't pussyfoot around or turn a blind eye to human nature." Ain't that the truth.

2000–1:

{ "Love and Theft" }

Sixteen days before his sixtieth birthday, Dylan returned to his once-familiar New York stomping ground to record his first album there since Infidels. *The studio he chose to make his home for a fortnight was deliberately retro. Clinton Recording Studios on Tenth Avenue was still set up to record analog, making its choice a clear statement of intent, as was Dylan's decision to produce the album himself (even if the tape logs credit Jeff Rosen in the role). For the first time since* Street-Legal, *Dylan had a precise idea of what songs he wanted to record. There would be no waste.*

Though Dylan had been keeping his new songs close to his chest—obliging me to organize them entirely by their recording date—he had evidently been thinking long and hard about what kind of record he wanted this time around, and whether he had anything left to say. Reminded in a January 1999 interview of the latter-day recordings of a musical hero, Skip James, he had told his interrogator, "If you listen to the records [James] made in the sixties, when they rediscovered him, you find that there's something missing. And what's missing is that interconnecting thread of the structure of the songs."

Determined not to make the same mistake with "Love and Theft," *Dylan took his own miscellany of "interconnecting threads" from songs he knew and wove them into an intricate tapestry that embraced everything from black and white movies to nursery rhymes to civil war lore to the novels of Mark Twain and F. Scott Fitzgerald, even drawing from an account of life as a yakuza, or Japanese gang member. It was an ambitious conceit, especially given his determination to record an album using analog sound for the first time in two decades.*

Not for the first time, his ambition proved greater than his artistry—"Love and Theft" was a patchwork quilt of borrowed ideas, and Dylan knew it. Hence, the little in-jokes with which he littered the lyrical trail. On the other hand, one has to acknowledge the bravura with which he approached his task. Previously, the editing process—before and during sessions—had generally expunged more derivative, less interesting debts. The reverse was now true. This time, Dylan positively celebrated every aspect of his cut-up canvas, even taking the album title from a 1993 book, Love & Theft: Blackface Minstrelsy and the American Working Class *by Eric Lott. He even bookended the collection with two tracks that copped not only their melodies, but also their arrangements from earlier recordings.*

Sticking resolutely to the m.o. of someone who knew, in the fullness of time, he would be hung as a thief, "Love and Theft" was all "interconnecting threads." The sum of its parts remained so much less than Dylan fondly imagined, even though his brazen plagiarism was initially celebrated as evidence of rekindled creativity (huh!) by many commentators for whom all popular music pre-Elvis was akin to some medieval mystery play. Dylan himself, evidently enjoying all the hubbub stirred up by such wholesale appropriation, couldn't wait to start reinforcing his conceit in concert . . .

{575} SUMMER DAYS

{576} TWEEDLE DEE & TWEEDLE DUM

{577} HONEST WITH ME

Published lyrics [#575–7]: Lyrics 04.

Known studio recordings [#575]: Clinton Recording Studios, NYC, May 8, 2001 [L+T—tk. 5].

Known studio recordings [#576]: Clinton Recording Studios, NYC, May 8–9, 2001—9 takes [L+T—tk. 9].

Known studio recordings [#577]: Clinton Recording Studios, NYC, May 9–10, 2001—6 takes [L+T—tk. 6].

First known performance [#575–7]: Spokane Arena, WA, October 5, 2001.

I knew after [*Time Out of Mind*] that when and if I ever committed myself to making another record, I didn't want to get caught short without up-tempo songs. A lot of my songs are slow ballads. I can gut-wrench a lot out of them. But if you put a lot of them on a record, they'll fade into one another . . . I blueprinted it this time to make sure I didn't get caught without up-tempo songs. —Rome press conference, July 23, 2001

That blueprint involved recording two derivative, up-tempo electric blues and a soft-shoe shuffle at the start of the sessions and building an album around them. On days one to three, Dylan recorded "Summer Days," "Tweedle Dee & Tweedle Dum," and "Honest with Me," in that order. This was because *"Love and Theft"* was his way of addressing unfinished business, revealing the other side of the coin Lanois had flipped on his behalf. It was also a return to recording the way he had back in the early eighties, when the whole tide of technology had been massing its forces against him.

Indeed, *"Love and Theft"* shares a lot with the much-maligned *Shot of Love*, not least Dylan's decision to use his touring band to make an album for the first time since those Rundown days. This time, though, he was looking to cut a track a day—literally. As engineer Chris Shaw relates: "There's twelve songs on *'Love and Theft,'* and we did twelve songs in twelve days, completed. Then we spent another ten days mixing it . . . 85 percent of the sound of that record is the band spilling into Bob's mike, because he'd sing live in the room with the band—without headphones . . . Bob wanted to get the live sound of the band he had at the time. Just get the whole band in the room playing."

Shaw, a Sony in-house engineer whose first Dylan session had been "Things Have Changed" in July 1999, was an analog-friendly antithesis of Lanois, i.e., an answer to Dylan's prayers. He even got complimented by the Album Vet, who told European journalists two months later, "On my last record, they put on all kinds of effects and overdubs afterwards, to make me sound like the way I do anyway. But on this record, we had a young engineer who knew exactly what to do. He got the point . . . [But then,] when you have an absolutely clear view of the arrangements you want, there is really nothing to produce."

Crucially, Dylan had decided to return to recording live with only the most marginal of safety nets. For the musicians, the option to redo parts did not really exist—not just because of technological restraints, but because Dylan had finally decided "soloing is not a big part of my records . . . Nobody buys them to hear solos. What I try to do [instead] is to make sure that the instrumental sections are dynamic and are extensions of the overall feeling of the song."

The *"Love and Theft"* musicians—already versed in the "stratagems, codes, and stability" Dylan brought to songs in concert—knew that they should concentrate on "the overall feeling of the song" and responded accordingly. Unfortunately, the one aspect of the sound that was often at odds with "the overall feeling of the song" was Dylan's own voice. Part of the problem was that, rather than replicating the working practice of *Shot of Love*, recorded when he was refreshed and raring to go, he was making the same mistake he had with that album's predecessor, *Saved*, coming straight off the road and recording an album.

After reminding himself of that inimitable Memphis musical stew at the Beale Street Music Festival on May 6, he arrived back in New York two days later to record "Summer Days" with a voice already in tatters from four decades of trying to emulate his musical idols, too many years on the unending road, and too few days" respite from his nightly ritual. Even the young engineer realized the vocals could present a problem, incautiously suggesting to *Uncut* in November 2008 that there were a number of alternate takes recorded at these sessions where "the vocal wasn't up to par, because Bob was just kind of still going through it." I don't know about the alternate takes, but the released takes of these three songs in particular feature some of the most desultory vocals the man had ever committed to tape.

Yet the songs were certainly worked on. "Tweedle Dee & Tweedle Dum" was subjected to some nine takes across two sessions, at least one of which (take four) topped six minutes; even "Honest with Me," as rudimentary as a roll in the hay, took some seven takes to shed a minute and a half from its seven-minute self (the first two—marked "r.o." on the reel— were apparently rolled over, though both were complete. Hopefully these were preserved on the live two-track DAT which was again running at the sessions[41]) before they found a "new drum groove" and stuck with it.

These two electric blues and the ersatz jazz of "Summer Days" not only established a working pattern, they also betrayed a methodology of appropriation that seeped into the very marrow of these songs, starting with the titles themselves (almost every song on the album was lifted from the lexicon of song and rhyme; the one exception was "Floater," whose working title "Too Much to Ask" had a more literary source). "Summer Days" became the first Charlie Patton reference on the album, being doubtless named after Patton's "Some Summer Day," while "Honest with Me" was bound to remind most listeners of Jimmy Reed's irresistible "Honest I Do." As for "Tweedle Dee & Tweedle Dum," it was the second time in eleven years that Dylan opened an album with a song title taken from a nursery rhyme, this one dating back to at least 1720 and famously quoted in Lewis Carroll's *Through the Looking Glass*:

> Tweedledum and Tweedledee
> Agreed to have a battle;
> For Tweedledum said Tweedledee
> Had spoiled his nice new rattle.
> Just then flew down a monstrous crow,
> As black as a tar-barrel;
> Which frightened both the heroes so,
> They quite forgot their quarrel.

"Tweedle Dee & Tweedle Dum," though it was recorded second, became the song chosen as an introduction to all that was to come. Fittingly, it displayed a working method short on inspiration and long on derivation. Dylan, though, wasn't about to become an apologist for his methodology. His way of describing this new way of composing to Robert Hilburn, from a fascinating 2004 conversation on songwriting, all but implied he was communing with the spirits of the great American songwriters, in the same way Elizabethan author George Chapman liked to commune with the spirit of Homer when translating his work into English:

I'm not a melodist. My songs are either based on old Protestant hymns or Carter Family songs or variations of the blues form . . . I'll take a song I know and simply start playing it in my head. That's the way I meditate . . . People will think they are talking to me and I'm talking back, but I'm not. I'm listening to the song in my head. At a certain point, some of the words will change and I'll start writing a song.

In the case of "Tweedle Dee & Tweedle Dum," his source was not any old Protestant hymn. It was a minor fifties hit for the pop duo Johnnie & Jack, entitled "Uncle John's Bongos," Dylan doing very little (if anything) to disguise his debt. Nor did his knowledge of the duo extend to this song alone. Within a month of these sessions, he would be opening the live set with their somewhat more memorable "Hummingbird." Here, he did not so much use Johnnie & Jack's 45 "as [a] departure point . . . that I change or dismantle from the inside" as graft his own words onto what was little more than a novelty song.

Even those words were no longer wholly his own unique spin on the collective canon of American song. As he put it to the assembled press in Rome that July, "I take notes. I retrieve them. I pull ideas together . . . I don't really do any writing. I don't sit down to write," which is a remarkably direct depiction of what he was now doing in the name of (his) art. In "Tweedle Dee & Tweedle Dum," there were lines which sounded like nothing that ever came from the man's pen. And after the hubbub surrounding his debts to movie dialogue in "Seeing the Real You at Last," he must surely have known his appropriations would not stay long below fans' radar.

And so it proved. The line, "Well, a childish dream is a deathless creed"—which always sounded like something lifted from a book of proverbs—turned out to be a direct quote from the American civil war poet Henry Timrod. Nor would it be the only time he felt like lifting a line or two from Timrod's poesy. At least the other allusion in "Tweedle Dee & Tweedle Dum" connected Timrod's quintessentially nineteenth-century imagery to his darker depiction of these malevolent twins. Dylan describes how "they walk among the stately trees / They know the secrets of the breeze," whereas Timrod had written of "the stately trees . . . shut within themselves . . . where lay fettered all the secrets of the breeze." Timrod continued to exercise an influence on this amateur historian of civil war rhetoric throughout this album and the next, finally prompting a 2006 article in the *New York Times* that questioned Dylan's motives for "disguising" any such debt to the lesser (known) visionary.

At least this unremittingly unpleasant song lives up to Dylan's claim to Mikal Gilmore that the songs on the album "deal with what many of my songs deal with—which is business, politics and war . . . It's not like the songs were written by . . . the man about town pretending to be happy." "Summer Days" also attempts to fuse the literary and the vernacular, but in such a stilted way that it leaves this listener cold. In keeping with the other song titles on *"Love and Theft,"* there is no obvious debt—save the title—to Patton's song. Rather, the melody sounds like a generic jitterbug rag tune to which Dylan set this collage of influences.

From the written page he has taken at least a couple of the threads which tie the song together. One, in verse five, constitutes the first of a dozen or so references seemingly lifted from John Bester's English translation of Japanese author Junichi Saga's *Confessions of a Yakuza*, a firsthand account of Nippon gangs. Where Saga asks, "D'you think I could call myself a yakuza if I couldn't stand up to some old businessman?" Dylan wonders, "What good are you anyway, if you can't stand up to some old businessman?" As to what excited Dylan so about Saga's saga, a close read of Bester's translation brings no illumination.

Dylan's other debt, stretched to an outlandish length to preserve the integrity of the allusion, comes from someone he had been referencing since at least 1971, F. Scott Fitzgerald, and his most celebrated work, *The Great Gatsby*. The relevant section—which probably also influenced "Floater"—warrants reproducing as is: "'You can't repeat the past.' 'Can't repeat the past?' he cried incredulously. 'Why of course you can!' He looked around him wildly, as if the past were lurking here in the shadow of his house, just out of reach." (A fuller discussion of the debt to Fitzgerald, and *The Great Gatsby* in particular, on *"Love and Theft"* can be found in Andrew Muir's *Troubadour*, pages 306–8.)

If the spirit of Fitzgerald's novel defined an age which provides the setting for "Summer Days," "Floater," and "Moonlight," Dylan is hoping said spirit can still inform the modern world. Hence, the allusions found in "Summer Days" to songs from said "golden age" like "Cotton-Eye Joe," "Hopped Up Mustang," and, last but by no means least, the traditional "Twenty-One Years," a song he recorded in St. Paul in 1960 and at the *World Gone Wrong* sessions in 1993 (and from which he took the line "I'm counting on you, babe, to give me a break"). "Summer Days" demonstrated that Dylan was now prepared to let such memorial impressions now crowd in.

The problem was that his editorial instincts were in almost as bad a state of disrepair as his voice. "Honest with Me," a gutbucket R&B tune that had seemingly just blown in from Chicago, "the city that never sleeps" (itself a reference to a 1953 noir film that was set in the Windy City), could have been an honest slice of down-home goodness on any album not so weighed down by the musically generic. But having restricted the permissible parameters of what his backing musicians could interject, Dylan decided *he* could go on as long as he liked—as if back in Nashville, and this the winter of '66.

"Honest with Me" might have begun life as a nice little protestation against a (specific) woman's perfidy ("You'd be honest with me, if only you knew . . . my feeling for you"), but by the time Dylan recut it on the tenth—having produced two takes at the previous day's session that were, according to the tape notes, "rockin' pretty good" and "more in the pocket"—he was obliged to resort to tradition in order to pad out the five six-line verses and provide him with the odd couplet ("I'm not sorry for nothing I've done / I'm glad I fought, I only wish we'd won," coming from the civil war song, "I'm a Good Ol' Rebel").

According to Augie Meyers—who also witnessed the tortuous *TOOM* sessions—Dylan was once again reworking lyrics at the sessions themselves, but this time he was not editing; he was *adding*. "[Dylan would] fool around for a while with a song, and then we'd cut it. And he'd say, 'I think I'm gonna write a couple more verses,' sit down and write five more verses. Each verse had six or eight lines. It's complicated stuff, and he was doing it right there."

The resultant songs were often without beginning or end and betrayed a general inconsistency of tone. Hence, perhaps, why so many of these songs—particularly the up-tempo ones—worked better in performance when Dylan could slur lesser lines and prune inferior verses, the words becoming blurred by the immediacy of the moment. These three songs certainly appealed to the singer on the road, Dylan racking up a staggering 661 performances of "Summer Days" (and 360 and 481 of the other two, respectively), by the end of 2008. By the end of the May 10 session, he had already ensured there was no danger of "get[ting] caught without up-tempo songs."

{578} LONESOME DAY BLUES

Published lyric/s: Lyrics 04.
*Known studio recordings: Clinton Recording Studios, NYC, May 11, 2001
[L+T—tk. 3].*
First known performance: La Crosse Center Arena, WI, October 24, 2001.

> I was [originally] using the ballad form. . . because I learned it in the folk
> circle . . . You can also tell the same story in a blues form . . . but once
> you get into production, you aren't going to tell much of the story at all.
> —Dylan, to Matt Damsker, September 1978

With "Lonesome Day Blues," Dylan made a concerted attempt
to use the blues to tell some immortal story with what, to his mind,
were archetypal figures (the soldier, the captain, the lover man, "the
longtime darling"). The musical structure alone ensured he would
fail—a basic twelve–bar blues was simply not designed to tell an
eleven-verse narrative, especially when the whole production forced
one to focus on that now-failing voice. And yet, according to Dylan,
there was an even longer narrative at one point: "If . . . I am going
in to record a song, I write more than I need. In the past that's been
a problem because I failed to use discretion at times. I have to guard
against that. On this album, 'Lonesome Day Blues' was twice as long
at one point."

The multitracks feature no such epic, though according to Chris
Shaw the first take did represent "the first time the band really got their
groove together, and Bob was just starting to sing it . . . As the song
progresses, you can hear him getting really into [it]." Shaw was hoping
this take might make *Tell Tale Signs*, before the decision was made to use
live versions of the two songs representing *"Love and Theft,"* "Lonesome
Day Blues" and "High Water." The February 2002 version of the former
has plenty of vim and verve, but it is no substitute for the subtlety of
thought that had once been the man's benchmark.

At least "Lonesome Day Blues" gave a thumbnail sketch of the
process Dylan was using and described thus, whereby he would "take a
song I know and simply start playing it . . . [and] at a certain point, some
of the words will change and I'll start writing a song." In this instance,

the point when the words began to change came some time after the first verse, lifted verbatim from Leroy Carr's "Blues Before Sunrise," which goes, "Today has been such a long and lonesome day / Been sittin' here thinkin' with my mind a million miles away."

The tune he began playing cleverly combined Howlin' Wolf's "Crying at Daybreak" with Muddy Waters's "Lonesome Day," presumably in the (forlorn) hope that the spirit of Chess might yet inhabit the song. However, there was no such musical debt to Blind Willie McTell's "Lonesome Day Blues," even if Dylan was indebted to that musical idol for a title he decided to make his own. Shame he couldn't kick the habit of showing off the breadth of his recent reading and movie viewing. Actually, the best joke in the song is a line from the classic W. C. Fields movie *The Fatal Glass of Beer*, "Weather not fit for man nor beast"—which in the movie always results in a bucket of water being thrown over the hapless star. Here it is used to convey the obstacles the song's narrator must overcome to get back home.

Elsewhere, Dylan delights in lifting yet more lines from those constant bedside companions Mark Twain's *The Adventures of Tom Sawyer* and Junichi Saga's *Confessions of a Yakuza*. The former provides a welcome alternative narrative. "My sister . . . run off and got married and never was heard of no more" acts as an undercurrent to the whole song, Twain going on to say, "I felt so lonesome I most wished I was dead. The stars was shining, and the leaves rustled in the woods ever so mournful . . . and the wind was trying to whisper something to me and I couldn't make out what it was." From Saga's more oriental home Dylan copped a less congruent attitude, "There was nothing sentimental about him—it didn't bother him at all that some of his pals had been killed" and an affected disinterest in others' opinions, "I don't know how it looked to other people, but I never even slept with her—not once."

Consciously or not, his use of the Twain texts seems both apposite and artistic, whereas the Saga stuff just comes across as stitched on. Nor was his (mis)use of *Confessions of a Yakuza* an isolated instance. The tenth verse in particular seems to have been interpolated by some mischievous monk to whom the task of transcribing another goddamn illuminated manuscript has started to wear on his nerves:

{ Still on the Road }

I'm going to spare the defeated, I'm going to speak to the crowd,
I'm going to teach peace to the conquered, I'm going to tame the proud.

Whether this is or isn't proof of an old man belatedly immersing himself in the classics, it is surely a conscious echo of a section from Virgil's *Aeneid*—"Remember Rome . . . this shall be thy task, to impose the ways of peace, to spare the vanquished, and to tame the proud by war." But again it fails to *fit* into a song that, for all its meandering seemed, until the penultimate verse, to be heading toward some kind of appropriately Dylanesque resolution. As it is, the moral of the song proves something of a disappointment: stop playing with yourself, darling; I'm coming home (or, as he puts it, "You're gonna need my help, sweetheart, you can't make love all by yourself").

{579} BYE AND BYE

Published lyric/s: Lyrics 04.
Known studio recordings: Clinton Recording Studios, NYC, May 12, 2001—8 takes [L+T—tk. 6].
First known performance: Wiltern Theatre, L.A., October 17, 2001.

> Many of these songs were written in some kind of "stream of consciousness" kind of mood, and I don't sit and linger, meditate on every line afterwards. My approach is just to let it happen. —Dylan, at press conference, July 2001

Between May 12 and 16, Dylan cut the four songs that stopped the album from becoming one long hard trawl through the Mississippi Delta: "Bye and Bye," "Floater," "Moonlight," and "Po' Boy," in that order, before returning us to the south just as the waters have begun to rise ("High Water"). "Bye and Bye" seems to have taken the most time and effort. The handful of takes that were transferred to the multis tell only a small part of the story, there being some eleven takes that were rolled over, some of which tried various different tempos (104, 106, and 110 beats per minute, the tape comments tell us), taking up one and a half DAT tapes, i.e., two and a half hours of tape (the DAT ID log is marked thirty-nine different times). The key of the song also changed from D-flat to B-flat, while it is attempted with and without "organ shuffle" (whatever that means). In the end, Dylan goes for the sixth of eight takes preserved on tape, in B-flat, and despite a long day at the coalface insists on beginning work on "Floater."

"Bye and Bye" as Dylan's chosen title lays another false trail, alluding to two songs he undoubtedly knew—both gospel standards—the one, "By and By" recorded by Elvis on *How Great Thou Art* (1967), the other, Blind Willie Johnson's "Bye and Bye Goin' to See the King," a song he rehearsed back in 1980. From this pair he took naught save perhaps the spirit of salvation found in Johnson's track, which infuses the *"Love and Theft"* song's final verse.

"I'm gonna baptize you in fire / So you can sin no more" alludes to both John the Baptist's prophecy that He would come and "baptize you with the Holy Ghost, and with fire" (Matthew 3:11) and J.C. Himself's admonishment to the fallen woman to "sin no more" (John 8:11). Yet such sentiments seem at odds with the rest of the song, which takes much of its tenor *and* tune from Billie Holiday's "Having Myself a Time." (The arrangement at least does enough with Holiday's original to suggest something more than a straight copy.) Chris Shaw was presumably referring to this very song when developing his thoughts on an aspect of Dylan's methodology at these sessions:

> He's always trying to find the arrangement that works best with the sentiment he's trying to express. He might say, "I'm kinda hearing this old Billie Holiday song." And so, we'll start with that: the band will actually start playing that song, try to get that sound, and then he'll go, "OK, and this is how my song goes."

"Bye and Bye" seems to be one instance where Dylan took heed of his own advice, using his "discretion" to prune the song down from more unwieldy origins, evinced in the one latter-day draft lyric to be included in the 2004 edition of *Lyrics*, a six-verse manuscript of this song on headed paper from the St. Regis Club, New York (which was probably where Dylan was staying during the recording sessions).

If this really was the lyric as it stood when he checked in to the exclusive club in early May, then Dylan meant it when he said the following July, "The tracks were not yet complete when we went into the studio. I had a general idea in mind, but not their finished form." The only parts of the finished song already in place are the opening couplets to verses one, two, and four, and a couple of other stray phrases, of which "Gonna establish my rule by civil war" appears in verse two on paper, but in the final verse on record.

By take six on May 12, the six verses will have become four, and the three bridges two, losing a part of the narrative concerned with someone hot on his trail (at one point he has admonished himself, "Gotta be quick on the trigger, practise a lot," while at another he is on the look out for a "low down scurvy ol' man / He'll stab you where you stand"). The unexpected introduction of a well-known character from a Shakespearean tragedy in verse five also suggests the threat may be greater than he first thought:

> Macbeth layin' on the couch, he got his sabres drawn, armies aligned,
> Writing poems to [make you] lose your mind.

However, for all its air of menace, this draft refrains from any allusion to the judgment to come. Rather, in the last verse, he has a different kind of trouble in mind: "Smokestack lightnin' shinin' like gold / Ingratitude just makes my blood run cold." The former line is Howlin' Wolf's; the latter line could be another allusion to Twain, specifically *The Mysterious Stranger*: "He turned on the boy and reproached him for his ingratitude, and then he fired up on his subject and turned his tongue and temper loose . . . The way the magician finished was awful; it made your blood run cold."

Feeling the need to prune a bridge or two, he also lost an allusion to another obscure jive 45, Billy Wilson's "Hen Pecked Boogie" and maybe one more from *The Adventures of Tom Sawyer* ("Tom listened a moment, but no *sound* disturbed the quiet . . . [just] the stillness, the solemnity that brooded in the *woods*, and the sense of loneliness"): "They doin' the hen-pecked boogie out on the north end of town, / Lord, at night in the woods you can't hear a sound." As it is, the released recording is almost entirely free of such allusions. Could it be he was worried he might be overdoing the references?

{580} FLOATER (TOO MUCH TO ASK)

Published lyric/s: Lyrics 04.
Known studio recordings: Clinton Recording Studios, NYC, May 12 and 14, 2001—5 takes [L+T—tk. 4].
First known performance: Orpheum Theater, Sioux City, IA, October 23, 2001.

I can imagine every situation in life as if I've done it, no matter what it might be: Whether it be like self-punishment or marrying my half-sister . . . I can feel all these things for some reason. —Dylan, to Karen Hughes, April 1978

"Floater (Too Much to Ask)"—or, as it was listed on the tape boxes, "Too Much to Ask (Floater)"—is definitely Dylan trying to stretch the parameters of his art, and it should be welcomed for that. It also has some lovely lines and a vocal that makes light of an unfamiliar structure, deftly disposing of any suspicion that he may have been looking to tread water on his first album of the new century. But for all its bravura as a performance piece, the song fails to engage or convince.

Its first problem stems from Dylan's decision to take as his musical template a song Bing Crosby had covered as early as 1932, "Snuggled on Your Shoulder." Having praised Crosby's phrasing as early as 1985, Dylan found that the more he investigated Crosby's work, the more he learned to appreciate it: "It never occurred to me [when I was young] that Bing Crosby was on the cutting edge twenty years before I was listening to him. I never heard *that* Bing Crosby." By 2001, he had fully immersed himself in "*that* Bing Crosby," but he was no longer vocally equipped to take on the king of crooners' mantle.

The effortless way Crosby could smooth out the roughest line in a song went against everything Dylan had been taught about phrasing by Lead Belly, Guthrie, and Johnson (in that order). And, as he would learn the hard way over these twelve days, you can't teach an old dog owner new tricks. "Floater" used up some twenty-nine DAT IDs before Dylan rewound to ID #25 (aka take four) for the album track, which he slowed down some 3 percent. Tempo was again an issue, as Dylan experimented with 121, 134, and 136 bpms. Most of the failed takes, though, were rolled over; and again, it took a day off, and a rethink, before he discovered what it was he wanted. In "Floater," rather than "trying to find the arrangement that works best with the sentiment he's trying to express," Dylan settled for largely replicating the 1932 snuggle song.

The tale he purports to tell, though murkier than most, is not entirely his own, having learned a lesson it took Ernest Hemingway to point out to F. Scott Fitzgerald: "The good parts of a book may be only something a writer is lucky enough to overhear, or it may be the wreck of his whole damn life—and one is as good as the other." At the time he was given such advice, Fitzgerald was hard at work on *The Great Gatsby*, from which Dylan probably took this song's "real" title, "Too Much to Ask." (In *Gatsby*, "I wouldn't ask too much of her" is the line before "You can't repeat the past," a line we know he borrowed.)

Like Fitzgerald, Dylan was actively engaged in creating a mythopoeic account of a fictional character with some awfully autobiographical attributes at the exact same time he was writing *"Love and Theft."* That project became the film *Masked and Anonymous*; as his coauthor Larry Charles confirmed in conversation, "[Yes,] he was working on 'Love and Theft' . . . In fact I had the privilege of going to the recording studio; and what happens is a lot of lines that didn't wind up in *Masked and Anonymous* winded [*sic*] up in 'Love and Theft,' and vice versa."

Visceral connections occur throughout the two projects. At one point, Dylan's film character talks about how his parents "were happy once, although it's hard to imagine now. Everything in their lives was infused with hope and meaning. Every thought, every emotion, still pure. It seems so long ago now . . ." which comes pretty close to replicating the underlying tone of perhaps the most moving—and certainly the best sung—verse in "Floater":

> My grandfather was a duck trapper
> He could do it with just dragnets and ropes
> My grandmother could sew new dresses out of old cloth
> I don't know if they had any dreams or hopes
> I had 'em once though, I suppose,
> To go along with all the ring dancin,"
> Christmas carols on all of the Christmas Eves
> I left all my dreams and hopes buried under tobacco leaves

For sure, Dylan thought he had found a new way of working. As he told one U.S. reporter between album and movie projects, "I'll take some of the stuff that people think is true and I'll build a story around that." Though he professed to be talking about his imminent autobiography, this approach is equally evident in the two works which preceded *Chronicles'* publication—ditto the way he elected to have a little fun with the archetypes of classical mythology. One hilarious vignette included in the *Masked and Anonymous* shooting script, but absent from the final cut, concerned a confrontation between Jack Fate and Oedipus (only identified in the script as "Blind Man"), where the latter comes across like a gate-crasher at a psychiatrists' convention:

> **Blind Man**: You don't know me, but I've heard of you. We have a lot in common. Pity me. I murdered my father in a scuffle, stabbed him in the neck. I married my mother in a lavish ceremony attended by hundreds. I put out my own eyes. I was forewarned that I would do this, and by golly, I did. All of the pieces of my life are not in good shape, but some things are in perfect order. It disgusted me when I had my fortune read and I was forewarned of what I was about to do. It was the last thing I ever thought would happen. I ran as far as I could to get away. I even ran to another country and I thought I was safe. I never thought it would happen to me, killing my father and marrying my mother. I wanted to turn and run and disappear. But to hear Dr. Freud tell it, I had it all planned out from the beginning. I'd strangle him if I could. He slandered me. He never met me. He made it all up. Dr. Freud, he wrote about me from cocaine hell . . . Psychotherapy, that great science, with no fixed laws. An entire industry based on cocaine fantasies and hallucinations.

It had been a while since Dylan had had to decide whether to apply his imagination pictorially or orally, but it would remain an issue as late as his 2009 interview with Bill Flanagan: "Say you wake up in a hotel room in Wichita and look out the window. A little girl is walking along the train tracks dragging a big statue of Buddha in a wooden wagon with a three-legged dog following behind. Do you reach for your guitar or your drawing pad?" (Though the question is credited to Flanagan, it reads like one of those Dylan rewrote while framing his e-mail answer.)

Also in the *M&A* film script was a cavalcade of characters from Shakespeare, transposed to unfamiliar surroundings (Prospero, Edgar, and Edmund each talk the vernacular, yet all conform to aspects of their Shakespearean selves in Dylan's brave new world). No surprise then that in "Floater" we have Romeo saying to Juliet, "You got a poor complexion, it don't give you an appearance of a youthful touch" and Juliet snapping back, "Why don't you just shove off if it bothers you so much" (a retort that actually comes verbatim from the Saga *Confessions* . . .). Meanwhile, Othello and Desdemona would become components of "Po' Boy."

This time, though, he was drawing a number of scenarios not from his imagination (or from Humphrey Bogart movies) but from the life and times of a real-life Japanese gangster from the first half of the twentieth century, Eiji Ijichi, a member of the yakuza who told his life story to Japanese doctor-author Junichi Saga shortly before his death. Over half of those lines in *"Love and Theft"* generally accepted as derived from Saga's book appear in "Floater," which is one way for Dylan to "take some of the stuff that people think is true and . . . build a story around that." In a song almost top-heavy with sayings, few are original to Dylan. "Age don't carry weight / It doesn't matter in the end" barely modifies the thoughts of Ijichi on the subject, "Age by itself just doesn't carry any weight." Likewise, it is Ijichi who says, "I'm not as cool or forgiving as I might have sounded" and who remembered how his "old man would sit there like a feudal lord."

When Dylan transposed such dialogue to his 2002 film, it fit a whole lot better (where it is Jack Fate's father, not Jack Frost, who presides over a political world). But it is *"Love and Theft"* which contains a character who really does say, "If you ever try to interfere with me, or cross my path again, you do so at the peril of your own life," a statement evidently gleaned from recent reading on the American Civil War, now transposed to "Floater" (it was said to Confederate General Braxton Bragg by Brigadier Nathan Bedford Forrest after the Battle of Chickamauga, when the Confederates again managed to snatch defeat from the jaws of victory). Again, the purpose of the exercise remains unclear. It may say everything about the interconnectedness of his working methods, but it tells us precious little about Dylan's worldview. And however much "Floater" jumped out on album, in concert it became little more than a sore-thumb shuffle.

{581} MOONLIGHT

Published lyric/s: Lyrics 04.

Known studio recordings: Clinton Recording Studios, NYC, May 15, 2001—4 takes [L+T—tk. 4 +insert].

First known performance: Key Arena, Seattle, WA, October 6, 2001.

When setting out to write "Moonlight," Dylan was again taking song ideas from the very font of Americana. "Meet Me by the Moonlight Alone" was one of A. P. Carter's famous hybrids, combining the traditional "Prisoner Song" with an early nineteenth-century English parlor song by Joseph Augustine Wade. First recorded by the Carter Family in May 1928, it became one of their most popular songs.

Dylan's own attempt to write a song along similar lines ended up more closely resembling a parlor song than Carter's grittier composition. Yet he seems to have enjoyed the experience, because he decided to continue the experiment on *Modern Times* (and, indeed, *Together Through Life*), trying to jam a phraseology bathed in traditional verities into a music-hall setting. It shows most obviously in those lines that manage to be both formulaic and inept. Phrases like "the masquerade of birds and bees"—a desperate rhyme for "cypress trees"—or "The trailing moss in mystic glow"—a line used by one bootlegger as an album title—are wincingly bad.

And the days when he could compensate for such lyrical lapses with a devastating vocal were fast receding, even if engineer Shaw has "really fond memories of recording . . . 'Moonlight' . . . I think the take that's on the record is the second take, the whole thing is completely live, vocals and all, not a single overdub, no editing, it all just flowed together at once." Not according to the track sheet, it wasn't. The take used was in fact number four, though another three had been done and rolled over. And according to the same sheet, there were two attempts at an ending insert, though whether they were then used is not clear. (Why even record them if the take "flowed together"?) I'm afraid, insert or not, I do not share Shaw's rose-tinted view of the song, though at least Dylan's decision to grace the song in early live performances with a nice harmonica intro was a smart one, making it sound like the product of an Appalachian parlor, rather than a London front room.

{582} PO' BOY

Published lyric/s: Lyrics 04.
*Known studio recordings: Clinton Recording Studios, NYC, May 16, 2001—3
takes [L+T—tk. 1].*
First known performance: Van Andel Arena, Grand Rapids, MI, November 6, 2001.

> There's some humor in my songs . . . I think there are funny things
> inside a lot of them . . . It's kind of mixed up so much that I wouldn't be
> one to just point and say, "This is funny." —Dylan, to Denise Worrell,
> November 1985

"Po' Boy"—recorded a couple of days after "Floater"—is very much
a continuation in both style and content. Its largest failing is that the
jokes herein are lamer—not to say telegraphed. The one exception,
"Calls down to room service, says 'Send up a room.'" he took, directly
or indirectly, from the Marx Brothers" 1938 *Room Service*, itself a celluloid version of a successful stage play. Like the W. C. Fields line in
"Lonesome Day Blues," it was essentially vaudeville humor (and therefore drawn from the same milieu as the musical influences he was keen
to display).

And just like "Floater," characters from one of Shakespeare's greatest
tragedies find themselves transposed to "Po' Boy," sharing the same
setting with our Japanese gangster in a song that has plenty of rhyme but
no clear reason. One verse, the seventh, is taken almost verbatim from
Saga's saga. Transposing the recollections of the yakuza—"My mother
. . . was the daughter of a wealthy farmer . . . [she] died when I was
eleven . . . My father was a traveling salesman . . . I never met him. [My
uncle] was a nice man, I won't forget him"—Dylan constructs a narrative
lifetimes removed from his own experiences (hence his sardonic claim
on the album's release that it "is completely autobiographical"). He was
also claiming that his twenty-first-century audience had learned to take
his work at face value: "My audience now . . . feel style and substance in
a more visceral way and let it go at that. Images don't hang [them] up.
Like if there's an astrologer with a criminal record in one of my songs
it's not going to make anybody wonder if the human race is doomed."
Could you blow just a little more smoke in my face, pleeze?!

The vignette involving Othello and his wife in verse five is, on the face of it, equally removed from his established worldview:

> Othello told Desdemona, "I'm cold, cover me with a blanket,
> By the way, what happened to that poisoned wine?'
> She said, "I gave it to you, [you] drank it."

This is more like the old Dylan of "I Dreamed I Saw St. Augustine" via "Desolation Row," disguising one archetype with another. He admitted to such a practice a couple of years later in *Chronicles*: "I have a problem sometimes remembering someone's real name, so I give them another one, something that more accurately describes them."

There is a *reason* why Dylan has transferred these two characters into this off-kilter ballad—they came from ballad lore all along. The real name of the man is either Lord Randall or Lord Henry, both characters being poisoned by their lover; the former of whom asks to lie down, the latter of whom asks if his wine has been spiked. Dylan had previously interpreted both ancient ballads, the latter as recently as 1993. So much for Dylan's contemporaneous claim that "Po' Boy" was a work of simple virtues, which "doesn't require . . . words. The ones I have written simply follow the melody and don't impose too much emotional rhetoric on it."

Having changed the setting to something more in keeping with the original "Po' Boy"—a traditional blues "covered" by the likes of Bukka White and Sonny Terry & Brownie McGhee—Dylan decided to produce a tapestry of mixed-up confusion that would serve to take our minds off the fact that "the human race is doomed" by reminding us that "mystery is a traditional fact." The song came pretty quickly, too. After a taped rehearsal, take one was a keeper, though it would appear that an insert comprising the last two verses was edited on the same day. Dylan then tried a bossa nova version, before sticking with what he already had.

For the first time at these sessions, Dylan had been leading by example, i.e., with guitar. As Shaw says, "We went in [to the sessions] thinking he was going to be playing guitar . . . Within two minutes, he abandoned the whole idea, wandered over to the piano, and never got off it . . . except for . . . 'High Water' and 'Po' Boy'." "High Water"—the next song he records—would continue to mess around with archetypal names, but its import was not so abstruse . . .

{583} HIGH WATER (FOR CHARLIE PATTON)

Published lyric/s: Lyrics 04.
Known studio recordings: Clinton Recording Studios, NYC, May 17, 2001—1 take [L+T—tk. 1+insert].
First known performance: Staples Center, L.A., October 19, 2001.

> My songs . . . remain contemporary. Something didn't have to fall out
> of the sky yesterday for it to be of these times. —Dylan, at Rome press
> conference, July 2001

Six weeks before he released his first album of the new century, Dylan gave a press conference to around a dozen European journalists who had previously been allowed a single listen to his latest album, due for release on September 11, 2001—the day when something really did "fall out of the sky," and the world stopped spinning on one axis and began spinning on quite another. If ever there was a song that captured that moment, not literally, but *prophetically*, it was Dylan's "High Water": "Nothing standing there . . . It's tough out there . . . Things are breaking up out there . . . It's bad out there / High water everywhere."

Back in May, "High Water" also marked the point in the sessions when Dylan raised his game. With just three songs left to record (which duly became four when someone remembered "Mississippi"), he stopped pretending he could be another Bing, realized never the Twain, and went back to doing what he did best, crafting something uniquely *his* out of everything his record player liked to play. This time his starting point was both propitious and apposite—Charlie Patton's two-part "High Water Everywhere."

Patton was writing in real time about something specific—the Great Mississippi Flood of 1927, which lasted for some eight months, and at one point covered some 27,000 square miles. In that time, the levees broke in 145 places. Not surprisingly, this catastrophe of almost biblical proportions inspired a number of songs from southern singers. Dylan preferred to make it a metaphor for every big flood, knowing full well it might be fire next time. As he was obliged to remind himself, he was not making a sequel to *World Gone Wrong*: "['*Love and Theft*'] is not an album I've recorded to please myself. If I really wanted to do that, I would record some Charlie Patton songs."

This time all the references stop short of being intrusive, though there's hardly a shortage of them. Patton himself gets a couple, notably the line "Bertha Mason shook it, broke it, and she hung it on the wall," which alludes to Patton's own "Shake It and Break It (But Don't Let It Fall Mama)"—and probably to Bertha Lee, Patton's wife. In fact, it seems Dylan can barely wait to start having fun with some of his favorite listening from yesteryear. In verse one, a name-check for Big Joe Turner sets him off, suggesting he was looking to cover more of that weird ol' America in five minutes than Greil Marcus managed in the whole of *Invisible Republic*:

> Big Joe Turner looking east and west from the dark room of his mind,
> He made it to Kansas City, Twelfth Street and Vine.

Cute. Dylan knows Turner made an album called *Kansas City Here I Come*, just as he knows Twelfth Street and Vine got a name-check in Wilbert Harrison's "Kansas City," a song he had covered himself. But for once there is nothing pasted on about this couplet. Turner paid his dues, just like Patton did. As with earlier songs at these sessions—but this time seamlessly—Dylan knowingly drops song titles into the "High Water" narrative (whether it's "Hopped Up Mustang," a Bill Romberger 45, or "I Believe I'll Dust My Broom," the quintessential Robert Johnson cut).

Other times, we get the odd snatch of a traditional lyric: "Judge says to the High Sheriff, I want him dead or alive" comes from a song Dylan last sang publicly when he was twenty years old, "Po' Lazarus"; "the cuckoo is a pretty bird, she warbles as she flies" comes from one he sang when just twenty-one, "The Cuckoo Is a Pretty Bird." (Actually, this is one line that smacks of having to find a rhyme, proving that even on this fine song he was sometimes knocking vainly at inspiration's door.)

Generally, though, the delights keep coming. "I'm no pig without a wig, I hope you treat me kind" hardly sounds like a nursery rhyme, but its source was another nineteenth-century childlike snatch, "Upon my word and honor / As I was going to Bonner / I met a pig without a wig / Upon my word and honor." Likewise, the line "Keeping away from the women, I'm giving them lots of room" is a clever play on the rhyming line ("I believe I'll dust my broom"), though only if one knows it comes from the traditional nagging song "Bald Headed End of a Broom" the chorus of which goes:

> Oh boys, stay away from the girls, I say,
> Oh give them lots of room.
> They'll find you and you'll wed,
> And they'll bang you till you're dead,
> With the bald-headed end of a broom.

But "High Water" is not just a composite of ghostly reminders from tradition's rich pageant; it is "filled with rambling ghosts and disturbed spirits . . . all screaming and forlorning. It's like they are caught in some weird web—some purgatory between heaven and hell and they can't rest," which is the way Dylan would later describe that whole "southern air" to Bill Flanagan. This is the same fetid air that suffuses both "High Water" and "Sugar Baby," the two most successful songs on *Love and Theft*"—along with the works of Tennessee Williams, another literary backdrop to everything good on the album.

Perhaps Dylan just worked on "High Water" longer and/or harder than the other songs he hoped might breathe the same air. The tape log suggests not. He got it in a single take and never went near it again, save to tinker with that elemental first take. Simple. Just not quite the whole story. The last song logged on the sixteenth was a two-and-a-half minute "bluegrass rehearsal." Though on first glance this appears to be a continuation of "Po' Boy," a bluegrass version of that cut seems a tad unlikely and, anyway, that song is done. The rehearsal take is rolled over (though hopefully preserved on DAT, ID#9). Next on the multi-track is that single version of "High Water" (though a DAT ID of #15 again suggests rehearsals may have been recorded live to DAT). This version is almost a minute longer than the released version, timed at five minutes, five seconds. It is also dated May 17 (though it is on a reel dated May 16). But nothing else is recorded that day, save for an eighty-second insert to "High Water" itself, which rather suggests that either the album was now done, or Dylan had yet to finish writing the couple of songs he still wanted to record.

As for "High Water," it would appear that—single take or not—Dylan redid parts of the song after the fact, specifically his own vocal (as Doug Sahm Band veteran Augie Meyers—recruited specifically for these sessions by Dylan—told *Rolling Stone*'s David Fricke: "Bob don't like to overdub much . . . [but] sometimes he'd overdub his voice. If he messed up [a vocal], he'd overdub a word or two"). He evidently changed more than a word or two, as on the one-inch digital mix reels for the album, a version mixed on the eighteenth is marked "High Water (old lyrics)" (and has the same timing as the live take). Another version is listed as "High Water #2" and is doubtless the version on the album. This was apparently a cut-up of an edit of an inserted dub of that first take. According to Shaw, "The verse order was changed quite a few times, literally hacking the tape up. He was like, 'Nah, maybe the third verse should come first.'"

The resultant version, released on the album, is terrific—as compelling musically as it is lyrically—but one would still love to hear how it sounded with an alternative/fuller lyric. When the opportunity arose, though—with the eighth volume in *The Bootleg Series*—a 2003 live version that wouldn't have been out of place on 1974's *Before the Flood* got the vote. As the man himself said back in 1980, "[Elvis] in 1969 . . . was just full-out power. There was nothing other than force behind that. I've fallen into that trap, too . . . It's a very thin line you have to walk to stay in touch with something once you've created it." By the time Dylan delivered the "High Water" included on *Tell Tale Signs*—a high-summer show in Canada—he was caught in that trap.

Yet "High Water" had been one of *the* outstanding performances at the intermittently impressive series of shows that came in the immediate aftermath of the album's 9/11 release. A vocal as understated as the album's was complemented by some lovely banjo picking by Larry Campbell, while the song itself was taken at an even more stately pace. Delivered to audiences of fellow Americans still in a collective state of shock, the song not only asserted its contemporary relevance, but was imbued with more ghosts than even Dylan could have imagined when he wrote it. Sadly, will alone has not enabled him to continue walking the same line. By 2002 Dylan had defaulted to "just full-out power."

{584} CRY A WHILE

Published lyric/s: Lyrics 04.
Known studio recordings: Clinton Recording Studios, NYC, May 18, 2001—2 takes [L+T—tk. 2].
First known performance: Sacramento Memorial Auditorium, CA, October 10, 2001.

> The old Chess records, the Sun records. . . I think that's my favorite sound for a record . . . I like . . . the intensity. The sound is uncluttered. There's power and suspense. The whole vibration feels like it could be coming from inside your mind. It's alive. It's right there. —Dylan, to Bill Flanagan, 2009

For the tenth song recorded at the *"Love and Theft"* sessions, Dylan returned to his "favorite sound," the one that came out of 2120 South Michigan Avenue, Chicago—fabled locale of Chess Studios when they had the likes of Chuck Berry, Sonny Boy Williamson, Howlin' Wolf, Otis Span, and Willie Dixon recording for them. In fact, the template for "Cry a While" featured no less than three of these gentlemen. Otis Span played piano and Willie Dixon plucked the bass on the March 1958 Sonny Boy Williamson session that resulted in "Your Funeral and My Trial."

As with the song that started this whole appropriation-as-art-form conceit—"Mississippi"—Dylan directly cops to his musical debt in the final couplet: "I might need a good lawyer, could be your funeral, my trial / Well, I cried for you, not it's your turn, you can cry awhile." And, like those guys, Dylan was determined to cut "Cry a While" in a couple of takes, max. Having conjured up usable first takes of both "Po' Boy" and "High Water" in the last couple of days, the man was on a roll and, sure 'nuff, he got the song on the second take, without a single roll over. Leonard would have been proud of him.

The song's conceptual debt did not, however, come from the Windy

City, though it could have come from any number of folk whose imprint was all over this album. "I Cried for You (Now It's Your Turn to Cry Over Me)" was the kind of standard that was bound to attract—and did—the likes of Billie Holiday, Bing Crosby, and Louis Armstrong. But it took Dylan to see that such a title suggested an electric blues, not a jazz standard.

Just to reinforce his stylistic switch, Dylan even dropped in a line from "The Dope Head Blues," a 1927 recording by his old friends, Lonnie Johnson and Victoria Spivey ("Feel like a fighting rooster, feeling better than I ever felt") and instituted (and kept) a tempo change at the start of it all, as if he had yet to decide which way the song should go. At the same time, he recovered his sense of humor, sending up the plot of a Donizetti opera with "It must have been Don Pasquale making a two A.M. booty call." He also satirized America's obsession with weight: "I'm longing for that sweet fat that sticks to your ribs" and perhaps dug into one of his Marx Brothers boxed sets for the line "Well, you bet on a horse, and it ran the wrong way." All things considered, "Cry a While" stands as the best of the songs on Dylan's 2001 album bearing a Chicago postmark.

{585} SUGAR BABY

Published lyric/s: Lyrics 04.
Known studio recordings: Clinton Recording Studios, NYC, May 19, 2001—7 takes [L+T—tk. 7].
First known performance: Spokane Arena, WA, October 5, 2001.

> Sam Cooke, the Coasters, Phil Spector, all that music was great but it didn't exactly break into my consciousness . . . As far as songwriting, I wanted to write songs like Woody Guthrie and Robert Johnson. Timeless and eternal. Only a few of those radio ballads still hold up. —Dylan, to Bill Flanagan, 2009

In a nutshell, Dylan here explains why so much of what he began playing on his weekly radio show, shortly after this album's release, has had so little direct bearing on his own art. The quest for the timeless and the eternal did, however, lead him to one of the most enduring of the "radio ballads" of the late twenties: "The Lonesome Road," recorded by Gene Austin using a tune he wrote with his longtime lyricist, Nat Shilkret. This masterful wrist-slasher not only provided Dylan with *"Love and Theft"*'s much-needed punch line ("Look up, look up, seek your Maker, 'fore Gabriel blows his horn"), but also gave him a way of using some original lyrics that had been lying around for five years or more ("Sugar Baby"'s opening couplet—"I got my back to the sun"— appeared first in the original 1996 demo for "Can't Wait"). One might even, unkindly, suggest that Shilkret managed in two verses what it took Dylan five to approximate:

> Look down, look down that lonesome road
> Before you travel on.
> Look up, look up and seek your maker
> 'fore Gabriel blows his horn.
> True love, true love, what have I done
> That you should treat me so,
> You caused me to walk and talk
> Like I never done before.

Dylan brought more than mere affection for Austin's original recording to the task at hand—he brought a copy of the 1928 recording, from which he evidently intended to cop the entire arrangement to "Sugar Baby." That it was Austin's quintessential version—and not any of the myriad cover versions by the likes of Frank Sinatra, Sam Cooke, or, again, Bing Crosby—a single listen to the (now out-of-copyright) original confirms. Which is not to say that Dylan hadn't become aware of the song from Cooke's snappy rendition on his 1958 debut solo album— as and when Sam's wondrous work managed to "break into [Dylan's] consciousness"—or from Sinatra, who used it to introduce each episode of his prime-time TV series in 1957–8.

But to hear that tolling bell and that doleful violin on the Austin 78 is to hear "Sugar Baby" in prototype. And if the musicians didn't have the same versing in old-time music that their employer did, Dylan made sure he introduced them to as much of it as time allowed, just as he had with

The Band back in 1967. Chris Shaw confirms that part of the recording process "on both '*Love and Theft*' and *Modern Times* [was when] Bob would sometimes come in with reference tracks, old songs, saying, 'I want the track to be like this.'" In "Sugar Baby"'s case, he definitely wanted more than the general vibe which had sufficed on everything recorded to date—he wanted them to travel down that same lonesome road.

And this took time. Only after twenty-eight DAT IDs and eleven multitrack takes (starting with ID #11), four of which he then rolled over, did they manage to replicate the Austin vibe respectfully enough for their old-school bandleader. Dylan knew this was a summation of everything he'd set out to say just eleven days earlier. Having probably redrafted this lyric at the last minute, to add filling to the last remaining sandwich from this odd smorgasbord—and after taking its closing line from Austin, and the opening lines from an earlier demo—the remainder of the song stuck to the same brief that had already informed most other songs recorded that fortnight.

Taking its title from the first track Dock Boggs recorded, back in 1927, Dylan made another reference to Huckleberry Finn, whose Aunt Sally wasn't really his aunt, and name-checked a Shelton Brooks song, "The Darktown Strutters Ball," which he presumably taught to The Band back in 1967 (they mention it on the sleeve of their seminal second album). But this time he wrote a lyric that actually lived up to the boast he made to Mikal Gilmore a few months later: "I've got enough superfluous lines in a lot of songs. But I've kind of passed that point." Between all these crowded memories, real and invented, Dylan duly inserted his own dolorous chorus:

> Sugar baby, get on down the road, ain't got no brains, no how,
> You went years without me—you might as well keep going now.

For a man who would be sixty in a matter of days—actually, three days after the last *L&T* recording session—"Sugar Baby" was a necessary big statement, even if he managed to sum up its message in a single sentence to Robert Hilburn later in the year: "Any day above the ground is a good day." And such was the power of this song that it was invariably greeted in concert with enough respectful awe for Dylan to spend seven or so minutes enunciating each and every last word, his affection only growing for what he had wrought.

Indeed, it slightly surprises me that Dylan did not use "Sugar Baby" at the end of *Masked and Anonymous*, reinforcing the sense that Judgment falls on everyone. That last line, delivered by a man on his knees, may not be one of his, but the setting is exactly right, reflecting a feeling that manages to be both painfully immediate and go way back. As he told *Rolling Stone*'s editor Jann Wenner after his next album closer reiterated these sentiments, "[The sense that] every day is a judgment . . . is instilled in me by the way I grew up; where I come from; early feelings."

{586} WAITIN' FOR YOU

Published lyric/s: Words Fill My Head

Known studio recordings: Sony Recording Studios, NYC, November 26, 2001 [DSYS].

First known performance: Brixton Academy, London, November 21, 2005.

"Waitin' for You" represents another oddity in the Dylan canon. Recorded specifically for the soundtrack of an equally odd film, *The Divine Secrets of the Ya-Ya Sisterhood*, it then popped up, wholly unexpectedly, in the live set, four years later, during another idiosyncratic London residency (alongside the likes of the Clash's "London Calling" and Fats Domino's "Blue Monday")—where it was even graced with a delightful little harmonica coda.

Unlike *"Love and Theft,"* "Waitin' for You" was recorded at Sony in New York, just two days after coming off another gruelling stint on the unending road. And again, it shows in a vocal that sounds like it has already taken a beating. The song itself is pleasant enough, though it is a long way short of the classic croon-tune which probably provided its trigger, Alec Wilder's "I'll Be Around." Indeed, Dylan's 2001 performance is some way short of his one-time-only acoustic version of the Wilder song at L.A.'s Greek Theatre in August 1988.

In Dylan's song, the refrain has become, "I'll be around, waitin'" for you"—rather than, "I'll be around till he's said good-bye"—but you get the drift. Again he takes liberties with a number of disparate sources, some obvious ("Another deal gone down, another man done gone," a two-for-one deal on borrowed song titles), others apposite (Webb Pierce's "Been So Long," from which he nicks a coupla lines), and one positively surreal—his first overt reference to Shelley, a poet he'd been citing for thirty years. And in the now usual way he takes a blender to them all. In one line he is name-checking a Bobby Vee song ("The Night with a Thousand Eyes"), in the next he is paraphrasing a line from Shelley's lyrical drama *Hellas* ("Hope may vanish, but can die not"). The overall effect is as mixed and as unsettling as the album which preceded it, but the post-9/11 reviews convinced him he could continue this experiment till his tour bus's wheels fall off and burn.

2002–6

{ Modern Times }

In days of yore, Dylan had been something of a master when it came to producing trilogies of albums that served as the building blocks for a greater whole—witness the three acoustic albums he recorded between 1962 and 1964, the great electric trio of 1965–66, that (anti-) romantic trio he completed between November 1973 and July 1975, and the so-called religious trilogy released in the years 1979–81. The album he recorded in February 2006 proved to be the last volume in a trilogy of albums all hewn from the same pre-rock era of influences.

Having been working from the same face for a decade now, he decided it was time to put it down for a while. But he fancied one last blast from the past, and Modern Times *was an album he had been working towards since the summer of 2002, when he rethought the template enough to make a major statement for someone else's film—Ron Maxwell's* Gods and Generals.

For the next three years he was silent about where he was heading, save for the single statement to Rolling Stone *at the time of his first volume of autobiography,* Chronicles *(2004), "You won't be surprised [by the next album]. The musical structure you're used to hearing—it might be rearranged a bit. [But] the songs themselves will speak to you." Two thousand five saw two more dry runs for the new album, Dylan swelling the soundtracks of lesser films again. But still, no album sessions.*

It took until February 2006 before he settled in for the long haul at Sony in New York, reconciled to the joys of digital, but trusting to his tour band again, leaving engineer Greg Shaw twiddling the knobs (or booting up Pro Tools). Given the tide of positive press which had greeted the disappointing "Love and

Theft," *Dylan was confident he had the songs to make a superior third instal-ment. And yet, the critical reaction was the least positive since* under the red sky—*even if it still fleetingly topped the charts both sides of the Atlantic. Few seemed to notice there was so much more attention to detail on* Modern Times *than its predecessor.*

And it was not just the more incisive lyrics or the greater range of the material. There was the voice, which in concert had started to resemble Clarence "Frogman" Henry's party-piece frog voice. With a little close miking, a respect-able break from the road beforehand (since the previous November), and songs that took account of his current range, not the one he had a decade earlier, the album proved a step in the right direction. Though still patchy, Modern Times' *peaks more closely resembled* Time Out of Mind's *than its piecemeal precursor. As if determined to prove there was still gas in the tank, Dylan returned to the studio just three months later to cut "Huck's Tune," a gorgeous lil' song wasted on another mediocre movie soundtrack, when it would have made* Modern Times—*still more than four months away from release—an even better way to say fare-thee-well for a while.*

{587} 'CROSS THE GREEN MOUNTAIN

Published lyric/s: Words Fill My Head.
Known studio recordings: Larrabee East, L.A., July 23, 2002 [G&G/TTS].

The inclusion of "'Cross the Green Mountain" as the last track on the two-CD edition of 2008's *Tell Tale Signs* rescued from relative obscurity the most audacious of the one-off sound track offerings which pepper Dylan's post-*TOOM* career. Released originally in February 2003 on the soundtrack album to *Gods and Generals*, the much gestated prequel to 1993's epic *Gettysburg*, the song suffered much the same fate as the film, which managed to make Dylan's own *Masked and Anonymous*—also released (and universally panned) later the same year—look like a roaring success.

Financed entirely by Ted Turner of Turner Classics, *Gods and Generals* apparently cost him personally close to seventy million dollars, taking barely twelve million at the box office. The problem—as Dylan could have told Turner—was the length, the film clocking in only twenty minutes shy of *Renaldo and Clara's* four hours. And in the same spirit, Dylan delivered an eight-minute song that features neither bridge nor chorus, but was instead an unrelenting account, verse by pitiless verse, of a world turned upside down. This time around, though, there is no suggestion that he has overdone it, for the song is as remorseless as war, as unforgiving as the heat of battle. The soldiers' tenuous hold on mortality drips from every line of a song set up in classic ballad fashion, as if 'twas but "a monstrous dream":

> Across the green mountain, I sat by the stream,
> Heaven blazing in my head, I dreamt a monstrous dream,
> Something came up out of the sea,
> Swept through the land of the rich and the free.

And yet, in a sense, this opening verse is at odds with the film's ostensible purpose—which was to provide the background to the defining battle of the civil war, Gettysburg, centering on the events surrounding Confederate General Stonewall Jackson. The song's narrative vantage point takes us back to Maxwell's *previous* civil war film, *Gettysburg*, based on Michael Sharra's Pulitzer winning novel, *The Killer Angels* (1974).

In Sharra's work of fiction, it is Lieutenant Colonel Arthur Lyon Fremantle, an ex-member of the Coldstream Guards observing on behalf of Queen Victoria, who travels with the Confederate Army to Gettysburg and there witnesses the second day of the battle in these terms: "Fremantle could feel the presence of that vast army . . . all those feet and wheels moving against the earth, moving in together like two waves meeting in a great ocean, like two avalanches coming down together on facing sides of a green mountain." And it is Fremantle who in the song appears to offer the following sentiment: "I watch and I wait and I listen while I stand / To the music that comes from a far better land." Dylan's own narrator, though, is not so dispassionate. He shares the Confederate comrades' point of view, as the final line of the song makes clear: "We loved each other more than we ever dared to tell."

The songsmith is in his element, happy to reveal an immersion in civil war lore that had already informed parts of *"Love and Theft"* (going on to imply in *Chronicles* that he read all this stuff back in 1961). Both civil war poet Henry Timrod (whose "Charleston" provides the opening line of verse three, "Along the dim Atlantic line") and Herman Melville are drafted to the cause. Melville's "The Scout Toward Aldie"—a depiction of the death of John Singleton Moseby, the guerilla leader of a rogue Confederate battalion who harassed the Union army relentlessly—informs the song at various points (the phrases, "brave blood to spill" and "The ravaged land was miles behind" both deriving from Ishmael's chronicler).

The tenor of Melville's poem—evidenced by his final verse in which "No joy remains for bard to sing; / And heaviest dole of all is this, / That other hearts shall be as gay / As hers that now no more shall spring"—probably served as a model for the song's valedictory tone, though Dylan adopts a more balladic phraseology. ("I dreamt a monstrous dream," "The bells of leavening have rung," and "A letter to Mother came today" all drawing from tradition's springboard.) The result achieves a commensurate pathos in a mere twelve four-line verses, before Dylan donates his best old-man-river vocal.

{588} TELL OL' BILL

Published lyric/s: Words Fill My Head.
Known studio recordings: Studio 4, Conshohocken, PA, June 17, 2005—14 takes [TTS—tk. 7] [NCS—tk. 14].

My terminology all comes from folk music. It doesn't come from . . . TV, or computers, or any of that stuff. It's embedded in the folk music of the English language. —Dylan, to Jann Wenner, 2007

Mid-June 2005, halfway through a thirty-two-date tour with Willie Nelson, Dylan used a two-day break from the road to cut his latest movie sound track offering, for an independent film, *North Country*, based on the life of a female miner who brought a sexual harassment suit in North Carolina. (Gee, wonder why that wasn't a summer blockbuster?!) It had been three years since he cut "'Cross the Green Mountain," but there was no sign of a sea change in his working method. The open-cast mining of American tradition for song titles, tunes, or passing references remained. "Tell Ol' Bill" took its title (and a single line) from a song first collected by Carl Sandburg in the 1920s, the nub of the traditional song being that there ain't no use trying to tell Bill anything, because he is dead:

> Tell old Bill when he comes home this morning,
> Tell old Bill when he comes home this evening,
> Tell old Bill when he comes home to leave them downtown gals alone,
> This evening, this morning, so soon.

Dylan knew the song well—indeed, he cut it for *Self Portrait* back in March 1970, though it went unused. However, in keeping with his usual methodology these days, the song that gave him his title was not his template for the one he wrote. That was provided by another old Carter Family favorite, "I Never Loved but One," from which Dylan took the basic melody and approach adopted on the sound track version, though not any specific lines ("I tried to find one smilin' face" is the closest, an allusion to the A. P. Carter couplet, "I look around but cannot trace / One welcome word or smiling face").

Like Carter, Dylan was looking to address the timeless preoccupations of traditional fare with words that came from within. Thus, verse six moves the death-bed setting of a "Barbara Allen" to modern times, with the bitterness between such a pair of ill-fated lovers intact:

> You trampled on me as you passed,
> Left the coldest kiss upon my brow,
> All my doubts and fears have gone at last,
> I've nothing more to tell you now.

For once, we have the evidence required to demonstrate that "Tell Ol' Bill" was one of those "songs . . . based on . . . Carter Family songs . . . [where] I'll take a song I know and . . . at a certain point . . . I'll start writing a [different] song." A tape of what appears to be the entire "Tell Ol' Bill" session has passed into general circulation and begins with something close to a Carteresque cover. Then, midsession, Dylan decides to go in a completely different direction.

After the fifth take, we hear Dylan suggest, "Maybe we should change it all, totally—change the melody, everything about it, [even] put it in a minor key . . . keep the same form though." Sure enough, the next take represents just such a turnaround. The words remain, but the entire mood of the performance has changed to something that, in a few months more, will become the *Modern Times* vibe. Meanwhile the vocals have lost any sense that the singer is straining to maintain its once-jaunty rhythm. The seventh take of the day—cut before Dylan complains that he has used up all the air in the place—shall end up on *Tell Tale Signs*, giving the song a whole new sound, and audience. Dylan perseveres, though, à la "Like a Rolling Stone." The version chosen for the sound-track CD comes from the end of the session (probably after the thirteenth and last take on the session tape), and only after Dylan has dropped his original eighth verse:

> From white to green, from brown to black,
> Not one more minute can I waste,
> They go too far, they drive me mad,
> At a slow and steady place.

In its place, Dylan sings of fatalistic "thunder-blasted trees"—an allusion to Poe's "To One in Paradise," which laments that "the light of Life is o'er! / No more—no more—no more / . . . Shall bloom the thunder-blasted tree"—presumably having the verse to hand. The autodidact was still building bookshelves.

{589} CAN'T ESCAPE FROM YOU

Published lyric/s: Words Fill My Head.
Known studio recordings: Westland Studios, Dublin, November 28–9, 2005 [TTS].

In the notes to *Tell Tale Signs*—where "Can't Escape from You" appears for the first time—Larry Sloman claims this is "one of the . . . most compelling songs Dylan has ever recorded." So compelling, in fact, that Dylan did not even bother to find a place for it on his next album, after the film for which it was originally intended failed to find the requisite financing. Quite what it is that Sloman finds compelling is a greater mystery than either the power of love or the mystery of death. Every line screams "outtake." It may even have so queered the pitch for its intended berth that the movie upped and died of its own accord.

Once again, Dylan seemed determined to try to cut a song when his vocal cords needed only rest and relaxation, recording it in Dublin barely a day after another year of unrelenting touring ran its course. One wonders if said sessions—which occupied two whole days—were a dry run for the *Modern Times* sessions three months later. If so, Dylan wisely scrapped anything he got, burying the tape deep in the vaults. Irrespective of whether—as Sloman asserts—its heaviest musical debt is to the Platters' "My Prayer," the song fails to adhere to the path that leads from "The Lonesome Road" to the "Highway of Regret." Even the curious instrumental coda is like the fitful sigh of an unwise lover at the end of his tether. As the man put it, midsong, "You've wasted all your power / You threw out the Christmas pie / Now you're withering like a flower / You'll play the fool and die." Thankfully, the next time he went in the studio, he had not only rested his vocal cords but had worked on at his lyrical craft . . .

590 songs in, I have had to resort to organizing the songs on Modern Times *in the order they appear on the album, because no information available enables me to put the songs in the order they were recorded at the sessions, let alone the order they were written in. So near, and yet . . .*

{590} THUNDER ON THE MOUNTAIN

Published lyric/s: Words Fill My Head; bobdylan.com.
Known studio recordings: Sony Recording Studios, NYC, February 2006 [MT].
First known performance: Seattle Center, WA, October 13, 2006.

> Songs I can fill . . . up with symbolism and metaphors. When you write a book [like *Chronicles*] . . . it can't be misinterpreted. —Dylan, to David Gates, September 2004

"Thunder on the Mountain," the opening track on *Modern Times*, continues a disappointing run of openers to Dylan albums that now goes all the way back to 1985's *Empire Burlesque*. Once again, he dispenses another dozen-verse dirge set against some imminent conflict, this one surrounded by portents like "thunder on the mountain and . . . fires on the moon."[42] Unlike the immensely effective "'Cross the Green Mountain," this one has been set to a generic R&B tune, suggesting we are in store for *"Love and Theft"* Pt. 2. And again it contains those ubiquitous lifts from the blues lexicon (in this case, Robert Johnson's "Honeymoon Blues," Leroy Carr's "Getting All Wet," and Kokomo Arnold's "Mean Old Twister," the last of which he both name-checks and purloins a line from—"Look like something bad gonna happen, you better roll your airplane down"). He also throws in another of his colored herrings, name of Alicia Keys (the young R&B singer, who was indeed born in Hell's Kitchen).

At least Dylan sings the whole thing with a certain gusto, as if something is really on his mind. It seems he may have got religion—or faith—again ("We degrade faith by talking about religion."—Dylan, 2007). Sacrifice lies at the very heart of a song in which the narrator sees the signs in the sky—and on the wall ("The writing on the wall, come read it, come see what it say")—prompting him to prepare to do battle for what he believes, knowing that "some sweet day I'll stand beside my king."

The song title itself could well be a reference to a passage in Exodus where Moses, having received God's commandments on Sinai, delivers them to the people: "And it came to pass . . . that there were thunders and lightnings, and a thick cloud on the mount, and the voice of the trumpet exceeding loud; so that all the people . . . trembled. And Moses brought forth the people out of the camp . . . and they stood at the nether part of the mount. And mount Sinai was altogether on a smoke, because the Lord descended upon it in fire: . . . and the whole mount quaked greatly. And when the voice of the trumpet sounded long, and waxed louder and louder, Moses spake, and God answered him" (19:16–19).

If Dylan intends to establish such a connection, his assertion in the third line that he's "gonna grab my trombone and blow" may be his way of joining the "voice of the trumpet." The final couplet of the song certainly suggests he recently leafed through Psalms (69:20) ("I looked for some to take pity, but there was none") and has heard the last trumpet blow—"The hammer's on the table, the pitchfork's on the shelf, / For the love of God, you ought to take pity on yourself."

{591} SPIRIT ON THE WATER

Published lyric/s: Words Fill My Head; bobdylan.com.
Known studio recordings: Sony Recording Studios, NYC, February 2006 (MT).
First known performance: Cox Arena, San Diego, CA, October 22, 2006.

"Spirit on the Water" seems to provide another worrying presentiment that the lessons of *"Love and Theft"* have not sunk in. Save for the opening couplet and the penultimate verse—which appear to come from an entirely different song—the whole shebang comes across like another consciously anachronistic parlor song that perversely owes more to the works of Sonny Boy Williamson than Stephen Foster. (He takes two lines each from "Black Gal Blues" and "Sugar Mama Blues," respectively: "Lord knows I'm wild about you, black gal, / You ought to be a fool about me" and "They are braggin' 'bout your sugar, sugar mama, / Been braggin' all over town.")

The opening image, though, "Spirit on the water / Darkness on the face of the deep," again sees Dylan drawing overtly on familiar verses from the Bible—"In the beginning . . . darkness was upon the face of the deep, And the Spirit of God moved upon the face of the waters" (Genesis 1:1–2). If the song promptly detours into conventional "miss you, babe" fare, there are occasional clues that the narrator is (again) caught in a bind of biblical proportions ("been trampling through mud / Praying to the powers above . . ."; "From east to west, ever since the world began . . ."). However, it is only in the penultimate verse that we discover we have been dealing with a man in a long black coat who's been driven into the land of Nod:

> I wanna be with you in paradise
> And it seems so unfair.
> I can't go to paradise no more
> I killed a man back there.

We seem to have retraced our footsteps to the beginning of the big black book, when Cain was driven "from the face of the earth; and from Thy face . . . hid" (Genesis 4:14) for the murder of his brother; or maybe back to Minnesota, where an impressionable teenager watched James Dean's angst-driven performance in *East of Eden* over and over again, before returning home to reexperience Johnny Cash intoning his way through "Folsom Prison Blues." The song certainly has mystery written all over it. It meant something to the songwriter, though, who initially injected an extra notch of vocal commitment in performance.

{592} ROLLIN' & TUMBLIN'

Published lyric/s: Words Fill My Head; bobdylan.com.
Known studio recordings: Sony Recording Studios, NYC, February 2006 [MT].
First known performance: Memorial Coliseum, Portland, OR, October 14, 2006.

> I'm not familiar with rock music. It's not something that I feel assimilated into . . . It doesn't get to the point quick enough. —Dylan, to Jann Wenner, 2007

His 2006 album only really slipped into gear when Dylan decided to "interpret" the blues standard "Rollin' & Tumblin'." Perhaps it was the legacy he was consciously addressing—and hopefully enhancing—that made the man inject more of himself here, but his version barely even acknowledges the efforts of Canned Heat and Cream, bypassing the rock tradition (and all those lead guitar breaks) entirely, going straight to the source for *feel*, and direct to Chess for *sound*.

To reach that source—as Dylan knew all too well—he was obliged to sail past Muddy Waters, Sleepy John Estes, and Robert Johnson to that tabula rasa of a bluesman, Hambone Willie Newbern, who cut "Roll & Tumble Blues" in Atlanta one March day in 1929. Hambone, who manages to make Robert Johnson's life and music seem positively well-documented, recorded just six tracks over two days before purportedly being beaten to death in a prison fight. He had been playing the song, a Mississippi standard, since at least 1917, complete with that immortal opening stanza, "I rolled and I tumbled and I cried the whole night long / Arose this mornin', mama, and I didn't know right from wrong."

Its influence was both immediate and profound. Robert Johnson recorded two variations of it, "If I Had Possession Over Judgment Day" and "Travelin' Riverside Blues," while the somnambulant John Estes reworked it as "The Girl I Love, She Got Long Curly Hair." But it was Muddy Waters who really made his name with the song—which he copyrighted to himself after cutting it twice in 1950, once as part of Baby Face Leroy Foster's trio and once in his own name. However, his claim on the song failed to fool contemporaries, even if it made Morgan a great deal from the covers which were an inevitable by-product of the blues-rock boom. Elmore James cut his own variant in early 1960, credited to one Robinson.

This time Dylan had no intention of washing his hands in Muddy Waters's—as he had back in 1986 when attempting the song at the *Knocked Out Loaded* sessions. Adopting one specific "variation of the blues form," he knew that "at a certain point, some of the words will change." Sure enough, save for that opening verse (which also tips its hat to Lil' Son Jackson's "Gambler Blues"), the lyric is the product of a lifetime spent living the blues. As with the preceding *Modern Times* cuts, "Rollin' and Tumblin'"'s narrator is troubled by the prospect of that dreadful day, and again women seem to be at the root of his concerns: "Some young lazy slut has charmed away my brain" (ponder and relish the lascivious way he sings this line).

And so, after swearing he "ain't gonna touch on another one for years," he dispenses some much-needed advice in "her" direction: "Sooner or later, you too shall burn." And just in time. By the ninth verse, an avenging Christ seems to have entered the frame. After all, who else would claim "I've been conjuring up all these long dead souls from their crumbling tombs" save the One who shall have possession over Judgment Day ("Death . . . delivered up the dead . . . and they were judged every man according to their works" [Revelation 20:13])?

It was presumably a predetermined act on Dylan's part that he should set the most personal of lyrics on his new album to a derivative, even Johnsonesque blues. And despite the nature of its debt, there is an almost shocking lack of Delta imagery in the song. When he does actually draw from the Delta, he is sending up the tradition—i.e., he "get[s] up in the dawn and go[es] down and lay[s] in the shade" or sees "the risin' sun return," but at no point does he wake up in the morning and/or dust his broom.

With this song he blew away any concerns that he would again take his songs "in the studio and hav[e] it be beaten up and whacked *around* and come out with some kind of incoherent thing which didn't have any resonance," which is how he put it later that year. He need not have worried. The recording makes its point while steering well clear of the blues-rock clichés. Unfortunately, in concert it was not so lucky, becoming one more crowd-pleasing mindless boogie in a set still dominated by *"Love and Theft"* songs to a disturbing degree.

{593} WHEN THE DEAL GOES DOWN

Published lyric/s: Words Fill My Head; bobdylan.com.
Known studio recordings: Sony Recording Studios, NYC, February 2006 *[MT]*.
First known performance: Pacific Coliseum, Vancouver, BC, October 11, 2006.

> ["When the Deal Goes Down"] demands all your attention. There's no song you're listening to that's influencing it . . . All you can do is hang on and hope you do it justice. —Bob Dylan, 2007

Though the one composition *directly* influencing "When the Deal Goes Down" was the early thirties Bing Crosby melody "Where the Blue of the Night (Meets the Gold of the Day)," it was his ongoing references to the works of Henry Timrod in this song, reported in the *New York Times*, that prompted another public debate about the scale and significance of all that Dylan was continuing to appropriate. As often with these kinds of debates, it was the bean counters who won the day, pointing out half a dozen possible (and in a couple of cases, rather tenuous) debts to the nineteenth-century versifier, without recognizing the distinct purpose to which Dylan put them.

A beautiful song on the transience of life, thanks in equal measure to that manufactured melody and Dylan's own fatalistic vocal, "When the Deal Goes Down" lends itself to a phrase like "More frailer than the flowers, these precious hours" far more than Timrod's "A Rhapsody of a Southern Winter Night." Whereas Timrod's elegant but vapid versifying—"A round of precious hours. / Oh! here, where in that summer noon I basked, / And strove, with logic frailer than the flowers . . ."—is concerned with torpor, Dylan makes it about *mortality*. Likewise, the opening couplet of the 2006 song—"In the still of the night, in the world's ancient light / Where wisdom grows up in strife"—does appear to take imagery from Timrod's "Retirement" ("There is a wisdom that grows up in strife"). But it is Dylan who gives it that proverbial generality—implying that only through strife are we likely to arrive at illumination. Timrod's poem rather suggested the reverse.

What Dylan seems to be taking from Timrod's verse is that uniquely southern fin de siècle air which, in tandem with this appropriated melody, helps convey a lost world. When he lampoons "moon in June"–type imagery with "The moon gives light [pregnant pause] And it shines by night / Well, I scarcely feel the glow," he morphs into that southern gentleman who, on the night when a visiting Oscar Wilde felt prompted to comment on how fine the moon was, observed, "Ah, but you should have seen it before the [civil] war."

Equally apposite is Dylan's use of the title phrase itself, a commonplace of the blues from Charlie Patton's "Don't Let Your Deal Go Down" via Robert Johnson's "Last Fair Deal Gone Down," to deal with death itself (by implication, he is *not* making a deal with the devil). Indeed, for the first time in a quarter of a century, Dylan appears to be directly addressing fellow believers ("We all wear the same thorny crown") with lines that can be equally directed at Him or her ("You come to my eyes like a vision from the skies"; "I owe my heart to you, and that's sayin' it true"). "When the Deal Goes Down," like life, may be brief, but it shines with an ancient light.

{594} SOMEDAY BABY

Published lyric/s: Words Fill My Head x2; bobdylan.com [*MT* take only].
Known studio recordings: Sony Recording Studios, NYC, February 2006
[MT—1 take] [TTS—1 take].

Dylan fans can—and do—endlessly debate the point at which the man's choice of what to release went from idiosyncratic to perverse (and even plain bizarre). As I have suggested elsewhere, perversity seems to me to have been a mainstay of the album selection process since the year dot ("The House Carpenter"'s absence from the debut LP!?). But nothing quite prepares one for the *Tell Tale Signs* outtake of "Someday Baby," which, compared to the version preferred for *Modern Times*, is not so much night and day as heaven and hell. Whereas there is a real communing with the spirit of the blues on the "alternate" take, the album take is little more than a lazy appropriation of someone else's shtick. And yet, it is the alternate take which was the afterthought, the diversion down a dirt road Dylan should have gone in the first place, as Chris Shaw revealed to *Uncut*:

> On both [the last two albums], Bob would sometimes come in with reference tracks, old songs . . . So on *Modern Times*, there's the Muddy Waters track ["Trouble No More"] that became "Someday Baby" . . . [*Tell Tale Signs* has] the slow, kind of gospel version of "Someday Baby." That was when he was getting frustrated with the "Muddy Waters" version not coming together. After dinner, he walked back into the room and George Receli, his drummer, was tapping out that groove. Bob sat down at the piano, and all of a sudden they came up with *that* version. We raced to record that. It was only done for one or two takes . . . [because] he was still stuck on the Muddy Waters version.

Dylan's debt to the Muddy Waters song "Trouble No More"—as well as its close cousin "I Can't Be Satisfied," another of Morgan's songs, which he performed at shows in fall 1992—was there for all to hear on *Modern Times*, especially for those listeners who knew his performance of this blues standard with the G. E. Smith combo at the famous four-hour Toad's show in January 1990. Yet it seems strange that a man who talked about using old songs as "blueprints" or "departure points" should cling so tenaciously to this particular template a mere two songs after he had taken another Muddy Waters favorite, "Rollin' & Tumblin'," as the merest blueprint to a radical reinterpretation.

And, as we now know, there was a better alternative on the same two-inch reel. The *Tell Tale Signs* set includes track sheets for "Someday Baby" and "Ain't Talkin'," the only solid information we have as to how these sessions went down. Taken in tandem with the two outtakes, they confirm another of Shaw's recollections: "Bob had a lot of ideas to sort through, there were a lot of different versions of each song he had to settle on before he could decide where he wanted them to go . . . There was [also] a lot more lyric writing he had to deal with. Bob never has a shortage of ideas where song lyrics are concerned."

Not only is the "Someday Baby" outtake entirely different in feel, it is almost another song lyrically. Of the eleven verses on the outtake, just five are replicated on the (nine-verse) album cut, and some of the ones lost are real diamonds-in-the-rough mix:

> You made me eat a ton of dust.
> You're potentially dangerous, and not worthy of trust,
> *Someday baby, you ain't gonna worry po' me any more.*
>
> Little by little, bit by bit,
> Every day I'm coming home with a different grip . . .
>
> Gonna blow out your mind, and make you pure,
> I've taken about as much as I can endure.

Even those five shared verses convey nuances a world apart from the other released performance. The way Dylan sings "I don't want to brag, but I'll wring your neck" raises the hairs on one's neck, in part because he uses that great deadpan, "Man with No Name" voice. But it also comes hard on the heels of a series of verses where the threat of violence is never far away (note the last one above). On the album take, Dylan is more concerned with threatening to turf her out than matching her blow for blow.

Insistence lies at the heart of this overpowering outtake. The groove, courtesy of Receli, is relentless, but so is Dylan's piano-driven vocal (the *TTS* mix unduly mutes that piano). One can't help but relish the way he leans on the title line at the end of every verse—"Someday baby—you ain't gonna worry—po' me—any*maw*"—the one line he copped from the Muddy Waters "original" (Waters himself probably took the line from an earlier Lightnin' Hopkins song, which shares its title with Dylan's).

The *Tell Tale* "Someday Baby" is one of the great Dylan studio vocals—I mean, period—as worthy in its way as "Every Grain of Sand" or "Stuck Inside of Mobile" and, considering its recording date, probably the greater achievement. That dying voice within, which in concert the year before sounded like it was not so much on its last legs as already sitting in a wheelchair, on this track picks itself up and walks.

Why then did Dylan reach for the Zimmer frame when he could still hit his stride like this? The track sheet suggests Dylan dug what he had done enough to let guitarist Denny Freeman apply "guitar o[ver]dubs," even allowing a further "revisiting [of] solos," while someone, maybe even Dylan, redrew his way of "playing [the] lick." The one thing he had generally adhered to throughout his recording career was recognizing when *he* had delivered the goods. He must have known the two takes were chalk and cheese. Yet these days, or so he claims, "I don't sit and meditate on every line afterwards. My approach is just to let it happen and then reject the things that don't work."

Perhaps it was his obsession with tempo and mood changes that now overrode the actual, qualitative differences between takes. Having seized control of his sessions after *Time Out of Mind*, he was in no mood to listen to more objective counsel. As he put it back in 2001, "I have always taken care with my records but now I no longer *trust* anyone." And, in 2009, "It saves a lot of time . . . translating my own ideas directly, rather than having them go through somebody else. I know my form of music better than anyone else would."

In his mind, the more up-tempo "Trouble No More" version of "Someday Baby" was probably a necessary counterbalance to the more sedate fare either side—"When the Deal Goes Down" and "Workingman's Blues #2." And he was no longer interested in getting into a fight over whether something filled some specific slot, or even redefined the parameters of what he had done to date. Dare one suggest, he might even have got a kick out of departing from the blueprint, only to use his return ticket when it came time to choose.

{595} WORKINGMAN'S BLUES #2

Published lyric/s: Words Fill My Head; bobdylan.com.
Known studio recordings: Sony Recording Studios, NYC, February 2006 [MT].
First known performance: Pacific Coliseum, Vancouver, BC, October 11, 2006.

"Workingman Blues #2" seems to have been another song where Dylan was unsure which set of verses or arrangement to use. In this case, it barely warranted the effort. There is a laziness that manifests itself in the way Dylan wanders from thought to thought, resorting to the lexicon to fill in any blanks, as if he's still working through *Love and Theft*." If his concern was too many "samey" songs stacked atop each other, he could easily have cut his cloth accordingly. As it is, he was set to deliver another album which topped the hour mark.

Again, he starts with someone else's song title—Merle Haggard's "Working Man Blues," a number one on the *Billboard* country charts in July 1969 and a song he enthuses about on his Theme Time Radio Hour—a fact he acknowledges with that "#2" and a last line of the chorus which quotes Haggard's own burden, "Sing a little bit of these workingman's blues." But that chorus bears a greater resemblance to Big Joe Williams's 1957 rerecording of "Meet Me in the Bottom," with its repeated refrain, "Meet me in the bottom, bring me my boots and shoes," a line Willie Dixon barely changed when recrafting it into "Down in the Bottom" for a 1961 Howlin' Wolf Chess session. Dylan does little more with Williams's lines to make "Well, meet me at the bottom, don't lag behind, / Bring me my boots and shoes."

He also seems to have been listening to his copies of Woody Guthrie's "Hobo's Lullaby" ("Can't you hear the steel rail humming") and Robert Johnson's "They're Red Hot" ("She sleeps in the kitchen with her feet in the hall")—though the selfsame line also appears in "Talkin' Blues," a song he redrafted as "I Shall Be Free" a lifetime ago. And our friend poet Timrod provides at least one line: "to feed my soul with thought" (from his love poem "To Thee"). But it is all rather lackluster, as if Dylan expects this random assortment of clichés to do the work for him ("You are dearer to me than myself, [as] you yourself can see" may originate with Ovid, but it is a cliché nonetheless). Nor does the sub–"Standing in the Doorway" melody do the song and singer any favors, leaving fans to discern various lyrical changes in concert as a necessary diversion from the unsettling thought that this might be all he's got left in the tank.

{596} BEYOND THE HORIZON

Published lyric/s: Words Fill My Head; bobdylan.com.
Known studio recordings: Sony Recording Studios, NYC, February 2006 [MT].
First known performance: Austin, TX, September 15, 2007.

Temporarily bereft of ideas, Dylan again reworked the crooners" canon to produce "Floater"'s natural sequel, "Beyond the Horizon." This time he sails awfully close to the wind, taking as his tune template a composition barely out of copyright, Jimmy Kennedy and Hugh Williams's "Red Sails in the Sunset," another song Bing made his own with a hugely popular 1935 recording, ahead of the likes of Louis Armstrong, Nat King Cole, the Platters, Fats Domino, and even the Beatles (who gave it the Ramones treatment during one of their Star Club residencies). Dylan's title he presumably derived from one of Hank Williams's, "Beyond the Sunset."

As well as continuing his practice of inserting the occasional in-joke into the lyric—like name-checking Crosby's 1945 movie, *The Bells of St. Mary's* and Cole Porter's classic song "Easy to Love"—he happily alludes to a song recorded at Big Pink, Bruce "Utah" Phillips's "Rock, Salt and Nails," with the line, "Down in the valley, the water runs cold."[43] Whereas Phillips remembers it as a place where he "first listened to the lies you told," Dylan grafts the image to something more positive, if prosaic: "Beyond the horizon, someone prayed for your soul."

Unfortunately, Dylan seems to have very little idea what to say next, though he is fully determined to run the full gamut of romantic stereotypes—it is "the long hours of twilight," then it is "round about midnight," finally it is "the soft light of morning." He will follow her "through flame and through fire," and "through countries and kingdoms," just to find somewhere he can shake free of all these tautologies. And then it is all over, and he is on to the next song of regret, which on an album of contrasts proves to be among his finest . . .

{597} NETTIE MOORE

Published lyric/s: Words Fill My Head; bobdylan.com.
Known studio recordings: Sony Recording Studios, NYC, February 2006 [MT].
First known performance: ARCO Arena, Sacramento, CA, October 18, 2006.

I love those old piano ballads. In my hometown walking down dark streets on quiet summer nights you would sometimes hear parlor tunes coming out of doorways and open windows. Somebody's mother or sister playing "A Bird in a Guilded Cage" off of sheet music. —Dylan, to Bill Flanagan, 2009.

Back in 1962, the twenty-one-year-old Dylan preferred to send up the songs churned out in Tin Pan Alley, in his intro to "Bob Dylan's Blues." At the time, he was probably unaware just how beholden heroes like Jimmie Rogers and the Carter Family were to the music halls and parlor songs of the nineteenth century for many of their "authentic" hillbilly songs. By 1997, when he journeyed back to songs made "time out of mind," he had already covered his first Stephen Foster song ("Hard Times" on *Good as I Been to You*), and in 2001 he recorded a song—"Moonlight"—directly influenced by A. P. Carter's take on an old English parlor song.

In such a context, his attempt to rework lines from another nineteenth-century parlor song into something fitting for the twenty-first century seems less of a leap. But a leap it is. "Nettie Moore" comes out of nowhere—a restoration to full power at a time when fitful brown-outs and periods of full-on darkness had become the norm. And Dylan knew he had pulling off something special, telling Jonathan Lethem, "['Nettie Moore'] troubled me the most, because I wasn't sure I was getting it right. Finally, I could see what the song is about. This is coherent, not just a bunch of random verses. I knew I wanted to record this. I was pretty hyped up on the melodic line."

That melodic line was not the one that accompanied the first printing of the parlor ballad, "The Little White Cottage, or Gentle Nettie Moore" in September 1857, a song that apparently required three persons to complete, with the lyric credited to Marshall S. Pike Esq., who on the basis of this lyric was a purveyor of the finest twaddle a music publisher could buy outright. The first verse alone should have ensured that each set of sheet music sold came with its own sick bag: "In a little white cottage, where the trees are evergreen, / And the climbing roses blossom by the door; / I've often sat and listen'd to the music of the birds, / And the gentle voice of charming Nettie Moore." But it is the chorus that interests us, especially those first two lines which somehow lit a spark within Dylan's recalcitrant muse:

> O! I miss you Nettie Moore,
> And my happiness is o'er,
> While a spirit sad around my heart has come;

And the busy days are long,
And the nights are lonely now,
For you've gone from our little cottage home.

One would like to know whether this was indeed one of those songs the young Robert heard in Hibbing "walking down dark streets on quiet summer nights." It has certainly been extracted from the same saccharin mine as "The Drunkard's Son," the first song we have in Bobby Zimmerman's hand (see Volume One). Yet Dylan does something extraordinary with this chorus, from which he lifts just the opening couplet (complete with the formulaic "o'er'"; "over" being such an annoyingly tough rhyme), showing Pike the poetaster how you actually convey something real in a verse of rhyme:

> Winter's gone, the river's on the rise,
> I loved you then and ever shall,
> But there's no one left here to tell,
> The world has gone black before my eyes.

Despair had always brought the best out of Dylan, and "Nettie Moore" is no exception. But it is a despair infused with hope for the world to come (the same despair/hope which had previously prompted him to start performing "Halleluiah, I'm Ready to Go" as a concert opener). For the first time in quite a while he had his King James to hand when trying to render something coherent out of what might otherwise have become yet another "bunch of random verses." Thus, in verse eight, the judge who is "coming in, everybody rise / Lift up your eyes" is surely the man Himself, the exhortation being a direct quote from Isaiah (51:6): "Lift up your eyes to the heavens, and look upon the earth beneath: for the heavens shall vanish away like smoke, and the earth shall wax old like a garment, and they that dwell therein shall die in like manner: but my salvation shall be for ever." Likewise, a similar exhortation in the final verse—"I'll stand in faith and raise / The voice of praise"—may directly refer to a chapter in 2 Chronicles (5:13), "They lifted up their voice . . . and praised the Lord, saying, For he is good; for his mercy endureth for ever."

"Nettie Moore" equally implies that our man is paying for a life of sin—he may even be the "Lost John sittin' on a railroad track" in line one (another one from the lexicon, "Lost John" was both the title and opening line of a well-known traditional song). From the very first verse, where Dylan also introduces a line from Robert Johnson's "Hellhound on My Trail" ("Blues fallin' down like hail"), judgment and damnation straddle the land. The singer duly admits he "got a pile of sins to pay for," even name-checking Frankie and Albert, characters from an infamous murder immortalized in a traditional ballad Dylan recently covered on *Good as I Been to You*. He suggests Frankie may still be "raising hell," but the narrator himself is "beginning to believe what the scriptures tell." Elsewhere he references W. C. Handy's "Yellow Dog Blues" ("I've gone where the Southern crosses the Yellow Dog"), a line Handy himself culled from the first blues song he ever heard.

Our singer, another God-fearin' killer who seems to believe in an eye for an eye, is telling us we best beware: "'Fore you call me any dirty names, you'd better think twice." The only thing real in his life had been gentle Nettie Moore, to whom he professes his love in the chorus, and, mythical or not, under whose spell even Dylan seems to have fallen. The hoots of approval that greeted the song in performance suggest his fans felt the same way. They too had missed the coherence of a narrative that is "not just a bunch of random verses."

{598} THE LEVEE'S GONNA BREAK

Published lyric/s: Words Fill My Head.

Known studio recordings: Sony Recording Studios, NYC, February 2006 [MT].

First known performance: Wachovia Spectrum, Philadelphia, PA, November 18, 2006.

Long before he learned the true meaning of the line "Won't be water, but fire next time," Dylan had allowed a dam full of "flood" songs to seep into his psyche. One of the songs he considered recording for his first album—performing it at Carnegie Recital Hall the first week in November 1961—was Bessie Smith's memorable "Backwater Blues" (aka "It Rained Five Days"). In the garage of his backing band's gaudy West Saugerties home, in the summer of 1967, he deconstructed John

Lee Hooker's "Tupelo Blues" in a way that showed he already knew life was but a joke.

And in 2001, he resurrected the spirit of Charlie Patton's master-piece, "High Water Everywhere Parts 1 & 2" with his own "High Water (for Charlie Patton)." The one "flood" song he hadn't yet recorded, or reworked—even though it had been a favorite of his since at least the time of the first album—was Memphis Minnie's memorable 1929 recording of the traditional "When the Levee Breaks" ("Back then, I was listening to Son House, Lead Belly, the Carter family, Memphis Minnie, and death romance ballads." —Dylan, 2009):

> If it keeps on raining levee's gonna break,
> And the water gonna come; and we'll have no place to stay.
> I worked on the levee, mama, both night and day,
> I ain't got nobody to keep the water away.

Long before "When the Levee Breaks" was even a twinkle in the eye of Led Zeppelin's music publisher, Dylan('s girlfriend, Suze Rotolo) had the song on a long-player, *Blues Fell This Morning: Rare Recordings of Southern Blues Singers*, an album that, according to a recognizable scrawl across the top of the rear sleeve of her (recently auctioned) copy, was "Made for and about Bob Dylan." The earnest young scribbler had also added the observation "Hand read by Bob Dylan" below Paul Oliver's sleeve notes. As such, he learned the following:

> For those who live in the plantation country of the river bottoms of the Brazos or the Yazoo-Mississippi Delta, the risk or loss of life and possessions through flooding is as great [as fire]. It is not possible to prevent the Mississippi floods; it is only possible to exert some measure of control over them by the construction of levees . . . But as Kansas Joe McCoy and his erstwhile partner Memphis Minnie convey with the dramatic urgency of their guitar rhythms, disaster follows swiftly when the levee breaks.

By 2005, such songs were part of the very fabric of Dylan's art, but what surely pushed Minnie's mournful blues to the forefront of his—and, indeed, most Americans'—consciousness were the events of Labor Day weekend, when Hurricane Katrina hit New Orleans. The levees (constructed with mud!) did indeed break, and Memphis Minnie's 1929 recording—courtesy of its position as closing track on Zeppelin's iconic fourth album—acquired renewed resonance on the radio. But while modern-day broadside balladeers took it as another opportunity to bust the president's balls, Dylan wasn't looking for no "photo op." with the homeless and the hopeless. He had a more timely message he was looking to convey.

For him, the message had changed very little since 1967, when he first sang, "If you go down in the flood, it's gonna be your fault," a feeling he reiterates here every time he opens a verse with Memphis Minnie's "If it keeps on raining levee's gonna break" and adds his own "Everybody says that this is the day only the Lord could make." The next but one time he quotes Minnie, he is delivering another double-edged message: "Some of these people don't know which road to take."

The sixth and final time he restates what was already obvious to anyone not in the National Guard—"If it keeps on raining levee's gonna break"—the next line comes straight from the Good Book: "Some people still sleepin'," some people are wide awake." Coming from the very man who wrote "When You Gonna Wake Up," such a line was bound to remind believers and nonbelievers alike of Romans (13:11), "Now it is high time to awake out of sleep: for now is our salvation nearer than when we believed." It could also be alluding to the section in 1 Thessalonians (5:9–10) that speaks of obtaining "salvation by our Lord Jesus Christ, who died for us, that, whether we wake or sleep, we should live together with him."

Either way, Dylan was back in an apocalyptic frame of mind, even at one point spouting the precepts of those millennialists who believe Christ will set up his kingdom for a thousand years *before* the final judgment: "Few more years of hard work, then there'll be a thousand years of happiness."

Elsewhere, he reserves a more mocking tone for those who believe "riches and salvation can be waiting behind the next bend in the road." He knows they ain't. Hats off, then, to Dylan for not taking the path of least resistance and spouting the kind of platitudes generally found on latter-day Neil Young albums. "The Levee's Gonna Break" reminded one and all of a greater reality—it ain't if, it's when—and in the process led listeners to another song set on that lonesome road . . .

{599} AIN'T TALKIN'

Published lyric/s: Words Fill My Head
Known studio recordings: Sony Recording Studios, NYC, February 2006 [MT—1 tk.] [TTS—1 tk.].
First known performance: City Center, NYC, November 20, 2006.

> You're talking to a person that feels like he's walking around in the ruins of Pompeii . . . A song is a reflection of what I see all around me all the time. —Dylan, to Mikal Gilmore, October 2001

> [On *Modern Times*] I just let the lyrics go, and when I was singing them, they seemed to have an ancient presence. —Dylan, to Jonathan Lethem, August 2006

"Sugar Baby" had been the most recent of Dylan's grand statements on the run-out groove [*sic*] of his assorted waxings. "Ain't Talkin'" once again adhered to these long-established rules but dug deeper still. This time, the process of immersing himself in the narrative was long and laborious. Thanks to *Tell Tale Signs*, though, it is possible to follow a step or two behind our hero as he walks "through this weary world of woe" (a nod to the traditional "Wayfaring Stranger"). For once, the alternate take of "Ain't Talkin'" on this archival volume is not there because it overshadows the "original," but because it casts a necessary shadow over it, illuminating the process by which Dylan arrived at his most effective album closer since "Shooting Star."

In an interview to promote his next offering, Dylan talked about how "a lot of . . . singers lose who they are after a while. You sing 'I'm a lineman for the county,' enough times and you start to scamper up poles." To him, it was important not to "confuse singers and performers with actors." Well, on the outtake version of "Ain't Talkin'," he is still acting the part, whereas on the album, he has started "scamper[ing] up poles," as it were. And until he *became* that person, he wasn't prepared to let the song lie. This probably explains why, as engineer Shaw points out, "The sessions for *Modern Times* went a little slower; it took maybe a month."

In the case of "Ain't Talkin'," the recording spread over at least two sessions because the track sheet included in both the two- and three-CD versions of *Tell Tale Signs* (though it is only clearly legible in the former) tells us that before they began recording, they "listen[ed] to old keeper take," i.e., from the previous session. This earlier take could well be the one on the 2008 set, given that Dylan ends up scrapping the second part of the song and writing something more coherent. On the other hand, references to "Bob Ordering Lyrics" and "Checking Lyrics" at a couple of points on the session sheet could suggest any reworking took place in situ.

I doubt it. He has, after all, thrown out three entire verses, rewritten three choruses, and figured out an entirely new ending, while at the same time dampening down the arrangement itself so that the focus is resolutely on the voice and the words. As he told Mikal Gilmore after his previous album, "My problem in writing songs has always been how to tone down the rhetoric in using the language." Lost in the process this time are a couple of compelling verses and an attendant chorus:

> It's the first new day of a grand and glorious Autumn,
> The queen of Love is coming across the grass,
> None dare call her anything but madam,
> No one flirts with her or even makes a pass.

> Ain't talking, just walking, standing outside the gates of wrath,
> Heart burning still yearning, take a little trip down the primrose path.

> I got the worst old feeling, and it's getting stronger,
> I'm worn out with public service, I'm beginning to crack,
> I won't stay on any longer,
> I'll avenge my father's death and then I'll step back.

Lyrically, though, the outtake peters out, merely repeating the opening verse in which he finds that even in "the mystic garden" there can be ruffians ready to hit one "from behind." The album take, though, comes up with an ending containing its own mystic connotation:

> As I walked out in the mystic garden,
> On a hot summer day, a hot summer lawn,
> Excuse me, ma'am, I beg your pardon,
> There's no one here, the gardener is gone.

On an album replete with biblical references, it seems unlikely Dylan would invoke a "mystic garden" and a mysterious disappearance—"the gardener is gone"—as its final image and *not* be alluding to Mary's discovery of Christ's empty tomb (she comes upon a person whom she mistakes for the gardener (as opposed to J.C.), who enquires, "Why are you crying? Who is it you are looking for?" One could interpret the last line of the song in a negative way—i.e., He has not risen again—but it would go against the whole thrust of the song, which contains its own fair share of biblical allusions, direct ("I'm a-tryin' to love my neighbor and do good unto others") and indirect ("I practice a faith that's been long abandoned / Ain't no altars on this long and lonesome road").

In "Ain't Talkin'," his faith is being tested like never before, but it would be some kind of sick joke if he took the sentiments of a Stanley Brothers song ("Highway of Regret") and used it to advocate apostasy. As it is, "Ain't talking, just walking, / Down that highway of regret . . ." just about sums it up for someone for whom "the fire [has] gone out, but the light is never dyin'." Having eventually nailed it in the studio, Dylan held back from unboxing this precious cargo in concert until the final concert of 2006, a special bonus show at New York's relatively intimate Civic Center. When he did unveil it, though, it had all "the language and the identity I use . . . [and] know . . . so well."

{600} HUCK'S TUNE

Published lyric/s: Words Fill My Head

Known studio recordings: Criteria Studios, Miami, FL, May 12–13, 2006 [LYS] [TTS].

> A song, you can keep it with you, you can hum it, you can go over things
> when you're out and around, you can keep it in your mind.
> —Dylan, to Jann Wenner, 2007

When in May 2006 Dylan returned to Criteria, the Miami studio where he cut his first all-original album of the post–G. E. Smith era, it had been less than three months since he completed his third album during those nine years. Yet perhaps the symbolism was lost on him. He had just finished another six-week stint on the Never Ending Tour at the Hard Rock in Hollywood, Florida, and he had a new song he wanted to record, and just knew somewhere they could do it. Maybe the song simply came to him on the road and he wanted to catch it quick. Even at the age of sixty-five, he could still claim—as he did to a *Sunday Times* reporter eighteen months earlier—"I do get caught up in writing. Every time I come up with a new song it's like the first rose of May."

"Huck's Tune" fully warranted any enthusiasm Dylan still brought to the process forty-five years after he entered his first pukka recording studio (and a matter of months before Sony sold off their last real recording studio in New York City). Indeed, it was precisely what *Modern Times* really needed to get rid of its three deadweights (tracks once, five, and six), and still produce an album-length CD. Instead Dylan donated the song to another forgettable flick, *Lucky You*, where it languished a while longer, before being scooped up and preserved on the eighth *Bootleg Series*, where it served as further evidence that the three albums recorded in the past decade were not the be-all and end-all of his recent studio output.

The song itself is an indulgent delight, Dylan constructing myriad reasons why he's "gonna have to put you down for a while." And though the vocal may have been reined in to reflect the contracting range of recent years, it fully manages to sound as worldly wise as the words of wisdom that cavort off the page and onto tape. Using one of his favorite rhyming schemes—that internal rhyme in line three—to maximum effect, he almost comes up with more quotable lines in a five-minute song than he managed on the whole of *"Love and Theft"*:

> When I kiss your lips, the honey drips . . .
> The short and the tall are coming to the ball . . .
> You're as fine as wine, I ain't handing you no line . . .
> I'm stacked high to the roof, and I'm not without proof . . .

And finally, to reflect (and repeat) the film's own gambling motif, he repeats, "The game's gotten old, the deck's gone cold . . ." One imagines he had a certain amount of fun capturing this one. The band also exude all the confidence that comes from already completing an album with Bob the bandleader, adding layers of textured sound Dylan could store away for the next installment in the never-ending story. For now, he had done what he needed to do. It was time to put it down for a while.

IIIII ENDNOTES IIIIII

1. Krogsgaard's sessionography suggests the one take of "Tangled Up in Blue" recorded on the sixteenth was incomplete. The tape box clearly marks it as complete. So it could be the one on *The Bootleg Series 1–3*, except that the AFM sheet clearly says that this was one of the songs recorded with Deliverance, and the single additional guitar and bass sure sounds like something that comes from the seventeenth or nineteenth (when he rerecorded the song). That said, the recording dates on the 1991 set are generally accurate (though it manages to give the mix date for two *Shot of Love* outtakes, rather than recording date).

2. "Chance is the fool's name for fate" is the catchphrase in the Astaire-Rogers 1934 movie *The Gay Divorcee*, to which Dylan is alluding in the first four lines of verse two.

3. I am dating the last *Desire* session to July 31, when "Sara" was recorded, although there was a session on August 1 which, according to Sloman, was a listening session. There is, however, a song called "Devito's Song" credited to August 1 in the Sony database.

4. John Bauldie first made the connection in his article on "Isis" in *Endless Road #1*, reiterating it in his monograph on *Desire* in the Wanted Man Study Series.

5. Three songs from the December 2, 1978, show—"Mr. Tambourine Man," "Changing of the Guards," and "Masters of War"—were shown on Italian TV to tie in with the release of *At Budokan*. Both prebroadcast and aired versions of the footage circulate in collectors' circles.

6. The album lyric sheet, included with promotional copies and in certain non-English-speaking countries, lays out "Where Are You Tonight?" (and indeed "Changing of the Guards") quite differently from *Lyrics*, where each trio of verses appears as a single, elongated verse that bears little relationship to the way it is sung. On the album lyric sheet, it is given as three four-line verses, a five-line bridge, three more verses, five-line bridge, four four-line verses, and a final five-line bridge. Immeasurably superior.

7. According to Michael Krogsgaard's sessionography, the song was recorded at the last *Street-Legal* session on May 1, but the original reference tape from which the circulating tape derives dates it to May 2, which makes a lot more sense. Of course, he could have done it at both.

8. The second line, as printed in *Lyrics*, is quite different: "Just say that I trusted in God and Christ was in me."

9. "Caribbean Wind," "The Groom's Still Waiting," "Let's Keep It Between Us," and "Yonder Comes Sin" were all copyrighted on October 27, 1980; "Every Grain of Sand" was copyrighted on October 7, 1980. The last of these was recorded on September 23, so a recording date of early to mid-October for the other four tracks would be about right.

{ Endnotes }

10. There is a song on the two extant soundchecks from April 1980, in Toronto and Montreal, that could well be a lost original. The quality of both tapes is pretty atrocious, but he appears to be singing "They Talk About Me," or even "They Talk About Jesus."

11. In the copyrighted transcript from October 1980 the first line is given as "told her about Jesus, told her about the man," but this is not what Dylan sings at either the rehearsal or the Warfield.

12. In the 1985 *Lyrics*, the "redeemed men" have become "Arabian men," and the night "arises," not "arrives." Both are clearly mistranscriptions.

13. In the lyric published in *Telegraph #10*, he is treated "like a snake," not "like a slave."

14. The recording date given in the generally accurate *Bootleg Series 1–3* notes—May 11—is almost certainly wrong, as that was a mixing session.

15. The May 12 sequence was as follows: Shot Of Love*. Heart of Mine. Property of Jesus*. Lenny Bruce*. Watered-Down Love*. Dead Man, Dead Man. In the Summertime*. Magic. Trouble. Every Grain of Sand*. Angelina.

    Asterisked tracks appeared on the finished album, though edited in the case of "Watered-Down Love." Also significantly "trimmed" for the album release were "Shot of Love," "Dead Man, Dead Man," and "In the Summertime."

16. Arthur Rosato's list of songs scheduled to be recorded for *Shot of Love* comes in three parts. Parts one and two constitute one list, with the songs in list one bracketed. The songs in list three were added at a later date (I surmise on or around April 23):

    I: Shot of Love. Grain of Sand. You Changed My Life. Need a Woman. Borrowed Time. Movin (or ?Wait + See). Angelina. Is It Worth It. Gonna Love Her Anyway. Groom Still Waiting. Almost Persuaded.

    II: In the Summertime. You Can't Make It on Your Own. Rockin' Boat. The King Is on the Throne. Fur Slippers. Straw Hat. Well Water. All the Way. More to This Than Meets the Eye. It's All Dangerous to Me. My Oriental Home. Walking on Eggs. Caribbean Wind. Ah Ah Ah Ah. Let's Keep It Between Us. She's Not for You.

    III: Property of Jesus. Magic. Don't Take Yourself Away. Be Careful. Trouble. Bolero (Heart of Mine). Watered Down-Love. Dead Man.

17. According to the Krogsgaard sessionography, the March 31 session was devoted entirely to "Caribbean Wind" (though Fred Tackett has suggested "Groom's Still Waiting" was also recorded then). During the day, there were eight attempts at the former song, the first five all listed as incomplete (one breakdown and four "long false starts"). The last three were all full takes, with the penultimate take marked "w/ electric guitar," the final take as being with "acoustic guitar." Leaving aside the sheer unlikelihood of the version on *Biograph* and the one on the unauthorized *Genuine Bootleg Series Vol. 1* set being consecutive takes, given the massive lyrical rewrites and drastic rearrangement of tempo *and* time-signature, the one on the latter set, with its crystal clear "acoustic guitar" intro, is surely that final March 31 take. So unless one can construct a credible case for Dylan rewriting the entire song *twice* at a single session, I think we should accept that the version on *Biograph* was recorded later—as the boxed-set credits themselves aver.

18. Though, by his own admission, Krogsgaard's own details for the April 23, 1981, session are incomplete, he still chooses to omit information included in *Recording Sessions*, based on hearing a fuller tape. The songs he omits are as follows: Shot of Love. Mystery Train. instrumental fragment. Half as Much. Groom's Still Waiting at the Altar. Dead Man, Dead Man.

19. The released cut has a vocal punch-in here. Dylan originally sings, "Smokin' over [some of] the tracks."

20. Though recorded in 1949, the album was not released until October 1972.

21. "St. James Infirmary" appears in the original track listing for this 1956 session, obtained by Sam Charters, with a spoken preface (just like "Dyin' Crapshooters Blues"), yet did not appear on the released version. Michael Gray fails to resolve this question in the expansive discography to his book on Blind Willie McTell and an inquiry for clarification failed to elicit a reply. Some scholar.

22. Two of these were copyrighted as part of a 1985 compilation: "Dark Groove" and "Don't Fly Unless It's Safe."

23. Dylan seems to have been singularly unhelpful with his song titles at the sessions, the engineer logging songs under the following titles: "There's a Woman," "Sometimes Satan," "By the Way That's a Cute Hat," "Brooklyn Anthem," and "Too Late" as opposed to "License to Kill," "Man of Peace," "Sweetheart Like You," "Clean Cut Kid," and "Foot of Pride," which is how they were later copyrighted.

24. "Go 'Way Little Boy" was copyrighted on August 6, 1984. "Driftin' Too Far From Shore," "Who Loves You," and the two instrumentals, "Firebird" and "Wolf," were copyrighted exactly a week later.

25. Jay Cocks, the person entrusted with writing a script, insists that the project is still not dead.

26. Missing from the track information Krogsgaard obtained for the Cherokee sessions— and by no means alone in this—are the session details for "Tight Connection to My Heart." The song was apparently subject to overdubs by the girl singers in New York in mid-January 1985, but these can only have taken place *after* Dylan recorded his own vocal track. It is possible that this could have taken place in New York earlier in January, especially as he clearly used elements of the basic track for "Someone's Got a Hold of My Heart" on the new recording—the song is still logged as "Hold of My Heart" when it receives the girl singer overdubs, and Mick Taylor, Sly Dunbar, and Robbie Shakespeare all receive credits for their 1983 contributions to the finished track. But it seems more likely that Dylan did his vocal in L.A., presumably at Cherokee.

27. It would appear that "Seeing the Real You at Last" was recorded at least twice. According to Krogsgaard's sessionograpy, it was one of three tracks recorded with "unknown recording dates" at Cherokee Studios in late December (twenty-second) 1984 and January 28 and 30, 1985. It is also given the specific recording date of January 28, and the session lineup of Campbell, Epstein, Heffington, and one John Paruolo. Presumably, it was also attempted on either December 22 or January 30.

28. There are two versions of "Straight as in Love" in circulation, both complete, and evidently done one after the other. These presumably date from the fourteenth. But according to the track sheet, these were takes six and seven, so there were five takes done earlier the same day, or on February 12, when Dylan was also at Cherokee Studios.

29. Dylan, in keeping with previous practice, allows an aural double meaning to one couplet by singing the word "buck" like "book," as in "for the love of a lousy book, I watched them die."

30. The Heartbreakers were in Dallas, Texas, on June 19, as part of the *True Confessions* tour, so they clearly were not in L.A., doing further recordings on "Got My Mind Made Up." This must have been a mix session, done without their direct participation.

31. The March 28 session, according to Krogsgaard, was a pukka recording session, with Dylan and the house band recording full, in-studio versions of "Political World," "Disease of Conceit," and "Where Teardrops Fall" (almost certainly "What Was It You Wanted" mislabeled), as well as overdubbing "Disease of Conceit" and "Dignity," from March 8 and 13 respectively. The three songs supposedly recut on this day—if we accept "What Was It You Wanted" as one of them—were all originally recorded March 8, yet none of the recut songs ended up on *Oh Mercy* (whatever the sessionographer says). We also know "Political World" was subject to vocal overdubs and reediting after its initial recording. To my mind, the most likely scenario is that this session was entirely for fixing up earlier recordings, the start of a series of overdub sessions that ran to mid-April.

32. "God knows I need you" is what Dylan sings on the original, 1989 recording. "God knows you ain't pretty" is the 1990 rewrite.

33. The track sheet for the released version of "Ring Them Bells" does not say March 7, but rather March ?, so it could be that the song was recorded earlier, and the date was not logged accurately. If the track sheet was Krogsgaard's source for the session date, its attribution must be open to question.

34. According to Krogsgaard's sessionography, Dylan cut three versions of "Where Teardrops Fall" at the March 28 session, picking the second take for the album and then doing new vocals on March 30, April 3, and April 8. However, he had already attributed the released cut to a session on March 21–22, to which overdubs were added on April 15 and 16. I suspect the March 28 song to be a re-recording/overdubbing of "What Was It You Wanted," using the version recorded on March 21 as its basis. That song was certainly given a new vocal, and other minor overdubs, between the original session and its eventual release. It also has the right combination of musicians, which "Where Teardrops Fall" does not.

35. "Ring Them Bells" would appear to be the only song on *Oh Mercy* to feature a live vocal, though the existence of another version on *Tell Tale Signs* tells us he still reworked it at least once.

36. Instrumental overdub sessions apparently ran from April 30 to May 4 and May 8 to 10, with two more on the fourteenth and twenty-fifth. Dylan's presence at some of these sessions is documented, and by then he was immersed in the Wilburys project.

37. The track sheets to "Dirt Road Blues," "Red River Shore," "Can't Wait," "All I Ever Loved Is You," "Stayed in Mississippi," "Dreamin' of You," and "Doing Alright" from *Time Out of Mind* and "Someday Baby" and "Ain't Talkin'" from *Modern Times* are partly or wholly reproduced in the *Tell Tale Signs* booklet.

38. The four songs on the album that use Oxnard "basic tracks" appear to be as follows: "Standing in the Doorway," "Million Miles," "Can't Wait," and "Highlands."

39. The first part of the line comes from a song Dylan covered as early as 1962, "I've Been a Moonshiner"; the latter part is an archaic expression, drawn from the military.

40. These last two lines also reappear in "Standing in the Doorway."

41. The tape logs for *"Love and Theft,"* save for the first two songs recorded, give DAT ID numbers for most takes, including those that are subsequently rolled over. These ID numbers are always higher than the number of takes logged, even when one takes into account those rolled over (the take numbers on the multis only referring to those takes *preserved* on two-inch tape). I interpret this to mean that there were several (largely incomplete) takes for each song preserved only on DAT, as the song was worked on by the musicians prior to rolling two-inch tape. These DAT IDs would doubtless also include false starts and breakdowns so the 35 DAT IDs on "Bye and Bye," say, do not mean thirty-five takes, just that there were a lot more attempts than the seven takes preserved on the multitracks.

42. Dylan is probably alluding to Norman Mailer's *Of a Fire on the Moon*, his 1971 book about the space program, in the opening line of "Thunder on the Mountain."

43. What Utah Phillips sings is "Down in some hollow, where the water runs cold," but Dylan again applies the double allusion. Here it is to the traditional song "Down in the Valley," more commonly known as "The Birmingham Jail."

▌▌▌ ACKNOWLEDGMENTS ▌▌▌

Once again I am obliged to outwardly genuflect to those ever-generous Dylan scholars and archivists Mitch Blank, Glen Dundas, and Ian Woodward for putting a number of necessary building blocks in place for me.

This time around I also had to marshal a number of sainted souls to confirm, deny, embellish, or discard aspects of the session information we have relied on to date. In each case they brought firsthand testimony to the process and helped nudge me incrementally closer to the facts. So, from across the years, salutations to you all: Ellen Bernstein, Joel Bernstein, Debbie Gold, Andy Goldstein, George Hechter, Don Heffington, Reid Kopel, Kevin Odegard, Arthur Rosato, Larry Sloman, and Winston Watson.

Thanks, too, to David Bristow for never voicing concern about when he is likely to get half of his Dylan book collection back. Ditto Peter Doggett and his papers.

My good friend Glenn Korman at Sony in New York was again responsive to every factual query about the various studio sessions, no matter how busy.

The Dylan office has again proved honorable and professional at every turn. Especial thanks to Jeff Rosen, to whom I owe a dedication one of these days.

Yuval Taylor and Leo Hollis, my editors at A Cappella and Constable & Robinson respectively, have endured this mammoth project to the bittersweet end and have kept it on the production rails come rain or shine. Muchas gracias.

The book was copyedited by a Dylan expert of many years standing, the upstanding Peter Vincent. His input has ensured an altogether error-free edition.

Artur Jarosinski generously and promptly provided all the material from his once active website devoted to the various sources Dylan may have purloined from for the lyrics to his 2001 and 2006 albums, an invaluable resource that should be more commonly available.

And finally gratitude too to those other hardy souls who have endured me talking, arguing, ranting about various aspects of the project in the cafes at night: Andrew Muir, Jonathan Cott, Raymond Foye, Jonathan Lethem, and Mike Decapite, I thank you all.

Oh, and just in case anyone thinks I'm mellowing with age, this book is *not* dedicated to John Wesley Harding, aka Wes Stace. You got a lotta nerve, but precious little talent, ol' buddy.

IIIII A SELECT BIBLIOGRAPHY IIIII

I again refer readers looking for a more completist bibliography of Dylan publications to my biography *Behind the Shades: Take Two (2000)* and my chronology *Dylan Day-By-Day (1995)*. Please note: (pp) = privately published.

1. Dylan's own writings.

"An Observation Revisited," *Photography* #1 (Summer 1976) [attributed to R. Zimmerman]

Chronicles (Simon & Schuster, 2004)

Drawn Blank (Random House, 1994)

"Four Songs," lyric sheets accompanying Special Rider demos, 1976–81 (including "Yonder Comes Sin" and "Need a Woman").

In His Own Write [ed. Michael Krogsgaard] (pp, 1980 + insert of 1979–80 lyrics)

In His Own Write 2 [ed. John Tuttle] (pp, 1990)

In His Own Write 3 [ed. John Tuttle] (pp, 1992)

Lyrics (Knopf, 1985)

Lyrics (Knopf, 2004)

Masked & Anonymous shooting script [with Larry Charles].

The Songs of Bob Dylan 1966–75 (Knopf, 1976)

Words to His Songs (pp, 1971)

Words Fill My Head (pp, 1991)

Untitled playscript, Margolis & Moss mss., circa 1964.

2. Dylan interviews.

The primary resource for Dylan interviews is a four-volume bookleg collection published in the mid-nineties by "Dr. Filth." Entitled *The Fiddler Now Upspoke* Vols. 1-4, it covers 99 percent of the interviews given up to 1995. For more information, readers are referred to the *Behind the Shades: Take Two* bibliography.

The post-1995 interviews also utilized are as follows (in order of publication):

September 28, 1997—Pareles, Jon: the *New York Times*.

September 29, 1997—Gundersen, Edna: *USA Today*.

October 6, 1997—Gates, David: *Newsweek*.

November 15, 1997—Jackson, Alan: *The Times Magazine*.

December 14, 1997—Hilburn, Robert: *Los Angeles Times*.

February 1998—Kaganski, Serge: *Mojo*.

March 1999—Engleheart, Murray: *Guitar World*.

September 10, 2001—Gundersen, Edna: *USA Today*

{ A Select Bibliography }

September 17, 2001—Farley, Christopher John: *Time*.
November 22, 2001—Gilmore, Mikal: *Rolling Stone*.
September 26, 2004—Preston, John: *The Sunday Telegraph*.
October 4, 2004—Gates, David: *Newsweek*.
December 9, 2004—Scaggs, Austin: *Rolling Stone*.
February 2006—Hilburn, Robert: *Guitar World Acoustic*. [Interview from 2004.]
September 7, 2006—Lethem, Jonathan: *Rolling Stone*.
May 3, 2007—Wenner, Jann: *Rolling Stone*.
June 6, 2008—Jackson, Alan: *The Times*.
April 2009—Flanagan, Bill: online on bobdylan.com.
May 14, 2009—Brinkley, Douglas: *Rolling Stone*.

3. Dylan fanzines. [*—now defunct]

Zimmerman Blues* #1–10.
Look Back* #1–27.
Endless Road* #1–7.
Occasionally* #1–5.
The Telegraph* #1–56.
Homer, the slut* #1–11.
Judas!* #1–19.
Isis #1–147.
The Bridge #1–19.
On The Tracks #1–24.

4. The biographies.

Heylin, Clinton—*Behind the Shades: Take Two* (Viking, 2000).
Scaduto, Anthony—*Bob Dylan* (Grosset & Dunlap, 1971).
Shelton, Robert—*No Direction Home* (New English Library, 1986).
Sounes, Howard—*Down the Highway* (2001).
Spitz, Bob—*Dylan: A Biography* (McGraw-Hill, 1988).

5. Main reference sources.

Cable, Paul—*Bob Dylan: The Unreleased Recordings* (Dark Star, 1978).
Cartwright, Bert—*The Bible in the Lyrics of Bob Dylan* (Wanted Man, 1985; revised ed., 1992).
Dundas, Glen—*Tangled Up in Tapes* (pp, various eds.).
Dunn, Tim—*The Bob Dylan Copyright Files 1962–1995* (pp, 1996).
Heylin, Clinton—*Rain Unravelled Tales: A Rumorography* (pp, 1984).
Heylin, Clinton—*The Recording Sessions 1960–1994* (Penguin, 1996).
Heylin, Clinton—*A Life in Stolen Moments: Dylan Day by Day* (Schirmer, 1996).
Wenner, Jann (ed.)—Rolling Stone *Cover to Cover: The First Forty Years* (1967–2006) (DVD-ROM, Bondi, 2007).

{ A Select Bibliography }

6. Other reference sources.

Balfour, Victoria—*Rock Wives* (Beech Tree, 1986).

Barker, Derek (ed.)—*Isis: A Bob Dylan Anthology* (Helter Skelter, 2001).

Bowden, Betsy—*Performed Literature: Words and Music by Bob Dylan* (Indiana University Press, 1982).

Flanagan, Bill—*Written in My Soul* (Contemporary, 1986).

Garrett, Pat—*The Authentic Life of Billy, the Kid* (University of Oklahoma Press, 2000).

Gilmour, Michael J.—*Tangled Up in the Bible: Bob Dylan & Scripture* (Continuum, 2004).

Gray, Michael—*Song & Dance Man* (Hart-Davis, 1972)
   —*Song & Dance Man III: The Art of Bob Dylan* (Cassell, 2000)
   —*Hand Me My Travelin' Shoes: In Search of Blind Willie McTell* (Bloomsbury, 2007)

Hedin, Benjamin—*Studio A: The Bob Dylan Reader* (Norton, 2004).

Hinton, Brian—*Album File & Complete Discography* (Cassell, 2006).

Muir, Andrew—*Troubadour: Early and Late Songs of Bob Dylan* (Woodstock Publications, 2003).

Odegard, Kevin and Andy Gill—*A Simple Twist of Fate: Bob Dylan and the Making of Blood on the Tracks* (Da Capo, 2004).

Pickering, Stephen—*Bob Dylan Approximately* (David McKay, 1974).

Sloman, Larry—*On the Road with Bob Dylan* (Bantam, 1978).

Webster, Patrick—*Friends & Other Strangers* (pp, 1985).

Williams, Paul—*Performing Artist Vol. 2: The Middle Years 1974–86* (Underwood-Miller, 1992).
   —*Performing Artist Vol. 3: 1986–1990 and Beyond* (Omnibus, 2004).
   —*What Happened?* (And Books, 1979).*
   —*One Year Later* (pp, 1981).*

[*—both monographs reproduced in *Bob Dylan: Watching the River Flow* (Omnibus, 1996)]

Zollo, Paul—*Songwriters on Songwriting* (Da Capo, 1997).

7. Folksong resources.

Atkinson, David &c.—*Roots & Branch #1* (EFDSS, 1999).

Dett, R. Nathaniel—*Religious Folk-Songs of the Negro* (Hampton Institute Press, 1927).

Lomax, John & Alan—*American Ballads & Folk Songs* (Dover, 1994).

Ramsay, Allan—*Tea-Table Miscellany* (1871 edition).

Silber, Irwin and Fred—*Folksingers Wordbook* (Oak, 1973).

Work, John W.—*American Negro Songs & Spirituals* (Bonanza, 1940).

The Editors—*The Collected Reprints from Sing Out! 1959–64 & 1964–73* (Sing Out, 1990).

8. Miscellaneous articles.

Bangs, Lester—"Dylan's Dalliance with Mafia Chic," *Creem*, [April] 1976.

Barker, Derek—Interview with Jacques Levy, *Isis* #90.
   —The Story of the Hurricane, *Isis* #91.
   —Interview with Jim Dickinson, *Isis* #73.

Bauldie, John—"The Oppression of Knowledge," in *All Across the Telegraph* (ed. Bauldie and Gray) (Sidgwick & Jackson, 1987).

{ A Select Bibliography }

Briggs, Keith and Alex van Der Tuuk—sleeve notes to *The Definitive Charlie Patton* three-CD set (Catfish, 2001).

Charlesworth, Chris—"Dylan's write hand man," *Melody Maker*, January 24, 1976.

Charters, Samuel—sleeve notes to *The Complete Blind Willie Johnson* two-CD set (Legacy, 1993).

Chase, Donald—Interview with Richard Marquand, *Datebook* (San Francisco Chronicle), November 23, 1986.

Cooper, Chris—Interview with Helena Springs, *Endless Road* #7.

Doggett, Pete—Interview with Don Was, *Record Collector* #215.

Evans, David—sleeve notes to *The Definitive Blind Willie McTell* two-CD set (Legacy, 1994).

Heylin, Clinton—Saved! Parts 1-3, *The Telegraph* #28–30.

Jones, Peter—Interview with Allen Ginsberg, *Goldmine*, September 8, 1989.

Kato, Masato—Interview with Fred Tackett, *The Bridge* #4.

Kent, Nick—review of *Shot of Love*, NME, August 15, 1981.

Kopel, Reid—Interview with Don Was, *The Telegraph* #37.

Lindley, John—"Movies Inside His Head," in *The Telegraph* #25.

Love, Damien et al.—Tell Tale Signs Special, *Uncut* # 138 [+ online edition, where the relevant interviews were reproduced in unedited form].

Oliver, Paul—*Blues Fell This Morning* LP sleeve notes (Phillips BBL 7369).

Rich, Motoko—"Who's This Guy Dylan . . . ?" in the *New York Times*, September 14, 2006.

9. Literary resources.

The Bible (King James edition).

Case, Paul Foster—*The Oracle of the Tarot: A Course on Tarot Divination* (pp, 1933).

Fitzgerald, F. Scott—*The Great Gatsby* (Scribner, 1925).

Henderson, T.F. & W.E. Henley—*The Poetry of Robert Burns*, 4 vols. (Edinburgh, 1896).

Lindsey, Hal—*The Late Great Planet Earth* (Lakeland, 1981).

—*Satan Is Alive and Well* (Bantam, 1974).

Lott, Eric—*Love and Theft: Blackface Minstrelsy & the American Working Class* (Oxford UP, 1995).

Petrarch, Francesco—*Canzoniere* (Carcanet, 2000)

Saga, Jun'ichi [trans. John Bester]—*Confessions of a Yakuza: A Life in Japan's Underworld* (Kodansha International, 1995).

Shepard, Sam—Fool to Love *and Other Plays* (Bantam, 1984).

10. DVDs.

The Gunfighter (20th Century Fox, 2008).

Pat Garrett and Billy the Kid (Warner, 2006).

Wonder Boys (Uca, 2000).

Masked & Anonymous (Columbia Tristar, 2004).

▌▌▌▌▌ COPYRIGHT INFORMATION ▌▌▌▌▌

{ Copyright Information }

{ Copyright Information }

{ Copyright Information }

{ Copyright Information }

{ Copyright Information }

{ Copyright Information }

{ Copyright Information }

{ Copyright Information }

‖‖‖ INDEX OF BOB DYLAN SONGS ‖‖‖

{ Song Index }

{ Song Index }

▌▌▌ GENERAL INDEX ▌▌▌
(see also INDEX OF BOB DYLAN SONGS)

{ General Index }

{ General Index }

{ General Index }

{ General Index }

{ General Index }